Hadoop in Practice

Hadoop in Practice

ALEX HOLMES

MANNING
SHELTER ISLAND

For online information and ordering of this and other Manning books, please visit
www.manning.com. The publisher offers discounts on this book when ordered in quantity.
For more information, please contact

Special Sales Department
Manning Publications Co.
20 Baldwin Road
PO Box 261
Shelter Island, NY 11964
Email: orders@manning.com

⊖ Recognizing the importance of preserving what has been written, it is Manning's policy to have
the books we publish printed on acid-free paper, and we exert our best efforts to that end.
Recognizing also our responsibility to conserve the resources of our planet, Manning books
are printed on paper that is at least 15 percent recycled and processed without the use of
elemental chlorine.

 Manning Publications Co.
20 Baldwin Road
PO Box 261
Shelter Island, NY 11964

Development editor: Cynthia Kane
Copyeditors: Bob Herbtsman, Tara Walsh
Proofreader: Katie Tennant
Typesetter: Gordan Salinovic
Illustrator: Martin Murtonen
Cover designer: Marija Tudor

ISBN 9781617290237
Printed in the United States of America
1 2 3 4 5 6 7 8 9 10 – MAL – 17 16 15 14 13 12

To Michal, Marie, Oliver, Ollie, Mish, and Anch

brief contents

contents

3   Data serialization—working with text and beyond   83

PART 3   BIG DATA PATTERNS 137

4   Applying MapReduce patterns to big data   139

5   Streamlining HDFS for big data   169

6 Diagnosing and tuning performance problems 194

11 Programming pipelines with Pig 359

12 Crunch and other technologies 394

13 Testing and debugging 410

preface

I first encountered Hadoop in the fall of 2008 when I was working on an internet crawl and analysis project at Verisign. My team was making discoveries similar to those that Doug Cutting and others at Nutch had made several years earlier regarding how to efficiently store and manage terabytes of crawled and analyzed data. At the time, we were getting by with our home-grown distributed system, but the influx of a new data stream and requirements to join that stream with our crawl data couldn't be supported by our existing system in the required timelines.

After some research we came across the Hadoop project, which seemed to be a perfect fit for our needs—it supported storing large volumes of data and provided a mechanism to combine them. Within a few months we'd built and deployed a Map-Reduce application encompassing a number of MapReduce jobs, woven together with our own MapReduce workflow management system onto a small cluster of 18 nodes. It was a revelation to observe our MapReduce jobs crunching through our data in minutes. Of course we couldn't anticipate the amount of time that we'd spend debugging and performance-tuning our MapReduce jobs, not to mention the new roles we took on as production administrators—the biggest surprise in this role was the number of disk failures we encountered during those first few months supporting production!

As our experience and comfort level with Hadoop grew, we continued to build more of our functionality using Hadoop to help with our scaling challenges. We also started to evangelize the use of Hadoop within our organization and helped kick-start other projects that were also facing big data challenges.

The greatest challenge we faced when working with Hadoop (and specifically MapReduce) was relearning how to solve problems with it. MapReduce is its own flavor of parallel programming, which is quite different from the in-JVM programming that we were accustomed to. The biggest hurdle was the first one—training our brains to think MapReduce, a topic which the book *Hadoop in Action* by Chuck Lam (Manning Publications, 2010) covers well.

After you're used to thinking in MapReduce, the next challenge is typically related to the logistics of working with Hadoop, such as how to move data in and out of HDFS, and effective and efficient ways to work with data in Hadoop. These areas of Hadoop haven't received much coverage, and that's what attracted me to the potential of this book—that of going beyond the fundamental word-count Hadoop usages and covering some of the more tricky and dirty aspects of Hadoop.

As I'm sure many authors have experienced, I went into this project confidently believing that writing this book was just a matter of transferring my experiences onto paper. Boy, did I get a reality check, but not altogether an unpleasant one, because writing introduced me to new approaches and tools that ultimately helped better my own Hadoop abilities. I hope that you get as much out of reading this book as I did writing it.

acknowledgments

First and foremost, I want to thank Michael Noll, who pushed me to write this book. He also reviewed my early chapter drafts and helped mold the organization of the book. I can't express how much his support and encouragement has helped me throughout the process.

I'm also indebted to Cynthia Kane, my development editor at Manning, who coached me through writing this book and provided invaluable feedback on my work. Among many notable "Aha!" moments I had while working with Cynthia, the biggest one was when she steered me into leveraging visual aids to help explain some of the complex concepts in this book.

I also want to say a big thank you to all the reviewers of this book: Aleksei Sergeevich, Alexander Luya, Asif Jan, Ayon Sinha, Bill Graham, Chris Nauroth, Eli Collins, Ferdy Galema, Harsh Chouraria, Jeff Goldschrafe, Maha Alabduljalil, Mark Kemna, Oleksey Gayduk, Peter Krey, Philipp K. Janert, Sam Ritchie, Soren Macbeth, Ted Dunning, Yunkai Zhang, and Zhenhua Guo.

Jonathan Seidman, the primary technical editor, did a great job reviewing the entire book shortly before it went into production. Many thanks to Josh Wills, the creator of Crunch, who kindly looked over the chapter that covers that topic. And more thanks go to Josh Patterson, who reviewed my Mahout chapter.

All of the Manning staff were a pleasure to work with, and a special shout-out goes to Troy Mott, Katie Tennant, Nick Chase, Tara Walsh, Bob Herbstman, Michael Stephens, Marjan Bace, and Maureen Spencer.

Finally, a special thanks to my wife, Michal, who had to put up with a cranky husband working crazy hours. She was a source of encouragement throughout the entire process.

about this book

Doug Cutting, Hadoop's creator, likes to call Hadoop the kernel for big data, and I'd tend to agree. With its distributed storage and compute capabilities, Hadoop is fundamentally an enabling technology for working with huge datasets. Hadoop, to me, provides a bridge between structured (RDBMS) and unstructured (log files, XML, text) data, and allows these datasets to be easily joined together. This has evolved from traditional use cases, such as combining OLTP and log files, to more sophisticated uses, such as using Hadoop for data warehousing (exemplified by Facebook) and the field of data science, which studies and makes new discoveries about data.

This book collects a number of intermediary and advanced Hadoop examples and presents them in a problem/solution format. Each of the 85 techniques addresses a specific task you'll face, like using Flume to move log files into Hadoop or using Mahout for predictive analysis. Each problem is explored step by step and, as you work through them, you'll find yourself growing more comfortable with Hadoop and at home in the world of big data.

This hands-on book targets users who have some practical experience with Hadoop and understand the basic concepts of MapReduce and HDFS. Manning's *Hadoop in Action* by Chuck Lam contains the necessary prerequisites to understand and apply the techniques covered in this book.

Many techniques in this book are Java-based, which means readers are expected to possess an intermediate-level knowledge of Java. An excellent text for all levels of Java users is *Effective Java, Second Edition*, by Joshua Bloch (Addison-Wesley, 2008).

Roadmap

This book has 13 chapters divided into five parts.

Part 1 contains a single chapter that's the introduction to this book. It reviews Hadoop basics and looks at how to get Hadoop up and running on a single host. It wraps up with a walk-through on how to write and execute a MapReduce job.

Part 2, "Data logistics," consists of two chapters that cover the techniques and tools required to deal with data fundamentals, getting data in and out of Hadoop, and how to work with various data formats. Getting data into Hadoop is one of the first roadblocks commonly encountered when working with Hadoop, and chapter 2 is dedicated to looking at a variety of tools that work with common enterprise data sources. Chapter 3 covers how to work with ubiquitous data formats such as XML and JSON in MapReduce, before going on to look at data formats better suited to working with big data.

Part 3 is called "Big data patterns," and looks at techniques to help you work effectively with large volumes of data. Chapter 4 examines how to optimize MapReduce join and sort operations, and chapter 5 covers working with a large number of small files, and compression. Chapter 6 looks at how to debug MapReduce performance issues, and also covers a number of techniques to help make your jobs run faster.

Part 4 is all about "Data science," and delves into the tools and methods that help you make sense of your data. Chapter 7 covers how to represent data such as graphs for use with MapReduce, and looks at several algorithms that operate on graph data. Chapter 8 describes how R, a popular statistical and data mining platform, can be integrated with Hadoop. Chapter 9 describes how Mahout can be used in conjunction with MapReduce for massively scalable predictive analytics.

Part 5 is titled "Taming the elephant," and examines a number of technologies that make it easier to work with MapReduce. Chapters 10 and 11 cover Hive and Pig respectively, both of which are MapReduce domain-specific languages (DSLs) geared at providing high-level abstractions. Chapter 12 looks at Crunch and Cascading, which are Java libraries that offer their own MapReduce abstractions, and chapter 13 covers techniques to help write unit tests, and to debug MapReduce problems.

The appendixes start with appendix A, which covers instructions on installing both Hadoop and all the other related technologies covered in the book. Appendix B covers low-level Hadoop ingress/egress mechanisms that the tools covered in chapter 2 leverage. Appendix C looks at how HDFS supports reads and writes, and appendix D covers a couple of MapReduce join frameworks written by the author and utilized in chapter 4.

Code conventions and downloads

All source code in listings or in text is in a `fixed-width font like this` to separate it from ordinary text. Code annotations accompany many of the listings, highlighting important concepts.

All of the text and examples in this book work with Hadoop 0.20.x (and 1.x), and most of the code is written using the newer org.apache.hadoop.mapreduce MapReduce APIs. The few examples that leverage the older org.apache.hadoop.mapred package are usually the result of working with a third-party library or a utility that only works with the old API.

All of the code used in this book is available on GitHub at https://github.com/alexholmes/hadoop-book as well as from the publisher's website at www.manning.com/HadoopinPractice.

Building the code depends on Java 1.6 or newer, git, and Maven 3.0 or newer. Git is a source control management system, and GitHub provides hosted git repository services. Maven is used for the build system.

You can clone (download) my GitHub repository with the following command:

```
$ git clone git://github.com/alexholmes/hadoop-book.git
```

After the sources are downloaded you can build the code:

```
$ cd hadoop-book
$ mvn package
```

This will create a Java JAR file, target/hadoop-book-1.0.0-SNAPSHOT-jar-with-dependencies.jar. Running the code is equally simple with the included bin/run.sh.

If you're running on a CDH distribution, the scripts will run configuration-free. If you're running on any other distribution, you'll need to set the HADOOP_HOME environment variable to point to your Hadoop installation directory.

The bin/run.sh script takes as the first argument the fully qualified Java class name of the example, followed by any arguments expected by the example class. As an example, to run the inverted index MapReduce code from chapter 1, you'd run the following:

```
$ hadoop fs -mkdir /tmp
$ hadoop fs -put test-data/ch1/* /tmp/

# replace the path below with the location of your Hadoop installation
# this isn't required if you are running CDH3
export HADOOP_HOME=/usr/local/hadoop

$ bin/run.sh com.manning.hip.ch1.InvertedIndexMapReduce \
  /tmp/file1.txt /tmp/file2.txt output
```

The previous code won't work if you don't have Hadoop installed. Please refer to chapter 1 for CDH installation instructions, or appendix A for Apache installation instructions.

Third-party libraries

I use a number of third-party libraries for the sake of convenience. They're included in the Maven-built JAR so there's no extra work required to work with these libraries. The following table contains a list of the libraries that are in prevalent use throughout the code examples.

Common third-party libraries

Library	Link	Details
Apache Commons IO	http://commons.apache.org/io/	Helper functions to help work with input and output streams in Java. You'll make frequent use of the IOUtils to close connections and to read the contents of files into strings.
Apache Commons Lang	http://commons.apache.org/lang/	Helper functions to work with strings, dates, and collections. You'll make frequent use of the StringUtils class for tokenization.

Datasets

Throughout this book you'll work with three datasets to provide some variety for the examples. All the datasets are small to make them easy to work with. Copies of the exact data used are available in the GitHub repository in the directory https://github.com/alexholmes/hadoop-book/tree/master/test-data. I also sometimes have data that's specific to a chapter, which exists within chapter-specific subdirectories under the same GitHub location.

NASDAQ FINANCIAL STOCKS

I downloaded the NASDAQ daily exchange data from Infochimps (see http://mng.bz/xjwc). I filtered this huge dataset down to just five stocks and their start-of-year values from 2000 through 2009. The data used for this book is available on GitHub at https://github.com/alexholmes/hadoop-book/blob/master/test-data/stocks.txt.

The data is in CSV form, and the fields are in the following order:

```
Symbol,Date,Open,High,Low,Close,Volume,Adj Close
```

APACHE LOG DATA

I created a sample log file in Apache Common Log Format (see http://mng.bz/L4S3) with some fake Class E IP addresses and some dummy resources and response codes. The file is available on GitHub at https://github.com/alexholmes/hadoop-book/blob/master/test-data/apachelog.txt.

NAMES

The government's census was used to retrieve names from http://mng.bz/LuFB and is available at https://github.com/alexholmes/hadoop-book/blob/master/test-data/names.txt.

Getting help

You'll no doubt have questions when working with Hadoop. Luckily, between the wikis and a vibrant user community your needs should be well covered.

The main wiki is located at http://wiki.apache.org/hadoop/, and contains useful presentations, setup instructions, and troubleshooting instructions.

The Hadoop Common, HDFS, and MapReduce mailing lists can all be found on http://hadoop.apache.org/mailing_lists.html.

Search Hadoop is a useful website that indexes all of Hadoop and its ecosystem projects, and it provides full-text search capabilities: http://search-hadoop.com/.

You'll find many useful blogs you should subscribe to in order to keep on top of current events in Hadoop. This preface includes a selection of my favorites:

- Cloudera is a prolific writer of practical applications of Hadoop: http://www.cloudera.com/blog/.
- The Hortonworks blog is worth reading; it discusses application and future Hadoop roadmap items: http://hortonworks.com/blog/.
- Michael Noll is one of the first bloggers to provide detailed setup instructions for Hadoop, and he continues to write about real-life challenges and uses of Hadoop: http://www.michael-noll.com/blog/.

There are a plethora of active Hadoop Twitter users who you may want to follow, including Arun Murthy (@acmurthy), Tom White (@tom_e_white), Eric Sammer (@esammer), Doug Cutting (@cutting), and Todd Lipcon (@tlipcon). The Hadoop project itself tweets on @hadoop.

Author Online

Purchase of *Hadoop in Practice* includes free access to a private web forum run by Manning Publications where you can make comments about the book, ask technical questions, and receive help from the author and other users. To access and subscribe to the forum, point your web browser to www.manning.com/HadoopinPractice or www.manning.com/holmes/. These pages provide information on how to get on the forum after you are registered, what kind of help is available, and the rules of conduct on the forum.

Manning's commitment to our readers is to provide a venue where a meaningful dialogue between individual readers and between readers and the author can take place. It's not a commitment to any specific amount of participation on the part of the author, whose contribution to the book's forum remains voluntary (and unpaid). We suggest you try asking him some challenging questions, lest his interest stray!

The Author Online forum and the archives of previous discussions will be accessible from the publisher's website as long as the book is in print.

About the author

ALEX HOLMES is a senior software engineer with over 15 years of experience developing large-scale distributed Java systems. For the last four years he has gained expertise in Hadoop solving big data problems across a number of projects. He has presented at JavaOne and Jazoon and is currently a technical lead at VeriSign.

Alex maintains a Hadoop-related blog at http://grepalex.com, and is on Twitter at https://twitter.com/grep_alex.

About the cover illustration

The figure on the cover of *Hadoop in Practice* is captioned "A young man from Kistanja, Dalmatia." The illustration is taken from a reproduction of an album of Croatian traditional costumes from the mid-nineteenth century by Nikola Arsenovic, published by the Ethnographic Museum in Split, Croatia, in 2003. The illustrations were obtained from a helpful librarian at the Ethnographic Museum in Split, itself situated in the Roman core of the medieval center of the town: the ruins of Emperor Diocletian's retirement palace from around AD 304. The book includes finely colored illustrations of figures from different regions of Croatia, accompanied by descriptions of the costumes and of everyday life.

Kistanja is a small town located in Bukovica, a geographical region in Croatia. It is situated in northern Dalmatia, an area rich in Roman and Venetian history. The word *mamok* in Croatian means a bachelor, beau, or suitor—a single young man who is of courting age—and the young man on the cover, looking dapper in a crisp, white linen shirt and a colorful, embroidered vest, is clearly dressed in his finest clothes, which would be worn to church and for festive occasions—or to go calling on a young lady.

Dress codes and lifestyles have changed over the last 200 years, and the diversity by region, so rich at the time, has faded away. It is now hard to tell apart the inhabitants of different continents, let alone of different hamlets or towns separated by only a few miles. Perhaps we have traded cultural diversity for a more varied personal life—certainly for a more varied and fast-paced technological life.

Manning celebrates the inventiveness and initiative of the computer business with book covers based on the rich diversity of regional life of two centuries ago, brought back to life by illustrations from old books and collections like this one.

Part 1

Background
and fundamentals

Part 1 of this book contains chapter 1, which looks at Hadoop's components and its ecosystem. The chapter then provides instructions for installing a pseudo-distributed Hadoop setup on a single host, and includes a system for you to run all of the examples in the book. Chapter 1 also covers the basics of Hadoop configuration, and walks you through how to write and run a Map-Reduce job on your new setup.

Hadoop in a heartbeat

This chapter covers

- Understanding the Hadoop ecosystem
- Downloading and installing Hadoop
- Running a MapReduce job

We live in the age of big data, where the data volumes we need to work with on a day-to-day basis have outgrown the storage and processing capabilities of a single host. Big data brings with it two fundamental challenges: how to store and work with voluminous data sizes, and more important, how to understand data and turn it into a competitive advantage.

Hadoop fills a gap in the market by effectively storing and providing computational capabilities over substantial amounts of data. It's a distributed system made up of a distributed filesystem and it offers a way to parallelize and execute programs on a cluster of machines (see figure 1.1). You've most likely come across Hadoop as it's been adopted by technology giants like Yahoo!, Facebook, and Twitter to address their big data needs, and it's making inroads across all industrial sectors.

Because you've come to this book to get some practical experience with Hadoop and Java, I'll start with a brief overview and then show you how to install Hadoop and run a MapReduce job. By the end of this chapter you'll have received

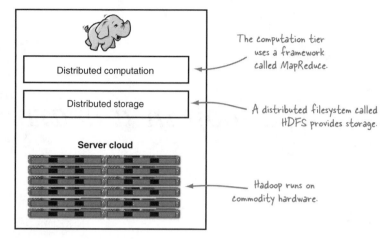

Figure 1.1   The Hadoop environment

a basic refresher on the nuts and bolts of Hadoop, which will allow you to move on to the more challenging aspects of working with Hadoop.[1]

Let's get started with a detailed overview of Hadoop.

1.1   *What is Hadoop?*

Hadoop is a platform that provides both distributed storage and computational capabilities. Hadoop was first conceived to fix a scalability issue that existed in Nutch,[2] an open source crawler and search engine. At the time Google had published papers that described its novel distributed filesystem, the Google File System (GFS), and MapReduce, a computational framework for parallel processing. The successful implementation of these papers' concepts in Nutch resulted in its split into two separate projects, the second of which became Hadoop, a first-class Apache project.

In this section we'll look at Hadoop from an architectural perspective, examine how industry uses it, and consider some of its weaknesses. Once we've covered Hadoop's background, we'll look at how to install Hadoop and run a MapReduce job.

Hadoop proper, as shown in figure 1.2, is a distributed master-slave architecture[3] that consists of the Hadoop Distributed File System (HDFS) for storage and MapReduce for computational capabilities. Traits intrinsic to Hadoop are data partitioning and parallel computation of large datasets. Its storage and computational capabilities scale with the addition of hosts to a Hadoop cluster, and can reach volume sizes in the petabytes on clusters with thousands of hosts.

In the first step in this section we'll examine the HDFS and MapReduce architectures.

---

[1] Readers should be familiar with the concepts provided in Manning's *Hadoop in Action* by Chuck Lam, and *Effective Java* by Joshua Bloch.

[2] The Nutch project, and by extension Hadoop, was led by Doug Cutting and Mike Cafarella.

[3] A model of communication where one process called the master has control over one or more other processes, called slaves.

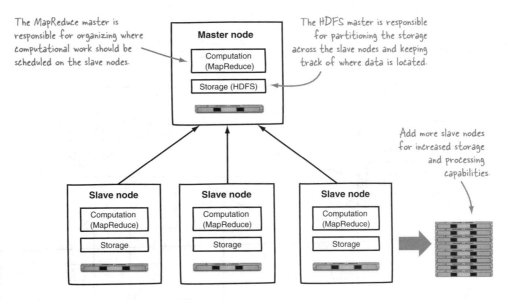

Figure 1.2 High-level Hadoop architecture

1.1.1 Core Hadoop components

To understand Hadoop's architecture we'll start by looking at the basics of HDFS.

HDFS

HDFS is the storage component of Hadoop. It's a distributed filesystem that's modeled after the Google File System (GFS) paper.[4] HDFS is optimized for high throughput and works best when reading and writing large files (gigabytes and larger). To support this throughput HDFS leverages unusually large (for a filesystem) block sizes and data locality optimizations to reduce network input/output (I/O).

Scalability and availability are also key traits of HDFS, achieved in part due to data replication and fault tolerance. HDFS replicates files for a configured number of times, is tolerant of both software and hardware failure, and automatically re-replicates data blocks on nodes that have failed.

Figure 1.3 shows a logical representation of the components in HDFS: the Name-Node and the DataNode. It also shows an application that's using the Hadoop filesystem library to access HDFS.

Now that you have a bit of HDFS knowledge, it's time to look at MapReduce, Hadoop's computation engine.

MAPREDUCE

MapReduce is a batch-based, distributed computing framework modeled after Google's paper on MapReduce.[5] It allows you to parallelize work over a large amount of

---

[4] See the Google File System, http://research.google.com/archive/gfs.html.
[5] See MapReduce: Simplified Data Processing on Large Clusters, http://research.google.com/archive/mapreduce.html.

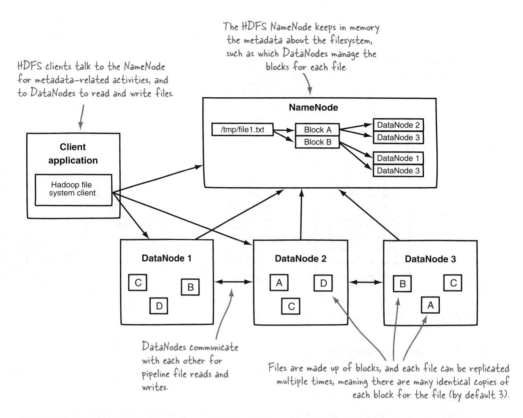

Figure 1.3   HDFS architecture shows an HDFS client communicating with the master NameNode and slave DataNodes.

raw data, such as combining web logs with relational data from an OLTP database to model how users interact with your website. This type of work, which could take days or longer using conventional serial programming techniques, can be reduced down to minutes using MapReduce on a Hadoop cluster.

The MapReduce model simplifies parallel processing by abstracting away the complexities involved in working with distributed systems, such as computational parallelization, work distribution, and dealing with unreliable hardware and software. With this abstraction, MapReduce allows the programmer to focus on addressing business needs, rather than getting tangled up in distributed system complications.

MapReduce decomposes work submitted by a client into small parallelized map and reduce workers, as shown in figure 1.4. The map and reduce constructs used in MapReduce are borrowed from those found in the Lisp functional programming language, and use a shared-nothing model[6] to remove any parallel execution interdependencies that could add unwanted synchronization points or state sharing.

---

[6] A shared-nothing architecture is a distributed computing concept that represents the notion that each node is independent and self-sufficient.

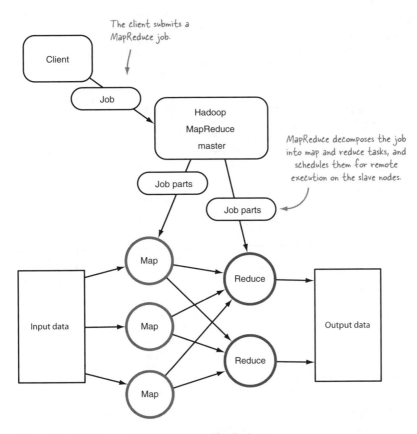

The client submits a
MapReduce job.

MapReduce decomposes the job
into map and reduce tasks, and
schedules them for remote
execution on the slave nodes.

Figure 1.4   A client submitting a job to MapReduce

The role of the programmer is to define map and reduce functions, where the map function outputs key/value tuples, which are processed by reduce functions to produce the final output. Figure 1.5 shows a pseudo-code definition of a map function with regards to its input and output.

The map function takes as input a key/value pair, which
represents a logical record from the input data source.
In the case of a file, this could be a line, or if the
input source is a table in a database, it could be a row.

```
map(key1, value1) ⟶ list(key2, value2)
```

The map function produces zero or more output key/value pairs for
that one input pair. For example, if the map function is a filtering
map function, it may only produce output if a certain condition is
met. Or it could be performing a demultiplexing operation, where a
single input key/value yields multiple key/value output pairs.

Figure 1.5   A logical view of the map function

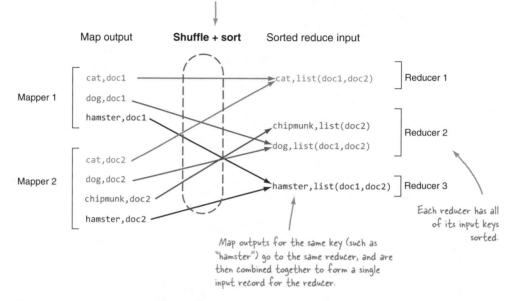

The shuffle and sort phases are responsible for two primary activities: determining the reducer that should receive the map output key/value pair (called partitioning); and ensuring that, for a given reducer, all its input keys are sorted.

Map outputs for the same key (such as "hamster") go to the same reducer, and are then combined together to form a single input record for the reducer.

Each reducer has all of its input keys sorted.

Figure 1.6   MapReduce's shuffle and sort

The power of MapReduce occurs in between the map output and the reduce input, in the shuffle and sort phases, as shown in figure 1.6.

Figure 1.7 shows a pseudo-code definition of a reduce function.

Hadoop's MapReduce architecture is similar to the master-slave model in HDFS. The main components of MapReduce are illustrated in its logical architecture, as shown in figure 1.8.

With some MapReduce and HDFS basics tucked under your belts, let's take a look at the Hadoop ecosystem, and specifically, the projects that are covered in this book.

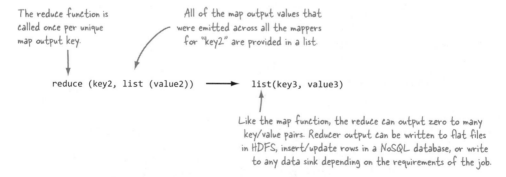

The reduce function is called once per unique map output key.

All of the map output values that were emitted across all the mappers for "key2" are provided in a list.

Like the map function, the reduce can output zero to many key/value pairs. Reducer output can be written to flat files in HDFS, insert/update rows in a NoSQL database, or write to any data sink depending on the requirements of the job.

Figure 1.7   A logical view of the reduce function

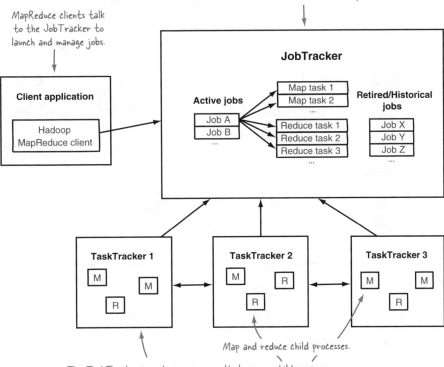

The JobTracker coordinates activities across the slave TaskTracker processes. It accepts MapReduce job requests from clients and schedules map and reduce tasks on TaskTrackers to perform the work.

MapReduce clients talk to the JobTracker to launch and manage jobs.

The TaskTracker is a daemon process that spawns child processes to perform the actual map or reduce work. Map tasks typically read their input from HDFS, and write their output to the local disk. Reduce tasks read the map outputs over the network and write their outputs back to HDFS.

Map and reduce child processes.

Figure 1.8 MapReduce logical architecture

1.1.2 *The Hadoop ecosystem*

The Hadoop ecosystem is diverse and grows by the day. It's impossible to keep track of all of the various projects that interact with Hadoop in some form. In this book the focus is on the tools that are currently receiving the greatest adoption by users, as shown in figure 1.9.

MapReduce is not for the faint of heart, which means the goal for many of these Hadoop-related projects is to increase the accessibility of Hadoop to programmers and nonprogrammers. I cover all of the technologies listed in figure 1.9 in this book and describe them in detail within their respective chapters. In addition, I include descriptions and installation instructions for all of these technologies in appendix A.

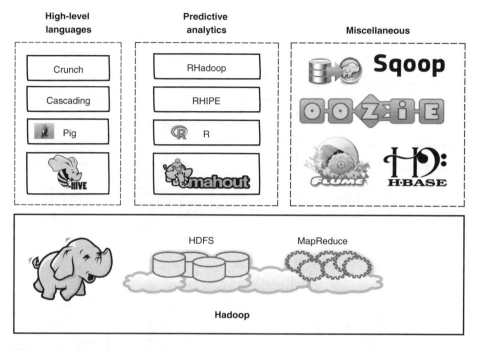

Figure 1.9   Hadoop and related technologies

Let's look at how to distribute these components across hosts in your environments.

1.1.3   *Physical architecture*

The physical architecture lays out where you install and execute various components. Figure 1.10 shows an example of a Hadoop physical architecture involving Hadoop and its ecosystem, and how they would be distributed across physical hosts. ZooKeeper requires an odd-numbered quorum,[7] so the recommended practice is to have at least three of them in any reasonably sized cluster.

For Hadoop let's extend the discussion of physical architecture to include CPU, RAM, disk, and network, because they all have an impact on the throughput and performance of your cluster.

The term *commodity hardware* is often used to describe Hadoop hardware requirements. It's true that Hadoop can run on any old servers you can dig up, but you still want your cluster to perform well, and you don't want to swamp your operations department with diagnosing and fixing hardware issues. Therefore, commodity refers to mid-level rack servers with dual sockets, as much error-correcting RAM as is affordable, and SATA drives optimized for RAID storage. Using RAID, however, is strongly discouraged on the DataNodes, because HDFS already has replication and error-checking built-in; but on the NameNode it's strongly recommended for additional reliability.

---

[7] A quorum is a High Availability (HA) concept that represents the minimum number of members required for a system to still remain online and functioning.

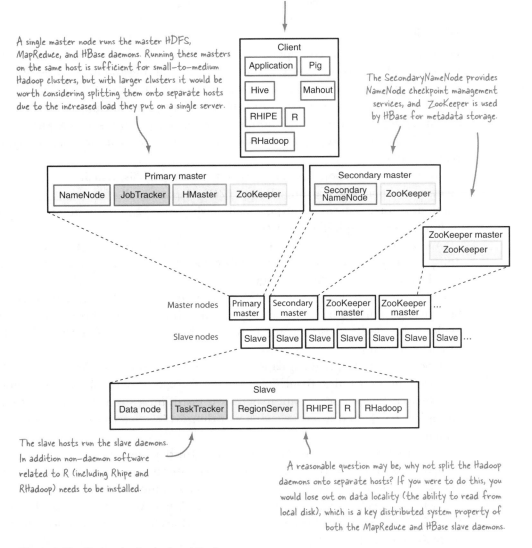

Figure 1.10   Hadoop's physical architecture

From a network topology perspective with regards to switches and firewalls, all of the master and slave nodes must be able to open connections to each other. For small clusters, all the hosts would run 1 GB network cards connected to a single, good-quality switch. For larger clusters look at 10 GB top-of-rack switches that have at least multiple 1 GB uplinks to dual-central switches. Client nodes also need to be able to talk to all of the master and slave nodes, but if necessary that access can be from behind a firewall that permits connection establishment only from the client side.

After reviewing Hadoop's physical architecture you've likely developed a good idea of who might benefit from using Hadoop. Let's take a look at companies currently using Hadoop, and in what capacity they're using it.

1.1.4 *Who's using Hadoop?*

Hadoop has a high level of penetration in high-tech companies, and is starting to make inroads across a broad range of sectors, including the enterprise (Booz Allen Hamilton, J.P. Morgan), government (NSA), and health care.

Facebook uses Hadoop, Hive, and HBase for data warehousing and real-time application serving.[8] Their data warehousing clusters are petabytes in size with thousands of nodes, and they use separate HBase-driven, real-time clusters for messaging and real-time analytics.

Twitter uses Hadoop, Pig, and HBase for data analysis, visualization, social graph analysis, and machine learning. Twitter LZO-compresses all of its data, and uses Protocol Buffers for serialization purposes, all of which are geared to optimizing the use of its storage and computing resources.

Yahoo! uses Hadoop for data analytics, machine learning, search ranking, email antispam, ad optimization, ETL,[9] and more. Combined, it has over 40,000 servers running Hadoop with 170 PB of storage.

eBay, Samsung, Rackspace, J.P. Morgan, Groupon, LinkedIn, AOL, Last.fm, and StumbleUpon are some of the other organizations that are also heavily invested in Hadoop. Microsoft is also starting to work with Hortonworks to ensure that Hadoop works on its platform.

Google, in its MapReduce paper, indicated that it used its version of MapReduce to create its web index from crawl data.[10] Google also highlights applications of MapReduce to include activities such as a distributed grep, URL access frequency (from log data), and a term-vector algorithm, which determines popular keywords for a host.

The organizations that use Hadoop grow by the day, and if you work at a Fortune 500 company you almost certainly use a Hadoop cluster in some capacity. It's clear that as Hadoop continues to mature, its adoption will continue to grow.

As with all technologies, a key part to being able to work effectively with Hadoop is to understand its shortcomings and design and architect your solutions to mitigate these as much as possible.

1.1.5 *Hadoop limitations*

Common areas identified as weaknesses across HDFS and MapReduce include availability and security. All of their master processes are single points of failure, although

---

[8] See http://www.facebook.com/note.php?note_id=468211193919.

[9] Extract, transform, and load (ETL) is the process by which data is extracted from outside sources, transformed to fit the project's needs, and loaded into the target data sink. ETL is a common process in data warehousing.

[10] In 2010 Google moved to a real-time indexing system called Caffeine: http://googleblog.blogspot.com/2010/06/our-new-search-index-caffeine.html.

you should note that there's active work on High Availability versions in the community. Security is another area that has its wrinkles, and again another area that's receiving focus.

HIGH AVAILABILITY

Until the Hadoop 2.x release, HDFS and MapReduce employed single-master models, resulting in single points of failure.[11] The Hadoop 2.x version will eventually bring both NameNode and JobTracker High Availability (HA) support. The 2.x NameNode HA design requires shared storage for NameNode metadata, which may require expensive HA storage. It supports a single standby NameNode, preferably on a separate rack.

SECURITY

Hadoop does offer a security model, but by default it's disabled. With the security model disabled, the only security feature that exists in Hadoop is HDFS file and directory-level ownership and permissions. But it's easy for malicious users to subvert and assume other users' identities. By default, all other Hadoop services are wide open, allowing any user to perform any kind of operation, such as killing another user's MapReduce jobs.

Hadoop can be configured to run with Kerberos, a network authentication protocol, which requires Hadoop daemons to authenticate clients, both user and other Hadoop components. Kerberos can be integrated with an organization's existing Active Directory, and therefore offers a single sign-on experience for users. Finally, and most important for the government sector, there's no storage or wire-level encryption in Hadoop. Overall, configuring Hadoop to be secure has a high pain point due to its complexity.

Let's examine the limitations of some of the individual systems.

HDFS

The weakness of HDFS is mainly around its lack of High Availability, its inefficient handling of small files, and its lack of transparent compression. HDFS isn't designed to work well with random reads over small files due to its optimization for sustained throughput. The community is waiting for append support for files, a feature that's nearing production readiness.

MAPREDUCE

MapReduce is a batch-based architecture, which means it doesn't lend itself to use cases that need real-time data access. Tasks that require global synchronization or sharing of mutable data aren't a good fit for MapReduce, because it's a shared-nothing architecture, which can pose challenges for some algorithms.

ECOSYSTEM VERSION COMPATIBILITIES

There also can be version-dependency challenges to running Hadoop. For example, HBase only works with a version of Hadoop that's not verified as production ready, due to its HDFS sync requirements (*sync* is a mechanism that ensures that all writes to a stream have been written to disk across all replicas). Hadoop versions 0.20.205 and

---

[11] In reality, the HDFS single point of failure may not be terribly significant; see http://goo.gl/1iSab.

newer, including 1.x and 2.x, include sync support, which will work with HBase. Other challenges with Hive and Hadoop also exist, where Hive may need to be recompiled to work with versions of Hadoop other than the one it was built against. Pig has had compatibility issues, too. For example, the Pig 0.8 release didn't work with Hadoop 0.20.203, requiring manual intervention to make them work together. This is one of the advantages to using a Hadoop distribution other than Apache, as these compatibility problems have been fixed.

One development worth tracking is the creation of BigTop (http://incubator .apache.org/projects/bigtop.html), currently an Apache incubator project, which is a contribution from Cloudera to open source its automated build and compliance system. It includes all of the major Hadoop ecosystem components and runs a number of integration tests to ensure they all work in conjunction with each other.

After tackling Hadoop's architecture and its weaknesses you're probably ready to roll up your sleeves and get hands-on with Hadoop, so let's take a look at how to get the Cloudera Distribution for Hadoop (CDH)[12] up and running on your system, which you can use for all the examples in this book.

1.2   *Running Hadoop*

The goal of this section is to show you how to run a MapReduce job on your host. To get there you'll need to install Cloudera's Hadoop distribution, run through some command-line and configuration steps, and write some MapReduce code.

1.2.1   *Downloading and installing Hadoop*

Cloudera includes the Cloudera Manager, a full-blown service and configuration management tool that works well for provisioning Hadoop clusters with multiple nodes. For this section we're interested in installing Hadoop on a single host, so we'll look at the individual packages that Cloudera offers. CDH includes OS-native installation packages for top-level Linux distributions such as RedHat, Debian, and SUSE, and their derivatives. Preinstalled CDH also includes tarball and Virtual Machine images. You can view all of the available options at http://www.cloudera.com/hadoop/.

Let's look at the instructions for installation on a RedHat-based Linux system (in this case you'll use CentOS). Appendix A includes the installation instructions for both the CDH tarball and the Apache Hadoop tarball.

RedHat uses packages called *RPMs* for installation, and Yum as a package installer that can fetch RPMs from remote Yum repositories. Cloudera hosts its own Yum repository containing Hadoop RPMs, which you'll use for installation.

You'll follow the pseudo-distributed installation instructions.[13] A pseudo-distributed setup is one where all of the Hadoop components are running on a single host. The first thing you need to do is download and install the "bootstrap" RPM, which will update your local Yum configuration to include Cloudera's remote Yum repository:

---

[12] I chose CDH for this task because of its simple installation and operation.

[13] See https://ccp.cloudera.com/display/CDHDOC/Installing+CDH3+on+a+Single+Linux+Node+in+Pseudo-distributed+Mode.

You need to run the wget and rpm commands as root. →

```
$ sudo -s
$ wget http://archive.cloudera.com/redhat/cdh/cdh3-repository-1.0-1.noarch.rpm
$ rpm -ivh cdh3-repository-1.0-1.noarch.rpm
```

Next, you'll import Cloudera's RPM signing key so that Yum can verify the integrity of the RPMs that it downloads:

Note that we had to split this command across two lines, so you use the "\\" character to escape the newline. ←

```
$ rpm --import \
    http://archive.cloudera.com/redhat/cdh/RPM-GPG-KEY-cloudera
```

The last step is to install the pseudo-distributed RPM package, which has dependencies on all the other core Hadoop RPMs. You'll also install Pig, Hive, and Snappy (which is contained in the Hadoop native package), because you'll be using them in this book:

```
$ yum install hadoop-0.20-conf-pseudo hadoop-0.20-native \
    hadoop-pig hadoop-hive
```

You've completed your installation of Hadoop. For this book you'll also be working with Oozie, HBase, and other projects, but you'll find instructions for these technologies in their respective sections.

> **Java versions**
>
> Hadoop requires version 1.6 update 8, or newer, of the Oracle Java Development Kit (JDK) on the host, which you can download from the Java SE Downloads (http://www.oracle.com/technetwork/java/javase/downloads/index.html) page.

You've installed the basics—it's time to learn how to configure Hadoop. Let's go over some basic commands so you can start and stop your cluster.

1.2.2 Hadoop configuration

After you've completed the installation instructions in the previous section, your software is ready for use without editing any configuration files. Knowing the basics of Hadoop's configuration is useful, so let's briefly touch upon it here. In CDH the Hadoop configs are contained under /etc/hadoop/conf. You'll find separate configuration files for different Hadoop components, and it's worth providing a quick overview of them in table 1.1.

Table 1.1   Hadoop configuration files

Filename	Description
hadoop-env.sh	Environment-specific settings go here. If a current JDK isn't in the system path you'll want to come here to configure your JAVA_HOME. You can also specify JVM options for various Hadoop components here. Customizing directory locations such as the log directory and the locations of the master and slave files is also performed here, although by default you shouldn't have to do any of what was just described in a CDH setup.
core-site.xml	Contains system-level Hadoop configuration items, such as the HDFS URL, the Hadoop temporary directory, and script locations for rack-aware Hadoop clusters. Settings in this file override the settings in core-default.xml. The default settings can be seen at http://hadoop.apache.org/common/docs/r1.0.0/core-default.html.
hdfs-site.xml	Contains HDFS settings such as the default file replication count, the block size, and whether permissions are enforced. To view the default settings you can look at http://hadoop.apache.org/common/docs/r1.0.0/hdfs-default.html. Settings in this file override the settings in hdfs-default.xml.
mapred-site.xml	HDFS settings such as the default number of reduce tasks, default min/max task memory sizes, and speculative execution are all set here. To view the default settings you can look at http://hadoop.apache.org/common/docs/r1.0.0/mapred-default.html. Settings in this file override the settings in mapred-default.xml.
masters	Contains a list of hosts that are Hadoop *masters*. This name is misleading and should have been called *secondary-masters*. When you start Hadoop it'll launch NameNode and JobTracker on the local host from which you issued the start command, and then SSH to all the nodes in this file to launch the SecondaryNameNode.
slaves	Contains a list of hosts that are Hadoop slaves. When you start Hadoop it will SSH to each host in this file and launch the DataNode and TaskTracker daemons.

The *site* XML files (those with *site* in their filenames) will grow as you start customizing your Hadoop cluster, and it can quickly become challenging to keep track of what changes you've made, and how they relate to the default configuration values. To help with this the author has written some code[14] that will compare the default and site files and indicate what properties have changed, as well as let you know about properties you may have misspelled. Some example output of the utility is included in the following code, which shows a few of the differences between the CDH core-default.xml and the core-site.xml files:

```
core-default.xml
Site file:  core-site.xml
                       Name   Final   Default              Site
              fs.default.name  false  file:///  dfs://localhost:8020
      fs.har.impl.disable.cache  false  true                 null
  hadoop.proxyuser.oozie.groups    -      -                    *
```

---

[14] https://github.com/alexholmes/hadoop-book/blob/master/src/main/java/com/manning/hip/ch1/
ConfigDumper.java.

The Cloudera team has researched[15] more advanced techniques using static and dynamic methods to determine what options are supported in Hadoop, as well as discrepancies between application and Hadoop configurations.

1.2.3 Basic CLI commands

Let's rattle through the essentials you need to get up and running. First, start your cluster. You'll need sudo access for your user to run this command (it launches the Hadoop services via init.d scripts):

```
$ for svc in /etc/init.d/hadoop-0.20-*; do sudo $svc start; done
```

All the daemon log files are written under /var/log/hadoop. For example, the NameNode file is written to hadoop-hadoop-namenode-<HOSTNAME>.log, and this can be a useful file to look at if you have problems bringing up HDFS. You can test that things are up and running in a couple of ways. First try issuing a command to list the files in the root directory in HDFS:

```
$ hadoop fs -ls /
```

Pathname expansions

You wouldn't think that the simple Hadoop filesystem command to list directory contents would have a quirk, but it does, and it's one that has bitten many a user, including the author, on numerous occasions. In bash and other shells it's normal to affix the * wildcard to filesystem commands, and for the shell to expand that prior to running a program. You would therefore (incorrectly) assume that the command `hadoop fs -ls /tmp/*` would work. But if you run this, and /tmp exists in your filesystem, your shell will expand the path based on the contents of /tmp on your local filesystem, and pass these filenames into Hadoop. At this point Hadoop will attempt to list files in HDFS that reside on your local system. The workaround is to prevent path expansion from occurring by enclosing the path in double quotes—this would become `hadoop fs -ls "/tmp/*"`.

If this works, HDFS is up and running. To make sure MapReduce is up and running you'll need to run a quick command to see what jobs are running:

```
$ hadoop job -list
0 jobs currently running
JobId    State    StartTime    UserName    Priority    SchedulingInfo
```

---

[15] See http://www.cloudera.com/blog/2011/08/automatically-documenting-apache-hadoop-configuration/.

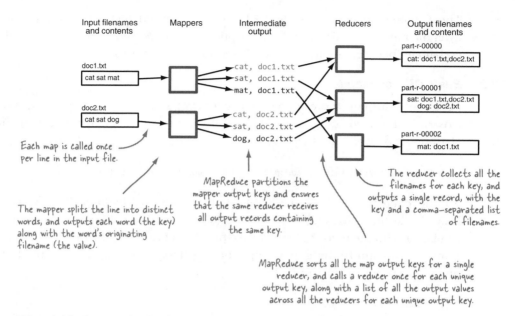

Figure 1.11 An example of an inverted index being created in MapReduce

Good, things seem to be in order. If you're curious about what commands you can issue from the command line take a look at http://hadoop.apache.org/common/docs/r1.0.0/file_system_shell.html for HDFS commands and http://hadoop.apache.org/common/docs/r1.0.0/commands_manual.html#job for MapReduce job commands.

Finally, to stop your cluster the process is similar to how you start it:

```
$ for svc in /etc/init.d/hadoop-0.20-*; do sudo $svc stop; done
```

With these essentials under your belt your next step is to write a MapReduce job (don't worry, it's not word count) that you can run in your new cluster.

1.2.4 *Running a MapReduce job*

Let's say you want to build an inverted index. MapReduce would be a good choice for this task because it can work on the creation of indexes in parallel, and as a result is a common MapReduce use case. Your input is a number of text files, and your output is a list of tuples, where each tuple is a word and a list of files that contain the word. Using standard processing techniques this would require you to find a mechanism to join all the words together. A naïve approach would be to perform this join in memory, but you may run out of memory if you have large numbers of unique keys. You could use an intermediary datastore such as a database, but that would be inefficient.

A better approach would be to tokenize each line and produce an intermediary file containing a word per line. Each of these intermediary files can then be sorted.

The final step would be to open all the sorted intermediary files and call a function for each unique word. This is what MapReduce does, albeit in a distributed fashion.

Figure 1.11 walks you through an example of a simple inverted index in MapReduce. Let's start by defining your mapper. Your reducers need to be able to generate a line for each word in your input, so your map output key should be each word in the input files so that MapReduce can join them all together. The value for each key will be the containing filename, which is your document ID. The following shows the mapper code:

When you extend the MapReduce mapper class you specify the key/value types for your inputs and outputs. You use the MapReduce default InputFormat for your job, which supplies keys as byte offsets into the input file, and values as each line in the file. Your map emits Text key/value pairs.

```java
public static class Map
      extends Mapper<LongWritable, Text, Text, Text> {
```

A Text object to store the document ID (filename) for your input.

```java
   private Text documentId;
```

To cut down on object creation you create a single Text object, which you'll reuse.

```java
   private Text word = new Text();
```

This method is called once at the start of the map and prior to the map method being called. You'll use this opportunity to store the input filename for this map.

Extract the filename from the context.

```java
   @Override
   protected void setup(Context context) {
      String filename =
         ((FileSplit) context.getInputSplit()).getPath().getName();
      documentId = new Text(filename);
   }
```

This map method is called once per input line; map tasks are run in parallel over subsets of the input files.

```java
   @Override
   protected void map(LongWritable key, Text value,
                     Context context)
      throws IOException, InterruptedException {
      for (String token :
            StringUtils.split(value.toString())) {
```

For each word your map outputs the word as the key and the document ID as the value.

Your value contains an entire line from your file. You tokenize the line using StringUtils (which is far faster than using String.split).

```java
         word.set(token);
         context.write(word, documentId);
      }
   }
}
```

The goal of your reducer is to create an output line for each word, and a list of the document IDs in which the word appears. The MapReduce framework will take care of calling your reducer once per unique key outputted by the mappers, along with a list of document IDs. All you need to do in your reducer is combine all the document IDs together and output them once in the reducer, as you can see in the next code block.

Much like your Map class you need to specify both the input and output key/value classes when you define your reducer.

```
public static class Reduce
    extends Reducer<Text, Text, Text, Text> {
private Text docIds = new Text();
public void reduce(Text key, Iterable<Text> values,
                   Context context)
    throws IOException, InterruptedException {

    HashSet<Text> uniqueDocIds = new HashSet<Text>();

    for (Text docId : values) {

        uniqueDocIds.add(new Text(docId));
    }

    docIds.set(new Text(StringUtils.join(uniqueDocIds, ",")));

    context.write(key, docIds);
    }
}
```

The reduce method is called once per unique map output key. The Iterable allows you to iterate over all the values that were emitted for the given key.

Iterate over all the DocumentIDs for the key.

Add the document ID to your set. The reason you create a new Text object is that MapReduce reuses the Text object when iterating over the values, which means you want to create a new copy.

Keep a set of all the document IDs that you encounter for the key.

Your reduce outputs the word, and a CSV-separated list of document IDs that contained the word.

The last step is to write the driver code that will set all the necessary properties to configure your MapReduce job to run. You need to let the framework know what classes should be used for the map and reduce functions, and also let it know where your input and output data is located. By default MapReduce assumes you're working with text; if you were working with more complex text structures, or altogether different data storage technologies, you would need to tell MapReduce how it should read and write from these data sources and sinks. The following source shows the full driver code:

Your input is 1 or more files, so create a sub-array from your input arguments, excluding the last item of the array, which is the MapReduce job output directory.

```
public static void main(String... args) throws Exception {

    runJob(
        Arrays.copyOfRange(args, 0, args.length - 1),
        args[args.length - 1]);
}

public static void runJob(String[] input, String output)
    throws Exception {
    Configuration conf = new Configuration();
    Job job = new Job(conf);

    job.setJarByClass(InvertedIndexMapReduce.class);

    job.setMapperClass(Map.class);

    job.setReducerClass(Reduce.class);

    job.setMapOutputKeyClass(Text.class);
    job.setMapOutputValueClass(Text.class);

    Path outputPath = new Path(output);
```

The Configuration container for your job configs. Anything that's set here is available to your map and reduce classes.

The Job class setJarByClass method determines the JAR that contains the class that's passed-in, which beneath the scenes is copied by Hadoop into the cluster and subsequently set in the Task's classpath so that your Map/Reduce classes are available to the Task.

If the map output key/value types differ from the input types you must tell Hadoop what they are. In this case your map will output each word and file as the key/value pairs, and both are Text objects.

Set the Map class that should be used for the job.

Set the Reduce class that should be used for the job.

Set the map output value class.

Set the HDFS input files for your job. Hadoop expects
multiple input files to be separated with commas.

```
FileInputFormat.setInputPaths(job, StringUtils.join(input, ","));
```

Set the HDFS output
directory for the job.

```
FileOutputFormat.setOutputPath(job, outputPath);
```

```
outputPath.getFileSystem(conf).delete(outputPath, true);
```

Tell the JobTracker to run
the job and block until
the job has completed.

```
job.waitForCompletion(true);
}
```

Delete the existing HDFS output directory if it
exists. If you don't do this and the directory
already exists the job will fail.

Let's see how your code works. You'll work with two simple files. First, you need to
copy the files into HDFS:

Copy file1.txt and
file2.txt into HDFS.

```
$ hadoop fs -put test-data/ch1/file*.txt /
$ hadoop fs -cat /file1.txt
cat sat mat
$ hadoop fs -cat /file2.txt
cat sat dog
```

Dump the contents of the HDFS
file /file1.txt to the console.

Dump the contents of
the HDFS file /file2.txt
to the console.

Next, run your MapReduce code. You'll use a shell script to run it, supplying the two
input files as arguments, along with the job output directory:

```
$ export JAVA_HOME=<path to your JDK bin directory>
$ bin/run.sh com.manning.hip.ch1.InvertedIndexMapReduce \
  /file1.txt /file2.txt output
```

When your job completes you can examine HDFS for the job output files, and also
view their contents:

```
$ hadoop fs -ls output/
Found 3 items
output/_SUCCESS
output/_logs
output/part-r-00000

$ hadoop fs -cat output/part-r-00000
cat     file2.txt,file1.txt
dog     file2.txt
mat     file1.txt
sat     file2.txt,file1.txt
```

You may be curious about where the map and reduce log files go. For that you need
to know the job's ID, which will take you to the logs directory in the local filesystem.
When you run your job from the command line, part of the output is the job ID,
as follows:

```
...
INFO mapred.JobClient: Running job: job_201110271152_0001
...
```

With this ID in hand you can navigate to the directory on your local filesystem, which contains a directory for each map and reduce task. These tasks can be differentiated by the *m* and *r* in the directory names:

```
$ pwd
/var/log/hadoop-0.20/userlogs/job_201110271152_0001
$ ls -l
attempt_201110271152_0001_m_000000_0
attempt_201110271152_0001_m_000001_0
attempt_201110271152_0001_m_000002_0
attempt_201110271152_0001_m_000003_0
attempt_201110271152_0001_r_000000_0
```

Within each of the directories in the previous code there are three files, corresponding to standard out, standard error, and the system log (output from both the infrastructure task code, as well as any of your own log4j logging):

```
$ ls attempt_201110271152_0001_m_000000_0
stderr   stdout   syslog
```

Remember that in the pseudo-distributed setup everything's running on your local host, so it's easy to see everything in one place. On a true distributed cluster these logs

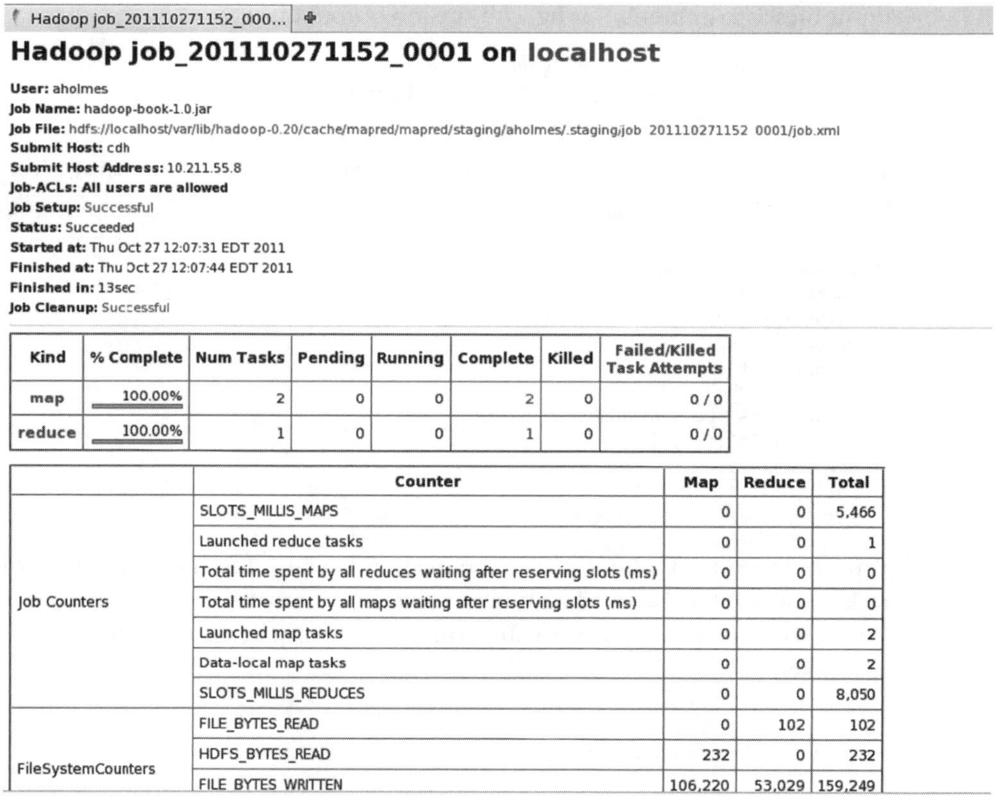

Hadoop job_201110271152_000... ✛

Hadoop job_201110271152_0001 on localhost

User: aholmes
Job Name: hadoop-book-1.0.jar
Job File: hdfs://localhost/var/lib/hadoop-0.20/cache/mapred/mapred/staging/aholmes/.staging/job_201110271152_0001/job.xml
Submit Host: cdh
Submit Host Address: 10.211.55.8
Job-ACLs: All users are allowed
Job Setup: Successful
Status: Succeeded
Started at: Thu Oct 27 12:07:31 EDT 2011
Finished at: Thu Oct 27 12:07:44 EDT 2011
Finished in: 13sec
Job Cleanup: Successful

Kind	% Complete	Num Tasks	Pending	Running	Complete	Killed	Failed/Killed Task Attempts
map	100.00%	2	0	0	2	0	0 / 0
reduce	100.00%	1	0	0	1	0	0 / 0

	Counter	Map	Reduce	Total
	SLOTS_MILLIS_MAPS	0	0	5,466
	Launched reduce tasks	0	0	1
	Total time spent by all reduces waiting after reserving slots (ms)	0	0	0
Job Counters	Total time spent by all maps waiting after reserving slots (ms)	0	0	0
	Launched map tasks	0	0	2
	Data-local map tasks	0	0	2
	SLOTS_MILLIS_REDUCES	0	0	8,050
	FILE_BYTES_READ	0	102	102
FileSystemCounters	HDFS_BYTES_READ	232	0	232
	FILE_BYTES_WRITTEN	106,220	53,029	159,249

Figure 1.12   The Hadoop JobTracker user interface

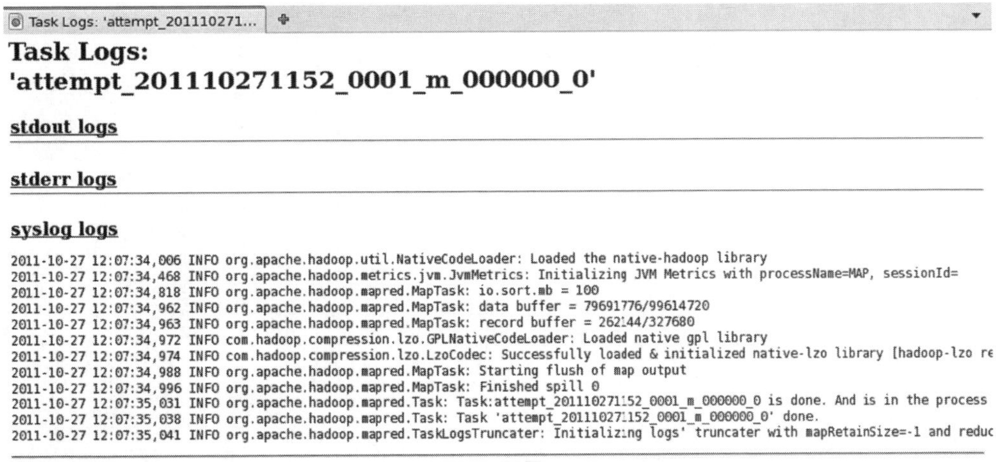

Figure 1.13 The Hadoop TaskTracker user interface

will be local to the remote TaskTracker nodes, which can make it harder to get to them. This is where the JobTracker and TaskTracker UI step in to provide easy access to the logs. Figures 1.12 and 1.13 show screenshots of the JobTracker summary page for your job, and the TaskTracker UI for one of the map tasks. In CDH you can access the JobTracker UI at http://localhost:50030/jobtracker.jsp.

This completes your whirlwind tour of how to run Hadoop.

1.3 *Chapter summary*

Hadoop is a distributed system designed to process, generate, and store large datasets. Its MapReduce implementation provides you with a fault-tolerant mechanism for large-scale data analysis. Hadoop also excels at working with heterogeneous structured and unstructured data sources at scale.

In this chapter, we examined Hadoop from functional and physical architectural standpoints. You also installed Hadoop and ran a MapReduce job.

The remainder of this book is dedicated to providing real-world techniques to solve common problems you encounter when working with Hadoop. You'll be introduced to a broad spectrum of subject areas, starting with HDFS and MapReduce, Pig, and Hive. You'll also look at data analysis techniques and explore technologies such as Mahout and Rhipe.

In chapter 2, the first stop on your journey, you'll discover how to bring data into (and out of) Hadoop. Without further ado, let's get started.

Part 2

Data logistics

If you've been thinking about how to work with Hadoop in production settings, this part of the book covers the first two hurdles you'll need to jump. These chapters detail the often-overlooked yet crucial topics that deal with data management in Hadoop.

Chapter 2 looks at ways to manage moving large quantities of data into and out of Hadoop. Examples include working with relational data in RDBMSs, structured files, and HBase.

The focus of chapter 3 is on ways to work with data stored in different formats, such as XML and JSON, which paves the way to a broader examination of data formats such as Thrift and Avro that work best with big data and Hadoop.

Moving data in and out of Hadoop

This chapter covers

- Understanding key design considerations for data ingress and egress tools
- Techniques for moving log files into HDFS and Hive
- Using relational databases and HBase as data sources and data sinks

Moving data in and out of Hadoop, which I'll refer to in this chapter as data *ingress* and *egress*, is the process by which data is transported from an external system into an internal system, and vice versa. Hadoop supports ingress and egress at a low level in HDFS and MapReduce. Files can be moved in and out of HDFS, and data can be pulled from external data sources and pushed to external data sinks using MapReduce. Figure 2.1 shows some of Hadoop's ingress and egress mechanisms.

The fact that your data exists in various forms and locations throughout your environments complicates the process of ingress and egress. How do you bring in data that's sitting in an OLTP (online transaction processing) database? Or ingress log data that's being produced by tens of thousands of production servers? Or work with binary data sitting behind a firewall?

27

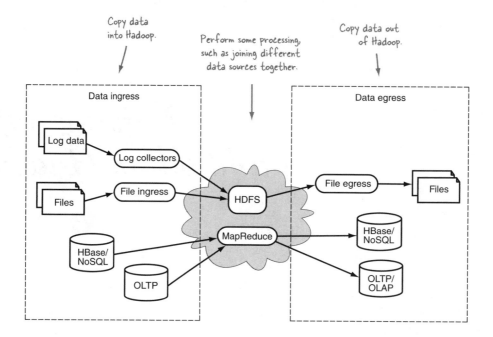

Figure 2.1   Hadoop data ingress and egress transports data to and from an external system to an internal one.

Further, how do you automate your data ingress and egress process so that your data is moved at regular intervals? Automation is a critical part of the process, along with monitoring and data integrity responsibilities to ensure correct and safe transportation of data.

In this chapter we'll survey the tools that simplify the process of ferrying data in and out of Hadoop. We'll also look at how to automate the movement of log files, ubiquitous data sources for Hadoop, but which tend to be scattered throughout your environments and therefore present a collection and aggregation challenge. In addition, we'll cover using Flume for moving log data into Hadoop, and in the process we'll evaluate two competing log collection and aggregation tools, Chukwa and Scribe.

We'll also walk through how to move relational data in and out of Hadoop. This is an emerging usage pattern where you can use Hadoop to join data sitting in your databases with data ingressed from other sources, such as log files, and subsequently push result data back out to databases. Finally, we'll cover how to use Sqoop for database ingress and egress activities, and we'll look at how to ingress and egress data in HBase.

We'll cover a lot of ground in this chapter, and it's likely that you have specific types of data you need to ingress or egress. If this is the case, feel free to jump directly to a particular section that provides the details you need. In addition, if you're looking for lower-level HDFS ingress and egress options, take a look at appendix B where I cover using tools such as WebHDFS and Hoop.

Let's start things off with a look at key ingress and egress system considerations.

2.1 Key elements of ingress and egress

Moving large quantities of data in and out of Hadoop has logistical challenges that include consistency guarantees and resource impacts on data sources and destinations. Before we dive into the techniques, however, we need to discuss the design elements to be aware of when working with data ingress and egress.

IDEMPOTENCE

An idempotent operation produces the same result no matter how many times it's executed. In a relational database the inserts typically aren't idempotent, because executing them multiple times doesn't produce the same resulting database state. Alternatively, updates often are idempotent, because they'll produce the same end result.

Any time data is being written idempotence should be a consideration, and data ingress and egress in Hadoop is no different. How well do distributed log collection frameworks deal with data retransmissions? How do you ensure idempotent behavior in a MapReduce job where multiple tasks are inserting into a database in parallel? We'll examine and answer these questions in this chapter.

AGGREGATION

The data aggregation process combines multiple data elements. In the context of data ingress this can be useful because moving large quantities of small files into HDFS potentially translates into NameNode memory woes, as well as slow MapReduce execution times. Having the ability to aggregate files or data together mitigates this problem, and is a feature to consider.

DATA FORMAT TRANSFORMATION

The data format transformation process converts one data format into another. Often your source data isn't in a format that's ideal for processing in tools such as MapReduce. If your source data is multiline XML or JSON form, for example, you may want to consider a preprocessing step. This would convert the data into a form that can be split, such as a JSON or an XML element per line, or convert it into a format such as Avro. Chapter 3 contains more details on these data formats.

RECOVERABILITY

Recoverability allows an ingress or egress tool to retry in the event of a failed operation. Because it's unlikely that any data source, sink, or Hadoop itself can be 100 percent available, it's important that an ingress or egress action be retried in the event of failure.

CORRECTNESS

In the context of data transportation, checking for correctness is how you verify that no data corruption occurred as the data was in transit. When you work with heterogeneous systems such as Hadoop data ingress and egress tools, the fact that data is being transported across different hosts, networks, and protocols only increases the potential for problems during data transfer. Common methods for checking correctness of raw data such as storage devices include Cyclic Redundancy Checks (CRC), which are what HDFS uses internally to maintain block-level integrity.

RESOURCE CONSUMPTION AND PERFORMANCE

Resource consumption and performance are measures of system resource utilization and system efficiency, respectively. Ingress and egress tools don't typically incur significant load (resource consumption) on a system, unless you have appreciable data volumes. For performance, the questions to ask include whether the tool performs ingress and egress activities in parallel, and if so, what mechanisms it provides to tune the amount of parallelism. For example, if your data source is a production database, don't use a large number of concurrent map tasks to import data.

MONITORING

Monitoring ensures that functions are performing as expected in automated systems. For data ingress and egress, monitoring breaks down into two elements: ensuring that the process(es) involved in ingress and egress are alive, and validating that source and destination data are being produced as expected.

On to the techniques. Let's start with how you can leverage Hadoop's built-in ingress and egress mechanisms.

2.2   *Moving data into Hadoop*

The first step in working with data in Hadoop is to make it available to Hadoop. As I mentioned earlier in this chapter, there are two primary methods that can be used for moving data into Hadoop: writing external data at the HDFS level (a data push), or reading external data at the MapReduce level (more like a pull). Reading data in MapReduce has advantages in the ease with which the operation can be parallelized and fault tolerant. Not all data is accessible from MapReduce, however, such as in the case of log files, which is where other systems need to be relied upon for transportation, including HDFS for the final data hop.

In this section we'll look at methods to move source data into Hadoop, which I'll refer to as *data ingress*. I'll use the data ingress design considerations in the previous section as the criteria to examine and understand the different tools as I go through the techniques.

We'll look at Hadoop data ingress across a spectrum of data sources, starting with log files, then semistructured or binary files, then databases, and finally HBase. We'll start by looking at data ingress of log files.

> **Low-level Hadoop ingress mechanisms**
>
> This section will focus on high-level data ingress tools that provide easy and automated mechanisms to get data into Hadoop. All these tools use one of a finite set of low-level mechanisms, however, which Hadoop provides to get data in and out. These mechanisms include Hadoop's Java HDFS API, WebHDFS, the new Hadoop 0.23 REST API, and MapReduce. An extensive evaluation of these mechanisms and tools is outside the scope of this chapter, but I provide them for reference in appendix B.

2.2.1 *Pushing log files into Hadoop*

Log data has long been prevalent across all applications, but with Hadoop came the ability to process the large volumes of log data produced by production systems. Various systems produce log data, from network devices and operating systems to web servers and applications. These log files all offer the potential for valuable insights into how systems and applications operate as well as how they're used. What unifies log files is that they tend to be in text form and line-oriented, making them easy to process.

In this section we'll look at tools that can help transport log data from source to HDFS. We'll also perform a deep dive into one of these tools and look at how to transport system log files into HDFS and Hive. I'll provide what you need to know to deploy, configure, and run an automated log collection and distribution infrastructure, and kick-start your own log data-mining activities.

COMPARING FLUME, CHUKWA, AND SCRIBE

Flume, Chukwa, and Scribe are log collecting and distribution frameworks that have the capability to use HDFS as a data sink for that log data. It can be challenging to differentiate between them because they share the same features.

FLUME

Apache Flume is a distributed system for collecting streaming data. It's an Apache project in incubator status, originally developed by Cloudera. It offers various levels of reliability and transport delivery guarantees that can be tuned to your needs. It's highly customizable and supports a plugin architecture where you can add custom data sources and data sinks.

Figure 2.2 shows Flume's architecture.

CHUKWA

Chukwa is an Apache subproject of Hadoop that also offers a large-scale mechanism to collect and store data in HDFS. And it's also in incubator status. Chukwa's reliability

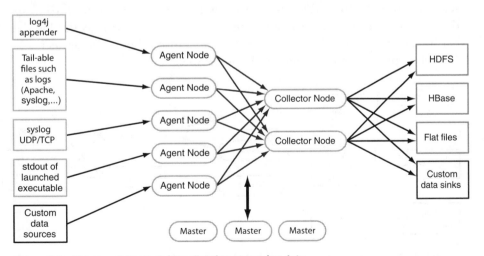

Figure 2.2 Flume architecture for collecting streaming data

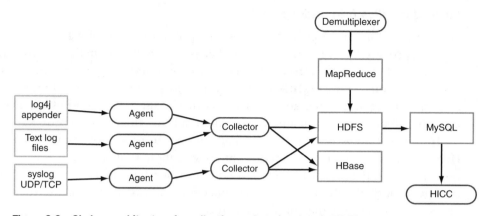

Figure 2.3   Chukwa architecture for collecting and storing data in HDFS

model supports two levels: end-to-end reliability, and fast-path delivery, which minimizes latencies. After writing data into HDFS Chukwa runs a MapReduce job to demultiplex the data into separate streams. Chukwa also offers a tool called Hadoop Infrastructure Care Center (HICC), which is a web interface for visualizing system performance.

Figure 2.3 shows Chukwa's architecture.

SCRIBE

Scribe is a rudimentary streaming log distribution service, developed and used heavily by Facebook. A scribe server that collects logs runs on every node and forwards them to a central Scribe server. Scribe supports multiple data sinks, including HDFS, regular filesystems, and NFS. Scribe's reliability comes from a file-based mechanism where the server persists to a local disk in the event it can't reach the downstream server.

Unlike Flume or Chukwa, Scribe doesn't include any convenience mechanisms to pull log data. Instead the onus is on the user to stream the source data to the Scribe server running on the local system. For example, if you want to push your Apache log files, you would need to write a daemon that tails and forwards the log data to the Scribe server. Figure 2.4 shows Scribe's architecture. The Scribe project is hosted on GitHub at https://github.com/facebook/scribe.

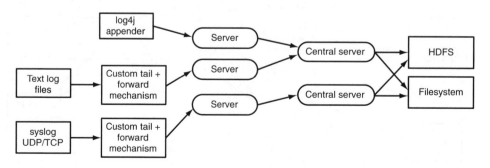

Figure 2.4   Scribe architecture also pushes log data into HDFS.

Table 2.1   Feature comparison of log collecting projects

Project	Centralized configuration	Reliability	Failover	Level of documentation	Commercial support	Popularity (number of mailing list messages from 08/11/2011)
Flume	Yes	Yes • Best effort • Disk failover • End-to-end	Yes • None • Manually configurable • Automated configuration	High	Yes (Cloudera)	High (348)
Chukwa	No	Yes • Fast • End-to-end	Yes • None • Manually configurable • Automated	Low	No	Medium (85)
Scribe	No	Yes • Disk-based (not end-to-end)	No	Low	No	Medium (46)

Each of these three tools can fulfill the criteria of providing mechanisms to push log data into HDFS. Table 2.1 compares the various tools based on features such as reliability and configuration.

From a high-level perspective there's not much feature difference between these tools, other than that Scribe doesn't offer any end-to-end delivery guarantees. It's also clear that the main downside for Chukwa and Scribe is their limited user documentation. Their mailing list activities were also moderate.

I had to pick one of these three tools for this chapter, so I picked Flume. My reasons for selecting Flume include its centralized configuration, its flexible reliability and failover modes, and also the popularity of its mailing list.

Let's look at how you can deploy and set up Flume to collect logs, using a problem/solution scenario. I'll continue to introduce techniques in this manner throughout the rest of this chapter.

TECHNIQUE 1 **Pushing system log messages into HDFS with Flume**

You have a bunch of log files being produced by multiple applications and systems across multiple servers. There's no doubt there's valuable information to be mined out of these logs, but your first challenge is a logistical one of moving these logs into your Hadoop cluster so that you can perform some analysis.

Problem

You want to push all of your production server system log files into HDFS.

Solution

For this technique you'll use Flume, a data collection system, to push a Linux log file into HDFS. We will also cover configurations required to run Flume in a distributed environment, as well as an examination of Flume's reliability modes.

Discussion

Figure 2.5 shows a full-fledged Flume deployment, and its four primary components:

- *Nodes*—Flume data paths that ferry data from a data source to a data sink. Agents and Collectors are simply Flume Nodes that are deployed in a way to efficiently and reliably work with a large number of data sources.
- *Agents*—Collect streaming data from the local host and forward it to the Collectors.
- *Collectors*—Aggregate data sent from the Agents and write that data into HDFS.
- *Masters*—Perform configuration management tasks and also help with reliable data flow.

This figure also shows data sources and data sinks. Data sources are streaming data origins whose data you want to transport to a different destination. Examples include application logs and Linux system logs, as well as nontext data that can be supported with custom data sources. Data sinks are the destination of that data, which can be HDFS, flat files, and any data target that can be supported with custom data sinks.

You'll run Flume in pseudo-distributed mode, which means you'll run the Flume Collector, Agent, and Master daemons on your single host. The first step is to install Flume, the Flume Master, and the Flume Node packages from the CDH3 Installation Guide.[1] After you've installed these packages, start up the Master and Agent daemons:

```
$ /etc/init.d/flume-master start
$ /etc/init.d/flume-node start
```

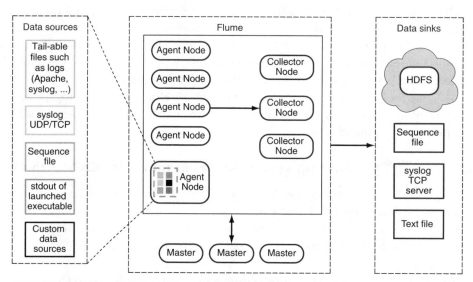

Figure 2.5   Example of Flume deployment for collecting streaming data

---

[1] Appendix A contains installation instructions and additional resources for working with Flume.

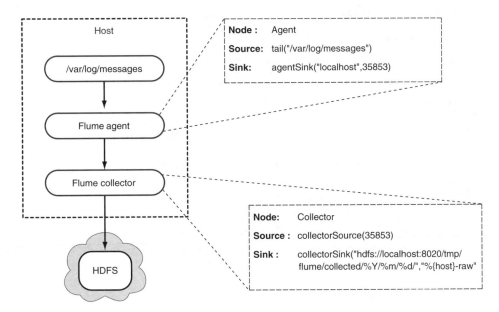

Figure 2.6 Data flow from /var/log/messages into HDFS

The data source in this exercise is the file /var/log/messages, the central file in Linux for system messages, and your ultimate data destination is HDFS. Figure 2.6 shows this data flow, and the Agent and Collector configuration settings you'll use to make it work.

By default, Flume will write data in Avro JSON format, which we'll discuss shortly. You'll want to preserve the original format of your syslog file, so you'll need to create and edit flume-site.xml and indicate the raw output format. The file should look like this:

```
$ cat /etc/flume/conf/flume-site.xml
<?xml version="1.0"?>
<?xml-stylesheet type="text/xsl"  href="configuration.xsl"?>
<configuration>
  <property>
    <name>flume.collector.output.format</name>
    <value>raw</value>
  </property>
</configuration>
```

If you've set up your cluster with LZO compression, you'll need to create a flume-env.sh file and set the directory that contains the native compression codecs:

```
$ cp /usr/lib/flume/bin/flume-env.sh.template \
  /usr/lib/flume/bin/flume-env.sh
$ vi /usr/lib/flume/bin/flume-env.sh
# add the following line for 64-bit environments
export JAVA_LIBRARY_PATH=/usr/lib/hadoop/lib/native/Linux-amd64-64
# or the following line for 32-bit environments
export JAVA_LIBRARY_PATH=/usr/lib/hadoop/lib/native/Linux-i386-32
```

Table 2.2   Flume UI endpoints

Daemon	URL
Flume Master	http://localhost:35871
Flume Node (Agent)	http://localhost:35862
Flume Node (Collector)	http://localhost:35863

You'll also need to copy the LZO JAR into Flume's lib directory:

```
$ cp /usr/lib/hadoop/lib/hadoop-lzo-0.4.1* /usr/lib/flume/lib/
```

Flume runs as the flume user, so you need to make sure that it has permissions to read any data source files (such as files under /var/log, for example).

Previously, when you launched the Flume Master and Node you were a Node short. Let's launch another Node, which you'll name collector, to perform the Collector duties:

```
$ flume node_nowatch -n collector
```

Each of the Flume daemons have embedded web user interfaces. If you've followed the previous instructions, table 2.2 shows the locations where they'll be available.

The advantage of using a Flume Master is that you can make configuration changes in a central location, and they'll be pulled by the Flume Nodes. There are two ways you can make configuration changes in the Flume Master: using the UI or the Flume shell. I'll show the configuration in the UI.

You'll need to configure the Agent and Collector Nodes according to the setup illustrated in figure 2.6. You'll connect to the Flume Master UI, and select the config menu from the top, as highlighted in figure 2.7. The drop-down box contains all of the Nodes, and you'll select the Agent node. The Agent node has the same name as

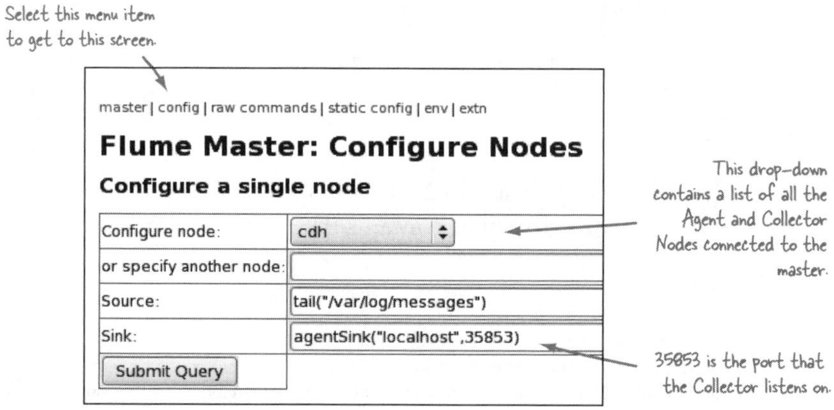

Figure 2.7   Flume Agent Node configuration to follow

master | config | raw commands | static config | env | extn

Flume Master: Configure Nodes

Configure a single node

Configure node:	Choose from list ⬍
or specify another node:	
Source:	collectorSource(35853)
Sink:	collectorSink("hdfs://localhost:8020/tmp/flume/collected/%Y/%m/%d/", "%{host}-raw")
Submit Query	

Figure 2.8 Flume Collector Node configuration to follow

the hostname that you're running on—in my case *cdh*. You should see one other Node in the drop-down called *collector*, which you'll configure next. For the Agent Node, you'll specify that the data source is a tail of the syslog file and the data sink is the port that your Collector will run on.

Now select the Collector from the drop-down, and in a similar fashion, set the data source, which is the local port that you'll listen on, and the data sink, which is the final destination in HDFS for your log data. Figure 2.8 shows the configuration.

The main Flume Master screen displays all of the Nodes and their configured data sources and sinks, as shown in figure 2.9.

All the actions you just performed can be executed in the Flume shell. Here's an example of how you can view the same information that you just saw in the UI. To better identify the text you entered, the shell prompts are surrounded by square brackets. Your first command is connect ... to connect to the Flume Master on port 35873 (the

Flume Master

Version: 0.9.4-cdh3u2, runknown
Compiled: 20111013-2105 by jenkins

ServerID: 0

Servers localhost

Node status

logical node	physical node	host name	status	version	last seen delta (s)	last seen
cdh	cdh	cdh	ACTIVE	Sun Nov 20 15:15:50 EST 2011	3	Sun Nov 20 15:25:06 EST 2011
collector	collector	cdh	ACTIVE	Sun Nov 20 15:17:22 EST 2011	0	Sun Nov 20 15:25:08 EST 2011

Node configuration

Node	Version	Flow ID	Source	Sink	Translated Version	Translated Source	Translated Sink
cdh	Sun Nov 20 15:15:50 EST 2011	default-flow	tail("/var/log/messages")	agentSink("localhost",35853)	Sun Nov 20 15:15:50 EST 2011	tail("/var/log/messages")	agentSink("localhost", 35853)
collector	Sun Nov 20 15:17:22 EST 2011	default-flow	collectorSource(35853)	collectorSink("hdfs://localhost:8020 /tmp/flume/collected/%Y/%m/%d/, "%{host}-raw")	Sun Nov 20 15:17:22 EST 2011	collectorSource(35853)	collectorSink("hdfs://localhost:8020/tmp/flume /collected/%Y/%m/%d/, "%{host}-raw")

Physical/Logical Node mapping

physical node	logical node
collector	collector
cdh	cdh

Figure 2.9 The main screen in the Flume Master UI after the configuration of your Nodes

default Flume Master port), and your second command is getconfigs, which dumps the current configuration for the Nodes:

```
$ flume shell
[flume (disconnected)] connect localhost:35873
[flume localhost:35873:45678] getconfigs
NODE        FLOW            SOURCE                     SINK
collector default-flow collectorSource(35853)       collectorSink(...)
cdh            default-flow tail("/var/log/messages") agentSink(...)
```

After you make the configuration changes in the UI, they'll be picked up by the Flume Nodes after a few seconds. The Agent will then start to pipe the syslog file, and feed the output to the Collector, which in turn will periodically write output into HDFS. Let's examine HDFS to check on the progress:

```
$ hadoop fs -lsr /tmp/flume
/tmp/flume/collected
/tmp/flume/collected/2011
/tmp/flume/collected/2011/11
/tmp/flume/collected/2011/11/20
/tmp/flume/collected/2011/11/20/cdh-raw20111120-133115126-...
/tmp/flume/collected/2011/11/20/cdh-raw20111120-134449503-...
/tmp/flume/collected/2011/11/20/cdh-raw20111120-135653300-...
...
```

We went through a whole lot of work without discussing some of the key concepts involved in setting up the data pipeline. Let's go back now and inspect the previous work in detail. The first thing we'll look at is the definition of the data source.

FLUME DATA SOURCES

A data source is required for both the Agent and Collector Nodes; it determines where they collect their data. The Agent Node's data source is your application or system data that you want to transfer to HDFS, and the Collector Node's data source is the Agent's data sink. Figure 2.10 shows a subset of data sources supported by the Agent Node.

As you can see, Flume supports a number of Agent sources, a complete list of which can be viewed on the Cloudera website http://archive.cloudera.com/cdh/3/flume/UserGuide/index.html#_flume_source_catalog. Figure 2.7 uses the tail data

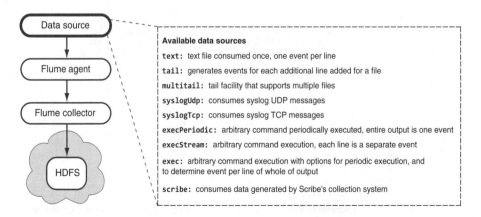

Figure 2.10   Flume Agent Node data sources supported by the Agent Node

Table 2.3   Flume Agent data sink reliability modes

Acronym	Description
E2E (end to end)	Guarantees that once an event enters Flume, the event will make its way to the end data sink.
DFO (disk failover)	Events are persisted on local disk in the event that a failure occurs when attempting to transmit the event to the downstream Node. Acknowledgement messages sent from downstream Nodes result in the persisted data being removed.
BE (best effort)	Events are dropped in the event of failed communication with a downstream Node.

source as an example, which works well for text files that are appended and rotated, specifying the file whose output you want to capture: `tail("/var/log/messages")`.

You can configure the `tail` data source to emit the complete file as events, or just start from the current end of the file. The default is to read the whole file. The `multi-tail` data source accepts a list of filenames, and the tailDir takes a directory name with a regular expression to filter files that should be tailed.

Flume also supports TCP/UDP data sources that can receive logs from syslog. Their data source names are `syslogUdp` for syslogd, and `syslogTcp` for syslog-ng.

In addition, Flume can periodically execute a command and capture its output as an event for processing, via the `execPeriodic` data source. And the `exec` data source gives you more control, allowing you to specify if each line of the processes output should be considered a separate message, or if the whole output should be considered the message. It also can be run periodically.

Flume supports a variety of other data sources out of the box as well, and it can be extended with a custom data source, as documented at http://archive.cloudera.com/cdh/3/flume/UserGuide/index.html#_arbitrary_data_flows_and_custom_architectures.

AGENT SINKS

Agent sinks are destinations for an Agent's data source. Flume offers three different levels of reliability guarantees, which are summarized in table 2.3.

Flume also has three levels of availability, as described in table 2.4. Figure 2.11 shows how the Flume failover options work. These reliability and availability modes are combined to form nine separate Agent sink options, as shown in figure 2.12.

Table 2.4   Flume failover options

Failover mode	Description
None	Configure each Agent to write to a single Collector. If the Collector goes down, the Agent waits until it comes back up again.
Manually specified failover	Configure each Agent with one or more Collectors in addition to the primary. If the primary Collector fails, the events will be routed to backup Collectors.
Automatic failover	In this mode the Flume Master will allocate failover Collectors for Agents whose Collectors fail. The advantage is that Flume balances the Agent/Collector event links to ensure that individual Collectors aren't overwhelmed. This rebalancing also occurs in normal situations where Collectors are added and removed.

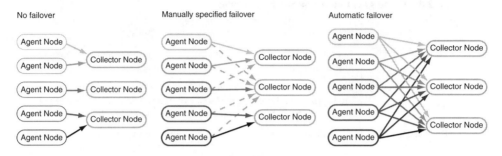

Figure 2.11 Flume failover architecture shows the three levels available.

All of these Agent sinks take as arguments the Collector Node host, and the port that it's listening on. In the example in figure 2.7 I utilized the default agentSink option, which guarantees end-to-end delivery, but has no failover support. The Collector is running on the same host, on port 35853:

```
agentSink("localhost",35853)
```

FLUME COLLECTOR DATA SINK
Flume contains a single Collector data sink, called collectorSink, which you'll configure to write to a directory on a local disk or HDFS. The sink takes two parameters: the directory, and the filename prefix for files written in that directory. Both of these arguments support the Flume functionality called *output bucketing*, which permits some macro substitutions. Let's review how to configure the Collector sink:

```
collectorSink("hdfs://localhost:8020/tmp/flume/collected/%Y/%m/%d/","%{host}-raw")
```

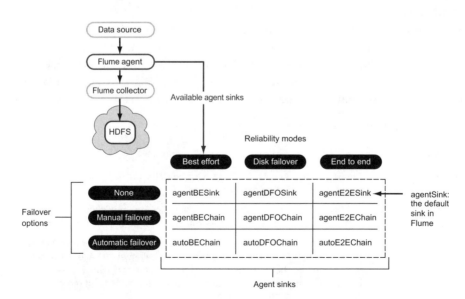

Figure 2.12 Flume Agent sinks that are available

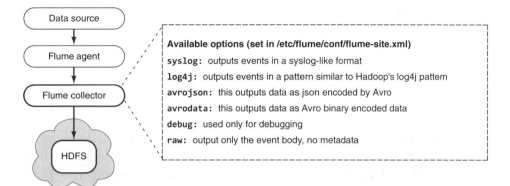

Figure 2.13 Flume Collector data sink supports a variety of output formats.

The %Y, %m, and %d are date escape sequences that are substituted with the date at which the event was received. The %{host} is substituted with the agent host that generated the event. A full list of the escape sequences is available at http://archive.cloudera.com/cdh/3/flume-0.9.1+1/UserGuide.html#_output_bucketing.

The Collection data sink supports a variety of output formats for events, some of which are shown in figure 2.13.

Earlier in this chapter you created a flume-site.xml file and specified raw as your output format. By default Flume chooses avrojson, an example of which is shown in the following code. The body field contains the raw contents of a single line from the syslog:

```
{
  "body":"Nov 20 13:25:40 cdh aholmes: Flume test",
  "timestamp":1321813541326,
  "pri":"INFO",
  "nanos":2748053914369042,
  "host":"cdh",
  "fields": {
    "AckTag":"20111120-132531557-0500.2748044145743042.00000145",
    "AckType":"msg",
    "AckChecksum":"\u0000\u0000\u0000\u00004\u0002?g",
    "tailSrcFile":"messages",
    "rolltag":"20111120-132532809-0500.2748045397574042.00000021"
  }
}
```

This approach uses Flume to show how to capture syslog appends and write them into HDFS. You can use this same approach for a variety of line-based text files.

Summary

We've used Flume on a single machine, using the default configuration settings, which assumes everything runs on the local host and on standard ports. In a fully distributed setup the Node hosts would need to specify where the Flume Master is located in flume-site.xml, as the next example demonstrates. Consult the user guide for more details at http://goo.gl/8YNsU.

```
<?xml version="1.0"?>
<?xml-stylesheet type="text/xsl"  href="configuration.xsl"?>

<configuration>
  <property>
    <name>flume.master.servers</name>
    <value>flume-master1,flume-master2,flume-master3</value>
  </property>
</configuration>
```

How do you determine the number of Flume masters that you should run? Let's say you want to be able to support the failure of two master Flume nodes. To figure out the number of Flume masters you should run, take the number of Flume master nodes that could fail, double it, and add 1. Flume uses an embedded ZooKeeper in each of the Master daemons, but you can configure it to use an external ZooKeeper if one already exists in your environment.

If you're capturing Apache logs, you can configure the web server to launch a Flume ad hoc Node and pipe the log output directly to Flume. If that Node is talking to a remote Collector, then, unfortunately, the client Node can't be configured for automatic failover or end-to-end reliability, because the Node can't be managed by the Flume Master. The workaround to this is to have the ad hoc Node forward to a local Flume Agent Node, which can have these reliability and failover properties.

Flume also includes a log4j appender, and you can find more details on this at http://archive.cloudera.com/cdh/3/flume/UserGuide/index.html#_logging_via_log4j_directly.

Using Flume for log distribution has many advantages over its peers, primarily because of its high level of documentation, its ease of use, and its customizable reliability modes.

We've looked at an automated way to shuttle log data into HDFS. But now imagine that the data you want to move into Hadoop isn't log data, but instead data that these tools have a harder time working with, such as semistructured or binary files.

2.2.2   *Pushing and pulling semistructured and binary files*

You've learned how to use log collecting tools like Flume to automate moving data into HDFS. But these tools don't support working with semistructured or binary data out of the box. This section looks at techniques to help you automate moving such files into HDFS.

Production networks typically have network silos where your Hadoop clusters are segmented away from other production applications. In such cases it's possible that your Hadoop cluster isn't able to pull data from other data sources, leaving you only the option to push data into Hadoop.

You need a mechanism to automate the process of copying files of any format into HDFS, similar to the Linux tool rsync. The mechanism should be able to compress files written in HDFS and offer a way to dynamically determine the HDFS destination for data partitioning purposes.

An automated mechanism to copy files into HDFS

Existing file transportation mechanisms such as Flume, Scribe, and Chukwa are geared towards supporting log files. What if you have different file formats for your files, such as semistructured or binary? If the files were siloed in a way that the Hadoop slave nodes couldn't directly access, then you couldn't use Oozie to help with file ingress either.

Problem

You need to automate the process by which files on remote servers are copied into HDFS.

Solution

The HDFS File Slurper open source project can copy files of any format in and out of HDFS. This technique covers how it can be configured and used to copy data into HDFS.

Discussion

You can use the HDFS File Slurper project that I wrote[2] to assist with your automation. The HDFS File Slurper is a simple utility that supports copying files from a local directory into HDFS and vice versa. Figure 2.14 provides a high-level overview of the Slurper (my nickname for the project), with an example of how you can use it to copy files. The Slurper reads any files that exist in a source directory and optionally consults with a script to determine the file placement in the destination directory. It then writes the file to the destination, after which there's an optional verification step. Finally, the

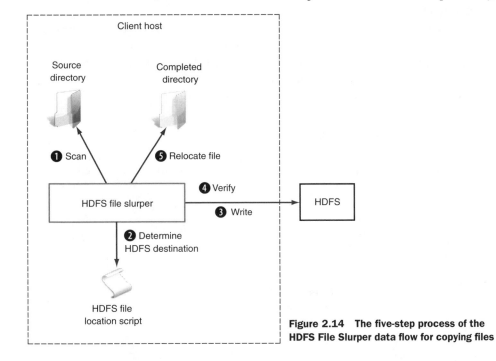

Figure 2.14 The five-step process of the HDFS File Slurper data flow for copying files

---

2 See https://github.com/alexholmes/hdfs-file-slurper.

Slurper moves the source file to a completed folder upon successful completion of all of the previous steps.

With this technique there are a few challenges you need to make sure you address:

- How do you effectively partition your writes to HDFS so that you don't lump everything into a single directory?
- How do you determine that your data is ready in HDFS for processing in order to avoid reading files that are mid-copy?
- How do you automate regular execution of your utility?

The first step is to download and build the code. The following assumes that you have git, Java, and version 3.0 or newer of Maven installed locally:

```
$ git clone git://github.com/alexholmes/hdfs-file-slurper.git
$ cd hdfs-file-slurper/
$ mvn package
```

Next you'll need to untar the tarball that the build created under /usr/local:

```
$ sudo tar -xzf target/hdfs-slurper-<version>-package.tar.gz \
  -C /usr/local/

$ sudo ln -s /usr/local/hdfs-slurper-<version> /usr/local/hdfs-slurper
```

CONFIGURATION

Before you can run the code you'll need to edit /usr/local/hdfs-slurper/conf/slurper-env.sh and set the Java home and Hadoop home directories.

The Slurper comes bundled with a /usr/local/hdfs-slurper/conf/slurper.conf, which contains details on the source and destination directory, along with other options. The file contains the following default settings, which you can change:

A name for the data being transferred. This is used for the log filename when launched via the Linux init daemon management system, which we'll cover shortly.

```
DATASOURCE_NAME = test
```

The source directory. Any files that are moved into here are automatically copied to the destination directory (with an intermediary hop to the staging directory).

The work directory. Files from the source directory are moved into this directory before the copy to the destination starts.

```
SRC_DIR = file:/tmp/slurper/in
```

```
WORK_DIR = file:/tmp/slurper/work
```

After the copy has completed, the file is moved from the work directory into the complete directory. Alternatively the REMOVE_AFTER_COPY setting can be used to delete the source file, in which case the COMPLETE_DIR setting shouldn't be supplied.

```
COMPLETE_DIR = file:/tmp/slurper/complete
```

Any errors encountered during the copy result in the source file being moved into this directory.

ERROR_DIR = file:/tmp/slurper/error

Staging directory. Files are first copied into this directory in the destination file system, and then the slurper performs an atomic move into the destination after the file has been copied.

DEST_DIR = hdfs:/tmp/slurper/dest

Final destination directory for source files.

DEST_STAGING_DIR = hdfs:/tmp/slurper/stage

You'll notice that all of the directory names are HDFS URIs. HDFS distinguishes between different filesystems in this way. The file:/ URI denotes a path on the local filesystem, and the hdfs:/ URI denotes a path in HDFS. In fact, the Slurper supports any Hadoop filesystem, as long as you configure Hadoop to use it.

RUNNING

Let's use the default settings, create a local directory called /tmp/slurper/in, write an empty file into it, and run the utility. If you're running your environment on a Hadoop distribution other than CDH, the HADOOP_HOME environment variable needs to be set with the location of your Hadoop installation:

```
$ mkdir -p /tmp/slurper/in
$ touch /tmp/slurper/in/test-file.txt

$ cd /usr/local/hdfs-slurper/
$ bin/slurper.sh  --config-file conf/slurper.conf

Copying source file 'file:/tmp/slurper/work/test-file.txt'
to staging destination 'hdfs:/tmp/slurper/stage/1354823335'

Moving staging file 'hdfs:/tmp/slurper/stage/1354823335'
to destination 'hdfs:/tmp/slurper/dest/test-file.txt'

File copy successful, moving source
file:/tmp/slurper/work/test-file.txt to completed file
file:/tmp/slurper/complete/test-file.txt

$ hadoop fs -ls /tmp/slurper/dest
/tmp/slurper/dest/test-file.txt
```

A key feature in the Slurper's design is that it doesn't work with partially written files. Files must be atomically moved into the source directory (file moves in both the Linux[3] and HDFS filesystems are atomic). Alternatively, you can write to a filename that starts with a period (.), which is ignored by the Slurper, and after the file write completes, you'd rename the file to a name without the period prefix.

Another key consideration with the Slurper is the assurance that files being copied are globally unique. If they aren't, the Slurper will overwrite that file in HDFS, which is likely an undesirable outcome.

---

[3] Moving files is atomic only if both the source and destination are on the same partition. In other words, moving a file from a NFS mount to a local disk results in a copy, which isn't atomic.

DYNAMIC DESTINATION PATHS

The previous approach works well if you're working with a small number of files that you're moving into HDFS on a daily basis. But if you're dealing with a large volume of files you want to think about partitioning them into separate directories. This has the benefit of giving you more finely grained control over the input data for your MapReduce jobs, as well as helping with the overall organization of your data in the filesystem (you wouldn't want all the files on your computer to reside in a single flat directory).

How can you have more dynamic control over the destination directory and the filename that the Slurper uses? The Slurper configuration file (slurper.conf) has a SCRIPT option (which is mutually exclusive of the DEST_DIR option), where you can specify a script that can provide that dynamic mapping of the source files to destination files.

Let's assume that the files you're working with contain a date in the filename, and you've decided that you want to organize your data in HDFS by date. Let's write a script that can perform this mapping activity. The following example is a Python script that does this:

```python
#!/usr/bin/python

import sys, os, re

# read the local file from standard input
input_file=sys.stdin.readline()

# extract the filename from the file
filename = os.path.basename(input_file)

# extract the date from the filename
match=re.search(r'([0-9]{4})([0-9]{2})([0-9]{2})', filename)

year=match.group(1)
mon=match.group(2)
day=match.group(3)

# construct our destination HDFS file
hdfs_dest="hdfs:/data/%s/%s/%s/%s" % (year, mon, day, filename)

# write it to standard output
print hdfs_dest,
```

Now you can update /usr/local/hdfs-slurper/conf/slurper.conf, set SCRIPT, and comment out DEST_DIR, which results in the following changes to the file:

```
# DEST_DIR = hdfs:/tmp/slurper/dest

SCRIPT = /usr/local/hdfs-slurper/bin/sample-python.py
```

Run the Slurper again and see what happens:

```
$ touch /tmp/slurper/in/apache-20110202.log

$ bin/slurper.sh  --config-file conf/slurper.conf

Copying source file 'file:/tmp/slurper/work/apache-2011-02-02.log' to
staging destination 'hdfs:/slurper/staging/1787301476'

Moving staging file 'hdfs:/slurper/staging/1787301476' to destination
'hdfs:/slurper/in/2011-02-02/apache-2011-02-02.log'
```

COMPRESSION AND VERIFICATION

What if you want to compress the output file in HDFS, and also verify that the copy is correct? You'd need to use the COMPRESSION_CODEC option, whose value, CompressionCodec classname, also needs to be used. The Slurper also supports verification, which rereads the destination file after the copy has completed, and ensures that the checksum of the destination file matches the source file. If you want to configure the Slurper to use Snappy for compression and verify the copy, you'd update the slurper.conf file and add the following lines:

```
COMPRESSION_CODEC = org.apache.hadoop.io.compress.SnappyCodec

VERIFY = true
```

Let's run the Slurper again:

```
$ touch /tmp/slurper/in/apache-20110202.log

$ bin/slurper.sh  --config-file conf/slurper.conf

Verifying files
CRC's match (0)
Moving staging file 'hdfs:/tmp/slurper/stage/535232571'
to destination 'hdfs:/data/2011/02/02/apache-20110202.log.snappy'
```

CONTINUOUS OPERATION

Now that you have the basic mechanics in place, your final step is to run your tool as a daemon, so that it continuously looks for files to transfer. To do this, you'll use a script called bin/slurper-inittab.sh, which is designed to work with the inittab respawn.[4] This script won't create a PID file or perform a nohup—because neither makes sense in the context of respawn since inittab is managing the process—and uses the DATA-SOURCE_NAME configuration value to create the log filename. This means that multiple Slurper instances can all be launched with different config files logging to separate log files.

Summary

The Slurper is a handy tool for data ingress from a local filesystem to HDFS. It also supports data egress by copying from HDFS to the local filesystem. It can be useful in

---

[4] Inittab is a Linux process management tool that you can configure to supervise and restart a process if it goes down. See http://unixhelp.ed.ac.uk/CGI/man-cgi?inittab+5 .

situations where MapReduce doesn't have access to the filesystem, and the files being transferred are in a form that doesn't work with tools such as Flume.

Now let's look at automated pulls, for situations where MapReduce has access to your data sources.

TECHNIQUE 3   Scheduling regular ingress activities with Oozie

If your data is sitting on a filesystem, web server, or any other system accessible from your Hadoop cluster, you'll need a way to periodically pull that data into Hadoop. While tools exist to help with pushing log files and pulling from databases (which we'll cover in this chapter), if you need to interface with some other system, it's likely you'll need to handle the data ingress process yourself.

There are two parts to this data ingress process: the first is how you import data from another system into Hadoop, and the second is how you regularly schedule the data transfer.

Problem

You want to automate a daily task to download content from an HTTP server into HDFS.

Solution

Oozie can be used to ingress data into HDFS, and can also be used to execute post-ingress activities such as launching a MapReduce job to process the ingressed data. An Apache project, Oozie started life inside Yahoo. It's a Hadoop workflow engine that manages data processing activities. For our scenario Oozie has a coordinator engine that can start workflows based on data and time triggers.

Discussion

In this technique, you perform a download of a number of URLs every 24 hours using Oozie to manage the workflow and scheduling. The flow for this technique is shown in figure 2.15.

You'll install Oozie from the instructions in Appendix A.

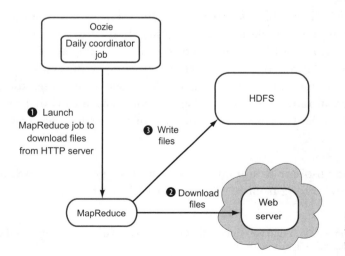

Figure 2.15   Three-step data flow for Oozie ingress to manage workflow and scheduling

You'll use Oozie's data triggering capabilities to kick off a MapReduce job every 24 hours. Oozie has the notion of a coordinator job, which can launch a workflow at fixed intervals. The first step is to look at the coordinator XML configuration file. This file is used by Oozie's Coordination Engine to determine when it should kick off a workflow. Oozie uses the JSP expression language to perform parameterization, as you'll see in the following code. Create a file called coordinator.xml with the content shown in the next listing.[5]

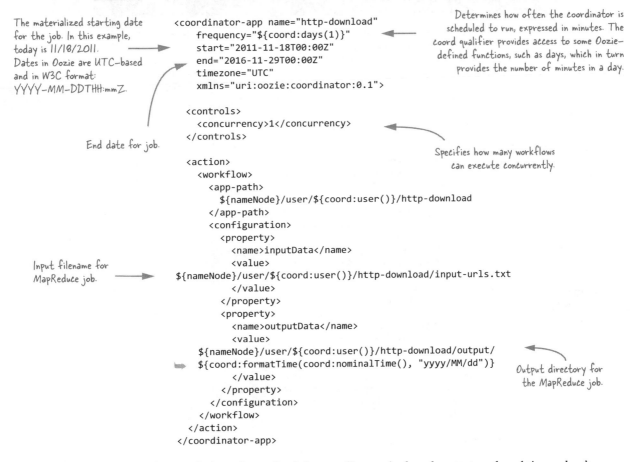

Oozie uses JSP to perform parameterization

The materialized starting date for the job. In this example, today is 11/18/2011. Dates in Oozie are UTC-based and in W3C format: YYYY-MM-DDTHH:mmZ.

Determines how often the coordinator is scheduled to run, expressed in minutes. The coord qualifier provides access to some Oozie-defined functions, such as days, which in turn provides the number of minutes in a day.

End date for job.

Specifies how many workflows can execute concurrently.

Input filename for MapReduce job.

Output directory for the MapReduce job.

```xml
<coordinator-app name="http-download"
    frequency="${coord:days(1)}"
    start="2011-11-18T00:00Z"
    end="2016-11-29T00:00Z"
    timezone="UTC"
    xmlns="uri:oozie:coordinator:0.1">

  <controls>
    <concurrency>1</concurrency>
  </controls>

  <action>
    <workflow>
      <app-path>
        ${nameNode}/user/${coord:user()}/http-download
      </app-path>
      <configuration>
        <property>
          <name>inputData</name>
          <value>
${nameNode}/user/${coord:user()}/http-download/input-urls.txt
          </value>
        </property>
        <property>
          <name>outputData</name>
          <value>
${nameNode}/user/${coord:user()}/http-download/output/
${coord:formatTime(coord:nominalTime(), "yyyy/MM/dd")}
          </value>
        </property>
      </configuration>
    </workflow>
  </action>
</coordinator-app>
```

What can be confusing about Oozie's coordinator is that the start and end times don't relate to the actual times that the jobs will be executed. Rather, they refer to the dates that will be materialized for the workflow. This is useful in situations where you have

[5] **GitHub source**—https://github.com/alexholmes/hadoop-book/blob/master/src/main/oozie/ch2/http-download/coordinator.xml

data being generated at periodic intervals, and you want to be able to go back in time up to a certain point and perform some work on that data. In this example, you don't want to go back in time, but instead want to schedule a job periodically every 24 hours going forward. However, you won't want to wait hours until the next day, so you can set the start date to be yesterday, and the end date to be some far-off date in the future.

Next you'll need to define the actual workflow, which will be executed for every interval in the past, and going forward when the wall clock reaches an interval. To do this, create a file called workflow.xml, with the content shown here.[6]

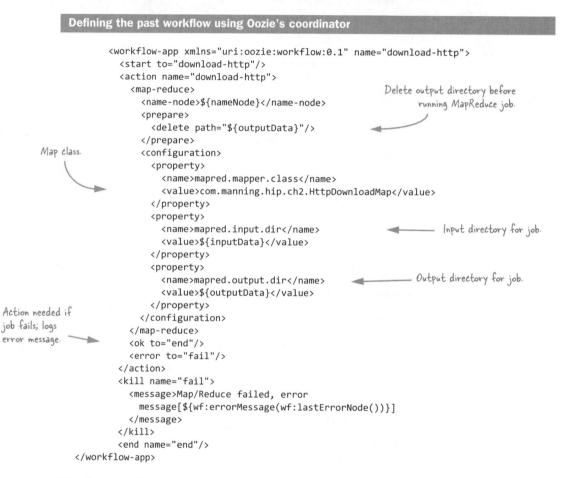

Defining the past workflow using Oozie's coordinator

```
<workflow-app xmlns="uri:oozie:workflow:0.1" name="download-http">
  <start to="download-http"/>
  <action name="download-http">
    <map-reduce>
      <name-node>${nameNode}</name-node>
      <prepare>
        <delete path="${outputData}"/>          Delete output directory before
      </prepare>                                  running MapReduce job.
      <configuration>
        <property>                               Map class.
          <name>mapred.mapper.class</name>
          <value>com.manning.hip.ch2.HttpDownloadMap</value>
        </property>
        <property>
          <name>mapred.input.dir</name>          Input directory for job.
          <value>${inputData}</value>
        </property>
        <property>
          <name>mapred.output.dir</name>         Output directory for job.
          <value>${outputData}</value>
        </property>
      </configuration>
    </map-reduce>
    <ok to="end"/>                               Action needed if
    <error to="fail"/>                           job fails; logs
  </action>                                       error message.
  <kill name="fail">
    <message>Map/Reduce failed, error
      message[${wf:errorMessage(wf:lastErrorNode())}]
    </message>
  </kill>
  <end name="end"/>
</workflow-app>
```

The last step is to define your properties file, which specifies how to get to HDFS, MapReduce, and the location of the two XML files previously identified in HDFS. Create a file called job.properties, as shown in the following code:

[6] **GitHub source**—https://github.com/alexholmes/hadoop-book/blob/master/src/main/oozie/ch2/ http-download/workflow.xml

```
nameNode=hdfs://localhost:8020
jobTracker=localhost:8021
queueName=default

oozie.coord.application.path=${nameNode}/user/${user.name}
                            /http-download
```

HDFS location of two xml files.

In the previous snippet, the oozie.coord.application.path value is the HDFS location of the coordinator.xml and workflow.xml files that you wrote earlier in this chapter. Now you need to copy the XML files, your input file, and the JAR file containing your MapReduce code into HDFS:

```
$ hadoop fs -put src/main/oozie/ch2/http-download http-download
$ hadoop fs -put test-data/ch2/http-download/input/* http-download/
$ hadoop fs -mkdir http-download/lib
$ hadoop fs -put \
  target/hadoop-book-1.0.0-SNAPSHOT-jar-with-dependencies.jar \
  http-download/lib/
```

Finally, run your job in Oozie:

```
$ oozie job -config src/main/oozie/ch2/http-download/job.properties \
  -run
job: 0000000-111119163557664-oozie-oozi-C
```

You can use the job ID to get some information about the job:

```
$ oozie job -info 0000000-111119163557664-oozie-oozi-C
Job ID : 0000000-111119163557664-oozie-oozi-C
------------------------------------------------------------------
Job Name : http-download
App Path : hdfs://user/aholmes/http-download/coordinator.xml
Status   : RUNNING
------------------------------------------------------------------
ID                                          Status    Nominal Time
0000000-111119163557664-oozie-oozi-C@1   SUCCEEDED 2011-11-18 00:00
------------------------------------------------------------------
0000000-111119163557664-oozie-oozi-C@2    SUCCEEDED 2011-11-19 00:00
------------------------------------------------------------------
```

This output tells you that the job resulted in two runs, and you can see the nominal times for the two runs. The overall state is RUNNING, which means that the job is waiting for the next interval to occur. When the overall job has completed (after the end date has been reached), the status will transition to SUCCEEDED.

Because the job ran twice you should confirm that there are two output directories in HDFS corresponding to the two materialized dates:

```
$ hadoop fs -ls http-download/output/2011/11
/user/aholmes/http-download/output/2011/11/18
/user/aholmes/http-download/output/2011/11/19
```

If you wish to stop the job, use the -suspend option:

```
$ oozie job -suspend 0000000-111119163557664-oozie-oozi-C
```

As long as the job is running, it'll continue to execute until the end date, which in this example has been set as the year 2016.

Summary

I showed you one example of the use of the Oozie coordinator, which offers cron-like capabilities to launch periodic Oozie workflows. The Oozie coordinator can also be used to trigger a workflow based on data availability. For example, if you had an external process, or even MapReduce generating data on a regular basis, you could use Oozie's data-driven coordinator to trigger a workflow, which could aggregate or process that data.

In this section we covered two automated mechanisms that can be used for data ingress purposes. The first technique covered a simple tool, the HDFS File Slurper, which automates the process of pushing data into HDFS. The second technique looked at how Oozie could be used to periodically launch a MapReduce job to pull data into HDFS or MapReduce.

These techniques are particularly helpful in situations where the data you're working with is in a binary or semistructured form, or is only accessible via interfaces such as HTTP or FTP.

At this point in our review of data ingress we've looked at pushing log files, pushing files from regular filesystems, and pulling files from web servers. Another data source that will be of interest to most organizations is relational data sitting in OLTP databases. Next up is a look at how you can access that data.

2.2.3 Pulling data from databases

Most organizations' crucial data exists across a number of OLTP databases. The data stored in these databases contains information about users, products, and a host of other useful items. If you want to analyze this data the traditional mechanism for doing so would be to periodically copy that data into a OLAP data warehouse.

Hadoop has emerged to play two roles in this space: as a replacement to data warehouses, and as a bridge between structured and unstructured data and data warehouses. Figure 2.16 shows the second role in play, where Hadoop is used as a large-scale joining and aggregation mechanism prior to export to an OLAP system (a commonly used platform for business intelligence applications).

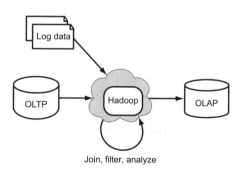

Figure 2.16   Using Hadoop for data ingress, joining, and egress to OLAP

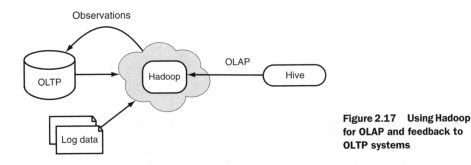

Figure 2.17 Using Hadoop for OLAP and feedback to OLTP systems

Facebook is an example of an organization that has successfully utilized Hadoop and Hive as an OLAP platform to work with petabytes of data. Figure 2.17 shows an architecture similar to that of Facebook's. This architecture also includes a feedback loop into the OLTP system, which can be used to push discoveries made in Hadoop, such as recommendations for users.

In either of the usage models shown in the previous figures, you need a way to bring relational data into Hadoop, and to also export it into relational databases. In the next techniques we'll cover two mechanisms you can use for database ingress. The first uses some built-in MapReduce classes, and the second provides an easy-to-use tool that removes the need for you to write your own code.

TECHNIQUE 4   Database ingress with MapReduce

Imagine you had valuable customer data sitting in a relational database. You used one of the previous techniques to push log data containing user activity from your web servers into HDFS. You now want to be able to do some analytics on your log data, and tie it back with your users in your relational database. How do you move your relational data into HDFS?

Problem

You want to import relational data using MapReduce.

Solution

This technique covers using the DBInputFormat class to import relational data into HDFS. It also looks at mechanisms to guard against too many concurrent connections to your relational database.

Discussion

MapReduce contains DBInputFormat and DBOutputFormat classes, which can be used to read and write data from databases via JDBC. Figure 2.18 shows the classes you'll use.

You'll work with stock data (more details about stock data are contained in the preface to this book). In chapter 3 I'll go into more details on the Writable interface and an implementation of the Writable called StockPriceWritable, which represents the stock data. The DBInputFormat class requires a bean representation of the table being imported, which implements both the Writable and DBWritable interfaces.

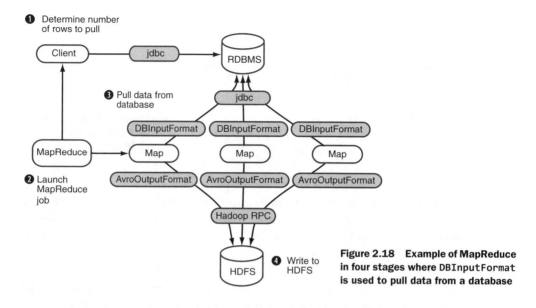

Figure 2.18   Example of MapReduce in four stages where `DBInputFormat` is used to pull data from a database

Because you'll also need to implement the `DBWritable` interface, you'll do so by extending the `StockPriceWritable` class, as shown in the following code.[7]

Extending the `StockPriceWritable` class

Array of table column names.

```
public class StockRecord extends StockPriceWritable
    implements Writable, DBWritable {
  private final static SimpleDateFormat sdf =
    new SimpleDateFormat("yyyy-MM-dd");
  public static String [] fields = { "symbol", "quote_date",
    "open_price", "high_price", "low_price", "close_price",
    "volume", "adj_close_price"};

  @Override
  public void readFields(ResultSet resultSet)
    throws SQLException {
    int idx=2;
    setSymbol(resultSet.getString(idx++));
    setDate(sdf.format(resultSet.getDate(idx++)));
    setOpen(resultSet.getDouble(idx++));
    setHigh(resultSet.getDouble(idx++));
    setLow(resultSet.getDouble(idx++));
    setClose(resultSet.getDouble(idx++));
    setVolume(resultSet.getInt(idx++));
    setAdjClose(resultSet.getDouble(idx));
  }
}
```

The implementation of the `DBWritable` interface's `readFields` method, which supplies a JDBC ResultSet. Read the values from it and set the bean properties.

---

[7] **GitHub source**—https://github.com/alexholmes/hadoop-book/blob/master/src/main/java/com/manning/hip/ch2/StockRecord.java

```
@Override
public void write(PreparedStatement statement)
    throws SQLException {
  int idx=1;
  statement.setString(idx++, getSymbol());
  try {
    statement.setDate(idx++,
        new Date(sdf.parse(getDate()).getTime()));
  } catch (ParseException e) {
    throw new SQLException("Failed to convert String to date", e);
  }
  statement.setDouble(idx++, getOpen());
  statement.setDouble(idx++, getHigh());
  statement.setDouble(idx++, getLow());
  statement.setDouble(idx++, getClose());
  statement.setInt(idx++, getVolume());
  statement.setDouble(idx, getAdjClose());
}
}
```

The implementation of the DBWritable interface's write method, which supplies a JDBC PreparedStatement. Write the bean properties to the statement.

Note that the array of column names in the previous code will be used later in your MapReduce configuration.

The MapReduce job, shown in the following listing,[8] will import from one table and write data into HDFS in Avro form.[9]

MapReduce job using `DBInputFormat` to import data from a relational database into HDFS

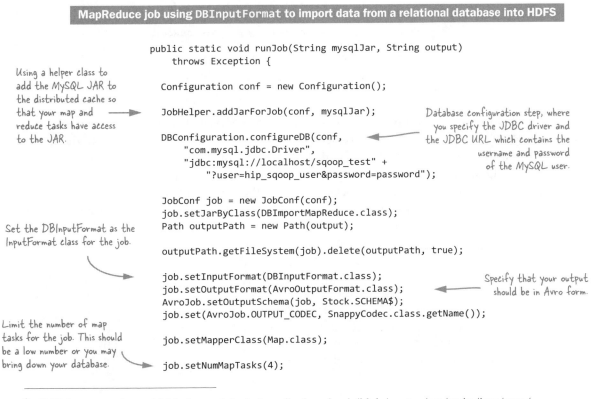

```
public static void runJob(String mysqlJar, String output)
    throws Exception {

  Configuration conf = new Configuration();

  JobHelper.addJarForJob(conf, mysqlJar);

  DBConfiguration.configureDB(conf,
      "com.mysql.jdbc.Driver",
      "jdbc:mysql://localhost/sqoop_test" +
          "?user=hip_sqoop_user&password=password");

  JobConf job = new JobConf(conf);
  job.setJarByClass(DBImportMapReduce.class);
  Path outputPath = new Path(output);

  outputPath.getFileSystem(job).delete(outputPath, true);

  job.setInputFormat(DBInputFormat.class);
  job.setOutputFormat(AvroOutputFormat.class);
  AvroJob.setOutputSchema(job, Stock.SCHEMA$);
  job.set(AvroJob.OUTPUT_CODEC, SnappyCodec.class.getName());

  job.setMapperClass(Map.class);

  job.setNumMapTasks(4);
```

Using a helper class to add the MySQL JAR to the distributed cache so that your map and reduce tasks have access to the JAR.

Database configuration step, where you specify the JDBC driver and the JDBC URL which contains the username and password of the MySQL user.

Set the DBInputFormat as the InputFormat class for the job.

Specify that your output should be in Avro form.

Limit the number of map tasks for the job. This should be a low number or you may bring down your database.

---

[8] **GitHub source**—https://github.com/alexholmes/hadoop-book/blob/master/src/main/java/com/manning/hip/ch2/DBImportMapReduce.java

[9] Avro is a data serialization library that we'll discuss in detail in chapter 3.

```
            job.setNumReduceTasks(0);
```
You want a map-only job, so set the reducers to 0.

```
            job.setMapOutputKeyClass(AvroWrapper.class);
            job.setMapOutputValueClass(NullWritable.class);

            job.setOutputKeyClass(AvroWrapper.class);
            job.setOutputValueClass(NullWritable.class);

            FileOutputFormat.setOutputPath(job, outputPath);
```

Specify your class that implements DBWritable, and also indicate the query to fetch the rows, as well as the query to determine the number of rows to fetch.

```
            DBInputFormat.setInput(
                job,
                StockRecord.class,
                "select * from stocks",
                "SELECT COUNT(id) FROM stocks");

            JobClient.runJob(job);
        }

        public static class Map implements
                Mapper<LongWritable, StockRecord,
                        AvroWrapper<Stock>, NullWritable> {

            public void map(LongWritable key,
                            StockRecord value,
                            OutputCollector<AvroWrapper<Stock>,
                                            NullWritable> output,
                            Reporter reporter) throws IOException {
                output.collect(
                    new AvroWrapper<Stock>(writableToAvro(value)),
                    NullWritable.get());
            }
        }
    }
```

Convert your Stock in Writable form into the Avro form and emit in your mapper.

Before you can continue, you'll need access to a MySQL database and have the MySQL JDBC JAR available.[10] You have access to a script (see note) that will create the necessary MySQL user and schema, and load the data for this technique. The script creates a hip_sqoop_user MySQL user, and creates a sqoop_test database with three tables: stocks, stocks_export, and stocks_staging. It then loads the stocks sample data (more details in the preface) into the stocks table. All of these steps are performed by running the following command:

```
$ bin/prep-sqoop-mysql.sh
```

Scripts, source code, and test data

All of the code in this book, sample data, and scripts (such as run.sh) to run the code are contained in the GitHub repository at https://github.com/alexholmes/hadoop-book. The preface has instructions to download, build, and run the examples.

---

[10] MySQL installation instructions can be found in appendix A, if you don't already have it installed. That section also includes a link to get the JDBC JAR.

Here's a quick peek at what the script did with the following MySQL client commands:

```
$ mysql
mysql> use sqoop_test;
mysql> show tables;
+----------------------+
| Tables_in_sqoop_test |
+----------------------+
| stocks               |
| stocks_export        |
| stocks_staging       |
+----------------------+
3 rows in set (0.00 sec)
mysql> select * from stocks;
+----+--------+------------+------------+------------+-----------+---
| id | symbol | quote_date | open_price | high_price | low_price |...
+----+--------+------------+------------+------------+-----------+---
|  1 | AAPL   | 2009-01-02 |      85.88 |      91.04 |     85.16 |...
|  2 | AAPL   | 2008-01-02 |     199.27 |     200.26 |    192.55 |...
|  3 | AAPL   | 2007-01-03 |      86.29 |      86.58 |      81.9 |...
    ...
```

Now you're ready to run your MapReduce job. The utility run.sh will launch the DBImportMapReduce MapReduce job, as shown in the following code:

Add MySQL JDBC JAR to Hadoop
classpath so it's available in client code.

Fully qualified Java
class you'll run.

Script to use
throughout book to run
your examples.

```
$ export HADOOP_CLASSPATH=<mysql-connector-jar>
$ bin/run.sh \
    com.manning.hip.ch2.DBImportMapReduce \
    <mysql-connector-jar> \
    output
```

Output directory
for MapReduce job.

MySQL JDBC JAR to use to
communicate with MySQL server.

The result of this MapReduce job is a number of Avro files in the job output directory containing the results of the SQL query. The AvroStockFileRead class, which we'll examine in chapter 3, can be used to view the contents of the Avro files:

```
$ hadoop fs -ls output
/user/aholmes/output/part-00000.avro
/user/aholmes/output/part-00001.avro
/user/aholmes/output/part-00002.avro
/user/aholmes/output/part-00003.avro

$ bin/run.sh com.manning.hip.ch3.avro.AvroStockFileRead \
    output/part-00000.avro

MSFT,2001-01-02,44.13,45.0,42.88,43.38,82413200,17.73
MSFT,2000-01-03,117.37,118.62,112.0,116.56,53228400,47.64
YHOO,2009-01-02,12.17,12.85,12.12,12.85,9514600,12.85
    ...
```

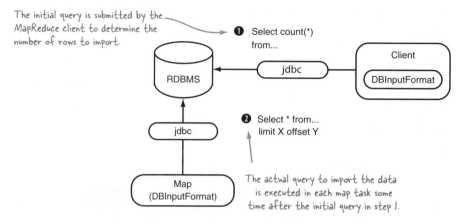

The initial query is submitted by the MapReduce client to determine the number of rows to import.

❶ Select count(*) from...

jdbc

RDBMS

Client

DBInputFormat

jdbc

❷ Select * from... limit X offset Y

Map (DBInputFormat)

The actual query to import the data is executed in each map task some time after the initial query in step 1.

Figure 2.19   The two-step process of SQL queries used for import

There's one file per map task and each contains a subset of the data that has been imported.

Summary

There are several important considerations to bear in mind when using this technique. First, you need to make sure that you don't run with too many map tasks, because bombarding your database with thousands of concurrent reads will probably bring the DBA knocking on your door.

You should also ensure that your import and count queries are idempotent. Figure 2.19 illustrates the time differences between when the initial count query is executed as part of job submission and the subsequent queries from the map tasks. If data in the table being exported is inserted or deleted, you'll likely get duplicate records and potentially worse side effects. Therefore, either perform the import against an immutable table, or carefully choose your queries to guarantee that the results won't change during the import.

As the figure 2.19 indicates, because multiple mappers will be running with differing LIMIT and OFFSET settings, the query should be written in a way that will ensure consistent and repeatable ordering in mind, which means that the query needs to leverage a unique key, such as a primary key.

Phew! Importing data from a relational database seems more involved than it should be—which makes you wonder if there's a better way to perform the import.

TECHNIQUE 5   Using Sqoop to import data from MySQL

The previous technique required a fair amount of work as you had to implement the Writable and DBWritable interfaces, and then write a MapReduce job to perform the import. Surely there's an easier way to import relational data!

Problem

You want to load relational data into your cluster and ensure your writes are efficient and at the same time idempotent.

Solution

In this technique, we'll look at how to use Sqoop as a simple mechanism to bring relational data into Hadoop clusters. We'll walk through the process of importing data from MySQL into Sqoop. We'll also cover methods for using the regular connector, as well as how to do bulk imports using the fast connector.

Discussion

Sqoop is a relational database import and export system. It was created by Cloudera, and is currently an Apache project in incubation status.

When you perform an import, Sqoop can write to HDFS, Hive, or HBase, and for exports it can do the reverse. Importing is broken down into two activities: connecting to the data source to gather some statistics, and then firing off a MapReduce job, which performs the actual import. Figure 2.20 shows these steps.

Sqoop has the notion of *Connectors*, which contain the specialized logic to read and write to external systems. Sqoop comes with two classes of connectors: a *common connector* for regular reads and writes, and a *fast connector* that uses database-proprietary batch mechanisms for efficient imports. Figure 2.21 shows these two classes of connectors and the databases that they support.

To get started, you'll need to install Sqoop, and the instructions for this are covered in appendix A. I recommend you read these instructions because they also contain steps for installing Sqoop dependencies, such as MySQL JDBC drivers. We covered

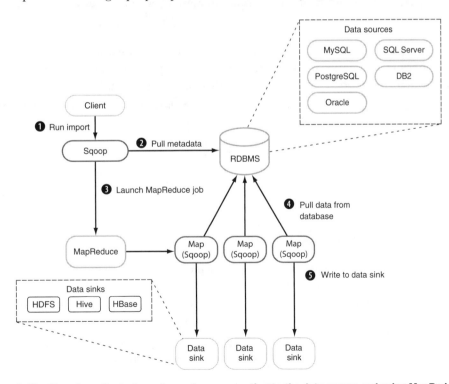

Figure 2.20   Five-stage Sqoop import overview: connecting to the data source and using MapReduce to write to a data sink

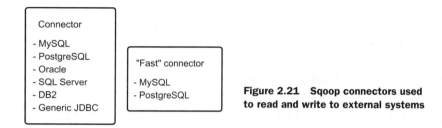

Figure 2.21   **Sqoop connectors used to read and write to external systems**

how to get MySQL installed and configured with the database, tables, and users in the previous technique, so if you haven't already done this step, go back and follow those instructions as well.

The first Sqoop command will be a basic import, where you'll specify connection information about your MySQL database, and the table you want to export:

```
$ sqoop import --username hip_sqoop_user --password password \
    --connect jdbc:mysql://localhost/sqoop_test --table stocks
```

MYSQL TABLE NAMES
MySQL table names in Linux are case sensitive. Make sure that the table name you supply in the Sqoop commands is also case sensitive.

It's generally not a good idea to have database passwords as arguments to a script because that allows other users to see your password using commands, such as ps, when the import is occurring. It'll also enter your shell history file. A best practice to follow is to write the password in Sqoop's option file and ensure that only you have read permissions on it:

```
$ cat > ~/.sqoop_import_options.txt << EOF
import
--username
hip_sqoop_user
--password
password
EOF
$ chmod 700 ~/.sqoop_import_options.txt
```

Sqoop also supports a -P option, which when present will result in you being prompted for the password.

Run the command again, this time specifying the options file you've created:

```
$ hadoop fs -rmr stocks
$ sqoop --options-file ~/.sqoop_import_options.txt \
    --connect jdbc:mysql://localhost/sqoop_test --table stocks
```

You may wonder why you had to delete the stocks directory in HDFS before rerunning the import command. Sqoop by default uses the table name as the destination in HDFS for the MapReduce job that it launches to perform the import. If you run the same command again, the MapReduce job will fail because the directory already exists. Let's take a look at the stocks directory in HDFS:

```
$ hadoop fs -ls stocks
624 2011-11-24 11:07 /user/aholmes/stocks/part-m-00000
644 2011-11-24 11:07 /user/aholmes/stocks/part-m-00001
642 2011-11-24 11:07 /user/aholmes/stocks/part-m-00002
686 2011-11-24 11:07 /user/aholmes/stocks/part-m-00003

$ hadoop fs -cat stocks/part-m-00000
1,AAPL,2009-01-02,85.88,91.04,85.16,90.75,26643400,90.75
2,AAPL,2008-01-02,199.27,200.26,192.55,194.84,38542100,194.84
3,AAPL,2007-01-03,86.29,86.58,81.9,83.8,44225700,83.8
...
```

IMPORT DATA FORMATS

Sqoop has imported your data as comma-separated text files. It supports a number of other file formats, which can be activated with the arguments listed in table 2.5. If you're importing large amounts of data you may want to use a file format such as Avro, which is a compact data format, and use it in conjunction with compression. The following example uses the Snappy compression codec in conjunction with Avro files:

```
$ hadoop fs -rmr stocks
$ sqoop --options-file ~/.sqoop_import_options.txt \
       --as-avrodatafile \
       --compress \
       --compression-codec org.apache.hadoop.io.compress.SnappyCodec\
       --connect jdbc:mysql://localhost/sqoop_test  \
       --table stocks
```

Note that the compression that's supplied on the command line must be defined in the config file, core-site.xml, under the property io.compression.codecs. The Snappy compression codec requires you to have the Hadoop native libraries installed. See chapter 5 for more details on compression setup and configuration.

You can introspect the structure of the Avro file to see how Sqoop has laid out the records by using an Avro dumper tool that I created. Sqoop uses Avro's GenericRecord

Table 2.5 Sqoop arguments that control the file formats of import commands

Argument	Description
--as-avrodatafile	Data is imported as Avro files.
--as-sequencefile	Data is imported as SequenceFiles.
--as-textfile	The default file format, with imported data as CSV text files.

for record-level storage (more details on that in chapter 3). If you run your generic Avro dumper utility against the Sqoop-generated files in HDFS you'll see the following:

```
$ bin/run.sh com.manning.hip.ch3.avro.AvroGenericFileDumper \
  stocks/part-m-00000.avro
{"id": 1, "symbol": "AAPL", "quote_date": "2009-01-02",
 "open_price": 85.88, "high_price": 91.04, "low_price": 85.16,
 "close_price": 90.75, "volume": 26643400, "adj_close_price": 90.75}
...
```

> **Using Sqoop in conjunction with SequenceFiles**
>
> One of the things that makes SequenceFiles hard to work with is that there isn't a generic way to access data in a SequenceFile. You must have access to the Writable class that was used to write the data. In Sqoop's case it code-generates this file. This introduces a major problem: if you move to a newer version of Sqoop, and that version modifies the code generator, there's a good chance your older, code-generated class won't work with SequenceFiles generated with the newer version of Sqoop. You'll either need to migrate all of your old SequenceFiles to the new version, or have code which can work with different versions of these SequenceFiles. Due to this restriction I don't recommend using SequenceFiles with Sqoop. If you're looking for more information on how SequenceFiles work, run the Sqoop import tool and look at the stocks.java file that's generated within your working directory.

In reality you'll more likely want to periodically import a subsection of your tables based on a query. But what if you want to import all of the Apple and Google stocks in 2007 and stick them into a custom HDFS directory? The following code shows how you would do this with Sqoop:

Store your query in variable query. The $CONDITIONS is a Sqoop macro that must be present in the WHERE clause of the query. It's used by Sqoop to substitute LIMIT and OFFSET options when issuing mySql queries.

Bash by default performs globbing, meaning that it'll expand wildcards like "*". You use this command to turn this off so that the next line generates the SQL correctly.

```
$ hadoop fs -rmr 2007-stocks
$ GLOBIGNORE=*
$ read -d '' query << "EOF"
select * from stocks
where symbol in ("AAPL", "GOOG")
  and quote_date between "2007-01-01" AND "2007-12-31"
  AND $CONDITIONS
EOF

$ sqoop --options-file ~/.sqoop_import_options.txt \
    --query "$query" \
    --split-by id \
    --target-dir /user/aholmes/2007-stocks \
    --connect jdbc:mysql://localhost/sqoop_test
```

This argument must be supplied so that Sqoop can determine which table column to use for splitting.

The `--query` SQL shown in the previous snippet can also be used to include only a subset of the columns in a table to be imported.

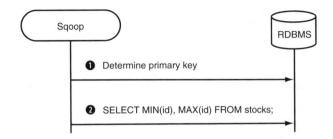

Figure 2.22 Sqoop preprocessing in two steps to determine query splits

DATA SPLITTING

How is Sqoop able to parallelize imports across multiple mappers?[11] In figure 2.20 I showed how Sqoop's first step is to pull metadata from the database. It inspects the table being imported to determine the primary key and runs a query to determine the lower and upper bounds of the data in the table (shown in figure 2.22). A somewhat even distribution of data within the minimum and maximum keys is assumed by dividing the delta by the number of mappers. Each mapper is then fed a unique query containing a range of the primary key.

You can configure Sqoop to use a nonprimary key with the `--split-by` argument. This can be useful in situations where the primary key doesn't have an even distribution of values between the min and max values. For large tables, however, you need to be careful that the column specified in `--split-by` is indexed to ensure optimal import times.

You can use the `--boundary-query` argument to construct an alternative query to determine the minimum and maximum values.

INCREMENTAL IMPORTS

You can also perform incremental imports. Sqoop supports two types, *append*, which works for numerical data that's incrementing over time, such as auto-increment keys; and *lastmodified*, which works on timestamped data. In both cases you need to specify the column using `--check-column`, the mode via the `--incremental` argument (the value must be either `append` or `lastmodified`), and finally, the actual value to use to determine the incremental changes, `--last-value`. Using the example, if you want to import stock data that's newer than January 1, 2005, you'd do the following:

```
$ hadoop fs -rmr stocks
$ sqoop --options-file ~/.sqoop_import_options.txt \
  --check-column "quote_date" \
  --incremental "lastmodified" \
  --last-value "2005-01-01" \
  --connect jdbc:mysql://localhost/sqoop_test \
  --table stocks
...
```

---

[11] By default Sqoop runs with four mappers. The number of mappers can be controlled with the `--num-mappers` argument.

```
tool.ImportTool:  --incremental lastmodified
tool.ImportTool:  --check-column quote_date
tool.ImportTool:  --last-value 2011-11-24 14:49:56.0
tool.ImportTool: (Consider saving this with 'sqoop job --create')
...
```

SQOOP JOBS AND THE METASTORE

You can see in the command output the last value that was encountered for the increment column. How can you best automate a process that can reuse that value? Sqoop has the notion of a *job*, which can save this information and reuse it in subsequent executions:

```
$ sqoop job --create stock_increment -- import \
  --append \
  --check-column "quote_date" \
  --incremental "lastmodified" \
  --last-value "2005-01-01" \
  --connect jdbc:mysql://localhost/sqoop_test \
  --username hip_sqoop_user \
  --table stocks
```

This merely saves the notion of this command as a job in something called the Sqoop *metastore*. A Sqoop metastore keeps track of all jobs. By default, the metastore is contained in your home directory under .sqoop, and is only used for your own jobs. If you want to share jobs, you would need to install a JDBC-compliant database and use the --meta-connect argument to specify its location when issuing job commands.

The job create command executed in the previous example didn't do anything other than add the job to the metastore. To run the job you need to explicitly execute it as shown here:

List all jobs in →
the metastore.

```
$ sqoop job --list
Available jobs:
  stock_increment
```

Executes your job. →

```
$ sqoop job --exec stock_increment
```

Shows metadata
information about
your job.

```
$ sqoop job --show stock_increment
...
incremental.last.value = 2011-11-24 15:09:38.0
...
```

The metadata includes the last value of your incremental column. This is actually the time that the command was executed, and not the last value seen in the table. If you're using this feature, make sure that the database server and any clients interacting with the server (including the Sqoop client) have their clocks synced with the Network Time Protocol (NTP).

Unfortunately, the --options-file argument, which referred to your local file with your username and password, doesn't work with jobs in Sqoop. The password also can't be specified when creating the job. Sqoop will instead prompt for the password when running the job. To make this work in an automated script you need to use Expect, a Linux automation tool, to supply the password from a local file when it detects Sqoop prompting for a password. The source of an Expect script that works with Sqoop is on GitHub at http://goo.gl/yL4KQ.

FAST MYSQL IMPORTS

What if you want to bypass JDBC altogether and use the fast MySQL Sqoop connector for a high-throughput load into HDFS? This approach uses the `mysqldump` utility shipped with MySQL to perform the load. You must make sure that `mysqldump` is in the PATH of the user running the MapReduce job. To enable use of the fast connector you must specify the `--direct` argument:

```
$ hadoop fs -rmr stocks
$ sqoop --options-file ~/.sqoop_import_options.txt \
    --direct \
    --connect jdbc:mysql://localhost/sqoop_test \
    --table stocks
```

What are the disadvantages of fast connectors? First, only MySQL and PostgreSQL are currently supported. Fast connectors also only work with text output files—specifying Avro or SequenceFile as the output format of the import won't work.

IMPORTING TO HIVE

The final step in this technique is to use Sqoop to import your data into a Hive table. The only difference between an HDFS import and a Hive import is that the Hive import has a postprocessing step where the Hive table is created and loaded, as shown in figure 2.23.

When data is loaded into Hive from an HDFS file or directory, such as in the case of Sqoop Hive imports (step 4 in the figure diagram), for the sake of efficiency, Hive moves the directory into its warehouse rather than copying the data (step 5). The HDFS directory that the Sqoop MapReduce job writes to won't exist after the import.

Hive imports are triggered via the `--hive-import` argument. Just like with the fast connector, this option isn't compatible with the `--as-avrodatafile` and `--as-sequence-file` options.

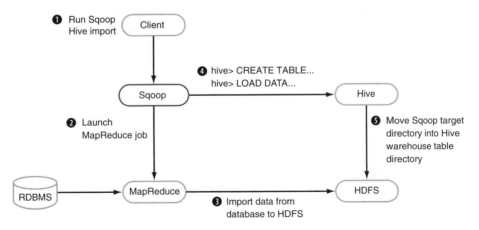

Figure 2.23   The five-stage Sqoop Hive import sequence of events

```
$ hadoop fs -rmr stocks
$ sqoop --options-file ~/.sqoop_import_options.txt \
    --hive-import \
    --connect jdbc:mysql://localhost/sqoop_test \
    --table stocks

$ hive
hive> select * from stocks;
OK
1 AAPL  2009-01-02  85.88  91.04   85.16   90.75  26643400   90.75
2 AAPL  2008-01-02 199.27 200.26  192.55  194.84  38542100  194.84
3 AAPL  2007-01-03  86.29  86.58   81.9    83.8   44225700   83.8
4 AAPL  2006-01-03  72.38  74.75   72.25   74.75  28829800   74.75
...
```

> **Importing strings containing Hive delimiters**
>
> You'll likely have downstream processing issues if you're importing columns that can contain any of Hive's delimiters (\n, \r and \01 characters). You have two options in such cases: either specify `--hive-drop-import-delims`, which will remove conflicting characters as part of the import, or specify `--hive-delims-replacement`, which will replace them with a different character.

If the Hive table already exists the data will be appended to the existing table. If this isn't the desired behavior, you can use the `--hive-overwrite` argument to indicate that the existing table should be replaced with the imported data.

Data in Hive can also be compressed. Since the LZOP compression codec is the only splittable codec[12] in Hadoop (see chapter 5 for details), it's the codec that should be used for Hive compression. The following example shows how to use the `--hive-overwrite` in conjunction with enabling LZOP compression. For this to work you'll need to have built and installed LZOP on your cluster, since it isn't bundled with Hadoop (or CDH) by default. Refer to chapter 5 for more details.

```
$ hive
hive> drop table stocks;

$ hadoop fs -rmr stocks

$ sqoop --options-file ~/.sqoop_import_options.txt \
    --hive-import \
    --hive-overwrite \
    --compress \
    --compression-codec com.hadoop.compression.lzo.LzopCodec \
    --connect jdbc:mysql://localhost/sqoop_test \
    --table stocks
```

---

[12] bzip2 is also a splittable compression codec which can be used in Hadoop, but its write performance is so poor that in practice it's rarely used.

Finally, you can use the `--hive-partition-key` and the `--hive-partition-value` to create different Hive partitions based on the value of a column being imported. For example, if you want to partition your input by date, you would do the following:

```
$ hive
hive> drop table stocks;

$ hadoop fs -rmr stocks

$ read -d '' query << "EOF"
SELECT id, quote_date, open_price
FROM stocks
WHERE symbol = "AAPL" AND $CONDITIONS
EOF

$ sqoop --options-file ~/.sqoop_import_options.txt \
    --query "$query" \
    --split-by id \
    --hive-import \
    --hive-table stocks \
    --hive-overwrite \
    --hive-partition-key symbol \
    --hive-partition-value "AAPL" \
    --connect jdbc:mysql://localhost/sqoop_test \
    --target-dir stocks

$ hadoop fs -lsr /user/hive/warehouse
/user/hive/warehouse/stocks/symbol=AAPL/part-m-00000
/user/hive/warehouse/stocks/symbol=AAPL/part-m-00001
...
```

Now, the previous example isn't optimal by any means. Ideally, a single import would be able to create multiple Hive partitions. Because you're limited to specifying a single key and value, you'd need to run the import once per unique partition value, which is laborious. You'd be better off importing into a nonpartitioned Hive table, and then retroactively creating partitions on the table after it had been loaded.

Also, the SQL query that you supply to Sqoop must also take care of filtering out the results, such that only those that match the partition are included. In other words, it would have been useful if Sqoop would have updated the WHERE clause with symbol = "AAPL" rather than having to do this yourself.

Summary

Obviously, for Sqoop to work your Hadoop cluster nodes need to have access to the MySQL database. Common sources of error are either misconfiguration or lack of connectivity from the Hadoop nodes. It's probably wise to log on to one of the Hadoop nodes and attempt to connect to the MySQL server using the MySQL client, and/or attempt access with the mysqldump utility (if using a fast connector).

Another important note when using a fast connector is that it's assumed that mysqldump is installed on each Hadoop node, and is in the PATH of the user running the map tasks.

2.2.4 *HBase*

Our final foray into the area of moving data into Hadoop is a look at HBase. HBase is a real-time, column-oriented database, and is often either co-located on the same hardware that serves as your Hadoop cluster, or is in close proximity to a Hadoop cluster. Being able to work with HBase data directly in MapReduce, or push it into HDFS, is one of the huge advantages when picking HBase as a solution.

I'll present two techniques in this section, the first focusing on how to import HBase data into HDFS, and the second on how to use HBase as a data source for a MapReduce job.

In this first technique I'll show you how to use a tool that HBase is bundled with to save an HBase table into HDFS.

TECHNIQUE 6   **HBase ingress into HDFS**

What if you had some customer data sitting in HBase that you wanted to leverage in MapReduce in conjunction with data in HDFS? You could write a MapReduce job which takes as input the HDFS dataset and pulls data directly from HBase in your map or reduce code. But in some cases it may be more useful to take a dump of the data in HBase into HDFS directly, especially if you plan to utilize that data in multiple MapReduce jobs and the HBase data is immutable, or changes infrequently.

Problem

How do you get HBase data into HDFS?

Solution

HBase includes an Export class that can be used to import HBase data into HDFS in SequenceFile format. This technique also walks through code that can be used to read the imported HBase data.

Discussion

Before we get started with this technique you first need to get HBase up and running.[13]

To be able to import data from HBase you also need to load some data into HBase. The loader I wrote creates an HBase table called stocks_example with a single column family, details. You'll store the HBase data as Avro binary-serialized data. I won't show the code here, but it's available on GitHub (https://github.com/alexholmes/hadoop-book/blob/master/src/main/java/com/manning/hip/ch2/HBaseWriteAvroStock.java).

Let's run the loader and use it to load the sample stock data into HBase:

```
$ bin/run.sh com.manning.hip.ch2.HBaseWriteAvroStock \
    test-data/stocks.txt
```

You can use the HBase shell to look at the results of the load. The list command, without any arguments, will show you all of the tables in HBase, and the scan command, with a single argument, will dump all of the contents of a table:

---

[13] Appendix A contains installation instructions and additional resources for working with HBase.

```
$ hbase shell

hbase(main):012:0> list
stocks_example
1 row(s) in 0.0100 seconds

hbase(main):007:0> scan 'stocks_example'
ROW                  COLUMN+CELL
AAPL2000-01-03       column=details:stockAvro, timestamp=1322315975123,...
AAPL2001-01-02       column=details:stockAvro, timestamp=1322315975123,...
...
```

With your data in place you're ready to export it to HDFS. HBase comes with an
org.apache.hadoop.hbase.mapreduce.Export class, which will dump an HBase table. An
example use of the Export class is shown in the following snippet, where you're exporting the whole HBase table:

HDFS directory
where exported
table is written.

```
$ bin/run.sh org.apache.hadoop.hbase.mapreduce.Export \
              stocks_example \
              output
```

HBase table
to export.

The Export class also supports exporting only a single column family, and can also
compress the following output:

Set the compression codec, in
this case Snappy. Snappy's a
good fit here since the
SequenceFile internally applies
the compression, and the
compressed content doesn't
need to be split.

Specify column family
to be exported.

```
$ bin/run.sh org.apache.hadoop.hbase.mapreduce.Export \
    -D hbase.mapreduce.scan.column.family=details \
    -D mapred.output.compress=true \
    -D mapred.output.compression.codec=\
org.apache.hadoop.io.compress.SnappyCodec \
    stocks_example output
```

Indicates the output
should be compressed.

The Export class writes the HBase output in the SequenceFile format, where the HBase
rowkey is stored in the SequenceFile record key using org.apache.hadoop.hbase
.io.ImmutableBytesWritable, and the HBase value is stored in the SequenceFile record
value using org.apache.hadoop.hbase.client.Result. What if you want to process that
exported data in HDFS? The following code shows an example of how you would read
the HBase SequenceFile and extract the Avro stock records.[14]

Reading the HBase SequenceFile to extract Avro stock records

```
...
import static com.manning.hip.ch2.HBaseWriteAvroStock.*;

public class HBaseExportedStockReader {
  public static void main(String... args) throws IOException {
    read(new Path(args[0]));
  }
```

---

[14] **GitHub source**—https://github.com/alexholmes/hadoop-book/blob/master/src/main/java/com/
manning/hip/ch2/HBaseExportedStockReader.java

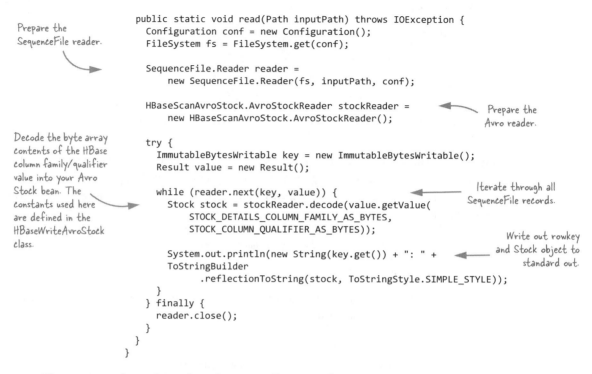

Prepare the
SequenceFile reader.

Decode the byte array
contents of the HBase
column family/qualifier
value into your Avro
Stock bean. The
constants used here
are defined in the
HBaseWriteAvroStock
class.

Prepare the
Avro reader.

Iterate through all
SequenceFile records.

Write out rowkey
and Stock object to
standard out.

```
public static void read(Path inputPath) throws IOException {
  Configuration conf = new Configuration();
  FileSystem fs = FileSystem.get(conf);

  SequenceFile.Reader reader =
      new SequenceFile.Reader(fs, inputPath, conf);

  HBaseScanAvroStock.AvroStockReader stockReader =
      new HBaseScanAvroStock.AvroStockReader();

  try {
    ImmutableBytesWritable key = new ImmutableBytesWritable();
    Result value = new Result();

    while (reader.next(key, value)) {
      Stock stock = stockReader.decode(value.getValue(
          STOCK_DETAILS_COLUMN_FAMILY_AS_BYTES,
          STOCK_COLUMN_QUALIFIER_AS_BYTES));

      System.out.println(new String(key.get()) + ": " +
      ToStringBuilder
          .reflectionToString(stock, ToStringStyle.SIMPLE_STYLE));
    }
  } finally {
    reader.close();
  }
}
```

You can run the code against the HDFS directory that you used for the export and view
the results:

```
$ bin/run.sh com.manning.hip.ch2.HBaseExportedStockReader \
  output/part-m-00000
AAPL2000-01-03: AAPL,2000-01-03,104.87,...
AAPL2001-01-02: AAPL,2001-01-02,14.88,...
AAPL2002-01-02: AAPL,2002-01-02,22.05,...
...
```

The HBaseExportedStockReader class is able to read and dump out the contents of the
SequenceFile used by HBase's Export class.

Summary

Exporting data from HBase into HDFS is made easier with the built-in HBase Export
class. But what if you don't want to write HBase data into HDFS, but instead want to
process it directly in a MapReduce job? Let's look at how to use HBase as a data source
for a MapReduce job.

> ### TECHNIQUE 7   MapReduce with HBase as a data source

The built-in HBase exporter writes out HBase data using SequenceFile, which isn't supported by programming languages other than Java, and doesn't support schema evolution. It also only supports a Hadoop filesystem as the data sink. If you want to have

more control over HBase data extracts, you may have to look beyond the built-in HBase facilities.

Problem

What if you want to operate on HBase directly within your MapReduce jobs without an intermediary step of copying the data into HDFS?

Solution

HBase has a `TableInputFormat` class that can be used in your MapReduce job to pull data directly from HBase. You will use this `InputFormat` to write Avro files in HDFS.

Discussion

The following listing shows a MapReduce job that uses `TableInputFormat` to read data from HBase. This listing writes the data into HDFS in Avro form.[15]

Importing HBase data into HDFS using MapReduce

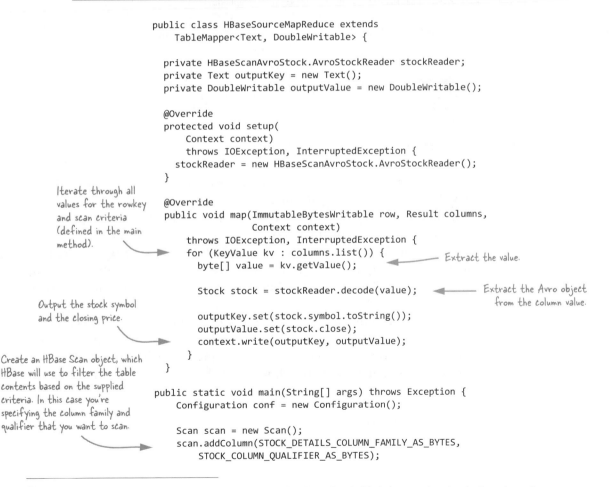

```
public class HBaseSourceMapReduce extends
    TableMapper<Text, DoubleWritable> {

  private HBaseScanAvroStock.AvroStockReader stockReader;
  private Text outputKey = new Text();
  private DoubleWritable outputValue = new DoubleWritable();

  @Override
  protected void setup(
      Context context)
      throws IOException, InterruptedException {
    stockReader = new HBaseScanAvroStock.AvroStockReader();
  }

  @Override
  public void map(ImmutableBytesWritable row, Result columns,
                  Context context)
      throws IOException, InterruptedException {
    for (KeyValue kv : columns.list()) {
      byte[] value = kv.getValue();

      Stock stock = stockReader.decode(value);

      outputKey.set(stock.symbol.toString());
      outputValue.set(stock.close);
      context.write(outputKey, outputValue);
    }
  }

  public static void main(String[] args) throws Exception {
    Configuration conf = new Configuration();

    Scan scan = new Scan();
    scan.addColumn(STOCK_DETAILS_COLUMN_FAMILY_AS_BYTES,
      STOCK_COLUMN_QUALIFIER_AS_BYTES);
```

Iterate through all values for the rowkey and scan criteria (defined in the main method).

Extract the value.

Extract the Avro object from the column value.

Output the stock symbol and the closing price.

Create an HBase Scan object, which HBase will use to filter the table contents based on the supplied criteria. In this case you're specifying the column family and qualifier that you want to scan.

---

[15] **GitHub source**—https://github.com/alexholmes/hadoop-book/blob/master/src/main/java/com/ manning/hip/ch2/HBaseSourceMapReduce.java

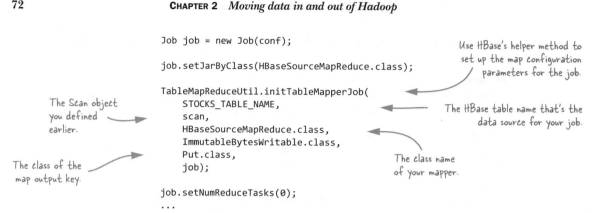

```
Job job = new Job(conf);

job.setJarByClass(HBaseSourceMapReduce.class);

TableMapReduceUtil.initTableMapperJob(
    STOCKS_TABLE_NAME,
    scan,
    HBaseSourceMapReduce.class,
    ImmutableBytesWritable.class,
    Put.class,
    job);

job.setNumReduceTasks(0);
...
```

Use HBase's helper method to set up the map configuration parameters for the job.

The Scan object you defined earlier.

The HBase table name that's the data source for your job.

The class name of your mapper.

The class of the map output key.

You can run this MapReduce job as follows:

```
$ bin/run.sh com.manning.hip.ch2.HBaseSourceMapReduce output
```

A quick peek in HDFS should tell you whether or not your MapReduce job worked as expected:

```
$ hadoop fs -cat output/part*
AAPL    111.94
AAPL    14.88
AAPL    23.3
```

This output confirms that the MapReduce job works as expected.

Summary

The `TableInputFormat` class examines HBase and creates an input split for each HBase table region. If there are ten HBase regions, ten map tasks will execute. It also includes the server that hosts the region in the input split, which means that the map tasks will be scheduled to execute on the same nodes as the HRegionServer hosting the data. This gives you locality at the HBase level and at the HDFS level. Data being read from the region will likely be coming from local disk, since after some time all of a region's data will be local to it. This all assumes that the HRegionServers are running on the same hosts as the DataNodes.

That concludes our examination of how to move data into Hadoop. We covered a broad area of data types, including log data, binary data, and relational data. We also looked at tools that help to automate data ingress in production environments.

With data ingress techniques covered, we'll switch to the subject of moving data out of Hadoop.

2.3 *Moving data out of Hadoop*

After data has been brought into Hadoop it will likely be joined with other datasets to produce some results. At this point either that result data will stay in HDFS for future access, or it will be pushed out of Hadoop. An example of this scenario would be one where you pulled some data from an OLTP database, performed some machine learning activities on that data, and then copied the results back into the OLTP database for use by your production systems.

In this section we'll cover how to automate moving regular files from HDFS to a local filesystem. We'll also look at data egress to relational databases and HBase. To start off we'll look at how to copy data out of Hadoop using the HDFS Slurper.

2.3.1 *Egress to a local filesystem*

In section 2.2.2, we looked at two mechanisms to move semistructured and binary data into HDFS, the HDFS File Slurper open source project, and Oozie to trigger a data ingress workflow. The challenge to using a local filesystem for egress (and ingress for that matter) is that map and reduce tasks running on clusters won't have access to the filesystem on a specific server. You need to leverage one of the following three broad options for moving data from HDFS to a filesystem:

1 Host a proxy tier on a server, such as a web server, which you would then write to using MapReduce.
2 Write to the local filesystem in MapReduce and then as a postprocessing step trigger a script on the remote server to move that data.
3 Run a process on the remote server to pull data from HDFS directly.

The third option is the preferred approach because it's the simplest and most efficient, and as such is the focus of this section. We'll look at how you can use the HDFS Slurper to automatically move files from HDFS out to a local filesystem.

TECHNIQUE 8 Automated file copying from HDFS

Let's say you have files being written in HDFS by MapReduce and you want to automate their extraction to a local filesystem. This kind of feature isn't supported by any Hadoop tools, so you have to look elsewhere for this task.

Problem
How do you automate moving files from HDFS to a local filesystem?

Solution
The HDFS File Slurper can also be used to copy files from HDFS to a local filesystem. This technique covers how to configure and run the HDFS File Slurper.

Discussion

The goal here is to use the HDFS File Slurper project[16] to assist with the automation. We covered the HDFS File Slurper in detail in section 2.2.2—please read that section before continuing with this technique. The HDFS Slurper also supports moving data from HDFS out to a local directory. All you need to do is flip around the source and destination directories, as you can see from the following subsection of the Slurper's configuration file:

```
SRC_DIR = hdfs:/tmp/slurper/in
WORK_DIR = hdfs:/tmp/slurper/work
COMPLETE_DIR = hdfs:/tmp/slurper/complete
ERROR_DIR = hdfs:/tmp/slurper/error
DEST_STAGING_DIR = file:/tmp/slurper/stage
DEST_DIR = file:/tmp/slurper/dest
```

You'll notice that not only is the source directory in HDFS, but also the work, complete, and error directories are there. The reason for this is that you need to be able to atomically move files between directories without incurring the expensive overhead of copying the files across filesystems.

Summary

At this point you may wonder how you can trigger the Slurper to copy a directory that was just written with a MapReduce job. When a MapReduce job completes successfully it creates a file called _SUCCESS in the job output directory. This would seem like the perfect trigger to kick off an egress process to copy that content to a local filesystem. As it turns out Oozie has a mechanism that can trigger a workflow when it detects these Hadoop "success" files, but again the challenge here is that any work performed by Oozie is performed in MapReduce, and therefore it can't be used to perform the transfer directly.

You could write your own script, which polls HDFS for completed directories and then triggers a file copy process. That file copy process could be the Slurper, or a simple *hadoop fs -get* command, if the source files need to be kept intact.

In the next topic we'll look at writing data from Hadoop out to relational databases.

2.3.2 *Databases*

Databases are usually the target of Hadoop data egress in one of two circumstances: either when you move data back into production databases to be used by production systems, or when you move data into OLAP databases to perform business intelligence and analytics functions.

In this section we'll use Apache Sqoop to export data from Hadoop to a MySQL database. Sqoop is a tool that simplifies database imports and exports. Sqoop is covered in detail in technique 5.

We'll walk through the process of exporting data from HDFS to Sqoop. We'll also cover methods using the regular connector, as well as how to do bulk imports using the fast connector.

---

[16] See https://github.com/alexholmes/hdfs-file-slurper.

Using Sqoop to export data to MySQL

Hadoop excels at performing operations at scales which defeat most relational databases, so it's common to extract OLTP data into HDFS, perform some analysis, and then export it back out to a database.

Problem

How do you write data to relational databases, and at the same time ensure that writes are idempotent?

Solution

This technique covers how Sqoop can be used to export text files to a relational database, and also looks at how it can be configured to work with files with custom field and record delimiters. We also cover idempotent exports to make sure that failed exports don't leave your database in an inconsistent state.

Discussion

This technique assumes you've already followed the instructions in technique 4 to install MySQL and create the schema.

Sqoop exports require that the database table you're exporting into already exists. Sqoop can support both inserts and updates of rows in the table.

Exporting data to a database shares many of the arguments that we examined in the import section. The differences are that exports require the `--export-dir` argument to determine the HDFS directory to export. You'll also create another options file for exports to keep from insecurely supplying the password on the command line:

```
$ cat > ~/.sqoop_export_options.txt << EOF
export
--username
hip_sqoop_user
--password
password
--connect
jdbc:mysql://localhost/sqoop_test
EOF
$ chmod 700 ~/.sqoop_export_options.txt
```

The first step will be to export data from MySQL to HDFS to ensure you have a good starting point, as seen in the following commands:

```
$ hadoop fs -rmr stocks
$ sqoop --options-file ~/.sqoop_import_options.txt \
   --connect jdbc:mysql://localhost/sqoop_test --table stocks
```

The result of the Sqoop import is a number of CSV files in HDFS, as you can see in the following code:

```
$ hadoop fs -cat stocks/part-m-00000 | head
1,AAPL,2009-01-02,85.88,91.04,85.16,90.75,26643400,90.75
2,AAPL,2008-01-02,199.27,200.26,192.55,194.84,38542100,194.84
...
```

For the Sqoop export from HDFS to MySQL, you'll specify that the target table should be stocks_export and that it should export data in the HDFS directory stocks:

```
$ sqoop --options-file ~/.sqoop_export_options.txt \
    --export-dir stocks \
    --table stocks_export
```

By default, Sqoop exports will perform an INSERT into the target database table. It can support updates with the --update-mode argument. A value of updateonly means that if there's no matching key, the updates will fail. A value of allowinsert results in an insert if a matching key doesn't exist. The table column name that's used to perform the update is supplied in the --update-key argument. The following example indicates that only an update should be attempted, using the primary key for the update:

```
$ sqoop --options-file ~/.sqoop_export_options.txt \
    --update-mode updateonly \
    --update-key id \
    --export-dir stocks \
    --table stocks_export
```

INPUT DATA FORMATTING

Several options are available that you can use to override the default Sqoop settings, which can be used to parse the input data. Table 2.6 shows these options.

IDEMPOTENT EXPORTS

The Sqoop map tasks that perform the exports use multiple transactions for their database writes. If a Sqoop export MapReduce job fails, your table could contain partial writes. For idempotent database writes Sqoop can be instructed to perform the MapReduce writes to a staging table. After successful job completion, the staging table

Table 2.6 Formatting options for input data

Argument	Default	Description
--input-enclosed-by	(None)	The field enclosing character. Every field must be enclosed with this character. (If the field enclosing character can occur inside a field, the --input-optionally-enclosed-by option should be used to enclose that field.)
--input-escaped-by	(None)	Escape character, where the next character is extracted literally, and isn't parsed.
--input-fields-terminated-by	','	The field separator.
--input-lines-terminated-by	'\n'	The line terminator
--input-optionally-enclosed-by	(None)	The field enclosing character. This argument is the same as --input-enclosed-by, except that it's applied only to fields that contain the field separator character. For example, in CSV it's common for fields to be enclosed by double quotes only when they contain commas.

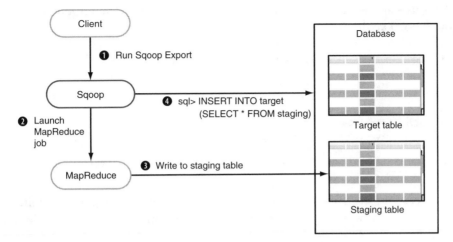

Figure 2.24   Sqoop four-stage sequence of events, which helps ensure idempotent writes

is moved to the target table in a single transaction, which is idempotent. You can see the sequence of events in figure 2.24.

In the following example the staging table is stocks_staging, and you're also telling Sqoop to clear it out before the MapReduce job starts, with the --clear-staging-table argument:

```
$ sqoop --options-file ~/.sqoop_export_options.txt \
        --export-dir stocks \
        --table stocks_export \
        --staging-table stocks_staging \
        --clear-staging-table
```

DIRECT EXPORTS
You used the fast connector in the import technique, which was an optimization that used the mysqldump utility. Sqoop exports also support using the fast connector, which uses the mysqlimport tool. All of the nodes in your cluster need to have mysqlimport installed and available in the PATH of the user that's used to run MapReduce tasks. And as with the import, the --direct argument enables utilization of the fast connectors:

```
$ sqoop --options-file ~/.sqoop_export_options.txt \
        --direct \
        --export-dir stocks \
        --table stocks_export
```

IDEMPOTENT EXPORTS WITH MYSQLIMPORT
Sqoop doesn't support using fast connectors in conjunction with a staging table, which is how idempotent writes are achieved with regular connectors. But it's still possible to achieve idempotent writes with fast connectors with a little extra work at your end. You need to use the fast connector to write to a staging table, and then trigger

the insert statement, which atomically copies the data into the target table. The steps would look like the following:

```
$ sqoop --options-file ~/.sqoop_export_options.txt \
        --direct \
        --export-dir stocks \
        --table stocks_staging

$ mysql --host=localhost \
        --user=hip_sqoop_user \
        --password=password \
        -e "INSERT INTO stocks_export (SELECT * FROM stocks_staging)"\
        sqoop_test
```

This breaks the earlier rule about exposing credentials on the command line, but it's easy to write a wrapper script that can read these settings from a configuration file.

Summary

Sqoop provides a more simplified usage model compared to using the DBInputFormat format classes that are provided in MapReduce. But using the DBInputFormat classes will give you the added flexibility to transform or preprocess your data in the same MapReduce job that performs the database export. The advantage of Sqoop is that it doesn't require you to write any code, and has some useful notions, such as staging, to help you achieve your idempotent goals.

The final step in this section and in the chapter is to look at HBase ingress and egress.

2.3.3   HBase

Apache HBase is a distributed key/value, column-oriented data store. In section 2.2.4 we looked at how to import data from HBase into HDFS, as well as how to use HBase as a data source for a MapReduce job. In this section we'll do the reverse, looking at how to bulk load data from HDFS into HBase, as well as use HBase as a data sink in a MapReduce job.

In this technique we'll look at how to write a MapReduce job to pull data from HBase and write it back into HBase.

TECHNIQUE 10   HDFS egress to HBase

Let's say that you serve some real-time data from your website from HBase, and use Hadoop in your back office for data analytics. You periodically join your data in HBase with some other data sources (such as log files), perform some analytics, and then you want to push the results back into HBase.

Problem

How do you move data from HDFS into HBase?

Solution

In this technique you will use the HBase Export class to export HDFS SequenceFiles to HBase.

Discussion

HBase comes with an `org.apache.hadoop.hbase.mapreduce.Export` class, which will load HBase tables from HDFS. You'll first need to create a table for the import using the HBase shell:

```
$ hbase shell

hbase(main):015:0> create 'stocks_example_import', 'details'
0 row(s) in 1.0590 seconds
```

You'll import the same data that you exported from HBase in section 2.2.4. In that section you discovered that the built-in HBase export process wrote SequenceFiles into HDFS, and similarly, the HBase import tool requires that the HDFS data being imported into HBase be in the same format. The following snippet shows the command for the HBase import:

The HBase table used for import.

```
$ bin/run.sh org.apache.hadoop.hbase.mapreduce.Import \
    stocks_example_import \
    output
```

HDFS directory whose contents will be imported.

You can use the HBase shell to verify that the write was successful:

```
$ hbase shell

hbase(main):017:0> scan 'stocks_example_import'
ROW               COLUMN+CELL
AAPL2000-01-03    column=details:stockAvro, timestamp=1322315975123,
                  value=\x08AAPL\x142000-01-03H...
AAPL2001-01-02    column=details:stockAvro, timestamp=1322315975123,
                  value=\x08AAPL\x142001-01-02\xC3\...

...
```

The output verifies your import was successful.

Summary

This technique is a useful way to load data without having to write any code, but you must have your data in SequenceFile form, which has disadvantages, including no support for schema evolution.

Being able to write to HBase from your MapReduce jobs means you'll need to write code, but in doing so you aren't tied to having your data in a specific file format, as we'll examine next.

TECHNIQUE 11   **Using HBase as a data sink in MapReduce**

Imagine you're working with HDFS data that you want to load into HBase. That data is most likely not in the SequenceFile format required by the HBase Import class, and generating data in that format requires adding an additional step to your MapReduce workflow code. Instead, it's more convenient to write directly from MapReduce into HBase.

Problem

How can you write to HBase directly from your MapReduce jobs?

Solution

MapReduce can be used to export HDFS data to HBase with the HBase TableOutput-
Format class.

Discussion

HBase provides a TableOutputFormat class that uses HBase as a data sink in MapReduce.
You'll read in regular text data in the mapper and convert them into Put classes that
the OutputFormat uses to write to HBase, as shown next.[17]

Writing to HBase from your MapReduce jobs

```
public class HBaseSinkMapReduce
    extends Mapper<LongWritable, Text, StockPriceWritable, Put> {
    public static String STOCKS_IMPORT_TABLE_NAME =
        "stocks_example_import";

    @Override
    protected void map(LongWritable key, Text value,
                        Context context)
        throws IOException, InterruptedException {

        StockPriceWritable stock =
            StockPriceWritable.fromLine(value.toString());

        byte[] rowkey = Bytes.add(
            Bytes.toBytes(stock.getSymbol()),
            Bytes.toBytes(stock.getDate()));

        Put put = new Put(rowkey);

        byte[] colValue = Bytes.toBytes(stock.getClose());
        put.add(STOCK_DETAILS_COLUMN_FAMILY_AS_BYTES,
            STOCK_COLUMN_QUALIFIER_AS_BYTES,
            colValue
        );
        context.write(stock, put);
    }

    public static void main(String[] args) throws Exception {
        Configuration conf = new Configuration();

        createTableAndColumn(conf, STOCKS_IMPORT_TABLE_NAME,
            STOCK_DETAILS_COLUMN_FAMILY_AS_BYTES);

        Job job = new Job(conf);

        job.setJarByClass(HBaseSinkMapReduce.class);
```

Create a new Put object and specify the rowkey in the constructor.

Write out the key and value. The key is ignored by the HBase TableOutputFormat, but it's useful to distribute the keys across all the reduces that will perform the HBase writes.

---

[17] **GitHub source**—https://github.com/alexholmes/hadoop-book/blob/master/src/main/java/com/
manning/hip/ch2/HBaseSinkMapReduce.java

```
TableMapReduceUtil.initTableReducerJob(       ◄─────  Use HBase's helper method to
    STOCKS_IMPORT_TABLE_NAME,                         set up the reduce configuration
    IdentityTableReducer.class,                             parameters for the job.
    job);
...
```

You can run this MapReduce jobs as follows:

```
$ hadoop fs -put test-data/stocks.txt stocks.txt

$ bin/run.sh com.manning.hip.ch2.HBaseSinkMapReduce stocks.txt output
```

As before, HBase should tell you whether or not your MapReduce job worked as expected:

```
hbase(main):054:0> scan 'stocks_example_import'
ROW                COLUMN+CELL
AAPL2000-01-03     column=details:stockAvro, timestamp=1322315975123,
                   value=@[\xFC(\xF5\xC2\x8F
AAPL2001-01-02     column=details:stockAvro, timestamp=1322315975123,
                   value=@-\xC2\x8F\(\xF5\xC3
...
```

The output indicates the egress to HBase worked.

Summary
MapReduce is a great way to move data into HBase. Unlike when exporting data into databases where you'll need to limit the number of MapReduce tasks that write in parallel, with HBase your write throughput can be much higher, as highly parallel writes is one of HBase's primary architectural features.

When you perform highly parallelized writes to HBase, however, you should be aware that they can lead to a phenomenon called *Region Hotspotting*, where all the writes are sent to a single Region server. This can happen in cases where you're writing row keys that are similar to each other, such as timeseries data, which will likely be routed to a single Region server. A common best practice to avoid this includes hashing the keys so that the keys are randomly distributed across the key space.

We've now concluded this examination of Hadoop egress tools. We covered how you can use the HDFS Slurper to move data out to a filesystem, how to use Sqoop for idempotent writes to relational databases, and we wrapped up this section with a look at ways to egress Hadoop data into HBase.

2.4 Chapter summary

Moving data in and out of Hadoop is a critical part of the Hadoop architecture. In this chapter we covered a broad spectrum of techniques that you can use to automate data ingress and egress, and that work with a variety of data sources.

Hadoop has a number of built-in mechanisms that can facilitate ingress and egress operations, such as the embedded NameNode HTTP server, and the upcoming

WebHDFS and Hoop interfaces. But these are low-level mechanisms, and they don't provide complete systems to manage the entire ingress and egress process. This chapter focused on higher-level tools that you can easily integrate and automate.

We looked at how to use Oozie to periodically schedule a workflow that used MapReduce to pull data from a web server. We compared and contrasted various log collection frameworks and showcased how Flume could be used to push data into HDFS and Hive. We also looked at how Sqoop could be used for relational database ingress and egress, and wrapped up with a look at HBase imports and exports.

MapReduce's model for computational parallelism offers its own unique challenges when working with various file formats, so the focus in the next chapter will be on how to work with common file formats such as XML and JSON, as well as helping you pick file formats better suited for life in Hadoop, such as SequenceFiles and Avro.

Data serialization—
working with text
and beyond

This chapter covers

- Working with text, XML, and JSON
- Understanding SequenceFiles, Avro, and Protocol Buffers
- Working with custom data formats

MapReduce offers straightforward, well-documented support for working with simple data formats such as log files. But the use of MapReduce has evolved beyond log files to more sophisticated data serialization formats—such as text, XML, and JSON—to the point that its documentation and built-in support runs dry. The goal of this chapter is to document how to work with common data serialization formats, as well as to examine more structured serialization formats and compare their fitness for use with MapReduce.

Imagine that you want to work with the ubiquitous data serialization formats XML and JSON. These formats work in a straightforward manner in most programming languages, with several tools available to help you with marshalling, unmarshalling, and validating where applicable. Working with XML and JSON in MapReduce, however, poses two equally important challenges. First, though MapReduce requires classes that can support reading and writing a particular data serialization format, there's a good chance it doesn't have such classes to support the serialization format you're working with. Second, MapReduce's power lies in its ability to parallelize reading your input data. If your input files are large (think hundreds of megabytes or more), it's crucial that the classes reading your serialization format be able to split your large files so multiple map tasks can read them in parallel.

We'll start this chapter by tackling the problem of how to work with serialization formats such as XML and JSON. Then we'll compare and contrast data serialization formats that are better suited to working with big data. I'll also show how to use these serialization formats with MapReduce. The final hurdle is when you need to work with a file format that's proprietary, or a less common file format for which no read/write bindings exist in MapReduce. I'll show you how to write your own classes to read/ write your file format.

Data serialization support in MapReduce is a property of the input and output classes that read and write MapReduce data. Let's start with an overview of how MapReduce supports data input and output.

This chapter assumes you're familiar with XML and JSON data formats. Wikipedia provides some good background articles on XML and JSON, if needed. You should also have some experience writing MapReduce programs and understand the basic concepts of HDFS and MapReduce input and output. Chuck Lam's book, *Hadoop in Action* from Manning, represents a good resource on this topic.

3.1   *Understanding inputs and outputs in MapReduce*

Your data might be XML files sitting behind a number of FTP servers, text log files sitting on a central web server, or Lucene indexes[1] in HDFS. How does MapReduce support reading and writing to these different serialization structures across the various storage mechanisms? You'll need to know the answer in order to support a specific serialization format.

Figure 3.1 shows the high-level data flows through MapReduce and identifies the actors responsible for various parts of the flow. On the input side you see that some work (*Create split*) is performed outside of the map phase, and other work is performed as part of the map phase (*Read split*). All of the output work is performed in the reduce phase (*Write output*).

---

[1] Apache Lucene is an information retrieval project that stores data in an inverted index data structure optimized for full-text search. More information is available at http://lucene.apache.org/.

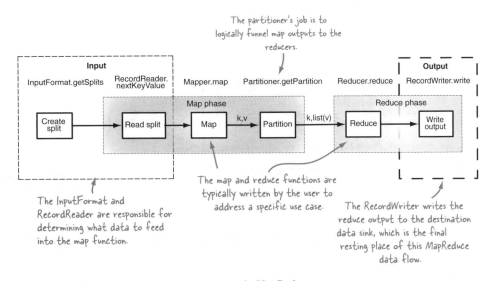

Figure 3.1 High-level input and output actors in MapReduce

Figure 3.2 shows the same flow with a map-only job. In a map-only job the MapReduce framework still uses the OutputFormat and RecordWriter classes to write the outputs directly to the data sink.

Let's walk through the data flow and describe the responsibilities of the various actors. As we do this, we'll also look at the relevant code from the built-in TextInput-Format and TextOutputFormat classes to better understand the concepts. The Text-InputFormat and TextOutputFormat classes read and write line-oriented text files.

3.1.1 Data input

The two classes that support data input in MapReduce are InputFormat and Record-Reader. The InputFormat class is consulted to determine how the input data should be

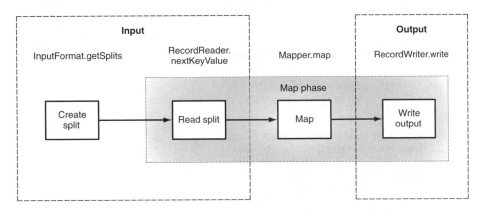

Figure 3.2 Input and output actors in MapReduce with no reducers

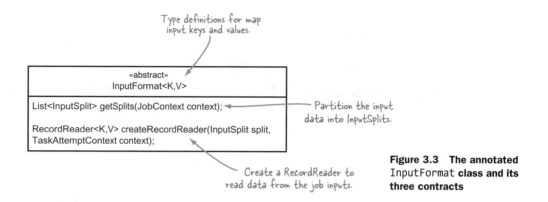

Type definitions for map input keys and values.

Partition the input data into InputSplits.

Create a RecordReader to read data from the job inputs.

Figure 3.3   The annotated `InputFormat` **class and its three contracts**

partitioned for the map tasks, and the `RecordReader` performs the reading of data from the inputs.

INPUTFORMAT

Every job in MapReduce must define its inputs according to contracts specified in the `InputFormat` abstract class. `InputFormat` implementers must fulfill three contracts: first, they describe type information for map input keys and values; next, they specify how the input data should be partitioned; and finally, they indicate the `RecordReader` instance that should read the data from source. Figure 3.3 shows the `InputFormat` class and how these three contracts are defined.

Arguably the most crucial contract is that of determining how to divide the input data. In MapReduce nomenclature these divisions are referred to as *input splits*. The input splits directly impact the map parallelism because each split is processed by a single map task. Working with an `InputFormat` that is unable to create multiple input splits over a single data source (such as a file) will result in a slow map phase because the file will be processed sequentially.

The `TextInputFormat` class (view source at http://goo.gl/VOMcJ) provides an implementation of the `InputFormat` class's `createRecordReader` method but delegates the calculation of input splits to its parent class, `FileInputFormat`. The following code shows the relevant parts of the `TextInputFormat` class:

```
public class TextInputFormat
           extends FileInputFormat<LongWritable, Text> {

  @Override
  public RecordReader<LongWritable, Text>
    createRecordReader(InputSplit split,
                       TaskAttemptContext context) {
    String delimiter = context.getConfiguration().get(
        "textinputformat.record.delimiter");
    byte[] recordDelimiterBytes = null;
    if (null != delimiter)
      recordDelimiterBytes = delimiter.getBytes();
```

The parent class, FileInputFormat, provides all of the input split functionality.

The default record delimiter is newline, but it can be overridden with textinputformat.record.delimiter.

```
    return new LineRecordReader(recordDelimiterBytes);
  }
...
```
◄────── Construct the RecordReader to read the data from the data source.

The code in `FileInputFormat` (source at http://goo.gl/mQfq1) to determine the input splits is a little more complicated. A simplified form of the code is shown in the following example to portray the main elements of this method:

```
public List<InputSplit> getSplits(JobContext job
                             ) throws IOException {
  List<InputSplit> splits = new ArrayList<InputSplit>();
  List<FileStatus>files = listStatus(job);
  for (FileStatus file: files) {
    Path path = file.getPath();

    BlockLocation[] blkLocations =
      FileSystem.getFileBlockLocations(file, 0, length);

    long splitSize = file.getBlockSize();

    while (splitsRemaining()) {
      splits.add(new FileSplit(path, ...));
    }
  }
  return splits;
}
```

The listStatus method determines all the input files for the job.

Retrieve all of the file blocks.

The size of the splits is the same as the block size for the file. Each file can have a different block size.

Create a split for each file block and add it to the result.

The following code is an example of how you specify the `InputFormat` to use for a MapReduce job:

```
job.setInputFormatClass(TextInputFormat.class);
```

RECORDREADER
The `RecordReader` class is used by MapReduce in the map tasks to read data from an input split and provide each record in the form of a key/value pair for use by mappers. A task is commonly created for each input split, and each task has a single `RecordReader` that's responsible for reading the data for that input split. Figure 3.4 shows the abstract methods you must implement.

As shown in a previous section, the `TextInputFormat` class created a `LineRecordReader` to read records from the input splits. The `LineRecordReader` directly extends the `RecordReader` class and leverages the `LineReader` class to read lines from the input split. The `LineRecordReader` uses the byte offset in the file for the map key and the contents of the line for the map value. I've included a simplified version of the `LineRecordReader` in the following example (source at http://goo.gl/iIS59):

```
public class LineRecordReader
          extends RecordReader<LongWritable, Text> {
  private LineReader in;
```

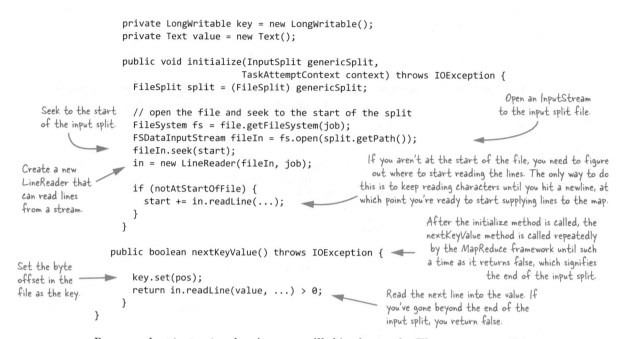

```java
private LongWritable key = new LongWritable();
private Text value = new Text();

public void initialize(InputSplit genericSplit,
                       TaskAttemptContext context) throws IOException {
  FileSplit split = (FileSplit) genericSplit;

  // open the file and seek to the start of the split
  FileSystem fs = file.getFileSystem(job);
  FSDataInputStream fileIn = fs.open(split.getPath());
  fileIn.seek(start);
  in = new LineReader(fileIn, job);

  if (notAtStartOfFile) {
    start += in.readLine(...);
  }
}

public boolean nextKeyValue() throws IOException {
  key.set(pos);
  return in.readLine(value, ...) > 0;
}
}
```

Seek to the start of the input split.

Create a new LineReader that can read lines from a stream.

Open an InputStream to the input split file.

If you aren't at the start of the file, you need to figure out where to start reading the lines. The only way to do this is to keep reading characters until you hit a newline, at which point you're ready to start supplying lines to the map.

After the initialize method is called, the nextKeyValue method is called repeatedly by the MapReduce framework until such a time as it returns false, which signifies the end of the input split.

Set the byte offset in the file as the key.

Read the next line into the value. If you've gone beyond the end of the input split, you return false.

Because the LineReader class is easy, we'll skip that code. The next step will be a look at how MapReduce supports data outputs.

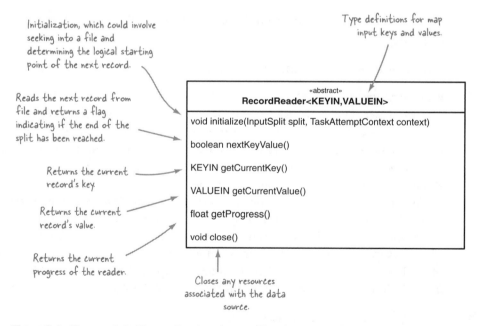

Initialization, which could involve seeking into a file and determining the logical starting point of the next record.

Reads the next record from file and returns a flag indicating if the end of the split has been reached.

Returns the current record's key.

Returns the current record's value.

Returns the current progress of the reader.

Type definitions for map input keys and values.

Closes any resources associated with the data source.

```
«abstract»
RecordReader<KEYIN,VALUEIN>

void initialize(InputSplit split, TaskAttemptContext context)

boolean nextKeyValue()

KEYIN getCurrentKey()

VALUEIN getCurrentValue()

float getProgress()

void close()
```

Figure 3.4   The annotated RecordReader class and its abstract methods

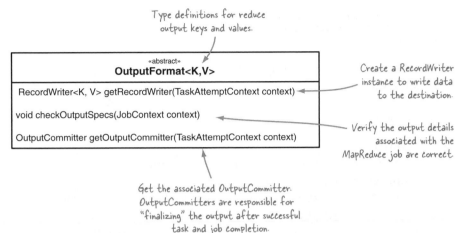

Type definitions for reduce output keys and values.

Create a RecordWriter instance to write data to the destination.

Verify the output details associated with the MapReduce job are correct.

Get the associated OutputCommitter. OutputCommitters are responsible for "finalizing" the output after successful task and job completion.

Figure 3.5 The annotated `OutputFormat` **class**

3.1.2 *Data output*

MapReduce uses a similar process for supporting output data as it does for input data. Two classes must exist, an OutputFormat and a RecordWriter. The OutputFormat performs some basic validation of the data sink properties, and the RecordWriter writes each reducer output to the data sink.

OUTPUTFORMAT

Much like the InputFormat class, the OutputFormat class, as shown in figure 3.5, defines the contracts that implementers must fulfill, including checking the information related to the job output, providing a RecordWriter, and specifying an output committer, which allows writes to be staged and then made "permanent" upon task and/or job success. Please refer to chapter 5 for more details on output committing.

Just like the TextInputFormat, the TextOutputFormat also extends a base class, FileOutputFormat, which takes care of some complicated logistics such as output committing, which we'll cover further in this chapter. For now let's take a look at the work the TextOutputFormat is performing (source at http://goo.gl/8ab7Z):

```
public class TextOutputFormat<K, V> extends FileOutputFormat<K, V> {
  public RecordWriter<K, V>            getRecordWriter(TaskAttemptContext job
                         ) throws IOException, InterruptedException {
    boolean isCompressed = getCompressOutput(job);

    String keyValueSeparator= conf.get(
      "mapred.textoutputformat.separator", "\t");

    Path file = getDefaultWorkFile(job, extension);

    FileSystem fs = file.getFileSystem(conf);
    FSDataOutputStream fileOut = fs.create(file, false);
```

The default key/value separator is the tab character, but this can be changed with the mapred.textoutputformat.separator configuration setting.

Creates a unique filename for the reducer in a temporary directory.

Creates the output file.

Returns a
RecordWriter
used to write to
the file.

```
                          return new LineRecordWriter<K, V>(
                              fileOut, keyValueSeparator);
              }
```

The following code is an example of how you specify the OutputFormat that should be used for a MapReduce job:

```
job.setOutputFormatClass(TextOutputFormat.class);
```

RECORDWRITER

You'll use the RecordWriter to write the reducer outputs to the destination data sink. It's a simple class, as figure 3.6 illustrates.

The TextOutputFormat returned a LineRecordWriter object (LineRecordWriter is an inner class of TextOutputFormat) to perform the writing to file. A simplified version of that class (source at http://goo.gl/8ab7Z) is shown in the following example:

```
    protected static class LineRecordWriter<K, V>   extends RecordWriter<K, V> {

      protected DataOutputStream out;

      public synchronized void write(K key, V value)
        throws IOException {

        writeObject(key);
        out.write(keyValueSeparator);
        writeObject(value);
        out.write(newline);
      }

      private void writeObject(Object o) throws IOException {
        out.write(o);
      }
```

Write out the key,
separator, value,
and newline.

Write out the
Object to the
output stream.

While on the map side it's the InputFormat that determines how many map tasks are executed, on the reducer side the number of tasks is solely based on the value for

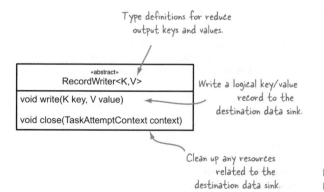

Type definitions for reduce
output keys and values.

Write a logical key/value
record to the
destination data sink.

Clean up any resources
related to the
destination data sink.

**Figure 3.6   The annotated
RecordWriter class overview**

`mapred.reduce.tasks` set by the client (or if it isn't set, the value is picked up from mapred-site.xml, or mapred-default.xml if it doesn't exist in the site file).

Now that you know what's involved in working with input and output data in MapReduce, it's time to apply that knowledge to solving some common data serialization problems. Your first step in this data serialization journey is to learn how to work with file formats such as XML.

3.2 *Processing common serialization formats*

XML and JSON are industry-standard data interchange formats. Their ubiquity in the technology industry is evidenced by their heavy adoption in data storage and exchange.

3.2.1 *XML*

XML has existed since 1998 as a mechanism to represent data that's readable by machine and human alike. It became a universal language for data exchange between systems. It's employed by many standards today such as SOAP and RSS, and used as an open data format for products such as Microsoft Office.

TECHNIQUE 12 **MapReduce and XML**

While MapReduce comes bundled with an `InputFormat` that works with text, it doesn't come with one that supports XML. Working on a single XML file in parallel in MapReduce is tricky because XML doesn't contain a synchronization marker in its data format.

Problem

You want to work with large XML files in MapReduce and be able to split and process them in parallel.

Solution

Mahout's `XMLInputFormat` can be used to work with XML files in HDFS with MapReduce. It reads records that are delimited by a specific XML begin and end tag. This technique also covers how XML can be emitted as output in MapReduce output.

Discussion

MapReduce doesn't contain built-in support for XML, so we'll turn to another Apache project, Mahout, a machine learning system, to provide an XML `InputFormat`. To showcase the XML `InputFormat`, let's write a MapReduce job that uses Mahout's XML `InputFormat` to read property names and values from Hadoop's configuration files. The first step will be to set up the job configuration:

```
conf.set("xmlinput.start", "<property>");

conf.set("xmlinput.end", "</property>");

job.setInputFormatClass(XmlInputFormat.class);
```

Define the string form of the XML start tag. Your job is taking Hadoop config files as input, where each configuration entry uses the property tag.

Define the string form of the XML end tag.

Set the Mahout XML input format class.

Looking at the previous code, it quickly becomes apparent that Mahout's XML Input-Format is rudimentary; you need to tell it an exact sequence of start and end XML tags that will be searched in the file. Looking at the source of the InputFormat confirms this:[2]

```
private boolean next(LongWritable key, Text value)
    throws IOException {
  if (fsin.getPos() < end && readUntilMatch(startTag, false)) {
    try {
      buffer.write(startTag);
      if (readUntilMatch(endTag, true)) {
        key.set(fsin.getPos());
        value.set(buffer.getData(), 0, buffer.getLength());
        return true;
      }
    } finally {
      buffer.reset();
    }
  }
  return false;
}
```

Next you need to write a mapper to consume Mahout's XML InputFormat. The XML element in Text form has been supplied, so you'll need to use an XML parser to extract content from the XML.

A mapper to work with XML

```
public static class Map extends Mapper<LongWritable, Text,
    Text, Text> {

  @Override
  protected void map(LongWritable key, Text value,
                     Mapper.Context context)
      throws
      IOException, InterruptedException {
    String document = value.toString();
    System.out.println("'" + document + "'");
    try {
      XMLStreamReader reader =
          XMLInputFactory.newInstance().createXMLStreamReader(new
              ByteArrayInputStream(document.getBytes()));
      String propertyName = ";
      String propertyValue = ";
      String currentElement = ";
      while (reader.hasNext()) {
        int code = reader.next();
        switch (code) {
          case START_ELEMENT:
            currentElement = reader.getLocalName();
```

---

[2] **GitHub source**—https://github.com/alexholmes/hadoop-book/blob/master/src/main/java/com/manning/hip/ch3/xml/XmlInputFormat.java

```
            break;
          case CHARACTERS:
            if (currentElement.equalsIgnoreCase("name")) {
              propertyName += reader.getText();
            } else if (currentElement.equalsIgnoreCase("value")) {
              propertyValue += reader.getText();
            }
            break;
        }
      }
      reader.close();
      context.write(propertyName.trim(), propertyValue.trim());
    } catch (Exception e) {
      log.error("Error processing '" + document + "'", e);
    }
  }
}
```

The map is given a Text instance, which contains a String representation of the data between the start and end tags. In this code you use Java's built-in Streaming API for XML (StAX) parser to extract the key and value for each property and output them. If you run the MapReduce job against Cloudera's core-site.xml and use the HDFS cat command to show the output, you'll see the following output:

```
$ hadoop fs -put $HADOOP_HOME/conf/core-site.xml core-site.xml

$ bin/run.sh com.manning.hip.ch3.xml.HadoopPropertyXMLMapReduce \
  core-site.xml output

$ hadoop fs -cat output/part*
fs.default.name hdfs://localhost:8020
hadoop.tmp.dir /var/lib/hadoop-0.20/cache/${user.name}
hadoop.proxyuser.oozie.hosts *
hadoop.proxyuser.oozie.groups *
```

This output shows that you've successfully worked with XML as an input serialization format with MapReduce. Not only that—you can support huge XML files since the InputFormat supports splitting XML.

WRITING XML

Having successfully read XML, the next question is how do you write XML? In your reducer you have callbacks that occur before and after your main reduce method is called, which you can use to emit a start and end tag, as shown in the following example.[3]

---

[3] **GitHub source**—https://github.com/alexholmes/hadoop-book/blob/master/src/main/java/com/manning/hip/ch3/xml/SimpleXmlOutputMapReduce.java

A reducer to emit start and end tags

```
public static class Reduce
    extends Reducer<Text, Text, Text, Text> {

  @Override
  protected void setup(
      Context context)
      throws IOException, InterruptedException {
    context.write(new Text("<configuration>"), null);
  }

  @Override
  protected void cleanup(
      Context context)
      throws IOException, InterruptedException {
    context.write(new Text("</configuration>"), null);
  }

  private Text outputKey = new Text();
  public void reduce(Text key, Iterable<Text> values,
                     Context context)
      throws IOException, InterruptedException {
    for (Text value : values) {
      outputKey.set(constructPropertyXml(key, value));

      context.write(outputKey, null);
    }
  }

  public static String constructPropertyXml(Text name, Text value) {
    StringBuilder sb = new StringBuilder();
    sb.append("<property><name>").append(name)
        .append("</name><value>").append(value)
        .append("</value></property>");
    return sb.toString();
  }
}
```

Use the setup method to write the root element start tag.

Use the cleanup method to write the root element end tag.

Construct a child XML element for each key/value combination provided in the reducer.

Emit the XML element.

This could also be embedded in an OutputFormat, but I'll leave that as an exercise for the reader. Writing an OutputFormat class is covered in section 3.4.1.

PIG

If you want to work with XML in Pig, the Piggybank library (a user-contributed library of useful Pig code, detailed in chapter 10) contains an XMLLoader. It works in a way similar to this technique and captures all of the content between a start and end tag, supplying it as a single byte array field in a Pig tuple.

HIVE

Currently, no means exists for working with XML in Hive. You would have to write a custom SerDe,[4] which we'll cover in chapter 10.

---

[4] SerDe is a shortened form of Serializer/Deserializer, and is the mechanism that allows Hive to read and write data in HDFS.

Summary

Mahout's XML InputFormat certainly helps you work with XML. But it's sensitive to an exact string match of both the start and end element names. If the element tag can contain attributes with variable values, or the generation of the element can't be controlled and could result in XML namespace qualifiers being used, then this approach may not work for you. Also problematic will be situations where the element name you specify is used as a descendant child element.

If you have control over the XML laid out in the input, this exercise can be simplified by having a single XML element per line. This will let you use the built-in MapReduce text-based InputFormats (such as TextInputFormat), which treat each line as a record and split accordingly to preserve that demarcation.

Another option worth considering is that of a preprocessing step, where you could convert the original XML into a separate line per XML element, or convert it into an altogether different data format such as a SequenceFile or Avro, both of which solve the splitting problem for you.

A streaming class called StreamXmlRecordReader also allows you to work with XML in your streaming code.

Now that you have a handle on how to work with XML, let's tackle another popular serialization format, JSON.

3.2.2 JSON

JSON shares the machine- and human-readable traits of XML, and has existed since the early 2000s. It's less verbose than XML, and doesn't have the rich typing and validation features available in XML.

TECHNIQUE 13 MapReduce and JSON

Imagine you have some code that's downloading JSON data from a streaming REST service and every hour writes a file into HDFS. The data amount that's being downloaded is large, so each file being produced is multiple gigabytes in size.

You've been asked to write a MapReduce job that can take as input these large JSON files. What you have here is a problem in two parts: first, MapReduce doesn't come with an InputFormat that works with JSON. Second, how does one even go about splitting JSON? Figure 3.7 shows the problem with splitting JSON. To split files, given a random offset in a file, you'll need to be able to determine the start of the next JSON element. This is made more challenging when working with JSON because it's a hierarchical data format and the same element name can be used in multiple levels, as shown in the figure.

JSON is harder to partition into distinct segments than a format such as XML because JSON doesn't have a token (like an end tag in XML) to denote the start or end of a record.

```
{
    "created_at" : "Thu, 29 Dec 2011 21:46:01 +0000",
    "from_user" : "xxx",
    "text" : "Lorem ipsum dolor sit amet",
    "children" : [
        {
            "created_at": "Thu, 29 Dec 2011 21:46:01 +0000",
            "username": "yyy"
        },
        {
            "created_at": "Thu, 29 Dec 2011 21:46:01 +0000",
            "username": "zzz"
        }
    ]
},
{
    "created_at" : "Mon, 26 Dec 2011 21:18:37 +0000",
    "from_user" : "xxx",
    "text" : "consectetur adipisicing elit",
    "children" : [
        {
            "created_at": "Thu, 29 Dec 2011 21:46:01 +0000"
        },
        {
            "created_at": "Thu, 29 Dec 2011 21:46:01 +0000"
        }
    ]
}
```

Input split N

Figure 3.7   Example of issue with JSON and multiple input splits

Problem
You want to work with JSON inputs in MapReduce and also ensure that input JSON files can be partitioned for concurrent reads.

Solution
The Elephant Bird `LzoJsonInputFormat` input format is used as a basis to create an input format class to work with JSON elements. This technique also covers another approach using my open source project that can work with multiline JSON.

Discussion
Elephant Bird,[5] an open source project that contains some useful utilities for working with LZOP compression, has an `LzoJsonInputFormat` that can read JSON, though it requires that the input file be LZOP-compressed. You'll use the Elephant Bird code as a template for your own JSON `InputFormat`, which doesn't have the LZOP compression requirement.

We're cheating with this solution, which assumes that each JSON record is on a separate line. My `JsonInputFormat` is simple and does nothing other than construct and return a `JsonRecordReader`, so we'll skip over that code. The `JsonRecordReader` emits `LongWritable`, `MapWritable` key/value pairs to the mapper, where the `MapWritable` is a map of JSON element names and their values. Let's take a look at how this

---

[5]   See https://github.com/kevinweil/elephant-bird.

RecordReader works. It leverages the LineRecordReader, which is a built-in MapReduce reader that emits a record for each line. To convert the line to a MapWritable, the reader uses the following method:[6]

```
public static boolean decodeLineToJson(JSONParser parser, Text line,
                                       MapWritable value) {
  try {
    JSONObject jsonObj = (JSONObject)parser.parse(line.toString());
    for (Object key: jsonObj.keySet()) {
      Text mapKey = new Text(key.toString());
      Text mapValue = new Text();
      if (jsonObj.get(key) != null) {
        mapValue.set(jsonObj.get(key).toString());
      }

      value.put(mapKey, mapValue);
    }
    return true;
  } catch (ParseException e) {
    LOG.warn("Could not json-decode string: " + line, e);
    return false;
  } catch (NumberFormatException e) {
    LOG.warn("Could not parse field into number: " + line, e);
    return false;
  }
}
```

The reader uses the json-simple[7] parser to parse the line into a JSON object, and then iterates over the keys and puts the keys and values into a MapWritable. The mapper is given the JSON data in LongWritable, MapWritable pairs and can process the data accordingly. You can view this basic code for the MapReduce job in the GitHub repository.

I'll demonstrate this technique using the following JSON:

```
{
  "results" :
    [
      {
        "created_at" : "Thu, 29 Dec 2011 21:46:01 +0000",
        "from_user" : "grep_alex",
        "text" : "RT @kevinweil: After a lot of hard work by ..."
      },
      {
        "created_at" : "Mon, 26 Dec 2011 21:18:37 +0000",
        "from_user" : "grep_alex",
        "text" : "@miguno pull request has been merged, thanks again!"
      }
    ]
}
```

---

[6] **GitHub source**—https://github.com/alexholmes/hadoop-book/blob/master/src/main/java/com/manning/hip/ch3/json/JsonInputFormat.java

[7] See http://code.google.com/p/json-simple/.

Because this technique assumes a JSON object per line, the following shows the JSON file you'll work with:

```
{"created_at" : "Thu, 29 Dec 2011 21:46:01 +0000","from_user" : ...
{"created_at" : "Mon, 26 Dec 2011 21:18:37 +0000","from_user" : ...
```

Now copy the JSON file into HDFS and run your MapReduce code. The MapReduce code writes each JSON key/value as the job output:

```
$ hadoop fs -put test-data/ch3/singleline-tweets.json \
  singleline-tweets.json

$ bin/run.sh com.manning.hip.ch3.json.JsonMapReduce \
  singleline-tweets.json output

$ hadoop fs -cat output/part*
text        RT @kevinweil: After a lot of hard work by ...
from_user   grep_alex
created_at  Thu, 29 Dec 2011 21:46:01 +0000
text        @miguno pull request has been merged, thanks again!
from_user   grep_alex
created_at  Mon, 26 Dec 2011 21:18:37 +0000
```

WRITING JSON

An approach similar to what we looked at in section 3.2.1 for writing XML could also be used to write JSON.

PIG

Elephant Bird contains a JsonLoader and an LzoJsonLoader, which you can use to work with JSON in Pig. These loaders work with line-based JSON. Each Pig tuple contains a chararray field for each JSON element in the line.

HIVE

Hive contains a DelimitedJSONSerDe, which can serialize JSON, but, unfortunately, not deserialize it, so you can't load data into Hive using this SerDe.

Summary

This solution assumes that the JSON input is structured with a line per JSON object. How would you work with JSON objects that are across multiple lines? An experimental project on GitHub[8] works with multiple input splits over a single JSON file. This approach searches for a specific JSON member and retrieves the containing object.

You can also review a Google Code project called hive-json-serde,[9] which can support both serialization and deserialization.

As you can see, using XML and JSON in MapReduce is kludgy and has rigid requirements about how to lay out your data. Support for these two formats in MapReduce is also complex and error prone, since neither lends itself naturally to splitting. Clearly you need to look at alternative file formats that have built-in support for splittability.

---

[8] A multiline JSON InputFormat: https://github.com/alexholmes/json-mapreduce.

[9] See http://code.google.com/p/hive-json-serde/.

The next step is to compare more sophisticated file formats, which are better suited to working with MapReduce, such as Avro and SequenceFiles.

3.3 Big data serialization formats

Unstructured text works well when you're working with scalar or tabular data. Semi-structured text formats such as XML and JSON can model more sophisticated data structures that include composite fields, or hierarchical data. But when you're working with big data volumes you'll need serialization formats with compact serialized forms that natively support partitioning and have schema evolution features.

In this section we'll compare the serialization formats that work best with big data in MapReduce, and follow up with how you can use them with MapReduce.

3.3.1 Comparing SequenceFiles, Protocol Buffers, Thrift, and Avro

It's important to make certain considerations when choosing a file format. I've selected the following criteria based on my belief that these are the important characteristics for big data serialization:

- *Code generation*—The ability to generate Java classes and utilities that can be used for serialization and deserialization.
- *Versioning*—The ability for the file format to support backward or forward compatibility.
- *Language support*—The programming languages supported by the library.
- *Transparent compression*—The ability for the file format to handle compressing records internally.
- *Splittability*—The ability of the file format to support multiple input splits.
- *Native support in MapReduce*—The input/output formats that support reading and writing files in their native format (that is, produced directly from the data format library).
- *Pig and Hive support*—The Pig Store and Load Functions (referred to as *Funcs*) and Hive SerDe classes to support the data format.

Table 3.1 compares three data serialization frameworks to see how they stack up against each other. Additional background on these technologies is provided in the succeeding section. Now let's look at each of these formats in more detail.

SEQUENCEFILE

The SequenceFile format was created to work with MapReduce, Pig, and Hive, and therefore integrates well with all of those tools. Its shortcomings are mainly its lack of code generation and versioning support, as well as limited language support.

Table 3.1 Feature comparison of data serialization frameworks

Library	Code generation	Versioning	Language support	Transparent compression	Splittable	Native support in MapReduce	Pig and Hive support
SequenceFile	No	No	Java, Python	Yes	Yes	Yes	Yes
Protocol Buffers	Yes (optional)	Yes	C++, Java, Python, Perl, Ruby	No	No	No	No
Thrift	Yes (mandatory)	Yes	C, C++, Java, Python, Ruby, Perl	No[a]	No	No	No
Avro	Yes (optional)	Yes	C, C++, Java, Python, Ruby, C#	Yes	Yes	Yes	Pig only (Hive coming soon, see HIVE-895)

[a] Thrift does support compression, but not in the Java library.

PROTOCOL BUFFERS

The Protocol Buffers format has been used heavily by Google for interoperability. Its strengths are its versioning support and compact binary format. Downsides include its lack of support in MapReduce (or in any third-party software) for reading files generated by Protocol Buffers serialization. Not all is lost, however; we'll look at how Elephant Bird uses Protocol Buffers serialization within a higher-level container file in section 3.3.3.

THRIFT

Thrift was developed at Facebook as a data serialization and RPC framework. It doesn't have support in MapReduce for its native data serialization format, though it can support different wire-level data representations, including JSON and various binary encodings. Thrift also includes an RPC layer with various types of servers, including a nonblocking implementation. We'll ignore the RPC capabilities for this chapter and focus on the data serialization.

AVRO

The Avro format was Doug Cutting's creation to help address the shortcomings of SequenceFiles. Based on certain evaluation criteria, Avro seems to be the best fit as a data serialization framework in Hadoop. SequenceFile is a close second, due to its inherent compatibility with Hadoop (it was designed for use with Hadoop).

You can review a useful project at https://github.com/eishay/jvm-serializers/wiki/, which runs various benchmarks to compare file formats based on items such as serialization and deserialization times. It contains benchmarks for Avro, Protocol Buffers, and Thrift, along with a number of other frameworks.

After looking at how the various data serialization frameworks compare, we'll dedicate the next few sections to showing you how you can work with them. We'll start things off with a look at SequenceFiles.

3.3.2 SequenceFiles

Because SequenceFiles were created for use with MapReduce, arguably they offer the highest level of integration support in conjunction with MapReduce, Pig, and Hive. SequenceFiles are a splittable binary file format that stores data in the form of key/value pairs. All SequenceFiles share the same header format, as shown in figure 3.8.

SequenceFiles come in three types, which vary based on how you apply compression. In addition, each type has its own corresponding `Writer` classes.

UNCOMPRESSED

Uncompressed SequenceFiles are written using the `SequenceFile.Writer` class. No advantage exists for this over the compressed formats, since compression generally reduces your storage footprint and is more efficient for reads and writes. The file format is shown in figure 3.9.

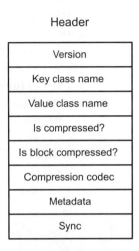

Header

Figure 3.8 Sequence-File header format

RECORD-COMPRESSED

Record compression SequenceFiles are written using the `SequenceFile.RecordCompress-Writer` class. When a record is added to the SequenceFile, it's immediately compressed and written to the file. The disadvantage to this approach is that your compression ratio will suffer compared to block compression. This file format is shown, along with uncompressed SequenceFiles, in figure 3.9.

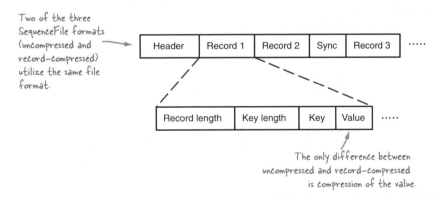

Two of the three SequenceFile formats (uncompressed and record-compressed) utilize the same file format.

The only difference between uncompressed and record-compressed is compression of the value.

Figure 3.9   Record-based SequenceFile format and its uncompressed SequenceFiles

BLOCK-COMPRESSED

Block-compression SequenceFiles are written using the SequenceFile.BlockCompress-Writer class. By default the block size is the same as the HDFS block size, although this can be overridden. The advantage to this compression is that it's more aggressive; the whole block is compressed, rather than at the record level. Data isn't written until it reaches the block size, at which point the whole block is compressed, resulting in good overall compression. The file format is shown in figure 3.10.

You only need one Reader class (SequenceFile.Reader) to read all three types of SequenceFiles. Even the Writer is abstracted because you can call SequenceFile.create-Writer to choose the preferred format and it returns a base class that can be used for writing regardless of compression.

SequenceFiles have a pluggable serialization framework. Written keys and values must have a related org.apache.hadoop.io.serializer.Serializer and Deserializer for marshalling and unmarshalling. Hadoop comes with four serializers: Avro, Java, Tether (for binary data contained within a TetherData class), and Writable[10] (the default serializer).

> **Custom SequenceFile serialization**
>
> If you want your SequenceFile to contain objects that aren't Writable or Serializable, you'll need to implement your own Serializer and register it. You register it by updating core-site.xml and appending the class name of the custom serialization implementation to the io.serializations property.

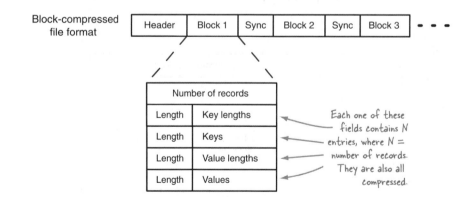

Figure 3.10   Block-based SequenceFile format

---

[10] Writable is an interface in Hadoop used to support general-purpose data serialization, and is used for sending data across the wire between Hadoop components. Yahoo has a good introduction to Writables at http://developer.yahoo.com/hadoop/tutorial/module5.html#writable.

SequenceFiles are splittable because a synchronization marker is written approximately every 6 KiB (1 kibibyte = 1024 bytes) in the file for record-based files, and before every block for block-based files.

Now let's look at how to use SequenceFiles in MapReduce.

TECHNIQUE 14 **Working with SequenceFiles**

Working with text in MapReduce can start to get tricky when you have to support complex types of data, which may include nonscalar data types such as lists or dictionaries. Dealing directly with large text files also means that you have to manage compression yourself, which can be a burden in MapReduce.

Problem

You want to work with a structured file format in MapReduce that you can use to model complex data structures, and that also supports compression and splittable inputs.

Solution

This technique looks at how the SequenceFile file format can be leveraged from both standalone applications as well as MapReduce.

Discussion

The SequenceFile format offers a high level of integration with computational tools such as MapReduce, and can also model complex data structures. We'll examine how to read and write SequenceFiles, and also use them with MapReduce, Pig, and Hive.

We'll work with the stock data for this technique. The most common serialization method used with SequenceFiles are `Writable`, so we'll create a `Writable` to represent the stock data. The key elements of writing a complex `Writable` are extending the `Writable` class and defining serialization/deserialization methods, as shown here.[11]

A `Writable` implementation to represent a stock price

```
public class StockPriceWritable
    implements WritableComparable<StockPriceWritable>, Cloneable  {
  String symbol;
  String date;
  double open;
  double high;
  double low;
  double close;
  int volume;
  double adjClose;

  @Override
  public void write(DataOutput out) throws IOException {      ◄─── Write out the fields of this
    WritableUtils.writeString(out, symbol);                        Writable in byte form to
    WritableUtils.writeString(out, date);                          the output stream.
```

---

[11] **GitHub source**—https://github.com/alexholmes/hadoop-book/blob/master/src/main/java/com/manning/hip/ch3/StockPriceWritable.java

```
      out.writeDouble(open);
      out.writeDouble(high);
      out.writeDouble(low);
      out.writeDouble(close);
      out.writeInt(volume);
      out.writeDouble(adjClose);
    }

    @Override
    public void readFields(DataInput in) throws IOException {
      symbol = WritableUtils.readString(in);
      date = WritableUtils.readString(in);
      open = in.readDouble();
      high = in.readDouble();
      low = in.readDouble();
      close = in.readDouble();
      volume = in.readInt();
      adjClose = in.readDouble();
    }

    public static StockPriceWritable fromLine(String line)
        throws IOException {
      CSVParser parser = new CSVParser();
      String[] parts = parser.parseLine(line);

      StockPriceWritable stock = new StockPriceWritable(
          parts[0], parts[1], Double.valueOf(parts[2]),
          Double.valueOf(parts[3]),
          Double.valueOf(parts[4]),
          Double.valueOf(parts[5]),
          Integer.valueOf(parts[6]),
          Double.valueOf(parts[7])
      );
      return stock;
    }
  }
```

Read the fields from byte form into the Writable fields. Note that this method reads fields in the same order as they were written in the write method.

A helper method to engineer a StockPriceWritable from a CSV line. This uses the open source OpenCSV project to parse the CSV.

Now that you have your Writable you'll need to write some code that will create a SequenceFile. You'll read your stocks file from the local disk, create the StockWritable, and write it to your SequenceFile, using the stock symbol as your key:[12]

```
  public static void write(File inputFile, Path outputPath)
      throws IOException {
    Configuration conf = new Configuration();
    FileSystem fs = FileSystem.get(conf);

    SequenceFile.Writer writer =
        SequenceFile.createWriter(fs, conf, outputPath, Text.class,
            StockPriceWritable.class,
            SequenceFile.CompressionType.BLOCK,
            new DefaultCodec());
    try {
      Text key = new Text();
      for (String line : FileUtils.readLines(inputFile)) {
```

Create a new SequenceFile writer, specifying that you want block-level compression. Also set the types for the keys and values that you'll be writing, in this case Text and IntWritable. Any Hadoop compression codec can be used with SequenceFiles; see chapter 5 for more details on compression.

Read all the lines in the input file and then split them into key/value pairs.

---

[12] **GitHub source**—https://github.com/alexholmes/hadoop-book/blob/master/src/main/java/com/manning/hip/ch3/seqfile/SequenceFileStockWriter.java

```
            StockPriceWritable stock =
              StockPriceWritable.fromLine(line);
            key.set(stock.getSymbol());

            key.set(stock.getSymbol());
            writer.append(key,stock);
          }
        } finally {
          writer.close();
        }
      }
```

Append a record to the SequenceFile. → (points to `key.set`/`writer.append` lines)

Create the StockPriceWritable instance, using the fromLine helper method in the StockPriceWritable class.

Great, now how do you go about reading the files created with your writer?

Create a reader that can read records from the SequenceFile. Note that you don't need to specify that you used block–level compression in the file or what key/value types are contained in the file.

```
SequenceFile.Reader reader =
  new SequenceFile.Reader(fs, inputPath, conf);

try {
  Text key = new Text();
  StockPriceWritable value = new StockPriceWritable();

  while (reader.next(key, value)) {
    System.out.println(key + "," + value);
  }
} finally {
  reader.close();
}
```

The next method on the reader returns true until it hits the end of the file. It also sets the key and value settings.

Now you need to prove that it works by writing and reading a file:

```
$ cat test-data/stocks.txt
AAPL,2009-01-02,85.88,91.04,85.16,90.75,26643400,90.75
AAPL,2008-01-02,199.27,200.26,192.55,194.84,38542100,194.84
AAPL,2007-01-03,86.29,86.58,81.90,83.80,44225700,83.80
...
$ bin/run.sh com.manning.hip.ch3.seqfile.SequenceFileStockWriter \
    test-data/stocks.txt  stocks.seqfile

$ bin/run.sh com.manning.hip.ch3.seqfile.SequenceFileStockReader \
  stocks.seqfile
AAPL,StockPriceWritable[symbol=AAPL,date=2009-01-02,open=85.88,...]
AAPL,StockPriceWritable[symbol=AAPL,date=2008-01-02,open=199.27,...]
AAPL,StockPriceWritable[symbol=AAPL,date=2007-01-03,open=86.29,...]
...
```

How would you process this SequenceFile in MapReduce? Luckily, both SequenceFile-InputFormat and SequenceFileOutputFormat nicely integrate with MapReduce. Remember earlier in this chapter when we talked about how the default SequenceFile serialization supported Writable classes for serialization? Because Writable is the native data format in MapReduce, using SequenceFiles with MapReduce is totally transparent. Let's see if you agree. The following code[13] shows a MapReduce job with an identity mapper and reducer:[14]

Specifies an output format for SequenceFiles.

```
Configuration conf = new Configuration();
Job job = new Job(conf);
job.setJarByClass(SequenceFileStockMapReduce.class);
job.setOutputKeyClass(Text.class);
job.setOutputValueClass(IntWritable.class);
job.setInputFormatClass(SequenceFileInputFormat.class);
job.setOutputFormatClass(SequenceFileOutputFormat.class);

SequenceFileOutputFormat.setCompressOutput(job, true);

SequenceFileOutputFormat.setOutputCompressionType(job,
    SequenceFile.CompressionType.BLOCK);
SequenceFileOutputFormat.setOutputCompressorClass(job,
    DefaultCodec.class);

FileInputFormat.setInputPaths(job, new Path(input));
Path outPath = new Path(output);
FileOutputFormat.setOutputPath(job, outPath);
outPath.getFileSystem(conf).delete(outPath, true);

job.waitForCompletion(true);
```

The SequenceFileInputFormat determines the type of Writable keys and values and emits these types as key/value pairs to the mapper.

Indicates that you want to compress output.

You want block-level compression (you can also set this to RECORD, BLOCK or NONE).

Set the compression codec that should be used; in this case you're using the default codec, which is the DEFLATE compression algorithm used by zip and gzip file formats.

Now let's run the identity MapReduce job against the stocks SequenceFile that you created earlier in this technique:

```
$ bin/run.sh com.manning.hip.ch3.seqfile.SequenceFileStockMapReduce \
    stocks.seqfile output
```

Because all it's doing is echoing the input to the output, you should see identical content in both files. Let's make sure that's the case by reading in the job output file(s). First of all, how do you verify that the output is a SequenceFile? Easy, just cat it—the first 3 bytes should be *SEQ*, followed by a fourth byte containing the SequenceFile version, which is then followed by the key and value classes:

Linux command to reset your terminal; useful after sending binary data to your screen.

```
$ hadoop fs -cat output/part*
SEQorg.apache.hadoop.io.Text&com.manning.hip.ch3.StockPriceWritable...
$ reset
```

Looks good. Now try using the SequenceFile reader code you wrote earlier to dump it to standard output:

---

[13] **GitHub source**—https://github.com/alexholmes/hadoop-book/blob/master/src/main/java/com/manning/hip/ch3/seqfile/SequenceFileStockMapReduce.java

[14] An identity function is a mathematical term to denote a function that returns the same value that was used as its argument. In MapReduce this means the same thing—the map identity function emits all the key/value pairs that it is supplied, as does the reducer, without any transformation or filtering. A job that doesn't explicitly set a map or reduce class results in Hadoop using a built-in identity function.

```
$ bin/run.sh com.manning.hip.ch3.seqfile.SequenceFileStockReader \
  output/part-r-00000
AAPL,StockPriceWritable[symbol=AAPL,date=2008-01-02,open=199.27,...]
AAPL,StockPriceWritable[symbol=AAPL,date=2007-01-03,open=86.29,...]
AAPL,StockPriceWritable[symbol=AAPL,date=2009-01-02,open=85.88,...]
...
```

That was easy. Because SequenceFiles are key/value based, and the default serialization data format for SequenceFiles is Writable, the use of SequenceFiles is 100 percent transparent to your map and reduce classes. We demonstrated this by using MapReduce's built-in identity map and reduce classes with the SequenceFile as input. The only work you had to do was to tell MapReduce to use the SequenceFile specific Input and Output format classes, which are built into MapReduce.

READING SEQUENCEFILES IN PIG

By writing your own Writable you created more work for yourself with non-MapReduce tools such as Pig. Pig works well with Hadoop's built-in scalar Writables such as Text and IntWritable, but doesn't have support for custom Writables. This will work well with MapReduce, but Pig's SequenceFileLoader won't work with your custom Writable, which means that you'll need to write your own Pig loader to process your files.

Your LoadFunc for Pig is straightforward, as shown in the next listing.[15] Please refer to chapter 11 for more details on how to write LoadFuncs.

A Pig loader function that converts a `StockPriceWritable` into a Pig tuple

```java
public class SequenceFileStockLoader extends FileInputLoadFunc {

  private SequenceFileRecordReader<Text, StockPriceWritable> reader;

  @Override
  public Tuple getNext() throws IOException {
    boolean next;
    try {
      next = reader.nextKeyValue();
    } catch (InterruptedException e) {
      throw new IOException(e);
    }

    if (!next) return null;

    Object value = reader.getCurrentValue();

    if (value == null) {
      return null;
    }
    if (!(value instanceof StockPriceWritable)) {
      return null;
    }
    StockPriceWritable w = (StockPriceWritable) value;
    return TupleFactory.getInstance().newTuple(Arrays.asList(
```

---

[15] **GitHub source**—https://github.com/alexholmes/hadoop-book/blob/master/src/main/java/com/manning/hip/ch3/seqfile/SequenceFileStockLoader.java

```
            w.getSymbol(), w.getDate(), w.getOpen(),
            w.getHigh(), w.getLow(), w.getClose(),
            w.getVolume(), w.getAdjClose()
    ));
  }

  @SuppressWarnings("unchecked")
  @Override
  public InputFormat getInputFormat() throws IOException {
    return new SequenceFileInputFormat<Text, StockPriceWritable>();
  }

  @SuppressWarnings("unchecked")
  @Override
  public void prepareToRead(RecordReader reader, PigSplit split)
      throws IOException {
    this.reader = (SequenceFileRecordReader) reader;
  }

  @Override
  public void setLocation(String location, Job job)
      throws IOException {
    FileInputFormat.setInputPaths(job, location);
  }
}
```

Installing and using Pig

Appendix A and chapter 11 contain details on installing and using Pig.

Let's try to load and dump the stock SequenceFile in Pig:

```
$ pig
grunt> REGISTER
        target/hadoop-book-1.0.0-SNAPSHOT-jar-with-dependencies.jar;
grunt> DEFINE SequenceFileStockLoader
            com.manning.hip.ch3.seqfile.SequenceFileStockLoader();
grunt> stocks = LOAD 'stocks.seqfile' USING SequenceFileStockLoader;
grunt> dump stocks;
(AAPL,2009-01-02,85.88,91.04,85.16,90.75,26643400,90.75)
(AAPL,2008-01-02,199.27,200.26,192.55,194.84,38542100,194.84)
(AAPL,2007-01-03,86.29,86.58,81.9,83.8,44225700,83.8)
(AAPL,2006-01-03,72.38,74.75,72.25,74.75,28829800,74.75)
(AAPL,2005-01-03,64.78,65.11,62.6,63.29,24714000,31.65)
...
```

That covers reading data into Pig, but what about writing data to SequenceFiles? We'll cover that in chapter 11.

HIVE

Hive contains built-in support for SequenceFiles but has two restrictions. First, it ignores the key portion of each record. Second, out of the box it only works with SequenceFile values that are Writable, and the way it supports them is to perform a toString() to convert the value into a Text form. In your case you have a custom

`Writable`, so you have to write a Hive SerDe, which deserializes your `Writable` into a form Hive can understand. The resulting DDL statement is as follows (the code for `StockWritableSerDe` is on GitHub at https://github.com/alexholmes/hadoop-book/ blob/master/src/main/java/com/manning/hip/ch3/StockWritableSerDe.java:

```
$ export HADOOP_CLASSPATH=\
<path-to-source>/target/hadoop-book-1.0.0-SNAPSHOT.jar

$ hive

hive> CREATE TABLE stocks (
  symbol    string,
  dates      string,
  open      double,
  high      double,
  low       double,
  close     double,
  volume    int,
  adjClose  double
)
ROW FORMAT SERDE 'com.manning.hip.ch3.StockWritableSerDe'
STORED AS SEQUENCEFILE;

hive> LOAD DATA INPATH 'stocks.seqfile' INTO TABLE stocks;

hive> select * from stocks;

AAPL 2009-01-02 85.88  91.04  85.16  90.75  26643400 90.75
AAPL 2008-01-02 199.27 200.26 192.55 194.84 38542100 194.84
AAPL 2007-01-03 86.29  86.58  81.9   83.8   44225700 83.8
AAPL 2006-01-03 72.38  74.75  72.25  74.75  28829800 74.75
AAPL 2005-01-03 64.78  65.11  62.6   63.29  24714000 31.65
...
```

We'll cover custom Hive SerDe examples in more detail in chapter 10.

Summary

SequenceFiles are useful in that they solve two problems that make using MapReduce challenging; they're natively splittable, and they also have built-in support for compression, which makes it transparent to the user. The thorn in the side of SequenceFiles is their lack of support outside of Java, which limits what other tools you can use with them. If your data mostly stays in HDFS, however, and is processed with MapReduce (or Hive/ Pig), SequenceFiles may be what you need.

Next up we'll examine how to integrate Protocol Buffers into MapReduce.

3.3.3 *Protocol Buffers*

Google developers invented Protocol Buffers to help them exchange data between services written in multiple languages in a compact and efficient manner. Protocol Buffers are now Google's de facto format for data—there are 48,162 different message types defined in Google across 12,183 `.proto` files.[16] They're used both in RPC systems and for persistent storage of data in a variety of storage systems.

---

[16] Protocol Buffers usage statistics taken from http://code.google.com/apis/protocolbuffers/docs/ overview.html

Protocol Buffers offer a compact and fast serialization format for semistructured data. You define the structure of your data in a .proto file and use Protocol Buffers' code generation capabilities to generate classes to access your data.

![TECHNIQUE 15] **Integrating Protocol Buffers with MapReduce**

The challenge to using Protocol Buffers in MapReduce is that currently no mechanism exists to work directly with files that are serialized with Protocol Buffers.[17]

Problem

You want to be able to read and write data encoded with Protocol Buffers in MapReduce.

Solution

Elephant Bird has a file format that can store Protocol Buffer encoded records. The Elephant Bird file format supports compression and splitability.

Discussion

We'll cover how you can use Protocol Buffers in your MapReduce jobs. We'll go through the steps to define a schema, generate Java classes from the schema, and then use your classes in a MapReduce job.

> **Installing Elephant Bird, LZOP, and Protocol Buffers**
>
> To work with Protocol Buffers and Elephant Bird, you'll need to download and install them as well as set up LZOP compression on your system. Elephant Bird requires Protocol Buffers version 2.3, and doesn't work with version 2.4 or later at this time.
>
> Appendix A contains installation instructions for all three libraries.

The key to this solution is Elephant Bird,[18] an open source project maintained by Twitter, which contains LZOP compression utilities. Elephant Bird contains Input and Output Formats that can write Protocol Buffers within an encapsulating file format. Twitter uses Protocol Buffers extensively[19] to store and work with data in MapReduce,

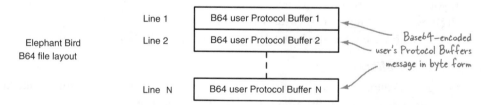

Figure 3.11   Elephant Bird line-based Protocol Buffers layout writes a Base64-encoded form per line.

---

[17] A MapReduce ticket asking for native Protocol Buffers support has been open since 2008. However, there's been little activity since the end of 2008 on this ticket. See https://issues.apache.org/jira/browse/MAPREDUCE-377.

[18] See https://github.com/kevinweil/elephant-bird.

[19] See http://engineering.twitter.com/2010/04/hadoop-at-twitter.html.

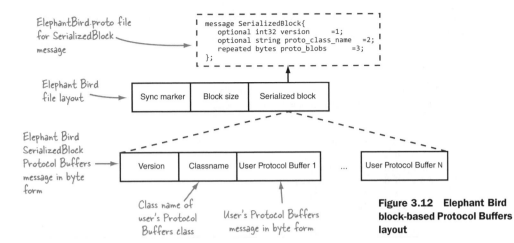

ElephantBird.proto file for SerializedBlock message

```
message SerializedBlock{
    optional int32 version       =1;
    optional string proto_class_name   =2;
    repeated bytes proto_blobs   =3;
};
```

Elephant Bird file layout

| Sync marker | Block size | Serialized block |

Elephant Bird SerializedBlock Protocol Buffers message in byte form

| Version | Classname | User Protocol Buffer 1 | ... | User Protocol Buffer N |

Class name of user's Protocol Buffers class

User's Protocol Buffers message in byte form

Figure 3.12 Elephant Bird block-based Protocol Buffers layout

and its developer contribution of this work to the open source world means you can leverage it for your technique.

Elephant Bird supports two encoding mechanisms for Protocol Buffers: line-oriented and block-based. The line-oriented mechanism, whose layout can be seen in figure 3.11, writes a Base64-encoded form of each Protocol Buffer record per line.

The second encoding option, block-based, as shown in figure 3.12, is an interesting format. It accumulates in memory the byte form of the Protocol Buffer (PB) objects being written, and then after a certain number of PB objects have accumulated (by default 100), it writes a logical block marker, followed by the block size, and then uses its own Protocol Buffer code-generated block (SerializedBlock) to use PB's serialization to write the PB object bytes to the stream. The block marker enables splittability. Both line-oriented and block-based formats are splittable.

Table 3.2 provides an overview of the classes related to each of the Protocol Buffers' encodings available in Elephant Bird.

Table 3.2 Elephant Bird encodings and related classes

Context	Line	Block
Reader	N/A	ProtobufBlockReader
Writer	N/A	ProtobufBlockWriter
Input Format	LzoProtobufB64LineInputFormat	LzoProtobufBlockInputFormat
Output Format	LzoProtobufB64LineOutputFormat	LzoProtobufBlockOutputFormat
Example Code	ProtobufMRExample	ProtobufMRExample

SCHEMA DEFINITION

Everything in Protocol Buffers starts with a .proto file, which is where you define your "messages" (which are types containing a number of uniquely numbered fields). These numbers are how Protocol Buffers identifies that particular field, and must never change for a given field. The next block of code is an example of a .proto file definition for your stock data:[20]

```
package proto;

option java_package = "com.manning.hip.ch3.proto";
option java_outer_classname = "StockProtos";

message Stock {
  required string symbol = 1;
  required string date = 2;
  required double open = 3;
  required double high = 4;
  required double low = 5;
  required double close = 6;
  required int32 volume = 7;
  required double adjClose = 8;
}

message StockAvg {
  required string symbol = 1;
  required double avg = 2;
}
```

CODE GENERATION

When your .proto file is ready, it's time to generate a Java-specific set of classes for your message types. The --java_out option specifies where the Java sources should be generated:

```
protoc --java_out=src/main/java/ \
       src/main/java/com/manning/hip/ch3/proto/stock.proto
```

MAPREDUCE

Now you have a number of generated files to start playing with Protocol Buffers. Next you'll write a MapReduce job that will calculate the stock averages for each company. Your MapReduce job will both consume and produce Protocol Buffer data. For this exercise you'll use the block-based Elephant Bird Protocol Buffers encoding.

First you'll need to generate an Elephant Bird block-encoded Protocol Buffers file. You need to load the stocks sample file, and write an LZOP-compressed Protocol Buffers file, as the following code shows.[21]

---

[20] **GitHub source**—https://github.com/alexholmes/hadoop-book/blob/master/src/main/java/com/manning/hip/ch3/proto/stock.proto

[21] **GitHub source**—https://github.com/alexholmes/hadoop-book/blob/master/src/main/java/com/manning/hip/ch3/proto/StockProtocolBuffersMapReduce.java

Your LZOP-compressed protocol buffers file

```
private static void generateInput(Configuration config,
                                  File inputFile,
                                  Path input) throws IOException {
    FileSystem hdfs = FileSystem.get(config);
    OutputStream os = hdfs.create(input);

    LzopCodec codec = new LzopCodec();
    codec.setConf(config);
    OutputStream lzopOutputStream =
        codec.createOutputStream(os);

    ProtobufBlockWriter<Stock> writer =
        new   ProtobufBlockWriter<Stock>(
            lzopOutputStream, Stock.class);

    for (String line : FileUtils.readLines(inputFile)) {
        Stock stock = createStock(line);
        writer.write(stock);
    }
    writer.finish();
    writer.close();
    IOUtils.closeStream(os);
}

static CSVParser parser = new CSVParser();

public static Stock createStock(String line) throws IOException {
    String parts[] = parser.parseLine(line);
    return Stock.newBuilder()
        .setSymbol(parts[0])
        .setDate(parts[1])
        .setOpen(Double.valueOf(parts[2]))
        .setHigh(Double.valueOf(parts[2]))
        .setLow(Double.valueOf(parts[2]))
        .setClose(Double.valueOf(parts[2]))
        .setVolume(Integer.valueOf(parts[6]))
        .setAdjClose(Double.valueOf(parts[2])).build();
}
```

Create an LZOP codec. Elephant Bird's Input and Output Formats mandate the use of LZOP.

Create an LZOP-compressed output stream.

Use Elephant Bird to create a Writer that will write the block-encoded Protocol Buffers object to the LZOP stream.

Create a Protocol Buffers Stock object from each input line.

Protocol Buffers objects are immutable and must be constructed with a Builder object.

In this example you'll pass the Protocol Buffers Stock object between the map and reduce functions. To do this you need to write your own class that extends Protobuf-Writable, and emits that in your map task:

```
public static class ProtobufStockWritable
    extends ProtobufWritable<Stock> {
  public ProtobufStockWritable() {
    super(new TypeRef<Stock>() {
    });
  }

  public ProtobufStockWritable(Stock m) {
    super(m, new TypeRef<Stock>() {
    });
  }
}
```

The map function emits the stock symbol and the entire Stock Protocol Buffers object as output. Notice that the Protocol Buffers Stock object is being passed to the mapper wrapped in a ProtobufWritable object:[22]

```
public static class PBMapper extends
    Mapper<LongWritable, ProtobufWritable<Stock>,
        Text, ProtobufStockWritable> {
  @Override
  protected void map(LongWritable key,
                  ProtobufWritable<Stock> value,
                  Context context) throws IOException,
      InterruptedException {
    context.write(
        new Text(value.get().getSymbol()),
        new ProtobufStockWritable(value.get()));
  }
}
```

The input to the Map function is the byte offset of the record in the input, and the wrapped Stock object.

The map emits the stock symbol and the original Protocol Buffers Stock object, wrapped in a ProtobufStockWritable.

The reducer function sums all of the prices for a stock symbol and emits the stock average:[23]

```
public static class PBReducer extends
    Reducer<Text, ProtobufStockWritable,
        NullWritable, ProtobufWritable> {
  private ProtobufWritable<StockAvg> stockAvg =
      new ProtobufWritable<StockAvg>();

  @Override
  protected void reduce(Text symbol,
                  Iterable<ProtobufStockWritable> values,
                  Context context) throws IOException,
      InterruptedException {
    double total = 0.0;
    double count = 0;
    for(ProtobufStockWritable d: values) {
      total += d.get().getOpen();
      count++;
    }

    StockAvg avg = StockAvg.newBuilder()
        .setSymbol(symbol.toString())
        .setAvg(total / count).build();
    stockAvg.set(avg);
    context.write(NullWritable.get(), stockAvg);
  }
}
```

The reduce input is the stock symbol and all of the related Stock objects.

Iterate over all of the Stock objects and sum the opening prices.

Build the Protocol Buffers StockAvg object using the Builder that was created as part of the Protocol Buffers code generation.

Output the StockAvg object. The RecordWriter used by the LzoProtobufBlockOutputFormat ignores the output key.

---

[22] **GitHub source**—https://github.com/alexholmes/hadoop-book/blob/master/src/main/java/com/manning/hip/ch3/proto/StockProtocolBuffersMapReduce.java

[23] **GitHub source**—https://github.com/alexholmes/hadoop-book/blob/master/src/main/java/com/manning/hip/ch3/proto/StockProtocolBuffersMapReduce.java

The final step is to set up the job configuration:

Indicates that you used the Elephant Bird input format class for block-based Protocol Buffers encoding.

Indicates that you used the Elephant Bird output format class for block-based Protocol Buffers encoding.

The map output key is the stock symbol, so use the Text type.

The map output value is the Stock Protocol Buffers object, and here you specify your custom class that you wrote earlier in this technique.

```
job.setMapOutputKeyClass(Text.class);

job.setMapOutputValueClass(ProtobufStockWritable.class);

job.setInputFormatClass(
    LzoProtobufBlockInputFormat
        .getInputFormatClass(Stock.class,
            job.getConfiguration()));

job.setOutputFormatClass(
    LzoProtobufBlockOutputFormat.getOutputFormatClass(
        StockAvg.class, job.getConfiguration()));
```

If you run this job it'll read your input text file containing stock details, create an LZOP-compressed input file, and run the MapReduce file, which will take that as input and create a final output in the form of an LZOP-compressed block-based Protocol Buffers file:

```
$ bin/run.sh com.manning.hip.ch3.proto.StockProtocolBuffersMapReduce \
    test-data/stocks.txt stocks.pb.lzo output-pb
```

Remember the .lzo extension

If you run the next example and don't specify your input filename to have an .lzo suffix, it'll be ignored by the MapReduce job.

You can dump the contents of the MapReduce output file using some reader code (source on GitHub at http://goo.gl/PEyUZ):

```
$ bin/run.sh \
    com.manning.hip.ch3.proto.StockAvgProtocolBuffersFileReader \
    output-pb/part-r-00000.lzo
StockAvg@5f0ab09f[symbol_=AAPL,avg_=68.631]
StockAvg@900bac2[symbol_=CSCO,avg_=31.148000000000003]
StockAvg@ee51b2c[symbol_=GOOG,avg_=417.47799999999995]
StockAvg@635aed57[symbol_=MSFT,avg_=44.63100000000001]
StockAvg@66941db6[symbol_=YHOO,avg_=69.333]
```

PROTOCOL BUFFERS AND PIG

Elephant Bird also contains a loader that can be used to read the LZOP-compressed Protocol Buffers data contained within Elephant Bird's serialization container.

LZOP with Pig requires you to export some Pig options so that the native Hadoop libraries are picked up correctly. Run the following command, and then copy the output string of the script prior to running Pig:

Run the script to generate the export command you need to run.

```
$ bin/pig-native-opts.sh
export PIG_OPTS="$PIG_OPTS -Djava.library.path=/usr/lib/..."

$ export PIG_OPTS="$PIG_OPTS -Djava.library.path=/usr/..."
```

Copy and paste the export command.

Now launch Pig and dump the contents of the LZOP-compressed Protocol Buffers file to standard out:

```
$ bin/pig-native-opts.sh

$ pig
grunt> REGISTER /usr/lib/pig/contrib/piggybank/java/piggybank.jar;
grunt> REGISTER
   target/hadoop-book-1.0.0-SNAPSHOT-jar-with-dependencies.jar;

grunt> DEFINE LzoProtobufBlockPigLoader
   com.twitter.elephantbird.pig.load.LzoProtobufBlockPigLoader
   ('com.manning.hip.ch3.proto.StockProtos$Stock');

grunt> raw = LOAD 'stocks.pb.lzo'
   USING LzoProtobufBlockPigLoader;

grunt> dump raw;

(AAPL,2009-01-02,85.88,85.88,85.88,85.88,26643400,85.88)
(AAPL,2008-01-02,199.27,199.27,199.27,199.27,38542100,199.27)
(AAPL,2007-01-03,86.29,86.29,86.29,86.29,44225700,86.29)
(AAPL,2006-01-03,72.38,72.38,72.38,72.38,28829800,72.38)
(AAPL,2005-01-03,64.78,64.78,64.78,64.78,24714000,64.78)
...
```

You need to use a $ character to specify the Stock inner class.

The Elephant Bird Pig loader made it easy to work with Protocol Buffers.

Summary

Elephant Bird contains some handy classes to help you work with Protocol Buffers. As I mentioned earlier, there are no InputFormat classes that will let you work with files natively serialized with Protocol Buffers. As you've seen, the way Elephant Bird enables you to work with Protocol Buffers is to introduce their own file format within which Protocol Buffers objects are serialized.

Using Elephant Bird's classes means you have to use LZOP; however, it would be possible to derive a version of their classes and remove the LZOP dependency.

No progress has been made as yet in MapReduce to provide native support for Protocol Buffers.[24] This would be ideal because it would allow users to work natively with Protocol Buffers serialized files.

Thrift is another data format, which, like Protocol Buffers, doesn't have out-of-the-box support with MapReduce. Again, Elephant Bird comes to the rescue for Thrift, which we'll take a look at in the next section.

---

[24] See https://issues.apache.org/jira/browse/MAPREDUCE-377.

3.3.4 *Thrift*

Facebook created Thrift to help with efficient data representation and transport. Facebook uses Thrift for a number of applications, including search, logging, and its ads platform.

Working with Thrift

As with Protocol Buffers, no InputFormats exist that can work with files generated directly from Thrift's data serialization library.

Problem

You want to use Thrift for data serialization and its code-generated beans to work with your data in MapReduce.

Solution

Elephant Bird has a file format that can store Thrift encoded records. The Elephant Bird file format supports compression and splitability.

Discussion

Similar to Protocol Buffers, Elephant Bird includes a Base64-encoded, line-based mechanism to serialize Thrift, as well as a block-based mechanism, which uses a Protocol Buffers generic container to write Thrift objects. This is the same block format shown in Protocol Buffers in figure 3.12.

SCHEMA DEFINITION

Thrift's schema has a lot in common with Protocol Buffers, which isn't surprising given the number of Google engineers who've joined Facebook. Compare the following schema[25] with the Protocol Buffers' schema you captured in section 3.3.3 to see the overlap:

```
namespace java com.manning.hip.ch3.thrift

struct Stock {
  1: string symbol,
  2: string date,
  3: double open,
  4: double high,
  5: double low,
  6: double close,
  7: i32 volume,
  8: double adjClose
}
struct StockAvg {
  1: string symbol,
  2: double avg
}
```

---

[25] **GitHub source**—https://github.com/alexholmes/hadoop-book/blob/master/src/main/java/com/manning/hip/ch3/thrift/stock.thrift

> **Thrift version and installation**
>
> Elephant Bird requires version 0.5 of Thrift, and it also has a dependency on LZOP compression. All of these libraries contain installation instructions you can find in appendix A.

Your next step is to generate the Java code. Thrift has a few options for the Java-generated code, including some Builder pattern semantics, where setters can return a reference to this, which you've enabled with the private-members=true setting:

```
$ thrift -o src/main/java/ --gen java:private-members=true \
src/main/java/com/manning/hip/ch3/thrift/stock.thrift
```

MAPREDUCE

Your MapReduce code looks almost identical to the Protocol Buffers code, because Elephant Bird uses the same methods for both formats. The only difference is you use the Thrift-specific classes to wrap your Thrift objects, and the ThriftWritable, Lzo-ThriftBlockInputFormat, and LzoThriftBlockOutputFormat classes to set the input and output classes. Other than that, the only change is in how you create the Thrift Stock object and write it into HDFS, which is as follows.[26]

The `Thrift` object used to write into HDFS

```
private static void generateInput(Configuration config,
                                  File inputFile,
                                  Path input) throws IOException {
  FileSystem hdfs = FileSystem.get(config);
  OutputStream os = hdfs.create(input);

  LzopCodec codec = new LzopCodec();
  codec.setConf(config);
  OutputStream lzopOutputStream = codec.createOutputStream(os);

  ThriftBlockWriter<Stock> writer =          ◄────  The ThriftBlockWriter will write out the Thrift
      new ThriftBlockWriter<Stock>(                 object in serialized form into a Protocol Buffers
          lzopOutputStream, Stock.class);           generic object, used in Elephant Bird as a general-
                                                     purpose storage mechanism for binary data.
  for (String line : FileUtils.readLines(inputFile)) {
    Stock stock = createStock(line);
    writer.write(stock);
  }

  writer.finish();
  writer.close();
  IOUtils.closeStream(os);
}
```

---

[26] **GitHub source**—https://github.com/alexholmes/hadoop-book/blob/master/src/main/java/com/manning/hip/ch3/thrift/ThriftStockMapReduce.java

```
public static Stock createStock(String line) throws IOException {
  String parts[] = parser.parseLine(line);
  return new Stock()
       .setSymbol(parts[0])
       .setDate(parts[1])
       .setOpen(Double.valueOf(parts[2]))
       .setHigh(Double.valueOf(parts[3]))
       .setLow(Double.valueOf(parts[4]))
       .setClose(Double.valueOf(parts[5]))
       .setVolume(Integer.valueOf(parts[6]))
       .setAdjClose(Double.valueOf(parts[7]));
}
```

Rather than a separate Builder class as in Protocol Buffers, Thrift uses Builder setters directly in the generated object.

You can review the complete code at GitHub. If you run the MapReduce code and examine the output data for the job you'll see the following:

```
$ bin/run.sh com.manning.hip.ch3.thrift.ThriftStockMapReduce \
    test-data/stocks.txt stocks.thrift.lzo output-thrift

...

$ bin/run.sh com.manning.hip.ch3.thrift.ThriftStockAvgFileReader \
   output-thrift/part-r-00000.lzo
StockAvg@774acfcd[symbol=AAPL,avg=68.631]
StockAvg@27b62aab[symbol=CSCO,avg=31.14]
StockAvg@28ab54eb[symbol=GOOG,avg=417.47]
StockAvg@8542529[symbol=MSFT,avg=44.63]
StockAvg@4c53ab04[symbol=YHOO,avg=69.33]
```

PIG
Elephant Bird also includes LzoThriftBlockPigLoader and LzoThriftBlockPigStorage to work with block-encoded Thrift, and classes to work with Base64, line-encoded Thrift as well.

Summary
Once again Elephant Bird has made it possible for you to work with Thrift data serialization. As with Protocol Buffers, your restriction in using Elephant Bird is that you're forced to use LZOP compression. But you should find it straightforward to copy and factor out the compression code if you don't want to use it.

Another item worth noting is that Elephant Bird doesn't supply Hive SerDe classes to allow you to work with Thrift in Hive.

Let's look at what's likely the most capable data serialization format of all our options, Avro.

3.3.5 *Avro*

Doug Cutting created Avro, a data serialization and RPC library, to help improve data interchange, interoperability, and versioning in MapReduce. Avro utilizes a compact binary data format—which you have the option to compress—that results in fast serialization times. While it has the concept of a schema, similar to Protocol Buffers, Avro improves on Protocol Buffers because it works natively with MapReduce. Avro has a

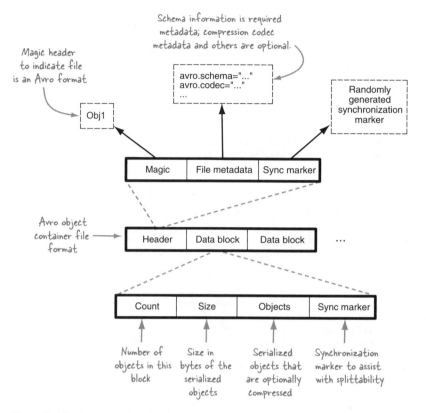

Figure 3.13   Avro container file format

mechanism to work with schema data that uses generic data types (an example of which can be seen in chapter 5).

The Avro file format is shown in figure 3.13. As you can see in this figure, the schema is serialized as part of the header, which makes deserialization simple, and loosens restrictions around users having to use the schema in some form when interacting with Avro for deserialization. Each data block contains a number of Avro records and by default is 16 KB in size.

With a firm understanding of Avro's file format under your belt, let's dive into the next technique.

TECHNIQUE 17   **Next-generation data serialization with MapReduce**

The holy grail of data serialization supports code generation, versioning, and compression, and has a high level of integration with MapReduce. Equally important is schema evolution, and that's the reason why Hadoop SequenceFiles aren't appealing—they don't support the notion of a schema or any form of data evolution.

Avro fits the bill on all fronts, but the problem you may quickly run into with Avro is that it has almost no documentation to help users understand how to use it.

Problem

You want to work with a data serialization library that works well with MapReduce and supports complex data types, code generation, and schema evolution.

Solution

Avro code-generation and MapReduce integration are covered in this technique. We also cover an examination of how Avro schema evolution works so that your code can support data serialized using different versions of your Avro schema.

Discussion

You can use Avro in one of two ways: either with code-generated classes or with its generic classes. In this technique we'll work with the code-generated classes, but you can see an example of how Avro's generic records are used in the small files technique in chapter 5. Since you'll take the code-generated route, everything starts with a schema. You'll continue to model the stock prices in this section, so the first step will be to create an Avro schema to represent an entry in the stock data:[27]

```
{
  "name": "Stock",
  "type": "record",
  "namespace": "com.manning.hip.ch3.avro.gen",
  "fields": [
      {"name": "symbol",    "type": "string"},
      {"name": "date",      "type": "string"},
      {"name": "open",      "type": "double"},
      {"name": "high",      "type": "double"},
      {"name": "low",       "type": "double"},
      {"name": "close",     "type": "double"},
      {"name": "volume",    "type": "int"},
      {"name": "adjClose",  "type": "double"}
  ]
}
```

Getting Avro

Appendix A contains instructions on how to get your hands on Avro.

Avro compilers come in two flavors: they can either compile a protocol file or a schema file. A protocol file supports both RPC messages and schema information, whereas a schema file can only support a single type. You'll use the schema compiler for this technique:

```
$ java -cp <Avro JARs> org.apache.avro.tool.Main compile schema \
        <path to avro schema> <path to put generated classes>
```

---

[27] **GitHub source**—https://github.com/alexholmes/hadoop-book/blob/master/src/main/java/com/manning/hip/ch3/avro/stock.avsc

For this example you would run this (note that the second command generates the code for a different schema file, stockavg.avsc):

```
$ java -cp \
  target/hadoop-book-1.0.0-SNAPSHOT-jar-with-dependencies.jar \
  org.apache.avro.tool.Main compile schema \
  src/main/java/com/manning/hip/ch3/avro/stock.avsc  src/main/java/
```

```
$ java -cp \
  target/hadoop-book-1.0.0-SNAPSHOT-jar-with-dependencies.jar \
  org.apache.avro.tool.Main compile schema \
  src/main/java/com/manning/hip/ch3/avro/stockavg.avsc  src/main/java/
```

Generated code will be put into package com.manning.hip.ch3.avro.gen. So how do you write Avro files from outside MapReduce?[28]

Writing Avro files from outside of MapReduce

```
static CSVParser parser = new CSVParser();

public static Stock createStock(String line) throws IOException {

    String parts[] = parser.parseLine(line);
    Stock stock = new Stock();

    stock.symbol = parts[0];
    stock.date = parts[1];
    stock.open = Double.valueOf(parts[2]);
    stock.high = Double.valueOf(parts[3]);
    stock.low = Double.valueOf(parts[4]);
    stock.close = Double.valueOf(parts[5]);
    stock.volume = Integer.valueOf(parts[6]);
    stock.adjClose = Double.valueOf(parts[7]);

    return stock;
}

public static void writeToAvro(File inputFile,
    OutputStream outputStream)
      throws IOException {
```

Create a writer that can write Avro's data file format.

```
    DataFileWriter<Stock> writer =
        new DataFileWriter<Stock>(
            new SpecificDatumWriter<Stock>())
          .setSyncInterval(1 << 20);
```

Override the default data block size from 16 KB to 1 MiB.

```
    writer.setCodec(CodecFactory.snappyCodec());
```

Specify that Snappy should be used to compress the data.

Indicate the schema that will be used.

```
    writer.create(Stock.SCHEMA$, outputStream);

    for(String line: FileUtils.readLines(inputFile)) {
      writer.append(createStock(line));
    }
```

Write each stock to the Avro file.

---

[28] **GitHub source**—https://github.com/alexholmes/hadoop-book/blob/master/src/main/java/com/manning/hip/ch3/avro/AvroStockFileWrite.java

```
    IOUtils.closeStream(writer);
    IOUtils.closeStream(outputStream);
  }
```

As you see, you can specify the compression codec that should be used to compress the data. In the example you're using Snappy, which, as shown in chapter 5, is the fastest codec for reads and writes. You also specified a larger data block size to show an example of how this can be done. Now how about reading the file you just wrote?[29]

```
public class AvroStockFileRead {

  public static void readFromAvro(InputStream is) throws IOException {
    DataFileStream<Stock> reader =
      new DataFileStream<Stock>(
          is,
          new SpecificDatumReader<Stock>(Stock.class));

    for (Stock a : reader) {
      System.out.println(ToStringBuilder.reflectionToString(a,
          ToStringStyle.SIMPLE_STYLE
      ));
    }

    IOUtils.closeStream(is);
    IOUtils.closeStream(reader);
  }

  public static void main(String... args) throws Exception {
    Configuration config = new Configuration();
    FileSystem hdfs = FileSystem.get(config);

    Path destFile = new Path(args[0]);

    InputStream is = hdfs.open(destFile);
    readFromAvro(is);
  }
}
```

Use Avro's file container deserialization class to read from an input stream.

Loop through the Stock objects and use the Apache Commons ToStringBuilder to help dump all the members to the console.

Let's first generate the Avro file, and then read it back:

```
$ bin/run.sh com.manning.hip.ch3.avro.AvroStockFileWrite \
  test-data/stocks.txt stocks.avro

$ bin/run.sh com.manning.hip.ch3.avro.AvroStockFileRead \
  stocks.avro
AAPL,2009-01-02,85.88,91.04,85.16,90.75,26643400,90.75
AAPL,2008-01-02,199.27,200.26,192.55,194.84,38542100,194.84
AAPL,2007-01-03,86.29,86.58,81.9,83.8,44225700,83.8
AAPL,2006-01-03,72.38,74.75,72.25,74.75,28829800,74.75
AAPL,2005-01-03,64.78,65.11,62.6,63.29,24714000,31.65
...
```

Reads the stocks.txt file from the local filesystem and writes the Avro output file stocks.avro to HDFS.

Reads the Avro file stocks.avro from HDFS and dumps the records to the terminal.

---

[29] **GitHub source**—https://github.com/alexholmes/hadoop-book/blob/master/src/main/java/com/manning/hip/ch3/avro/AvroStockFileRead.java

AVRO AND MAPREDUCE

The big question is, does Avro play nicely with MapReduce? Avro comes with some mapper and reducer classes that you can subclass to work with Avro. They're useful in situations where you want your mappers and reducers to exchange Avro objects. But if you don't have a requirement to pass Avro objects between your map and reduce tasks, you're better off using the Avro Input/Output Format classes directly, as you'll see in the following code, which produces an average of all of the opening stock values.

We'll start with a look at the job configuration. Your job is to consume stock data and produce stock averages, both in Avro formats. To do this you need to set the job configuration with the schema information for both schemas. You also need to specify Avro's Input and Output Format classes:[30]

Set the Avro schema for the input files that are to be processed.

Set the Avro schema for the job output files.

Set the compression codec for this job.

Indicate that the input data is Avro.

The output data is also Avro.

```
job.set(AvroJob.INPUT_SCHEMA, Stock.SCHEMA$.toString());

job.set(AvroJob.OUTPUT_SCHEMA, StockAvg.SCHEMA$.toString());

job.set(AvroJob.OUTPUT_CODEC, SnappyCodec.class.getName());

job.setInputFormat(AvroInputFormat.class);

job.setOutputFormat(AvroOutputFormat.class);
```

Next up is the Map class. Your map function simply extracts the necessary fields from the stock record and emits them to the reducer, with the stock symbol and the opening stock price as the key/value pairs:[31]

```
public static class Map
    implements
    Mapper<AvroWrapper<Stock>, NullWritable, Text, DoubleWritable> {

    @Override
    public void map(AvroWrapper<Stock> key,
                    NullWritable value,
                    OutputCollector<Text, DoubleWritable> output,
                    Reporter reporter) throws IOException {
        output.collect(new Text(key.datum().symbol.toString()),
            new DoubleWritable(key.datum().open));
    }

    @Override
    public void close() throws IOException {
    }

    @Override
    public void configure(JobConf job) {
    }
}
```

The Avro InputFormat supplies the Avro objects wrapped in an AvroWrapper object.

---

[30] **GitHub source**—https://github.com/alexholmes/hadoop-book/blob/master/src/main/java/com/manning/hip/ch3/avro/AvroStockMapReduce.java

[31] **GitHub source**—https://github.com/alexholmes/hadoop-book/blob/master/src/main/java/com/manning/hip/ch3/avro/AvroStockMapReduce.java

Finally, the reduce function sums together all of the stock prices for each stock, and outputs an average price:[32]

```
public static class Reduce
    implements Reducer<Text, DoubleWritable, AvroWrapper<StockAvg>,
    NullWritable> {

  @Override
  public void reduce(Text key,
                     Iterator<DoubleWritable> values,
                     OutputCollector<AvroWrapper<StockAvg>,
                         NullWritable> output,
                     Reporter reporter) throws IOException {
    double total = 0.0;
    double count = 0;
    while (values.hasNext()) {
      total += values.next().get();
      count++;
    }
    StockAvg avg = new StockAvg();
    avg.symbol = key.toString();
    avg.avg = total / count;
    output.collect(new AvroWrapper<StockAvg>(avg),
        NullWritable.get());
  }

  @Override
  public void close() throws IOException {
  }

  @Override
  public void configure(JobConf job) {
  }
}
```

The Avro OutputFormat expects AvroWrapper output.

Output the AvroWrapper containing your StockAvg instance.

You can run the MapReduce code as follows:

```
$ bin/run.sh com.manning.hip.ch3.avro.AvroStockMapReduce \
    stocks.avro output
```

Your MapReduce job is outputting a different Avro object (`StockAvg`) from the job input. You can verify that the job produced the output you expected by writing some code (not listed) to dump your Avro objects:

```
$ bin/run.sh com.manning.hip.ch3.avro.AvroStockAvgFileRead \
    output/part-00000.avro
StockAvg[symbol=AAPL,avg=68.631]
StockAvg[symbol=CSCO,avg=31.148000000000003]
StockAvg[symbol=GOOG,avg=417.47799999999995]
StockAvg[symbol=MSFT,avg=44.631]
StockAvg[symbol=YHOO,avg=69.333]
```

---

[32] **GitHub source**—https://github.com/alexholmes/hadoop-book/blob/master/src/main/java/com/manning/hip/ch3/avro/AvroStockMapReduce.java

If you want to use Avro's own mapper and reducer classes, take a look at their Java-docs[33] for examples of how to use them via the AvroJob helper class.

AVRO AND PIG

The 0.9 version of Pig contains support for AvroStorage,[34] which LinkedIn contributed. CDH currently only supports Pig 0.8.1, so to use Avro with Pig you'll need to move to the newer version. In the following code you load the stock data using Avro-Storage and dump it out:

```
$ bin/pig-native-opts.sh

$ pig
grunt> REGISTER /app/hadoop/lib/avro-1.6.1.jar;
grunt> REGISTER /app/pig-0.9.0/contrib/piggybank/java/piggybank.jar;
grunt> REGISTER /app/pig-0.9.0/build/ivy/lib/Pig/json-simple-1.1.jar;
grunt> REGISTER
  /app/pig-0.9.0/build/ivy/lib/Pig/jackson-core-asl-1.6.0.jar;

grunt> raw = LOAD 'stocks.avro'
  USING org.apache.pig.piggybank.storage.avro.AvroStorage
  AS (symbol: chararray, date: chararray, open: double,
      high:double, low: double, close: double, volume: int,
      adjClose: double);

grunt> DUMP raw;
(AAPL,2009-01-02,85.88,91.04,85.16,90.75,26643400,90.75)
(AAPL,2008-01-02,199.27,200.26,192.55,194.84,38542100,194.84)
(AAPL,2007-01-03,86.29,86.58,81.9,83.8,44225700,83.8)
(AAPL,2006-01-03,72.38,74.75,72.25,74.75,28829800,74.75)
(AAPL,2005-01-03,64.78,65.11,62.6,63.29,24714000,31.65)
...
```

AVRO AND HIVE

Currently, Hive doesn't support Avro, but there's an open ticket actively being worked on.[35]

Now that we've covered how Avro works with MapReduce, let's take a look at one of Avro's important features, schema evolution.

AVRO VERSIONING

Avro's backward and forward compatibility is supported by a number of features that help with schema evolution. It can support the following operations:

1 Removing fields
2 Renaming fields
3 Adding new fields

---

[33] See http://avro.apache.org/docs/current/api/java/org/apache/avro/mapred/package-summary.html.
[34] See https://cwiki.apache.org/confluence/display/PIG/AvroStorage.
[35] See https://issues.apache.org/jira/browse/HIVE-895.

Imagine that you want to update the Stocks schema to be the following:

```
"fields": [
{"name": "symbol",    "type": "string"},
{"name": "date",      "type": "string"},
{"name": "open",      "type": "double"},
{"name": "high",      "type": "double"},
{"name": "close",     "type": "double"},
{"name": "volume",    "type": "int"},
{"name": "adjustedClose",  "type": "double",
"aliases": ["adjClose"]},
{"name": "dailyAvg",  "type": "double", "default":0.0}
]
```

You renamed a field, but used Avro's aliasing capabilities to preserve the old name for backward and forward compatibility.

You added a new field, providing a default that will be used when reading older versions of the file.

With this second version of the Stock schema Avro can support code generated from your original version reading an Avro file serialized with the new version (forward compatibility) as well as vice versa (backward compatibility).

Summary

The previous technique demonstrated how easy and straightforward it is to use Avro with MapReduce and Pig. The main advantage of using a data serialization format such as SequenceFile over Avro is that it has Hive support. If Hive support is important to you, take a look at https://issues.apache.org/jira/browse/HIVE-895 to make sure it's available for use with Avro.

As in the previous technique and the technique for working with small files in chapter 5, Avro's flexibility in being able to work with code-generated files, as well as its built-in generic code via the GenericData.Record class, make it a useful tool.

Using Avro to store your data gives you a number of useful, free features, such as versioning support, compression, splittability, and code generation. It plays well with MapReduce and Pig, and I hope it will have Hive support soon, too.

We've covered working with common file formats, and working with various data serialization tools for tighter compatibility with MapReduce. It's time to look at how to support file formats that may be proprietary to your organization, or even public file formats for which no input or output formats exist to work with them in MapReduce.

3.4 Custom file formats

In any organization you'll typically find a plethora of custom or uncommon file formats that litter its data centers. There may be backend servers dumping out audit files in a proprietary format or old code or systems that write files using formats that aren't in common use any longer. If you want to work with such data in MapReduce you'll need to write your own input and output format classes to work with your data. This section walks you through that process.

3.4.1 Input and output formats

At the start of this chapter we took a high-level look at the functions of Input and Output Format classes in MapReduce. Input and Output classes are required to feed data to map functions, and to write the outputs of reduce functions.

Writing input and output formats for CSV

Imagine you have a bunch of data sitting around in CSV files and you're writing multiple MapReduce jobs that read and write data in CSV form. Because CSV is text, you could use the built-in `TextInputFormat` and `TextOutputFormat`, and handle parsing the CSV in your MapReduce code. However, this can quickly become tiring, and result in the same parsing code being copy-and-pasted across all of your jobs.

If you thought MapReduce had any built-in CSV input and output formats that could take care of this parsing, you'd be out of luck—there are none.

Problem

You want to write an input and output format to work with CSV.

Solution

You will see how CSV input and output formats can be crafted from scratch, and along the way understand key properties of these classes.

Discussion

We'll cover all of the steps required to write your own format classes to work with CSV input and output. CSV is one of the simpler file formats to work with, which will make it easier to focus on MapReduce format specifics, without having to think too much about the file format.

Your custom `InputFormat` and `RecordReader` classes will parse CSV files and supply the data to the mapper in a user-friendly format. You'll support a custom field separator for noncomma delimiters. Because you don't want to reinvent the wheel, you'll leverage the CSV parser in the open source OpenCSV[36] project, which will take care of quoted fields and ignoring separator characters in quoted fields.

> **Overview of** `InputFormat` **and** `OutputFormat`
>
> I provided a detailed overview of `InputFormat` and `OutputFormat` and their related classes at the start of this chapter that may be worth referencing prior to looking at the code in this technique.

THE INPUTFORMAT

Your first step is to define the `InputFormat`. The function of `InputFormat` is to validate the set of inputs supplied to the job, identify input splits, and create a `RecordReader` class to read input from the sources. The following code[37] reads the separator (if supplied) from the job configuration, and constructs a `CSVRecordReader`:

```
public class CSVInputFormat extends
        FileInputFormat<LongWritable, TextArrayWritable> {
```

---

[36] See http://opencsv.sourceforge.net/.

[37] **GitHub source**—https://github.com/alexholmes/hadoop-book/blob/master/src/main/java/com/manning/hip/ch3/csv/CSVInputFormat.java

```
public static String CSV_TOKEN_SEPARATOR_CONFIG =
    "csvinputformat.token.delimiter";

@Override
public RecordReader<LongWritable, TextArrayWritable>
createRecordReader(InputSplit split,
                   TaskAttemptContext context) {
  String csvDelimiter = context.getConfiguration().get(
    CSV_TOKEN_SEPARATOR_CONFIG);

  Character separator = null;
  if(csvDelimiter != null && csvDelimiter.length() == 1) {
    separator = csvDelimiter.charAt(0);
  }

  return new CSVRecordReader(separator);
}

@Override
protected boolean isSplitable(JobContext context, Path file) {
  CompressionCodec codec =
      new CompressionCodecFactory(context.getConfiguration())
          .getCodec(file);
  return codec == null;
}
```

Reads (optional) custom separator for the CSV.

Creates a RecordReader and returns it.

If the file is compressed, it's not splittable; otherwise it is. The FileInputFormat parent class takes care of determining splits (by using the HDFS block size).

InputFormat and compressed files

In the previous code you'll see that when the input is compressed, a flag is returned to indicate that it couldn't be split. The reason for doing this is that compression codecs aren't splittable, apart from LZOP. But splittable LZOP can't work with regular InputFormat classes—it needs special-case LZOP InputFormat classes to work with them. These details are covered in chapter 5.

Your InputFormat class is complete. You extended the FileInputFormat class, which contains code that calculates input splits along HDFS block boundaries, keeping you from having to handle calculating the input splits yourself. The FileInputFormat manages all of the input files and splits for you. Now let's move on to the RecordReader, which will require a little more effort.

The RecordReader class performs two main functions. It must first open the input source based on the input split it is supplied, and optionally seek into a specific offset in that input split. The second function of the RecordReader is to read individual records from the input source. In your case a logical record equates to a line in your CSV file, so you'll leverage the existing LineRecordReader class in MapReduce to handle working with the file. When it's initialized with the InputSplit, it will open the input file, seek to the start of the input split, and keep reading characters until it reaches the start of the next record, which in the case of a line means a newline. The following code shows a simplified version of the LineRecordReader.initialize method:

Extract the byte offset for the start of the input split.

Open an InputStream for the input file.

If the input split doesn't start at byte 0, seek to the starting byte.

Calculate the byte offset for the end of the input split.

Create a LineReader, which the LineRecordReader uses to read each line. The InputStream that was created, and on which a seek was performed, is passed in to the constructor of the LineReader.

If your input split didn't start at byte 0, read a line from your LineReader and discard it. When the FileInputFormat determines input splits, it splits across block boundaries, without consideration for line boundaries. To determine the true starting point from a random offset in a file, you must keep reading from that offset until a newline is reached, and only then can complete lines be returned.

```java
public void initialize(InputSplit genericSplit,
                       TaskAttemptContext context) throws IOException {
  start = split.getStart();
  end = start + split.getLength();
  final Path file = split.getPath();

  FileSystem fs = file.getFileSystem(job);
  FSDataInputStream fileIn = fs.open(split.getPath());
  boolean skipFirstLine = false;
  if (start != 0) {
    skipFirstLine = true;
    --start;
    fileIn.seek(start);
  }
  in = new LineReader(fileIn, job);

  if (skipFirstLine) {
    start += in.readLine(new Text(), 0,
              (int)Math.min((long)Integer.MAX_VALUE, end - start));
  }
}
```

The LineRecordReader returns key/value pairs for each line in LongWritable/Text form. Because you'll want to provide some functionality in the RecordReader, you need to encapsulate the LineRecordReader within your class. The RecordReader needs to supply a key/value pair representation of each record to the mapper, and in this case the key is the byte offset in the file, and the value is an array containing the tokenized parts of the CSV line:[38]

The RecordReader class's responsibility is to read records from the input file. It emits keys in the form of the file offset in the file, and the values are an array of tokens in the CSV line.

Create the CSV parser (courtesy of the OpenCSV project).

Leverage LineRecordReader to perform the heavy lifting. It will open the file specified in the InputSplit and seek to the start of the split.

```java
public static class CSVRecordReader
    extends RecordReader<LongWritable, TextArrayWritable> {
  private LineRecordReader reader;
  private TextArrayWritable value;
  private final CSVParser parser;

  public CSVRecordReader(Character csvDelimiter) {
    this.reader = new LineRecordReader();
    if (csvDelimiter == null) {
      parser = new CSVParser();
    } else {
      parser = new CSVParser(csvDelimiter);
    }
  }

  @Override
  public void initialize(InputSplit split,
                         TaskAttemptContext context)
      throws IOException, InterruptedException {
    reader.initialize(split, context);
  }
```

---

[38] **GitHub source**—https://github.com/alexholmes/hadoop-book/blob/master/src/main/java/com/manning/hip/ch3/csv/CSVInputFormat.java

Next, you need to provide methods to read the next record and to get at the key and value for that record.[39]

Methods for reading the next record and retrieving the key and value of the record

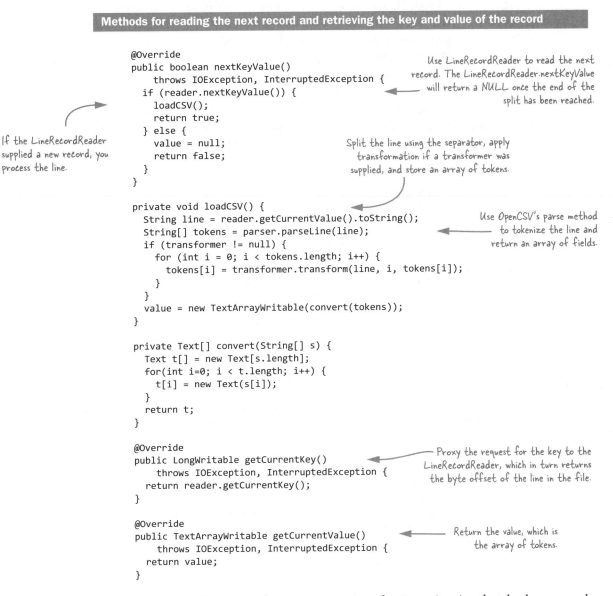

```
@Override
public boolean nextKeyValue()
    throws IOException, InterruptedException {
  if (reader.nextKeyValue()) {
    loadCSV();
    return true;
  } else {
    value = null;
    return false;
  }
}

private void loadCSV() {
  String line = reader.getCurrentValue().toString();
  String[] tokens = parser.parseLine(line);
  if (transformer != null) {
    for (int i = 0; i < tokens.length; i++) {
      tokens[i] = transformer.transform(line, i, tokens[i]);
    }
  }
  value = new TextArrayWritable(convert(tokens));
}

private Text[] convert(String[] s) {
  Text t[] = new Text[s.length];
  for(int i=0; i < t.length; i++) {
    t[i] = new Text(s[i]);
  }
  return t;
}

@Override
public LongWritable getCurrentKey()
    throws IOException, InterruptedException {
  return reader.getCurrentKey();
}

@Override
public TextArrayWritable getCurrentValue()
    throws IOException, InterruptedException {
  return value;
}
```

Use LineRecordReader to read the next record. The LineRecordReader.nextKeyValue will return a NULL once the end of the split has been reached.

If the LineRecordReader supplied a new record, you process the line.

Split the line using the separator, apply transformation if a transformer was supplied, and store an array of tokens.

Use OpenCSV's parse method to tokenize the line and return an array of fields.

Proxy the request for the key to the LineRecordReader, which in turn returns the byte offset of the line in the file.

Return the value, which is the array of tokens.

At this point, you've created an InputFormat and a RecordReader that both can work with CSV files. Now that you've completed the InputFormat, it's time to move on to the OutputFormat.

---

[39] **GitHub source**—https://github.com/alexholmes/hadoop-book/blob/master/src/main/java/com/manning/hip/ch3/csv/CSVInputFormat.java

OUTPUTFORMAT

OutputFormat classes follow a similar patter to InputFormat classes, where the Output-Format class handles the logistics around creating the output stream, and delegates the stream writes to the RecordWriter.

The CSVOutputFormat indirectly extends the FileOutputFormat class (via the Text-OutputFormat), which handles all of the logistics related to creating the output file-name, creating an instance of a compression codec (if compression was enabled), and output committing, which we'll discuss shortly.

That leaves the OutputFormat class with the tasks of supporting a custom field delimiter for your CSV output file, and also creating a compressed OutputStream if required. It must also return your CSVRecordWriter, which will write CSV lines to the output stream:[40]

```
public class CSVOutputFormat extends
    TextOutputFormat<TextArrayWritable, NullWritable> {
```

The OutputFormat expects keys as TextArrayWritable, and NullWritable values.

```
public static String CSV_TOKEN_SEPARATOR_CONFIG =
    "csvoutputformat.token.delimiter";
```

Define a configuration constant so that users can specify a custom CSV separator character.

```
@Override
public RecordWriter getRecordWriter(TaskAttemptContext job)
    throws IOException, InterruptedException {
  Configuration conf = job.getConfiguration();
  boolean isCompressed = getCompressOutput(job);

  String
      keyValueSeparator =
      conf.get(CSV_TOKEN_SEPARATOR_CONFIG, ",");
```

Read a custom separator from configuration, and if none exists use the default of a comma.

```
...
  if (!isCompressed) {
    FSDataOutputStream fileOut = fs.create(file, false);
    return new CSVRecordWriter(fileOut,
        keyValueSeparator);
```

Create an uncompressed output stream for the reducer and construct a CSVRecordWriter to write the reducer output.

```
  } else {
    FSDataOutputStream fileOut = fs.create(file, false);
    return new CSVRecordWriter(
        new DataOutputStream(codec.createOutputStream(fileOut)),
        keyValueSeparator);
  }
}
```

Create a compressed output stream using the configured compression codec for the job and construct a CSVRecordWriter to write the reducer output.

Your RecordWriter must write each record emitted by the reducer to the output destination. You require that the reducer output key is in array form representing each token in the CSV line, and you specify that the reducer output value must be a NullWritable,

---

[40] **GitHub source**—https://github.com/alexholmes/hadoop-book/blob/master/src/main/java/com/manning/hip/ch3/csv/CSVOutputFormat.java

which means that you don't care about the value part of the output. Let's take a look at
the CSVRecordWriter class. The constructor, which only sets the field separator and the
output stream, is excluded, as seen here.[41]

A RecordWriter that produces MapReduce output in CSV form

```
protected static class CSVRecordWriter
    extends RecordWriter<TextArrayWritable, NullWritable> {
  private static final String utf8 = "UTF-8";
  private static final byte[] newline;

  protected DataOutputStream out;
  private final String csvSeparator;

  @Override
  public void write(TextArrayWritable key, NullWritable value)
      throws IOException, InterruptedException {
    if (key == null) {
      return;
    }

    boolean first = true;
    for (Writable field : key.get()) {
      writeObject(first, field);
      first = false;
    }
    out.write(newline);
  }

  /**
   * Write the object to the byte stream, handling Text as a special
   * case.
   *
   * @param o the object to print
   * @throws IOException if the write throws, we pass it on
   */
  private void writeObject(boolean first, Writable o)
    throws IOException {

    if(!first) {
      out.write(csvSeparator.getBytes(utf8));
    }

    boolean encloseQuotes = false;
    if (o.toString().contains(csvSeparator)) {
      encloseQuotes = true;
    }

    if(encloseQuotes) {
      out.write("\".getBytes(utf8));
    }
    if (o instanceof Text) {
      Text to = (Text) o;
      out.write(to.getBytes(), 0, to.getLength());
```

The write method is called for each record emitted by the reducer. Iterate through all of the fields in the array and call the writeObject to handle writing the field to the output stream. When this is complete, write the newline string to the stream.

Write the CSV separator.

Write quotes if the field contains the separator character.

Write your field.

---

[41] **GitHub source**—https://github.com/alexholmes/hadoop-book/blob/master/src/main/java/com/
manning/hip/ch3/csv/CSVOutputFormat.java

```
    } else {
      out.write(o.toString().getBytes(utf8));
    }
    if(encloseQuotes) {
      out.write("\".getBytes(utf8));
    }
  }
}
```

Now you need to apply the new input and output format classes in a MapReduce job.

MAPREDUCE

Your MapReduce jobs will take CSV as input, and also produce CSV which is separated by colons, not commas. It'll perform identity map and reduce functions, which means that you won't be changing the data as it passes through MapReduce. Your input file will be delimited with the comma character, and your output file will be colon-separated. Your input and output format classes support the notion of custom delimiters via Hadoop configuration properties.

The MapReduce code is as follows:[42]

```
conf.set(CSVInputFormat.CSV_TOKEN_SEPARATOR_CONFIG, ",");
conf.set(CSVOutputFormat.CSV_TOKEN_SEPARATOR_CONFIG, ":");

Job job = new Job(conf);
job.setJarByClass(CSVMapReduce.class);
job.setMapperClass(Map.class);
job.setReducerClass(Reduce.class);
job.setInputFormatClass(CSVInputFormat.class);
job.setOutputFormatClass(CSVOutputFormat.class);

job.setMapOutputKeyClass(LongWritable.class);
job.setMapOutputValueClass(TextArrayWritable.class);

job.setOutputKeyClass(TextArrayWritable.class);
job.setOutputValueClass(NullWritable.class);
```

Indicate the separator character for the CSV input file.

Indicate the separator character for the CSV output file, which in this case is a colon.

Set the OutputFormat class.

Set the InputFormat class.

The map and reduce functions don't do much other than echo their inputs to output, but you'll include them so you can see how to work with the CSV in your MapReduce code:[43]

```
public static class Map
    extends Mapper<LongWritable, TextArrayWritable,
    LongWritable, TextArrayWritable> {

  @Override
  protected void map(LongWritable key, TextArrayWritable value,
                     Context context)
      throws
      IOException, InterruptedException {
    context.write(key, value);
```

You can see the TextArrayWritable being supplied as input to the mapper.

---

[42] **GitHub source**—https://github.com/alexholmes/hadoop-book/blob/master/src/main/java/com/manning/hip/ch3/csv/CSVMapReduce.java

[43] **GitHub source**—https://github.com/alexholmes/hadoop-book/blob/master/src/main/java/com/manning/hip/ch3/csv/CSVMapReduce.java

```
        }
    }

    public static class Reduce
        extends Reducer<LongWritable, TextArrayWritable,
        TextArrayWritable, NullWritable> {

      public void reduce(LongWritable key,
                         Iterable<TextArrayWritable> values,
                         Context context)
           throws IOException, InterruptedException {
          for (TextArrayWritable val : values) {
            context.write(val, NullWritable.get());
          }
        }
    }
}
```

Similarly the TextArrayWritable is also used as output.

If you run this input against a comma-delimited file, you can examine the mapper output and see if the results are as expected:

```
$ hadoop fs -put test-data/stocks.txt stocks.txt
$ bin/run.sh com.manning.hip.ch3.csv.CSVMapReduce stocks.txt output

$ hadoop fs -cat output/part*
AAPL:2009-01-02:85.88:91.04:85.16:90.75:26643400:90.75
AAPL:2008-01-02:199.27:200.26:192.55:194.84:38542100:194.84
AAPL:2007-01-03:86.29:86.58:81.90:83.80:44225700:83.80
...
```

You now have a functional `InputFormat` and `OutputFormat` that can consume and produce CSV output in MapReduce.

PIG AND HIVE

Pig's piggybank library contains a `CSVLoader` that can be used to load CSVs into tuples. It supports double-quoted fields in the CSV and provides each item as a `byte array`.

There's a GitHub project called csv-serde,[44] which has a Hive SerDe that can both serialize and deserialize CSV. As with the `InputFormat` example, it also uses the OpenCSV project for reading and writing the CSV.

Summary

This technique demonstrated how you can write your own MapReduce format classes to work with text-based data. Work is currently underway in MapReduce to add a CSV Input Format (see https://issues.apache.org/jira/browse/MAPREDUCE-2208).

Arguably, it would have been simpler to use the `TextInputFormat` and split the line in the mapper. But if you need to do this multiple times you're likely suffering from the copy-paste anti-pattern, since the same code to tokenize the CSV likely exists in multiple locations. If the code is written with code reuse in mind, you'd be covered.

We've covered how you can write your own IO format classes to work with a custom file format in MapReduce. Now we need to look at a crucial aspect of working with output formats—output committing.

---

[44] See https://github.com/ogrodnek/csv-serde.

3.4.2 *The importance of output committing*

In the CSV OutputFormat example earlier in this chapter, you extended FileOutput-Format, which takes care of "committing" output after the task has succeeded. Why do you need "commits" in MapReduce, and why should you care?

As a job and its tasks are executing, at some point they will start writing job output. Tasks and jobs can fail, they can be restarted, and they can also be speculatively executed.[45] To allow OutputFormats to correctly handle these scenarios, MapReduce has the notion of an OutputCommitter, which is a mechanism by which MapReduce invokes a callback when an individual task as well as the overall job have completed.

Most OutputFormats in MapReduce use FileOutputFormat, which uses FileOutput-Committer for its output committing. When the FileOutputFormat is initially consulted about the location of the output files, it delegates the decision of where the output should be located to the FileOutputCommitter, which in turn specifies that the output should go to a temporary directory under the job output directory (<job-output>/_temporary/<task-attempt-id>). Only after the overall task has completed will the FileOutputCommitter be notified, at which point the temporary output is moved to the job output directory. When the overall job has successfully completed the FileOutputCommitter is again notified, and this time it touches a file _SUCCESS in the job output directory, to help downstream processors know the job succeeded.

This is great if your data sink is HDFS, where you can leverage FileOutputFormat and its committing mechanism. Things start to get trickier when you're working with data sources other than files, such as a database. If in such cases idempotent writes (the same operation applied multiple times without changing the result) are necessary, you'll need to factor that into the design of your destination data store or your OutputFormat.

This topic was examined in more detail in chapter 2, which covers exporting data from Hadoop to databases.

3.5 *Chapter summary*

The goal for this chapter was to show you how to work with common file formats such as XML and JSON in MapReduce. We also looked at more sophisticated file formats such as SequenceFiles, Avro, and Protocol Buffers, which provide useful features for working with big data, such as versioning, compression, and complex data structures. We also walked you through the process of working with your own custom file formats to ensure they'll work in MapReduce.

At this point you're equipped to work with any file format in MapReduce. Now that you understand how to effectively work with files in HDFS and MapReduce, the next step is to look at patterns to help you effectively work with your data. That's next in chapter 4.

---

[45] Speculative execution is when MapReduce executes multiple tasks for the same input data, to guard against slow or misbehaving nodes slowing down the overall job. By default both map-side and reduce-side speculative execution is enabled. The mapred.map.tasks.speculative.execution and mapred.reduce.tasks.speculative.execution configuration parameters control this behavior.

Part 3

Big data patterns

Now that you've completed part 1, which introduced you to Hadoop, and part 2, which covered how to best move and store your data in Hadoop, you're ready to explore part 3 of this book, which examines the techniques you need to know to streamline your work with big data.

In chapter 4 we'll examine techniques to optimize MapReduce operations, such as joining and sorting on large datasets. These techniques make jobs run faster and allow for more efficient use of computational resources.

Chapter 5 applies the same principles to HDFS and looks at how to work with small files, as well as how compression can save you from many storage and computational headaches.

Finally, chapter 6 looks at how to measure, collect, and profile your MapReduce jobs and identify areas in your code and hardware that could be causing jobs to run longer than they should.

Applying MapReduce
patterns to big data

This chapter covers

- Learning how to join data with map-side and reduce-side joins
- Understanding how a secondary sort works
- Discovering how partitioning works and how to globally sort data

With your data safely in HDFS, it's time to learn how to work with that data in MapReduce. Previous chapters showed you some MapReduce snippets in action when working with data serialization. In this chapter we'll look at how to work effectively with big data in MapReduce to solve common problems.

MapReduce basics

If you want to understand the mechanics of MapReduce and how to write basic MapReduce programs, it's worthwhile to read *Hadoop in Action* by Chuck Lam.

MapReduce contains many powerful features, but in this chapter we'll focus on joining, sorting, and sampling. These three patterns are important because they're natural operations you'll want to perform on your big data, and the goal of your clusters should be to squeeze as much performance as possible from your MapReduce jobs.

The ability to join disparate and sparse data is a powerful MapReduce feature, but an awkward one in practice, so we'll also look at advanced techniques to optimize join operations with large datasets. Examples of joins include combining log files with reference data from a database and inbound link calculations on web graphs.

Sorting in MapReduce is also a black art, and we'll dive into the depths of MapReduce to understand how it works by examining two techniques that everyone will encounter at some point, secondary sort and total order sorting. We'll wrap things up with a look at *sampling* in MapReduce, which provides the opportunity to quickly iterate over a large dataset by working with a small subset of that data.

4.1 Joining

Joins are relational constructs you use to combine relations together (you're probably familiar with them in the context of databases). In MapReduce joins are applicable in situations where you have two or more datasets you want to combine. An example would be when you want to combine your users (which you extracted from your OLTP database) with your log files that contain user activity details. Scenarios where it would be useful to combine these datasets together include these:

- Data aggregations based on user demographics (such as differences in user habits between teenagers and users in their 30s)
- To send an email to users who haven't used the website for a prescribed number of days
- A feedback loop that examines a user's browsing habits, allowing your system to recommend previously unexplored site features to the user

All of these scenarios require you to join datasets together, and the two most common types of joins are inner joins and outer joins. *Inner joins* compare all tuples in relations *L* and *R*, and produce a result if a join predicate is satisfied. In contrast, *outer joins* don't require both tuples to match based on a join predicate, and instead can retain a record from *L* or *R* even if no match exists. Figure 4.1 shows the different types of joins.

In this section we'll look at three joining strategies in MapReduce that support the two most common types of joins (inner and outer). The three strategies perform the join either in the map phase or in the reduce phase by taking advantage of the MapReduce sort-merge architecture:

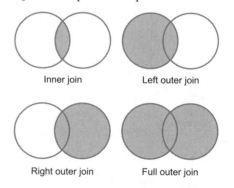

Inner join   Left outer join

Right outer join   Full outer join

Figure 4.1   Different types of joins shown as Venn diagrams used to combine relations together

1 *Repartition join*—A reduce-side join for situations where you're joining two or more large datasets together

2 *Replication join*—A map-side join that works in situations where one of the datasets is small enough to cache

3 *Semi-join*—Another map-side join where one dataset is initially too large to fit into memory, but after some filtering can be reduced down to a size that can fit in memory

After we cover these joining strategies, we'll include a decision tree so you can see what the best join strategy is for your situation.

4.1.1 *Repartition join*

A repartition join is a reduce-side join that takes advantage of MapReduce's sort-merge to group together records. It's implemented as a single MapReduce job, and can support an *N*-way join, where *N* is the number of datasets being joined.

The map phase is responsible for reading the data from the various datasets, determining the join value for each record, and emitting that join value as the output key. The output value contains data that you'll want to include when you combine datasets together in the reducer to produce the job output.

A single reducer invocation receives all of the values for a join key emitted by the map function and partitions the data into *N* partitions. After the reducer has read all of the input records for the join value and partitioned them in memory, it performs a Cartesian product across all partitions and emits the results of each join. Figure 4.2 shows the repartition join at a high level.

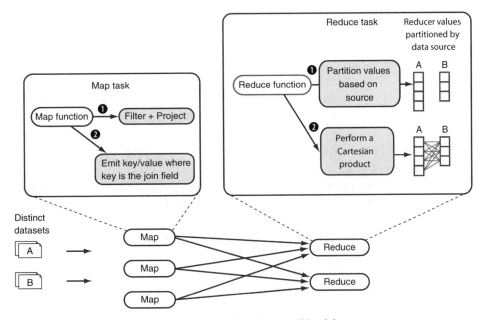

Figure 4.2 A basic MapReduce implementation of a repartition join

Filtering and projection

With a repartition join, and with MapReduce in general, it's a good idea to cut down on the amount of data sent between the map and reduce phases, because it's expensive to sort and transfer data between the two phases over a network. If reduce-side work can't be avoided, as in the case of the repartition join, a good practice is to filter and project as much as possible in the map phase. Filtering is the act of discarding map input records that you don't need to include in the job output. Projection is a relational algebra term and is used to cut down the fields sent to the reducer. For example, if you're working with user data and you only care about the results of the join containing the age of a user, your map task should only project (or emit) the age field, and not any of the other fields for the user.

TECHNIQUE 19   **Optimized repartition joins**

The book *Hadoop in Action* contains an example of how to implement a repartition join using the org.apache.hadoop.contrib.utils.join Hadoop contrib package. The contrib package does all of the heavy lifting and only requires a handful of methods to be implemented.

   The contrib implementation of the repartition join is not space efficient; it requires all of the output values for a given join value to be loaded into memory before it can perform the multiway join. It's more efficient to load the smaller of the datasets into memory and then iterate over the larger of datasets, performing the join along the way.

Problem

You want to perform a repartition join in MapReduce, but you want to do so without the overhead of caching all the records in the reducer.

Solution

This technique uses an optimized repartition join framework that caches just one of the datasets being joined to reduce the amount of data cached in the reducers.

Discussion

Appendix D includes an implementation of an optimized repartition join framework that's modeled after the org.apache.hadoop.contrib.utils.join contrib package. This optimized framework only caches records from the smaller of the two datasets to cut down on the memory overhead of caching all the records. Figure 4.3 shows the improved repartition join in action.

   Figure 4.4 shows a class diagram broken into two parts, with a generic framework and some sample implementation classes

   Users of the join framework must provide concrete implementations of the OptimizedDataJoinMapperBase and the OptimizedDataJoinReducerBase classes.

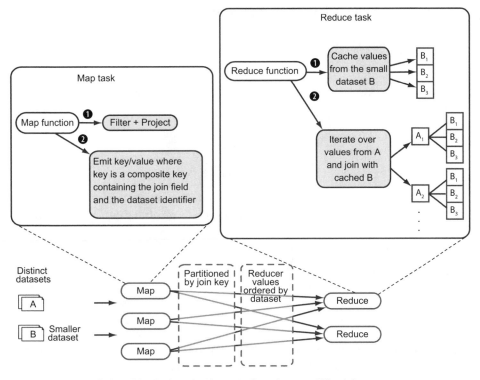

Figure 4.3   An optimized MapReduce implementation of a repartition join

Let's say you want to join together some user details and logs that contain information about user activity. The first step is to determine which of the two datasets is smaller in size. For a reasonably sized website with these two datasets it's likely that the user dataset will be smaller than the activity logs.

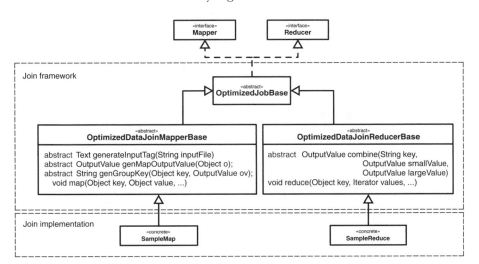

Figure 4.4   Class diagram showing main classes in the framework and sample implementation

The user data in the following example consists of the user's name, age, and state:

```
$ cat test-data/ch4/users.txt
anne     22    NY
joe      39    CO
alison   35    NY
mike     69    VA
marie    27    OR
jim      21    OR
bob      71    CA
mary     53    NY
dave     36    VA
dude     50    CA.
```

The user activity logs contain the user's name, the action performed, and the source IP address. This file would normally be a much larger file than the user's file:

```
$ cat test-data/ch4/user-logs.txt
jim      logout       93.24.237.12
mike     new_tweet    87.124.79.252
bob      new_tweet    58.133.120.100
mike     logout       55.237.104.36
jim      new_tweet    93.24.237.12
marie    view_user    122.158.130.90
```

First, you must provide the implementation of the `OptimizedDataJoinMapperBase` abstract class, which is called on the map side. The implementation class is responsible for creating the map output key and value, as well as informing the framework whether the current input split being worked on is the smaller of the datasets being joined:[1]

```
public class SampleMap extends OptimizedDataJoinMapperBase {

    private boolean smaller;

    @Override
    protected Text generateInputTag(String inputFile) {
        smaller = inputFile.contains("users.txt");
        return new Text(inputFile);
    }

    @Override
    protected String generateGroupKey(Object key,
                             OptimizedTaggedMapOutput output) {
        return key.toString();
    }
}
```

You hardcode the fact that the user's file is the smaller file.

This method needs to return a unique identifier for the supplied input file, so you echo back the filename.

This MapReduce job will use the KeyValueTextInputFormat, so the key contains the username, which is the join field.

---

[1] **GitHub source**—https://github.com/alexholmes/hadoop-book/blob/master/src/main/java/com/manning/hip/ch4/joins/improved/SampleMap.java

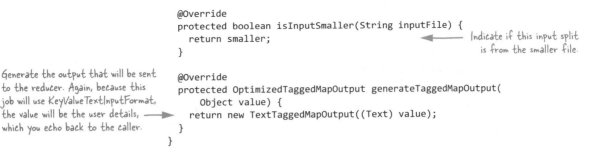

Indicate if this input split is from the smaller file.

```
@Override
protected boolean isInputSmaller(String inputFile) {
  return smaller;
}
```

Generate the output that will be sent to the reducer. Again, because this job will use KeyValueTextInputFormat, the value will be the user details, which you echo back to the caller.

```
@Override
protected OptimizedTaggedMapOutput generateTaggedMapOutput(
    Object value) {
  return new TextTaggedMapOutput((Text) value);
}
}
```

Next up, you'll write an implementation of the OptimizedDataJoinReducerBase abstract class, which is called on the reduce side. In this class you're passed a map output key and two map output values from different datasets, and you need to return the reduce output tuple:[2]

```
public class Reduce extends OptimizedDataJoinReducerBase {

    private TextTaggedMapOutput output = new TextTaggedMapOutput();
    private Text textOutput = new Text();

    @Override
    protected OptimizedTaggedMapOutput combine(String key,
                                    OptimizedTaggedMapOutput value1,
                                    OptimizedTaggedMapOutput value2) {
      if(value1 == null || value2 == null) {
        return null;
      }
      Object[] values = {
          smallValue.getData(), largeValue.getData()
      };
      textOutput.set(StringUtils.join(values, "\t"));
      output.setData(textOutput);
      return output;
    }
}
```

You're performing an inner join, so if any of the values are NULL, return a NULL, which will result in no reducer output.

Combine both of the values as the reducer output for the key.

Finally, the job driver code needs to indicate the InputFormat class and set up the secondary sort:[3]

```
job.setInputFormat(KeyValueTextInputFormat.class);

job.setMapOutputKeyClass(CompositeKey.class);
job.setMapOutputValueClass(TextTaggedMapOutput.class);
job.setOutputKeyClass(Text.class);
job.setOutputValueClass(Text.class);

job.setPartitionerClass(CompositeKeyPartitioner.class);
job.setOutputKeyComparatorClass(CompositeKeyComparator.class);
job.setOutputValueGroupingComparator(
    CompositeKeyOnlyComparator.class);
```

---

[2] **GitHub source**—https://github.com/alexholmes/hadoop-book/blob/master/src/main/java/com/manning/hip/ch4/joins/improved/SampleReduce.java

[3] **GitHub source**—https://github.com/alexholmes/hadoop-book/blob/master/src/main/java/com/manning/hip/ch4/joins/improved/SampleMain.java

You're ready to run the join:

```
$ hadoop fs -put test-data/ch4/users.txt users.txt
$ hadoop fs -put test-data/ch4/user-logs.txt user-logs.txt

$ bin/run.sh com.manning.hip.ch4.joins.improved.SampleMain \
    users.txt,user-logs.txt \                                      ◄─────── The files being joined
    output

$ hadoop fs -cat output/part*
bob      71    CA    new_tweet    58.133.120.100
jim      21    OR    logout       93.24.237.12
jim      21    OR    new_tweet    93.24.237.12
jim      21    OR    login        198.184.237.49
marie    27    OR    login        58.133.120.100
marie    27    OR    view_user    122.158.130.90
mike     69    VA    new_tweet    87.124.79.252
mike     69    VA    logout       55.237.104.36
```

If you refer back to the original files you joined, you can see that because you implemented an inner join, the output doesn't include entries for the users anne, alison, and others that weren't in the log file.

Summary

My join implementation improves on the Hadoop contrib join by buffering only the values of the smaller dataset. But it still suffers from the problem of all the data being transmitted between the map and reduce phases, which is an expensive network cost to incur.

Further, while the Hadoop contrib join package can support *N*-way joins, my implementation only supports two-way joins.

A simple mechanism to further reduce the memory footprint of the reduce-side join is to be aggressive about projections in the map function. Projection is the act of cutting down on the fields that the map emits. For example, if you're working with user data, and you only care about the result of the join containing the age of a user, then the map task should only project (or emit) the age field, and not any of the other fields for the user. This results in less network traffic between the map and reduce tasks, and also cuts down on the reducer memory overhead when performing the join.

My repartition join implementation supports filtering and projections, like the original join contrib package. Filtering is supported by allowing the genMapOutputValue method to return NULL, and projections are supported by allowing this same method to define the contents of the output value.

What if you want to avoid the overhead of sorting and transferring all of your data over the network to the reducer? The solution for this brings us to the two next join strategies, the replicated join and semi-join.

4.1.2   Replicated joins

A replicated join is a map-side join, and gets its name from its function—the smallest of the datasets is replicated to all the map hosts. The replicated join is predicated on the fact that one of the datasets being joined is small enough to be cached in memory. You'll use the distributed cache[4] to copy the small dataset to the nodes running the map tasks, and use the initialization method of each map task to load the small dataset into a hashtable. Use the key from each record fed to the map function from the large dataset to look up the small dataset hashtable, and perform a join between the large dataset record and all of the records from the small dataset that match the join value. Figure 4.5 shows how the replicated join works in MapReduce.

The implementation of the replicated join is straightforward, and you can see a demonstration in *Hadoop in Action*. Appendix D provides a generalized framework to perform replicated joins, which can work with data from any `InputFormat` and `Output-Format`. (We'll use this framework in the next technique.) This join framework dynamically determines whether the contents of the distributed cache or the input split should be cached, depending on which is smaller.

Is there a way to utilize map-side joins in cases where initially neither of the datasets are small enough to fit in memory? Time to look at semi-joins.

4.1.3   Semi-joins

Imagine a situation where you're working with two large datasets that you want to join, such as user logs and user data from an OLTP database. Neither of these datasets is small enough to cache in a map task's memory, so it would seem you'll have to resign

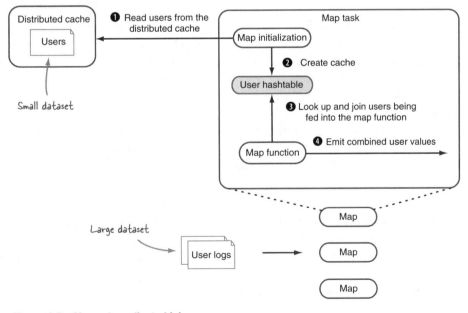

Figure 4.5   Map-only replicated join

---

[4] Hadoop's distributed cache copies files located on the MapReduce client host, or files in HDFS, to the slave nodes before any map or reduce tasks are executed on the nodes. Tasks can read these files from their local disk to use as part of their work.

yourself to performing a reduce-side join. Not necessarily—ask yourself this question: would one of the datasets fit into memory if you were to remove all records that didn't match a record from the other dataset? In the example there's a good chance that the users that appear in your logs are a small percentage of the overall set of users in your OLTP database, so by removing all the OLTP users that don't appear in your logs, you could get the dataset down to a size that fits into memory. If this is the case, the semi-join is the solution.

Figure 4.6 shows the three MapReduce jobs you'll execute to perform a semi-join. Let's look at what's involved in writing a semi-join.

TECHNIQUE 20   Implementing a semi-join

When faced with the challenge of joining two large datasets together, the obvious choice is to go with a repartition join, which leverages the full MapReduce framework to perform the join on the reduce-side. In fact, this may be your only option if you can't filter one of the datasets to a size that can be cached on the map side. However, if you believe that you could pare down one dataset to a manageable size, you may not have to use a repartition join.

Problem

You want to join large datasets together and at the same time avoid the overhead of the shuffle and sort phases.

Solution

In this technique you will use three MapReduce jobs to join two datasets together to avoid the overhead of a reducer-side join. This technique is useful in situations where you're working with large datasets, but a job can be reduced down to a size that can fit into the memory of a task by filtering out records that don't match the other dataset.

Discussion

For this technique you'll leverage the replicated join code I wrote (see appendix D) to implement the last two steps in the MapReduce job. In this technique you'll break down the three jobs illustrated in figure 4.6.

JOB 1

The function of the first MapReduce job is to produce a set of unique user names that exist in the logs files. You do this by having the map function perform a projection of the user name, and in turn use the reducers to emit the user name. To cut down on the amount of data transferred between the map and reduce phases, have the map task cache all of the user names in a HashSet and emit the values of the HashSet in the cleanup method. Figure 4.7 shows the flow of this job.

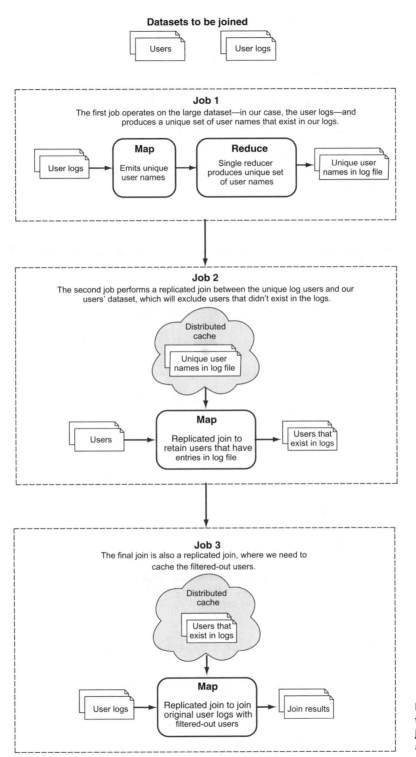

Figure 4.6 The three MapReduce jobs that comprise a semi-join

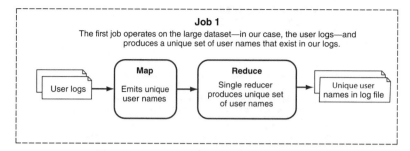

Figure 4.7   The first job in the semi-join produces a unique set of user names that exist in the log files.

The following code shows the MapReduce job:[5]

```java
public static class Map extends Mapper<Text, Text, Text, NullWritable> {
  private Set<String> keys = new HashSet<String>();          // Create the
                                                             // HashSet to cache
                                                             // the user names.
  @Override
  protected void map(Text key, Text value, Context context)
      throws IOException, InterruptedException {
    keys.add(key.toString());                               // Add the user
  }                                                          // name to the cache.

  @Override
  protected void cleanup(
      Context context)
      throws IOException, InterruptedException {
    Text outputKey = new Text();
    for(String key: keys) {
      outputKey.set(key);
      context.write(outputKey, NullWritable.get());         // Write out the
    }                                                       // user names.
  }
}

public static class Reduce
  extends Reducer<Text, NullWritable, Text, NullWritable> {
  @Override
  protected void reduce(Text key, Iterable<NullWritable> values,
                        Context context)
      throws IOException, InterruptedException {
    context.write(key, NullWritable.get());                 // Write out the
  }                                                         // user names.
}
```

The result of the first job is a unique set of users that appears in the log files.

JOB 2

The second step is an elaborate filtering MapReduce job, where the goal is to remove users from the user dataset that don't exist in the log data. This is a map-only job that

---

[5] **GitHub source**—https://github.com/alexholmes/hadoop-book/blob/master/src/main/java/com/manning/hip/ch4/joins/semijoin/UniqueHashedKeyJob.java

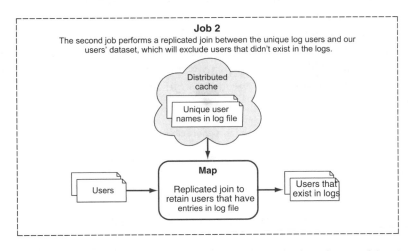

Figure 4.8   The second job in the semi-join removes users from the user dataset missing from the log data.

uses a replicated join to cache the user names that appear in the log files and join them with the user's dataset. The unique user's output from job 1 will be substantially smaller than the entire user dataset, which makes it the natural selection for caching. Figure 4.8 shows the flow of this job.

This is a good time to quickly look at the replicated join framework in appendix D. The framework has built-in support for KeyValueTextInputFormat and TextOutputFormat, and assumes that the key produced by the KeyValueTextInputFormat is the join key. As it happens, this is also how your data is laid out. You can see the class diagram for the framework in figure 4.9.

The GenericReplicatedJoin class performs the join. The first three methods in the GenericReplicatedJoin class, as shown in figure 4.9, are extensible and allow the

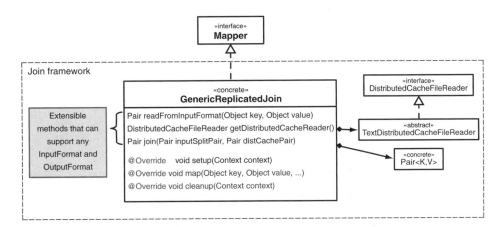

Figure 4.9   The replicated join framework illustrating the class diagram

behavior of the replicated join to be customized. The `readFromInputFormat` can be used to work with any `InputFormat`, and the `getDistributedCacheReader` method can be overridden to support any file formats in the distributed cache. For this step you're interested in the join method, which produces the output key and value for the job. The default implementation combines the values of both datasets to produce the final output value. You want to change this to output only the value from the user's table, as follows:[6]

```
public class ReplicatedFilterJob extends GenericReplicatedJoin {
  @Override
  public Pair join(Pair inputSplitPair, Pair distCachePair) {
    return inputSplitPair;
  }
}
```

You also need to add the files from job 1 into the distributed cache:

```
for(FileStatus f: fs.listStatus(uniqueUserStatus)) {
  if(f.getPath().getName().startsWith("part")) {
    DistributedCache.addCacheFile(
      f.getPath().toUri(), conf);
  }
}
```

That's it. Let's take a look at the complete driver code, which leverages the `GenericReplicatedJoin` class:

```
public class ReplicatedFilterJob extends GenericReplicatedJoin {
  public static void runJob(Path usersPath,
                            Path uniqueUsersPath,
                            Path outputPath)
      throws Exception {

    Configuration conf = new Configuration();

    for(FileStatus f: fs.listStatus(uniqueUsersPath)) {
      if(f.getPath().getName().startsWith("part")) {
        DistributedCache.addCacheFile(f.getPath().toUri(), conf);
      }
    }

    Job job = new Job(conf);

    job.setJarByClass(ReplicatedFilterJob.class);
    job.setMapperClass(ReplicatedFilterJob.class);

    job.setNumReduceTasks(0);

    job.setInputFormatClass(KeyValueTextInputFormat.class);

    outputPath.getFileSystem(conf).delete(outputPath, true);

    FileInputFormat.setInputPaths(job, usersPath);
```

---

[6]   **GitHub source**—https://github.com/alexholmes/hadoop-book/blob/master/src/main/java/com/manning/hip/ch4/joins/semijoin/ReplicatedFilterJob.java

```
    FileOutputFormat.setOutputPath(job, outputPath);

    if(!job.waitForCompletion(true)) {
      throw new Exception("Job failed");
    }
  }

  @Override
  public Pair join(Pair inputSplitPair, Pair distCachePair) {
    return inputSplitPair;
  }
}
```

The output of the second job is the filtered users that also existed in the log output.

JOB 3

In this final step you'll combine the filtered users produced from job 2 with the original user logs. Ostensibly, the filtered users are now small enough to stick into memory, allowing you to put them in the distributed cache. Figure 4.10 shows the flow of this job.

```
FileStatus usersStatus = fs.getFileStatus(usersPath);

for(FileStatus f: fs.listStatus(usersPath)) {
  if(f.getPath().getName().startsWith("part")) {
    DistributedCache.addCacheFile(                    ◄────  Add the filtered user files
      f.getPath().toUri(), conf);                            to the distributed cache.
  }
```

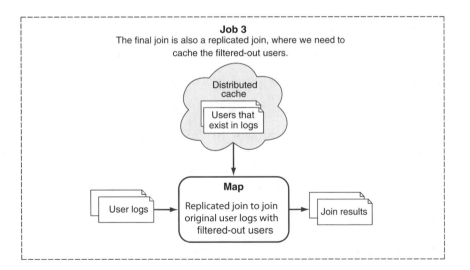

Figure 4.10   The third job in the semi-join combines the users produced from the second job with the original user logs.

Again you're using the replicated join to perform the join, but this time you won't tweak the behavior of the join method because you want the data from both datasets to appear in the final output.

Run the code and look at the output produced by each of the previous steps:

```
$ bin/run.sh com.manning.hip.ch4.joins.semijoin.Main \
    users.txt user-logs.txt output
```

```
$ hadoop fs -ls output
/user/aholmes/output/filtered
/user/aholmes/output/result
/user/aholmes/output/unique
```

◄──── *The output directory shows three subdirectories corresponding to the three jobs you ran.*

```
$ hadoop fs -cat output/unique/part*
bob
jim
marie
mike
```

◄──── *The output of the first job is the unique user names in the log file.*

```
$ hadoop fs -cat output/filtered/part*
mike   69  VA
marie  27  OR
jim    21  OR
bob    71  CA
```

◄──── *The second job output shows the users' file filtered by users that were in the log file.*

```
$ hadoop fs -cat output/result/part*
jim    logout     93.24.237.12      21  OR
mike   new_tweet  87.124.79.252  69  VA
bob    new_tweet  58.133.120.100 71  CA
mike   logout     55.237.104.36  69  VA
jim    new_tweet  93.24.237.12   21  OR
marie  view_user  122.158.130.90 27  OR
jim    login      198.184.237.49 21  OR
marie  login      58.133.120.100 27  OR
```

◄──── *The final output has the results of the join between the user logs and the filtered users.*

The output shows the logical progression of the jobs in the semi-join and the final join output.

Summary

In this technique we looked at how to use a semi-join to combine two datasets together. The semi-join construct involves more steps than the other joins, but it's a powerful way to leverage a map-side join even when working with large datasets (with the caveat that one of the datasets must be reduced to a size that fits in memory).

With the three join strategies in hand, you may be wondering which one you should use in what circumstance.

4.1.4 Picking the best join strategy for your data

Each of the join strategies we've covered has different strengths and weaknesses, so how do you determine which one is best suited for the data you're working with?

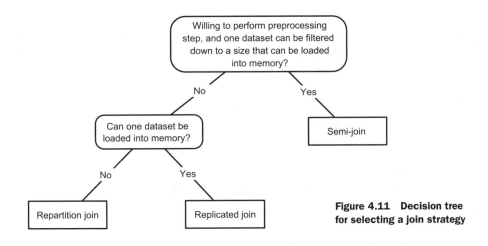

**Figure 4.11   Decision tree
for selecting a join strategy**

Figure 4.11 shows a decision tree you can use, which is modeled after the decision tree presented in the paper "A Comparison of Join Algorithms."[7]

I'll summarize the decision tree shown in the previous figure with the following three points:

- If one of your datasets is small enough to fit into a mapper's memory, the map-only replicated join is sufficient.
- If both datasets are large, and one dataset can be substantially reduced by prefiltering elements that don't match the other, the semi-join works well.
- If you can't preprocess your data and your data sizes are too large to cache, which means you have to perform the join in the reducer, repartition joins needs to be used.

It's possible to have reduce-side joins in MapReduce because MapReduce sorts and correlates the map output keys together. In the next section we'll look at common sorting techniques in MapReduce.

4.2   Sorting

MapReduce sorts data for two reasons: sorting allows MapReduce to group the map keys together so that reduce tasks can be called once per unique map key. And sorting allows users to sort job outputs when they have specific use cases that need sorting. Examples of these use cases include data analytical jobs where you want to see the top *N* most popular users or web pages.

In this section you'll look at two particular scenarios where you want to tweak the behavior of MapReduce sorting. First we'll look at the secondary sort, which allows you to sort values for a reducer key. Secondary sorts are useful when you want some data to arrive at your reducer ahead of other data, as in the case of the optimized repartition join earlier in this chapter. Secondary sorts are also useful if you want your

---

[7]   See http://pages.cs.wisc.edu/~jignesh/publ/hadoopjoin.pdf.

job output to be sorted by a secondary key. An example of this would be if you want to perform a primary sort of stock data by stock symbol, and then perform a secondary sort on the time of each stock quote during a day. Secondary sorts are used in many of the techniques in this book, ranging from optimizing the repartition join to graph algorithms such as friends-of-friends.

The second scenario we'll cover in this section looks at sorting data across all the reducer outputs. This is useful in situations where you want to extract the top or bottom *N* elements from a dataset.

4.2.1 Secondary sort

As you saw earlier in the joining section, you need secondary sorts to allow some records to arrive at a reducer ahead of other records. Secondary sorts require an understanding of both data arrangement and data flows in MapReduce. Figure 4.12 shows the three elements that impact data arrangement and flow (partitioning, sorting, and grouping) and how they're integrated into MapReduce.

The partitioner is invoked as part of the map output collection process, and is used to determine which reducer should receive the map output. The sorting RawComparator

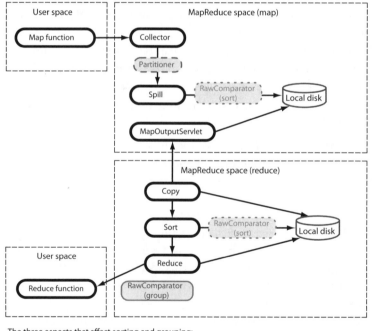

Figure 4.12   An overview of where sorting, partitioning, and grouping occur in MapReduce

is used to sort the map outputs within their respective partitions, and is used in both the map and reduce sides. Finally, the grouping RawComparator is responsible for determining the group boundaries across the sorted records.

The default behavior in MapReduce is for all three functions to operate on the entire output key emitted by map functions.

TECHNIQUE 21 Implementing a secondary sort

Secondary sorts are useful when you want some of the values for a unique map key to arrive at a reducer ahead of other values. I'll show the value of secondary sorting in other techniques in this book, such as the optimized repartition join, and the friends-of-friends algorithm in chapter 7.

Problem

You want to order values sent to a single reducer invocation for a natural key.

Solution

This technique covers writing your partitioner, sort comparator, and grouping comparator classes, which are required for secondary sort to work.

Discussion

In this technique we'll look at how to use secondary sort to order people's names. You'll use the primary sort to order people's last names, and secondary sort on their first names.

To support secondary sort you need to create a composite output key, which will be emitted by your map functions. The composite key will contain two parts:

1 The *natural key*, which is the key to use for joining purposes
2 The *secondary key*, which is the key to use to order all of the values sent to the reducer for the natural key

Figure 4.13 shows the composite key for your user. It also shows a composite value that provides reducer-side access to the secondary key.

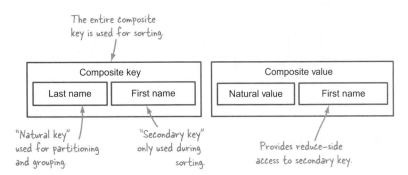

Figure 4.13 The user composite key and value

Let's go through the partitioning, sorting, and grouping phases and implement them for your user. But before that, you need to write your composite key class.

COMPOSITE KEY

The composite key contains both the first and last name. It extends WritableComparable, which is recommended for Writable classes that are emitted as keys from map functions:[8]

```
public class Person implements WritableComparable<Person> {

  private String firstName;
  private String lastName;

  @Override
  public void readFields(DataInput in) throws IOException {
    this.firstName = in.readUTF();
    this.lastName = in.readUTF();
  }

  @Override
  public void write(DataOutput out) throws IOException {
    out.writeUTF(firstName);
    out.writeUTF(lastName);
  }
...
```

Figure 4.14 shows the configuration names and methods to call to set the partitioning, sorting, and grouping classes, and it also shows what part of the composite key each class uses.

Let's look at the implementation code for each of these classes.

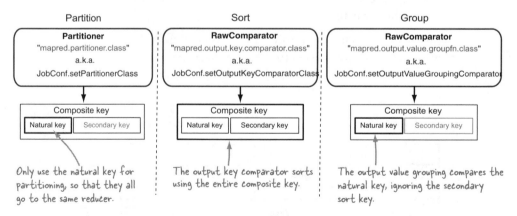

Figure 4.14 Partitioning, sorting, and grouping settings and key utilization

---

[8] **GitHub source**—https://github.com/alexholmes/hadoop-book/blob/master/src/main/java/com/manning/hip/ch4/sort/secondary/Person.java

PARTITIONER

The partitioner is used to determine which reducer should receive a map output record. The default MapReduce partitioner (HashPartitioner) calls the hashCode method of the output key and performs a modulo with the number of reducers to determine which reducer should receive the output. The default partitioner uses the entire key, which won't work for your composite key, because it will likely send keys with the same natural key value to different reducers. Instead, you need to write your own Partitioner, which partitions on the natural key.

The following code shows the Partitioner interface you must implement. The get-Partition method is passed the key, value, and the number of partitions:[9]

```
public interface Partitioner<K2, V2> extends JobConfigurable {
  int getPartition(K2 key, V2 value, int numPartitions);
}
```

Your partitioner will calculate a hash based on the last name in the Person class, and perform a modulo of that with the number of partitions (which is the number of reducers):

```
public class PersonNamePartitioner extends
    Partitioner<Person, Text> {

  @Override
  public int getPartition(Person key, Text value, int numPartitions) {
    return Math.abs(key.getLastName().hashCode() * 127) %
        numPartitions;
  }
}
```

SORTING

Both the map and reduce sides participate in sorting. The map-side sorting is an optimization to help make the reducer sorting more efficient. You want MapReduce to use your entire key for sorting purposes, which will order keys according to both the last name and the first name.

In the following example you can see the implementation of the WritableComparator, which compares users based on their last name and their first name:[10]

```
public class PersonComparator extends WritableComparator {
  protected PersonComparator() {
    super(Person.class, true);
  }

  @Override
  public int compare(WritableComparable w1, WritableComparable w2) {
```

---

[9] **GitHub source**—https://github.com/alexholmes/hadoop-book/blob/master/src/main/java/com/manning/hip/ch4/sort/secondary/PersonNamePartitioner.java

[10] **GitHub source**—https://github.com/alexholmes/hadoop-book/blob/master/src/main/java/com/manning/hip/ch4/sort/secondary/PersonComparator.java

```
    Person p1 = (Person) w1;
    Person p2 = (Person) w2;

    int cmp = p1.getLastName().compareTo(p2.getLastName());
    if (cmp != 0) {
      return cmp;
    }
      return p1.getFirstName().compareTo(p2.getFirstName());
  }
}
```

GROUPING

Grouping occurs when the reduce phase is streaming map output records from local disk. Grouping is the process by which you can specify how records are combined to form one logical sequence of records for a reducer invocation.

When you're at the grouping stage, all of the records are already in secondary-sort order, and the grouping comparator needs to bundle together records with the same last name:[11]

```
public class PersonNameComparator extends WritableComparator {

  protected PersonNameComparator() {
    super(Person.class, true);
  }

  @Override
  public int compare(WritableComparable o1, WritableComparable o2) {

    Person p1 = (Person) o1;
    Person p2 = (Person) o2;

    return p1.getLastName().compareTo(p2.getLastName());

  }
}
```

MAPREDUCE

The final steps involve telling MapReduce to use the partitioner, sort comparator, and group comparator classes:[12]

```
job.setPartitionerClass(PersonNamePartitioner.class);
job.setSortComparatorClass(PersonComparator.class);
job.setGroupingComparatorClass(PersonNameComparator.class);
```

---

[11] **GitHub source**—https://github.com/alexholmes/hadoop-book/blob/master/src/main/java/com/manning/hip/ch4/sort/secondary/PersonNameComparator.java
[12] **GitHub source**—https://github.com/alexholmes/hadoop-book/blob/master/src/main/java/com/manning/hip/ch4/sort/secondary/SortMapReduce.java

To complete this technique you need to write the map and reduce code. The mapper creates the composite key and emits that in conjunction with the first name as the output value.

The reducer produces output identical to the input:[13]

```java
public static class Map
    extends Mapper<Text, Text, Person, Text> {

  private Person outputKey = new Person();

  @Override
  protected void map(Text lastName, Text firstName, Context context)
      throws IOException, InterruptedException {
    outputKey.set(lastName.toString(), firstName.toString());
    context.write(outputKey, firstName);
  }
}

public static class Reduce
    extends Reducer<Person, Text, Text, Text> {

  Text lastName = new Text();
  @Override
  public void reduce(Person key, Iterable<Text> values,
                     Context context)
      throws IOException, InterruptedException {
    lastName.set(key.getLastName());
    for (Text firstName : values) {
      context.write(lastName, firstName);
    }
  }
}
```

You'll upload a small file with unordered names, and test whether the secondary sort code produces output sorted by first name:

```
$ hadoop fs -put test-data/ch4/usernames.txt .

$ hadoop fs -cat usernames.txt
Smith John
Smith Anne
Smith Ken

$ bin/run.sh com.manning.hip.ch4.sort.secondary.SortMapReduce \
  usernames.txt output

$ hadoop fs -cat output/part*
Smith Anne
Smith John
Smith Ken
```

---

[13] **GitHub source**—https://github.com/alexholmes/hadoop-book/blob/master/src/main/java/com/manning/hip/ch4/sort/secondary/SortMapReduce.java

The output is sorted as expected.

Summary

You saw how a secondary sort can be performed in MapReduce. Next we'll look at how to sort outputs across multiple reducers.

4.2.2   Total order sorting

You'll find a number of situations where you'll want to have your job output in total sort order. For example, if you want to extract the most popular URLs from a web graph you'll have to order your graph by some measure of popularity, such as Page-Rank. Or if you want to display a table in your portal of the most active users on your site, you need the ability to sort them based on some criteria such as the number of articles they wrote.

TECHNIQUE 22   Sorting keys across multiple reducers

We all know that the MapReduce framework sorts map output keys prior to feeding them to reducers. This sorting is only guaranteed within each reducer, and unless you specify a partitioner for your job, you will be using the default MapReduce partitioner, HashPartitioner, which partitions using a hash of the map output keys. This ensures that all records with the same map output key go to the same reducer, but the HashPartitioner doesn't perform total sorting of the map output keys across all the reducers. Knowing this, you may be wondering how you could use MapReduce to sort keys across multiple reducers so that you can easily extract the top and bottom *N* records from your data.

Problem

You want a total ordering of keys in your job outputs, but without the overhead of having to run a single reducer.

Solution

This technique covers use of the TotalOrderPartitioner class, a partitioner that is bundled with Hadoop, to assist in sorting output across all reducers. The partitioner ensures that output sent to the reducers is totally ordered, so as long as the reducer emits the same output key as the input key, total job output is guaranteed.

Discussion

Hadoop has a built-in partitioner called the TotalOrderPartitioner, which distributes keys to specific reducers based on a partition file. The partition file is a precomputed SequenceFile that contains *N*-1 keys, where *N* is the number of reducers. The keys in the partition file are ordered by the map output key comparator, and as such each key represents a logical range of keys. To determine which reducer should receive an output record, the TotalOrderPartitioner examines the output key, determines which range it falls into, and maps that range into a specific reducer.

Figure 4.15 shows the two parts of this technique. You need to create the partition file and then run your MapReduce job using the TotalOrderPartitioner.

First you'll use the InputSampler class, which samples the input files and creates the partition file. You can use one of two samplers, the RandomSampler class, which as the name

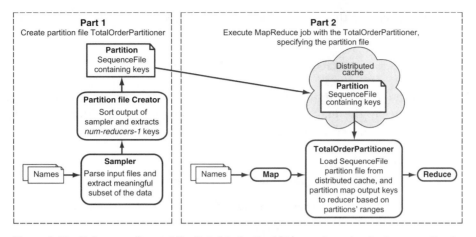

Figure 4.15   Using sampling and the `TotalOrderPartitioner` to sort output across all reducers

suggests picks random records from the input, and the `IntervalSampler` class, which for every *R* record includes the record in the sample. Once the samples have been extracted, they're sorted and then *N*-1 keys are written to the partition file, where *N* is the number of reducers. The `InputSampler` isn't a MapReduce job; it reads records from the `InputFormat` and produces the partition within the process calling the code.

The following code shows the steps you need to execute prior to calling the `InputSampler` function:[14]

```
int numReducers = 2;
Path input = new Path(args[0]);
Path partitionFile = new Path(args[1]);

InputSampler.Sampler<Text, Text> sampler =
    new InputSampler.RandomSampler<Text,Text>
        (0.1,
        10000,
        10);

JobConf job = new JobConf();

job.setNumReduceTasks(numReducers);

job.setInputFormat(KeyValueTextInputFormat.class);

job.setMapOutputKeyClass(Text.class);

job.setMapOutputValueClass(Text.class);

TotalOrderPartitioner.setPartitionFile(job, partitionFile);

FileInputFormat.setInputPaths(job, input);

InputSampler.writePartitionFile(job, sampler);
```

The probability that a key will be picked from the input.

The number of samples to extract from the input.

The maximum number of input splits that will be read to extract the samples.

Run the InputSampler code to sample and create the partition file. This code uses all the items set in the JobConf object to perform this task.

Set the number of reducers (which is used by the InputSampler when creating the partition file).

Set the InputFormat for the job, which the InputSampler uses to retrieve records from the input.

You also need to specify the map output key and value classes, even if the InputFormat explicitly types them.

Specify the location of the partition file.

Set the job input files.

---

[14] **GitHub source**—https://github.com/alexholmes/hadoop-book/blob/master/src/main/java/com/manning/hip/ch4/sort/total/TotalSortMapReduce.java

Next up is specifying that you want to use the `TotalOrderPartitioner` as the partitioner for your job:

```
job.setPartitionerClass(TotalOrderPartitioner.class);
```

For this technique you don't want to do any processing in your MapReduce job, so you'll not specify the map or reduce classes. This means the identity MapReduce classes will be used, so you're ready to run the code:

The input file containing the names to be sorted.

```
$ hadoop fs -put test-data/names.txt names.txt

$ bin/run.sh com.manning.hip.ch4.sort.total.TotalSortMapReduce \
names.txt \
large-names-sampled.txt \
output
```

The job output directory.

You ran with two reducers, so you have two part files in the output directory.

```
$ hadoop fs -ls output
/user/aholmes/output/part-00000
/user/aholmes/output/part-00001
```

You expect to see names starting with A's at the top of the first output file.

```
$ hadoop fs -cat output/part-00000 | head
AABERG
AABY
AADLAND
$ hadoop fs -cat output/part-00000 | tail
LANCZ
LAND
LANDA
$ hadoop fs -cat output/part-00001 | head
LANDACRE
LANDAKER
LANDAN
$ hadoop fs -cat output/part-00001 | tail
ZYSK
ZYSKOWSKI
ZYWIEC
```

The bottom of the first output file contains names starting with L, which is roughly halfway through the alphabet.

The top of the second output file continues with names that are lexicographically after the last name in the first file.

At the bottom of the second file are names starting with Z.

You can see from the results of the MapReduce job that the map output keys are indeed sorted across all the output files.

Summary

This technique used the `InputSampler` to create the partition file, which is subsequently used by the `TotalOrderPartitioner` to partition map output keys.

You could also use MapReduce to generate the partition file. An efficient way of doing this would be to write a custom `InputFormat` class that performs the sampling, and then output the keys to a single reducer, which in turn can create the partition file. This brings us to sampling, the last section of this chapter.

4.3 Sampling

Imagine you're working with a terabyte-scale dataset and you have a MapReduce application you want to test with that dataset. Running your MapReduce application against the dataset may take hours, and constantly iterating with code refinements and rerunning against it isn't an optimal workflow.

To solve this problem you look to sampling, which is a statistical methodology for extracting a relevant subset of a population. In the context of MapReduce, sampling provides an opportunity to work with large datasets without the overhead of having to wait for the entire dataset to be read and processed. This greatly enhances your ability to quickly iterate when developing and debugging MapReduce code.

TECHNIQUE 23   Reservoir sampling

You need to iterate over the development of a MapReduce job, and have a large dataset that you want to work with to iteratively test with. Working with the entire dataset takes a long time, and impedes your ability to rapidly work with your code.

Problem

You want to work with a small subset of a large dataset during the development of a MapReduce job.

Solution

You'll write an input format that can wrap the actual input format used to read data. The input format that you'll write can be configured with the number of samples that should be extracted from the wrapped input format.

Discussion

In this technique you'll use reservoir sampling[15] to choose samples. Reservoir sampling is a strategy that allows a single pass through a stream to randomly produce a sample. As such it's a perfect fit for MapReduce because input records are streamed from an input source. Figure 4.16 shows the algorithm for reservoir sampling.

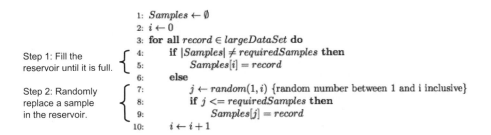

```
 1:  Samples ← ∅
 2:  i ← 0
 3:  for all record ∈ largeDataSet do
 4:      if |Samples| ≠ requiredSamples then
 5:          Samples[i] = record
 6:      else
 7:          j ← random(1, i) {random number between 1 and i inclusive}
 8:          if j <= requiredSamples then
 9:              Samples[j] = record
10:      i ← i + 1
```

Step 1: Fill the reservoir until it is full. {

Step 2: Randomly replace a sample in the reservoir. {

Figure 4.16   The reservoir sampling algorithm allows one pass through a stream to randomly produce a sample.

---

[15] See http://en.wikipedia.org/wiki/Reservoir_sampling.

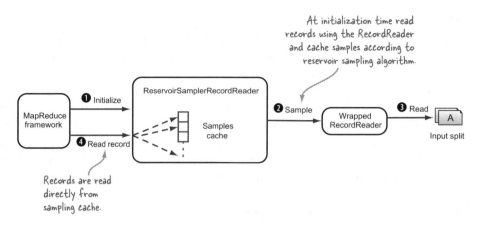

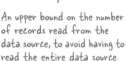

Figure 4.17   The `ReservoirSamplerRecordReader` in action

The input split determination and record reading will be delegated to wrapped Input-
Format and RecordReader classes. You'll write classes that provide the sampling functionality and wrap the delegated InputFormat and RecordReader classes.[16] Figure 4.17 shows
how the ReservoirSamplerRecordReader works.

The following code shows the ReservoirSamplerRecordReader:[17]

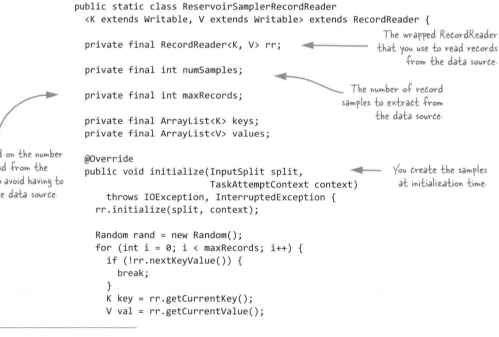

```
public static class ReservoirSamplerRecordReader
  <K extends Writable, V extends Writable> extends RecordReader {

  private final RecordReader<K, V> rr;          ◄── The wrapped RecordReader
                                                     that you use to read records
                                                     from the data source.
  private final int numSamples;                 ◄── The number of record
                                                     samples to extract from
  private final int maxRecords;                    the data source.

  private final ArrayList<K> keys;
  private final ArrayList<V> values;

  @Override
  public void initialize(InputSplit split,      ◄── You create the samples
                         TaskAttemptContext context)    at initialization time.
    throws IOException, InterruptedException {
  rr.initialize(split, context);

  Random rand = new Random();
  for (int i = 0; i < maxRecords; i++) {
    if (!rr.nextKeyValue()) {
      break;
    }
    K key = rr.getCurrentKey();
    V val = rr.getCurrentValue();
```

An upper bound on the number
of records read from the
data source, to avoid having to
read the entire data source.

---

[16] If you need a refresher on these classes, please review chapter 3 for more details.

[17] **GitHub source**—https://github.com/alexholmes/hadoop-book/blob/master/src/main/java/com/
manning/hip/ch4/sampler/ReservoirSamplerInputFormat.java

If you haven't collected the target number of samples, add the current record to your samples.

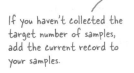

```
    if (keys.size() < numSamples) {
      keys.add(WritableUtils.clone(key, conf));
      values.add(WritableUtils.clone(val, conf));
    } else {
      int r = rand.nextInt(i);
      if (r < numSamples) {
        keys.set(r, WritableUtils.clone(key, conf));
        values.set(r, WritableUtils.clone(val, conf));
      }
    }
  }
 }
}
...
```

When you've collected the minimum number of samples, use the reservoir algorithm to determine if you should update existing samples with the current record.

To use the ReservoirSamplerInputFormat class in your code you'll use convenience methods to help set up the InputFormat and other parameters, as shown in the following code:[18]

This is the only required method that needs to be called, which sets the InputFormat to read the records from the data source.

```
ReservoirSamplerInputFormat.setInputFormat(job,
    TextInputFormat.class);

ReservoirSamplerInputFormat.setNumSamples(job, 10);

ReservoirSamplerInputFormat.setMaxRecordsToRead(job, 10000);

ReservoirSamplerInputFormat.
    setUseSamplesNumberPerInputSplit(job, true);
```

Set the maximum number of records that will be read from each input split to create the samples.

Set the number of samples to be extracted. This number is either across all input splits, or for each input split. The behavior is driven with the setUseSamplesNumberPerInputSplit method.

Determines whether the number of samples should be extracted per input split, or across all input splits. If set to false (the default), the number of samples is divided by the number of input splits.

You can see the sampling InputFormat in action by running an identity job against a large file containing names:

The input file has 88799 lines.

```
$ wc -l test-data/names.txt
88799 test-data/names.txt

$ hadoop fs -put test-data/names.txt names.txt

$ bin/run.sh com.manning.hip.ch4.sampler.SamplerJob \
    names.txt output

$ hadoop fs -cat output/part* | wc -l
10
```

Your sampling InputFormat sampled ten lines as per your job configuration.

You configured the ReservoirSamplerInputFormat to extract ten samples, and indeed the output file contained that number of lines.

---

[18] **GitHub source**—https://github.com/alexholmes/hadoop-book/blob/master/src/main/java/com/manning/hip/ch4/sampler/ReservoirSamplerInputFormat.java

Summary

Sampling support in MapReduce code can be a useful development and testing feature when engineers are running code against production-scale datasets. That begs the question: what's the best approach to integrate sampling support into an existing codebase? One approach would be to add a configurable option that would toggle the use of the sampling InputFormat, similar to the following code:

```
if(appConfig.isSampling()) {

  ReservoirSamplerInputFormat.setInputFormat(job,
    TextInputFormat.class);
  ...
} else {
  job.setInputFormatClass(TextInputFormat.class);
}
```

You can apply this sampling technique to any of the preceding sections as a way to work efficiently with large datasets.

4.4   *Chapter summary*

Joining and sorting are cumbersome tasks in MapReduce, and we spent this chapter learning about methods to optimize and ease their use. We looked at three different join strategies, two of which were on the map side, and one on the reduce side. The goal was to simplify joins in MapReduce, and as such I presented two frameworks that reduce the amount of user code required for joins.

We also covered sorting in MapReduce by examining how secondary sorts work, and how you can sort all of the output across all the reducers.

We'll cover a number of performance patterns and tuning steps in chapter 6, which will result in faster join and sorting times. But before we get there, we'll look at HDFS patterns to optimize storage and disk/network I/O in the next chapter.

Streamlining
HDFS for big data

This chapter covers
- Understanding how to work with small files
- Working with compression
- Choosing the best codec for splittability and performance

In the previous chapter we looked at how to work effectively with MapReduce and big data. You might tend to spend more time thinking about MapReduce because of its computational layer, but you shouldn't deprive HDFS of attention when wrestling with big data, because improvements to HDFS will pay great dividends in terms of performance with our MapReduce jobs.

In view of this, this chapter is dedicated to looking at ways to efficiently store and access big data in HDFS. The first subject I'll address is how to work with a large number of small files in HDFS. As you'll soon discover, the NameNode loads metadata about the filesystem into memory, which can cause memory-exhaustion problems with large numbers of small files. In this chapter we'll look at how to use Avro to work around this limitation.

Another big data pattern we'll look at is compression. Critical in Hadoop, compression isn't for the faint of heart. You need compression to maximize your storage capabilities, as well as for streamlining local disk reads and data transferred across your network between map and reduce tasks. Compression ideally would be transparent to HDFS users, but it isn't, and it's cumbersome and unintuitive to work with large, compressed files of common file formats. The bulk of this chapter, therefore, contains techniques to help you effectively use compression with large files.

> **Chapter prerequisites**
>
> This chapter assumes you have a basic understanding of HDFS concepts and you have experience working directly with HDFS. If you need to become familiar with the topic, pick up a copy of Hadoop in Action by Chuck Lam, which offers the background information you'll need on HDFS.

We'll start things off with a look at how to work with small files in HDFS.

5.1   *Working with small files*

Hearing the term *big data* conjures up images of large files that are gigabytes in size or more. But big data can also be a large number of small files. In fact, much of the data that you'll want to work with will be small—as an example, log files are frequently rotated when they reach megabytes in size. In this section we'll look at effective techniques for working with small files in HDFS.

TECHNIQUE 24   Using Avro to store multiple small files

Let's say that you're working on a project akin to Google Images, where you crawl the web and download image files from websites. Your project is internet-scale, so you're downloading millions of files and storing them individually in HDFS. Unfortunately, in doing so you'll be exposing some weaknesses in HDFS and MapReduce, including the following:

1. Hadoop's NameNode keeps all the HDFS metadata in memory for fast metadata operations. Yahoo! estimated[1] that each file on average occupies 600 bytes of space in memory, which translates to a metadata overhead of one billion files amounting to 60 GB, all of which needs to be stored in the NameNode's memory. That's a lot of memory for a single process, even with today's mid-tier server RAM capacities.

2. If your input to a MapReduce job is a large number of files, the number of mappers that will run (assuming your files are text or splittable) would be equivalent

---

[1] According to Yahoo! statistics, each block or node uses less than 200 bytes of memory, and on average each file occupies 1.5 blocks with a 3x replication factor. See http://developer.yahoo.com/blogs/hadoop/posts/2010/05/scalability_of_the_hadoop_dist/ and https://issues.apache.org/jira/browse/HADOOP-1687.

to the number of blocks that these files occupy. If you run a MapReduce job whose input is thousands or millions of files, then your job will spend more time at the kernel layer dealing with creating and destroying your map task processes than it will on its work.

3   Finally, if you're running in a controlled environment where there's a Scheduler, you may have a cap on the number of tasks your MapReduce job can use. Because each file (by default) results in least one map task, this could cause your job to be rejected by the Scheduler.

If at this point you're thinking you won't have this problem, think again. What percentage of your files are smaller than the HDFS block size?[2] And how much smaller are they, 50 percent, 70 percent, 90 percent? What if your big data project takes off and suddenly you need to be able to scale to handle datasets that are several orders of magnitude more in size? Isn't that why you use Hadoop in the first place? To scale you want to be able to add more nodes, then get back to your morning coffee, and not have to go back and redesign your use of Hadoop and deal with migrating your files. Thinking and preparing for this eventuality is best done early in your design phase.

Problem

You want to store a large number of files in HDFS, and do so without hitting the NameNode memory limits.

Solution

The easiest way to work with small files in HDFS is to package them into a larger containing file. For this technique you'll read all of the files in a directory stored on local disk and save them in a single Avro file in HDFS. You'll also see how to use the Avro file in MapReduce to process the contents of the original files.

Discussion

Figure 5.1 shows the first part of this technique, where you create the Avro file in HDFS. In doing so you create fewer files in HDFS, which means less data to be stored in NameNode memory, which also means you can store more stuff.

Avro is a data serialization and RPC library invented by Doug Cutting, the creator of Hadoop. He created Avro primarily to help improve data interchange, interoperability, and versioning in Hadoop. Avro has strong schema evolution capabilities that give it an advantage over competitors such as SequenceFiles. Avro and its competitors were covered extensively in chapter 3.

Let's take a look at the Java code in the following listing,[3] which will create the Avro file.

---

[2]   The default block size is 64 MB. Check the value of `dfs.block.size` to see what it's set to in your cluster.

[3]   **GitHub source**—https://github.com/alexholmes/hadoop-book/blob/master/src/main/java/com/manning/hip/ch5/SmallFilesWrite.java

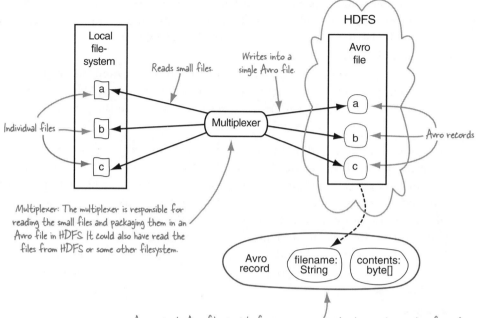

Figure 5.1   Storing small files in Avro allows you to store more.

Reads a directory containing small files and produces a single Avro file in HDFS

```java
public class SmallFilesWrite {

  public static final String FIELD_FILENAME = "filename";
  public static final String FIELD_CONTENTS = "contents";
  private static final String SCHEMA_JSON =
        "{\"type\": \"record\", \"name\": \"SmallFilesTest\", "
      + "\"fields\": ["
      + "{\"name\":\" + FIELD_FILENAME
      + "\", \"type\":\"string\"},"
      + "{\"name\":\" + FIELD_CONTENTS
      + "\", \"type\":\"bytes\"}]}";
  public static final Schema SCHEMA = Schema.parse(SCHEMA_JSON);

  public static void writeToAvro(File srcPath,
        OutputStream outputStream)
        throws IOException {
  DataFileWriter<Object> writer =
        new DataFileWriter<Object>(
            new GenericDatumWriter<Object>())
            .setSyncInterval(100);
```

Avro uses JSON to define the data structure schema, which in this example is defined in the SCHEMA_JSON variable. You define two fields per record: the filename you're storing, and the raw contents of the file.

Create an Avro writer.

Compress Avro content using the Snappy codec.

Associate the schema and output stream with the writer.

```
writer.setCodec(CodecFactory.snappyCodec());

writer.create(SCHEMA, outputStream);

for (Object obj :
        FileUtils.listFiles(srcPath, null, false)) {
  File file = (File) obj;
  String filename = file.getAbsolutePath();
  byte content[] = FileUtils.readFileToByteArray(file);

  GenericRecord record = new GenericData.Record(SCHEMA);

  record.put(FIELD_FILENAME, filename);

  record.put(FIELD_CONTENTS, ByteBuffer.wrap(content));

  writer.append(record);
  System.out.println(
          file.getAbsolutePath()
          + ": "
          + DigestUtils.md5Hex(content));
  }

  IOUtils.cleanup(null, writer);
  IOUtils.cleanup(null, outputStream);
}

public static void main(String... args) throws Exception {
  Configuration config = new Configuration();
  FileSystem hdfs = FileSystem.get(config);

  File sourceDir = new File(args[0]);
  Path destFile = new Path(args[1]);

  OutputStream os = hdfs.create(destFile);
  writeToAvro(sourceDir, os);
  }
}
```

For each file in the input directory, you create a new Avro record, specifying your schema. You then write the filename and contents to the record, using the names you defined in your schema.

GenericRecord is Avro's generic wrapper around a single record, defined by a schema.

Set the filename field for the record.

Set the raw file bytes in the record.

Write the record to the writer (and its associated stream, which in your case will write into HDFS).

As you're writing the file contents, you'll also produce an MD5 hash, so that later you can visually compare that your writing and reading is correct.

> **Compression dependency**
>
> To run the code in this chapter you'll need to have both the Snappy and LZOP compression codecs installed on your host. Please refer to appendix A for details on how to install and configure them.

Let's see what happens when you run this script against Hadoop's config directory:

```
$ bin/run.sh \
  com.manning.hip.ch5.SmallFilesWrite /etc/hadoop/conf test.avro
/etc/hadoop/conf/ssl-server.xml.example: cb6f1b218...
/etc/hadoop/conf/log4j.properties: 6920ca49b9790cb...
/etc/hadoop/conf/fair-scheduler.xml: b3e5f2bbb1d6c...
...
```

Looks promising—let's make sure that the output file is in HDFS:

```
$ hadoop fs -ls test.avro
2011-08-20 12:38 /user/aholmes/test.avro
```

To be sure everything's working as expected, you'll also write some code that will read the Avro file from HDFS, and output the MD5 hash for each file content:[4]

```java
public class SmallFilesRead {

private static final String FIELD_FILENAME = "filename";
private static final String FIELD_CONTENTS = "contents";

public static void readFromAvro(InputStream is) throws IOException {
  DataFileStream<Object> reader =
      new DataFileStream<Object>(
          is, new GenericDatumReader<Object>());

  for (Object o : reader) {

    GenericRecord r = (GenericRecord) o;

    System.out.println(
        r.get(FIELD_FILENAME) +
        ": " +
        DigestUtils.md5Hex(
            ((ByteBuffer) r.get(FIELD_CONTENTS)).array())));
  }
  IOUtils.cleanup(null, is);
  IOUtils.cleanup(null, reader);
}

public static void main(String... args) throws Exception {
  Configuration config = new Configuration();
  FileSystem hdfs = FileSystem.get(config);

  Path destFile = new Path(args[0]);

  InputStream is = hdfs.open(destFile);
  readFromAvro(is);
}
}
```

Loop through every record in the Avro file.

Create an Avro reader object by supplying the InputStream of the file in HDFS. Note that you don't need to supply schema information, because Avro encodes that in the Avro file.

Cast each record to a GenericRecord instance.

Retrieve the filename and contents from the record.

This code is simpler than the write. Because Avro writes the schema into every Avro file, you don't need to tell Avro information about the schema as part of deserialization. Let's give your code a spin:

```
$ bin/run.sh com.manning.hip.ch5.SmallFilesRead test.avro
/etc/hadoop/conf/ssl-server.xml.example: cb6f1b21...
/etc/hadoop/conf/log4j.properties: 6920ca49b9790c...
/etc/hadoop/conf/fair-scheduler.xml: b3e5f2bbb1d6...
...
```

The hashes are the same as those you generated with the write, so things are looking good.

---

[4] **GitHub source**—https://github.com/alexholmes/hadoop-book/blob/master/src/main/java/com/manning/hip/ch5/SmallFilesRead.java

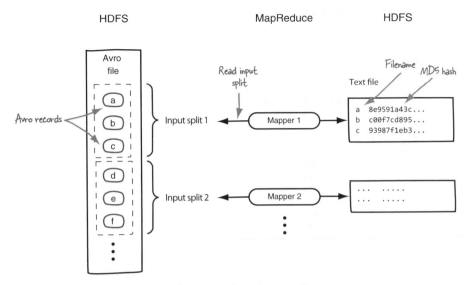

Figure 5.2   Map job to read Avro files and write out a text file

At this point you have Avro files in HDFS. Even though this chapter is about HDFS, the next thing you'll likely want to do is to process the files that you wrote in MapReduce. Let's segue and look at how to do that. You'll write a map-only MapReduce job that can read as input the Avro records and write out a text file containing the filenames and MD5 hashes of the file contents, as shown in figure 5.2.

The next listing[5] shows the code for this MapReduce job.

A MapReduce job that takes as input Avro files containing the small files

```
public class SmallFilesMapReduce {

    public static void main(String... args) throws Exception {
        JobConf job = new JobConf();
        job.setJarByClass(SmallFilesMapReduce.class);
        Path input = new Path(args[0]);
        Path output = new Path(args[1]);

        output.getFileSystem(job).delete(output, true);

        AvroJob.setInputSchema(job, SmallFilesWrite.SCHEMA);

        job.setInputFormat(AvroInputFormat.class);

        job.setOutputFormat(TextOutputFormat.class);

        job.setMapperClass(Map.class);

        FileInputFormat.setInputPaths(job, input);
```

Avro has a convenience method to help set the appropriate job configuration settings for Avro input files.

Set the Avro-specific InputFormat for your job.

---

5   **GitHub source**—https://github.com/alexholmes/hadoop-book/blob/master/src/main/java/com/manning/hip/ch5/SmallFilesMapReduce.java

```
        FileOutputFormat.setOutputPath(job, output);

        job.setNumReduceTasks(0);

        JobClient.runJob(job);
    }

    public static class Mapper implements
        Mapper<AvroWrapper<GenericRecord>, NullWritable,
            Text, Text> {
      @Override
      public void map(AvroWrapper<GenericRecord> key,
                      NullWritable value,
                      OutputCollector<Text, Text> output,
                      Reporter reporter) throws IOException {
        outKey.set(
          key.datum().get(
            SmallFilesWrite.FIELD_FILENAME).toString());
        outValue.set(DigestUtils.md5Hex(
          ((ByteBuffer) key.datum().get(SmallFilesWrite.FIELD_CONTENTS))
            .array()));

        output.collect(outKey, outValue);
      }
    }
}
```

Your Avro file uses the basic building-block GenericRecord objects, so you define this type as your input type for the mapper.

You extract your data from the GenericRecord using the simple get methods.

If you run this MapReduce job over the Avro file you created earlier, the job log files will contain your filenames and hashes:

```
$ bin/run.sh com.manning.hip.ch5.SmallFilesMapReduce test.avro output

$ hadoop fs -cat output/part*
```

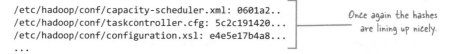

```
/etc/hadoop/conf/capacity-scheduler.xml: 0601a2..
/etc/hadoop/conf/taskcontroller.cfg: 5c2c191420...
/etc/hadoop/conf/configuration.xsl: e4e5e17b4a8...
...
```

Once again the hashes are lining up nicely.

In this technique it was assumed that you were working with a file format (such as image files) that couldn't be concatenated together. If your files can be concatenated, you should consider that option. If you go this route, try your best to make sure that the file size is at least as large as the HDFS block size to minimize the data stored in NameNode.

Summary

You could have used Hadoop's SequenceFile as a mechanism to hold your small files. SequenceFiles are a more mature technology, having been around longer than Avro files. But SequenceFiles are Java-specific and don't provide the rich interoperability and versioning semantics you get with Avro.

Google's Protocol Buffers, as well as Apache Thrift, which originated from Facebook, can also be used to store small files. But neither has the InputFormat that works with native Thrift or Protocol Buffers files.

Another approach you could use is to write the files into a zip file. The downsides to this approach are that you would have to write a custom InputFormat[6] to process the zip file, and zip files aren't splittable (as opposed to Avro and SequenceFiles). This could be mitigated by generating multiple zip files and attempting to make them close to the HDFS block size.

Hadoop also has a CombineFileInputFormat that can feed multiple input splits (across multiple files) into a single map task, which greatly decreases the number of map tasks needed to run.

In a similar vein you can also configure Hadoop to allow a single map task JVM to work on multiple tasks, reducing the expense of JVM cycling. The mapred.job .reuse.jvm.num.tasks by default is set to 1, which means one JVM will process one task, but you can configure to a larger number, or -1, such that there is no limit (for the same job).

You also could have created a tarball file containing all the files, and then produced a separate text file which contained the locations of the tarball file in HDFS. This text file would be supplied as the input to the MapReduce job, and the mapper would open the tarball directly. But that approach would circumvent the locality in MapReduce, because the mappers would be scheduled to execute on the node that contained the text file, and would therefore likely need to read the tarball blocks from remote HDFS nodes incurring unnecessary network IO.

Hadoop Archive files (HARs) are Hadoop files specifically created to solve the problem of small files. They are a virtual filesystem that sits on top of HDFS. The disadvantages of HAR files are that they can't be optimized for local disk access in MapReduce, and they can't be compressed.

Hadoop version 2.x supports HDFS Federation, where HDFS is partitioned into multiple distinct namespaces, with each independently managed by a separate NameNode. This in effect means that the overall impact of keeping block information in memory can be spread across multiple NameNodes, thereby supporting a much larger number of small files. Hortonworks has a good blog post that contains more details about HDFS Federation at http://hortonworks.com/an-introduction-to-hdfs-federation/.

Finally, MapR, which provides a Hadoop distribution, has its own distributed filesystem that supports large numbers of small files. Using MapR for your distributed storage is a big change to your system, so it's unlikely you'll move to MapR to mitigate this problem with HDFS.

You may encounter times when you'll want to work with small files in Hadoop, and using them directly would result in bloated NameNode memory use and MapReduce jobs that run slowly. This technique helped you mitigate these issues by packaging small files into larger container files. I picked Avro for this technique because of its

---

[6] There has been a ticket open since 2008 asking for a zip InputFormat implementation; see
https://issues.apache.org/jira/browse/MAPREDUCE-210.

support for splittable files, compression, and its expressive schema language, which will help with versioning.

What if you have the opposite problem, where your files are plenty big and you want to be more efficient about how you store your data? Can you compress data in Hadoop, and how does that work with things like MapReduce? Read on to find out.

5.2   *Efficient storage with compression*

Data compression is a mechanism to reduce the size of data to a more compact form to save on storage space and to make it more efficient to transfer the data. Compression is an important aspect of dealing with files, and becomes all the more important when dealing with the data sizes that Hadoop supports. Your goal with Hadoop is to be as efficient as possible when working with your data, and picking a suitable compression codec[7] will result in your jobs running faster and allow you to store more data in your cluster.

TECHNIQUE 25   **Picking the right compression codec for your data**

Using compression with HDFS isn't as transparent as it is on filesystems such as ZFS,[8] especially when dealing with compressed files that can be split (more on that later in this chapter). One of the advantages to working with file formats such as Avro and SequenceFiles is their built-in compression support, making compression almost completely transparent to users. But you lose that luxury when working with most other file formats.

Problem

You want to evaluate and determine the optimal compression codec for use with your data.

Solution

Snappy, a compression codec from Google, offers the best combination of compressed size and read/write execution times. However LZOP is the best codec when working with large compressed files that must support splittability.

Discussion

Let's kick things off with a quick look at the compression codecs available for use in Hadoop, shown in table 5.1.

---

[7] A compression codec is a programming implementation capable of reading and writing a given compression format.
[8] ZFS, short for Z File System, is a filesystem developed by Sun Microsystems that provides innovative features to enhance data integrity.

Table 5.1   Compression codecs

Codec	Background
Deflate	Deflate is similar to zlib, which is the same compression algorithm that gzip uses without the gzip headers.
gzip	The gzip file format consists of a header and a body, which contains a Deflate-compressed payload.
bzip2	bzip2 is a space-efficient compression codec.
LZO	LZO is a block-based compression algorithm that allows the compressed data to be split.
LZOP	LZOP is LZO with additional headers. At one time LZO/LZOP came bundled with Hadoop, but they have since been removed due to GPL licensing restrictions.
Snappy	Snappy (http://code.google.com/p/hadoop-snappy/) is a recent addition to codec options in Hadoop. It's Google's open source compression algorithm. Google uses it for compressing data in both MapReduce and BigTable.[a] Its main drawback, which is a significant one, is that it's not splittable. This won't matter if you work primarily with files that are smaller than or equal to the HDFS block size, but if you work with large files, your jobs won't perform as fast as they should. CDH3 bundles Snappy with the optional native Hadoop bits. At the time of this writing no production-ready version of Apache Hadoop contains support for Snappy, although it's been committed into the Hadoop core (see https://issues.apache.org/jira/browse/HADOOP-7206).

[a.] BigTable is Google's proprietary database system; see http://research.google.com/archive/bigtable.html.

To properly evaluate the codecs you first need to specify your evaluation criteria, which should be based in terms of functional and performance traits. For compression your criteria is likely to include the following:

- *Space/time trade-off*—Generally, the more intensive (and longer in duration), the better the compression ratio.
- *Splittability*—Can a compressed file be split for use by multiple mappers? If a compressed file can't be split, only a single mapper will be able to work on it. If that file spans multiple blocks, you'll lose out on data locality, because the map will likely have to read blocks from remote DataNodes incurring the overhead of network IO.
- *Native compression support*—Is there a native library that performs compression and decompression? This will usually out-perform a compression codec written in Java with no underlying native library support.

Running your own tests

When you're performing your own evaluation, I recommend you perform your tests using your data, and preferably on hosts similar to your production nodes. This way you'll have a good sense of the expected compression and runtimes for the codecs.

Table 5.2 Comparison of compression codecs

Codec	Extension	Licensing	Splittable	Java-only compression support	Native compression support
Deflate	.deflate	zlib	No	Yes	Yes
gzip	.gz	GNU GPL	No	Yes	Yes
bzip2	.gz	BSD	Yes [a]	Yes	No
lzo	.lzo_deflate	GNU GPL	No	No	Yes
lzop	.lzo	GNU GPL	Yes [b]	No	Yes
Snappy	.gz	New BSD	No	No	Yes

[a]. bzip2 is splittable, but splitting isn't supported in Hadoop until 1.1 (see https://issues.apache.org/jira/browse/HADOOP-4012).

[b]. LZOP files aren't natively splittable. You need to preprocess them to create an index file, which is then used by their respective CompressionCodec implementations to determine the file splits. We'll cover how you achieve this in a later section on LZOP.

Let's see how the compression codecs currently available compare with each other in table 5.2 (we'll cover the space/time comparison in the next section).

Now that you understand the codecs, how do they square up when looking at their space/time trade-offs? I generated a 128 MiB (one mebibyte is 2^{20} bytes) text file by concatenating the source code of Hadoop and various other open source libraries, and then used that to compare the codec run times and their compression sizes. The results of these tests can be seen in table 5.3.

Figure 5.3 shows the compressed sizes in bar graph form.

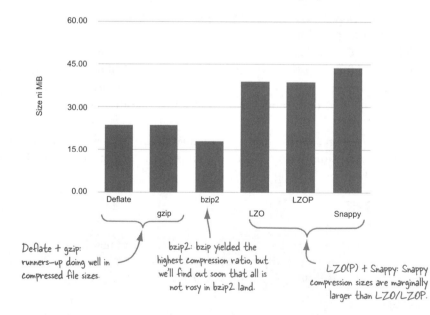

Figure 5.3 Compressed file sizes for a single 1GiB file. Smaller values are better.

Table 5.3　Performance comparison of compression codecs on a 128 MiB text file

Codec	Compression time (secs)	Decompression time (secs)	Compressed file size	Compressed percentage
Deflate	6.88	6.80	24,866,259	18.53%
gzip	6.68	6.88	24,866,271	18.53%
bzip2	3,012.34	24.31	19,270,217	14.36%
lzo	1.69	7.00	40,946,704	30.51%
lzop	1.70	5.62	40,946,746	30.51%
Snappy	1.31	6.66	46,108,189	34.45%

Figure 5.4 shows the compressed times in bar graph form. These times will vary significantly based on hardware, and are only supplied to give a sense of how they relate to each other.

What do the space and time results tell you? If squeezing as much data into your cluster as possible is your top priority, and you can live with long compression times, then bzip2 may be the right codec for you. If you want to compress your data but introduce the least amount of CPU overhead when it comes to reading and writing compressed files, you should look at Snappy. Anyone looking for a balance between compression and execution times would have to eliminate bzip2 from the picture.

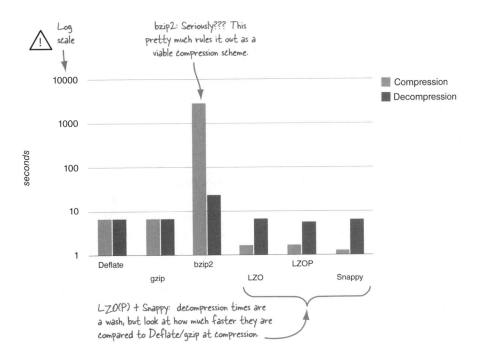

Figure 5.4　Compression and decompression times for a single 1GiB file. Smaller values are better.

Being able to split your compressed files is important, and here you have to choose between bzip2 and LZOP. The bzip2 times will likely cause most people to pause. Its only advantage over LZOP is that its Hadoop integration is much easier to work with than LZOP's. While LZOP is the natural winner here, as you'll see in the LZOP technique, it requires some effort to work with.

Summary

The best codec for you will depend on your criteria. Snappy is the most promising codec if you don't care about splitting your files, and LZOP is what you should be looking at if you want splittable files.

Bear in mind that compressed sizes will vary based on whether your file is text or binary, and its contents, so to get accurate numbers on your data it'll be worth your while to run similar tests against your own data.

Compressing data in HDFS has many benefits including reduced file sizes and faster MapReduce job runtimes. A number of compression codecs are available for use in Hadoop, and we evaluated them based on features and performance. Now you're ready to start using compression. Let's look at how to compress files and use them with tools such as MapReduce, Pig, and Hive.

TECHNIQUE 26   **Compression with HDFS, MapReduce, Pig, and Hive**

Because HDFS doesn't provide built-in support for compression, it can be a challenge to work with compression in Hadoop. The onus falls on you to figure out how to work with compressed files. Also, splittable compression isn't for the faint of heart, because it doesn't come out of the box with Hadoop.[9] If you're dealing with medium-size files that compress down to near the HDFS block size, this technique will be the quickest and simplest way to reap the benefits of compression in Hadoop.

Problem

You want to read and write compressed files in HDFS and also use them with MapReduce, Pig, and Hive.

Solution

Working with compressed files in MapReduce involves updating the MapReduce configuration file `mapred-site.xml` and registering the compression codec you are using. After you do this, working with compressed input files in MapReduce requires no additional steps, and producing compressed MapReduce output is a matter of setting `mapred.output.compress` and `mapred.output.compression.codec` MapReduce properties.

Discussion

The first step is to figure out how to read and write files using any of the codecs evaluated earlier in this chapter. All of the codecs detailed in this chapter are bundled with

---

[9] Technically, you can get out-of-the-box splittable compression with bzip2, but its performance traits, as shown earlier in this section, rule it out as a serious compression codec.

Hadoop except for LZO/LZOP and Snappy, so if you want to work with those three you'll need to download and build them yourself (I'll walk you through how to work with LZO/LZOP later in this section).

As you've learned, there are a number of compression codecs you can use. To use them you need to know their class names, which are covered in table 5.4.

Table 5.4 Codec classes

Codec	Class
Deflate	org.apache.hadoop.io.compress.DeflateCodec
gzip	org.apache.hadoop.io.compress.GzipCodec
bzip2	org.apache.hadoop.io.compress.BZip2Codec
lzo	com.hadoop.compression.lzo.LzoCodec
lzop	com.hadoop.compression.lzo.LzopCodec
Snappy	org.apache.hadoop.io.compress.SnappyCodec

HDFS

How would you compress an existing file in HDFS using any one of the codecs mentioned in the previous table? The following code supports doing that:[10]

You read the compression codec from your input arguments.

```
Configuration config = new Configuration();
FileSystem hdfs = FileSystem.get(config);

Class<?> codecClass = Class.forName(args[2]);

CompressionCodec codec = (CompressionCodec)
    ReflectionUtils.newInstance(codecClass, config);

InputStream is = hdfs.open(new Path(args[0]));
OutputStream os = hdfs.create(
    new Path(args[0] + codec.getDefaultExtension()));

OutputStream cos = codec.createOutputStream(os);

IOUtils.copyBytes(is, cos, config, true);

IOUtils.closeStream(os);
IOUtils.closeStream(is);
```

Construct an instance of the codec with the help of Hadoop's ReflectionUtils.

Each codec has a default extension (which was shown for each codec earlier in this section), and it's a best practice to use that extension when writing a compressed file.

Use the codec to create a compressed output stream.

You can use any standard Java OutputStream writing mechanism to write to your compressed stream; here you're using a utility provided by Hadoop.

---

[10] **GitHub source**—https://github.com/alexholmes/hadoop-book/blob/master/src/main/java/com/manning/hip/ch5/CompressedFileWrite.java

Codec caching

One of the overheads to using compression codecs is that they can be expensive to create. Using the Hadoop `ReflectionUtils` class will result in some of the reflection overhead associated with creating the instance being cached in `ReflectionUtils`, which should speed up subsequent creation of the codec. A better option would be to use the `CompressionCodecFactory`, which provides caching of the codecs themselves.

Reading this file is as simple as the write:[11]

```
InputStream is = hdfs.open(new Path(args[0]));

Class<?> codecClass = Class.forName(args[1]);
CompressionCodec codec = (CompressionCodec)
    ReflectionUtils.newInstance(codecClass, config);

InputStream cis = codec.createInputStream(is);

IOUtils.copyBytes(cis, System.out, config, true);

IOUtils.closeStream(is);
```

Use the codecs createInputStream to return an InputStream for reading.

Super simple. Now that you can create compressed files, let's look at how to work with them in MapReduce.

MAPREDUCE

To work with compressed files in MapReduce you need to set some configuration options for your job. For the sake of brevity let's assume identity[12] mappers and reducers in this example:[13]

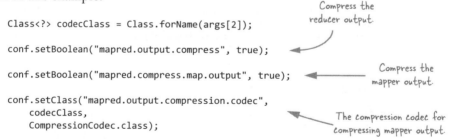

```
Class<?> codecClass = Class.forName(args[2]);

conf.setBoolean("mapred.output.compress", true);

conf.setBoolean("mapred.compress.map.output", true);

conf.setClass("mapred.output.compression.codec",
    codecClass,
    CompressionCodec.class);
```

Compress the reducer output.

Compress the mapper output.

The compression codec for compressing mapper output.

The only difference between a MapReduce job that works with uncompressed versus compressed IO are the three annotated lines in the previous example.

---

[11] **GitHub source**—https://github.com/alexholmes/hadoop-book/blob/master/src/main/java/com/manning/hip/ch5/CompressedFileRead.java

[12] An identity task is one that emits all of the input it receives as output, without any transformation or filtering.

[13] **GitHub source**—https://github.com/alexholmes/hadoop-book/blob/master/src/main/java/com/manning/hip/ch5/CompressedMapReduce.java

Not only can a job's input and output be compressed, but so can the intermediate map output, because it's spilled first to disk, and then eventually over the network to the reducer. The effectiveness of compressing the map output will ultimately depend on the type of data being emitted, but as a general rule you should see some job speed-up by making this change.

Why didn't you have to specify the compression codec for the input file? By default the `FileInputFormat` class uses the `CompressionCodecFactory` to determine if the input file extension matches any of the registered codecs. If it finds a codec that's associated with that file extension, it automatically uses that codec to decompress the input files.

How does MapReduce know which codecs to use? You need to specify the codecs in mapred-site.xml. The following code shows how to register all of the codecs we've evaluated. Remember that other than the gzip, Deflate, and bzip2, all the other compression codecs need to be built and available on your cluster before you can register them:

```
<property>
  <name>io.compression.codecs</name>
  <value>
    org.apache.hadoop.io.compress.GzipCodec,
    org.apache.hadoop.io.compress.DefaultCodec,
    org.apache.hadoop.io.compress.BZip2Codec,
    com.hadoop.compression.lzo.LzoCodec,
    com.hadoop.compression.lzo.LzopCodec,
    org.apache.hadoop.io.compress.SnappyCodec
  </value>
</property>
<property>
  <name>
    io.compression.codec.lzo.class
  </name>
  <value>
    com.hadoop.compression.lzo.LzoCodec
  </value>
</property>
```

Now that you've mastered compression with MapReduce, it's time to look higher up the Hadoop stack. As I'll show in chapters 10 and 11, Pig and Hive are higher-level languages that abstract away some of the complex details of MapReduce. Because compression can also be used in conjunction with Pig and Hive, let's see how you can mirror your MapReduce compression accomplishment using Pig and Hive.

PIG

If you're working with Pig, as with the MapReduce example, there's no extra work required to make Pig work with compressed input files. But if you're using a native compression with Pig, you'll need to make sure that the Pig JVM has the correct `java.library.path` set to load the native libraries. The following script is bundled with the code and can be executed to create the correct options to export to provide Pig access to the native libraries:

```
$ bin/pig-native-opts.sh
export PIG_OPTS="$PIG_OPTS -Djava.library.path=/usr/lib/..."

$ export PIG_OPTS="$PIG_OPTS -Djava.library.path=/usr/..."
```

Copy and paste the export command.

◄─── Run the script to generate the export command you need to run.

To have Pig work with compressed files all you need to do is specify the compression codec extension on the filename. Let's see how this works, starting with how to load compressed data. The following example gzips a file and loads it into Pig:

```
$ gzip -c /etc/passwd > passwd.gz
$ hadoop fs -put passwd.gz passwd.gz

$ pig
grunt> A = load 'passwd.gz' using PigStorage(':');

grunt> B = foreach A generate $0 as id;
grunt> DUMP B;
(root)
(bin)
(daemon)
...
```

Ending your filename with the .gz extension results in the underlying MapReduce OutputFormat recognizing the file as being gzipped, and using the appropriate compression codec to decompress the contents.

It's the same notion to write out a gzipped file—make sure to specify the extension for a compression codec. The following example stores the results of Pig relation B in a file in HDFS, and then copies them to the local filesystem to examine the contents:

```
grunt> STORE B INTO 'passwd-users.gz';

# Ctrl+C to break out of Pig shell

$ hadoop fs -get passwd-users.gz/part-m-00000.gz .

$ gunzip -c part-m-00000.gz
root
bin
daemon
...
```

That was straightforward—let's hope things are equally smooth with Hive.

HIVE

As with Pig, all you need to do is specify the codec extension when defining the filename:

```
hive> CREATE TABLE apachelog (...);

hive> LOAD DATA INPATH /user/aholmes/apachelog.txt.gz
      OVERWRITE INTO TABLE apachelog;
```

As with the Pig example, the .gz filename extension acts as a trigger for the appropriate compression codec for decompression.

The previous example loaded a gzipped file into Hive. In this situation Hive moves the file being loaded into Hive's warehouse directory and continues to use the raw file as its storage for the table. What if you want to create another table and also specify that it should be compressed? The following example achieves this by setting some Hive configs to enable MapReduce compression (because a MapReduce job will be executed to load the new table in the last statement):

```
hive> SET hive.exec.compress.output=true;
hive> SET hive.exec.compress.intermediate = true;
hive> SET mapred.output.compression.codec =
  org.apache.hadoop.io.compress.GzipCodec;

hive> CREATE TABLE apachelog_backup (...);

hive> INSERT OVERWRITE TABLE apachelog_backup SELECT * FROM apachelog;
```

You can verify that Hive is indeed compressing the storage for the new apachelog_backup table by looking at it in HDFS:

```
$ hadoop fs -ls /user/hive/warehouse/apachelog_backup
/user/hive/warehouse/apachelog_backup/000000_0.gz
```

It should be noted that Hive recommends using SequenceFile as the output format for tables, because SequenceFile blocks can be individually compressed.

Summary

This technique provides a quick and easy way to get compression running in Hadoop. It works well for files that aren't too large because it offers a fairly transparent way of working with compression in Hadoop.

If your compressed file sizes are much larger than the HDFS block size, read on for compression techniques that can split your files.

TECHNIQUE 27 Splittable LZOP with MapReduce, Hive, and Pig

Imagine that you're working with large text files which, even when compressed, are many times larger than the HDFS block size. To avoid having one map task process an entire large compressed file, you'll need to pick a compression codec that can support splitting that file.

LZOP fits the bill, but working with it is more complex than the example detailed in the previous technique, because LZOP is not in and of itself splittable. Wait, you may be thinking, didn't you state earlier that LZOP is splittable? LZOP is block-based, but you can't perform a random seek into an LZOP file and determine the next block starting point. This is the challenge we'll tackle with the following technique.

Problem

You want to use a compression codec that will allow MapReduce to work in parallel on a single compressed file.

Solution

In MapReduce, splitting large LZOP-compressed input files requires the use of LZOP-specific input format classes such as LzoInputFormat. The same principle applies when working with LZOP-compressed input files in both Pig and Hive.

Discussion

The LZOP compression codec is one of only two codecs that allow for compressed files to be split, and therefore can be worked on in parallel by multiple reducers. The other codec, bzip2, suffers from compression times that are so slow they arguably render the codec unusable. LZOP is also a good compromise between compression and speed.

> **What's the difference between LZO and LZOP?**
>
> Both LZO and LZOP codecs can be used with Hadoop. LZO is a stream-based compression store that doesn't have the notion of blocks or headers. LZOP has the notion of blocks (that are checksummed), and therefore is the codec you want to use if you want your compressed output to be splittable. Confusingly, the Hadoop codecs by default treat files ending with the .lzo extension to be LZOP-encoded, and files ending with the .lzo_deflate extension to be LZO-encoded. Also much of the documentation seems to use LZO and LZOP interchangeably. I'll attempt to be consistent and refer to LZOP throughout this book.

PREPARING YOUR CLUSTER FOR LZOP

Unfortunately, Hadoop doesn't bundle LZOP for licensing reasons.[14]

Getting all the prerequisites compiled and installed on your cluster is laborious, but rest assured there are detailed instructions in appendix A. To compile and run the code in this section you'll need to complete the instructions in the appendix.

READING AND WRITING LZOP FILES IN HDFS

Previously, we covered how to read and write compressed files in section 5.2. To perform the same activity with LZOP requires you to specify the LZOP codec in your code. This code is shown in the following listing.[15]

Methods to read and write LZOP files in HDFS

```
public static Path compress(Path src,
            Configuration config)
    throws IOException {
  Path destFile =
    new Path(
        src.toString() +
        new LzopCodec().getDefaultExtension()));
  LzopCodec codec = new LzopCodec();
  codec.setConf(config);

  FileSystem hdfs = FileSystem.get(config);
  InputStream is = null;
```

Use the compression codec's file extension (in this case .lzo) for the output filename.

Create an instance of the LZOP codec.

---

[14] LZOP used to be included with Hadoop, but with the work performed in Jira ticket https://issues.apache.org/jira/browse/HADOOP-4874 it was removed from 0.20 and newer releases due to LZOP's GPL licensing limiting its redistribution.

[15] **GitHub source**—https://github.com/alexholmes/hadoop-book/blob/master/src/main/java/com/manning/hip/ch5/LzopFileReadWrite.java

```
    OutputStream os = null;
    try {
      is = hdfs.open(src);
      os = codec.createOutputStream(hdfs.create(destFile));    ◀──── Use the codec to create
                                                                       an output stream.
      IOUtils.copyBytes(is, os, config);
    } finally {
      IOUtils.closeStream(os);
      IOUtils.closeStream(is);
    }
    return destFile;
  }

  public static void decompress(Path src, Path dest,
                                Configuration config)
      throws IOException {
    LzopCodec codec = new LzopCodec();
    codec.setConf(config);

    FileSystem hdfs = FileSystem.get(config);
    InputStream is = null;
    OutputStream os = null;
    try {                                                        Use the LZOP
      is = codec.createInputStream(hdfs.open(src));    ◀──── compression codec to
      os = hdfs.create(dest);                                  create an input
                                                                stream.
      IOUtils.copyBytes(is, os, config);
    } finally {
      IOUtils.closeStream(os);
      IOUtils.closeStream(is);
    }
  }
```

Let's write and read an LZOP file, and then make sure that LZOP utilities can work with the generated file:

```
$ hadoop fs -put $HADOOP_HOME/conf/core-site.xml \
    core-site.xml
$ bin/run.sh com.manning.hip.ch5.LzopFileReadWrite core-site.xml
```

The previous code will generate a core-site.xml.lzo file in HDFS. Now make sure you can use this LZOP file with the lzop binary. Install a lzop binary on your host (for RedHat and Centos you can install the rpm from http://pkgs.repoforge.org/lzop/lzop-1.03-1.el5.rf.x86_64.rpm). Copy the LZOP file from HDFS to local disk, uncompress it with the native lzop binary, and compare it with the original file:

```
$ hadoop fs -get core-site.xml.lzo /tmp/core-site.xml.lzo
$ lzop -l /tmp/core-site.xml.lzo
method          compressed   uncompr. ratio uncompressed_name
LZO1X-1             454          954  47.6% core-site.xml
$ cd /tmp
$ lzop -d core-site.xml.lzo
$ ls -ltr
-rw-r--r-- 1 aholmes aholmes     954 Sep 11 09:05 core-site.xml
-rw-r--r-- 1 aholmes aholmes     504 Sep 11 09:05 core-site.xml.lzo
$ diff core-site.xml $HADOOP_HOME/conf/core-site.xml
$
```

The diff verified that the file compressed with the LZOP codec could be decompressed with the lzop binary. Now that you have your LZOP file you need to index it so that it can be split.

CREATING INDEXES FOR YOUR LZOP FILES

Earlier I made the paradoxical statement that LZOP files can be split, but that they're not natively splittable. Let me clarify what that means—the lack of block-delimiting synchronization markers means you can't do a random seek into an LZOP file and start reading blocks. But because internally it does use blocks, all you need is a preprocessing step that can generate an index file containing the block offsets. The LZOP file is read in its entirety and block offsets are written to the index file as the read is occurring. The index file format, shown in figure 5.5, is a binary file containing a consecutive series of 64-bit numbers that indicate the byte offset for each block in the LZOP file.

You can create index files in one of two ways, as shown in the following two code snippets. If you want to create an index file for a single LZOP file, then this is a simple library call that will do this for you:

```
shell$ bin/run.sh
        com.hadoop.compression.lzo.lzoIndexer \
        /tmp/core-site.xml.lzo\
```

The following option works well if you have a large number of LZOP files and you want a more efficient way to generate the index files. The indexer runs a MapReduce job to create the index files. Both files and directories (which are scanned recursively for LZOP files) are supported:

```
shell$ bin/run.sh  \
        com.hadoop.copmression.lzo.DistributedLzoIndexer  \
        core.site.xml.lzo  \
        /path/to/lzop
```

Both ways depicted in the previous options will generate an index file in the same directory as the LZOP file. The index filename is the original LZOP filename suffixed

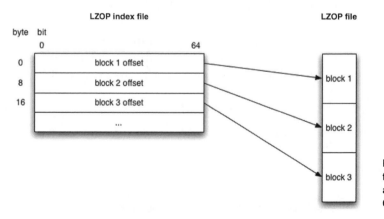

Figure 5.5   **LZOP index file is a binary containing a consecutive series of 64-bit numbers.**

with .index. Running the previous commands would have yielded the filename core-site.xml.lzo.index. Now let's look at how you would use the LzoIndexer in your Java code (this is copied from the main method of LzoIndexer). Using this code will result in the index file being created synchronously:

```
LzoIndexer lzoIndexer = new LzoIndexer(new Configuration());
for (String arg: args) {
  try {
    lzoIndexer.index(new Path(arg));
  } catch (IOException e) {
    LOG.error("Error indexing " + arg, e);
  }
}
```

With the DistributedLzoIndexer the MapReduce job will launch and run with *N* mappers, one for each .lzo file. No reducers are run, so the (identity) mapper via the custom LzoSplitInputFormat and LzoIndexOutputFormat writes the index files directly. To run the MapReduce job from your own Java code you can use the DistributedLzoIndexer code as an example.

You need the LZOP index files so that you can split LZOP files in your MapReduce, Pig, and Hive jobs. Now that you have the aforementioned LZOP index files, you can look at how to use them with MapReduce.

MAPREDUCE AND LZOP

After you've created index files for your LZOP files it's time to start using your LZOP files with MapReduce. Unfortunately, this brings us to the next challenge: none of the existing, built-in Hadoop-file-based Input Formats will work with splittable LZOP due to the need for specialized logic to handle input splits using the LZOP index file. You need specific InputFormat classes to work with splittable LZOP.

Todd Lipcon's LZOP library[16] provides an LzoTextInputFormat implementation for line-oriented LZOP-compressed text files with accompanying index files.[17]

The following code shows the required steps to configure the MapReduce job to work with LZOP. You would perform these steps for a MapReduce job that had text LZP inputs and outputs:

```
job.setInputFormatClass(LzoTextInputFormat.class);
job.setOutputFormatClass(TextOutputFormat.class);

job.getConfiguration().setBoolean("mapred.output.compress", true);
job.getConfiguration().setClass("mapred.output.compression.codec",
    LzopCodec.class, CompressionCodec.class);
```

In addition, compressing intermediary map output will also speed up the overall execution time of your MapReduce jobs:

---

[16] Todd Lipcon maintains the LZOP library for Cloudera. Todd's version is downstream of the master version maintained by Kevin Weil and other committers. Kevin's LZOP project is more actively developed and can be used for other Hadoop distributions, including Apache; see https://github.com/kevinweil/hadoop-lzo.

[17] The LZOP input formats work well with LZOP files that also don't have index files.

```
conf.setBoolean("mapred.compress.map.output", true);
conf.setClass("mapred.map.output.compression.codec",
     LzopCodec.class,
     CompressionCodec.class);
```

You can easily confgure your cluster to always compress your map output by editing hdfs-site.xml:

```
<property>
   <name>mapred.compress.map.output</name>
   <value>true</value>
 </property>
 <property>
   <name>mapred.map.output.compression.codec</name>
   <value>com.hadoop.compression.lzo.LzopCodec</value>
 </property>
```

The number of splits per LZOP file is a function of the number of LZOP blocks that the file occupies, not the number of HDFS blocks that the file occupies.

Now that we've covered MapReduce, let's look at how Pig and Hive can work with splittable LZOP.

PIG AND HIVE

Elephant Bird,[18] a project containing utilities to work with LZOP that Twitter maintains, provides a number of useful MapReduce and Pig classes to help work with LZOP. Elephant Bird has an `LzoPigStorage` class that works with text-based, LZOP-compressed data in Pig.

Hive can work with LZOP-compressed text files by using the `com.hadoop.mapred` `.DeprecatedLzoTextInputFormat` input format class found in both Todd Lipcon's and Kevin Weil's LZO project.

Summary

Working with splittable compression in Hadoop is tricky. If you're fortunate enough to be able to store your data in SequenceFiles or Avro, they offer the simplest way to work with files that can be easily compressed and split. If you want to compress other file formats and need them to be split, LZOP is the only real candidate.

As I mentioned earlier, the Elephant Bird project provides some useful LZOP input formats that will work with LZOP-compressed file formats such as XML, and also plain text. If you need to work with an LZOP-compressed file format that isn't supported by either Todd Lipcon's LZO project, or Elephant Bird, you'll have to write your own Input Format. This is a big hurdle for developers. I hope at some point Hadoop will be able to support compressed files with custom splitting logic so that end users don't have to write their own Input Formats for compression.

Compression is likely to be a hard and fast requirement for any production environment where resources are always scarce. Compression also allows faster execution times for your computational jobs, and so is a compelling aspect of storage. In the previous

---

[18] See appendix A for more details on Elephant Bird.

section I showed you how to evaluate and pick the codec best suited for your data. We also covered how to use compression with HDFS, MapReduce, Pig, and Hive. Finally, we tackled the tricky subject of splittable LZOP compression.

5.3 Chapter summary

Big data in the form of large numbers of small files brings to light a limitation in HDFS, and in this chapter we worked around this limitation by looking at how to package small files into larger Avro containers.

Compression is a key part of any large cluster, and we evaluated and compared the different compression codecs. I recommended codecs based on various criteria, and also showed how to compress and work with these compressed files in MapReduce, Pig, and Hive. We also looked at how to work with LZOP to achieve compression as well as blazing fast computation with multiple input splits.

This chapter and the previous chapter were dedicated to looking at techniques to work effectively with big data in MapReduce and HDFS. The next chapter covers techniques to diagnose and tune Hadoop to squeeze as much performance as you can out of your clusters.

Diagnosing and tuning performance problems

6

Imagine you wrote a new piece of MapReduce code and you're executing it on your shiny new cluster. You're surprised to learn that despite having a good-size cluster, your job is running significantly longer than you expected. You've obviously hit a performance issue with your job, but how do you figure out where the problem lies?

One of Hadoop's selling points when it comes to performance is that it scales horizontally. This means that adding nodes tends to yield a linear increase in throughput, and often in job execution times. So isn't the solution to your performance problem to add more nodes?

Maybe, but first let's poke around a little to understand the root cause of your poorly performing job. A plethora of problems may be causing your job to run slowly, including issues with your hardware, your code, or the data with which you're working. To get a handle on your performance problem, you'll need to follow a calculated and systematic approach to performance tuning, which is described in the following steps:

1 Ensure you have the monitoring and measurement capabilities required to gather metrics about your software and hardware.
2 Use these metrics to identify potential performance issues.
3 Tweak some configuration or code in an attempt to fix the perceived problem. To truly have a handle on the exact cause of the problem, change only one item at a time.
4 Re-execute the process and compare the metrics of the updated system with the previous metrics.

I've organized this chapter based on the previous steps. Many of the techniques in this chapter will show you how to isolate the cause of your performance problems in Hadoop. Because this information is so important, we'll spend the first half of the chapter looking at how to diagnose and measure the performance of your jobs. This structured approach helps you discover where your performance problems lie. The second half of this chapter focuses on techniques to improve job performance by covering topics such as skew mitigation and data serialization.

6.1   Measuring MapReduce and your environment

Before you can start performance tuning, you need to have the tools and processes in place to capture system metrics. You need these tools in order to gather and examine empirical data related to your MapReduce job and determine whether or not you're suffering from a performance problem.

In this section we'll look at the tools and metrics that Hadoop provides, and also touch upon monitoring as an additional tool in your performance tuning toolkit.

6.1.1   Tools to extract job statistics

A number of the techniques in this chapter rely on extracting job and task-level metrics from Hadoop. You can extract these statistics in one of three ways:

1 Use the JobTracker UI to view job and task counters.
2 Use the Hadoop CLI (command-line interface) to view job and task counters and other metrics from the job history.
3 Use my utilities, which also extract metrics from the job history.

The last two items are useful because they allow you to view both job and task metrics, as well as some aggregated statistics. Let's briefly look at how job history works, and how it's used by both the Hadoop CLI and my utilities.

JOB HISTORY AND THE CLI

For each job MapReduce generates a job statistics file, which contains task and job-level statistics. The easiest way to view a summary of the information in this file is to use the Hadoop CLI. Let's say you want to extract the metrics for a job where the output was written to an HDFS directory named output. You would supply that directory name to the CLI, as follows:

```
$ hadoop job -history output

Hadoop job: job_201112081615_0181
=====================================
Job tracker host name: localhost
Submitted At: 23-Dec-2011 08:55:22
Launched At: 23-Dec-2011 08:55:22 (0sec)
Finished At: 23-Dec-2011 08:55:37 (15sec)
Status: SUCCESS
Counters:

|Group Name  |Counter name        |Map Value |Reduce Value|Total    |
------------------------------------------------------------------
|FileSystem  |FILE_BYTES_READ     |0         |961,831     |961,831  |
|FileSystem  |HDFS_BYTES_READ     |696,068   |0           |696,068  |
|FileSystem  |FILE_BYTES_WRITTEN  |1,071,837 |1,071,519   |2,143,356|
|FileSystem  |HDFS_BYTES_WRITTEN  |0         |784,221     |784,221  |
...


Analysis
=========

Time taken by best performing map task 2sec
Average time taken by map tasks: 2sec
Worse performing map tasks:
TaskId          Timetaken
task_201112081615_0181_m_000001 2sec
...
```

The previous output is only a small subset of the overall output produced by the command, and it's worth executing it yourself to see the full metrics it exposes. This output is useful in quickly evaluating metrics such as average- and worst-task execution times.

Where does the job history file exist? Figure 6.1 shows its location.

The job history filename can be confusing because the file ends with a .jar extension, but it's a text file, marshalled with the JobHistory class. You can use the same class to reverse engineer a Java representation of this file. You can use the Hadoop CLI only to extract the job statistics from the HDFS output directory, but my utilities have support for that, as well as for extracting statistics from the NameNode log directory.

6.1.2 Monitoring

It's important to capture your CPU, memory, and network utilization as your jobs are running. The goal at this point is to ensure that you aren't overutilizing or underutilizing your hardware. If you're overutilizing your hardware, your systems are likely

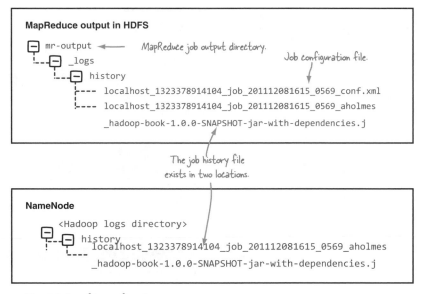

The job history filename format:
[host]_[epoch-of-jobtracker-start-millis]_[job-id]_[user]_[jar-filename]

Figure 6.1 The job history file location

spending a considerable amount of time competing for resources, be it CPU context switching or memory page swapping. Underutilization of your cluster means you're not leveraging all that you can from your hardware. With MapReduce your system resource utilization will be a function of the type of jobs you're running, and how CPU-bound or I/O-bound they are.

Being able to automatically track system utilization is crucial—without it you won't have a historical perspective on the normal performance traits of your hardware, nor will you be able to do useful things like provide alerts when you've reach undesired utilization levels. There are many fine tools that you can use for this, ranging from sar,[1] the built-in Linux utility that collects and reports on system activity, to more sophisticated tools such as Nagios and Ganglia. Ganglia[2] is an open source project designed to monitor clusters, and provides a rich user interface with useful graphs, some of which can be seen in figure 6.2. Ganglia has the added advantage of being able to pull statistics from Hadoop.[3]

---

[1] This IBM article discusses using sar and gnuplot to generate system activity graphs: http://www.ibm.com/developerworks/aix/library/au-gnuplot/index.html.

[2] See the Ganglia project page: http://ganglia.sourceforge.net/.

[3] The Hadoop wiki has basic instructions on Ganglia and Hadoop integration http://wiki.apache.org/hadoop/GangliaMetrics.

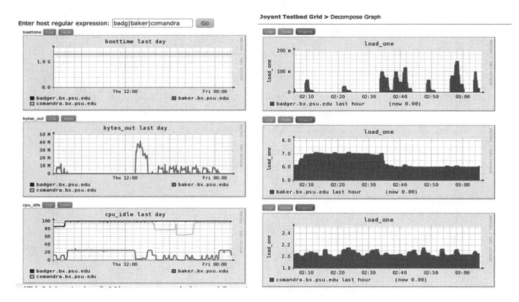

Figure 6.2   Ganglia screenshots showing CPU utilization for multiple hosts

6.2   *Determining the cause of your performance woes*

Let's say a job is taking a ridiculously long period of time to execute and you suspect something isn't quite right. In this section we'll cover how to isolate where that job is spending time. To do this we'll look at how to use built-in tools that Hadoop provides as well as some utilities I wrote.

> **System monitoring and Hadoop tasks**
>
> Hadoop 0.20.x doesn't have a built-in way to extract CPU and memory utilization for individual MapReduce tasks. But thanks to a change in version 0.22 (see https://issues.apache.org/jira/browse/MAPREDUCE-220), the CPU and memory utilization information will be written to the job history file, and will be visible in the Hadoop user interface.

6.2.1   *Understanding what can impact MapReduce job performance*

Before we delve into the techniques let's take a high-level look at what can adversely impact the performance of your job. You can break down the items that can impact your jobs into the following broad categories:

1 *Hadoop configuration*—Using the default Hadoop configurations on most server-grade hardware will result in an extremely underutilized cluster. Conversely, an incorrectly tuned configuration can also lead to performance issues such as swapping and CPU saturation.

2   *Map tasks*—The performance of map tasks is sensitive to unusually large or small data inputs. Inefficient user code can also have an impact.

3   *Reduce tasks*—Items such as data skew, the number of reducers, and unoptimized user code all can contribute to slow tasks.

4   *Hardware*—Badly behaving nodes and network issues will have a big impact on your cluster, particularly if it's not a large cluster.

We'll go through a number of common scenarios that cause your job to perform poorly. Each scenario will be a separate technique that shows how to identify the problem. The scenarios will be grouped together by the categories covered in an earlier section.

The decision tree in figure 6.3 describes the techniques to consider depending on different performance properties.

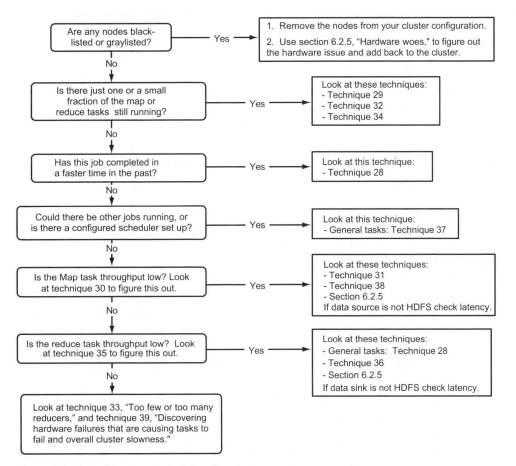

Figure 6.3   A decision tree for isolating MapReduce performance problems

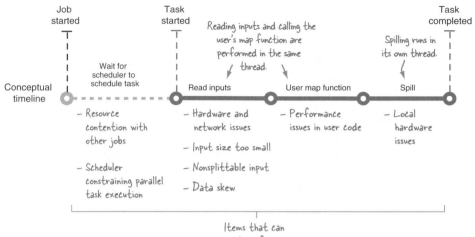

Figure 6.4   Map task timeline and impact on job performance

6.2.2   Map woes

Figure 6.4 shows the main units of work performed in the map task, and highlights areas that can have an impact on the performance of a job.

TECHNIQUE 28   Investigating spikes in input data

One cause of slow jobs may be that the data the job is working on has grown larger than expected. For example, if you're running a web log processing job, and on a particular day your website is overwhelmed with page hits, this will result in much larger-than-normal log files, which in turn slows down your MapReduce job.

Problem

You want to quickly evaluate if there are spikes in your map and reduce input sizes.

Solution

Use the JobTracker UI to compare the map input and output data sizes of the slow job with the input and output sizes of historical jobs.

Discussion

Go to the JobTracker UI and select the slow-running job. In the job summary screen you'll see job statistics similar to those shown in figure 6.5.

Compare these numbers with previous runs of the same job—if the previous runs have smaller input sizes, they could well be the reason why your job runs slowly.

Summary

Depending on what input data you're processing, it's possible there's a spike in the data volumes that has caused your job to work with larger-than-normal data sizes.

Counter	Map	Reduce	Total
FILE_BYTES_READ	2,023,432,350	1,100,414,378	3,123,846,728
HDFS_BYTES_READ	1,001,155,258	0	1,001,155,258
FILE_BYTES_WRITTEN	3,166,340,124	1,100,468,304	4,266,808,428
HDFS_BYTES_WRITTEN	0	1,099,102,302	1,099,102,302
Reduce input groups	0	9,901,036	9,901,036
Combine output records	0	0	0
Map input records	9,937,101	0	9,937,101
Reduce shuffle bytes	0	1,100,419,082	1,100,419,082
Reduce output records	0	9,937,101	9,937,101
Spilled Records	28,166,219	9,937,101	38,103,320
Map output bytes	1,080,540,164	0	1,080,540,164
Map input bytes	1,001,043,356	0	1,001,043,356
SPLIT_RAW_BYTES	79,284	0	79,284
Map output records	9,937,101	0	9,937,101
Combine input records	0	0	0
Reduce input records	0	9,937,101	9,937,101

The number of output bytes written to HDFS by the reducers.

The total number of input bytes for all the reducers.

This is the number of output bytes that mappers produced. Ideally, this is much smaller than the input bytes.

This is the number of input bytes that mappers read.

Figure 6.5   JobTracker UI showing HDFS and MapReduce statistics

---

TECHNIQUE 29   **Identifying map-side data skew problems**

It's natural for skewed data to exist. On the map side, data skew is typically the result of a handful of large unsplittable files or a large number of smaller files.

Problem

You want to determine if a job runs slowly due to skewed data.

Solution

Use the JobTracker UI to compare the input sizes across map tasks for the same job.

Discussion

Data skew manifests itself as a small number of tasks taking disproportionately longer to execute than most of the others. If you combine this with comparing the input sizes of the lingering tasks with the completed task input sizes, you'll have an almost fool-proof way of identifying data skew.

Figure 6.6 shows the steps to take to use the JobTracker UI to identify data skew.

Summary

Imagine that you've successfully used this technique to identify that your job, which is still executing, exhibits significant data skew. Your next step should be to try and mitigate the effects of skew in your job. Techniques 50 and 51 looks at potential causes of data skew and how to address them.

❶ Determine if there are lingering tasks.

Kind	% Complete	Num Tasks	Pending	Running	Complete	Killed	Failed/Killed Task Attempts
map	99.87%	786	0	1	785	0	0 / 0
reduce	33.29%	1	0	1	0	0	0 / 0

All map tasks have completed except for one. Click on the link to get to the views shown in the next step.

❷ Determine if the lingering task is working on a much larger input than other tasks.

Task	Complete	Status
task_201112081615_0568_m_000000	0.00%	hdfs://localhost/user/aholmes/input/large-file.txt.lzo:0+10000325739

The task list view shows the input file, the start byte offset, and the number of bytes to read. It's clear that the task that's still running has a much larger input to process.

Task	Complete	Status
task_201112081615_0568_m_000001	100.00%	hdfs://localhost/user/aholmes/input/file-1.txt:0+1329

❸ The task counters can provide the same information, which can help when working with data sources that aren't files. This also works well for diagnosing reducer skew.

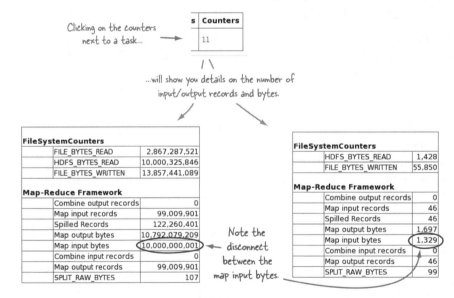

Clicking on the counters next to a task...

s	Counters
	11

...will show you details on the number of input/output records and bytes.

FileSystemCounters

FILE_BYTES_READ	2,867,287,521
HDFS_BYTES_READ	10,000,325,846
FILE_BYTES_WRITTEN	13,857,441,089

Map-Reduce Framework

Combine output records	0
Map input records	99,009,901
Spilled Records	122,260,401
Map output bytes	10,792,079,209
Map input bytes	10,000,000,001
Combine input records	0
Map output records	99,009,901
SPLIT_RAW_BYTES	107

Note the disconnect between the map input bytes.

FileSystemCounters

HDFS_BYTES_READ	1,428
FILE_BYTES_WRITTEN	55,850

Map-Reduce Framework

Combine output records	0
Map input records	46
Spilled Records	46
Map output bytes	1,697
Map input bytes	1,329
Combine input records	0
Map output records	46
SPLIT_RAW_BYTES	99

Figure 6.6   Determining data skew using the JobTracker UI

TECHNIQUE 30 Determining if map tasks have an overall low throughput

In this technique we'll try to determine if your map tasks have low throughput and we'll talk about likely issues that can cause low throughput.

Problem

You want to determine if a job runs slowly due to low task throughput.

Solution

Calculate the map task throughput using metrics from the JobTracker UI, or the job history metadata.

Discussion

You can calculate the map throughput for individual tasks by using the JobTracker to get at the task execution times. Figure 6.7 shows how to calculate throughput for map tasks.

The easiest way to get at the throughput statistics for all map tasks is to execute the TaskThroughput class (source: http://goo.gl/QQvvQ) against the job history file for your job, as shown in figure 6.8.

Summary

You've calculated the map task throughput, but how do you know if that number is low or high? If your tasks are reading all their data from their local nodes (as they ideally should be when working with HDFS and files that can be split), you would expect the throughput numbers to be close to the local disk read throughput. For jobs that read their inputs from a data source other than HDFS, this determination is harder, and requires knowledge about the read rate of the data source as well as network latencies that exist between the Hadoop nodes and the data source.

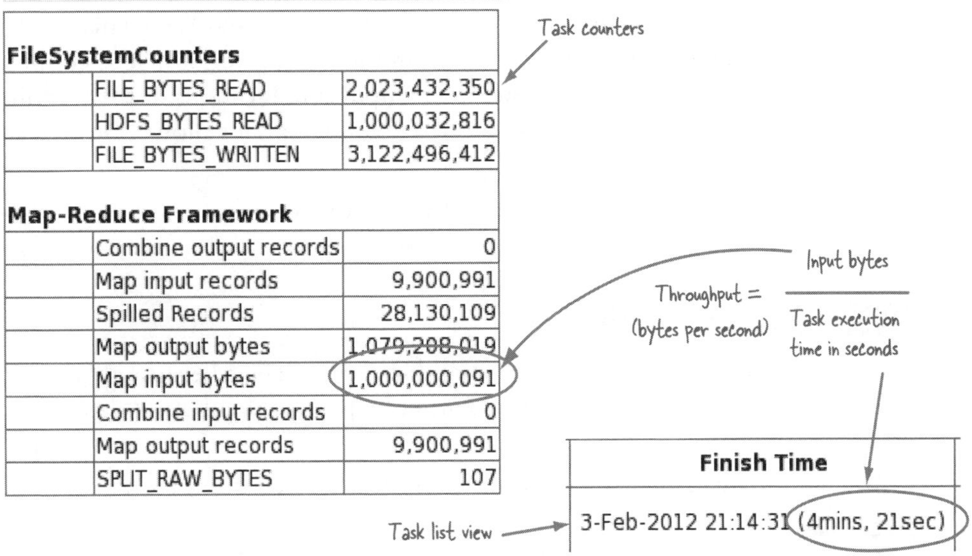

Figure 6.7 The map task throughputs calculated from the JobTracker UI

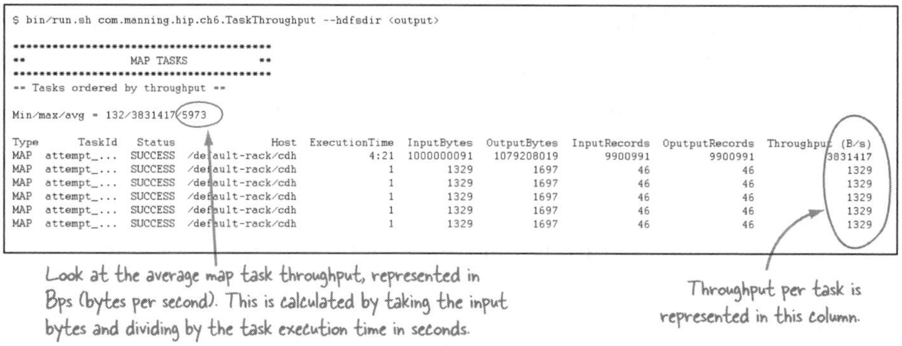

```
$ bin/run.sh com.manning.hip.ch6.TaskThroughput --hdfsdir <output>

**********************************************
**              MAP TASKS              **
**********************************************
-- Tasks ordered by throughput --

Min/max/avg = 132/3831417/5973

Type    TaskId    Status        Host    ExecutionTime   InputBytes   OutputBytes   InputRecords   OputputRecords   Throughput  (B/s)
MAP    attempt_...  SUCCESS  /default-rack/cdh      4:21    1000000091   1079208019      9900991         9900991            3831417
MAP    attempt_...  SUCCESS  /default-rack/cdh         1          1329         1697           46              46               1329
MAP    attempt_...  SUCCESS  /default-rack/cdh         1          1329         1697           46              46               1329
MAP    attempt_...  SUCCESS  /default-rack/cdh         1          1329         1697           46              46               1329
MAP    attempt_...  SUCCESS  /default-rack/cdh         1          1329         1697           46              46               1329
MAP    attempt_...  SUCCESS  /default-rack/cdh         1          1329         1697           46              46               1329
```

Look at the average map task throughput, represented in Bps (bytes per second). This is calculated by taking the input bytes and dividing by the task execution time in seconds.

Throughput per task is represented in this column.

Figure 6.8   The map task throughputs extracted from the job history file

Items that could contribute to low map task throughput include the following:

- The source files are significantly smaller than the HDFS block size, which means that you're spending more time starting and stopping tasks, and not enough time reading and processing inputs.
- The files being worked on aren't splittable, so you're having to incur network I/O to read file blocks from other nodes.
- A node's local disk or disk controller is running in a degraded mode that results in poor read and write performance. This is more likely to affect individual nodes as opposed to all the nodes.
- If the input data to your MapReduce isn't files in HDFS, you'll want to look into latency issues between your Hadoop nodes and your input data source.
- The map task reads its input from a different DataNode. This can be checked by looking at the map task details in the JobTracker, which in conjunction with all the task attempts also shows the input split locations. If the machine that the task is scheduled on isn't one of the input split locations, you're losing out on data locality.

Separate techniques will be discussed for all of the items listed that will help determine the exact cause of low map task throughput.

TECHNIQUE 31   Small files

Running a job over thousands of small files is inefficient because this results in thousands of Java task processes being spawned to process small input datasets.

Problem

You want to determine if a job runs slowly due to small input files.

Solution

Use the JobTracker UI or the job history metadata to inspect the size of your input splits.

hdfs://localhost/user/aholmes/input/file-10.txt:0+1329

hdfs://localhost/user/aholmes/input/file-100.txt:0+1329

hdfs://localhost/user/aholmes/input/file-101.txt:0+1329

hdfs://localhost/user/aholmes/input/file-102.txt:0+1329

hdfs://localhost/user/aholmes/input/file-103.txt:0+1329

hdfs://localhost/user/aholmes/input/file-104.txt:0+1329

hdfs://localhost/user/aholmes/input/file-105.txt:0+1329

hdfs://localhost/user/aholmes/input/file-106.txt:0+1329

hdfs://localhost/user/aholmes/input/file-107.txt:0+1329

Look at the input files and specifically the data range for each file. For example, here "0+1329" means that the file is only 1329 bytes, which is small.

Figure 6.9   The status column from the Hadoop map task list

Discussion

As you've seen in previous techniques, you can get an overall sense of the size of map task inputs by eyeballing the input files in the JobTracker's map task list for your job. Figure 6.9 shows an example of the map task list for a job with small input files.

Alternatively, the job statistics summarization tool, shown in figure 6.10, will show minimum, maximum, average, and median values for the input map bytes.

Summary

If the input files to a job are significantly smaller than the HDFS block size, it's likely that your cluster spends more effort starting and stopping Java processes than it spends performing work. If you're suffering from this problem you should consult chapter 5, where I explain various approaches you can take to work efficiently with small files.

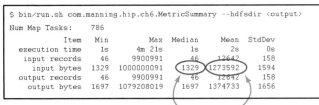

```
$ bin/run.sh com.manning.hip.ch6.MetricSummary --hdfsdir <output>
Num Map Tasks:    786
          Item    Min          Max    Median      Mean  StdDev
  execution time    1s       4m 21s        1s        2s      0s
   input records    46      9900991        46     12642     158
     input bytes  1329   1000000091      1329   1273592    1594
  output records    46      9900991        46     12642     158
    output bytes  1697   1079208019      1697   1374733    1656
```

Note: for small jobs the input and output byte values can be –1, which means no metrics were gathered by Hadoop.

Look at the median and mean (average) input sizes for the map tasks. If they are substantially smaller than the HDFS block size (as they are in this example because we're running with the default of 64MB), you will have to tune your inputs to extract better performance from your job.

Figure 6.10   Output of the job statistics tool

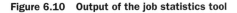

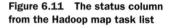

If a file appears just once in the list, and the data range is larger than the HDFS block size, you're likely dealing with a file that

a) Can't be split
b) Is being used with the wrong InputFormat.

Figure 6.11   The status column from the Hadoop map task list

---

TECHNIQUE 32   **Unsplittable files**

If your jobs are working with input files that can't be split (such as files compressed with certain codecs, or binary files that by nature aren't block-based), you'll lose out on HDFS locality and optimal parallelization of your data. In this technique we'll look at how to determine if this is impacting your jobs.

Problem

You want to determine if a job runs slowly due to unsplittable files.

Solution

Use the JobTracker UI or the job history metadata to determine if the size of your input splits are too large.

Discussion

You can eyeball the input files in the JobTracker's map task list for your job. Figure 6.11 shows an example of the map task list for a job with large input files that aren't being split.

Alternatively, the job statistics summarization tool, shown in figure 6.12, will show minimum, maximum, average, and median values for the input map bytes.

Use the JobTracker to view the list of map tasks, and calculate the average number of input bytes for each map task.

```
$ bin/run.sh com.manning.hip.ch6.MetricSummary --hdfsdir <output>

Num Map Tasks:    12

          Item        Min          Max         Median          Mean   StdDev
 execution time   1h 12m 5s    1h 43m 21s    1h 15m 31s    1h 23m 41s   5m 31s
  input records         12           12            12            12        0
    input bytes   73456344626  73456344626   73456344626   73456344626     0
 output records         12           12            12            12        0
   output bytes   73456344630  73456344630   73456344630   73456344630     0
```

Look at the median and mean (average) input sizes for the map tasks. If they are substantially larger than the HDFS block size (as they are in this example), you will have to investigate the cause.

Figure 6.12   The map task throughputs extracted from the job history

Summary

If the input files to a job are significantly larger than the HDFS block size, it's likely that you have a handful of slots in the cluster processing these large files, and a bunch of available slots that aren't being utilized to work in the inputs because the input files aren't split.

If this is happening to you, the first thing to consider is whether this is the expected behavior. This can be the case when you're working with a binary file that's not block-based and can't be split. This would also be the case when working with compressed files that can't be split, which is the case with nearly every compression codec apart from LZOP and bzip2. Table 5.2 in chapter 5 contains all of the Hadoop compression codecs and whether or not they can be split.

The other thing to watch out for is cases where this happens with LZOP files. LZOP files can be split, but there are two circumstances under which they will be treated as unsplittable:

1 There's no associated index file for the LZOP file, so the LZOP input format classes don't know how to split the file. If this is the case, refer to chapter 5 for instructions on how to create an index file.

2 You're not using an LZOP `InputFormat` to process the file. If you use a regular input format (such as the default `TextInputFormat`) for your job, it doesn't know how to split an LZOP file and as such will treat the whole file as a single split. You must use an input format whose name starts with Lzo, such as `LzoTextInputFormat`. See chapter 5 for more details.

This wraps up our look at map task performance. Next we'll look at `Reducer` task performance, and we'll follow that with some general task performance issues.

6.2.3 Reducer woes

Much like map tasks, reduce tasks have their own unique problems that can affect performance. Figure 6.13 shows the reduce task timeline with the units of work and potential areas impacting performance.

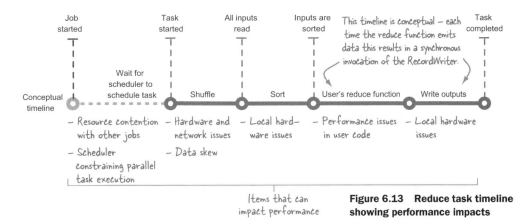

Figure 6.13 Reduce task timeline showing performance impacts

Kind	% Complete	Num Tasks	Pending	Running	Complete	Killed	Failed/Killed Task Attempts
map	99.87%	786	0	1	785	0	0 / 0
reduce	33.29%	1020	600	420	0	0	0 / 0

The number of reducers configured for the job. This can be changed by calling setNumReduceTasks or setting "mapred.reduce.tasks."

Figure 6.14   The number of reducers used for a job

In this section we'll look at how common problems can affect the performance of reducer tasks.

TECHNIQUE 33   **Too few or too many reducers**

For the most part, parallelism on the map side is automatically set, and is a function of your input files and the InputFormat you're using. But on the reduce side you have total control over the number of reducers for your job, and if that number is too small or too big, you're potentially not getting the most value out of your cluster.

Problem

You want to determine if a job runs slowly due to the number of reducers.

Solution

The JobTracker UI can be used to inspect the number of reducers running for your job.

Discussion

Use the JobTracker UI to look at the number of reducers for your job, as shown in figure 6.14. Use the JobTracker UI to look at the number of reducers for your job. This number should ideally be set to a number smaller than the number of reduce slots in your cluster. You can view the number of slots by going to the JobTracker UI, as shown in figure 6.15.

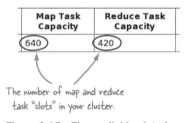

The number of map and reduce task "slots" in your cluster.

Figure 6.15   The available slots in your cluster using the JobTracker UI

Summary

There are circumstances where you can't avoid running with a small number of reducers, such as when you're writing to an external resource (such as a database) that you don't want to overwhelm.

A common anti-pattern in MapReduce is using a single reducer when you want job output to have total order, and not ordered within the scope of a reducer's output. This anti-pattern can be avoided with TotalOrderPartitioner, which we looked at in chapter 4.

If your job is writing to HDFS, you should make use of the available reduce slots in your cluster. You can easily determine this number by looking at the JobTracker, as I showed in this technique. The ideal number of reducers is equal to the number of reduce slots in your cluster—minus a few slots—so that if a certain percentage of nodes goes down you'll still be able to run all the reducers in parallel. If the number is significantly less than the number of available slots, you're likely not maximizing the parallelization of your work. If the number is greater than the number of reducers, your job execution time takes longer, because the additional number of reducers will need to execute after the first batch has completed.

Bear in mind this is a general and simple rule that works well when your cluster is running only a single job at a time. In reality there are likely to be multiple jobs running concurrently, which makes it harder to come up with the ideal number of reducers for your job. But the number of reduce slots works well as a general rule.

TECHNIQUE 34 Identifying reduce-side data skew problems

On the reduce side, data skew exists when there's a disproportionately large number of map output values for a key, or when some values are significantly large in size compared to others.

Problem

You want to determine if a job runs slowly due to skewed data.

Solution

Use the JobTracker UI to compare the shuffled bytes across the reducers in your job to determine whether some reducers are receiving the bulk of the mapper outputs. This technique also covers visualizing the map and reduce task runtimes to help understand potential data skew issues.

Discussion

As with map-side, reduce-side data skew manifests itself as a small number of tasks taking disproportionately longer to execute than most of the others. Figure 6.16 shows how you can use the JobTracker UI to identify data skew.

This approach works well for a quick sanity check on a potential data skew issue. Visually examining task execution times can get you there much faster, which prompted me to write a simple utility that provides task-level statistics, including the input/output record counts and the sizes of inputs and outputs in bytes. The output is broken into map and reduce sections, and each section contains three subsections, where results are ordered by execution time, number of input records, and the input size in bytes:

```
$ bin/run.sh com.manning.hip.ch6.DataSkewMetrics --hdfsdir output
```

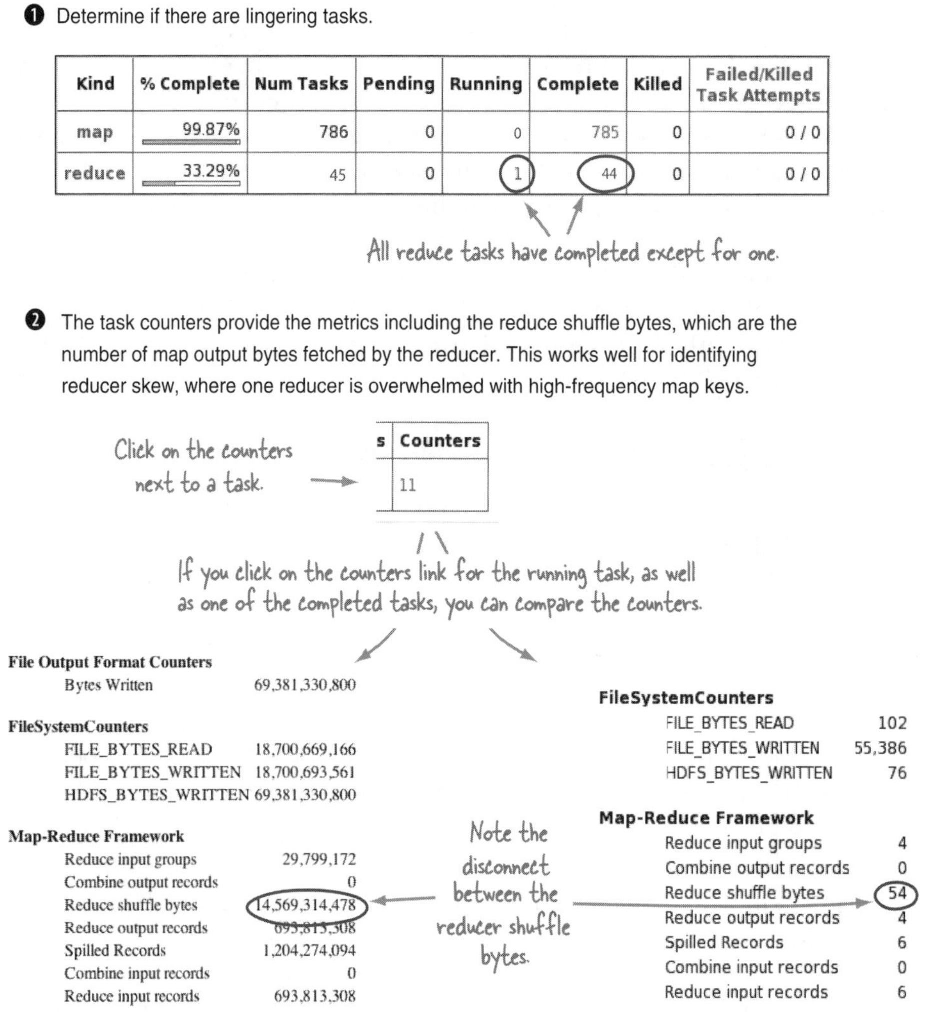

❶ Determine if there are lingering tasks.

Kind	% Complete	Num Tasks	Pending	Running	Complete	Killed	Failed/Killed Task Attempts
map	99.87%	786	0	0	785	0	0 / 0
reduce	33.29%	45	0	1	44	0	0 / 0

All reduce tasks have completed except for one.

❷ The task counters provide the metrics including the reduce shuffle bytes, which are the number of map output bytes fetched by the reducer. This works well for identifying reducer skew, where one reducer is overwhelmed with high-frequency map keys.

Click on the counters next to a task. ⟶

s	Counters
	11

If you click on the counters link for the running task, as well as one of the completed tasks, you can compare the counters.

File Output Format Counters
Bytes Written   69,381,330,800

FileSystemCounters
FILE_BYTES_READ   18,700,669,166
FILE_BYTES_WRITTEN   18,700,693,561
HDFS_BYTES_WRITTEN   69,381,330,800

Map-Reduce Framework
Reduce input groups   29,799,172
Combine output records   0
Reduce shuffle bytes   14,569,314,478
Reduce output records   693,813,308
Spilled Records   1,204,274,094
Combine input records   0
Reduce input records   693,813,308

Note the disconnect between the reducer shuffle bytes.

FileSystemCounters
FILE_BYTES_READ   102
FILE_BYTES_WRITTEN   55,386
HDFS_BYTES_WRITTEN   76

Map-Reduce Framework
Reduce input groups   4
Combine output records   0
Reduce shuffle bytes   54
Reduce output records   4
Spilled Records   6
Combine input records   0
Reduce input records   6

Figure 6.16   Determining data skew using the JobTracker

I also have a utility that will dump out a tab-separated file of task execution times (and input sizes), which you can use for plotting purposes to help eyeball problems. The following command will generate map and reduce times:

```
$ bin/run.sh com.manning.hip.ch6.DataSkewGnuplot --hdfsdir output
```

Figure 6.17 shows this data plotted. In this illustration you'll see that some map tasks are taking significantly longer than other tasks, but the reduce tasks all seem to be taking around the same amount of time.

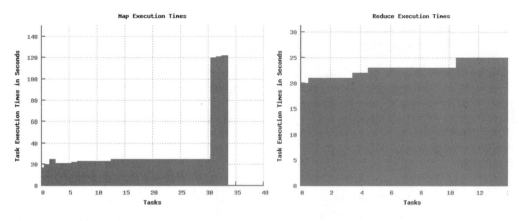

Figure 6.17   Map and reduce task execution times

Summary
When you've identified that you have reducer skew, your next step should be to try and mitigate the effects of skew in your job. Techniques 50 and 51 look at potential causes of data skew, and how they can be addressed.

TECHNIQUE 35   **Determining if reduce tasks have an overall low throughput**

Reduce tasks running slowly will contribute to the overall slowness of a MapReduce job. There are a variety of issues that could cause reduce tasks to run slowly, some related to the user's reduce code, and others related to hardware issues. The challenge is in identifying whether your reduce tasks are running slower than you should expect.

Problem
You want to determine if a job runs slowly due to low task throughput.

Solution
Use the JobTracker UI or the job history metadata to calculate the throughput of your reduce tasks.

Discussion
The reduce throughput can be calculated for individual tasks by using the JobTracker to get at the task execution times. Figure 6.18 shows how to calculate throughput for reduce tasks.

The easiest way to get at the throughput statistics for all the reduce tasks is to execute my script against the job history file for your job, as shown in figure 6.19.

Summary
You have four throughput metrics to examine from the task throughput script, which will help you isolate if one aspect of the reduce task is significantly slower than the other. In this technique you'll focus on the reduce throughput; in the next technique we'll look at the shuffle and sort phases.

File Output Format Counters
    Bytes Written   69,381,330,800 ◄——— Task counters

FileSystemCounters
    FILE_BYTES_READ   18,700,669,166
    FILE_BYTES_WRITTEN 18,700,693,561
    HDFS_BYTES_WRITTEN 69,381,330,800

Map-Reduce Framework

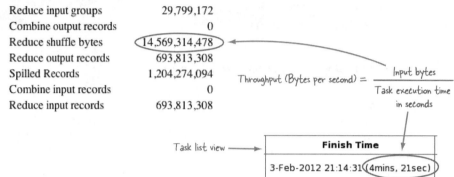

    Reduce input groups   29,799,172
    Combine output records   0
    Reduce shuffle bytes   14,569,314,478
    Reduce output records   693,813,308
    Spilled Records   1,204,274,094
    Combine input records   0
    Reduce input records   693,813,308

Figure 6.18 Calculating the throughput for a reduce task

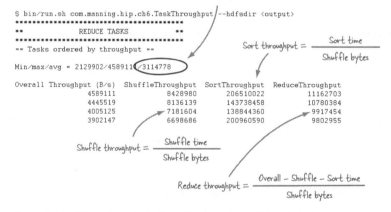

Figure 6.19 The reduce task throughputs extracted from job history

The reduce phase accounts for time taken to read the spilled map outputs on local disk, for the reduce code to operate, and for the reduce outputs to be written to the data sink. Items that could contribute to low reduce throughput include the following:

- Local disk issues can cause issues as the MapReduce framework reads the spilled local inputs and feeds them to the reduce code.
- Inefficiencies in the code.
- Network problems if the job output is HDFS.
- Latency or throughput issues if the data sink is not HDFS.

Separate techniques will be discussed for all of the items listed (apart from the last one) to help determine the exact cause of low reduce throughput.

TECHNIQUE 36   Slow shuffle and sort

The shuffle phase involves fetching the map output data from the TaskTrackers and merging them in the background. The sort phase, which is another merge, will merge the files together into a smaller number of files.

Problem

You want to determine if a job runs slowly due to the shuffle and sort phases.

Solution

Use the job history metadata to extract statistics around the shuffle and sort execution times.

Discussion

Figure 6.20 uses the job summary code to examine statistics around a job's shuffle and sort times, and looks at some areas for potential improvements in their times.

Summary

The simplest ways to cut down on shuffle and sort times is to use a combiner, and to compress your map outputs. Both approaches reduce the amount of data flowing between the map and reduce tasks and lessen the network and CPU/disk burden related to the shuffle and sort phases.

You can also tune a variety of configuration settings to increase the sort buffer size, as well as the number of threads used on the reduce side and map side to transfer map outputs. These are covered in section 6.4.2.

6.2.4   General task woes

In this section we'll look at problems that can affect both map and reduce tasks.

```
$ bin/run.sh com.manning.hip.ch6.MetricSummary --hdfsdir <output>
```

```
******************************************
**             REDUCE TASKS            **
******************************************

Num Reduce Tasks: 1

          Item         Min         Max      Median        Mean  StdDev
execution time       20m 5s      20m 5s      20m 5s      20m 5s      0s
   shuffle time    18m 29s     18m 29s     18m 29s     18m 29s      0s
      sort time         1s          1s          1s          1s      0s
 input records    9937101     9937101     9937101     9937101       0
   input bytes 1100419082  1100419082  1100419082  1100419082       0
output records    9937101     9937101     9937101     9937101       0
  output bytes 1099102302  1099102302  1099102302  1099102302       0
```

Look at the median and mean (average) shuffle and sort times for the reduce tasks...

 ... if they seem large (for the number of input bytes they're working on) then ...

❶ Check the "Hardware Woes" section to make sure that there aren't any network or disk issues on your nodes.

❷ Consider tuning the number of threads in the reduce tasks and TaskTracker processes.

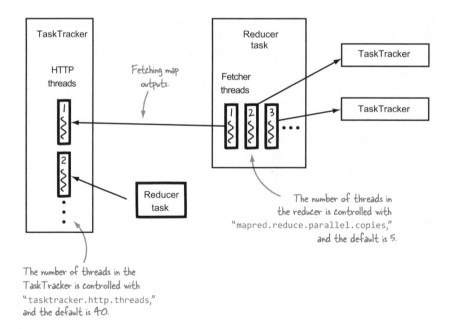

The number of threads in the reducer is controlled with "mapred.reduce.parallel.copies," and the default is 5.

The number of threads in the TaskTracker is controlled with "tasktracker.http.threads," and the default is 40.

Figure 6.20   Extracting shuffle and sort metrics for a MapReduce job

Competing jobs and scheduler throttling

Imagine that you've tuned your job such that the map tasks are all working on large files that can be split, and your number of reducers is set to the number of reduce slots configured in your cluster. Your job could still be running slowly due to other environmental issues, as you'll see in this next technique.

Problem

You want to determine if a job runs slowly due to other jobs running in the cluster.

Solution

Compare the number of executing reduce tasks with your Hadoop cluster's reduce task capacity.

Discussion

If, based on previous techniques, you believe you've configured your job correctly, and the per-task throughput numbers look good, then your job slowness could be due to competition for resources on the cluster. How can you make this determination? I have a couple of approaches to show you.

If the job is still running, go to the JobTracker and look at the number of concurrently executing map and reduce tasks for your job, and compare these numbers to the cluster capacity, as shown in figure 6.21.

The figure shows how you're clearly running with far fewer reducers than what's configured for the cluster.

Summary

The amount of parallelism available to you is a function of your cluster capacity, the other jobs running at the same time as your job, and any schedulers configured for your environment. You can use the JobTracker UI to determine if other jobs are running at the same time as yours. If this is the case, there's no simple solution to your job's throughput issues.

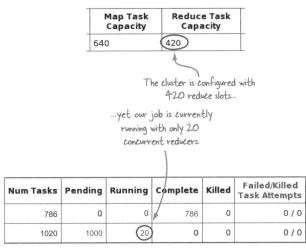

Map Task Capacity	Reduce Task Capacity
640	420

The cluster is configured with 420 reduce slots...

...yet our job is currently running with only 20 concurrent reducers.

Num Tasks	Pending	Running	Complete	Killed	Failed/Killed Task Attempts
786	0	0	786	0	0 / 0
1020	1000	20	0	0	0 / 0

Figure 6.21 Comparing the configured slots in your cluster with the number of tasks running

By default MapReduce uses a FIFO scheduler to determine how tasks should be scheduled if there are multiple jobs running at the same time. If someone else submitted a job ahead of your job, that job will have its tasks scheduled ahead of your tasks. Depending on the importance of your job you may want to use the Fair or Capacity Schedulers so that resources are more evenly distributed. These schedulers can also be set up in a way such that they will give more cluster resources to some jobs over other jobs.

TECHNIQUE 38   **Using stack dumps to discover unoptimized user code**

Inefficiencies in your code can slow down your jobs. For example, many of the Java String tokenization techniques you're accustomed to using are inefficient and can substantially increase the runtime of a job.

Problem

You want to determine if a job runs slowly due to inefficiencies in your code.

Solution

Determine the host and process ID of currently executing tasks, and take a number of stack dumps, which are subsequently examined, to narrow-down bottlenecks in your code.

Discussion

The challenge with this technique is that MapReduce versions 1.0.0 and earlier don't have metrics around how much time is spent in user code in the map and reduce phases. The best approach to understanding time that's being taken in your code is to update your code to time how long you spend in each task. But in this technique you want to get a rough sense of whether this is an issue without having to change code.

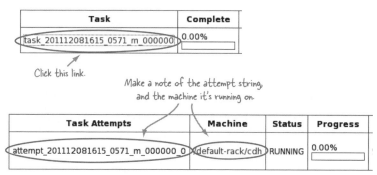

Figure 6.22   Determine the task attempt string.

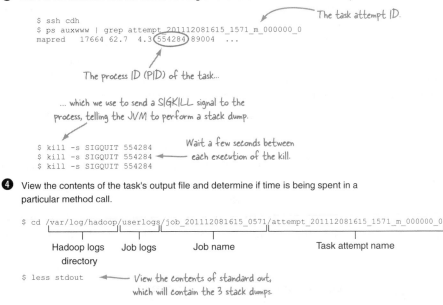

Figure 6.23   Take task stack dumps.

In an earlier technique we looked at how to calculate the throughput of map tasks. This calculation was a rough one based on the map execution times and the map input sizes. You can take the same approach to estimate the throughput of reduce tasks.

If you have user code that's not performing optimally, these throughput numbers will be low. But they can be low for a variety of reasons (which were covered in that technique), and not as a result of your code. Use the prior techniques to eliminate other potential issues in the cluster.

If you're doing something inefficient in your code, chances are that you'll be able to discover what it is by taking some stack dumps of the task process. Figure 6.22 shows how to identify the job and task details so that you can take the stack dumps.

Now that you know the job name, task name, and the host it's executing on, you can take your stack dumps and follow the next steps, as shown in figure 6.23.

Summary

Stack dumps are a primitive yet often effective means to discover where a Java process is spending its time, particularly if that process is CPU-bound. Clearly they're not as effective as using a profiler, which will more accurately pinpoint where time is being spent, but the advantage of stack dumps is that they can be performed on any running Java process, whereas if you were to use a profiler, you'd need to re-execute the process with the required profiling JVM settings—a nuisance in MapReduce.

When taking stack dumps, it's useful to take multiple dumps with some pauses in between successive dumps. This allows you to visually determine if the code execution stacks across multiple dumps are roughly in the same point. If this is the case, there's a good chance the code in the stack is what's causing the slowness.

If your code isn't in the same location across the different stack dumps, this doesn't necessarily indicate that there aren't inefficiencies. In this case the best approach is to profile your code or add some measurements in your code and rerun your job to get a more accurate breakdown of where time is being spent.

6.2.5   *Hardware woes*

Modern hardware is generally reliable with mean time to failure (MTTF) values that typically span multiple years. But when you're working with clusters, the overall MTTF drops significantly; clusters with hundreds of nodes should expect one failure or more per week. In this section we'll look at how to determine if your CPU, memory, disks, and networks are overutilized, and what you can do to bring them down to reasonable operating levels.

TECHNIQUE 39   **Discovering hardware failures**

Nodes can fail due to issues such as disk controller failures, disk space issues, and other hardware issues. It's also possible that a bug in Hadoop causes tasks to fail, although this is less likely. When this happens it can have an adverse effect on job execution times, particularly in smaller clusters. We'll look at how to determine if nodes are failing in your cluster.

Problem

You want to determine if a job runs slowly due to hardware problems, and you want to see if nodes are blacklisted or graylisted.

Solution

Use the JobTracker UI to check for nodes that are graylisted or blacklisted.

Discussion

Go to the JobTracker UI and check to see if there are any blacklisted or graylisted nodes. Figure 6.24 shows where you should look to keep tabs on nodes.

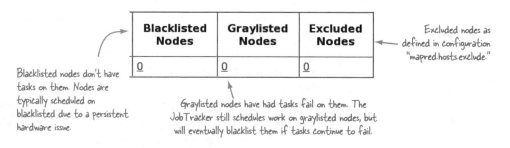

Figure 6.24   JobTracker UI showing node statuses

Summary
It's undesirable to have blacklisted or graylisted nodes, particularly in smaller clusters. Graylisted nodes that have transient or permanent failures will chew up job execution times due to failing tasks. Blacklisted nodes don't have any work scheduled on them and don't contribute to the cluster, and their removal from the cluster can have a significant impact on job performance.

If nodes are blacklisted or graylisted the cause of the problem can sometimes be determined by looking at task and TaskTracker or DataNode log files. In any case, Operations should be contacted to investigate the failing nodes.

It's good to set up monitoring for blacklisted and graylisted nodes so that you can quickly react to node failures. An example of a Nagios monitor that does this can be seen at http://goo.gl/R6deM. It uses curl to download the blacklisted web page from the JobTracker using http://127.0.0.1:50030/machines.jsp?type=blacklisted (this URL is intended to be fetched on the same host as the JobTracker) and checks that no blacklisted nodes exist.

TECHNIQUE 40   **CPU contention**

If your nodes are overutilized from a CPU perspective, your overall computational throughput suffers because the OS spends more time context switching than it does performing work.

Problem
You want to determine if a job runs slowly due to CPU overutilization.

Solution
Use the Linux tool vmstat to observe the CPU context switches.

Discussion
vmstat is an excellent tool to quickly gauge how busy a host is in terms of CPU utilization, I/O wait, and context switching. Figure 6.25 shows how it can be executed and explains some options.

The first row contains
averages since the last time   Display units in megabytes
the host was rebooted.   (1048576 bytes).

Sampling time
period in seconds.

```
$ vmstat -S M 5
procs -----------memory---------- ---swap-- -----io---- --system-- -----cpu------
 r  b   swpd   free   buff  cache   si   so    bi    bo   in    cs us sy id wa st
 1  0   1044     51     44    244    0    0    14    38    1     4  0  1 99  0  0
10  0   1044     51     44    244    0    0     6    30  109  1144  0  0 99  0  0
 9  0   1044     51     44    244    0    0     0    26  112  1169  0  1 99  0  0
10  0   1044     51     44    244    0    0     0    30  109  1150  0  1 99  0  0
...
```

Subsequent rows contain averages over the sample
period (apart from "procs" and "memory,"
which are instantaneous).

Figure 6.25 Executing vmstat and its options

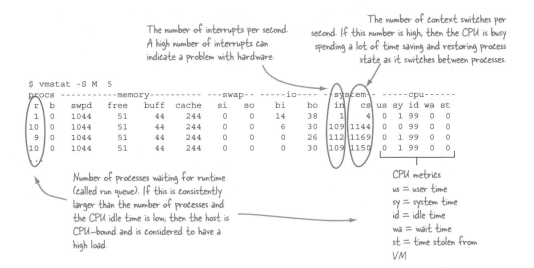

Figure 6.26 Annotated vmstat output helps you watch your host.

Figure 6.26 depicts some of the items you should watch.

Summary
The longer the Linux run queue, which is the number of processes waiting for CPU time, the more time the Linux kernel spends context switching from one process to another. Each context switch is expensive because it requires the CPU to save the state of the existing process and load the state of the next process. Therefore, excessive context switching means that you're possibly running too many tasks on your host. Remember that as a rule of thumb your mapred.tasktracker.map.tasks.maximum and mapred.tasktracker.reduce.tasks.maximum totaled should be around 120 percent of the logical cores on your host.

Sometimes the TaskTracker can become CPU pegged, which can cause high CPU loads on your server. Use top to determine if the TaskTracker is CPU bound, and if it is consider bouncing the TaskTracker process.

In addition, procinfo is a handy tool to use in situations where you want to figure out what devices are causing high interrupt numbers, and sar is useful for collecting and saving system data into files for later use. Finally, mpstat is useful because it gives statistics broken down by CPU, and not aggregated across all the CPUs, as other commands will do.

TECHNIQUE 41 Memory swapping

Swapping happens when you start exceeding the physical limits of memory on your hosts, which makes the OS start to use disk as an overflow mechanism for memory.

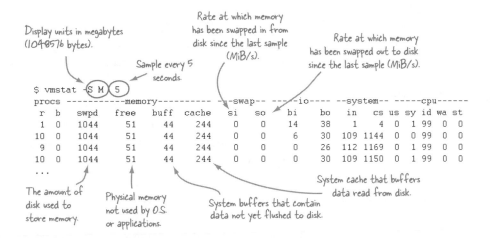

Figure 6.27 Executing `vmstat` to look at swapping

Reading and writing to disk is orders of magnitude slower than reading and writing to RAM, and therefore has a significant toll on the performance of a node.

Problem
You want to determine if a job runs slowly due to swapping.

Solution
Use the Linux tool `vmstat` to observe if memory is being swapped in and out of disk.

Discussion
Not only is `vmstat` useful for monitoring CPU behavior, as we saw in the previous technique, but it can also be used to examine whether your host is swapping to disk (and back). Figure 6.27 shows how it can be executed and explains some options.

Figure 6.28 looks at some of the items to watch.

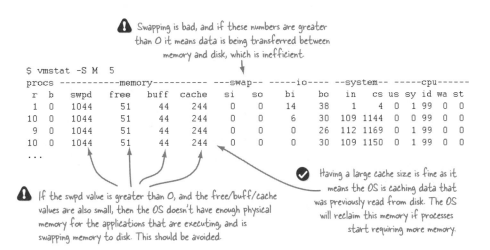

Figure 6.28 Annotated `vmstat` output to look at swapping

Summary

If you're using swap, you either need to add additional RAM to your host or look at reducing the number of concurrent map and reduce tasks running on the node (mapred.tasktracker.map.tasks.maximum and mapred.tasktracker.reduce.tasks.maximum).

TECHNIQUE 42   Disk health

A Hadoop cluster under load puts a lot of stress on disks and disk controllers. In this section we'll look at how to evaluate whether your drives are healthy, and also investigate if your drives have been remounted as read-only due to I/O errors.

Problem

You want to understand if a drive runs in degraded or read-only mode.

Solution

The Linux tool iostat can be used to look at drive request queues and IO wait times. Other Linux tools such as dmesg can help determine if a drive has gone into a read-only mode.

Discussion

Out of all the tools in Linux, iostat is the most comprehensive one for disk and device-level statistics. Figure 6.29 shows how it can be executed and explains some options.

Figure 6.30 looks at the output of iostat and highlights some of the items to watch for.

Another important thing to watch for is a filesystem going into read-only mode. This can happen due to bugs in disk or RAID controllers in Linux, and will debilitate the node. If this happens your TaskTracker and DataNode logs will contain errors complaining that they can't write to disk. You can also look at /var/log/messages,

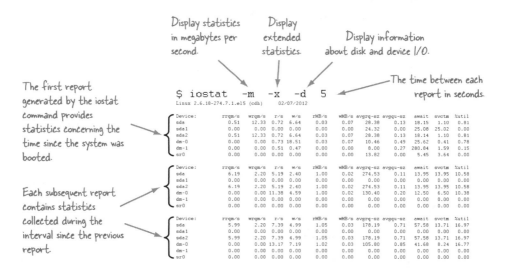

Figure 6.29   Executing iostat to evaluate drives

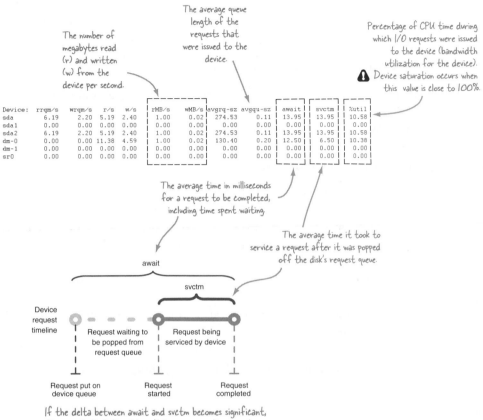

Figure 6.30 `iostat` output explained to evaluate drives

and use `dmesg` to check for messages about the filesystem being moved into a read-only state:

```
$ dmesg | grep read-only
```

Summary

Too much load on disks can cause read and write requests to get queued, increasing I/O wait times, which has the effect of slowing down a node. Further, the Linux kernel will mount drives as read-only if I/O errors related to the drive are encountered, which, depending on your drive setup, can cripple your node.

You can use `hdparm` to measure the sequential read rate of your hard disk. Replace `/dev/md1` with the name of your disk device (consult `/etc/fstab` for device names):

```
$ cat /etc/fstab
...
/dev/md5  /usr  ext3  defaults  1 2
...
```

```
$ sudo /sbin/hdparm -t /dev/md5

/dev/md5:
 Timing cached reads:    30656 MB in  1.99 seconds = 15405.72 MB/sec
 Timing buffered disk reads:  108 MB in  3.03 seconds =  35.63 MB/sec
```

If the DataNodes are exhibiting I/O wait issues, you may want to install additional hard drives on each node and configure dfs.data.dir to use multiple disks, which will spread the read and write load across them.

TECHNIQUE 43 Networking

A networking problem will have a big impact on the performance of MapReduce and HDFS, because both are heavily reliant on data transfer between nodes. In this technique we'll look at ways to ensure you've configured your nodes correctly, and also look at how you can test the network throughput between nodes.

Problem
You want to determine if a job runs slowly due to network issues.

Solution
Examining the output of the Linux tools ethtool and sar can help diagnose network mis-configurations.

Discussion
The first thing you need to check is that you've configured your ethernet card to run at the correct speed, and that it's running at full duplex (the ability of the network

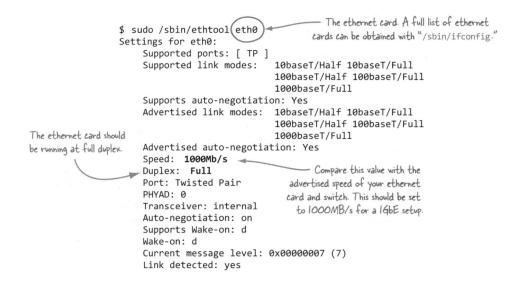

Figure 6.31 ethtool **command and output explained for your network**

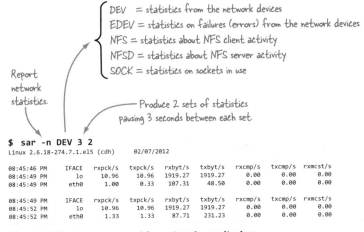

Figure 6.32 **sar command for network monitoring**

card and switch to send and receive data at the same time). Figure 6.31 shows how to use ethtool to get that information.

The ethtool command will give you the totals for items such as transmitted bytes. To view differences in network card metrics as they happen you can use sar, as shown in figure 6.32.

Figure 6.33 looks at the output of sar and highlights metrics that could indicate network issues.

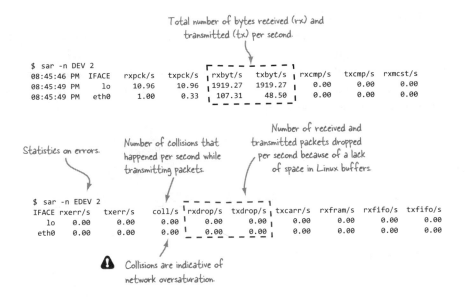

Figure 6.33 sar **command output explained for networks**

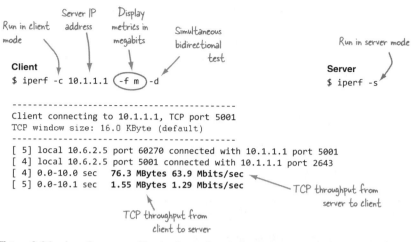

Figure 6.34 `iperf` **command for testing network throughput**

To test the network bandwidth between two hosts, you can use `iperf` (http://openmaniak.com/iperf.php), as shown in figure 6.34. CentOS RPMs are available at http://pkgs.repoforge.org/iperf/.

Summary

In this technique we looked at ways to verify that you configured your network cards correctly, and also looked at tools to capture network metrics. I also explained how to measure network bandwidth to test your network card and switches.

6.3 *Visualization*

In MapReduce it's useful to measure the execution time of the various MapReduce stages, as shown in figure 6.35.

Unfortunately, as of the 0.20.x release Hadoop doesn't measure and expose all of these stages. Figure 6.36 shows the execution times that are exposed in 0.20.x, and how they map to the MapReduce stages.

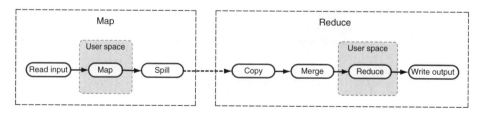

Figure 6.35 **The various stages of a MapReduce job**

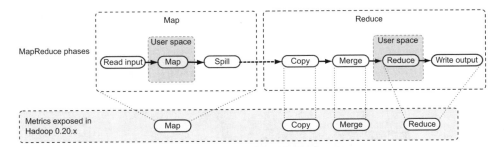

Figure 6.36   Mapping of MapReduce phases to what's measured in Hadoop 0.20.x

---

TECHNIQUE 44   **Extracting and visualizing task execution times**

We'll look at how to use the job history metrics to retrieve a timeline of the number of
tasks running during the course of the job execution. This can be useful both for performance tuning and from a comprehension-of-task-concurrency standpoint. Visually
examining your job can be useful in identify issues such as straggling tasks and low
task concurrency numbers.

Problem

You want to visualize the performance characteristics of a slow job rather than comb
through a bunch of numbers.

Solution

Metrics can be extracted from the job history metadata and plotted with graphing
software to visually inspect map, reduce, sort, and shuffle execution times.

Discussion

To execute your code you must determine the location of the history file for a job you
want to analyze, or the job output directory in HDFS must still exist (see section 6.1.1
for more details):

*The HDFS
output directory
of a job you
want to
visualize.*

```
$ bin/run.sh com.manning.hip.ch6.ExtractJobTaskTimeline \
    --hdfsdir output \
    2> src/main/gnuplot/ch6/tasksovertime.dat
```
*The tab-separated data file is written
to standard error, and here you pipe it
to a data file.*

*You change
directories to
the location of
your gnuplot
script.*

```
$ cd src/main/gnuplot/ch6/

$ gnuplot ./tasksovertime.pg
```
*Run gnuplot, which will generate a
PNG image file called mr.png.*

You're using the Linux graphing utility gnuplot[4] to plot your data in a stacked histogram form.

An example image file is illustrated in figure 6.37.

---

[4] See http://gnuplot.sourceforge.net/.

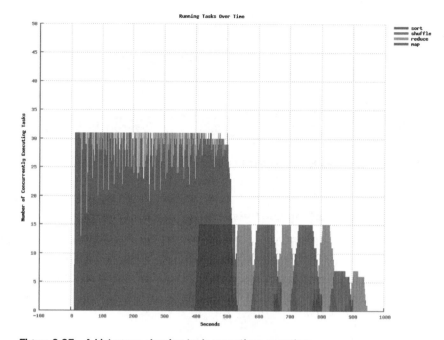

Figure 6.37   A histogram showing task executions over time

EVALUATING THE HISTOGRAM

With the histogram displayed, you now need to use it to narrow down where your performance problem may exist. There are two main things you should be looking out for. First, because the x-axis is the timeline for your job, you should use it to determine if there's a particular stage in MapReduce that's taking up a large part of the job execution time. This isn't an exact science, but if, for example, you have a CPU-bound process, you may see large periods of time spent executing your MapReduce code.

Second, the ideal MapReduce histogram is one where both the map and reduce phases have consistently high numbers of concurrent tasks. If there's a long tail in the map and reduce phases, this can indicate some data skew issues, where map and reduce tasks are receiving a disproportionate number of records.

Figure 6.38 shows three examples of task execution graphs, two of which have less-than-ideal patterns, and the third of which is the ideal graph.

Gnuplot version

Gnuplot version 4.4 was used to generate the graphs in this section. If you encounter syntax errors or appearance differences this may be a result of running a different version of gnuplot.

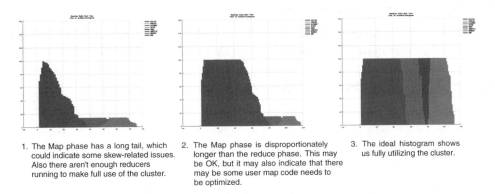

1. The Map phase has a long tail, which could indicate some skew-related issues. Also there aren't enough reducers running to make full use of the cluster.

2. The Map phase is disproportionately longer than the reduce phase. This may be OK, but it may also indicate that there may be some user map code needs to be optimized.

3. The ideal histogram shows us fully utilizing the cluster.

Figure 6.38   Examples of task execution graphs

Summary

Visualizing MapReduce job and task metrics is a useful way to examine and make observations about your data. I've compiled a number of other visualizations to be made from the history files, which can help you better understand your jobs, including the following:

- Plotting the start and end execution times for tasks, to give a sense of how long they're taking to run.
- Correlating the input and output data sizes with the amount of time it takes for a task to run.
- Plotting the number of tasks for each slave node executing over time to help identify hosts that aren't having many tasks allocated to them.

One of the challenges to working with the history file format is that it's unstructured. Hadoop 0.23 will remedy this with the enhancement described in MAPREDUCE-157 (see https://issues.apache.org/jira/browse/MAPREDUCE-157) and writes to the file in JSON form.

If your histogram indicates that your map and reduce code is taking a long time, your next step is to try and determine what's causing the slowdown in your application code.

This section and the previous section focused on helping identify potential performance problems while running a MapReduce job. The next section looks at solutions to common performance problems.

6.4   *Tuning*

In the previous sections we looked at how you could narrow down where your performance problems lie. This section is all about profiling and tuning your jobs to extract as much performance out of them as you can. We'll look at how to improve the performance of the shuffle and sort phases, and several other tips that will help cut down on your job execution times.

6.4.1   *Profiling MapReduce user code*

When you suspect that there's something awry in your map or reduce code that's causing slow execution times, it's time to break out the profiler.

<hr>

TECHNIQUE 45   **Profiling your map and reduce tasks**

<hr>

Profiling standalone Java applications is straightforward and well supported by a large
number of tools. In MapReduce you're working in a distributed environment running multiple map and reduce tasks, so it's less clear how you would go about profiling your code.

Problem

You suspect that there are inefficiencies in your map and reduce code, and need to
identify where they exist.

Solution

Use HPROF in combination with a number of MapReduce job methods such as set-
ProfileEnabled to profile your tasks.

Discussion

Hadoop has built-in support for the HPROF profiler, Oracle's Java profiler built into
the JVM. To get started you don't need to understand any HPROF settings—you
can call JobConf.setProfileEnabled(true) and Hadoop will run HPROF with the following settings:

```
-agentlib:hprof=cpu=samples,heap=sites,force=n,thread=y,verbose=n,file=%s
```

This will generate object allocation stacks sizes that are too small to be useful, so
instead you'll programmatically set custom HPROF parameters:

Enable →
profiling.
```
job.setProfileEnabled(true);

job.setProfileParams(
    "-agentlib:hprof=depth=8,cpu=samples,heap=sites,force=n," +
    "thread=y,verbose=n,file=%s");

job.setProfileTaskRange(true, "0,1,5-10");

job.setProfileTaskRange(false,"");

JobClient.runJob(job);
```

Specify the HPROF parameters. Here
you're running with a stack depth of
eight, to help you tie the bottom of
the stack to your user code.

You don't want to
profile any reduce
tasks, because
your example job
uses the identity
reducer.

This method sets the range of tasks that will be profiled.
This is useful because it allows you to profile a small subsection
of tasks for large jobs. As you can see, the grammar is flexible
and allows individual task numbers as well as ranges to be
defined. The first flag is a Boolean that indicates whether
the range is being specified for the map or reduce tasks.

The sample job profiled is quite simple. It parses a file containing IP addresses and
extracts the first octet from the IP and emits it as the output value:

```
public void map(LongWritable key, Text value,
                OutputCollector<LongWritable, Text> output,
```

```
                    Reporter reporter) throws IOException {
    String[] parts = value.toString().split("\\.");
    Text outputValue = new Text(parts[0]);
    output.collect(key, outputValue);
}
```

You'll upload a large(ish) file of IP addresses and run your job against it, with the previous profiling options set:

```
$ hadoop fs -put test-data/ch6/large-ips.txt .

$ bin/run.sh com.manning.hip.ch6.SlowJob \
  large-ips.txt output
```

```
$ ls -1
attempt_201112081615_0365_m_000001_0.profile
attempt_201112081615_0365_m_000000_0.profile
```

⟵ *The job copies the profile files from the remote TaskTrackers to the local filesystem of your job submission host.*

The HPROF option you used will create a text file that can be easily parsed. The file contains a number of stack traces, and at the bottom contains memory and CPU time accumulations, with references to stack traces that accounted for the accumulations. In the example you ran you'll look at the top two items, which accounted for the most CPU times, and correlate them with the code:

```
CPU SAMPLES BEGIN (total = 995) Sat Dec 24 18:26:15 2011
rank   self  accum   count trace method
   1  7.44%  7.44%      74 313153 java.lang.Object.<init>
   2  4.42% 11.86%      44 313156 java.lang.Object.<init>
   3  3.52% 15.38%      35 313176 java.lang.Object.<init>
   4  3.32% 18.69%      33 313132 java.util.regex.Pattern.compile
   5  2.81% 21.51%      28 313172 java.lang.Object.<init>
   6  2.61% 24.12%      26 313151 java.lang.Object.<init>
   7  2.61% 26.73%      26 313152 java.lang.Object.<init>
   8  2.51% 29.25%      25 313128 java.nio.HeapCharBuffer.<init>
```

⟵ *The stack trace that had the most accumulated time has a trace ID of 313153. You use this ID to search for the stack in the file.*

```
TRACE 313153: (thread=200001)
java.lang.Object.<init>(Object.java:20)
java.lang.String.<init>(String.java:636)
java.lang.String.substring(String.java:1939)
java.lang.String.subSequence(String.java:1972)
java.util.regex.Pattern.split(Pattern.java:1002)
java.lang.String.split(String.java:2292)
java.lang.String.split(String.java:2334)
com.manning.hip.ch6.SlowJob$Map.map(SlowJob.java:23)
```

⟵ *This is the stack trace for ID 313153. It looks like the String.split method is using a regular expression, which is slow.*

```
TRACE 313156: (thread=200001)
java.lang.Object.<init>(Object.java:20)
org.apache.hadoop.io.BinaryComparable.<init>(BinaryComparable.java:25)
org.apache.hadoop.io.Text.<init>(Text.java:80)
com.manning.hip.ch6.SlowJob$Map.map(SlowJob.java:24)
```

⟵ *The item that is the second-most utilized in the task is in the constructor of the Text object, and the overhead of creating the BinaryComparable. This is also something that you need to optimize.*

The two issues identified at the top of the CPU times, the String.split method and the Text constructor, are both addressed later in this section.

Summary

Running HPROF adds significant overhead to the execution of Java; it instruments Java classes to collect the profiling information as your code is executing. This isn't something you'll want to regularly run in production.

6.4.2 Configuration

You can tune a number of settings in Hadoop depending on your hardware resources, and the types of MapReduce jobs you are running, as you'll see in table 6.1.

Table 6.1 Configurations that can be tuned for improved performance

Process	Configuration	Default value	Notes
Map	io.sort.mb	100	The amount of memory reserved to store and sort map outputs, in megabytes. This should be approximately 70% of the map task's heap size.
Map	io.sort.record.percent	0.05	The percentage of io.sort.mb that's used to store metadata about the map outputs.
Map	io.sort.spill.percent	0.80	The percentage of the map output buffer after which the buffer will be spilled to disk.
Map	tasktracker.http.threads	40	The number of TaskTracker HTTP threads that are used to service reducer requests for map outputs. Recommended to be 80 for smaller clusters, and even higher for larger clusters with 1,000-plus nodes.
Map, Reduce	io.sort.factor	10	The number of files to merge together in a single pass. Larger clusters with 1,000-plus nodes can bump this up to 100.
Reduce	mapred.reduce.parallel.copies	5	The number of threads used in each reducer to fetch map outputs from TaskTrackers. Larger clusters with 1,000-plus nodes can bump this up to 20.
Reduce	fs.inmemory.size.mb	100	The amount of memory reserved to cache and merge fetched map outputs, in megabytes. This should be approximately 70% of the reducer's heap size.

Table 6.1   Configurations that can be tuned for improved performance *(continued)*

Process	Configuration	Default value	Notes
TaskTracker	mapred.tasktracker.map.tasks.maximum	2	The maximum number of concurrent map tasks that will be run by a Task-Tracker. This combined with the value for `mapred.task-tracker.reduce.tasks.maximum` should be approximately 120% of the number of logical cores on a node. This map task number should constitute 75% of this number, and `mapred.task-tracker.reduce.tasks.maximum` the remaining 25%. On sites with heterogeneous hardware this should be tuned for each node stereotype in the cluster.
TaskTracker	mapred.tasktracker.reduce.tasks.maximum	2	The maximum number of concurrent reduce tasks that will be run by a Task-Tracker. See `mapred.task-tracker.map.tasks.maximum` for details on what to set this to.
Map, Reduce	mapred.child.java.opts	-Xmx200m	Java options for map and reduce processes. *-Xmx* sets the maximum Java heap size for the process. This value should be tuned based on the work performed in the cluster. If your nodes are swapping, either `mapred.task-tracker.{map,reduce}.tasks.max imum` need to be tuned down, or this value needs to be decreased. Also consider setting `mapred.child.ulimit` to approximately twice the value of this setting; it will also cap the memory utilized by any processes launched by the map/reduce processes, such as when you're using streaming.
NameNode	dfs.namenode.handler.count	10	The number of threads that the NameNode uses to handle block-level requests from DataNodes. Larger clusters with 1,000-plus nodes can bump this up to 40.
DataNode	dfs.datanode.handler.count	3	The number of threads that the DataNode uses to handle block-level requests from other DataNodes.

6.4.3 Optimizing the shuffle and sort phase

The shuffle stage in MapReduce is an expensive one, which can incur high network utilization when transferring data between map and reduce tasks. The overhead of sorting and merging can also be significant. The goal of this section is to provide a number of techniques to help mitigate the overhead of the shuffle phase.

TECHNIQUE 46 **Avoid the reducer**

Reducers are useful mechanisms when you want to join data together, but they come at the expense of transferring data over the network.

Problem

You want to consider not using the reduce phase in MapReduce.

Solution

Set the MapReduce configuration parameter setNumReduceTasks to 0 to run a map-only job.

Discussion

The shuffle and sort phases are typically used to join data together. But as you saw in chapter 4, some joins can be performed on the map side if certain conditions hold true about your data. In such situations you can run a map-only job, with no reducers. This is easily accomplished by setting the number of reducers to 0:

```
job.setNumReduceTasks(0);
```

Summary

A map-only job uses the same OutputFormat that the reducer uses to write the job outputs, as shown in figure 6.39.

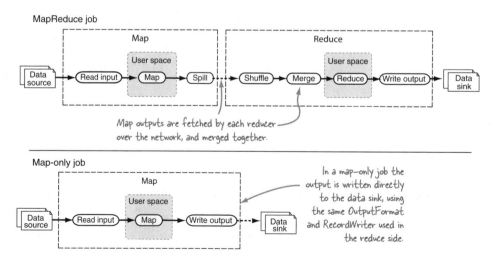

Figure 6.39   Comparing a MapReduce job with a map-only job.

If you can't run without a reducer in your job, the next step is to minimize the impact it has on your job execution time.

TECHNIQUE 47   Filter and project

Much of the data emitted from the map to the reduce tasks is transferred over the network, which is expensive.

Problem

You want to cut down on data being shuffled.

Solution

Reduce the size of the map output records, and aggressively omit records from being outputted by the mapper.

Discussion

Filtering and projecting are relational concepts to cut down on data being processed. These concepts also apply in MapReduce as a way to minimize the data that map tasks emit. Simple definitions of filtering and projection follow:

- Filtering is the process of removing entire records from the map emission.
- Projection cuts down on the record sizes by removing individual fields.

The following code is an example of both concepts in action:[5]

```
Text outputKey = new Text();
Text outputValue = new Text();


@Override
public void map(LongWritable key, Text value,
               OutputCollector<Text, Text> output,
               Reporter reporter) throws IOException {

  String v = value.toString();
  if (!v.startsWith("10.")) {                          Filter out
    String[] parts = StringUtils.split(v, ".", 3);     private IP addresses.
    outputKey.set(parts[0]);
    outputValue.set(parts[1]);                         Projection of the first two
    output.collect(outputKey, outputValue);            octets of the IP address.
  }
}
```

Summary

The use of filtering and projection are two of the easiest mechanisms that you can employ to dramatically reduce the runtime of your MapReduce jobs.

If you've ensured that you're performing as much filtering and projection as possible in your map task, the next step to the shuffle and sort optimization is to look at using the combiner. The combiner is another mechanism you can use to cut down on data traveling between map and reduce tasks.

---

[5] **GitHub source**—https://github.com/alexholmes/hadoop-book/blob/master/src/main/java/com/manning/hip/ch6/FilterProjectJob.java

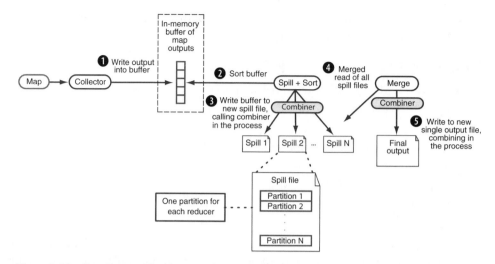

Figure 6.40   How the combiner is called in the context of the map task

---

TECHNIQUE 48   **Using the combiner**

The combiner is a powerful mechanism to aggregate data in the map phase to cut down on data sent to the reducer. It's a map-side optimization where your user code is invoked with a number of map output values for the same output key.

Problem

You're filtering and projecting your data, but your shuffle and sort are still taking longer than you want. How can you cut down on them even further?

Solution

Define a combiner and use the setCombinerClass method to set it for your job.

Discussion

The combiner is invoked on the map side as part of writing map output data to disk in both the spill and merge phases, as shown in figure 6.40. To help with grouping values together to maximize the effectiveness of a combiner, use a precursory sorting step in both phases prior to calling the combiner function.

Calling the setCombinerClass sets the combiner for a job, similar to how the map and reduce classes are set:

```
job.setCombinerClass(Combine.class);
```

Your combiner implementation must conform to the reducer specification. In this technique you'll build upon the IP filter and projection code that you wrote in the previous technique, and combine records together where the second octet is identical:[6]

---

[6]   **GitHub source**—https://github.com/alexholmes/hadoop-book/blob/master/src/main/java/com/manning/hip/ch6/CombineJob.java

```
public static class Combine
    implements Reducer<Text, Text, Text, Text> {

    @Override
    public void reduce(Text key, Iterator<Text> values,   ◄─────
                    OutputCollector<Text,
                          Text> output,
                    Reporter reporter) throws IOException {

        Text prev = null;
        while (values.hasNext()) {
          Text t = values.next();

          if (!t.equals(prev)) {     ◄─────
            output.collect(key, t);
          }
          prev = ReflectionUtils.copy(job, t, prev);   ◄─────
        }
    }
}
```

Much like a reducer, the combiner will be called with multiple values for the same key in situations where a block of map outputs contain the same key.

You only output a key/value pair if you detect a new value.

The MapReduce framework reuses the iterator value objects supplied to combiners/reducers, so you need to clone the value so that it's not overwritten.

It's important that if you have a combiner, the function is distributive. In figure 6.40 you saw that the combiner will be called multiple times for the same input key, and there are no guarantees about how the output values will be organized when they're sent to the combiner (other than that they were paired with the combiner key). A distributive function is one where the end result is identical regardless of how inputs were combined.

Summary

The combiner is a powerful tool in your MapReduce toolkit, as it helps cut-down on the amount of data transmitted over the network between the mappers and reducers. Another tool to improve the execution times of your MapReduce jobs are binary comparators, which we'll examine next.

TECHNIQUE 49 **Blazingly fast sorting with comparators**

When MapReduce is sorting or merging it leverages the RawComparator for the map output key to compare keys. Built-in Writable classes (such as Text and IntWritable) have byte-level implementations that are fast because they don't require the byte form of the object to be unmarshalled to Object form for the comparison. When writing your own Writable, it may be tempting to implement the WritableComparable interface, but this can lead to longer shuffle and sort phases because it requires Object unmarshalling from byte form for comparisons.

Problem

You have custom Writable implementations and you want to reduce the sort times for your jobs.

Solution

Write a byte-level comparator to ensure optimal comparisons during sorting.

Discussion

In MapReduce there are multiple stages where output keys are compared to each other when data is being sorted. To facilitate key sorting, all map output keys must implement the WritableComparable interface:

```
public interface WritableComparable<T>
  extends Writable, Comparable<T> {
}
```

If you look at the Person you created in section 4.2.1 in chapter 4, your implementation was as follows:[7]

```
public class Person implements WritableComparable<Person> {

  private String firstName;
  private String lastName;

  @Override
  public int compareTo(Person other) {
    int cmp = this.lastName.compareTo(other.lastName);
    if (cmp != 0) {
      return cmp;
    }
    return this.firstName.compareTo(other.firstName);
  }
  ...
```

The trouble with this Comparator is that MapReduce stores your intermediary map output data in byte form, and every time it needs to sort your data it has to unmarshall it into Writable form to perform the comparison. This unmarshalling is expensive because it recreates your objects for comparison purposes.

If you look at the built-in Writables in Hadoop, not only do they extend the WritableComparable interface, but they also provide their own custom Comparator that extends the WritableComparator class. The following code presents a subsection of the WritableComparator class:

```
public class WritableComparator implements RawComparator {

  public int compare(byte[] b1, int s1, int l1,
                     byte[] b2, int s2, int l2
                     ) {

    try {
      buffer.reset(b1, s1, l1);
      key1.readFields(buffer);
```

The second batch of arguments pertain to the second object being compared.

The b1 field contains a byte array, part of which contains the WritableComparable in byte form. The s1 field is the offset into the byte array where the WritableComparable object starts, and l1 is the number of bytes that the WritableComparable occupies in the byte array.

Unmarshall the first object into WritableComparable form. The class reuses the key1 instance so that it's not recreated.

---

[7] **GitHub source**—https://github.com/alexholmes/hadoop-book/blob/master/src/main/java/com/manning/hip/ch4/sort/secondary/Person.java

```
      buffer.reset(b2, s2, 12);
      key2.readFields(buffer);          ◄──────── Unmarshall the second object into
                                                  WritableComparable form.
    } catch (IOException e) {
      throw new RuntimeException(e);
    }

    return compare(key1, key2);         ◄──── Call a function to
  }                                            compare the objects.

  /** Compare two WritableComparables.
   *
   * <p> The default implementation uses the natural ordering,
   * calling {@link
   * Comparable#compareTo(Object)}. */
  @SuppressWarnings("unchecked")
  public int compare(WritableComparable a, WritableComparable b) {
    return a.compareTo(b);           The default implementation uses the
  }                          ◄────── WritableComparable's compare function.
  ...
}
```

To write a byte-level `Comparator` the compare method needs to be overridden. Let's look at how the `IntWritable` class implements this method:

```
public class IntWritable implements WritableComparable {

  public static class Comparator extends WritableComparator {
    public Comparator() {                              Override the
      super(IntWritable.class);            WritableComparator.compare method
    }                                          to provide an optimized version.

    public int compare(byte[] b1, int s1, int l1,
                       byte[] b2, int s2, int l2) {
      int thisValue = readInt(b1, s1);        Use the WritableComparator's
      int thatValue = readInt(b2, s2);           helper method to read the
      return (thisValue<thatValue ? -1 :       integer form of the first value.
        (thisValue==thatValue ? 0 : 1));
    }                                        Read the
  }                                          second value.

    static {
      WritableComparator.define(IntWritable.class,
        new Comparator());
    }
}
```

Register the WritableComparator. This tells MapReduce to use the WritableComparator implementation rather than the IntWritable's compareTo method for comparison.

The built-in `Writable` classes all provide `WritableComparator` implementations, which means you don't need to worry about optimizing the `Comparators` as long as your MapReduce job output keys use these built-in `Writables`. But if, as in the earlier example, you have a custom `Writable` that you use as an output key, you'll ideally provide a `WritableComparator`. We'll now revisit your `Person` class and look at how to do this.

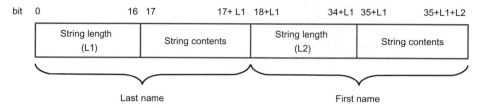

Figure 6.41   Byte layout of `Person`

In your `Person` class you had two fields, the first and last names. Your implementation stored them as strings, and used the DataOutput's `writeUTF` method to write them out:

```
private String firstName;
private String lastName;

@Override
public void write(DataOutput out) throws IOException {
  out.writeUTF(lastName);
  out.writeUTF(firstName);
}
```

The first thing you need to understand is how your `Person` object is represented in byte form, based on the previous code. The `writeUTF` method writes two bytes containing the length of the string, followed by the byte form of the string. Figure 6.41 shows how this information is laid out in byte form.

Assume that you want to perform a lexicographical comparison that includes both the last and first names, but you can't do this with the entire byte array because the string lengths are also encoded in the array. Instead, the `Comparator` needs to be smart enough to skip over the string lengths. The following code shows how to do this:[8]

```
@Override
public int compare(byte[] b1, int s1, int l1, byte[] b2, int s2,
                   int l2) {
  int lastNameResult = compare(b1, s1, b2, s2);

  if (lastNameResult != 0) {
    return lastNameResult;
  }

  int b1l1 = readUnsignedShort(b1, s1);

  int b2l1 = readUnsignedShort(b2, s2);

  return compare(b1, s1 + b1l1 + 2, b2, s2 + b2l1 + 2);
}
```

Compare the last name.

If the last name isn't identical, return the result of the comparison.

Read the size of the last name from the first byte array.

Read the size of the last name from the second byte array.

Return the result of the comparison on the first name.

---

[8] **GitHub source**—https://github.com/alexholmes/hadoop-book/blob/master/src/main/java/com/manning/hip/ch6/PersonBinaryComparator.java

Read the size of the UTF-8 string in byte array b1.

Read the size of the UTF-8 string in byte array b2.

Use the WritableComparator.compareBytes method to perform a lexicographical comparison of the UTF-8 binary data.

```
public static int compare(byte[] b1, int s1, byte[] b2, int s2) {
    int b1l1 = readUnsignedShort(b1, s1);

    int b2l1 = readUnsignedShort(b2, s2);

    return compareBytes(b1, s1 + 2, b1l1, b2, s2 + 2, b2l1);
}

public static int readUnsignedShort(byte[] b, int offset) {
    int ch1 = b[offset];
    int ch2 = b[offset + 1];
    return (ch1 << 8) + (ch2);
}
```

Summary

Using the writeUTF is limited because it can only support strings that contain less than 65,536 characters. This is probably fine for the scenario where you're working with people's names. If you need to work with a larger string, you should look at using Hadoop's Text class, which can support much larger strings. If you look at the Comparator inner class in the Text class you'll see that its binary string comparator works in a similar fashion to yours. Your approach could be easily extended to work with names represented with Text objects rather than Java String objects.

The next section in performance tuning is a look at how you can guard against the impact that data skews can have on your MapReduce jobs.

6.4.4   Skew mitigation

Data skews are natural occurrences in data. There are always outliers that will cause your data to be skewed, and these outliers can significantly impede the progress of your MapReduce jobs. Skews generally fall into one of the following categories:

1 *Skewed data frequencies*—Where there are a disproportionately large number of records in a dataset
2 *Skewed record sizes*—Where some records are significantly larger than the average record size

Data skews can exist on both the map and reduce sides. On the map side, skews can exacerbate matters when working with heterogeneous datasets. On the reduce side, the default MapReduce partitioner can create unintended data skew.

Skews are bad because the map and reduce tasks that operate on datasets that contain skews can take much longer to complete than other tasks. A secondary problem that arises with skewed data is that the memory consumption of tasks can be adversely affected. This is of concern when you're performing actions such as joins, which require data to be cached.

In this section we'll examine a number of techniques to help you identify what data is skewed, and how you can mitigate the effect. If you're looking to identify whether data skew exists in the first place, look at techniques 29 and 34 in sections 6.2.2 and 6.2.3.

Collecting skewed data

When using some of the earlier techniques, you may have determined that you have map or reduce data skew. The next step is to find out what keys are skewed. We'll focus on data skew issues on the reduce side resulting from a large number of values for specific map output keys.

Problem

You want to identify the map output keys that are causing data skews.

Solution

Add intelligence to your reduce method to log details about a larger number of map outputs for a given map output key.

Discussion

When you realize you have skewed data, it can be helpful to understand what keys are causing the skews. An easy way to do this is to keep track of the keys with the most values in your code. You can drop a configurable threshold into your code, and after you receive more values than your threshold, you dump out the key to the logs:[9]

```java
public static final String MAX_VALUES = "skew.maxvalues";

private int maxValueThreshold;

@Override
public void configure(JobConf job) {
  maxValueThreshold = job.getInt(MAX_VALUES, 100);          // Read the configurable number
}                                                            // of max values for a key.
@Override
public void reduce(Text key, Iterator<Text> values,
                   OutputCollector<Text,
                        Text> output,
                   Reporter reporter) throws IOException {
  int i = 0;
  while (values.hasNext()) {
    values.next();
    i++;
  }
  if (++i > maxValueThreshold) {                             // Dump the key name and the
    log.info("Received " + i + " values for key " + key);   // number of values to the log file.
  }
}
```

After you run your job you can look at the logs to determine what keys are skewed, and by how much.

---

[9] **GitHub source**—https://github.com/alexholmes/hadoop-book/blob/master/src/main/java/com/manning/hip/ch6/SkewLogsJob.java

Summary

Keeping track of your skewed data is an important step to better understanding your data, which in turn will help you when it comes to designing your MapReduce jobs. Next up is a look at how to guard against reducer skew.

TECHNIQUE 51 Reduce skew mitigation

Reducer skew is typically a result of a number of map output keys with disproportionately large numbers of associated map output values.

Problem

You want to look at ways to mitigate reduce-side data skew problems.

Solution

Examine a number of techniques to cut down on the risk of data skew, such as using custom partitioners and using map-side joins.

Discussion

In this solution we'll cover a variety of approaches to guard against reducer data skew.

SAMPLING AND RANGE PARTITIONING

The default partitioner in Hadoop partitions based on a hash of the map output key. This works great if your output keys have a somewhat even frequency distribution, but doesn't work so well if your data has skewed key frequencies.

What you need in such situations is a partitioner that operates based on some knowledge of your data. As part of examining the `TotalOrderPartitioner` in chapter 4, we looked at how you could precompute partition boundaries by randomly sampling data from your input data. The `TotalOrderPartitioner` provides a range partitioner that partitions the input keys based on these precomputed input key ranges. This same technique will work well at counteracting skewed key frequencies in your data.

CUSTOM PARTITIONING

An alternative approach to sampling and range partitioning would be to build a custom partitioner based on explicit knowledge of the output keys. For example, if you have a MapReduce job whose output keys are the words in a book, you would expect to see high frequency stopwords.[10] Your custom partitioner could send such output to a fixed set of reducers, and partition all other words to the remaining reducers.

COMBINER

Using a combiner can go a long way towards reducing both skewed key frequencies and skewed record sizes. The goal of the combiner is to aggregate and condense data if possible. We covered the combiner in technique 48.

---

[10] Stop words are common words frequently filtered out as part of natural language processing; see http://en.wikipedia.org/wiki/Stop_words.

MAP-SIDE JOINS AND SEMI-JOINS

If you're performing joins and the datasets being joined seem too large to cache for a map-side join, consider the joining techniques in chapters 4 and 7 that provide join optimizations to work with larger datasets.

SKEWED RECORD SIZES

Skewed record sizes in combination with any reduce- or map-side caching can be particularly problematic as they frequently result in the dreaded `OutOfMemoryError` exception in Java. You won't find any easy way to handle these situations. The `RecordReader` used by the `TextInputFormat` and `KeyValueTextInputFormat` classes can be configured to skip over lines of a certain length by setting `mapred.linerecordreader.maxlength` (the default setting has no limit). Similarly, in your map and reduce code you can choose to ignore values when a certain frequency has been crossed, as you saw when you looked at the contrib `org.apache.hadoop.contrib.utils.join` package, which in the reducer by default limits the number of values per cached dataset to 100.

Another approach is to consider using lossy data structures that compress data, such as Bloom filters, which are covered in chapter 7.

Summary

Next up we'll take a look at user space MapReduce code and constructs in Java that can have a detrimental impact on performance. We'll also look at some patterns to optimize your code.

6.4.5 *Optimizing user space Java in MapReduce*

MapReduce's execution patterns exercise code in different ways than what you may be accustomed to with other Java applications. This is largely due to the fact that the MapReduce framework is efficient at processing vast amounts of data, which results in map and reduce functions being called millions of times over short periods of times. The end result is that you frequently uncover undesired performance traits in common libraries, including Java's JDK.

> **Further reading**
>
> Joshua Bloch's excellent book *Effective Java* contains many useful tips to help write efficient Java code.

In technique 45 we uncovered how to profile MapReduce code to understand where your code is spending time. Using this technique we identified issues related to the following code:

```
public void map(LongWritable key, Text value,
                OutputCollector<LongWritable, Text> output,
                Reporter reporter) throws IOException {
    String[] parts = value.toString().split("\\.");
```

This was the line that was consuming most of the CPU for your job, as a result of the split method using a regular expression.

```
Text outputValue = new Text(parts[0]);
output.collect(key, outputValue);
}
```

This line was the second-biggest CPU hog as a result of constructing the Text object for every output that's emitted.

In this section we'll discuss the two issues discovered in the previous code (regular expressions in Java, and lack of code reuse), as well as some other general Java gotchas in MapReduce.

REGULAR EXPRESSIONS

Regular expressions in Java have a rich and flexible feature set. But the flexibility comes at the price of execution speed. The slowness of regular expressions in Java were exposed in technique 45, where the profile showed that most of the time in your map was spent in the `Pattern.split` code. As a general guideline, it's best to avoid regular expressions where possible in MapReduce applications. If they can't be avoided outright, it's still worth factoring out as many uses of them as possible.

STRING TOKENIZATION

Java's documentation recommends the use of the `String.split` and `Scanner` classes for string tokenization. You may be surprised to know that both classes use regular expressions behind the scenes, which as you've found out are slow. Ironically, the next step may be to fall back on the `StringTokenizer` class, use of which is discouraged in the class Javadocs comments in favor of the newer regular expression-based tokenizers. But the implementation of `StringTokenizer` isn't optimal, and benchmarks comparing all of the previous methods with the Apache commons `StringUtils` class in figure 6.42 show that using `StringUtils` is the way to go.

The benchmarks were produced with the 1.6.0_29 version of the JDK on OS X running on a quad-core 2.7 GHz CPU.

OBJECT REUSE

The second item taking up CPU times in your HPROF output was the following line in your code, which you were executing for each key/value pair fed into the map method:

```
Text outputValue = new Text(parts[0]);
```

The issue with this code is again a consequence of it being called many times. Object allocation in Java is expensive, incurring CPU overhead at construction time as well as during garbage collection. It's much more efficient to reuse objects where possible. The following shows how this code should be written to maximize reuse:

```
Text outputValue = new Text();
public void map(LongWritable key, Text value,
               OutputCollector<LongWritable, Text> output,
               Reporter reporter) throws IOException {
  String[] parts = StringUtils.split(value.toString(), "."));
  outputValue.set(parts[0]);
  output.collect(key, outputValue);
}
```

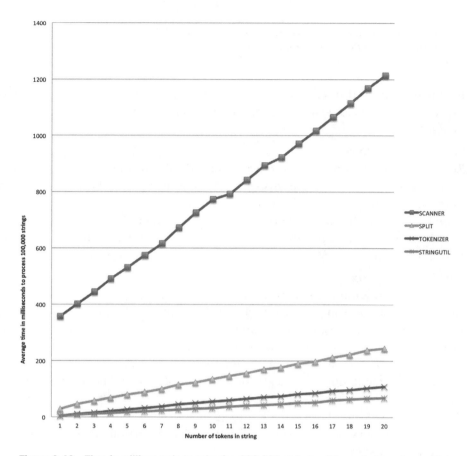

Figure 6.42   Time in milliseconds to tokenize 100,000 strings with varying numbers of tokens using the `Scanner`**,** `String.split`**,** `StringTokenizer`**, and Apache Commons** `StringUtils.split`

Hadoop also reuses objects in its own code, which results in a gotcha to watch out for in the reducer. When the reducer feeds data into the values iterator it reuses the objects. If you're caching any of the value data in the reducer you'll need to clone the object, as shown in the following code:

```
public static class Reduce
  extends Reducer<Text, Text, Text, Text> {

@Override
public void reduce(Text key, Iterable<Text> values,
                   Context context)
    throws IOException, InterruptedException {
  List<Text> cached = new ArrayList<Text>();
  for (Text value : values) {
    cached.add(WritableUtils.clone(
      value, context.getConfiguration()));
  }
}
}
```

WritableUtils is a Hadoop helper class that contains numerous methods to make working with Writable classes easier. The clone method uses Hadoop's serialization to make a copy of the Writable, so that your copy doesn't get overwritten by the MapReduce framework.

STRING CONCATENATION

One of the oldest rules in Java has always been that string concatenation using the plus operator should be avoided at all cost, which the following code example shows:

```
String results = a + b;
```

The reason it was discouraged is that older compilers would generate bytecode using the StringBuffer class, whose synchronization slowed down its execution. In recent years, however, the generated bytecode replaced StringBuffer with its nonsynchronized cousin StringBuilder. Does that mean that the plus operator is now safe to use? The answer is complicated, and is a *yes* in situations where the resulting String length is less than 16 characters. A detailed analysis of this topic is available at http://goo.gl/9NGe8, but the bottom line is that the safest bet is to use the StringBuilder class, and ideally use the constructor to preallocate enough space for the resulting String to avoid reallocation of the internal byte array in StringBuilder.

OBJECT OVERHEAD

Often you want to cache data in your map and reduce tasks, such as you saw in the map-side join techniques in chapter 4. In Java caching data is expensive, so let's briefly get a sense of how much space is taken up when working with common Strings and arrays. To start things off, what do you think is the memory usage of the following code?

```
ArrayList<String> strings = new ArrayList<String>();
strings.add("a");
string.add("b");
```

Let's go through the exercise of calculating the memory usage of the previous Array-List and its contents:

- Each Object in Java requires 8 bytes of housekeeping. Therefore the ArrayList starts off with 8 bytes in size.
- The ArrayList contains a single integer primitive field that occupies 4 bytes.
- The ArrayList uses an Object array to store the data. The memory used for each reference field is 4 bytes.
- The total memory usage for each Object must be a multiple of 8. Summing all the previous numbers together yields 16 bytes, so no rounding is required.

The ArrayList is occupying 24 bytes of memory and we've not yet stored anything in it. Let's look at the memory usage for the Object array within the ArrayList:

- An array requires 12 bytes of housekeeping because it requires 4 additional bytes to store the size of the array.
- Each element in the array requires 4 bytes for the object reference. There are two elements, so 2 x 4 = 8 bytes.
- Because the total memory usage for each Object must be a multiple of eight, and so far the Object array is using 12 + 8, round the usage up to 24 bytes.

So now there are 24 bytes for the ArrayList and 24 bytes for the Object array. Finally, you need to understand the memory usage of Strings in Java, which are calculated with the following formula:

$$\text{String memory usage in bytes*} = (numberOfCharacters \cdot 2) + 38$$

Again the result of this formula needs to be rounded up to the nearest multiple of 8. So each String occupies 40 bytes. The grand total of memory usage for storing the two strings in the ArrayList is 128 bytes!

　　The reason I went through this exercise is to build awareness of the overhead incurred in Java to cache data. This is also relevant in MapReduce because you often want to cache data, and it's useful to be able to accurately calculate the memory usage when caching data. More details for memory usage in Java can be seen at http://goo.gl/V8sZi.

6.4.6　*Data serialization*

How you store and transfer your data has an impact on performance. In this section we'll briefly look at data serialization best practices to squeeze the most performance out of Hadoop.

COMPRESSION

Compression is an important part of optimizing Hadoop. You can lessen your data storage footprint when job outputs are compressed and also accelerate the speed at which the data is ingested in a downstream MapReduce job. It's also important to compress the map outputs to reduce the network I/O between map and reduce tasks. We covered compression in detail in chapter 5.

BINARY FILE FORMATS

Much like compression, using binary file formats such as Avro and SequenceFiles results in a more compact representation of your data, and yields improved marshalling and unmarshalling times compared to storing data as text. I dedicated a large part of chapter 3 to working with these file formats.

　　Even when the end result of your work in MapReduce is a nonbinary file format, it's good practice to store your intermediate data in binary form so that you can reap the benefits of your data being in binary form. For example, if you have a MapReduce pipeline where you have a sequence of MapReduce jobs executing, you should consider using Avro or SequenceFile to store your individual job outputs. The last job that's producing the final results can use whatever output format is required for your use case, but intermediate jobs use a binary output format to speed up the writing and reading parts of MapReduce.

6.5 *Chapter summary*

In this chapter we covered the three essential ingredients necessary to tune a job in MapReduce:

1. Ensuring adequate measurement and understanding how to extract Map-Reduce and system performance metrics
2. Utilizing these metrics to narrow down potential performance problems
3. Fixing common performance problems by looking at MapReduce/HDFS configurations, optimizing MapReduce shuffle/sort phases, and also some user space MapReduce performance techniques

In part 4, we'll look at Hadoop in the context of data science, and how you can model complex data structures and perform data-mining activities over data.

Part 4

Data science

The ultimate challenge to working with Hadoop and big data is how to mine useful information about your data. The objective of this part of the book is to present techniques to address nontrivial questions asked about your data, and to create new insights into your data.

Data modeling and algorithms are the pillars on which data science is built, and chapter 7 examines how graphs can be represented and utilized in Map-Reduce to implement algorithms such as Friends-of-Friends and PageRank.

R is a tool data scientists use that has attained popularity through its large array of statistical and data-mining packages. Chapter 8 explores how R and Map-Reduce can work in concert to quickly bring data scientists to the Hadoop table.

Chapter 9 covers the three C's of Mahout: clustering, classification, and collaboration. These three topics offer different data mining approaches that work with MapReduce.

7

Utilizing data structures and algorithms

This chapter covers

- Representing data structures such as graphs and Bloom filters in MapReduce
- Applying algorithms such as PageRank and semi-joins to large amounts of data
- Learning how social network companies recommend making connections with people outside your network

In this chapter we'll look at how you can implement algorithms in MapReduce to work with internet-scale data. We'll focus on nontrivial data, which is commonly represented using graphs.

We'll also look at how you can use graphs to model connections between entities, such as relationships in a social network. We'll run through a number of useful algorithms that can be performed over graphs, such as the shortest path algorithm, friends-of-friends (FoF) to help expand the interconnectedness of a network, and PageRank, which looks at how to determine the popularity of web pages.

You'll learn how to use Bloom filters, whose unique space-saving properties make them handy to solve distributed system problems in P2P (peer-to-peer) and distributed databases. We'll also create Bloom filters in MapReduce, and then use them to optimize joins in MapReduce.

A chapter on scalable algorithms wouldn't be complete without mention of statistics and machine learning. These topics will be covered in chapters 8 and 9. In addition, sorting and joining algorithms are covered in chapter 4.

Let's kick things off with a look at how to model graphs in MapReduce.

7.1   *Modeling data and solving problems with graphs*

Graphs are mathematical constructs that represent an interconnected set of objects. They're used to represent data such as the hyperlink structure of the internet, social networks (where they represent relationships between users), and in internet routing to determine optimal paths for forwarding packets.

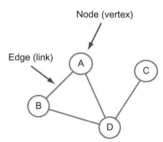

Figure 7.1   A small graph with nodes and edges

A graph consists of a number of nodes (formally called *vertices*) and links (informally called *edges*) that connect nodes together. Figure 7.1 shows a graph with nodes and edges.

The edges can be directed (implying a one-way relationship), or undirected. For example, you would use a directed graph to model relationships between users in a social network because relationships are not always bidirectional. Figure 7.2 shows examples of directed and undirected graphs.

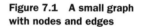

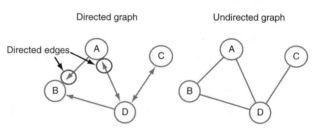

Figure 7.2   Directed and undirected graphs

Graphs can be cyclic or acyclic. In cyclic graphs it's possible for a vertex to reach itself by traversing a sequence of edges. In an acyclic graph it's not possible for a vertex to traverse a path to reach itself. Figure 7.3 shows examples of cyclic and acyclic graphs. To start working with graphs,

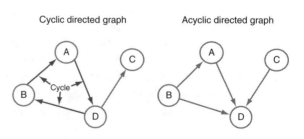

Figure 7.3   Cyclic and acyclic graphs

you'll need to be able to represent them in your code. So what are the common methods used to represent these graph structures?

7.1.1 Modeling graphs

Two common ways of representing graphs are with *adjacency matrices* and with *adjacency lists.*

ADJACENCY MATRIX

With an adjacency matrix, you represent a graph as an *N x N* square matrix *M*, where *N* is the number of nodes, and *Mij* represents an edge between nodes *i* and *j*.

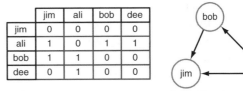

	jim	ali	bob	dee
jim	0	0	0	0
ali	1	0	1	1
bob	1	1	0	0
dee	0	1	0	0

Figure 7.4   An adjacency matrix representation of a graph

Figure 7.4 shows a directed graph representing connections in a social graph. The arrows indicate a one-way relationship between two people. The adjacency matrix shows how this graph would be represented.

The disadvantage of adjacency matrices are that they model both the existence and lack of a relationship, which makes them a dense data structure.

ADJACENCY LIST

Adjacency lists are similar to adjacency matrices, other than the fact that they don't model the lack of relationship. Figure 7.5 shows how you'd represent a graph using an adjacency list.

	jim	ali	bob	dee		
jim	0	0	0	0	→	jim ->
ali	1	0	1	1	→	ali -> jim, bob, dee
bob	1	1	0	0	→	bob -> jim, ali
dee	0	1	0	0	→	dee -> ali

Figure 7.5   An adjacency list representation of a graph

The advantage of the adjacency list is that it offers a sparse representation of the data, which is good because it requires less space. It also fits well when representing graphs in MapReduce because the key can represent a vertex, and the values are a list of vertices that denote a directed or undirected relationship node.

Next up we'll cover three graph algorithms starting off with the shortest path algorithm.

7.1.2 Shortest path algorithm

The shortest path algorithm is a common problem in graph theory, where the goal is to find the shortest route between two nodes. Figure 7.6 shows an example of this algorithm on a graph where the edges don't have a weight, in which case the shortest path is the

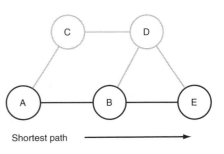

Figure 7.6   Example of shortest path between nodes A and E

path with the smallest number of hops, or intermediary nodes between the source and destination. Applications of this algorithm include traffic mapping software to determine the shortest route between two addresses, routers that compute the shortest path tree for each route, and social networks to determine connections between users.

TECHNIQUE 52   Find the shortest distance between two users

Dijkstra's algorithm is a shortest path algorithm commonly taught in undergraduate computer science courses. A basic implementation uses a sequential iterative process to traverse the entire graph from the starting node, as seen in the algorithm presented in figure 7.7.

The basic algorithm doesn't scale to graphs that exceed your memory sizes, and it's also sequential and not optimized for parallel processing.

Problem

You need to use MapReduce to find the shortest path between two people in a social graph.

Solution

Use an adjacency list to model a graph, and for each node store the distance from the original node, as well as a backpointer to the original node. Use the mappers to propagate the distance to the original node, and the reducer to restore the state of the graph. Iterate until the target node has been reached.

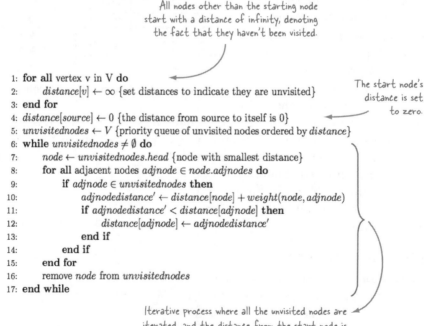

All nodes other than the starting node start with a distance of infinity, denoting the fact that they haven't been visited.

```
1:  for all vertex v in V do
2:      distance[v] ← ∞ {set distances to indicate they are unvisited}
3:  end for
4:  distance[source] ← 0 {the distance from source to itself is 0}
5:  unvisitednodes ← V {priority queue of unvisited nodes ordered by distance}
6:  while unvisitednodes ≠ ∅ do
7:      node ← unvisitednodes.head {node with smallest distance}
8:      for all adjacent nodes adjnode ∈ node.adjnodes do
9:          if adjnode ∈ unvisitednodes then
10:             adjnodedistance' ← distance[node] + weight(node, adjnode)
11:             if adjnodedistance' < distance[adjnode] then
12:                 distance[adjnode] ← adjnodedistance'
13:             end if
14:         end if
15:     end for
16:     remove node from unvisitednodes
17: end while
```

The start node's distance is set to zero.

Iterative process where all the unvisited nodes are iterated, and the distance from the start node is propagated through the graph by adding weights encountered when edges are traversed.

Figure 7.7   Pseudo-code for Dijkstra's algorithm

Discussion

Figure 7.8 shows a small social network, which you'll use for this technique. Your goal is to find the shortest path between Dee and Joe. There are four paths that you can take from Dee to Joe, but only one of them results in the fewest number of hops.

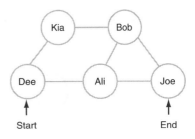

You'll implement a parallel breadth-first search algorithm to find the shortest path between two users. Because you're operating on a social network, you don't need to care about weights on your edges. The pseudo-code for the algorithm can be seen in figure 7.9.

Figure 7.8 Social network used in this technique

Figure 7.10 shows the algorithm iterations in play with your social graph. Just like Dijkstra's algorithm, you'll start with all the node distances set to infinite, and set the distance for the starting node, Dee, at zero. With each MapReduce pass, you'll determine nodes that don't have an infinite distance and propagate their distance values to their adjacent nodes. You continue this until you reach the end node.

You first need to create the starting point. This is done by reading in the social network (which is stored as an adjacency list) from file and setting the initial distance values. Figure 7.11 shows the two file formats, the second being the format that's used iteratively in your MapReduce code.

Map(node-name, node)
1: *emit(node-name, node)* {to preserve node}
2: **if** *node.distance* $\neq \infty$ **then** {process neighbors if the current node distance has been computed}
3:      *neighbor-distance* ← *node.distance* + 1
4:      **for all** adjacent nodes *adjnode* ∈ *node.adjnodes* **do**
5:          {output the adjacent node, the adjacent node's distance, and the path backpointer}
6:          emit (*adjnode.name*, [*neighbor-distance, node.backpointer+node.name*])
7:      **end for**
8: **end if**

Reduce(node-name, list-of-nodes)
1: *node.distance* ← ∞
2: *node.backpointer* ← *null*
3: **for all** *reducer-node* ∈ *nodes* **do**
4:      *distance* ← *reducer-node.distance*
5:      *backpointer* ← *reducer-node.backpointer*
6:      **if** *distance* < *node.distance* **then**
7:          *node.distance* ← *distance*
8:          *node.backpointer* ← *backpointer*
9:      **end if**
10: **end for**
11: *emit(node-name, node)*

Figure 7.9 Pseudo-code for breadth-first parallel search on graph using MapReduce

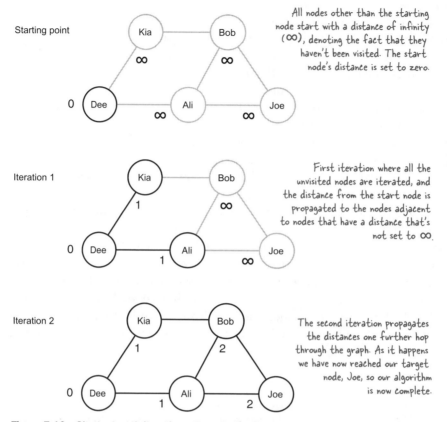

Figure 7.10   Shortest path iterations through the network

Figure 7.11   Original social network file format and MapReduce form optimized for algorithm

Your first step is to create the MapReduce form from the original file. The following listing shows the original input file, and the MapReduce-ready form of the input file generated by the transformation code:

```
$ cat test-data/ch7/friends-short-path.txt      ◀——— The input data.
dee  kia  ali
ali  dee  kia  bob  joe
joe  bob  ali
```

```
kia   ali   dee
bob   ali   joe

$ hadoop fs -cat output/input.txt
dee   0                kia   ali
ali   2147483647   dee   kia   bob   joe
joe   2147483647   bob   ali
kia   2147483647   ali   dee
bob   2147483647   ali   joe
```

The MapReduce-ready form of the input data, with the addition of a numeric that indicates the number of hops from the source node. The starting node is Dee, so she has a hop of 0. All other nodes use Integer.MAX_VALUE to indicate that they haven't been visited.

The code that generates the previous output is shown here:[1]

```
OutputStream os = fs.create(targetFile);
LineIterator iter = org.apache.commons.io.IOUtils
    .lineIterator(fs.open(file), "UTF8");
while (iter.hasNext()) {
  String line = iter.nextLine();

  String[] parts = StringUtils.split(line);

  int distance = Map.INFINITE;
  if (startNode.equals(parts[0])) {
    distance = 0;
  }

  IOUtils.write(parts[0] + '\t' +
    String.valueOf(distance) + "\t\t", os);

  IOUtils.write(StringUtils.join(parts, '\t',
    1, parts.length), os);
  IOUtils.write("\n", os);
}
```

Read each line from the original social network file.

If the current node is the starting node, set its distance to zero.

Set the default distance to the node to be infinite (which you represent with a Math.MAX_VALUE).

Write out the distance and an empty backpointer.

Write out the adjacent nodes (the friends).

The structure of the MapReduce data isn't changed across iterations of the algorithms; each job produces the same structure, which makes it easy to iterate, because the input format is the same as the output format.

Your map function will perform two major functions. First, it outputs all the node data to preserve the original structure of the graph. If you didn't do this, you couldn't make this an interactive process because the reducer wouldn't be able to reproduce the original graph structure for the next map phase. The second function of the map is, for all adjacent nodes, to output each adjacent node with its distance and a backpointer, if the node has a non-infinite distance number. The backpointer carries information about the nodes visited from the starting node, so that when you reach the end node you know the exact path that was taken to get there:[2]

```
@Override
protected void map(Text key, Text value, Context context)
    throws IOException, InterruptedException {
```

[1] **GitHub source**—https://github.com/alexholmes/hadoop-book/blob/master/src/main/java/com/manning/hip/ch7/shortestpath/Main.java
[2] **GitHub source**—https://github.com/alexholmes/hadoop-book/blob/master/src/main/java/com/manning/hip/ch7/shortestpath/Map.java

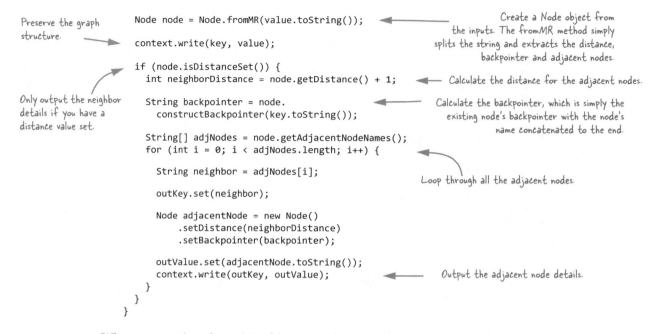

Preserve the graph structure.

Only output the neighbor details if you have a distance value set.

Create a Node object from the inputs. The fromMR method simply splits the string and extracts the distance, backpointer and adjacent nodes.

Calculate the distance for the adjacent nodes.

Calculate the backpointer, which is simply the existing node's backpointer with the node's name concatenated to the end.

Loop through all the adjacent nodes.

Output the adjacent node details.

```
Node node = Node.fromMR(value.toString());

context.write(key, value);

if (node.isDistanceSet()) {
  int neighborDistance = node.getDistance() + 1;

  String backpointer = node.
    constructBackpointer(key.toString());

  String[] adjNodes = node.getAdjacentNodeNames();
  for (int i = 0; i < adjNodes.length; i++) {

    String neighbor = adjNodes[i];

    outKey.set(neighbor);

    Node adjacentNode = new Node()
        .setDistance(neighborDistance)
        .setBackpointer(backpointer);

    outValue.set(adjacentNode.toString());
    context.write(outKey, outValue);
  }
 }
}
```

When outputting the original input node, as well as the adjacent nodes and the distances to them, the format (not contents) of the map output value are identical, to make it easier for your reducer to read the data. To do this you use a Node class to model the notion of a node, its adjacent nodes, and the distance from the starting node. Its toString method generates a string form of this data, which is used as the map output key, as shown in the following listing.[3]

The Node class, which will help with serialization in the MapReduce code

```
public class Node {
  private int distance = INFINITE;
  private String backpointer;
  private String[] adjacentNodeNames;

  public static int INFINITE = Integer.MAX_VALUE;
  public static final char fieldSeparator = '\t';

  public String constructBackpointer(String name) {
    StringBuilder backpointer = new StringBuilder();
    if (StringUtils.trimToNull(getBackpointer()) != null) {
      backpointers.append(getBackpointer()).append(":");
    }
    backpointer.append(name);
    return backpointer.toString();
  }
```

[3] **GitHub source**—https://github.com/alexholmes/hadoop-book/blob/master/src/main/java/com/manning/hip/ch7/shortestpath/Node.java

```java
@Override
public String toString() {
  StringBuilder sb = new StringBuilder();
  sb.append(distance)
      .append(fieldSeparator)
      .append(backpointer);

  if (getAdjacentNodeNames() != null) {
    sb.append(fieldSeparator)
        .append(StringUtils
            .join(getAdjacentNodeNames(), fieldSeparator));
  }
  return sb.toString();
}

public static Node fromMR(String value) throws IOException {
  String[] parts = StringUtils.splitPreserveAllTokens(
      value, fieldSeparator);
  if (parts.length < 2) {
    throw new IOException(
        "Expected 2 or more parts but received " + parts.length);
  }
  Node node = new Node()
      .setDistance(Integer.valueOf(parts[0]))
      .setBackpointer(StringUtils.trimToNull(parts[1]));
  if (parts.length > 2) {
    node.setAdjacentNodeNames(Arrays.copyOfRange(parts, 2,
        parts.length));
  }
  return node;
}
```

Your reducer's job is to calculate the minimum distance for each node, and to output the minimum distance, the backpointer, and the original adjacent nodes. The following listing shows this code.[4]

The reducer code for the shortest path algorithm

```java
public static enum PathCounter {
  TARGET_NODE_DISTANCE_COMPUTED,     ◄──  The counter enum you'll use to set the number
  PATH                                    of hops when you've reached the target node.
}

private Text outValue = new Text();
private String targetNode;

protected void setup(Context context)              Read the target node name
  throws IOException, InterruptedException {    ◄──  from the configuration.
  targetNode = context.getConfiguration().get(
      Main.TARGET_NODE);
}
```

---

[4] **GitHub source**—https://github.com/alexholmes/hadoop-book/blob/master/src/main/java/com/manning/hip/ch7/shortestpath/Reduce.java

```
public void reduce(Text key, Iterable<Text> values,
                   Context context)
    throws IOException, InterruptedException {

  int minDistance = Node.INFINITE;          ◄────── The initial minimum distance is infinite.

  Node shortestAdjacentNode = null;
  Node originalNode = null;

  for (Text textValue : values) {

    Node node = Node.fromMR(textValue.toString());   ◄──── Convert the input
                                                           value into a Node.

    if(node.containsAdjacentNodes()) {
      // the original data
      originalNode = node;              ◄────── If the node represents the original node
    }                                            (with adjacent nodes), preserve it.

    if(node.getDistance() < minDistance) {
      minDistance = node.getDistance();       ◄──── If the distance to this node from an
      shortestAdjacentNode = node;                 adjacent node is less than the minimum
    }                                                        distance, preserve it.
  }

  if(shortestAdjacentNode != null) {    ◄────── Store the minimum distance and
    originalNode.setDistance(minDistance);     backpointer from the adjacent node.
    originalNode.setBackpointer(
      shortestAdjacentNode.getBackpointer());
  }

  outValue.set(originalNode.toString());

  context.write(key, outValue);

  if (minDistance != Node.INFINITE &&          If the current node is the target node, and you
      targetNode.equals(key.toString())) {     have a valid distance value, you're done and you
    Counter counter = context.getCounter(    ◄──── indicate this by setting the distance and
        PathCounter.TARGET_NODE_DISTANCE_COMPUTED);    backpointer in MapReduce counters.
    counter.increment(minDistance);
    context.getCounter(PathCounter.PATH.toString(),
        shortestAdjacentNode.getBackpointer()).increment(1);
  }
 }
}
```

Write out your node. (annotation pointing to `context.write(key, outValue);`)

You're ready to run your code. You need to copy the input file into HDFS, and then kick off your MapReduce job, specifying the start node name (dee) and target node name (joe):

```
$ hadoop fs -put \
    test-data/ch7/friends-short-path.txt \
    friends-short-path.txt

$ bin/run.sh com.manning.hip.ch7.shortestpath.Main dee joe \
  friends-short-path.txt output

==========================================
= Shortest path found, details as follows.
=
= Start node:  dee
```

```
= End node:    joe
= Hops:        2
= Path:        dee:ali
==========================================


$ hadoop fs -cat output/2/part*
ali 1 dee dee kia bob joe
bob 2 dee:ali ali joe
dee 0 null kia ali
joe 2 dee:ali bob ali
kia 1 dee ali dee
```

The output of your job shows that the minimum hops between Dee and Joe is 2, and that Ali was the connecting node.

Summary

This exercise showed how a shortest path algorithm could be used to determine the minimum number of hops between two people in a social network. An algorithm related to the shortest path algorithm, called *graph diameter estimation*,[5] attempts to determine the average number of hops between nodes. This has been used to support[6] the notion of *six degrees of separation* in large social network graphs with millions of nodes.

The shortest path algorithm has multiple applications, but an arguably more useful and utilized algorithm in social networks is that of friends-of-friends (FoF).

7.1.3 Friends-of-friends

Social network sites such as LinkedIn and Facebook use the FoF algorithm to help users broaden their networks.

TECHNIQUE 53 Calculating FoFs

The Friends-of-friends (FoF) algorithm suggests friends that a user may know that aren't part of their immediate network. For the intent of this section and technique, consider a FoF to be in the 2nd degree network as shown in figure 7.12.

The key ingredient to success with this approach is to order the FoFs by the number of common friends, which increases the chances that the user knows the FoF.

Problem

You want to implement the FoF algorithm in MapReduce.

Solution

Two MapReduce jobs are required to calculate the FoFs for each user in a social network. The first job calculates the common friends for each user, and the second job sorts the common friends by the number of connections to your friends.

---

[5] See the PDF, "HADI: Fast Diameter Estimation and Mining in Massive Graphs with Hadoop," at http://goo.gl/Estxk.

[6] See "Four Degrees of Separation," at http://arxiv.org/abs/1111.4570.

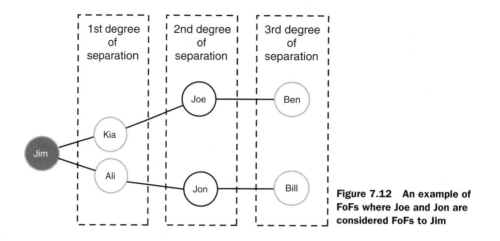

Figure 7.12   An example of FoFs where Joe and Jon are considered FoFs to Jim

Discussion

You should first look at an example graph and understand what results you're looking for. Figure 7.13 shows a network of people with Jim, one of the users, highlighted. In this graph Jim's FoFs are represented in bold (Dee, Joe, and Jon). Next to Jim's FoFs are the number of friends that the FoF and Jim have in common. Your goal here is to determine all the FoFs and order them by the number of fiends in common. Therefore, your expected results would have Joe as the first FoF recommendation, followed by Dee, and then Jon.

The text file to represent the social graph for this technique is shown here:

```
$ cat test-data/ch7/friends.txt
joe     jon     kia     bob     ali
kia     joe     jim     dee
dee     kia     ali
ali     dee     jim     bob     joe     jon
jon     joe     ali
bob     joe     ali     jim
jim     kia     bob     ali
```

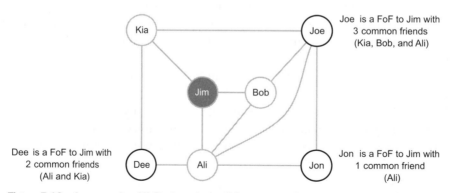

Figure 7.13   An example of FoF where Joe and Jon are considered FoFs to Jim

Map(node-name, node)

1: **for all** *adjnode* ∈ *node.adjacency-list* **do**
2:      *emit(lexicographically-ordered-tuple(node-name, adjnode.name), 1)*
3:      **for all** *adj2node* ∈ *node.adjacency-list* **do**
4:          **if** the *tuple(adjnode.name, adj2node.name)* hasn't already been
            emitted **then**
5:              *emit(lexicographically-ordered-tuple(adjnode.name, adj2node.name), 2)*

Reduce(tuple(node1.name, node2.name), [i₁, i₂, ...])

1: *common-friends ← 0*
2: *already-friends ← false*
3: **for all** *i* ∈ *counts[i₁, i₂, ...]* **do**
4:      **if** *i* = 1 **then**
5:          *already-friends ← true*
6:      *common-friends ← common-friends + 1*
7: **if** *already-friends* ≠ *true* **then**
8:      *emit(tuple(node1.name, node2.name), common-friends)*

Figure 7.14   The first MapReduce job, which calculates the common friends for each user

This algorithm requires you to write two MapReduce jobs. The first job, the pseudo-code for which is shown in figure 7.14, calculates the FoFs and counts the number of friends in common. The result of the job is a line for each FoF relationship excluding people who are already friends.

The output for executing this job against the graph in figure 7.13 is shown below:

```
ali   kia   3
bob   dee   1
bob   jon   2
bob   kia   2
dee   jim   2
dee   joe   2
dee   jon   1
jim   joe   3
jim   jon   1
jon   kia   1
```

Your second job needs to produce output such that for each user you should have a list of FoFs in order of common friends. Figure 7.15 shows the algorithm. You're using secondary sort to order a user's FoFs in order of common friends.

The output for executing this job against the output of the previous job can be seen here:

```
ali   kia:3
bob   kia:2,jon:2,dee:1
dee   jim:2,joe:2,jon:1,bob:1
jim   joe:3,dee:2,jon:1
joe   jim:3,dee:2
jon   bob:2,kia:1,dee:1,jim:1
kia   ali:3,bob:2,jon:1
```

$Map(tuple(node1.name, node2.name), common\text{-}friends)$
 1: $emit(tuple(node1.name, common\text{-}friends), tuple(node2.name, common\text{-}friends))$
 2: $emit(tuple(node2.name, common\text{-}friends), tuple(node1.name, common\text{-}friends))$

$Partitioner(tuple(node.name, common\text{-}friends))$
 1: partition by $node.name$

$Sort(tuple(node.name, common\text{-}friends))$
 1: sort by $tuple(node.name, common\text{-}friends)$

$Reduce(tuple(node.name, common\text{-}friends), [tuple_1, tuple_2, ...])$
 1: $potential\text{-}friends \leftarrow \emptyset$
 2: **for all** $t \in tuples[tuple_1, tuple_2, ...]$ **do**
 3:     $potential\text{-}friends_i \leftarrow tuple(t.name, t.common\text{-}friends)$
 4: $emit(node.name, potential\text{-}friends)$

Figure 7.15   The second MapReduce job, which sorts the common friends by the number of friends in common

Let's dive into the code in the following listing and look at the first MapReduce job, which calculates the FoFs for each user.[7]

Mapper and reducer implementations for FoF calculation

```
public static class Map
    extends Mapper<Text, Text, TextPair, IntWritable> {

  private TextPair pair = new TextPair();
  private IntWritable one = new IntWritable(1);
  private IntWritable two = new IntWritable(2);

  @Override
  protected void map(Text key, Text value, Context context)
      throws IOException, InterruptedException {
    String[] friends = StringUtils.split(value.toString());
    for (int i = 0; i < friends.length; i++) {
      pair.set(key.toString(), friends[i]);
      context.write(pair, one);

      for (int j = i + 1; j < friends.length; j++) {
        pair.set(friends[i], friends[j]);
        context.write(pair, two);
      }
    }
  }
}

public static class Reduce
    extends Reducer<TextPair, IntWritable, TextPair, IntWritable> {
```

Go through all the adjacent nodes in the graph (the users' friends).

For each friend, emit the fact that they're friends so that this relationship can be discarded in the reduce phase. The TextPair class lexicographically orders the two names so that for a given pair of users there'll be a single reducer key.

For each friend, go through the remaining friends and emit the fact that they're a FoF.

[7] **GitHub source**—https://github.com/alexholmes/hadoop-book/blob/master/src/main/java/com/manning/hip/ch7/friendsofafriend/CalcMapReduce.java

```
    private IntWritable friendsInCommon = new IntWritable();

    public void reduce(TextPair key, Iterable<IntWritable> values,
                       Context context)
        throws IOException, InterruptedException {

      int commonFriends = 0;
      boolean alreadyFriends = false;
      for (IntWritable hops : values) {
        if (hops.get() == 1) {
          alreadyFriends = true;
          break;
        }

        commonFriends++;
      }

      if (!alreadyFriends) {
        friendsInCommon.set(commonFriends);
        context.write(key, friendsInCommon);
      }
    }
  }
```

Ignore this relationship if the users are already friends.

Output the fact that they're FoFs, including a count of common friends. This also uses the TextPair class to lexicographically order the user names.

The job of the second MapReduce job in the following listing is to sort the FoFs such that you see FoFs with a higher number of mutual friends ahead of those that have a smaller number of mutual friends.[8]

Mapper and reducer implementations that sorts FoFs by the number of shared common friends

```
    public static class Map
        extends Mapper<Text, Text, Person, Person> {

      private Person outputKey = new Person();
      private Person outputValue = new Person();

      @Override
      protected void map(Text key, Text value, Context context)
          throws IOException, InterruptedException {
        String[] parts = StringUtils.split(value.toString());
        String name = parts[0];
        int commonFriends = Integer.valueOf(parts[1]);

        outputKey.set(name, commonFriends);
        outputValue.set(key.toString(), commonFriends);
        context.write(outputKey, outputValue);

        outputValue.set(name, commonFriends);
        outputKey.set(key.toString(), commonFriends);
        context.write(outputKey, outputValue);
      }
    }
```

Emit one half of the relationship.

Emit the other half of the relationship.

---

8 **GitHub source**—https://github.com/alexholmes/hadoop-book/blob/master/src/main/java/com/manning/hip/ch7/friendsofafriend/SortMapReduce.java

```
public static class Reduce
    extends Reducer<Person, Person, Text, Text> {

  private Text name = new Text();
  private Text potentialFriends = new Text();

  @Override
  public void reduce(Person key, Iterable<Person> values,
                     Context context)
    throws IOException, InterruptedException {

    StringBuilder sb = new StringBuilder();

    int count = 0;
    for (Person potentialFriend : values) {
      if(sb.length() > 0) {
        sb.append(",");
      }
      sb.append(potentialFriend.getName())
         .append(":")
         .append(potentialFriend.getCommonFriends());

      if (++count == 10) {
        break;
      }
    }

    name.set(key.getName());
    potentialFriends.set(sb.toString());
    context.write(name, potentialFriends);
  }
}
```

All the people in your list are sorted in order of common friends.

Only keep the top 10.

Emit the FoFs for the user.

I won't show the whole driver code, but to enable secondary sort, I had to write a few extra classes as well as inform the job to use the classes for partitioning and sorting purposes (for more details on how secondary sort works, look at chapter 4):

```
job.setPartitionerClass(PersonNamePartitioner.class);
job.setSortComparatorClass(PersonComparator.class);
job.setGroupingComparatorClass(PersonNameComparator.class);
```

You'll copy an input file containing the friend relationships into HDFS and then run your driver code to run your two MapReduce jobs. The last two arguments are the output directories for the two MapReduce jobs:

```
$ hadoop fs -put test-data/ch7/friends.txt .
$ bin/run.sh com.manning.hip.ch7.friendsofafriend.Main \
  friends.txt calc-output sort-output
```

After running your code you can look at the output in HDFS:

```
$ hadoop fs -cat sort-output/part*
ali   kia:3
bob   kia:2,jon:2,dee:1
dee   jim:2,joe:2,jon:1,bob:1
jim   joe:3,dee:2,jon:1
joe   jim:3,dee:2
jon   bob:2,kia:1,dee:1,jim:1
kia   ali:3,bob:2,jon:1
```

This output indeed verifies what you saw with your own eyes in figure 7.13, that Jim has three FoFs, and that they're ordered by the number of common friends.

Summary

This approach can be used not only as a recommendation engine to help users grow their networks, but also for informational purposes as the user is browsing the social network's website. For example, when you view people in LinkedIn, you'll be shown the degrees of separation between you and the person being viewed. Your approach can be used to precompute that information for two hops. To reproduce this for three hops (for example, to show friends-of-friends of a friend) you would need to introduce a third MapReduce job to compute the third hop from the output of the first job. This is left as an exercise for the reader!

To simplify your approach, you used a undirected graph, which implies that user relationships are bidirectional. Most social networks don't have such a notion, and the algorithm would need some minor tweaks to model this behavior.

This brings us to the final graph technique, which is how to use PageRank to calculate the popularity of web pages.

7.1.4 PageRank

PageRank was a formula introduced[9] by the founders of Google during their Stanford years in 1998. The paper discusses their overall approach to crawling and indexing the web, and includes as part of that a calculation, which they titled *PageRank*, which gives a score to each web page indicating the page's importance. This wasn't the first paper to introduce a scoring mechanism for web pages,[10] but it was the first to weigh scores propagated to each outbound link based on the total number of outbound links.

TECHNIQUE 54 **Calculate PageRank over a web graph**

Fundamentally, PageRank gives pages that have a large number of inbound links a higher score than pages that have a smaller number of inbound links. When evaluating the score

for a page, PageRank uses the scores for all the inbound links to calculate a page's PageRank. But it penalizes individual inbound links from sources that have a high number of outbound links by dividing that outbound link PageRank by the number of outbound links. Figure 7.16 presents a simple example of a web graph with three pages and their respective PageRank values.

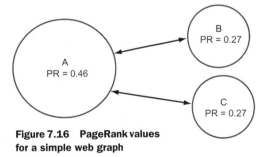

Figure 7.16   PageRank values for a simple web graph

---

9   See "The Anatomy of a Large-Scale Hypertextual Web Search Engine" at http://infolab.stanford.edu/pub/papers/google.pdf.

10 Before PageRank the HITS link analysis method was popular; see http://nlp.stanford.edu/IR-book/html/htmledition/hubs-and-authorities-1.html.

$$PageRank(n) = \frac{1-d}{|webGraph|} + d \sum_{i \in InboundLinks(n)} \frac{PageRank(i)}{|i.outboundLinks|}$$

Figure 7.17   The PageRank formula

Figure 7.17 shows the PageRank formula. In the formula, $|webGraph|$ is a count of all the pages in the graph, and d, set to 0.85, is a constant damping factor used in two parts. First, it denotes the probability of a random surfer reaching the page after clicking on many links (this is a constant equal to 0.15 divided by the total number of pages), and, second, it dampens the effect of the inbound link PageRanks by 85 percent.

Problem
You want to implement an the iterative PageRank graph algorithm in MapReduce.

Solution
PageRank can be implemented by iterating a MapReduce job until the graph has converged. The mappers are responsible for propagating node PageRank values to their adjacent nodes, and the reducers are responsible for calculating new PageRank values for each node, and for re-creating the original graph with the updated PageRank values.

Discussion
One of the advantages of PageRank is that it can be computed iteratively and applied locally. Every vertex starts with a seed value, with is 1 divided by the number of nodes, and with each iteration each node propagates its value to all pages it links to. Each vertex in turn sums up the value of all the inbound vertex values to compute a new seed value. This iterative process is repeated until such a time as convergence is reached. Convergence is a measure of how much the seed values have changed since the last iteration. If the convergence value is below a certain threshold, it means that there's been minimal change and you can stop the iteration. It's also common to limit the number of iterations in cases

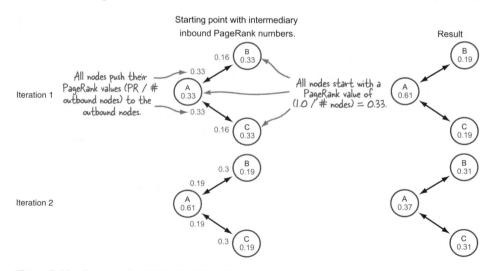

Figure 7.18   An example of PageRank iterations

$Map(node\text{-}name, node)$

1: $emit(node\text{-}name, node)$ {preserve the graph structure}

2: $outPageRank \leftarrow \dfrac{node.pageRank}{|node.adjacency\text{-}list|}$

3: **for all** $adjnode \in node.adjacency\text{-}list$ **do**

4:     $emit(adjnode.name, outPageRank)$

$Reduce(node\text{-}name, [node, inPageRank_1, inPageRank_2, ...])$

1: $sumInPageRanks \leftarrow 0$

2: $node \leftarrow null$

3: **for all** $i \in [node, inPageRank_1, inPageRank_2, ...]$ **do**

4:     **if** i isa $node$ **then**

5:         $node \leftarrow i$

6:     **else**

7:         $sumInPageRanks \leftarrow sumInPageRanks + i$

8: $m.pageRank \leftarrow sumInPageRanks$

9: $emit(node\text{-}name, node)$

Figure 7.19   PageRank decomposed into map and reduce phases

of large graphs where convergence takes too many iterations. Figure 7.18 shows two iterations of the PageRank against the simple graph you saw at the start of this technique.

Figure 7.19 shows the PageRank algorithm expressed as map and reduce parts. The map phase is responsible for preserving the graph as well as emitting the PageRank value to all the outbound nodes. The reducer is responsible for recalculating the new PageRank value for each node and including it in the output of the original graph.

In this technique you'll operate on the graph shown in figure 7.20. In this graph all the nodes have both inbound and output edges.

Your first step is to write the map task. The map task in the following listing has two primary functions: to preserve the graph structure and to propagate the PageRank number to each outbound node.[11]

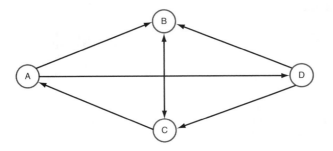

Figure 7.20   Sample web graph for this technique

---

[11] **GitHub source**—https://github.com/alexholmes/hadoop-book/blob/master/src/main/java/com/manning/hip/ch7/pagerank/Map.java

The PageRank mapper inverts the graph structure so the reducer can calculate PageRanks

```java
public class Map
    extends Mapper<Text, Text, Text, Text> {

  private Text outKey = new Text();
  private Text outValue = new Text();

  @Override
  protected void map(Text key, Text value, Context context)
      throws IOException, InterruptedException {

    context.write(key, value);          ⟵————— Emit the input to preserve the graph structure.

    Node node = Node.fromMR(value.toString());

    if(node.getAdjacentNodeNames() != null &&
        node.getAdjacentNodeNames().length > 0) {
      double outboundPageRank = node.getPageRank() /        ⟵ Calculate the outbound PageRank by
          (double)node.getAdjacentNodeNames().length;            dividing the node's PageRank with the
                                                                  number of outbound links.

      for (int i = 0; i < node.getAdjacentNodeNames().length; i++) {

        String neighbor = node.getAdjacentNodeNames()[i];

        outKey.set(neighbor);

        Node adjacentNode = new Node()
            .setPageRank(outboundPageRank);

        outValue.set(adjacentNode.toString());
        context.write(outKey, outValue);        ⟵————— For each outbound node, emit that
      }                                                  node name along with the PageRank.
    }
  }
}
```

The map task outputs two pieces of information: the original graph and the outbound PageRank values. Your reducer's job, as shown in the next listing, is to reconstruct the original graph and to update each node with a new PageRank value based on all the sum of inbound PageRank values.[12]

PageRank reducer that calculates new PageRank values

```java
public class Reduce
    extends Reducer<Text, Text, Text, Text> {

  public static final double CONVERGENCE_SCALING_FACTOR = 1000.0;
  public static final double DAMPING_FACTOR = 0.85;
  public static String CONF_NUM_NODES_GRAPH = "pagerank.numnodes";
  private int numberOfNodesInGraph;

  public static enum Counter {
    CONV_DELTAS
  }
```

---

[12] **GitHub source**—https://github.com/alexholmes/hadoop-book/blob/master/src/main/java/com/manning/hip/ch7/pagerank/Reduce.java

```
@Override
protected void setup(Context context)
   throws IOException, InterruptedException {
  numberOfNodesInGraph =
    context.getConfiguration().getInt(
      CONF_NUM_NODES_GRAPH, 0);
}

private Text outValue = new Text();

public void reduce(Text key, Iterable<Text> values,
                   Context context)
   throws IOException, InterruptedException {

  double summedPageRanks = 0;
  Node originalNode = new Node();

  for (Text textValue : values) {

    Node node = Node.fromMR(textValue.toString());

    if (node.containsAdjacentNodes()) {
      originalNode = node;
    } else {
      summedPageRanks += node.getPageRank();
    }
  }

  double dampingFactor =
      ((1.0 - DAMPING_FACTOR) / (double) numberOfNodesInGraph);

  double newPageRank =
      dampingFactor + (DAMPING_FACTOR * summedPageRanks);

  double delta = originalNode.getPageRank() - newPageRank;

  originalNode.setPageRank(newPageRank);

  outValue.set(originalNode.toString());

  context.write(key, outValue);

  int scaledDelta =
      Math.abs((int) (delta * CONVERGENCE_SCALING_FACTOR));

  context.getCounter(Counter.CONV_DELTAS)
    .increment(scaledDelta);
  }
}
```

Read the number of nodes in the graph from configuration.

If the node represents the original node, preserve that information.

The node represents the outbound node and PageRank, so add the PageRank to the total.

Calculate the new PageRank, taking into consideration the damping factor.

Write out the original graph information with the updated PageRank information.

Update the counter with the delta between the old and new PageRank values. This will be used for convergence testing in the driver code.

The final piece is a driver class that will keep launching the MapReduce job and read the counter from each job until you have convergence. This is as simple as dividing all the deltas between the node's old and new PageRank values by the number of nodes, and checking that they're below the desired threshold:[13]

---

[13] **GitHub source**—https://github.com/alexholmes/hadoop-book/blob/master/src/main/java/com/manning/hip/ch7/pagerank/Main.java

```
long summedConvergence = job.getCounters().findCounter(
    Reduce.Counter.CONV_DELTAS).getValue();
double convergence =
    ((double) summedConvergence /
        Reduce.CONVERGENCE_SCALING_FACTOR) /
        (double) numNodes;
```

If you push the web graph into HDFS and run your job, it will run for five iterations until the graph converges:

```
$ hadoop fs -put test-data/ch7/webgraph.txt .

$ bin/run.sh com.manning.hip.ch7.pagerank.Main webgraph.txt output
...
========================================
=  Num nodes:          4
=  Summed convergence: 11
=  Convergence:        0.00275
========================================
Convergence is below 0.01, we're done
```

You can look at the output of the last MapReduce job to see the PageRank values for each graph node:

```
$ hadoop fs -cat output/5/part*
A  0.14289417100694443  B  D
B  0.2864322672526042   C
C  0.36966846191406244  A  B  D
D  0.2010050998263889   B  C
```

According to your output, node C has the highest PageRank, followed by node B. Initially, this observation may be surprising given that B has three inbound links and C has just two. But if you look at who's linking to C, you can see that node B, who also has a high PageRank value, only has one outbound link to C, so node C gets B's entire PageRank score in addition to its other inbound PageRank score from node D. Therefore, node C's PageRank will always be higher than B's.

Summary

Although you did implement the PageRank formula, it was made simple by the fact that your graph was well connected, and that every node had outbound links. Pages with no outbound links are called *dangling pages*. Dangling pages pose a problem with the PageRank algorithm because they become *PageRank sinks*, because their PageRank values can't be further propagated through the graph. This in turn causes convergence problems because graphs that aren't strongly connected aren't guaranteed to converge.

There are various approaches to solving this problem. You could remove the dangling nodes before your PageRank iterations, and then add them back for a final PageRank iteration after the graph has converged. Or you could sum together the PageRank totals for all dangling pages and redistribute them across all the nodes in the graph. For a detailed examination of dealing with dangling pages, as well as advanced PageRank practices, see *Google's PageRank and Beyond* by Amy N. Langville and Carl Dean Meyer.

This concludes the section on graphs. As you learned, graphs are useful mechanisms to represent people in a social network and pages in a web graph. You used these models to find some useful information about your data, such as finding the shortest path between two points, and what web pages are more popular than others.

You crafted your own MapReduce code in the techniques—if you wanted to leverage a framework you could have used Giraph (http://incubator.apache.org/giraph/), which provides a vertex message-passing mechanism.

This brings us to the subject of the next section, Bloom filters. Bloom filters are a different kind of data structure from graphs. While graphs are used to represent entities and their relationships, Bloom filters are a mechanism to model sets and offer membership queries on their data, as you'll discover next.

7.2 *Bloom filters*

A Bloom filter is a data structure that offers a membership query mechanism where the answer to a lookup is one of two values: a definitive *no*, meaning that the item being looked up doesn't exist in the Bloom filter, or a *maybe*, meaning that there's a probability that the item exists. Bloom filters are popular due to their space efficiencies—representing the existence of N elements requires much less than N positions in the data structure, which is why the membership query can yield false positive results. The amount of false positives in a Bloom filter can be tuned, which we'll discuss shortly.

Bloom filters are used in BigTable and in HBase to remove the need to read blocks from disk to determine if they contain a key. They're also used in distributed network applications such as Squid to share cache details between its multiple instances without having to replicate the whole cache or incur a network I/O hit in the case of cache misses.

The implementation of Bloom filters is simple. They use a bit array of size m bits, where initially each bit is set to 0 (zero). They also contain k hash functions, which are used to map elements to k locations in the bit array.

To add an element into a Bloom filter, it's hashed k times, and a modulo of the hashed value and the size of the bit array is used to map the hashed value to a specific bit array location. That bit in the bit array is then toggled to 1 (one). Figure 7.21 shows three elements being added to a Bloom filter and their locations in the bit array.

To check the membership of an element in the Bloom filter, just like with the add operation, the element is hashed k times and each hash key is used to index into the bit array. A true response to the membership query is only returned in cases where all k bit array locations are set to 1. Otherwise, the response to the query is false. Figure 7.22 shows an example of a membership query where the item was previously added to the Bloom filter, and therefore all the bit array locations

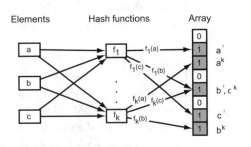

Figure 7.21 Adding elements to a Bloom filter

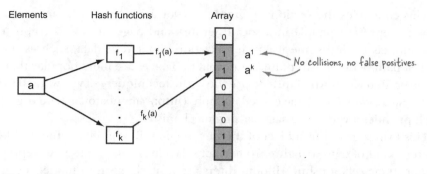

Figure 7.22   An example of a Bloom filter membership query that yields a true positive result

contained a 1. This is an example of a true positive membership result because the element had been previously added to the Bloom filter.

The next example shows how you can get a false positive result for a membership query. The element being queried is *d*, which hadn't been added to the Bloom filter. As it happens, all *k* hashes for *d* are mapped to locations that are set to 1 from other elements. This is an example of collision in the Bloom filter where the result is a false positive. Figure 7.23 shows this example in action.

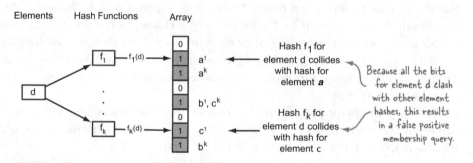

Figure 7.23   An example of a Bloom filter membership query that yields a false positive result

The probability of false positives can be tuned based on two factors: *m*, the number of bits in the bit array, and *k*, the number of hash functions. Or expressed another way, if you have a desired false positive rate in mind, and you know how many elements will be added to the Bloom filter, you can calculate the number of bits needed in the bit array with the equation in figure 7.24.

$$m = -\frac{n \ln p}{(\ln(2))^2}$$

m is required number of bits in the bit array to achieve the desired false probability rate of *p* for *n* inserted elements

n is the number of elements inserted

p is the desired false positive rate (0.01 means 1%)

Figure 7.24   Equation to calculate the desired number of bits for a Bloom filter bit array

$$k = \frac{m \ln(2)}{n}$$
  Figure 7.25 Equation to calculate the optimal number of hashes

The equation, shown in figure 7.25, assumes an optimal number of number of k hashes and that the hashes being produced are random over the range *[1..m]*.

Put another way, if you want to add 1 million elements into a Bloom filter with a 1 percent false positive rate of your membership queries, you'll need 9,585,058 bits or 1.2 megabytes with seven hash functions. This is around 9.6 bits for each element.

Table 7.1 shows the calculated number of bits per element depending on various false positive rates.

False positives	Bits required per element
2%	8.14
1%	9.58
0.1%	14.38

Table 7.1 Number of bits required per element based on differing false positives

With all that theory in your heads, you now need to turn your attention to the subject of how Bloom filters can be utilized in MapReduce.

TECHNIQUE 55 Parallelized Bloom filter creation in MapReduce

MapReduce is good for processing large amounts of data in parallel, and therefore is a good fit if you want to create a Bloom filter based on a large set of input data. For example, let's say you're a large internet social media organization with hundreds of millions of users, and you want to create a Bloom filter for a subset of users that are within a certain age demographic. How would you do this in MapReduce?

Problem

You want to create a Bloom filter in MapReduce.

Solution

Write a MapReduce job to create and output a Bloom filter using the Hadoop built-in `BloomFilter` class. The mappers are responsible for creating intermediary Bloom filters, and the single reducer combines them together to output a combined Bloom filter.

Discussion

Figure 7.26 shows what your technique will do. You'll write a mapper, which will process user data and create a Bloom filter containing users in a certain age bracket. The mappers will emit their Bloom filters, and a single reducer will combine them together. The final result is a single Bloom filter stored in HDFS in Avro form.

Hadoop comes bundled with an implementation of a Bloom filter in the form of the `org.apache.hadoop.util.bloom.BloomFilter` class, as seen in figure 7.27. Luckily, it's a `Writable`, which makes it easy to ship around in MapReduce. The `Key` class is used to represent an element, and it's simply a `Writable` container for a byte array.

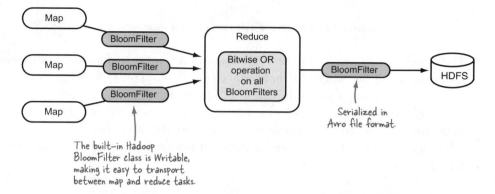

Figure 7.26   A MapReduce job to create a Bloom filter

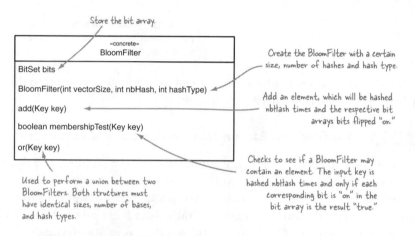

Figure 7.27   Hadoop's built-in BloomFilter class

The constructor requires that you tell it what hashing function to use. There are two implementations you can choose from: Jenkins and Murmur. They're both faster than cryptographic hashers such as SHA-1 and produce good distributions. Benchmarks indicate that Murmur has faster hashing times than Jenkins, so that's what you'll use.

Let's press on with the code. Your map function will operate on your user information, which is a simple key/value pair, where the key is the user name, and the value is their age:[14]

```
public static class Map implements
    Mapper<Text, Text, NullWritable, BloomFilter> {
  private BloomFilter filter =
    new BloomFilter(1000, 5, Hash.MURMUR_HASH);
  OutputCollector<NullWritable, BloomFilter> collector;
```

Create the BloomFilter with 1,000 bits, 5 hash functions using the Murmur hash.

---

[14] **GitHub source**—https://github.com/alexholmes/hadoop-book/blob/master/src/main/java/com/manning/hip/ch7/bloom/BloomFilterCreator.java

```
@Override
public void configure(JobConf job) {
}

@Override
public void map(Text key, Text value,
               OutputCollector<NullWritable, BloomFilter> output,
               Reporter reporter) throws IOException {

  int age = Integer.valueOf(value.toString());
  if (age > 30) {
    filter.add(new Key(key.toString().getBytes()));
  }
  collector = output;
}

@Override
public void close() throws IOException {
  collector.collect(NullWritable.get(), filter);
}
}
```

If the user's age is over 30, add the user name to your BloomFilter.

When the map function has executed over all the input data, output the BloomFilter to the reducer.

Why do you output the Bloom filter in the close method, and not output it for every record you process in the map method? You do this to cut down on the amount of traffic between the map and reduce phases; there's no reason to output a whole lot of data if you can combine them yourself on the map side and just emit a single `BloomFilter` per map.

Your reducer's job is to combine all the Bloom filters outputted by the mappers into a single Bloom filter. The unions are performed with the bitwise or method exposed by the `BloomFilter` class. When performing a union, all the `BloomFilter` attributes such as bit array size and number of hashes must be identical:[15]

```
public static class Reduce implements
    Reducer<NullWritable, BloomFilter,
            AvroWrapper<GenericRecord>, NullWritable> {
  private BloomFilter filter =
    new BloomFilter(1000, 5, Hash.MURMUR_HASH);
  OutputCollector<AvroWrapper<GenericRecord>, NullWritable>
      collector;

  @Override
  public void reduce(NullWritable key, Iterator<BloomFilter> values,
                     OutputCollector<AvroWrapper<GenericRecord>,
                         NullWritable> output,
                     Reporter reporter) throws IOException {
    while (values.hasNext()) {
      BloomFilter bf = values.next();

      filter.or(bf);
    }
    collector = output;
  }
```

Create an empty BloomFilter. It's important that all the constructor fields are identical to the ones you created in the mappers.

Extract the BloomFilter from the input.

Perform a union of the Bloom filters.

---

[15] **GitHub source**—https://github.com/alexholmes/hadoop-book/blob/master/src/main/java/com/manning/hip/ch7/bloom/BloomFilterCreator.java

```
    @Override
    public void close() throws IOException {
      collector.collect(                          ◄──────── Write the Bloom filter in Avro form.
          new AvroWrapper<GenericRecord>(
              AvroBytesRecord.toGenericRecord(filter)),
          NullWritable.get());
    }
  }
}
```

You'll upload your sample user file and kick off your job. When the job is complete, you'll dump the contents of the Avro file to view the contents of your `BloomFilter`:

```
$ hadoop fs -put test-data/ch7/user-ages.txt .
$ hadoop fs -cat user-ages.txt
anne    23
joe     45
alison  32
mike    18
marie   54

$ bin/run.sh com.manning.hip.ch7.bloom.BloomFilterCreator \
  user-ages.txt output

$ bin/run.sh com.manning.hip.ch7.bloom.BloomFilterDumper \
  output/part-00000.avro
{96, 285, 292, 305, 315, 323, 399, 446, 666, 667, 670, 703, 734, ...}
```

The `BloomFilterDumper` code simply unmarshalls the `BloomFilter` from the Avro file and calls the `toString()` method, which in turn simply calls the `BitSet.toString()` method, which outputs the offset for each bit which is "on."

Summary

You used Avro as a serialization format for the Bloom filter. You could have just as easily emitted the `BloomFilter` object itself in your reducer because it's a `Writable`.

You used a single reducer in this technique, which will scale well to jobs that use thousands of map tasks and `BloomFilters` whose bit array sizes are in the millions. If the time taken to execute the single reducer becomes long, you can run with multiple reducers to parallelize the Bloom filter unions and have a postprocessing step to combine them further into a single Bloom filter.

Another distributed method to create a Bloom filter would be to view the set of reducers as the overall bit array, and in the map phase perform the hashing and output the hashes. The partitioner would then partition the output to the relevant reducer that manages that section of the bit array. Figure 7.28 visually presents how this may look.

For code comprehensibility you hardcoded the `BloomFilter` parameters; in reality you'll want to either calculate them dynamically or move them into a configuration file. This technique resulted in the creation of a `BloomFilter`. This `BloomFilter` could be pulled out of HDFS and used in another system or it could be used directly in Hadoop, as you'll see in the next section.

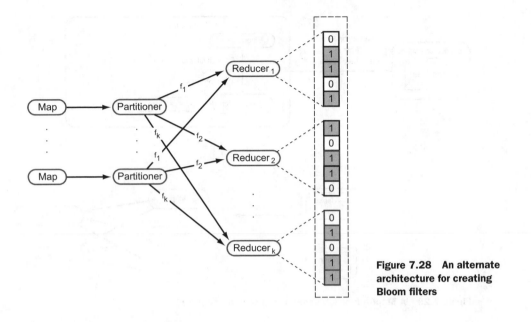

Figure 7.28   An alternate
architecture for creating
Bloom filters

TECHNIQUE 56   MapReduce semi-join with Bloom filters

In chapter 4 we looked at an implementation of a join, which used a semi-join as one of the steps to try and avoid performing a reduce-side join. The semi-join was performed using a HashMap to cache the smaller of the datasets. Bloom filters can replace a HashMap in the semi-join if you don't care about storing the contents of the dataset being cached, and you only care about whether the element on which you're performing the join exists or doesn't exist in the other dataset.

Problem
You want to perform an efficient semi-join in MapReduce.

Solution
Perform a semi-join by having the mappers load a Bloom filter from the Distributed Cache, and then filter results from the actual MapReduce data source by performing membership queries against the Bloom filter to determine which data source records should be emitted to the reducers.

Discussion
The key to this technique is to create a Bloom filter on a reasonably sized dataset. You'll extend the work you performed in the previous technique, where you created a Bloom filter on all users of a certain age. Imagine you wanted to join that set of users with all their tweets, which is a much larger dataset than the set of users.

Figure 7.29 shows how you would filter data in a mapper such that the join in MapReduce operates on a smaller set of the overall data.

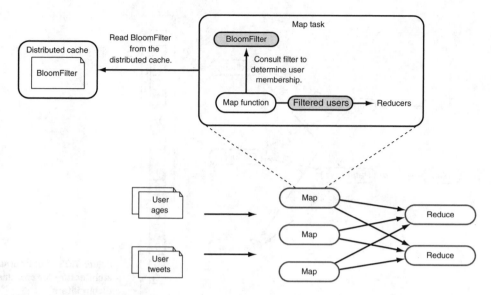

Figure 7.29   A MapReduce job using a map to join and filter

The code for the mapper is shown in the following listing:[16]

```
public static class Map extends Mapper<Text, Text, Text, Text> {
  BloomFilter filter;

  @Override
  protected void setup(
      Context context)
      throws IOException, InterruptedException {

    Path[] files = DistributedCache.getLocalCacheFiles(
      context.getConfiguration());
    filter = BloomFilterDumper.fromFile(
        new File(files[0].toString()));
  }

  @Override
  protected void map(Text key, Text value, Context context)
      throws IOException, InterruptedException {
    if(filter.membershipTest(
      new Key(key.toString().getBytes()))) {
      context.write(key, value);
    }
  }
}
```

Retrieve a list of the files in the distributed cache.

Extract the Bloom filter from the first file (assuming the distributed cache only contains a single file).

Check if the user (the key) is a member of your Bloom filter and, if it is, output it to the reducer.

---

[16] **GitHub source**—https://github.com/alexholmes/hadoop-book/blob/master/src/main/java/com/manning/hip/ch7/bloom/BloomJoin.java

The only additional item you need to perform in your MapReduce driver code is to add the Bloom filter file you created in the previous technique into the distributed cache, as follows:

```
DistributedCache.addCacheFile(bloomFilterPath.toUri(), conf);
```

Your MapReduce job doesn't have a reducer, so the map output will be written to HDFS. How about you launch your job and verify the output?

```
$ hadoop fs -put test-data/ch7/user-tweets.txt .
```
Copy the user tweets into HDFS (the user age file was copied in the previous technique).

```
$ bin/run.sh com.manning.hip.ch7.bloom.BloomJoin \
    user-ages.txt,user-tweets.txt \
    output2 \
    output/part-00000.avro
```
The two datasets being joined, the user ages, and the user tweets.

The Bloom filter file created in the previous technique.

```
$ hadoop fs -cat output2/part* | awk '{print $1}' | sort | uniq
alison
joe
marie
```

A peek at the output of the job in HDFS verifies that it only contains users *joe, alison,* and *marie,* who were present in the Bloom filter.

Summary

This technique only works in situations where one of the datasets being joined is small enough to be expressed in a Bloom filter. In the example, you were joining tweets with users, in which case the users could easily be represented with a Bloom filter.

Why would you not have used a hashtable rather than a Bloom Filter to represent the users? To construct a Bloom filter with a false positive rate of 1 percent, you need just 9.8 bits for each element in the data structure. Compare this with the best-case use of a HashSet containing integers, which require 8 bytes. Or if you were to have a HashSet that only reflected the presence of an element that ignores collision, you end up with a Bloom filter with a single hash, yielding higher false positives.

Version 0.10 of Pig will include support for Bloom filters in a similar mechanism to what I've presented here. Details can be viewed in the JIRA ticket at https://issues.apache.org/jira/browse/PIG-2328.

This concludes our examination of Bloom filters in MapReduce. In this section you learned that Bloom filters offer good space-constrained set membership capabilities. We looked at how you could create Bloom filters in MapReduce, and you also applied that code to a subsequent technique, which helped you optimize a Map-Reduce semi-join.

7.3   *Chapter summary*

Most of the algorithms laid out in this chapter are straightforward. What makes things interesting is how they're applied in MapReduce in ways that enable you to efficiently work with large datasets.

The two main data structures presented were graphs—good for modeling relationships—and Bloom filters, which excel at compact set membership. With graphs we looked at how you would use them to model social networks and web graphs, and went through some algorithms such as FoFs and PageRank to mine out interesting facts about your data.

With Bloom filters we looked at how to use MapReduce to create a Bloom filter in parallel, and then apply that Bloom filter to optimize a semi-join operation in MapReduce.

We've only scratched the surface in this chapter with regard to how data can be modeled and processed. Other chapters cover algorithms related to sorting and joins (chapter 4), statistics (chapter 8), and machine learning (chapter 9).

Integrating R and Hadoop for statistics and more

This chapter covers

- Integrating your R scripts with MapReduce and Streaming
- Understanding Rhipe, RHadoop, and R + Streaming

R is a statistical programming language for performing data analysis and graphing the results. The capabilities of R[1] let you perform statistical and predictive analytics, data mining, and visualization functions on your data. Its breadth of coverage and applicability across a wide range of sectors (such as finance, life sciences, manufacturing, retail, and more) make it a popular tool.

A data scientist who's working with Hadoop likely has an existing arsenal of homegrown and external R packages that they leverage. Rewriting these packages

---

[1] R contains built-in as well as user-created packages which can be accessed via CRAN, its package distribution system; see (http://cran.r-project.org/web/packages/).

in Java (or any other high-level MapReduce language) would be onerous and would be the antithesis to rapid development. What you need is a way to use R in conjunction with Hadoop and bridge the gap between Hadoop and the huge database of information that exists in R.

Much of the data you work with exists in text form, such as tweets from Twitter, logs, and stock records. In this chapter we'll look at how you can use R to calculate some simple average-based calculations on some text-based stock data. In doing so we'll highlight how you can use R with three different integration approaches: R with Streaming, Rhipe, and RHadoop. By the end of the chapter you'll understand the various ways that R can be integrated with Hadoop and pick the best approach for your application.

> **R and statistics**
>
> The focus of this chapter is on integrating R with Hadoop. For more details on R, consult the Manning book *R in Action* (August 2011, http://www.manning.com/kabacoff/). To get up to speed (or as a refresher) on statistics, I recommend the book *Statistics: A Gentle Introduction*, http://www.sagepub.com/books/Book235514.

8.1 Comparing R and MapReduce integrations

In this section we'll evaluate the three different methods you'll use in this chapter to integrate R with MapReduce. I picked these three approaches due to their popularity and differing approaches to solving the same problem, that of combining R and Hadoop together.

1. *R + Streaming*—With this approach, you use MapReduce to execute R scripts in the map and reduce phases.
2. *Rhipe*—Rhipe is an open source project which allows MapReduce to be closely integrated with R on the client side.
3. *RHadoop*—Like Rhipe, RHadoop also provides an R wrapper around MapReduce so that they can be seamlessly integrated on the client side.

Table 8.1 compares these three options with each other.

Table 8.1 Comparing R and MapReduce integration options

Criteria	R + Streaming	Rhipe	RHadoop
License	R is a combination of GPL-2 and GPL-3. Streaming is integrated into Hadoop, which is Apache 2.0.	Apache 2.0.	Apache 2.0.

Table 8.1   Comparing R and MapReduce integration options *(continued)*

Criteria	R + Streaming	Rhipe	RHadoop
Installation complexity	Easy. The R package needs to be installed on each DataNode, but packages are available on publicly available Yum repositories for easy installation.	High. R must be installed on each DataNode, in conjunction with Protocol Buffers, and Rhipe itself. To do so requires building Protocol Buffers, and the Rhipe installation isn't seamless and can require some hacking to get it to work.	Moderate. R must be installed on each DataNode, and RHadoop has dependencies on other R packages. But these packages can be installed with CRAN, and the RHadoop installation, while not via CRAN, is straight-forward.
Client-side integration with R	None. You need to use the Hadoop command-line to launch a Streaming job, and specify as arguments the map-side and reduce-side R scripts.	High. Rhipe is an R library which handles running a MapReduce job when the appropriate function is called. Users simply write native R map and reduce functions in R, and Rhipe takes care of the logistics of transporting them and invoking them from the map and reduce tasks.	High. RHadoop is also an R library, where users define their map and reduce functions in R.
Underlying technologies used	Streaming.	Rather than using Streaming, Rhipe instead uses its own map and reduce Java functions, which stream the map and reduce inputs in Protocol Buffers encoded form to a Rhipe C executable, which uses embedded R to invoke the user's map and reduce R functions.	RHadoop is a simple, thin wrapper on top of Hadoop and Streaming. Therefore, it has no proprietary MapReduce code, and has a simple wrapper R script which is called from Streaming and in turn calls the user's map and reduce R functions.

So which tool should you pick? As we go through the techniques, you may find that one approach lends itself more to your situation than others. Table 8.2 represents the author's opinion on which tool performs best.

Before we start diving into these technologies, let's take a few minutes to look at some R basics so that your techniques don't look too alien.

Table 8.2   Areas where R and MapReduce approaches work well, and where they don't

Approach	Works well in these situations	Things to bear in mind
R and Streaming	You want advanced control over your MapReduce functions such as partitioning and sorting.	Hard to invoke directly from existing R scripts, as opposed to the other approaches.
Rhipe	You want access to R and MapReduce without leaving R.	Requires proprietary Input and Output Formats to work with the Protocol Buffers encoded data.
RHadoop	You want access to R and MapReduce without leaving R. You also want to work with existing MapReduce Input and Output Format classes.	There needs to be sufficient memory to store all the reducer values for a unique key in memory; values aren't streamed to the reducer function.

8.2   *R fundamentals*

In this section we'll quickly look at some R basics to get R installed on your system, and a reference guide to help understand the basic R language constructs and types.

INSTALLATION

Follow instructions in appendix A to install R. Care should be taken to install R in the same directory on all the nodes. Also make sure that all nodes are running the same version of R.

STARTING R AND RUNNING YOUR FIRST COMMAND

Starting R couldn't be simpler:

```
$ R
> min(1:5)
[1] 1
```

R is started by simply running R from the command line.

Calculate the minimum number in a sequence between 1 and 5.

If the result of a function or operation in R isn't assigned to a variable, by default it's printed on the console.

QUICK EXAMPLES

We'll look at a handful of R basics to help you understand the techniques in this chapter, as detailed in figure 8.1.

In R, vectors are the most useful data structure because most of the numerical functions support them. Figure 8.2 presents some R vector basics.

R supports other data structures such as matrices, arrays, data frames, and factors. This chapter focuses mostly on using vectors (because the examples in this chapter

Variables

```
> x <- 2

> print(x)
[1] 2

> y = 5
> y <- toString(mean(c(1:5)))

> z <- c(3:5)

> ls()
[1] "x"  "y"  "z"

> ls.str()
x :  num 2
y :  chr "3"
z :  int [1:3] 3 4 5

> rm(x)
> ls()
[1] "y"  "z"
```

Assign 2 to the local variable x.

Writes the contents of x to standard out.

R is dynamically typed so we can reassign data of a different type to y.

Assign a vector containing a sequence of numbers from 3 to 5 to variable z

List all the variables in the workspace.

List the variables, types and values in the workspace.

Remove variable x from the environment.

Figure 8.1   Examples of R variables in use

Vectors

```
> x <- c(1, 2*4, "5", TRUE)          ◄——— Create a vector of strings.
```

Because we're mixing types R coerces all the data into strings.

```
> x <- c(x, 10, 4:6)                 ◄——— Add elements to the end of the vector.

> x[2:4]                             ◄——— Extract a range of elements from index 2 to 4.
[1] "8" "5" "TRUE"

> x[-(2:4)]                          ◄——— Extract all elements from the vector
[1] "1" "10" "4" "5" "6"                   excluding elements 2 to 4.

> x <- as.numeric (x)                ◄——— Convert the string vector into a numerical
Warning message:                           vector and remove non-numerics.
NAs introduced by coercion           ◄
```

This message means that elements which couldn't be converted into numerics now exist as the special NA symbol.

```
> print(x <- x[! is.na (x)])
[1] 1  8  5 10  4  5  6
```

Calculate summary statistics on vector x

The is.na returns a vector of TRUE or FALSE elements which we use to remove NAs from x

```
> summary (x)
 Min. 1st Qu.  Median    Mean 3rd Qu.    Max.
1.000   4.500   5.000   5.571   7.000  10.000

> unlist (lapply (c(1:3),  function (y) y+1))   ◄——— Generate a new vector with all the
                                                      values incremented by one.
```

An anonymous function that is executed against each element

unlist converts a list (the result of lapply) into a vector. Not all numerical functions in R support lists, so it's generally best to keep your data in vectors.

lapply allows you to perform a function on each element of x, which is either a vector or list. The result is a list of the same length as x

```
> sapply (c(1:3),  function (y) y+1)   ◄——— The same as lapply, but conveniently
[1] 2 3 4                                    returns a vector rather than a list
```

Figure 8.2   Examples of R vectors and functions

only use vectors), so we won't get into the details on these other data structures. To sink your teeth into R, take a look at *R in Action* from Robert Kabacoff (http://www .manning.com/kabacoff/).

We've looked at some simple examples of how to get up and running with R. It's time to introduce Hadoop into the equation and look at how you can use R in combination with Hadoop Streaming.

8.3   *R and Streaming*

With Hadoop Streaming, you can write map and reduce functions in any programming or scripting language that supports reading data from standard input and writing to standard output. In this section we'll look at how you can get Streaming to work directly with R in two steps, first in a map-only job, and then in a full MapReduce job. You'll be working with stock data and performing simple calculations. The goal is to show how the integration of R and Hadoop can be made with Streaming.

8.3.1   *Streaming and map-only R*

Just like with regular MapReduce, you can have a map-only job in Streaming and R. Map-only jobs make sense in situations where you don't care to join or group your data together in the reducer.

TECHNIQUE 57   **Calculate the daily mean for stocks**

In this technique you'll look at how Hadoop Streaming and R can be used on your stock data to calculate the daily means for each stock symbol.

Problem

You want to integrate R and MapReduce, and you don't need to join your data, or sort your outputs.

Solution

Use R and Hadoop Streaming to process data in a map-only job.

Discussion

In this technique you'll work on the stock CSV file, which contains the following elements for each stock:

```
Symbol,Date,Open,High,Low,Close,Volume,Adj Close
```

A subset of the contents of the file can be viewed here:

```
$ head -6 test-data/stocks.txt
AAPL,2009-01-02,85.88,91.04,85.16,90.75,26643400,90.75
AAPL,2008-01-02,199.27,200.26,192.55,194.84,38542100,194.84
AAPL,2007-01-03,86.29,86.58,81.90,83.80,44225700,83.80
AAPL,2006-01-03,72.38,74.75,72.25,74.75,28829800,74.75
AAPL,2005-01-03,64.78,65.11,62.60,63.29,24714000,31.65
AAPL,2004-01-02,21.55,21.75,21.18,21.28,5165800,10.64
```

In your job, you'll calculate the daily mean for each line using the open and close prices. The R script to perform that task is shown here:[2]

Identify the R process name that's used to execute this script. →

```
#! /usr/bin/env Rscript

options(warn=-1)

sink("/dev/null")
```

Disable warnings so they don't pollute your output.

← *This sink function controls the destination of output. Because your code is being used in Hadoop Streaming, you want control over what's written to standard output. Therefore, you redirect all R output (such as output that could be generated by third-party functions) to /dev/null until later in your code.*

---

[2]   **GitHub source**—https://github.com/alexholmes/hadoop-book/tree/master/src/main/R/ch8/stock_day_avg.R

Open a handle to the process standard input.

```r
input <- file("stdin", "r")
```

Read a line from standard input. n is the number of lines that should be read. You set the warn to FALSE because you don't receive an EOF when reading from standard input. If you hit an empty line, you take that to mean you've hit the end of the input.

```r
while(length(currentLine <-
        readLines(input, n=1, warn=FALSE)) > 0) {
```

Split the string using a comma as the separator, and flatten the resulting list into a vector.

```r
  fields <- unlist(strsplit(currentLine, ","))
```

Create a vector and add to it the stock open and close prices in numeric form.

```r
  lowHigh <- c(as.double(fields[3]), as.double(fields[6]))
```

```r
  mean <- mean(lowHigh)
```

Calculate the mean of the open and close prices.

```r
  sink()
```

```r
  cat(fields[1], fields[2], mean, "\n", sep="\t")
```

Concatenate the stock symbol, date, and mean prices for the day and write them to standard output.

Calling sink with no arguments restores the output destination so that you can write your data to standard output.

```r
  sink("/dev/null")
}
close(input)
```

Redirect all R output to /dev/null.

Summary

Figure 8.3 shows how Streaming and R work together in a map-only job.

Any MapReduce code can be challenging to test, but the great thing about using Hadoop Streaming code is that it's very easy to test on the command line without having to involve MapReduce at all. The following shows how the Linux cat utility (a simple

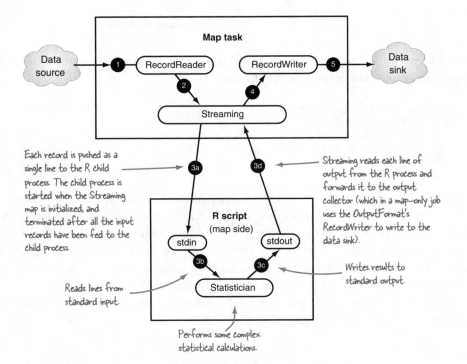

Each record is pushed as a single line to the R child process. The child process is started when the Streaming map is initialized, and terminated after all the input records have been fed to the child process.

Streaming reads each line of output from the R process and forwards it to the output collector (which in a map-only job uses the OutputFormat's RecordWriter to write to the data sink).

Reads lines from standard input.

Writes results to standard output.

Performs some complex statistical calculations.

Figure 8.3 The R and Streaming map-only data flow

utility to write the contents of a file to standard output) can be used to quickly test your R script to make sure the output is what you expect:

```
$ cat test-data/stocks.txt | src/main/R/ch8/stock_day_avg.R
AAPL  2009-01-02  88.315
AAPL  2008-01-02  197.055
AAPL  2007-01-03  85.045
AAPL  2006-01-03  73.565
...
```

That output looks good, so you're ready to run this in a Hadoop job:

Copy the stocks data into HDFS.

```
$ export HADOOP_HOME=/usr/lib/hadoop
```
Set the location of your Hadoop installation. This should be a fully qualified path.

```
$ ${HADOOP_HOME}/bin/hadoop fs -rmr output
```
Remove the output directory in HDFS. If the directory doesn't exist this will generate a warning that can be ignored.

```
$ ${HADOOP_HOME}/bin/hadoop fs -put test-data/stocks.txt \
  stocks.txt
```

```
$ ${HADOOP_HOME}/bin/hadoop \
  jar ${HADOOP_HOME}/contrib/streaming/*.jar \
  -D mapreduce.job.reduces=0 \
  -inputformat org.apache.hadoop.mapred.TextInputFormat \
  -input stocks.txt \
  -output output \
  -mapper `pwd`/src/main/R/ch8/stock_day_avg.R \
  -file `pwd`/src/main/R/ch8/stock_day_avg.R
```

You're running a map-only job, so set the number of reducers to 0.

Identify the input file for the job.

Set the output directory for the job.

Specify that you want to run the Streaming JAR. This should be a fully qualified path.

Specify the InputFormat for the job.

Tell Streaming the location of the executable that should be executed in the map phase.

Specify that the R executable should be copied into the distributed cache and made available to the map tasks.

You can perform a simple cat that shows you that the output is identical to what you produced when calling the R script directly:

```
$ hadoop fs -cat output/part*
AAPL  2009-01-02  88.315
AAPL  2008-01-02  197.055
AAPL  2007-01-03  85.045
AAPL  2006-01-03  73.565
...
```

You may have noticed that you used TextInputFormat, which emits a key/value tuple where the key is the byte offset in the file, and the value contains the contents of a line. But in your R script you were only supplied the value part of the tuple. This is an optimization in Hadoop Streaming, where if it detects you're using TextInputFormat it ignores the key from the TextInputFormat. If you want the key supplied to your script, you can set the stream.map.input.ignoreKey Hadoop configuration to true.

Figure 8.4 shows some Streaming configuration settings, which can be used to customize map inputs and outputs.

By default the input keys and values are separated by the tab character.
To override this value, use the following configuration key. In this example
you're telling Streaming to use the comma as the separator string:

```
-D stream.map.input.field.separator=","
```

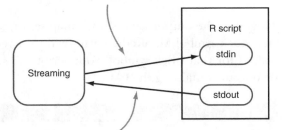

To extract the key/value pair from a line of output from a script, Streaming
will split using the tab character. This can be overridden with the following
configuration key:

```
-D stream.map.output.field.separator=","
```

Streaming will split the output line based on the first occurrence of
`stream.map.output.field.separator` to determine which part is the key and
value. If instead you wanted to split on the third instance of the separator
character you would specify the above setting in your job:

```
-D stream.num.map.output.key.fields=3
```

**Figure 8.4   Streaming
configurations for map tasks**

Now that we've covered how to use R and Streaming for a map-only job, let's see how
to get R working with a full map and reduce job.

8.3.2   Streaming, R, and full MapReduce

We'll now look at how you can integrate R with a full-blown MapReduce job. You'll
build upon what you've learned about using Streaming and a map-side R function,
and introduce a reduce-side function. In doing so you'll learn how Hadoop Streaming
supplies map output keys and the list of map output value tuples to the standard input
of the R function, and how the R function outputs are collected.

TECHNIQUE 58   Calculate the cumulative moving average for stocks

The previous technique calculated the daily mean for each stock symbol, and you'll
use the MapReduce framework to group together all of the daily means for each stock
symbol across multiple days, and then calculate a cumulative moving average (CMA)
over that data.

Problem

You want to integrate R and Streaming in both the map and reduce sides.

Solution

Use R and Hadoop Streaming to process data in mappers and reducers.

Discussion

If you recall the map-side technique, the map R script emitted tab-separated output with the following fields:

```
Symbol  Date  Mean
```

MapReduce will sort and group together the output keys of your map script, which is the stock symbol. For each unique stock symbol MapReduce will feed your reduce R script with all the map output values for that stock symbol. Your script will sum the means together and emit a single output containing the CMA.[3]

The R script emits a single output

```
#! /usr/bin/env Rscript
options(warn=-1)
sink("/dev/null")

outputMean <- function(stock, means) {          A simple R function that takes as input the stock
  stock_mean <- mean(means)                      symbol and a vector of means. It calculates the CMA
  sink()                                         and writes the symbol and CMA to standard output.
  cat(stock, stock_mean, "\n", sep="\t")
  sink("/dev/null")
}

input <- file("stdin", "r")

prevKey <- "
means <- numeric(0)

while(length(currentLine <- readLines(input, n=1, warn=FALSE)) > 0) {

  fields <- unlist(strsplit(currentLine, "\t"))

  key <- fields[1]                          Read the key, which is the stock symbol.
  mean <- as.double(fields[3])

  if( identical(prevKey, ") || identical(prevKey, key)) {
    prevKey <- key
    means <- c(means, mean)
  } else {
    outputMean(prevKey, means)
    prevKey <- key
    means <- c(means, mean)                When you find a new key it means you've hit a new map
  }                                         output key. This means it's time to call the function to
}                                           calculate the CMA and write the output to standard out.

if(!identical(prevKey, ")) {
  outputMean(prevKey, means)
}

close(input)
```

Read the mean from the input.

---

[3] **GitHub source**—https://github.com/alexholmes/hadoop-book/tree/master/src/main/R/ch8/stock_cma.R

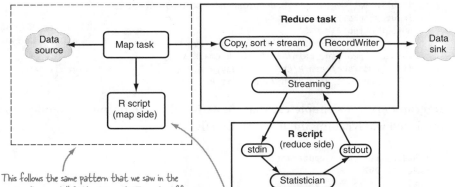

This follows the same pattern that we saw in the previous "map-only" R Streaming job. The only difference is that the output isn't written to the OutputFormat, and instead is collected and spilled to disk, awaiting fetch commands from reducer tasks.

These are two separate scripts, one for the map side, and the other for the reduce side.

The reduce script is supplied each map output record on a separate line. The map output key and value are separated by tab by default. Map output keys are grouped together, so our code needs to read the input line by line, and when we see a change in the input key we can process all the values for that key.

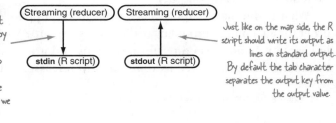

Just like on the map side, the R script should write its output as lines on standard output. By default the tab character separates the output key from the output value.

Figure 8.5   The R and Streaming MapReduce data flow

Summary

Figure 8.5 shows how Streaming and your R script work together on the reduce side. The beauty of Streaming is that you can easily test it with streaming Linux commands:

```
$ cat test-data/stocks.txt | src/main/R/ch8/stock_day_avg.R | \
  sort --key 1,1 | src/main/R/ch8/stock_cma.R
AAPL  68.997
CSCO  49.94775
GOOG  123.9468
MSFT  101.297
YHOO  94.55789
```

That output looks good, so you're ready to run this in a Hadoop job:

```
$ export HADOOP_HOME=/usr/lib/hadoop

$ ${HADOOP_HOME}/bin/hadoop fs -rmr output

$ ${HADOOP_HOME}/bin/hadoop fs -put test-data/stocks.txt stocks.txt
$ ${HADOOP_HOME}/bin/hadoop \
  jar ${HADOOP_HOME}/contrib/streaming/*.jar \
```

```
-inputformat org.apache.hadoop.mapred.TextInputFormat \
-input stocks.txt \
-output output \
-mapper `pwd`/src/main/R/ch8/stock_day_avg.R \          Specify the map R script (the same script
-reducer `pwd`/src/main/R/ch8/stock_cma.R \              you ran in the previous map-only technique).
-file `pwd`/src/main/R/ch8/stock_day_avg.R \          Set the reduce R script.
-file `pwd`/src/main/R/ch8/stock_cma.R
```

You can perform a simple `cat` that shows you that the output is identical to what you produced when calling the R script directly:

```
$ hadoop fs -cat output/part*
AAPL   68.997
CSCO   49.94775
GOOG   123.9468
MSFT   101.297
YHOO   94.55789
```

Figure 8.6 shows some Streaming configuration settings, which can be used to customize reduce inputs and outputs.

What if the map output values need to be supplied to the reducer in a specific order for each map output key (called *secondary sort*)? You encountered secondary sort in chapters 4 and 7 when performing joins and graph operations. Secondary sort in Streaming can be achieved by using the `KeyFieldBasedPartitioner`, as shown here:

```
$ export HADOOP_HOME=/usr/lib/hadoop

$ ${HADOOP_HOME}/bin/hadoop fs -rmr output               You specify that Streaming
                                                         should consider both the
$ ${HADOOP_HOME}/bin/hadoop fs -put test-data/stocks.txt stocks.txt    stock symbol and date to be
                                                         part of the map output key.
$ ${HADOOP_HOME}/bin/hadoop \
  jar ${HADOOP_HOME}/contrib/streaming/*.jar \
  -D stream.num.map.output.key.fields=2 \
  -D mapred.text.key.partitioner.options=-k1,1\        Specify that MapReduce should partition
  -inputformat org.apache.hadoop.mapred.TextInputFormat \    output based on the first token in the
  -input stocks.txt \                                   map output key, which is the stock symbol.
  -output output \
  -mapper `pwd`/src/main/R/ch8/stock_day_avg.R \
  -reducer `pwd`/src/main/R/ch8/stock_cma.R \            Specify the partitioner for the job,
  -partitioner \                                         KeyFieldBasedPartitioner, which will parse
      org.apache.hadoop.mapred.lib.KeyFieldBasedPartitioner \   the mapred.text.key.partitioner.options
  -file `pwd`/src/main/R/ch8/stock_day_avg.R           to determine what to partition.
```

For additional Streaming features such as more control over sorts, please look at the Hadoop streaming documentation.[4]

We've looked at how you can use R in combination with Streaming to calculate the means over your stock data. One of the disadvantages of this approach is that this can't be easily integrated into client-side R scripts. This is the problem that Rhipe and RHadoop solve. Let's first take a look at Rhipe.

---

[4] See http://hadoop.apache.org/common/docs/r1.0.3/streaming.html.

To set a custom input key/value separator string, use the following
configuration key. The default is the tab character:

```
-D stream.reduce.input.field.separator=","
```

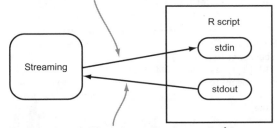

To set a custom output key/value separator string, use the following
configuration key. The default is the tab character:

```
-D stream.reduce.output.field.separator=","
```

Set the number of `stream.reduce.output.field.separator` separators,
which delimit the output key form the output value. The default is 1:

```
-D stream.num.reduce.output.key.fields=3
```

**Figure 8.6 Streaming
configurations for reduce tasks**

8.4   *Rhipe—Client-side R and Hadoop working together*

Rhipe, short for *R and Hadoop Integrated Processing Environment*, is an open source project
that, as the name suggests, provides a closer integration of R and Hadoop than what you
saw with R and Streaming. In R and Streaming you used the command line to launch
a Hadoop job, whereas with Rhipe you can actually work with MapReduce directly in R.

Before we get started, you'll need to follow the instructions in appendix A to install
Rhipe and its dependencies on the Hadoop nodes in your cluster.

TECHNIQUE 59   Calculating the CMA using Rhipe

In this technique you'll again implement the CMA of each stock symbol, just like you
did with R and Streaming. But in this technique you'll use Rhipe and see how you can
achieve tight integration of R and Hadoop.

Problem

You want to seamlessly leverage Hadoop from your R code.

Solution

This technique shows how Rhipe allows you to write client-side R code that can launch
a MapReduce job. It also takes a look at how Rhipe R callbacks are used in the scope
of Rhipe MapReduce jobs.

Discussion

The Rhipe script to calculate the stock CMA is shown next. Notice that the MapReduce
integration is fully baked into Rhipe, which makes it easy to integrate MapReduce into
your existing R scripts and processes:[5]

---

[5] **GitHub source**—https://github.com/alexholmes/hadoop-book/tree/master/src/main/R/ch8/
stock_cma_rhipe.R

```
#! /usr/bin/env Rscript                           Load the Rhipe library into memory.
library(Rhipe)

rhinit(TRUE,TRUE)                   Initialize Rhipe.

map <- expression({                               Define the map expression that's
  process_line <- function(currentLine) {         executed in the map task.
    fields <- unlist(strsplit(currentLine, ","))
    lowHigh <- c(as.double(fields[3]), as.double(fields[6]))
    rhcollect(fields[1], toString(mean(lowHigh)))         The Rhipe function rhcollect is called to
  }                                                       emit key/value tuples from the map phase.
  lapply(map.values, process_line)
})
                                    The reduce expression consists of three parts. The pre block is called for each unique
reduce <- expression(               map output key, prior to the values for the key being supplied to the reduce block.
  pre = {                           The map output key is contained in the variable reduce.key (not used in this code).
    means <- numeric(0)
  },                                The reduce block is called containing a vector of values in reduce.values. This is
                                    called multiple times if the number of values for a key is greater than 10,000.
  reduce = {
    means <- c(means, as.numeric(unlist(reduce.values)))
  },

  post = {
    rhcollect(reduce.key, toString(mean(means)))         Just like in the map expression, the
  }                                                      rhcollect function is called to emit the
)                                                        output key and value pair.

input_file <- "stocks.txt"
output_dir <- "output"

job <- rhmr(                        The rhmr function is used to set up the job.
  jobname  = "Rhipe CMA",
  map      = map,
  reduce   = reduce,
  ifolder  = input_file,
  ofolder  = output_dir,
  inout    = c("text", "sequence")
)                                   Launch the MapReduce job.

rhex(job)
```

Summary

As opposed to your R with Streaming technique, with Rhipe you can execute the R
script directly, which in turn will launch the MapReduce job:

```
$ hadoop fs -put test-data/stocks.txt /tmp/stocks.txt
$ export HADOOP_BIN=/usr/lib/hadoop/bin
$ src/main/R/ch8/stock_cma_rhipe.R
```

The stock_cma_rhipe.R script can be
executed directly because it starts with a
shebang indicating to the shell that it should
be executed by Rscript, the R runtime.

To try and understand how Rhipe works, and how your R code is integrated with Rhipe,
we'll walk through the series of steps in a Rhipe workflow, starting with a look at the main
parts of your R script, and how the MapReduce job is triggered, as shown in figure 8.7.

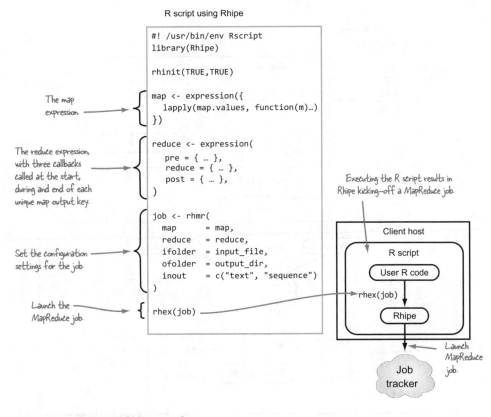

R script using Rhipe

```
#! /usr/bin/env Rscript
library(Rhipe)

rhinit(TRUE,TRUE)

map <- expression({
  lapply(map.values, function(m)…)
})

reduce <- expression(
  pre = { … },
  reduce = { … },
  post = { … },
)

job <- rhmr(
  map      = map,
  reduce   = reduce,
  ifolder  = input_file,
  ofolder  = output_dir,
  inout    = c("text", "sequence")
)

rhex(job)
```

The map expression.

The reduce expression, with three callbacks called at the start, during and end of each unique map output key.

Set the configuration settings for the job.

Launch the MapReduce job.

Executing the R script results in Rhipe kicking-off a MapReduce job.

Client host

R script

User R code

rhex(job)

Rhipe

Launch MapReduce job.

Job tracker

Figure 8.7   High-level Rhipe overview

Next we'll look at how Rhipe works in the context of MapReduce tasks, starting with the map task (as shown in figure 8.8).

Now we'll see how Rhipe works on the reduce side (as shown in figure 8.9).

Rhipe also contains a number of functions that can be used to read and write to HDFS. More information on those functions can be seen at http://saptarshiguha .github.com/RHIPE/functions.html#hdfs-related.

One area to watch out for in Rhipe is that it doesn't use Streaming and instead uses its own map and reduce functions and its own Input/Output Format classes. As a result, it can't use other Input/Output Format classes, which you may already have in place to work with your data formats.

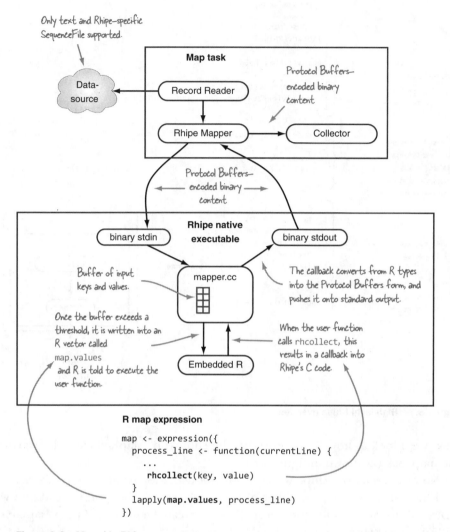

Figure 8.8 Map-side Rhipe

That concludes our look at Rhipe, which offers an integration of R and Hadoop into client-side R scripts. The final section takes a look at RHadoop, which also offers a client-side integration of R and Hadoop, albeit in a more lightweight way.

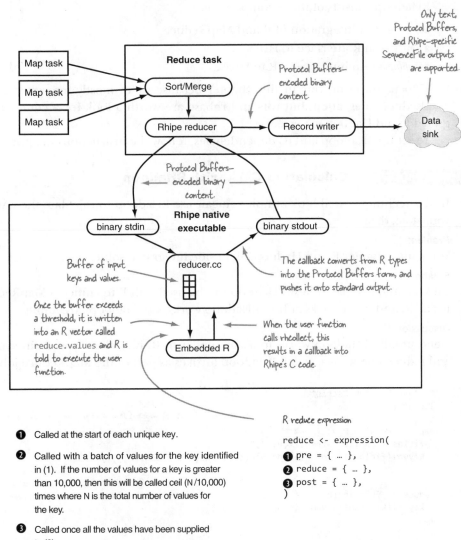

Only text,
Protocol Buffers,
and Rhipe-specific
SequenceFile outputs
are supported.

Protocol Buffers—
encoded binary
content.

Protocol Buffers—
encoded binary
content.

Buffer of input
keys and values.

The callback converts from R types
into the Protocol Buffers form, and
pushes it onto standard output.

Once the buffer exceeds
a threshold, it is written
into an R vector called
reduce.values and R is
told to execute the user
function.

When the user function
calls rhcollect, this
results in a callback into
Rhipe's C code.

❶ Called at the start of each unique key.

❷ Called with a batch of values for the key identified
in (1). If the number of values for a key is greater
than 10,000, then this will be called ceil (N/10,000)
times where N is the total number of values for
the key.

❸ Called once all the values have been supplied
to (2).

R reduce expression

```
reduce <- expression(
❶ pre = { … },
❷ reduce = { … },
❸ post = { … },
)
```

Figure 8.9   Reduce-side Rhipe

8.5   *RHadoop—a simpler integration of client-side R and Hadoop*

RHadoop is an open source project created by Revolution Analytics, which provides
another approach to integrating R and Hadoop. Just like Rhipe, RHadoop allows
MapReduce interactions directly from within your R code.

RHadoop consists of three components:

1 *rmr*—The integration of R and MapReduce
2 *rdfs*—An R interface to HDFS
3 *rhbase*—An interface in R to HBase

We'll focus on using rmr in this chapter because we're mostly interested in R and MapReduce integration, but rdfs and rhbase are worth a look for a completely integrated R and Hadoop experience.

To set up RHadoop and its dependencies, follow the instructions in appendix A.

TECHNIQUE 60   **Calculating CMA with RHadoop**

In this technique we'll look at how you can use RHadoop to calculate the CMA using your stock data.

Problem

You want a simpler R and Hadoop client-side integrated solution.

Solution

This technique looks at how RHadoop can be used with R to launch a MapReduce job inside R, and it also looks at how RHadoop works with Hadoop Streaming.

Discussion

Conceptually, RHadoop works in a way similar to Rhipe, where you define your map and reduce operations, which RHadoop invokes as part of the MapReduce job:[6]

```
#! /usr/bin/env Rscript            ⟵ Load the rmr library.
library(rmr)

map <- function(k,v) {      ⟵  Define a map function, which takes a key/value pair as input. The keyval
  fields <- unlist(strsplit(v, ","))      function is called for each key/value output tuple that the map emits.
  keyval(fields[1], mean(as.double(c(fields[3], fields[6]))))
}

reduce <- function(k,vv) {        ⟵  The reduce function, which is called once
  keyval(k, mean(as.numeric(unlist(vv))))       for each unique map key, where k is the
}                                                   key, and v is a list of values.

kvtextoutputformat = function(k,v) {    ⟵  You define your own reduce output key/value separator.
  paste(c(k,v, "\n"), collapse = "\t")
}

mapreduce(                     ⟵  Run a MapReduce job.
  input = "stocks.txt",
  output = "output",
  textinputformat = rawtextinputformat,
  textoutputformat = kvtextoutputformat,
  map = map,
  reduce = reduce)
```

---

[6] **GitHub source**—https://github.com/alexholmes/hadoop-book/tree/master/src/main/R/ch8/ stock_cma_rmr.R

Summary

To execute the code in this technique, you'd run the following commands:

```
$ HADOOP_HOME=<Hadoop installation directory>
$ $HADOOP_HOME/bin/hadoop fs -put test-data/stocks.txt stocks.txt

$ src/main/R/ch8/stock_cma_rmr.R

$ hadoop fs -cat output/part*
CSCO 30.8985
MSFT 44.6725
AAPL 68.997
GOOG 419.943
YHOO 70.971
```

rmr is different from Rhipe in that it uses Hadoop Streaming. Figure 8.10 shows you how your code correlates to the MapReduce job execution.

One of the interesting features of rmr is that it makes the R client-side environment available to the map and reduce R functions executed in MapReduce. What this means is that the map and reduce functions can reference variables outside of the scope of their respective functions, which is a huge boon for R developers.

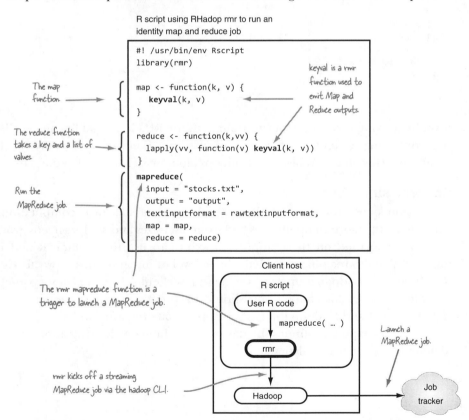

Figure 8.10   rmr and client-side interactions

rmr has another neat trick up its sleeve in that it can essentially work seamlessly with MapReduce inputs and outputs. In your technique, the input to your job was already in HDFS, and you didn't interact with the output of your job in R. But rmr has support for writing R variables directly to HDFS, using them as inputs to the MapReduce job and, after the job has completed, loading them back into an R data structure. This isn't the approach you'll want to take when working with large volumes of data, but nonetheless is great for prototyping and testing with smaller datasets:

```
$ R
> library(rmr)
> small.ints = to.dfs(1:10)          ◄─────  Create a numeric sequence of 1 to 10, and
                                              store the resulting vector in HDFS.

> out = mapreduce(                    ◄─────  The result from the MapReduce job is a closure that
          input = small.ints,                 can be used to read the results back out of HDFS.
          map = function(k,v) keyval(v, v^2))
...
> result = from.dfs(out)
> print(result)
[[1]]                                 ◄─────  Read the job outputs from HDFS.
[[1]]$key
[1] 10

[[1]]$val
[1] 100

attr(,"rmr.keyval")
[1] TRUE

...
```

If you're looking for additional rmr examples, the RHadoop wiki has an excellent tutorial containing examples of logical regression, K-means and more at https://github.com/RevolutionAnalytics/RHadoop/blob/master/rmr/pkg/docs/tutorial.md.

8.6   *Chapter summary*

The fusion of R and Hadoop allows for large-scale statistical computation, which becomes all the more compelling as both your data sizes and analysis needs grow. In this chapter we focused on three approaches you can use to combine R and Hadoop together. R and Streaming provided a basic level of integration, and we also looked at the Rhipe and RHadoop frameworks, which allow client-side R and Hadoop integration.

After reading this chapter you should have enough information to choose the right level of R and Hadoop integration appropriate for your project.

The next chapter continues the data science theme by looking at how you can use Mahout for predictive analytics.

Predictive
analytics with Mahout

9

This chapter covers

- Using recommenders to make product suggestions
- Spam email classification with naïve Bayes
- Clustering to identify trends or patterns in data

Predictive analytics is the field of deriving information from current and historical data. It's one of the main tools in a data scientist's tool belt, whose job is to examine large datasets (often called *big data* these days) and derive meaningful insights from that data, optimally in the form of new products. Predictive analytics can be broken down into three broad categories:

- *Recommender*—Recommender systems suggest items based on past behavior or interest. These items can be other users in a social network, or products and services in retail websites.
- *Classification*—Classification (otherwise known as *supervised learning*) infers or assigns a category to previously unseen data, based on discoveries made from some prior observations about similar data. Examples of classification include email spam filtering and detection of fraudulent credit card transactions.

- *Clustering*—A clustering system (also known as *unsupervised learning*) groups data together into clusters. It does so without learning the characteristics about related data. Clustering is useful when you're trying to discover hidden structures in your data, such as user habits.

Mahout is a machine learning library which includes implementations of these three classes of predictive analytics techniques. Many of its algorithms have MapReduce implementations, which is the focus of this chapter, and this is where Mahout comes into its own—its ability to work with huge datasets that other predictive analytics tools can't support. In fact Mahout only starts to make sense if you're working with datasets that number in the millions or more.

In this chapter we'll look at the Mahout MapReduce implementations of recommenders, classifiers, and clusterers. You'll use recommenders to recommend movies similar to movies that users have already rated; you'll write a classifier that can filter out spam emails; and, finally, we'll look at how you can use clustering to discover structure in your data.

We'll get things started with a look at recommenders.

9.1   Using recommenders to make product suggestions

Recommender systems, which are also known as *collaborative filtering (CF)* systems, are the computer equivalent of you asking your friends for a restaurant recommendation. The more recommendations you receive from your friends, the higher the probability that you'll go there. In the online world you see recommender engines in play every day—most social and retail websites recommend new people for you to interact with, or a new product for you to buy.

There are two types of collaborative recommenders: user-based recommenders and item-based recommenders:

- *User-based recommenders* look at users similar to a target user, and use their collaborative ratings to make predictions to the target user.
- *Item-based recommenders* look at similar items, and use this information to recommend items that are related to items previously used by a target user.

You can see the results of recommenders in action in figure 9.1.

Figure 9.1   Examples of recommenders that suggest other users of interest in a social network, and movies that a user may be interested in watching

Both types of recommender systems need to be able to determine the degree of similarity between users or items, so we first need to look at how similarity metrics work.

9.1.1 *Visualizing similarity metrics*

In both user- and item-based recommenders, the system needs to find similar users or items. They do this by comparing users or items with each other to arrive at a similarity score. Popular measures that can calculate these scores include Euclidean distance and Pearson's correlation. These algorithms operate on numerical data, where the data points are vector-like (points in space).

The Euclidean distance is the most commonly used distance measure, and can be seen in figure 9.2, which shows how the Euclidean distance calculation works.

The Euclidean distance is in a family of related distance measures, which also includes the Manhattan distance (the distance between two points measured along axes at right angles). These measures are all similar in how they calculate distances, and as such switching from one to the other is not likely to significantly change results.

Correlation-based measures, however, are less concerned with the distance between points in a dataset and care more about similarity, which is the degree of linear relationship between two variables. Pearson's correlation is widely used in science to measure the dependencies between two variables. Its advantage over the Euclidean

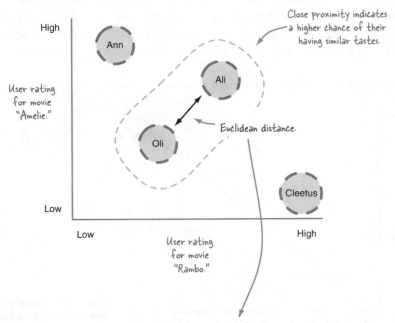

If $p = (p_1, p_2)$ and $q = (q_1, q_2)$, then the Euclidean distance is:

$$d(p, q) = \sqrt{(p_1 - q_1)^2 + (p_2 - q_2)^2}$$

Figure 9.2 A plot showing user preferences for two movies, and how the Euclidean distance is calculated

distance is that it can be used to find correlations between users even if one user tends to give higher scores than another user, assuming that, in general, they like and dislike the same movies. Figure 9.3 illustrates this correlation.

Pearson's correlation will result in a number between -1 and 1, which is an indicator of how much two series of numbers move proportionate to each other, and exhibits a linear relationship. A value of 1 indicates the highest correlation and -1 the lowest. Figure 9.3 shows an example of a highly correlated relationship. The math behind Pearson's correlation is more complex than the Euclidean distance, and is outside of the scope of this chapter, but if you're interested you can read more details at http://en.wikipedia.org/wiki/Pearson_product-moment_correlation_coefficient.

Mahout can support the Euclidean and Pearson's similarity measures for both user-based and item-based recommenders. Mahout supports additional similarity measures for item-based recommenders such as the Tanimoto coefficient.[1] All the user-based and item-based similarity implementations can be seen by searching for implementations of the `UserSimilarity` and `ItemSimilarity` interfaces.

Next we'll look at the dataset you'll use in this section on recommenders.

9.1.2   *The GroupLens dataset*

GroupLens is a research lab in the Department of Computer Science and Engineering at the University of Minnesota. They perform research into recommender systems, among other research areas, and provide a dataset of 1 million ratings from 6,000 users on 4,000 movies at http://www.grouplens.org/node/12. Here you'll download this data and prepare it in a format that can be used by the Mahout recommender engines.

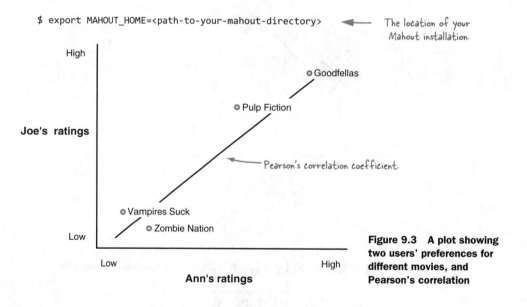

Figure 9.3   **A plot showing two users' preferences for different movies, and Pearson's correlation**

---

[1] See http://en.wikipedia.org/wiki/Jaccard_index#Tanimoto_Similarity_and_Distance.

> **Mahout installation**
>
> Follow the instructions in appendix A to install Mahout on your system before executing the instructions in this section.

```
$ cd $MAHOUT_HOME          ◄──────  The location of your
$ mkdir -p corpus/grouplens-1m      Mahout installation.
$ cd corpus/grouplens-1m
$ curl -O http://www.grouplens.org/system/files/ml-1m.zip
$ unzip ml-1m.zip
Archive:  ml-1m.zip
   creating: ml-1m/
  inflating: ml-1m/movies.dat
  inflating: ml-1m/ratings.dat
  inflating: ml-1m/README
   creating: __MACOSX/
   creating: __MACOSX/ml-1m/
  inflating: __MACOSX/ml-1m/._README
  inflating: ml-1m/users.dat
```

The ratings file contains data in the following format:

```
UserID::MovieID::Rating::Timestamp

- UserIDs range between 1 and 6040
- MovieIDs range between 1 and 3952
- Ratings are made on a 5-star scale (whole-star ratings only)
- Timestamp is represented in seconds since the epoch
- Each user has at least 20 ratings
```

You can see an example from the top of the file:

```
$ head -n 5 ml-1m/ratings.dat
1::1193::5::978300760
1::661::3::978302109
1::914::3::978301968
1::3408::4::978300275
1::2355::5::978824291
```

This isn't quite in the format that you need for Mahout, which expects CSV-delimited format as you see next:

```
UserID,ItemID,Value
```

You can write a simple awk script to convert the GroupLens data into CSV form:

```
$ awk -F"::" '{print $1","$2","$3}' ml-1m/ratings.dat > ratings.csv
```

Your data is now in a form that you can use in the techniques in this section.

9.1.3   *User-based recommenders*

Mahout doesn't have a way to run user-based recommenders in MapReduce because the user-based recommender is only designed to work within a single JVM. Because user-based recommenders aren't relevant for this book, we'll skip them and move on to look at item-based recommenders. If you're curious about user-based recommenders, the book *Mahout in Action*, by Owen et al., covers them in detail.

9.1.4   *Item-based recommenders*

Item-based recommenders calculate recommendations based on items, and not users. The goal is the same as that of user-based recommenders—recommend items that the user will hopefully be interested in. But rather than look at similarities between users, item-based recommenders look at similarities between items. Because the item rating is the only data point to go by, this combined with what examining all items that all users rate are the data points used to make the item predictions.

Because item similarities tend to be less volatile than user similarities, they lend themselves more to precomputation, which can speed up the recommender operation. The item-based recommender in Mahout supports a distributed execution model, so that it can be computed using MapReduce. The distributed recommender will be the focus of this section.

Let's use figure 9.4 to walk through a simple example of item recommendation.

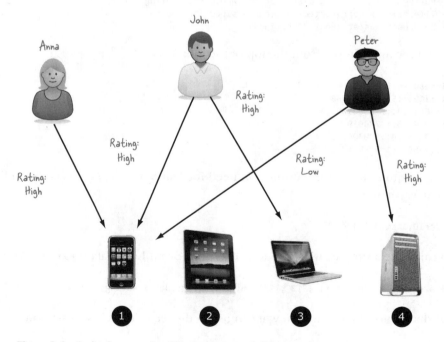

Figure 9.4   A simple example of item recommendation

To recommend items for Anna, item recommendation looks at other items that co-occur with items Anna reviews (items 3 and 4), determines their similarity (based on reviewer ratings), and then ranks them by multiplying Anna's rating with the similarity rating for other items. In this example, item 3 would have a higher predicted value than 4, because John rated 1 and 3 as high, but Peter rated 1 as low.

Let's now look at how you can get the distributed item-based recommender working.

TECHNIQUE 61　**Item-based recommenders using movie ratings**

How would you use the GroupLens movie rating dataset to recommend movies for three users in the dataset using MapReduce?

Problem

You have a large number of user item preferences and you want to recommend additional items to users in a scalable fashion.

Solution

Use Mahout's MapReduce item-based recommender in combination with the GroupLens data to make movie recommendations. Mahout's item recommender uses 10 MapReduce jobs to perform this recommendation, which perform functions such as data preparation, similarity co-occurrence calculations, and calculating the final recommendations.

Discussion

The distributed item-based recommender requires two inputs: the recommendations file and a file of user IDs for which item recommendations will be generated. Let's go ahead and create the file of user IDs (you'll select the first three IDs from the ratings file), and then push both files into HDFS:

```
$ cat > user-ids.txt << EOF
1
2
3
EOF

$ hadoop fs -put user-ids.txt ratings.csv .
```

You're now ready to run the item-based recommender:

```
$ export MAHOUT_HOME=<path-to-your-mahout-directory>
$ export HADOOP_HOME=<path-to-your-hadoop-directory>
$ $MAHOUT_HOME/bin/mahout   \
    recommenditembased \
     -Dmapred.reduce.tasks=10 \
    --similarityClassname SIMILARITY_PEARSON_CORRELATION \
    --input ratings.csv \
    --output item-rec-output \
    --tempDir item-rec-tmp \
    --usersFile user-ids.txt
```

When the job completes you can view the output in HDFS. The output format consists of the user ID, followed by a comma-separated list of item IDs and their related scores:

```
$ hadoop fs -cat item-rec-output/part*
1    [1566:5.0,1036:5.0,1033:5.0,1032:5.0,1031:5.0,1030:5.0,3107:5.0,
     3114:5.0,1026:5.0,1025:5.0]
2    [2739:5.0,3811:5.0,3916:5.0,2:5.0,10:5.0,11:5.0,16:5.0,3793:5.0,
     3791:5.0,3789:5.0]
3    [1037:5.0,1036:5.0,2518:5.0,3175:5.0,3108:5.0,10:5.0,1028:5.0,
     3104:5.0,1025:5.0,1019:5.0]
```

> ### HADOOP_HOME **environment variable**
>
> You must export the HADOOP_HOME environment variable to refer to the location of your local install of Hadoop (/usr/lib/hadoop for CDH-packaged installations, and /usr/local/hadoop for installations that followed the tarball instructions in appendix A). Mahout uses this variable to discover your Hadoop cluster settings. If this step is omitted, Mahout will use the local filesystem for storage, and run MapReduce jobs on your client host.

Summary

Running the distributed item-based recommender resulted in ten MapReduce jobs being executed. The jobs and a quick description of them can be seen in figure 9.5.

The distributed implementation of an item-based recommender creates a co-occurrence matrix to associate similar items together. It does this by combining items with similar ratings from each user, and then counting the number of times that each pair of items was rated by all the users. It then predicts the ratings for unknown items by multiplying the users' ratings for an item with all the item's co-occurrences, and then sorts all these item predictions and retains the top K as recommendations.

So far you've been focused on the item-based recommender where items are entities such as movies or products. You could also have used this approach to recommend users. Existing user relationships could be modeled by replacing item IDs with user IDs. The rating value itself could then become a constant, or if desired you could also use it to model the level of friendship (for example, if two users commonly interact their rating could be higher than those that don't).

Mahout also comes with another distributed item-based recommender called the *slope-one recommender*, which is a simpler recommender that just requires two MapReduce jobs. It doesn't use a similarity algorithm to measure the similarity of items, and instead performs a simple average of the difference between rating values. Take a look at the SlopeOneAverageDiffsJob class if you're interested in more details.

In this section you learned how user-based and item-based recommenders work, and you looked in detail at how a MapReduce item-based recommender could be

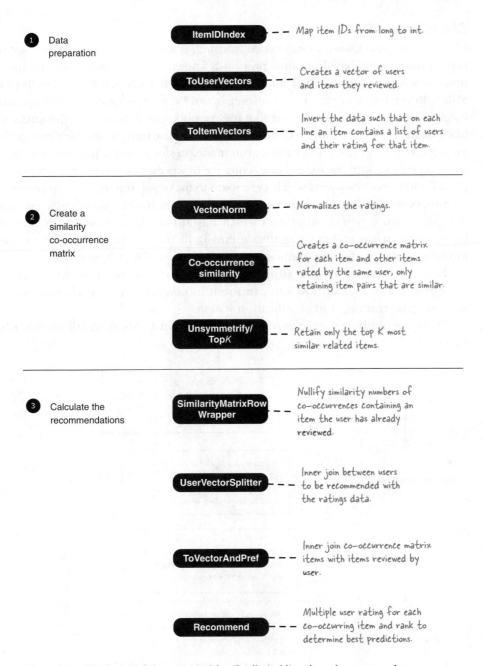

Figure 9.5 MapReduce jobs executed for distributed item-based recommender

used to make movie recommendations. You'll now move into the second section in a three-part sections on predictive analytics, and look at how you can use classification to make movie predictions.

9.2 *Classification*

Classification, also known as supervised learning, is a fancy term for a system that makes predictions on data based on some previously known data. As humans we do this all the time—when you see an email titled "REQUEST FOR URGENT BUSINESS RELATION-SHIP," do you eagerly open it? The answer is, no. Prior experience has told you that the combination of words, and the fact that they're uppercase, means that this email is most likely spam. This is an example of human supervised learning, where your current behavior is a result of previous observations you made on similar data. You may not have seen an email subject with the exact same sequence of words, but you've seen enough examples of similar email subjects which were spam to make you immediately suspicious.

Supervised learning works in exactly the same way. In the case of email spam detection, you train a system using data which has already been labeled (or marked) as being either spam or ham (legitimate email) to build a model, and then use that model to make predictions about emails that the system hasn't seen before.

In this section we'll look at one of the simpler supervised learning algorithms, naïve Bayes, and look at how you can use it in conjunction with Hadoop to build a scalable spam training and classification system.

There are multiple steps involved in building such a system, which are described in figure 9.6.

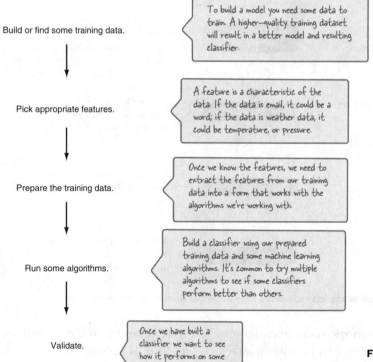

Build or find some training data.

> To build a model you need some data to train. A higher-quality training dataset will result in a better model and resulting classifier.

Pick appropriate features.

> A feature is a characteristic of the data. If the data is email, it could be a word; if the data is weather data, it could be temperature, or pressure.

Prepare the training data.

> Once we know the features, we need to extract the features from our training data into a form that works with the algorithms we're working with.

Run some algorithms.

> Build a classifier using our prepared training data and some machine learning algorithms. It's common to try multiple algorithms to see if some classifiers perform better than others.

Validate.

> Once we have built a classifier we want to see how it performs on some test data.

Figure 9.6   The steps involved in building a supervised learning model

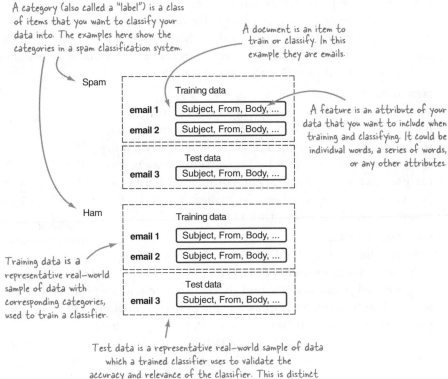

A category (also called a "label") is a class of items that you want to classify your data into. The examples here show the categories in a spam classification system.

A document is an item to train or classify. In this example they are emails.

A feature is an attribute of your data that you want to include when training and classifying. It could be individual words, a series of words, or any other attributes.

Training data is a representative real-world sample of data with corresponding categories, used to train a classifier.

Test data is a representative real-world sample of data which a trained classifier uses to validate the accuracy and relevance of the classifier. This is distinct from the data used to train the classifier.

Figure 9.7 Classification term definitions

Some of the terms you just saw will be used throughout this section, and are defined in figure 9.7 using email spam classification as an example.

Two additional terms also need to be defined:

- *Training*—The process by which categorized documents are used to build a model, which can be used by a classifier to categorized unseen documents.
- *Classifier*—A classifier uses a model extracted from the training data to make predictions about unseen documents or datasets.

Before we dive into the Hadoop side of supervised learning, we'll walk through building a handmade classifier using a simple training dataset to get an idea of the overall process.

9.2.1 Writing a homemade naïve Bayesian classifier

We just identified the five steps it takes to build a classifier. You'll apply these five steps to write your own naïve Bayes spam classifier. To classify emails, a naïve Bayes classifier examines words that occur in emails and checks to see if they're more likely to occur in spam or ham categories. If a word is used frequently in an email, and the spam category has also observed a high frequency of that word (and the ham category has seen the word less frequently), then the word is deemed to be more spam than ham. Bayes theorem comes into play once each word has had a spam and ham probability calculated, and combines them together to form the overall email probability of ham or spam.

Your first task is to find some data to train your classifier.

FINDING SOME TRAINING DATA

The two hardest parts of building a classifier happen to be the first two steps. When it comes to training data, your classifier is only as good as the data used to train it. Lucky for you there are some high-quality datasets you can use when working with spam. For now we'll just conjure up a few example subject lines which you'll use for training data, which you can see in figure 9.8.

Label	Email subject
Ham	windyhill roofing estimate
Ham	quick hadoop meetup
Spam	cheap quick xanax
Spam	quick easy money

Figure 9.8   A small training dataset for spam

SELECTING FEATURES

After you have a set of training data that you're happy with, you can start examining that data for attributes that you want to use for training. This is called *feature selection*, and there's a whole science around this one topic. The goal of feature selection is to pick features that you believe will increase the ability of your classifier to separate data between the different categories.

When building an email classifier, there are several attributes within an email that can be used as features, such as the contents of the subject line, other email header data points, and the body of the email. As an example, the date the email was sent doesn't lend itself to being a feature because there's nothing about the date that can be used to separate ham from spam. But the email subject and body can definitely contain text that can be used to help identify spam.

The text in the email subject and body are useful, but should all the words be used as features? The short answer is, no. You don't want words that commonly appear in the English language (referred to in text mining circles as *stopwords*) to be used as features because they'll appear in every single email. Similarly, you don't want words that are rare and only appear in a handful of emails because they won't help with classification, either.

For now let's assume that your data only consists of the email subject line.

DATA PREPARATION

Now that you know what features you're interested in, you need to prepare the data for training. You're working with the naïve Bayes classifier, which can work with data in text form, so you don't need to manipulate or transform your data. Therefore, all you need to do is feed your training data to your classifier:

```
Classifier c = new Classifier();

c.train("ham windyhill roofing estimate");
c.train("ham quick hadoop meetup");
c.train("spam cheap quick xanax");
c.train("spam quick easy money");
```

TRAINING A CLASSIFIER

For naïve Bayes, training is a matter of reading in the documents for each category, and for each document extracting the words and calculating for each word the probability of that word in the category. To start with you need to split up the words for the training document and extract the category and the associated words:

```java
public static class Classifier {
  Map<String, Category> categories = new HashMap<String, Category>();

  public void train(String document) {
    String[] parts = StringUtils.split(document);    ◄──── Tokenize the string into words.

    String category = parts[0];    ◄──── The first token is the category name.

    List<String> words = Arrays.asList(    ◄──── The rest of the tokens are words
        Arrays.copyOfRange(parts, 1, parts.length));         from the email subject line.
    Category cat = categories.get(category);
    if (cat == null) {
      cat = new Category(category);
      categories.put(category, cat);
    }
    cat.train(words);    ◄──── Tell the Category instance to train using the words.

    for (Category c : categories.values()) {
      c.updateProbability(numDocuments);    ◄──── Tell all the categories to recalculate
    }                                                  their probabilities.
  }
}
```

Next you need to model the notion of a category, and keep track of the words in the category, the number of times you saw the word in the category, and the number of documents that were used to train the category:

```java
public static class Category {
  String label;
  int numDocuments;
  double categoryProbability;
  Map<String, MutableInt> features =
      new HashMap<String, MutableInt>();

  void train(List<String> words) {
    numDocuments++;    ◄──── Keep a count of the number of
    for (String word : words) {         documents used to train this category.
      MutableInt i = features.get(word);
      if (i == null) {
        i = new MutableInt(0);
        features.put(word, i);
      }
      i.increment();    ◄──── Keep a count of the number of times
    }                         you've seen a word in this category.
  }

  void updateProbability(int totalDocuments) {              Calculate the probability that a
    categoryProbability = (double) numDocuments /    ◄──── randomly selected document will
        (double) totalDocuments;                     be in this category. This is used later as
  }                                                      part of the classification process.
}
```

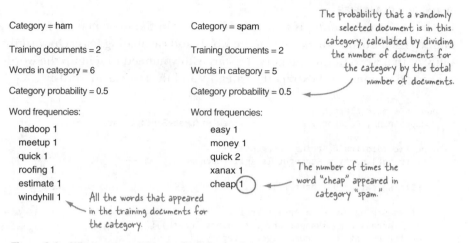

Figure 9.9   What your model looks like after training

After you've trained your classifier with the four documents, your classifier contains all the data it needs for classification. Figure 9.9 shows the data that you have in your classifier after you've finished training.

RUNNING A CLASSIFIER

You've built a model of the training data and you're now ready to use it to classify some new emails. There are two parts to your naïve Bayes classifier: first you need to extract the words from the email and calculate the probability that the words exist in each category. Then you multiply these probabilities to form the overall probability for each category. Figure 9.10 shows how Bayes' theorem is used in text classification.

When you see a new email subject, you need to calculate the probability of each word being in a category. The probability is expressed numerically between 0 and 1, where 1 indicates a probability of 100 percent. To calculate this number, you take the number of times a word appears in the category and divide it by the total number of documents for the category. The following code shows this probability being calculated for a word in a specific category:

```
public static class Category {
  int numDocuments;
  Map<String, MutableInt> features =
      new HashMap<String, MutableInt>();

  double weightedProbability(String word) {
    MutableInt i = features.get(word);
return (i == null ? 0.1 : (i.doubleValue() /
        (double) numDocuments));
  }
  ...
}
```

Take the example of the word *quick*: in the spam category it appeared twice, and there were two documents used to train the spam category, so the probability is (2/2) = 1.

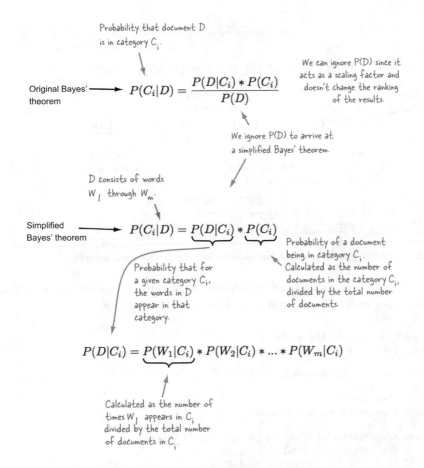

Probability that document D
is in category C_i.

Original Bayes'
theorem $\longrightarrow$ $P(C_i|D) = \dfrac{P(D|C_i) * P(C_i)}{P(D)}$

We can ignore P(D) since it
acts as a scaling factor and
doesn't change the ranking
of the results.

We ignore P(D) to arrive at
a simplified Bayes' theorem.

D consists of words
W_1 through W_m.

Simplified $\longrightarrow$ $P(C_i|D) = \underbrace{P(D|C_i)} * \underbrace{P(C_i)}$
Bayes' theorem

Probability that for
a given category C_i,
the words in D
appear in that
category.

Probability of a document
being in category C_i.
Calculated as the number of
documents in the category C_i,
divided by the total number
of documents.

$$P(D|C_i) = \underbrace{P(W_1|C_i)} * P(W_2|C_i) * \ldots * P(W_m|C_i)$$

Calculated as the number of
times W_1 appears in C_i
divided by the total number
of documents in C_i.

Figure 9.10   Bayes' theorem and how it applies to text classification

The same word appeared once in the ham category, so its probability in the ham category is (1/2) = 0.5. These values will be used as the value of P(W|C) in the Bayes formula, which you'll see shortly.

So you have the probability that each individual word is in a category, but how do you calculate the probability of the overall document being in a category? Bayes comes to the rescue with a theorem into which you can plug your word probabilities, as you see in figure 9.10.

Figure 9.11 shows how you would use your naïve Bayes classifier to calculate probabilities of membership to spam and ham categories.

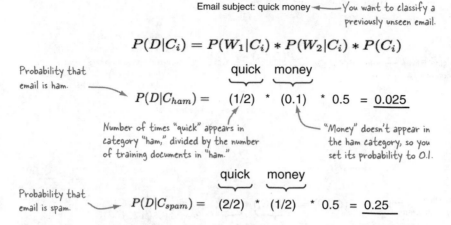

Figure 9.11   **Calculating spam and ham probabilities for an example email subject**

The following code calculates the probability of the input document belonging to each of the categories using the naïve Bayes formula you just saw:

```
public void classify(String words) {
  String[] parts = StringUtils.split(words);

  for (Category c : categories.values()) {
    double p = 1.0;
    for (String word : parts) {
      p *= c.weightedProbability(word);
    }
    System.out.println("Probability of document '" + words +
        "' for category '" + c.label +
        "' is " + (p * c.categoryProbability));
  }
}
```

If you run your code, you'll see the same values that you calculated by hand earlier:

```
$ bin/run.sh com.manning.hip.ch9.HomegrownNBClassifier
Category = ham, numDocs = 2, categoryProbability = 0.5
  hadoop 1
  meetup 1
  quick 1
  roofing 1
  estimate 1
  windyhill 1
Category = spam, numDocs = 2, categoryProbability = 0.5
  easy 1
  money 1
  quick 2
  xanax 1
  cheap 1

Probability of document 'quick money' for category 'ham' is 0.025
Probability of document 'quick money' for category 'spam' is 0.25
```

In real life your classifier wouldn't work because of the small amount of training documents. You'd ideally want a large and equal number of spam and ham documents for training purposes. Let's move on to look at how you'd do that with Mahout.

9.2.2 A scalable spam detection classification system

Classification in Mahout can be executed sequentially or via MapReduce. All of the Mahout supervised learning algorithms can be executed in MapReduce, but only a few of them have parallel execution models. Naïve Bayes is one of them.[2]

TECHNIQUE 62 **Using Mahout to train and test a spam classifier**

How would you train a spam classifier using MapReduce and see how well it performs on unseen emails?

Problem

You have a large spam corpus and you want to build a spam classifier.

Solution

Use Mahout's MapReduce naïve Bayes classifier on the Spam Assassin corpus to train a model, and then test its effectiveness on unseen emails.

Discussion

For this technique you'll use the SpamAssassin corpus, which can be downloaded from http://spamassassin.apache.org/publiccorpus/. You'll use this corpus both to train your classifier and to test it to see how well it performs at detecting spam. Your first step is to download and extract the spam and ham datasets:

```
$ cd $MAHOUT_HOME
$ mkdir -p corpus/spam-assassin          Create a directory for your corpus.
$ cd corpus/spam-assassin          Download the spam and ham corpora.
$ curl -O \
  http://spamassassin.apache.org/publiccorpus/20021010_spam.tar.bz2
$ curl -O \
  http://spamassassin.apache.org/publiccorpus/20021010_easy_ham.tar.bz2

$ tar xjf 20021010_spam.tar.bz2          Extract the downloaded tarballs.
$ tar xjf 20021010_easy_ham.tar.bz2

$ ls -1 spam/* | wc -l          Each email is contained in a
501                             separate file—list the number of
$ ls -1 easy_ham/* | wc -l      emails that are spam and ham.
2551
```

You now need to separate the corpus into a testing set and training set. The training set will be used to build the classifier model, and the testing set will be classified with

---

[2] Mahout uses an implementation of naïve Bayes based on the paper "Tackling the Poor Assumptions of Naïve Bayes Text Classifiers"; see http://people.csail.mit.edu/jrennie/papers/icml03-nb.pdf.

the model to gauge the accuracy of the model. In creating the training corpus, you're careful to use the same number of spam and ham emails, which will help with the performance of your classifier:

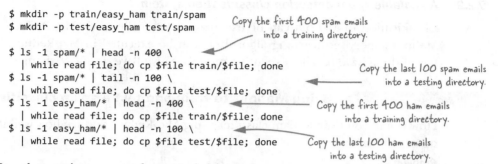

```
$ mkdir -p train/easy_ham train/spam
$ mkdir -p test/easy_ham test/spam

$ ls -1 spam/* | head -n 400 \
  | while read file; do cp $file train/$file; done
$ ls -1 spam/* | tail -n 100 \
  | while read file; do cp $file test/$file; done
$ ls -1 easy_ham/* | head -n 400 \
  | while read file; do cp $file train/$file; done
$ ls -1 easy_ham/* | head -n 100 \
  | while read file; do cp $file test/$file; done
```

Copy the first 400 spam emails into a training directory.

Copy the last 100 spam emails into a testing directory.

Copy the first 400 ham emails into a training directory.

Copy the last 100 ham emails into a testing directory.

Now that you've separated your training set from your test set, you need to convert it into a form that the training code can work with. The data as it stands right now consists of a file for each email, and the format you want to convert it into contains an email (or document) per line, with the category name as the first token in the line. Mahout has a built-in tool that can perform that conversion for you, which you'll run on both the training and test set. After you're done, copy the data into HDFS:

```
$ export HADOOP_HOME=/usr/lib/hadoop

$ $MAHOUT_HOME/bin/mahout prepare20newsgroups \
  -p train/ \
  -o train_mahout/        \
  -a org.apache.mahout.vectorizer.DefaultAnalyzer  \
  -c UTF-8

$ $MAHOUT_HOME/bin/mahout prepare20newsgroups \
  -p test/ \
  -o test_mahout/        \
  -a org.apache.mahout.vectorizer.DefaultAnalyzer  \
  -c UTF-8

$ hadoop fs -put train_mahout  test_mahout
```

You must export HADOOP_HOME so that the prepped data is stored in HDFS. If you don't do this, the data will be written to the local filesystem.

Convert the training data into a form which will work when training the classifier.

Convert the test data into the same form as the training data, which also works with the classifier.

Copy the prepared data into HDFS in preparation for training and testing.

Now that your data is in a form that can be used by the training tool, you can run that tool to generate the model:

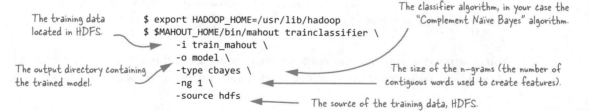

The training data located in HDFS.

The output directory containing the trained model.

```
$ export HADOOP_HOME=/usr/lib/hadoop
$ $MAHOUT_HOME/bin/mahout trainclassifier \
    -i train_mahout \
    -o model \
    -type cbayes \
    -ng 1 \
    -source hdfs
```

The classifier algorithm, in your case the "Complement Naïve Bayes" algorithm.

The size of the n-grams (the number of contiguous words used to create features).

The source of the training data, HDFS.

When the training has completed it persists the model into several subdirectories under the model directory in HDFS. You can now run the classifier on your test data by specifying the location of your model:

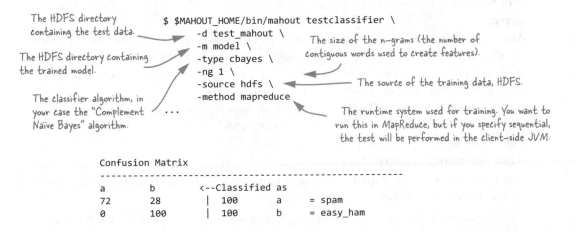

The HDFS directory containing the test data.

The HDFS directory containing the trained model.

The classifier algorithm, in your case the "Complement Naïve Bayes" algorithm.

```
$ $MAHOUT_HOME/bin/mahout testclassifier \
  -d test_mahout \
  -m model \
  -type cbayes \
  -ng 1 \
  -source hdfs \
  -method mapreduce
  ...
```

The size of the n-grams (the number of contiguous words used to create features).

The source of the training data, HDFS.

The runtime system used for training. You want to run this in MapReduce, but if you specify sequential, the test will be performed in the client-side JVM.

```
Confusion Matrix
-------------------------------------------------------
a       b       <--Classified as
72      28      |  100      a       = spam
0       100     |  100      b       = easy_ham
```

The output of the `testclassifier` command shows something called a *confusion matrix*, which is telling you that the classifier correctly identified 72 spam emails as being spam, and incorrectly identified 28 spam emails as ham. Your classifier also was able to be 100 percent accurate at classifying ham emails.

Summary

In this technique we looked at how we could use Mahout to train and test a spam classifier—let's look at them in more detail.

TRAINING

The scalability that can be achieved with training in Mahout comes at a high cost, as highlighted in figure 9.12, which shows all the MapReduce jobs that must execute to train the model.

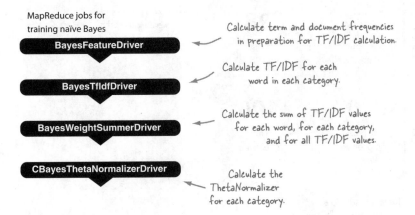

MapReduce jobs for training naïve Bayes

BayesFeatureDriver — Calculate term and document frequencies in preparation for TF/IDF calculation.

BayesTfIdfDriver — Calculate TF/IDF for each word in each category.

BayesWeightSummerDriver — Calculate the sum of TF/IDF values for each word, for each category, and for all TF/IDF values.

CBayesThetaNormalizerDriver — Calculate the ThetaNormalizer for each category.

Figure 9.12   Jobs executed during training of naïve Bayes classifier

When training the model, you can play with the -ng argument, which specifies the size of the n-grams extracted from the training data. You ran with it set to 1, which means every word was an independent feature, but the overall accuracy of the classifier can improve with larger values.

TESTING

When you completed testing your classifier, you were presented with something called a *confusion matrix*. A confusion matrix is used to visualize the performance of your classifier, and tells you how well your model works. Let's look at the confusion matrix and try and make head or tail of the output (see figure 9.13).

The MapReduce naïve Bayes training comes into its own when you're working with large training sets (hundreds of thousands and more) which start hitting the memory limits of a single host.

ONLINE AND OFFLINE CLASSIFICATION

There are two options available to use when using your classifier to classify documents—online and offline:

- In online mode you're responding to a classification request in real time, such as a backend REST API. In this case you can use the Mahout BayesAlgorithm and InMemoryBayesDatastore to load the model from the filesystem and perform inline classification.

- Offline mode would be suited to cases where you want to classify millions of documents. In this situation you'd write a MapReduce job that performed a function similar to Mahout's testing code. You should look at the BayesClassifierDriver class and use the code there to write your own MapReduce classifier.

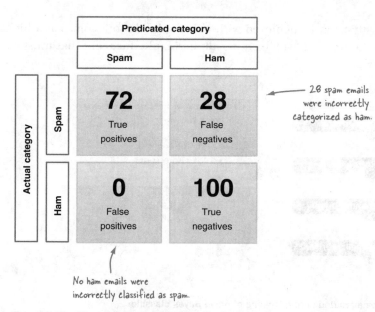

Figure 9.13 The confusion matrix from the test results

9.2.3 Additional classification algorithms

Mahout contains other classification algorithms (in various stages of completion), which are outlined in table 9.1.

For more details on these algorithms take a peek at https://cwiki.apache.org/MAHOUT/algorithms.html.

Your final predictive analytics technique is a look at clustering, a series of algorithms whose goal is to group data together and help you make new discoveries about your data.

Table 9.1 Mahout classification algorithms

Algorithm	Description
Logistic regression	Logistic regression is a model used for prediction of the probability of occurrence of an event. It makes use of several predictor variables that may be either numerical or categories.
Support Vector Machines	As with naïve Bayes, Support Vector Machines (or SVMs) can be used to solve the task of assigning objects to classes. But the way this task is solved is completely different to the setting in naïve Bayes.
Neural Network	Neural Networks are a means for classifying multidimensional objects.
Hidden Markov Models	Hidden Markov Models are used in multiple areas of machine learning, such as speech recognition, handwritten letter recognition, or natural language processing.

9.3 Clustering with K-means

In the previous section we looked at supervised learning, where a classifier is built with some data which was previously categorized. Clustering is an example of an unsupervised learning technique, where no such categorized data is used to build the model. Clustering is different from classification and recommenders: the goal of classification and recommenders is to make predictions about some data, such as whether or not a web page is in a sports category, or whether a user is likely to enjoy a book they've not read before. The goal of clustering is to partition data into a number of clusters so that data in each cluster is more similar to each other than to data in other clusters.

To help you understand clustering, figure 9.14 shows an example of data which you can see is tightly grouped into three distinct clusters. The goal of clustering is to identify these clusters so that you can make new discoveries about your data. In this figure it's obvious that these clusters exist, but in reality your data isn't likely to be so well separated, and this is where clustering can help you find groupings of data leading to previously unknown observations.

Clustering has many applications in fields such as marketing, to find groups of customers with similar behaviors, and biology, to classify plants and animals, and so on.

Mahout has a number of clustering algorithms, but we'll look at K-means, one of the simpler algorithms.

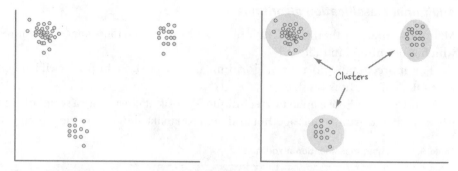

Figure 9.14   Example of how a clustering algorithm would partition data

9.3.1   *A gentle introduction*

K-means is the oldest and simplest clustering algorithm. With K-means you tell the K-means algorithm ahead of time how many clusters you're looking for (the *K* in K-means). The K-means process starts with the initial placement of the *K* cluster centroids. The initial K centroids can either be randomly located or specifically placed. Randomly located centroids will likely give different results, and therefore the recommendation is that centroids are located as far away from each other as possible.

Once the initial centroids have been placed, K-means follows an iterative algorithm whereby each data point is associated to the nearest cluster centroid, and then the cluster centroids are repositioned relative to all the data points. This process repeats until such a time as the cluster centroids don't move, at which time the clusters are considered to have converged.

To determine the distances between data points and the cluster centroids, clustering supports most of the similarity metrics that you saw in the recommenders section, such as Euclidean distance, Tanimoto, and Manhattan.

A high-level algorithm for K-means is as follows:

1. Model the objects that you want to cluster into *N* dimensions.
2. Place the *K* centroids into the space represented by the objects.
3. Using a distance metric, assign each object to the centroid that is closest to it.
4. Recalculate the position of the *K* centroids.
5. Repeat steps 3 and 4 until either (a) the *K* centroids don't move/converge beyond a certain threshold, or (b) the maximum number of iterations has been reached.

Figure 9.15 shows this algorithm in play with a two-dimensional space.

Now that you understand the basics of K-means, let's look at how you can use it in Mahout.

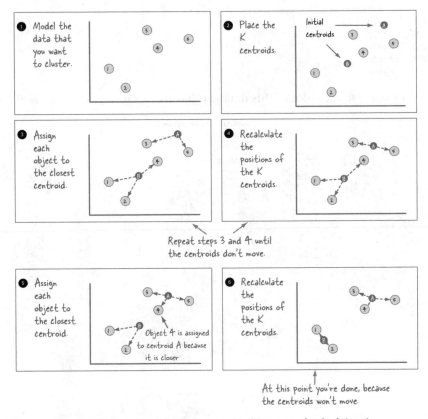

Figure 9.15   A walk-through of the K-means algorithm on a simple dataset

9.3.2   *Parallel K-means*

As with many algorithms in Mahout, K-means also has both sequential (in-memory) and parallel (MapReduce) implementations. In this section we'll look at the parallel implementation of K-means.

TECHNIQUE 63   **K-means with a synthetic 2D dataset**

How would you execute parallel K-means on a simulated dataset from http:// cs.joensuu.fi/sipu/datasets/, which has 3,000 data points containing 20 clusters?

Problem

You want to detect clusters using K-means.

Solution

Use Mahout's MapReduce K-means algorithm to cluster data together and observe the importance of the placement of the initial centroids.

Discussion

The synthetic data is a series of two-dimensional data points that represent twenty synthetic clusters:

```
$ head -n 5 test-data/ch9/synthetic.txt
54620    43523
52694    42750
53253    43024
54925    42624
54973    43980
```

If you produce a scatter plot of this data you'll see output similar to figure 9.16.[3]

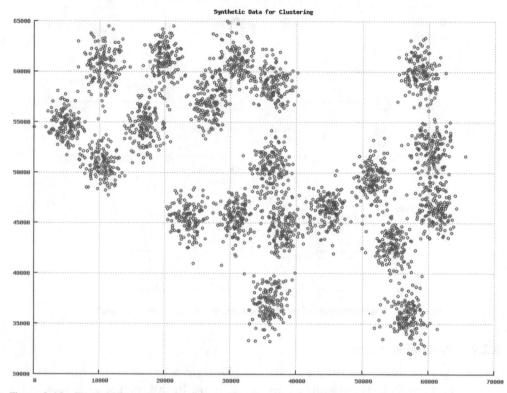

Figure 9.16   The 3,000 synthetic 2D data points shown in a scatter plot

You need to convert the synthetic 2D data into the SequenceFile format required by Mahout for clustering:

```
public static void write(File inputFile, Path outputPath)
    throws IOException {
  Configuration conf = new Configuration();
  FileSystem fs = FileSystem.get(conf);

  SequenceFile.Writer writer =
      SequenceFile.createWriter(fs, conf, outputPath,
        NullWritable.class,
        VectorWritable.class,
```

The SequenceFile key is ignored by the algorithm. In nonsynthetic use this would be used to store an identifier for the record.

The value is a VectorWritable, which is a Mahout type.

---

[3] **GitHub source**—https://github.com/alexholmes/hadoop-book/tree/master/src/main/java/com/manning/hip/ch9/Synthetic2DClusteringPrep.java

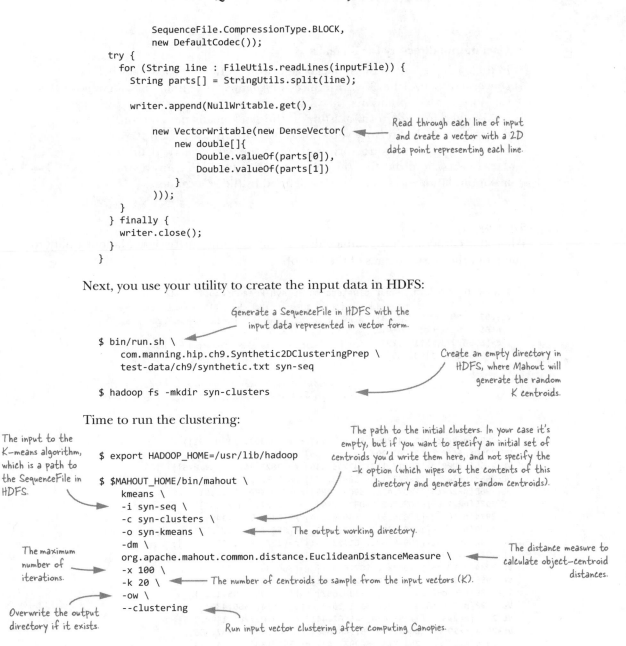

```
                SequenceFile.CompressionType.BLOCK,
                new DefaultCodec());
    try {
      for (String line : FileUtils.readLines(inputFile)) {
        String parts[] = StringUtils.split(line);

        writer.append(NullWritable.get(),

            new VectorWritable(new DenseVector(
                new double[]{
                    Double.valueOf(parts[0]),
                    Double.valueOf(parts[1])
                }
            )));
      }
    } finally {
      writer.close();
    }
}
```

Read through each line of input and create a vector with a 2D data point representing each line.

Next, you use your utility to create the input data in HDFS:

Generate a SequenceFile in HDFS with the input data represented in vector form.

```
$ bin/run.sh \
    com.manning.hip.ch9.Synthetic2DClusteringPrep \
    test-data/ch9/synthetic.txt syn-seq

$ hadoop fs -mkdir syn-clusters
```

Create an empty directory in HDFS, where Mahout will generate the random K centroids.

Time to run the clustering:

The input to the K-means algorithm, which is a path to the SequenceFile in HDFS.

The path to the initial clusters. In your case it's empty, but if you want to specify an initial set of centroids you'd write them here, and not specify the −k option (which wipes out the contents of this directory and generates random centroids).

```
$ export HADOOP_HOME=/usr/lib/hadoop

$ $MAHOUT_HOME/bin/mahout \
    kmeans \
    -i syn-seq \
    -c syn-clusters \
    -o syn-kmeans \
    -dm \
    org.apache.mahout.common.distance.EuclideanDistanceMeasure \
    -x 100 \
    -k 20 \
    -ow \
    --clustering
```

The output working directory.

The distance measure to calculate object–centroid distances.

The number of centroids to sample from the input vectors (K).

The maximum number of iterations.

Overwrite the output directory if it exists.

Run input vector clustering after computing Canopies.

This will start an iterative sequence of MapReduce jobs until such a time as the clusters converge, or you hit the maximum number of iterations. When the clustering has completed there should be a number of directories in HDFS that contain output for each of the MapReduce iterations.

Final output directory for K-means

In the example below, the K-means algorithm iterated for 22 times before it converged, hence the *22* in the directory name. The number of iterations can vary across executions (because initial centroids are randomly calculated); therefore, perform a listing in the syn-kmeans directory in HDFS to determine which directory you should use with the mahout clusterdump command (it will be the directory containing the word *final*). If this directory doesn't exist, it means that the algorithm wasn't able to converge before the maximum number of iterations, as defined by the -x argument.

Summary

When the clustering has completed, you can use the clusterdump Mahout utility to dump out the cluster details of the last job:

```
$ $MAHOUT_HOME/bin/mahout clusterdump -s syn-kmeans/clusters-22-final
```

clusterdump writes out a line for each cluster. VL indicates that the cluster has converged, and CL means that the cluster hasn't converged.

```
VL-2976{
  n=65
  c=[8906.923, 51193.292]
  r=[955.286, 1163.688]
}
```

The cluster centroid.

The number of data points connected to this cluster, which for this cluster is 65.

The radius of the cluster, expressed as a standard deviation of the distance from the centroid to all 65 data points in the cluster.

```
VL-2997{n=88 c=[11394.705, 50557.114] r=[920.032, 1179.291]}
VL-2950{n=464 c=[39502.394, 42808.983] r=[4022.406, 4273.647]}
VL-2956{n=900 c=[57117.122, 47795.646] r=[3623.267, 7669.076]}
VL-2963{n=307 c=[28842.176, 58910.573] r=[2532.197, 2463.770]}
VL-2968{n=24 c=[12087.458, 59659.125] r=[610.980, 587.461]}
VL-2973{n=21 c=[9767.762, 60524.619] r=[334.271, 680.851]}
VL-2974{n=149 c=[17056.611, 54574.094] r=[1424.306, 1499.089]}
VL-2979{n=15 c=[13094.200, 61833.467] r=[654.127, 769.270]}
VL-2982{n=152 c=[19948.691, 61123.151] r=[1272.827, 1526.470]}
VL-2983{n=282 c=[36355.816, 54751.617] r=[1492.798, 4144.325]}
VL-2984{n=13 c=[8319.385, 58726.923] r=[866.362, 745.068]}
VL-2985{n=13 c=[10221.231, 62308.692] r=[499.819, 494.718]}
VL-2986{n=6 c=[11515.167, 63330.667] r=[573.996, 795.132]}
VL-2990{n=6 c=[8507.333, 63171.167] r=[862.534, 506.489]}
VL-2993{n=295 c=[27153.434, 45502.441] r=[3910.728, 1400.395]}
VL-2994{n=19 c=[10641.105, 57988.000] r=[506.490, 1047.906]}
VL-2995{n=14 c=[8254.714, 60997.643] r=[552.130, 481.433]}
VL-2998{n=145 c=[4732.103, 54700.310] r=[1308.754, 1182.706]}
VL-2999{n=22 c=[10977.409, 61125.545] r=[513.230, 369.197]}
```

If you superimpose these clusters on top of the original scatterplot, you can see how well the algorithm worked. Note that the clusters will vary based on the initial centroids, so your results will differ from those presented here (see figure 9.17).

Mahout didn't do a great job of picking initial random cluster locations (denoted with gray crosses).

Because of the initial poor cluster locations, only a handful of them account for the majority of the actual clusters.

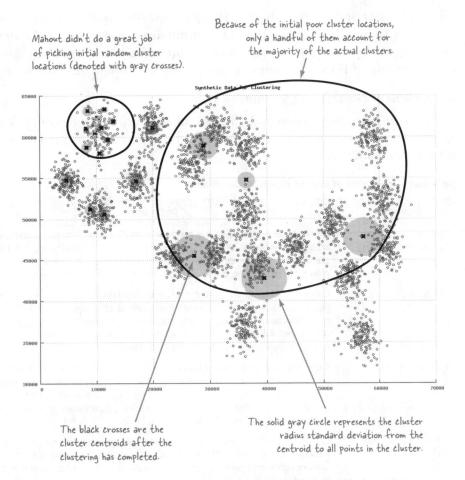

The black crosses are the cluster centroids after the clustering has completed.

The solid gray circle represents the cluster radius standard deviation from the centroid to all points in the cluster.

Figure 9.17 The initial and ending cluster centroids plotted against the input data

Clustering is sensitive to the initial locations of the centroids; if they had been more randomly distributed, the clustering algorithm would have identified more of the clusters.

In this simplified example, you only worked with data in two dimensions, which is easy to visualize and vectorize. Working in two dimensions means that you can only work with two features, because each dimension represents a single feature. If you want to work with *n* features, you need *n* dimensions, which the Mahout Vector classes all support. An example would be working with text, where each unique word is considered a separate feature, and therefore a dimension.

9.3.3   *K-means and text*

Because K-means works with vectorized data, if you want to use K-means with text data (such as clustering on the Reuters news collection) you need to vectorize that data prior to using it with Mahout. How you do this is outside of the scope of this book, but you can look at and execute the $MAHOUT_HOME/examples/bin/build-reuters.sh (this script is bundled with the Mahout distribution), which takes the Reuters news collection, vectorizes it and then runs K-means over that data. *Mahout in Action* (Owen et al., Manning, 2011) also contains a section that goes through this exercise in detail.

9.3.4 *Other Mahout clustering algorithms*

Mahout contains other clustering algorithms, some of which can be seen in table 9.2. A complete list can be viewed at https://cwiki.apache.org/confluence/display/MAHOUT/Algorithms.

Table 9.2   An overview of Mahout clustering algorithms

Algorithm	Description
Hierarchical clustering/ Top Down clustering	Hierarchical clustering is the process or finding bigger clusters, and also the smaller clusters inside the bigger clusters. Top Down clustering is a type of hierarchical clustering. It tries to find bigger clusters first and then does fine-grained clustering on these clusters—hence the name *Top Down*.
Canopy clustering	Canopy clustering is a simple, fast, and surprisingly accurate method for grouping objects into clusters. Canopy clustering is often used as an initial step in more rigorous clustering techniques, such as K-means clustering. By starting with an initial clustering, the number of more expensive distance measurements can be significantly reduced by ignoring points outside of the initial canopies.
Fuzzy K-means	Fuzzy K-means (also called Fuzzy C-means) is an extension of K-means, the popular simple clustering technique. While K-means discovers hard clusters (a point belong to only one cluster), Fuzzy K-means is a more statistically formalized method and discovers soft clusters where a particular point can belong to more than one cluster with certain probability.
Latent Dirichlet Allocation (LDA)	Latent Dirichlet Allocation (Blei et al., http://www.cs.princeton.edu/~blei/papers/BleiNgJordan2003.pdf, 2003) is a powerful learning algorithm for automatically and jointly clustering words into *topics* and documents into mixtures of topics.

9.4   *Chapter summary*

After reading this chapter, you should be able to understand and apply three predictive analytics algorithms, specifically item-based recommenders, naïve Bayes classification, and K-means clustering. All these algorithms exist to help you better understand and leverage data in your systems, whether as mechanisms to help recommendation products or services to your users; or as ways to classify new data coming into your system (such as email spam detection); or even to help you find out new facts about your existing data, as in the case of clustering.

This brings to a close part 4, the series of chapters related to data science. In part 5, we'll look at tools and approaches that make life that much easier when working with Hadoop, which I've dubbed, "Taming the elephant."

Part 5

Taming the elephant

Part 5 is called "Taming the elephant," and it's dedicated to examining languages, tools, and processes that make it easier to work with MapReduce. Why is *elephant* in the title? Hadoop was created by Doug Cutting, who named the framework after his son's yellow stuffed elephant.

Chapter 10 dives into Hive, a SQL-like domain-specific language that's one of the most accessible interfaces when you work with MapReduce.

Pig, covered in chapter 11, offers a good compromise as an abstracted MapReduce language that can bump down into Java code when you need a lower level of access to Hadoop.

Chapter 12 targets programmers who want to integrate MapReduce with existing Java applications. You'll learn about Crunch and Cascading, two technologies offering abstractions that let you hide some of the boilerplate code you just can't avoid with raw MapReduce.

Chapter 13, the final chapter, examines how you can tame MapReduce code using different approaches to unit testing. It also looks at how you can debug any MapReduce job, and offers some anti-patterns you'd best avoid.

Hacking with Hive

10

This chapter covers

- Learning how serialization and deserialization works in Hive
- Writing a UDF to use the distributed cache
- Optimizing your joins for faster query execution times
- Using the EXPLAIN command to understand how Hive is planning your work

Working with MapReduce is nontrivial and has a steep learning curve, even for Java programmers. Over the course of the next three chapters, we'll look at technologies that lower the barrier of entry to MapReduce.

Let's say that it's nine o'clock in the morning and you've been asked to generate a report on the top ten countries that generated visitor traffic over the last month. And it needs to be done by noon. Your log data is sitting in HDFS ready to be used. Are you going to break out your IDE and start writing Java MapReduce code? Not likely. This is where languages such as Hive come into play. Hive, with its SQL-like syntax, allows you to write and start executing MapReduce jobs in the same time that it would take you to write your main method in Java.

335

Hive is one of the easiest to use of the high-level MapReduce frameworks. It's essentially a Hadoop data warehouse tool, which in some organizations (such as Facebook) has replaced traditional RDBMS-based data warehouse tools. Hive owes much of its popularity to the fact that its language is essentially SQL, and as such is accessible to those who've had some exposure to SQL in the past.

Hive was originally an internal Facebook project that eventually tenured into a full-blown Apache project. It was created to sim-

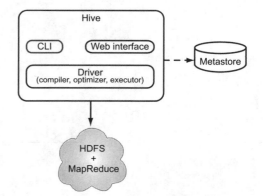

Figure 10.1 The Hive high-level architecture

plify access to MapReduce by exposing a SQL-based language for data manipulation. The Hive architecture can be see in figure 10.1.

In this chapter we'll look at practical examples of how you can use Hive to work with Apache web server logs. We'll look at different ways you can load and arrange data in Hive to optimize how you access that data. We'll also look at some advanced join mechanisms and other relational operations such as grouping and sorting. We'll kick things off with a brief introduction to Hive.

10.1 Hive fundamentals

To understand Hive fundamentals, Chuck Lam's book *Hadoop in Action* should be consulted. In this section we'll skim through some Hive basics.

10.1.1 Installation

Appendix A contains installation instructions for Hive.

10.1.2 Metastore

Hive maintains metadata in a metastore, which is stored in a relational database. This metadata contains information about what tables exist, their columns, privileges, and more.

By default Hive uses Derby to store the metastore, which is an embedded Java relational database. Because it's embedded, Derby can't be shared between users, and as such it can't be used in a multiuser environment where the metastore needs to be shared. Appendix A should be consulted on how to use MySQL as a metastore in multiuser shared environments.

10.1.3 Databases, tables, partitions, and storage

Hive can support multiple databases, which can be used to avoid table name collisions (two teams or users that have the same table name) and to allow separate databases for different users or products.

A Hive table is a logical concept that's physically comprised of a number of files in HDFS. Tables can either be internal—where Hive organizes them inside a warehouse directory, which is controlled by the `hive.metastore.warehouse.dir` property whose default value is `/user/hive/warehouse` (in HDFS); or external—in which case Hive doesn't manage them. Internal tables are useful if you want Hive to manage the complete lifecycle of your data including the deletion, whereas external tables are useful when the files are being used outside of Hive.

Tables can be partitioned, which is a physical arrangement of data associated with each partition into distinct subdirectories for each unique partitioned key. Partitions can be static and dynamic, and we'll look at both cases later in this section.

10.1.4 Data model

Hive supports the following types:

- *Signed integers*—`BIGINT` (8 bytes), `INT` (4 bytes), `SMALLINT` (2 bytes), and `TINYINT` (1 byte)
- *Floating point numbers*—`FLOAT` (single precision) and `DOUBLE` (double precision)
- *BOOLEAN*—`TRUE` or `FALSE`
- *String*—Sequence of characters in a specified character set
- *Maps*—Associative arrays with a collection of key/value pairs where keys are unique
- *Arrays*—Indexable lists, where all elements must be the same type
- *Structs*—Complex types that contain elements

10.1.5 Query language

Hive's query language supports much of the SQL specification, along with Hive-specific extensions, some of which are covered in this section. The full list of statements supported in Hive can be viewed at https://cwiki.apache.org/confluence/display/Hive/LanguageManual.

10.1.6 Interactive and noninteractive Hive

The Hive shell provides an interactive interface:

```
$ hive
hive> SHOW DATABASES;
OK
default
Time taken: 0.162 seconds
```

Hive in noninteractive mode lets you execute scripts containing Hive commands. Note that you used the `-S` option so that only the output of the Hive command was written to the console:

```
$ cat hive-script.ql
SHOW DATABASES;

$ hive -S -f hive-script.ql
default
```

Another noninteractive feature is the -e option, which lets you supply a Hive command as an argument:

```
$ hive -S -e "SHOW DATABASES"
default
```

If you're debugging something in Hive and you want to see more detailed output on the console output, you can use the following command to run Hive:

```
$ hive -hiveconf hive.root.logger=INFO,console
```

That concludes our brief introduction to Hive. Next we'll look at how you can use Hive to mine interesting data from your log files.

10.2   *Data analytics with Hive*

The goal with this section is to walk through a practical application of Hive and use it to showcase several intermediary Hive features. For an example, imagine that you're working at a company that provides online movie streaming services, and you want to perform some basic data analytics (mapping out the top movie categories for each country) on your user log data.

Along the way you'll learn intermediary Hive features such as how to write a SerDe (serializer/deserializer) to parse log data, partition Hive tables, write a user-defined function to geolocate the IP addresses, and some advanced joining options.

10.2.1   *Serialization and deserialization*

Serialization and deserialization, or SerDe as it's known in Hive speak, is what allows Hive to read data from a table (deserialization), and also to write it into HDFS (serialization). In addition to a number of built-in SerDe classes, Hive supports custom SerDe implementations.

TECHNIQUE 64   **Loading log files**

Imagine that you had a number of Apache logs files that you wanted to work with in Hive. The first step is to create a table into which they can be loaded.

Problem

You have log files that you want to load into a Hive table, and using the default Hive SerDe class won't tokenize it correctly.

Solution

Use the RegexSerDe bundled with Hive and define a regular expression that can be used to parse the contents of Apache log files. This technique also looks at how serialization and deserialization works in Hive, and how to write your own SerDe to work with log files.

Discussion

Let's assume that you have logs being written into HDFS under the directory /data/logs/*YYYMMDD*, and you want to calculate daily analytics on the data. First you'll need to create a table to represent the data. Assume that you don't want Hive to manage the table storage for you, so it will be an external table.

Hive comes with a contrib RegexSerDeclass, which can tokenize your logs:

```
hive> CREATE EXTERNAL TABLE logs_20120101 (
        host STRING,
        identity STRING,
        user STRING,
        time STRING,
        request STRING,
        status STRING,
        size STRING)
    ROW FORMAT SERDE 'org.apache.hadoop.hive.contrib.serde2.RegexSerDe'
    WITH SERDEPROPERTIES (
      "input.regex" =
        "([^ ]*) ([^ ]*) ([^ ]*) (-|\\[[^\\]]*\\])
        ([^ \"]*|\"[^\"]*\") (-|[0-9]*) (-|[0-9]*)",

      "output.format.string"="%1$s %2$s %3$s %4$s %5$s %6$s %7$s"
    )
    STORED AS TEXTFILE LOCATION '/data/logs/20120101/';
```

The regular expression used to match and extract groups that are mapped to the table columns. Also note that there's a single space separator where the regular expression is split across two lines.

Determines the order and formatting of the table when it's being written.

You'll copy some data into that directory:

```
$ hadoop fs -put test-data/ch10/hive-log.txt /data/logs/20120101/
```

A quick test will tell you if the data's being correctly handled by the SerDe. Since the RegexSerDe class is part of the Hive contrib, you'll need to register the JAR so that it's copied into the distributed cache and can be loaded by the MapReduce tasks:

```
hive> add jar $HIVE_HOME/lib/hive-contrib-0.7.1-cdh3u2.jar;
hive> SELECT host, request FROM logs_20120101 LIMIT 10;

89.151.85.133    "GET /movie/127Hours HTTP/1.1"
212.76.137.2     "GET /movie/BlackSwan HTTP/1.1"
74.125.113.104   "GET /movie/TheFighter HTTP/1.1"
212.76.137.2     "GET /movie/Inception HTTP/1.1"
127.0.0.1        "GET /movie/TrueGrit HTTP/1.1"
10.0.12.1        "GET /movie/WintersBone HTTP/1.1"
```

CDH Hive is installed under /usr/lib/hive. You should substitute $HIVE_HOME with the location of your Hive installation because Hive doesn't expand environment variables.

If you're seeing nothing but NULL values in the output, it's probably because you have a missing space in your regular expression. Ensure that the regex in the CREATE statement looks like figure 10.2.

When a table is being read in Hive, as in the case of the SELECT you just executed, Hive uses information you specified when creating the table to materialize rows and

```
"input.regex" =
  "([^ ]*) ([^ ]*) ([^ ]*) (-|\\[[^\\]]*\\]) ([^ \"]*|\"[^\"]*\") (-|[0-9]*) (-|[0-9]*)",
        ↑        ↑       ↑              ↑                        ↑          ↑
      space    space   space          space                   space      space
```

Figure 10.2 CREATE table regex showing spaces

fields from the table. As you can see in figure 10.3, deserialization involves the Input-
Format reading records from the data source; the deserializer is responsible for converting the record produced by the InputFormat into a Java object (of any type); and
the ObjectInspector is the bridge between Hive's type system and the object produced
by the deserializer. If you don't specify an InputFormat or SerDe class, Hive treats inputs
as text and deserializes records from the file using LazySimpleSerDe.

Hive doesn't restrict how rows and fields in Hive are represented, and only
requires that an ObjectInspector exists that knows how to extract fields from the
objects returned by the deserializer. Hive has built-in ObjectInspectors to support Java
primitives as well as collections of Java primitives, which are commonly used in deseri-
alizers, as in the case of the RegexSerDe class.

The SerDe and ObjectInspector concepts means that it's really easy to work natively
with serialized data forms such as Avro and Protocol Buffers, since they don't need to
be converted to a Hive-specific format.

You can examine how the RegexSerDe works to learn about how you would write
your own SerDe. RegexSerDe implements the SerDe interface, which in turn implements
Deserializer and Serializer (not pictured). See figure 10.4.[1]

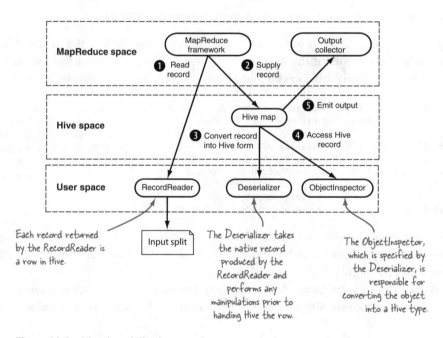

Figure 10.3   Hive deserialization overview

[1] **Hive Subversion source**—http://svn.apache.org/viewvc/hive/tags/release-0.8.1/contrib/src/java/org/
apache/hadoop/hive/contrib/serde2/RegexSerDe.java?view=co

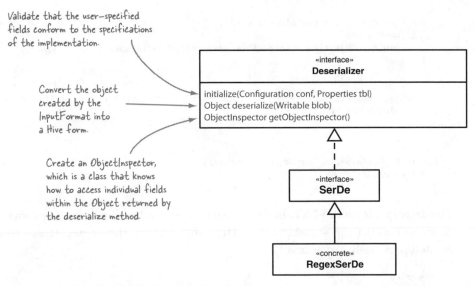

Figure 10.4   Hive Deserialization class diagram

Let's look at the RegexSerDe implementation of the three methods in the Deserializer interface, starting with the initialize and getObjectInspector methods. We'll simplify the code to highlight the key concepts:

```
@Override
public void initialize(Configuration conf, Properties tbl)
    throws SerDeException {

  inputRegex = tbl.getProperty("input.regex");

  String columnNameProperty = tbl.getProperty(
                  Constants.LIST_COLUMNS);
  String columnTypeProperty = tbl.getProperty(
                  Constants.LIST_COLUMN_TYPES);

  inputPattern = Pattern.compile(inputRegex, ...);

  List<String> columnNames = Arrays.asList(
    columnNameProperty.split(","));

  List<TypeInfo> columnTypes = TypeInfoUtils
    .getTypeInfosFromTypeString(columnTypeProperty);

  for (int c = 0; c < numColumns; c++) {
    if (!columnTypes.get(c).equals(TypeInfoFactory.stringTypeInfo)) {
      throw new SerDeException(...);
    }
  }

  List<ObjectInspector> columnOIs = new ArrayList<ObjectInspector>(
      columnNames.size());
```

Read the regular expression from the table definition.

Read the column names from the table definition.

Read the column types from the table definition.

Construct the Java Pattern object, which will be used in the deserialize method.

Tokenize the column names.

Tokenize the column types.

Ensure that each column type is a String.

```
  for (int c = 0; c < numColumns; c++) {          Create a primitive ObjectInspector for each field.
    columnOIs.add(
      PrimitiveObjectInspectorFactory.javaStringObjectInspector);
  }

  rowOI =                                          Create a structure
      ObjectInspectorFactory.getStandardStructObjectInspector(    ObjectInspector for the row that
      columnNames, columnOIs);                     works with List and Array-based
}                                                  representations of rows.

@Override
public ObjectInspector getObjectInspector() throws SerDeException {
  return rowOI;
}
```

The deserialize method is called for each record produced by the RecordReader, and it needs to convert the Writable into a Hive object which the ObjectInspector class you created previously can access:[2]

```
@Override
public Object deserialize(Writable blob) throws SerDeException {

  Text rowText = (Text) blob;          Convert the Writable into a Text object.

  Matcher m = inputPattern.matcher(rowText.toString());

  // If do not match, ignore the line, return a row with all nulls.
  if (!m.matches()) {
    return null;                       If the regular expression didn't match the record, return null.
  }

  // Otherwise, return the row.
  for (int c = 0; c < numColumns; c++) {
    try {                                    For each group in the regular expression, set the appropriate
      row.set(c, m.group(c + 1));            column in the array—the row is a reusable ArrayList that was
    } catch (RuntimeException e) {           created in the initialize method, which was omitted for brevity.
      row.set(c, null);
    }
  }                          Set a null if you ran out of groups.
  return row;
}
```

Figure 10.5 shows the serialization interface in Hive. If you don't specify an Output-Format or SerDe class, Hive writes output as text and serializes records from the file using LazySimpleSerDe.[3]

---

[2] **Hive Subversion source**—http://svn.apache.org/viewvc/hive/tags/release-0.8.1/contrib/src/java/org/apache/hadoop/hive/contrib/serde2/RegexSerDe.java?view=co

[3] **Hive Subversion source**—http://svn.apache.org/viewvc/hive/tags/release-0.8.1/contrib/src/java/org/apache/hadoop/hive/contrib/serde2/RegexSerDe.java?view=co

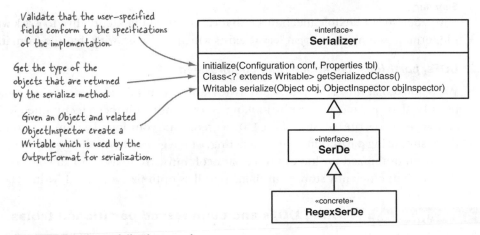

Validate that the user-specified fields conform to the specifications of the implementation.

Get the type of the objects that are returned by the serialize method.

Given an Object and related ObjectInspector create a Writable which is used by the OutputFormat for serialization.

Figure 10.5   Hive serialization overview

The following code shows the implementations of the Serialized interface in the RegexSerDe class, with some unimportant code removed to help with readability:

```
@Override
public Class<? extends Writable> getSerializedClass() {
  return Text.class;
}
```
Tell Hive that your serialize method produces Text objects.

```
Object[] outputFields;
Text outputRowText;

@Override
public Writable serialize(Object obj, ObjectInspector objInspector)
    throws SerDeException {

  StructObjectInspector outputRowOI =
    (StructObjectInspector) objInspector;
  List<? extends StructField> outputFieldRefs = outputRowOI
      .getAllStructFieldRefs();

  for (int c = 0; c < numColumns; c++) {
    Object field = outputRowOI
      .getStructFieldData(obj, outputFieldRefs.get(c));
    ObjectInspector fieldOI = outputFieldRefs.get(c)
      .getFieldObjectInspector();
    StringObjectInspector fieldStringOI = (StringObjectInspector)
      fieldOI;
    outputFields[c] =
      fieldStringOI.getPrimitiveJavaObject(field);
  }

  String outputRowString = String.format(
    outputFormatString, outputFields);

  outputRowText.set(outputRowString);
  return outputRowText;
}
```
Extract the individual ObjectInspector for each field in the table.

Use the ObjectInspector to extract the column.

Create the output line using all the columns with the format defined in the output.format.string, which is set in the SerDe properties.

Summary

Hive's SerDe is a flexible mechanism that can be used to extend Hive to work with any file format, as long as an `InputFormat` exists which can work with that file format.

10.2.2 *UDFs, partitions, bucketing, and compression*

We've looked at how Hive reads and writes tables, so it's time to start doing something useful with your data. Since we're looking to cover more advanced techniques, we'll look at how you can write a custom Hive UDF to geolocate your logs. In doing so, you'll write the results using partitioning and bucketing, which gives you the ability to store the data in a form optimized for lookup by certain columns. We'll also look at compression so that you can efficiently store your data, as well as optimize your read/write IO.

TECHNIQUE 65   **Writing UDFs and compressed partitioned tables**

Your next step is to geolocate the IP address from the logs and write a subset of the log details to a new internal Hive table. This table will use partitions to determine how the data is laid out in HDFS. The partitions should be organized in a way to optimize common queries such that the queries don't need to process data in the entire table. In your case, you want to perform lookups by day and country; therefore, you'll use a static partition to organize the log data by day, and a secondary dynamic partition to store data by country.

Problem

How do you write a custom function in Hive, and work with compressed partitioned tables?

Solution

Learn how to write a UDF in Hive, and how static and dynamic partitions and buckets work.

Discussion

The following HiveQL creates a table which you'll partition by date as well as by country. To allow you to sample data from this table, it's defined that it should be bucketed into 256 buckets (more on that shortly). This table will become large over time because every day you'll be adding additional data into the table, so you're storing it using `SequenceFile` as the storage format, and you'll also compress the data within the SequenceFile (which you'll see shortly):

```
hive> DROP TABLE viewed_movies;
hive> CREATE TABLE viewed_movies (
        host STRING,
        movie STRING)
      PARTITIONED BY (dt string, country string)
      CLUSTERED BY(movie) INTO 64 BUCKETS
      STORED AS SEQUENCEFILE;
```

You have two partitions: dt is the date, and country is the two-digit country code.

Bucketing is a mechanism that helps you with sampling data from your table. Here you're specifying that you want each partition to consist of 64 buckets.

You'll geolocate the IP addresses from the logs table using the free geolocation database from MaxMind. Download the free country geolocation database,[4] unzip it, and copy the GeoIP.dat file under /tmp/.

Next you'll use a UDF to geolocate the IP address from the log table that you created in the previous technique, and use the country code as a dynamic partition. The date will be a static partition.

The difference between static and dynamic partitions is that with a static partition, the name of the partition is hardcoded in the insert statement, whereas with a dynamic partition, Hive will automatically determine the partition based on the value of the partition field:

Dynamic partitions needs to be explicitly enabled in Hive.

Earlier you specified that the viewed_movies was a bucketed table with 64 buckets. Bucketed tables are optimized for sampling because without them extracting a sample from a table requires a full table scan. Whenever you write to a bucketed table, you need to make sure that you either set hive.enforce.bucketing to true, or set mapred.reduce.tasks to the number of buckets.

```
hive> SET hive.exec.dynamic.partition=true;

hive> SET hive.enforce.bucketing = true;

hive> ADD jar
  /usr/lib/hive/lib/hive-contrib-0.7.1-cdh3u2.jar;

hive> ADD jar
<path>/target/hadoop-book-1.0.0-SNAPSHOT-jar-with-dependencies.jar;

hive> ADD file /tmp/GeoIP.dat;

hive> CREATE temporary function country_udf AS
  'com.manning.hip.ch10.GeolocUDF';

hive> CREATE temporary function movie_udf AS
  'com.manning.hip.ch10.ExtractMovieUDF';

hive> SET hive.exec.compress.output=true;

hive> SET hive.exec.compress.intermediate = true;

hive> SET mapred.output.compression.codec =
        org.apache.hadoop.io.compress.SnappyCodec;

hive> INSERT OVERWRITE TABLE viewed_movies
      PARTITION (dt='2012-01-01', country)
      SELECT host, movie_udf(request),
        country_udf(host, "GeoIP.dat")
      FROM logs_20120101;

hive> SELECT * from viewed_movies;
OK
89.151.85.133    127Hours     2012-01-01   GB
212.76.137.2     BlackSwan    2012-01-01   RU
```

Add the geolocation data file into the distributed cache.

Add the JAR containing your UDF so that it can be used in MapReduce.

Define country_udf as the alias for your geolocation UDF and specify the class name.

Enable compression for MapReduce job outputs.

Define an alias for your movie UDF, which extracts the movie name from the URL path.

Enable compression for intermediate map outputs.

Use the Snappy compression codec.

An example of both a static (the dt column) and dynamic (the country column) partitions in action.

Call your UDF specifying the field on which it should operate (the host column from the logs table), and the filename of the geolocation data file, which is in the distributed cache.

---

[4] See http://www.maxmind.com/app/geoip_country.

```
212.76.137.2    Inception      2012-01-01  RU
74.125.113.104  TheFighter     2012-01-01  US
127.0.0.1       TrueGrit       2012-01-01

__HIVE_DEFAULT_PARTITION__
10.0.12.1       WintersBone    2012-01-01  __HIVE_DEFAULT_PARTITION__
```

The __HIVE_DEFAULT_PARTITION__ is used to store records whose dynamic partition column value is NULL, or the empty string.

PARTITIONS, BUCKETS, AND PHYSICAL LAYOUT

If you examine the output of running the previous commands, you'll see the partitions that were used as part of the insert. The SHOW PARTITIONS command can also show you all the partitions for a table:

```
Loading data to table default.viewed_movies partition
 Loading partition {dt=2012-01-01, country=GB}
 Loading partition {dt=2012-01-01, country=RU}
 Loading partition {dt=2012-01-01, country=US}
 Loading partition {dt=2012-01-01, country=__HIVE_DEFAULT_PARTITION__}
6 Rows loaded to viewed_movies
OK

hive> SHOW PARTITIONS viewed_movies;
OK
dt=2012-01-01/country=GB
dt=2012-01-01/country=RU
dt=2012-01-01/country=US
dt=2012-01-01/country=__HIVE_DEFAULT_PARTITION__
```

Using partitions and buckets also changes the physical storage characteristics of your table. A separate directory is used to store each partition, and is nested according to how many partitions you have. The number of buckets that you specified (in conjunction with setting the number of reducers or enabling Hive to autodetect that number based on setting hive.enforce.bucketing to true) also determines how may files are stored in the partition.

Figure 10.6 shows how your table is laid out in HDFS.

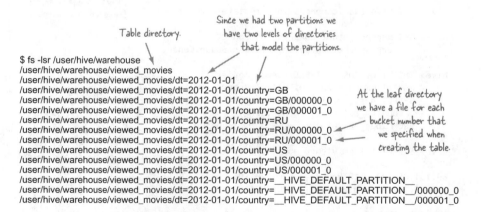

Figure 10.6   Layout in HDFS of a Hive partitioned table

BUCKETS AND SAMPLING

Earlier you used CLUSTERED BY(movie) INTO 64 BUCKETS when creating your table and set hive.enforce.bucketing = true when loading data into your table. This is called *bucketing*, and the reason you want to do this is that it will help optimize sample operations, as you see in the following example:

The value 64 in the BUCKET ... OUT OF ...
must be the same as the number of buckets
specified in the table creation DDL.

```
SELECT * FROM viewed_movies
TABLESAMPLE(BUCKET 1 OUT OF 64 ON movie);
```

If you didn't have buckets, your TABLESAMPLE would have to look like the following HiveQL, which would incur a full table scan:

```
SELECT * FROM viewed_movies
TABLESAMPLE(BUCKET 1 OUT OF 64 ON rand());
```

But this approach has the upside in that it allows you to dynamically size how large you want your sample to be. If you used buckets when creating the table, you would be stuck with whatever bucket size you specified at that time.

UDFS

It's time to look at your UDF. When writing a UDF there are two implementation options, either extend the UDF class, or implement the GenericUDF class, as seen in figure 10.7. The main differences between them are that the GenericUDF class can work with arguments that are complex types, and they are more efficient because the UDF class requires Hive to use reflection for discovery and invocation.

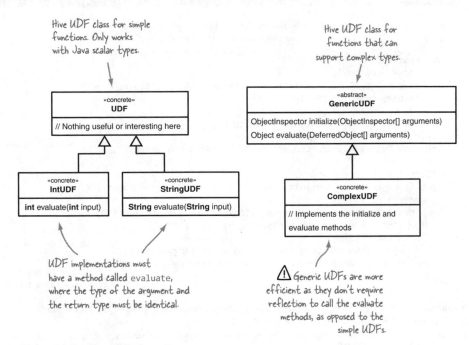

Figure 10.7 Hive UDF class diagram

We'll first look at the simple UDF that extracted the movie name from the URL. You'll extend the UDF class to see how it works:[5]

```java
public class ExtractMovieUDF extends UDF {
  private Text result = new Text();
  public Text evaluate(final Text t) {
    if (t == null) { return null; }
    String s = t.toString();
    String[] parts = StringUtils.split(s, " ");
    if(parts.length != 3) {
      return null;
    }
    String path = parts[1];

    if(!path.startsWith("/movie/")) {
      return null;
    }
    result.set(path.substring(7));
    return result;
  }
}
```

Looking at the UDF class, there aren't actually any methods to override to implement the function. Hive actually uses reflection to find methods whose names are evaluate and matches the arguments used in the HiveQL function call. Hive can work with both the Hadoop Writables and the Java primitives, but it's recommended to work with the Writables since they can be reused.

This UDF works on the request field, which you split into three parts: the HTTP method, the resource (which is the URL path), and the protocol.

Ignore URLs that don't pertain to the movie part of your website.

Extract the text after the leading movie path, which contains your movie title.

Next we'll look at the geolocation UDF, which you'll implement using the `GenericUDF` class.[6]

The geolocation UDF

The Description annotation is used to provide usage information in the Hive shell (you'll see how this works following this code).

```java
@Description(
    name = "country",
    value = "_FUNC_(ip, geolocfile) - Returns the geolocated " +
            "country code for the IP"
)
public class GeolocUDF extends GenericUDF {
  private LookupService geoloc;
  private ObjectInspectorConverters.Converter[] converters;

  @Override
  public ObjectInspector initialize(ObjectInspector[] arguments) {
    converters =
      new ObjectInspectorConverters.Converter[arguments.length];
    for (int i = 0; i < arguments.length; i++) {
      converters[i] =
        ObjectInspectorConverters.getConverter(arguments[i],
        PrimitiveObjectInspectorFactory.javaStringObjectInspector);
```

The geolocation lookup class.

Converters, which you'll use to convert the input types to the types you want to operate with.

Create a converter that you can use in the evaluate method to convert all the arguments (which in your case are the IP address and geolocation file) from their native type into Java Strings.

---

[5] **GitHub source**—https://github.com/alexholmes/hadoop-book/blob/master/src/main/java/com/manning/hip/ch10/ExtractMovieUDF.java

[6] **GitHub source**—https://github.com/alexholmes/hadoop-book/blob/master/src/main/java/com/manning/hip/ch10/GeolocUDF.java

```
      }
      return PrimitiveObjectInspectorFactory           ◄──────  Specify that the return type for the UDF
        .getPrimitiveJavaObjectInspector(                       (in other words the evaluate function) will be
           PrimitiveObjectInspector.PrimitiveCategory.STRING);                a Java String.
  }

  @Override
  public Object evaluate(GenericUDF.DeferredObject[] arguments) {

    Text ip = (Text) converters[0].convert(arguments[0].get());
    Text filename = (Text) converters[1].convert(arguments[1].get());

    return lookup(ip, filename);           ◄──────────    After retrieving the IP address and
  }                                                       geolocation filename from the arguments, call
                                                              a function to perform the geolocation.
  protected String lookup(Text ip, Text filename)
                       throws HiveException {
    try {                                            Load the geolocation data file
      if (geoloc == null) {                          from the distributed cache.
        URL u = getClass().getClassLoader() ◄──
        .getResource(filename.toString());
        geoloc =                 ◄──────────────    Create an instance of the MaxMind Lookup class.
            new LookupService(u.getFile(),
                           LookupService.GEOIP_MEMORY_CACHE);
      }
                               ◄──────   Perform the geolocation and extract the country code.
      String countryCode =
        geoloc.getCountry(ip.toString()).getCode();

      if ("--".equals(countryCode)) {
        return null;
      }

      return countryCode;    ◄──────   Return the country code.
    } catch (IOException e) {
      throw new HiveException("Caught IO exception", e);
    }
  }
                                             Creates a string that's used in situations
  @Override                                  such as exceptions to provide some context
  public String getDisplayString(String[] children) { ◄──   on how the UDF was being invoked.
    assert (children.length == 2);
    return "country(" + children[0] + ", " + children[1] + ")";
  }
}
```

The Description annotation, which we used to annotate the GeolocUDF class in the previous listing, can be viewed in the Hive shell with the DESCRIBE FUNCTION command:

```
hive> DESCRIBE FUNCTION country;
OK
country(ip, geolocfile) - Returns the geolocated country code
for the IP
```

Summary
Although the UDF we looked at operates on scalar data, Hive also has something called a *UDAF*, which allows more complex processing capabilities over aggregated data. You can see more information around writing a UDAF on the Hive wiki at https://cwiki.apache.org/Hive/genericudafcasestudy.html.

Hive also has UDTFs, which operate on scalar data but can emit more than one output for each input. See the GenericUDTF class for more details.

10.2.3 *Joining data together*

Much like SQL, a join in Hive combines records from two tables by using values common to each. As you saw in chapter 4, joins in MapReduce were fairly complex, especially when working with joins such as map-side joins. Joins in Hive abstract away the complexities that you saw when working with MapReduce joins in chapter 4. But when working with big data, you need to understand what Hive is doing behind the scenes and what optimizations are available to streamline your joins.

TECHNIQUE 66 **Tuning Hive joins**

The overall goal of your data analytics is to provide the top movie categories for each country. So far you have a Hive table containing geolocated IP addresses and movie titles. You now need to combine your movie titles with another Hive table that also contains movie titles in addition to the category for the movie. This will require a join, so we'll look at how joins can be optimized much like we did for MapReduce in chapter 4.

Problem

Your Hive joins are running slower than expected, and you want to learn what options you have to speed them up.

Solution

Look at how you can optimize Hive joins with *repartition joins*, *replication joins*, and *semi-joins*.

Discussion

We'll cover three type of joins in Hive: the repartition join, which is the standard reduce-side join; the replication join which is the map-side join; and the semi-join which only cares about retaining data from one table.

REPARTITION JOINS

Repartition joins are essentially equi-joins (inner or outer joins) executed in the reduce side. You can see how they work in MapReduce in figure 10.8.

For this technique let's suppose that you have another table which contains category information for your movies:

```
hive> CREATE TABLE movie_categories (
          title STRING,
          category STRING)
      ROW FORMAT DELIMITED
      FIELDS TERMINATED BY ' '
      LINES TERMINATED BY '\n'
      STORED AS TEXTFILE;

hive> LOAD DATA LOCAL INPATH
          'test-data/ch10/hive-movie-categories.txt'
          OVERWRITE INTO TABLE movie_categories;
```

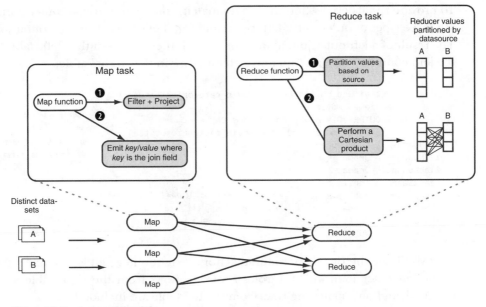

Figure 10.8 A repartition join

The following query will join the movie title from your `viewed_movies` and newly created `movie_categories` tables. This is an example of an inner join, which only returns results for rows where both tables have the same join value:

```
hive> SELECT * FROM viewed_movies;
89.151.85.133    127Hours      2012-01-01  GB
212.76.137.2     BlackSwan     2012-01-01  RU
212.76.137.2     Inception     2012-01-01  RU
74.125.113.104   TheFighter    2012-01-01  US
127.0.0.1        TrueGrit      2012-01-01  __HIVE_DEFAULT_PARTITION__
10.0.12.1        WintersBone   2012-01-01  __HIVE_DEFAULT_PARTITION__

hive> SELECT * from movie_categories;
127Hours      Adventure
127Hours      Drama
BlackSwan     Drama
BlackSwan     Thriller
TheFighter    Drama
13Assassins   Action

hive> SET mapred.reduce.tasks=2;        ⬅──── Set the number of reducers for the job.

hive> SELECT viewed_movies.movie, movie_categories.category
      FROM viewed_movies
      JOIN movie_categories ON ⬅────   Indicate that you're joining the viewed_movies table
          (viewed_movies.movie = movie_categories.title);    with the movie_categories table,
127Hours      Adventure                              and specify the columns that
127Hours      Drama                            should be joined (viewed_movies.movie and
BlackSwan     Drama                                    movie_categories.title).
BlackSwan     Thriller
TheFighter    Drama
```

To provide results even when there's no match, you need to use an outer join. There are three types of outer joins: left, right, and full. Let's look at the left outer join first. The result of a left outer join always contains all the rows from the "left" table, even if the join condition doesn't find any matching row in the "right" table:

```
hive> SELECT viewed_movies.movie, movie_categories.category
      FROM viewed_movies
      LEFT OUTER JOIN movie_categories ON
          (viewed_movies.movie = movie_categories.title);
127Hours     Adventure
127Hours     Drama
BlackSwan    Drama
BlackSwan    Thriller
Inception    NULL
TheFighter   Drama
TrueGrit     NULL
WintersBone  NULL
```

A left outer join includes all rows from the viewed_movies table regardless of whether or not they have a matching row in the movie_categories table.

You have some movies that don't have categories, in which case with a left outer join they'll have a NULL value for the category field.

Next you'll see the right outer join in action. A right outer join is essentially the same as the left outer join, with the roles reversed. Rows from the right table are always returned, and only matching rows from the left table are included:

```
hive> SELECT viewed_movies.movie, movie_categories.category,
            movie_categories.title
      FROM viewed_movies
      RIGHT OUTER JOIN movie_categories ON
          (viewed_movies.movie = .movie_categories.title);
NULL         Action     13Assassins
BlackSwan    Drama      BlackSwan
BlackSwan    Thriller   BlackSwan
TheFighter   Drama      TheFighter
TheFighter   Drama      TheFighter
127Hours     Adventure  127Hours
127Hours     Drama      127Hours
```

A right outer join includes all rows from the movie_categories tables, and only matching rows from the viewed_movies table.

Because all the rows from the movie_categories are included, rows that don't have a matching entry in the viewed_movies table will contain a NULL value for any columns from that table.

And, finally, we'll look at the full outer join. In this join rows from both tables are always included, even if there's no match:

```
hive> SELECT viewed_movies.movie, movie_categories.category,
            movie_categories.title
      FROM viewed_movies
      FULL OUTER JOIN movie_categories ON
          (viewed_movies.movie = movie_categories.title);
NULL         Action     13Assassins
BlackSwan    Drama      BlackSwan
BlackSwan    Thriller   BlackSwan
TheFighter   Drama      TheFighter
TheFighter   Drama      TheFighter
TrueGrit     NULL       NULL
WintersBone  NULL       NULL
127Hours     Adventure  127Hours
127Hours     Drama      127Hours
Inception    NULL       NULL
```

A full outer join includes all rows from both tables regardless of whether there is a match.

Just like with the left and right outer joins, any rows that fail to match will contain NULL values for the table with no corresponding entry.

Table ordering in joins

In joins, it's important that the largest table is the last table in your Hive statement. This is because in the MapReduce implementation of the join, Hive caches matching rows from all the other tables, and then streams the last table, just like the optimized repartition join in chapter 4.

REPLICATED JOINS

A replicated join is a map-side join where a small table is cached in memory and the big table is streamed. You can see how it works in MapReduce in figure 10.9.

To perform a replicated join, there's a hint you can give to Hive to indicate which table is small and should be cached:

```
hive> SELECT /*+ MAPJOIN(movie_categories) */
         viewed_movies.movie, movie_categories.category
      FROM viewed_movies
      JOIN movie_categories
      ON viewed_movies.movie = movie_categories.title;
```

The hint which triggers the map join and also tells Hive which table (movie_categories) to cache.

Replicated join limitations

Only inner joins are currently supported with replicated joins.

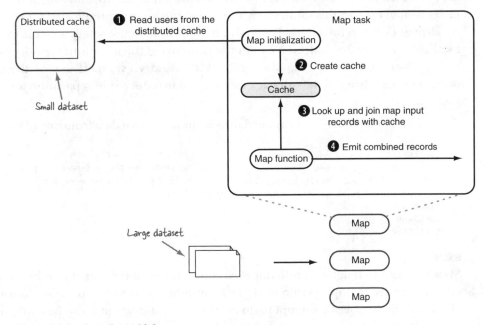

Figure 10.9 A replicated join

The `MAPJOIN` is merely a hint, and Hive will only perform a map-side join if the following conditions are met:

1. The files in the small tables are smaller than the value specified in `hive .mapjoin.smalltable.filesize`, whose default value is set at 25 MB.

2. The memory utilization of loading the small table must be less than `hive .mapjoin.localtask.max.memory.usage`, which is set at 0.90 (90 percent) by default.

Isn't Hive smart enough to automatically convert a repartition join into a replicated join if one of the tables is small enough? As it turns out, it is, but this behavior isn't enabled by default. Let's revisit your original inner join and see how you can enable Hive's automatic replicated join capabilities:

```
hive> SET hive.auto.convert.join = true;
```
Enable Hive's automatic join optimization to convert repartition joins to replicated joins if one of the tables is small enough.

```
hive> SELECT viewed_movies.movie, movie_categories.category
      FROM viewed_movies
      JOIN movie_categories
      ON viewed_movies.movie = movie_categories.title;
...
Mapred Local Task Succeeded. Convert the Join into MapJoin
...
```
This output tells you that Hive decided to go ahead and use a replicated join.

So this begs the question: what criteria does Hive use to determine if a table is small enough to warrant using a replicated join? It compares the sizes of the tables in the join operation with `hive.smalltable.filesize` (this is different than the `hive.mapjoin.smalltable.filesize` that you saw earlier), whose default value 25 MB, and only if one of the tables is smaller than this value will it attempt to perform the replicated join.

Hive goes a step further and actually attempts to load the small table into a simple local task to verify that indeed it can fit the contents of the table into memory (see the earlier discussion of `hive.mapjoin.localtask.max.memory.usage`). If any of these steps don't succeed, Hive will default back to the regular reduce-side repartition join.

SEMI-JOINS

A semi-join is one where you only need the results to contain data from one of the tables:

```
hive> SELECT  viewed_movies.movie
      FROM viewed_movies
      LEFT SEMI JOIN movie_categories
      ON viewed_movies.movie = movie_categories.title;
127Hours
BlackSwan
TheFighter
```
In a semi-join you can't have the result contain any fields from the right-hand side of the join, which in your case is the movie_categories table.

SKEW

Skew can lead to lengthy MapReduce execution times since a small number of reducers may receive a disproportionately large number of records for some join values. Hive, by default, doesn't attempt to do anything about this, but it can be configured to detect skew and optimize joins on skewed keys:

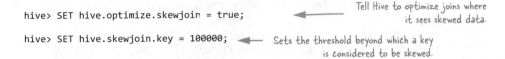

```
hive> SET hive.optimize.skewjoin = true;
```
Tell Hive to optimize joins where
it sees skewed data.

```
hive> SET hive.skewjoin.key = 100000;
```
Sets the threshold beyond which a key
is considered to be skewed.

So what happens when Hive detects skew? You can see the additional step that Hive adds in figure 10.10, where skewed keys are written to HDFS and processed in a separate MapReduce job.

It should be noted that this skew optimization only works with reduce-side repartition joins, not map-side replication joins.

Summary

This technique covered a wide variety of joining options in Hive. Your goal was to join movie titles and their categories together, and assuming that your movie category table can fit into memory, the best join option would have been an inner replicated join.

10.2.4 Grouping, sorting, and explains

Grouping is a relational operation used to group a set of rows together and perform an aggregate function on them, and you'll use it to group movie categories together. You'll then use sorting to order them by the number of IPs that viewed that movie category, thus giving you the most popular categories first. When you're done, you'll look at Hive's EXPLAIN keyword, which can be used to figure out the query plan for your query.

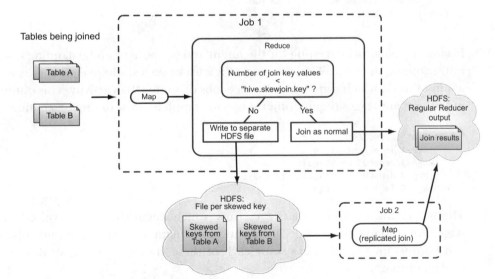

Figure 10.10   Hive skew optimization

The original goal of this section was to produce the top movie categories for a country. Let's go ahead and write the query which will produce this result:

```
hive> SET hive.optimize.skewjoin = false;
hive> SELECT movie_categories.category, count(1) AS cnt
      FROM viewed_movies
      JOIN movie_categories ON
          (viewed_movies.movie = movie_categories.title)
      WHERE viewed_movies.country = "RU"
      GROUP BY movie_categories.category
      ORDER BY cnt DESC;
```

Search for the top categories in Russia. Your table is partitioned by country, which speeds up your query because only files contained in these partitions will be loaded.

Order the results by the number of movies in each category, so the most popular category is the first result.

Why didn't you use SORT BY for sorting the results? SORT BY only sorts results within a reducer, so if your job is running with multiple reducers, you won't get total ordering. But ORDER BY does give you total ordering across all the reducers.

Three MapReduce jobs are executed to satisfy the above query. Why so many? Much like with regular databases, grouping and sorting are expensive operations in Hive. So how can you figure out what each of the MapReduce jobs are doing? That's where EXPLAIN comes into play. You can prefix the SELECT with EXPLAIN and see how Hive is distributing work across the various MapReduce jobs.

The EXPLAIN output first contains the abstract syntax tree, which is simply a tokenized tree representation of the query:

```
ABSTRACT SYNTAX TREE:
(TOK_QUERY (TOK_FROM (TOK_JOIN (TOK_TABREF
(TOK_TABNAME viewed_movies)) (TOK_TABREF
(TOK_TABNAME movie_categories)) (= (.
...
```

It's not particularly interesting for the intent and purpose of understanding how Hive is distributing the work. The next output is a list of stages, where each stage describes a unit of work, which can be MapReduce jobs or some HDFS activity. This output also indicates if any stages require other stages to complete prior to their execution:

```
STAGE DEPENDENCIES:
  Stage-1 is a root stage
  Stage-2 depends on stages: Stage-1
  Stage-3 depends on stages: Stage-2
  Stage-0 is a root stage
```

The last chunk of data is the stage plans, which detail the steps involved in each stage. For a MapReduce stage it indicates information about the inputs, operators, and outputs for the job. Let's study each of these concepts before we dive into the explain output:

- MapReduce inputs can be either a single or multiple Hive tables, or the output from a previous MapReduce job.

- Hive operators are internal constructs which perform some action on data being passed through the map or reduce phases. Hive has operators for joining, filtering, grouping, and so on. Hive can chain multiple operators together within a map or reduce phase to efficiently combine operations together, as you'll see shortly.
- MapReduce outputs will include information about what fields are included in the output, as well as the `OutputFormat` class used to write the output.

Let's look at the output of the first stage, which is a MapReduce job. We'll tackle the map phase first:

```
Stage: Stage-1
  Map Reduce
    Alias -> Map Operator Tree:
      movie_categories
        TableScan
          alias: movie_categories          ◄──── This tells you that the movie_categories
          Reduce Output Operator                  table is one of the input tables for the job.
            key expressions:
                  expr: title ◄───              This tells you that the map is emitting an
                  type: string                  output key/value tuple where the key is the
            sort order: +                                                  movie title.
            Map-reduce partition columns:
                  expr: title  ◄────── The title, which is the output key, is being used for partitioning.
                  type: string
            tag: 1
            value expressions:
                  expr: category ◄──── The output value is the movie category.
                  type: string
      viewed_movies  ◄───── This section shows details for the viewed_movies table. The output
        TableScan                 key/value tuples are the movie title and country, respectively.
          alias: viewed_movies
          Reduce Output Operator
            key expressions:
                  expr: movie
                  type: string
            sort order: +
            Map-reduce partition columns:
                  expr: movie
                  type: string
            tag: 0
            value expressions:
                  expr: country
                  type: string
```

That wasn't so hard to parse. Let's hope the reducer output is as simple to understand:

```
Reduce Operator Tree:  The first operation on the reduce side is a join, and by looking
  Join Operator ◄────       down a couple of lines you can see that it's an inner join.
    condition map:
        Inner Join 0 to 1
    condition expressions:
      0 {VALUE._col3}
```

```
   1 {VALUE._col1}
handleSkewJoin: false
outputColumnNames: _col3, _col7
Filter Operator       ◄──────── This operator is filtering results based on your
  predicate:                    criteria that only results from Russia be included.
      expr: (_col3 = 'RU')
      type: boolean
  Select Operator     ◄──────── The select operator does nothing other than pass
    expressions:                        through data to the next operator.
          expr: _col7
          type: string
    outputColumnNames: _col7
  Group By Operator   ◄──── This group is a localized group within all the rows for a given join key.
    aggregations:          You're grouping on the movie category, so the output of this group is the
          expr: count()    category name and a count of the number of rows with the same category.
    bucketGroup: false
    keys:
          expr: _col7
          type: string
    mode: hash
    outputColumnNames: _col0, _col1
  File Output Operator ◄── The last step indicates that the output is being written to
    compressed: true             file and the output format used to perform the write.
    GlobalTableId: 0
    table:
     input format:  org.apache.hadoop.mapred.
                    SequenceFileInputFormat
     output format: org.apache.hadoop.hive.ql.io.
                    HiveSequenceFileOutputFormat
```

That reducer output was a lot more complex to understand. There were five operators chained together which joined, filtered, grouped, and emitted the key/value output tuple for the job, where the key is the movie category, and the value is a localized count of movies that were encountered as part of the join.

What do the other two MapReduce jobs do? The first MapReduce job groups the movie categories in the reducer and creates an aggregated count for each category. The second job simply sorts all the results by the number of movies for each category. So the group and sort in your query each incurred the expense of an additional MapReduce job.

10.3   *Chapter summary*

Hive is a great tool for nonprogrammers and programmers alike who are versed in using SQL. In this chapter I showed you a number of useful techniques related to loading and working with log data in Hive. We focused on understanding how Hive manages data in internal and external tables, and also looked at advanced topics such as join customization and user-defined functions.

The next high-level language we'll look at is Pig, which also offers a simple way to interact with Hadoop.

11

Programming
pipelines with Pig

This chapter covers

- Customizing data loading in Pig
- Data analysis with log data
- Storing data in a compact format with SequenceFiles
- Effective workflow and performance techniques

Pig is a platform that offers a high-level language with rich data analysis capabilities, making it easy to harness the power of MapReduce in a simplified manner.

Pig started life in Yahoo! as a research project to aid in working rapidly with MapReduce for prototyping purposes, and a year later was externalized into an Apache project. It uses its own language called PigLatin to model and operate on data. It's extensible with its user-defined functions (UDFs), which allow users to bump down to Java when needed for fine-grained control over loading, manipulating, and storing data. External programs such as shell scripts, binaries, and other programming languages can interact with Pig.

We'll work with web server log data in this chapter, and use this data to follow through the typical Pig process flow. The techniques will cover different methods to load data, effective practices to operate on your data, such as some data analysis functions, and finally how to store results in HDFS. After you have these techniques down, we'll identify some tricks for optimizing Pig workflows during development and testing phases, and also examine some performance techniques to ensure speedy job execution.

This chapter isn't meant to serve as an introduction to Pig. It's instead aimed at users who've already experienced working with Pig. To understand Pig fundamentals, you should consult Chuck Lam's book, *Hadoop in Action*.

We'll start with some very brief Pig basics and then jump into the thick of things with some log parsing.

11.1 Pig fundamentals

To understand Pig fundamentals, you should consult Chuck Lam's book *Hadoop in Action*. In this section we'll quickly skim through some Pig basics.

11.1.1 Installation

Appendix A contains installation instructions for Pig.

11.1.2 Architecture

The Pig architecture is presented in figure 11.1. Pig consists of a shell, which allows for interactive command execution, PigLatin, its data flow language, and its execution engine, which translates the PigLatin commands into MapReduce execution plans and executes them.

We'll quickly step through PigLatin, Pig's programming language, and specifically its type system, functions, and operators. After that we'll be ready to move on to some techniques.

11.1.3 PigLatin

Pig's language is called *PigLatin*, and is used to model data flows in Pig. PigLatin has functions and operators that support many of the relational SQL constructs you saw in Hive, such as joining, grouping, and sorting. More details on PigLatin can be viewed on the Apache wiki page at http://hadoop.apache.org/pig/docs/r0.7.0/piglatin_ref1.html.

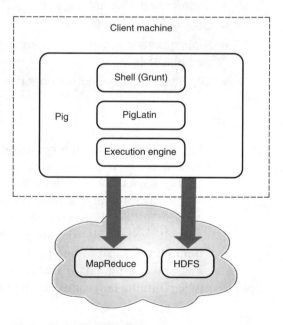

Figure 11.1   The Pig architecture

11.1.4 Data types

PigLatin contains a small number of scalar, array, and composite data types. Scalars in PigLatin are integers, longs, floats, and doubles. Array types are string or byte arrays. Composite types are limited to *tuples*, ordered list fields, *bags*, unordered sets of tuples, and *maps*, sets of key/value pairs.

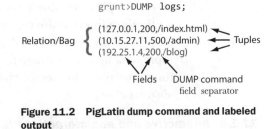

Figure 11.2 PigLatin dump command and labeled output

You'll hear the terms *relation* and *bag* used interchangeably in Pig. Relation is simply a synonym for bag, or a set of tuples. Figure 11.2 shows the Pig `dump` command, which writes the contents of a relation to standard output, and identifies some of these concepts.

Tuples in Pig consist of an ordered list of fields. Fields can be explicitly typed or remain untyped. By default Pig will treat all fields as byte arrays, unless a function, or the user, specifies a type for each field. PigLatin provides you with a mechanism to view the type information for a given relation with the `describe` keyword.

11.1.5 Operators and functions

Operators in PigLatin are language constructs used to load, operate on, and store data. They can be broadly broken into different categories, such as relational, arithmetic, and others. Relational operators are used in PigLatin to perform activities that are similar to relational database SQL constructs, such as joining, grouping, and filtering your data. A complete list of all the operators is available on the Pig website at http://pig.apache.org/docs/r0.9.1/basic.html.

Functions in Pig are callable units of work that can be referenced in the context of specific operators. Pig has a number of built-in functions and also allows users to define their own functions, called user-defined functions (UDFs) in Pig terminology. Functions are grouped into one of four types, each related to a specific operator in whose context they can be used:

1 *Load functions*—These are used in conjunction with the LOAD operator, and are responsible for unmarshalling data from either HDFS or some external source into Pig's Tuple form. These functions must implement methods defined in the `org.apache.pig.LoadFunc` abstract class.

2 *Evaluation functions*—These are used in conjunction with the FOREACH operator, and manipulate data to produce modified output. Examples include mathematical functions, string functions, and bag/tuple functions. These functions must implement methods defined in the `org.apache.pig.EvalFunc` abstract class.

3 *Filter functions*—These, used in conjunction with the FILTER operator, filter out input data and produce an output relation, which is a subset of the input.

There's only one built-in filter function called IsEmpty, which filters out any bag or map tuples that don't contain any fields. These functions must implement methods defined in the org.apache.pig.FilterFunc abstract class.

4 *Store functions*—These, used in conjunction with the STORE operator, store Pig tuple data in some storage format, either in HDFS or an external source. These functions must implement methods defined in the org.apache.pig.StoreFunc abstract class.

11.1.6 *Interactive and noninteractive Pig*

The Pig shell, called Grunt, provides an interactive interface:

```
$ pig
grunt> logs = LOAD 'log.txt';
grunt> DUMP logs;
...
```

Pig can be used in noninteractive mode to execute scripts containing PigLatin commands:

```
$ cat pig-script.pig
logs = LOAD 'log.txt';
DUMP logs;
$ pig -f pig-script.pig
```

Another noninteractive feature is the -e option, which lets you supply a Pig command as an argument:

```
$ pig -d ERROR -e "logs = LOAD 'log.txt'; DUMP logs;"
```

The -d ERROR is an option that turns off the verbose logging and only shows error output.

With this whirlwind tour of Pig completed, it's time to move on to look at some advanced Pig techniques!

11.2 *Using Pig to find malicious actors in log data*

We'll highlight some advanced Pig techniques by walking through an real-life application of Pig. We'll work with Apache web server logs, which contain details about how your website is being used, and attempt to mine some interesting data that could suggest misuse of your website.

Along the way we'll look at how to write user-defined functions to load and operate on data, and also see how streaming and the distributed cache can be utilized. Figure 11.3 shows the pipeline that we'll go through, where each pipe will be a separate technique.

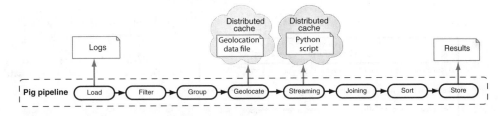

Figure 11.3 Pig Pipeline to find malicious website activities

11.2.1 Loading data

To work with data in Pig, the first thing you need to do is load data from a source, and Pig has a LOAD function that does just that. In this section you'll skip straight into writing your own load function. Writing custom Pig loaders is useful in situations where you're working with data formats for which Pig loader doesn't exist, or if you want to provide rich capabilities to a loader such as schema details, and custom parsing features. Adding schema details to loaders is useful because it means that users of your loaders won't have to define the schema every time they work with your loader. Tuning a loader to work with a specific file format removes the parsing onus from downstream users, freeing up their time to solve problems. This chapter focuses on web server log data, so we'll look at writing a loader for them.

TECHNIQUE 67 Schema-rich Apache log loading

If you look at the Apache Pig mailing lists, you'll see that working with web server log files is a common use of Pig. You'll use this technique both to show how a custom loader in Pig works, and at the same time provide a fully featured log loader that will make working with log data a whole lot simpler.

Problem

The existing log loader in Piggybank, a repository of user-submitted UDFs, does provide a CommonLogLoader to load Apache's Common Log Format. But it doesn't provide rich parsing capabilities, doesn't define schema information, and is slow as a result of regular expressions.

Solution

Learn how Pig loads data with LoadFuncs, and write your own, which loads Apache log files. Discover how to use the REGISTER and DEFINE statements to register and define an alias for your LoadFunc, and how to use your LoadFunc in combination with the LOAD statement.

Discussion

Your goal here is to create a more useful log file loader. Your loader needs to be able to perform the following:

- Simple string tokenization for rapid parsing.

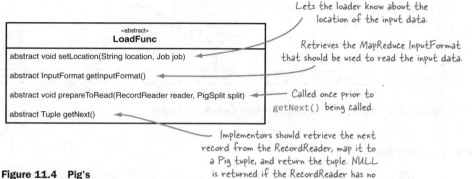

Figure 11.4   Pig's LoadFunc abstract class

- Expose a Pig schema for your log tuple, which means that users don't need to define field names and types.
- Denormalize some of the fields to help with downstream processing.
- Substitute the Apache token denoting no data (-) for NULLs.

In Pig terminology, code that handles reading input and converting it into Pig tuple form is called a LoadFunc, short for load function. Pig has an abstract class called Load-Func that has a number of methods that must be provided by concrete subclasses, as seen in figure 11.4.

The LoadFunc is tightly integrated with Hadoop's InputFormat class; reading data from source is delegated to the InputFormat, and the concrete LoadFunc is responsible for converting it from the InputFormat's key/value form to Pig's tuple form. Pig provides a FileInputLoadFunc class that extends LoadFunc, and is the basis for most Pig Load-Funcs that are file-based, including yours.

Let's take a look at how you tell Pig what InputFormat it should use. In your case, you've defined your own InputFormat class, which will parse the log file (available on GitHub at http://goo.gl/1qT7M):[1]

```
public class TypedCommonLogLoader extends FileInputLoadFunc
  implements LoadMetadata, TypedCommonLogLoaderConstants {

  protected CommonLogInputFormat.CommonLogRecordReader in = null;

  private ArrayList<Object> tuple = null;
  private TupleFactory tupleFactory = TupleFactory.getInstance();

  @Override
  public InputFormat getInputFormat() throws IOException {
    return new CommonLogInputFormat();
  }
}
```

---

[1] **GitHub source**—https://github.com/alexholmes/hadoop-book/blob/master/src/main/java/com/manning/hip/ch11/TypedCommonLogLoader.java

The getNext method in the following listing pops records from the input data using the RecordReader, which in your case is each line of your log file. Because your InputFormat already deals with parsing the line, all you need to do here is grab your data from your RecordReader, and set the equivalent Pig fields.[2]

The Apache log file Pig LoadFunc, which creates Pig tuples

```
@Override
public Tuple getNext() throws IOException {

  tuple = new ArrayList<Object>(11);        ◄─── You use an ArrayList to set individual fields. Here you're
                                                  creating it and presetting the size to the number of fields.
  for (int i = 0; i < 11; i++) {
    tuple.add(null);
  }

  try {                                            If the RecordReader has reached the end of the input
    if (!in.nextKeyValue()) {     ◄───            split, you return NULL to indicate to Pig that you've
      return null;                                         completed reading from source.
    }
    setTuple(in.getCurrentValue());    ◄───  Call your setTuple method with the value from your RecordReader.
                                                  Your RecordReader gives you a Java Bean representing the log line.
    return tupleFactory.newTupleNoCopy(tuple);   ◄───  TupleFactory is a factory that can engineer Tuples
  } catch (InterruptedException e) {                        from various representations, including an ArrayList.
    int errCode = 6018;
    String errMsg = "Error while reading input";
    throw new ExecException(errMsg, errCode,
      PigException.REMOTE_ENVIRONMENT, e);
  }
}

private void setTuple(CommonLogEntry entry) throws IOException {   ◄───  You set each field in your
  tuple.set(0, entry.getRemoteAddress());                                    ArrayList using the
  tuple.set(1, entry.getRemoteLogname());                                  CommonLogEntry member
  tuple.set(2, entry.getUserId());                                                variables.
  tuple.set(3, entry.getTime());
  tuple.set(4, entry.getRequestLine());
  tuple.set(5, entry.getStatusCode());
  tuple.set(6, entry.getObjSize());
  tuple.set(7, entry.getMethod());
  tuple.set(8, entry.getResource());
  tuple.set(9, entry.getProtocol());
  tuple.set(10, entry.getEpoch());
}
```

The advantage of creating an InputFormat that performs the parsing for you (as opposed to using a TextInputFormat and parsing the lines in your LoadFunc directly) is that you can also leverage the InputFormat directly in MapReduce, if you decide to optimize your code later.

You also want your loader to specify type information about your fields. To do this you need to implement the LoadMetadata interface and specify an ordered list of your

---

[2] **GitHub source**—https://github.com/alexholmes/hadoop-book/blob/master/src/main/java/com/manning/hip/ch11/TypedCommonLogLoader.java

field names and related type information. In the following code[3] the field names are simply references to string literals you've defined in a `TypedCommonLogLoaderConstants` interface for ease of use:

```java
@Override
public ResourceSchema getSchema(String location, Job job)
 throws IOException {
 return new ResourceSchema(new Schema(
   Arrays.asList(
     new Schema.FieldSchema(REMOTE_ADDR, DataType.CHARARRAY),
     new Schema.FieldSchema(REMOTE_LOGNAME, DataType.CHARARRAY),
     new Schema.FieldSchema(USERID, DataType.CHARARRAY),
     new Schema.FieldSchema(TIME, DataType.CHARARRAY),
     new Schema.FieldSchema(REQUEST_LINE, DataType.CHARARRAY),
     new Schema.FieldSchema(STATUS_CODE, DataType.LONG),
     new Schema.FieldSchema(OBJ_SIZE, DataType.LONG),
     new Schema.FieldSchema(METHOD, DataType.CHARARRAY),
     new Schema.FieldSchema(RESOURCE, DataType.CHARARRAY),
     new Schema.FieldSchema(PROTOCOL, DataType.CHARARRAY),
     new Schema.FieldSchema(EPOCH, DataType.LONG)
   )));
 }
```

When your `LoadFunc` has been created, you need to register the JAR that contains the class with Pig, specify an alias (to prevent finger strain from repetitively typing in package names), and then load using the `LOAD` operator:

```
$ hadoop fs -put test-data/apachelog.txt apachelog.txt

$ pig

grunt> REGISTER
target/hadoop-book-1.0.0-SNAPSHOT-jar-with-dependencies.jar;
grunt> DEFINE LogLoader com.manning.hip.ch11.TypedCommonLogLoader();
grunt> logs = LOAD 'apachelog.txt' USING LogLoader;
grunt> describe logs;

logs: {remoteAddr: chararray,
  remoteLogname: chararray,userid: chararray,time:
  chararray,requestLine: chararray,statusCode: long,objSize: long,
  method: chararray,resource: chararray,protocol: chararray,
  epoch: long}

grunt> dump logs;

(240.12.0.2,,,[23/Jun/2009:10:40:54 +0300],GET / HTTP/1.1,500,612,...)
(240.12.0.2,,,[23/Jun/2009:10:40:54 +0300],GET /favicon.ico HTTP/...)
(242.0.22.2,,,[23/Jun/2009:10:54:51 +0300],GET / HTTP/1.1,200,34,...)
(242.0.22.2,,,[23/Jun/2009:10:54:51 +0300],GET /favicon.ico HTTP/...)
...
```

---

[3] **GitHub source**—https://github.com/alexholmes/hadoop-book/blob/master/src/main/java/com/manning/hip/ch11/TypedCommonLogLoader.java

You're done! Now your data is loaded with field names and types defined by your LoadFunc. Let's perform a simple operation and count the number of requests for each HTTP status code, which can be used to validate that the majority of requests are successful and, if not, serve as a starting point for further diagnosis into potential misuses of your websites:

```
grunt> grpd = GROUP logs BY statusCode;
grunt> cntd = FOREACH grpd GENERATE group, COUNT(logs);
grunt> dump cntd;
(200,10)
(404,9)
(500,2)
```

Summary
You could have chosen to use the CommonLogLoaderLoadFunc supplied by Piggybank. Consider the Pig code you would write to use this LoadFunc:

```
grunt> REGISTER ./contrib/piggybank/java/piggybank.jar;
grunt> REGISTER ./build/ivy/lib/Pig/joda-time-1.6.jar;
grunt> DEFINE CustomFormatToISO
org.apache.pig.piggybank.evaluation.datetime.convert.
CustomFormatToISO();
grunt> DEFINE ISOToUnix
org.apache.pig.piggybank.evaluation.datetime.convert.ISOToUnix();

grunt> logs = LOAD 'apachelog.txt'
      USING org.apache.pig.piggybank.storage.apachelog.CommonLogLoader;

grunt> dump logs;
(127.0.0.1,-,-,10/Apr/2007:10:39:11 +0300,GET,/,HTTP/1.1,500,606)
(127.0.0.1,-,-,10/Apr/2007:10:39:11 +0300,GET,/favicon.ico,HTTP/...)
(139.12.0.2,-,-,10/Apr/2007:10:40:54 +0300,GET,/,HTTP/1.1,500,612)
...

grunt> epoch = foreach logs generate
   (long) ISOToUnix(CustomFormatToISO($3, 'dd/MMM/yyyy:hh:mm:ss Z'));
grunt> describe epoch
epoch: {org.apache.pig....customformattoiso_13_14: long}

grunt> dump epoch
(1176190751000)
(1176190751000)
(1176190854000)
(1176190854000)
```

Using the CommonLogLoader, you would need to define your own schema, handle the Apache no-data character (-), and, if you wanted to work with the date in epoch form, perform that conversion. Your LoadFunc contained all these features, which makes it easy to work with the tuples it produced.

In your LoadFunc, you could have left the schema definition (using the AS construct) to the user. But this would have meant that the schema would have to be defined each time the data's loaded, so it's best to let the LoadFunc specify the schema. The only time that it may be better not to specify the schema in the LoadFunc is if you're dealing with a dynamic schema that varies between tuples. There's no requirement in Pig that all tuples in a bag contain the same fields; in this sense Pig supports sparse data.

I just showed how to load data into Pig, which was an important prerequisite to working with that data. Now that the data is loaded, the next step is to perform a number of Pig operations on your data.

11.2.2 *Filtering and projection*

Filters provide a mechanism to reduce a relation into a subset of tuples, and projection is a way to reduce the number of fields being worked on. There's a reason that we'll cover them in the first manipulation technique; they're one of the most effective techniques to reduce the amount of data you work with. Less data in the Pig pipeline means faster execution times, which is a win for you!

TECHNIQUE 68   Reducing your data with filters and projection

We'll look at some filtering methods you can apply to your log data.

Problem

How do you remove tuples from a relation?

Solution

Use the FOREACH operator for projection to cut down on the data you are working with. This technique also covers the FILTER operator to remove unwanted records and writing your own UDF to perform custom filtering.

Discussion

Let's study projection and filtering in detail.

PROJECTION

Projection gives you the ability to reduce the fields being operated on with the FOREACH operator. In this example, you're looking for malicious user activity, and so you're interested in agents that may be looking for certain URLs on your web server that don't exist. So you only really care about retaining the IP address, HTTP response code, and the resource, which you can achieve with the following statement:

```
projected_logs = FOREACH logs GENERATE remoteAddr, statusCode, resource;
```

FILTERING

Your goal with filtering is to remove log entries that originated from inside your organization, and to only retain log entries that resulted in a 404 HTTP response code. Assume that all internal IP addresses are private.[4] Luckily, Pig supports regular expression matching, which you can use for this technique. For the 20-bit private IP addresses (in the range 172.16.0.0–172.31.255.255) you'll need to use a more complex regular expression:

---

[4] See http://en.wikipedia.org/wiki/Private_network#Private_IPv4_address_spaces.

The FILTER operator selects tuples based on the condition that follows the operation.

```
filtered_logs =
FILTER projected_logs
BY (NOT
 (remoteAddr MATCHES '10\\..*' OR
  remoteAddr MATCHES '192\\.168\\..*' OR
  remoteAddr MATCHES
      '(172\\.1[6-9]\\..*)|(172\\.2[0-9]\\..*)|(172\\.3[0-1]\\..*)'
))
AND statusCode >= 400;
```

The MATCHES keyword is used to denote that a regular expression match should be performed. With a match the expression must match the entire string. The \\. is used to denote a period in the IP address, since by default a period (.) is a wildcard in a regular expression; hence the \\ escapes it.

If you need a more sophisticated filtering capability for your data, the filter function can work in conjunction with a UDF to reduce the dataset. Let's suppose that you want to optimize the filter you just wrote to not use regular expressions, and to package it so that it can be easily reused. You'd need to write a custom Java UDF that extended Pig's FilterFunc. The UDF will be supplied each tuple in the relation, and you need to return a Boolean indicating if the tuple should exist in the result relation, as you see here:[5]

```java
public class IsPrivateIP extends FilterFunc {

    protected List<Range<Long>> ipRanges;

    public IsPrivateIP() {
      ipRanges = new ArrayList<Range<Long>>();
      ipRanges.add(getRange("10.0.0.0", "10.255.255.255"));v
      ipRanges.add(getRange("172.16.0.0", "172.31.255.255"));
      ipRanges.add(getRange("192.168.0.0", "192.168.255.255"));
    }

    @Override
    public List<FuncSpec> getArgToFuncMapping()
       throws FrontendException {
      List<FuncSpec> funcList = new ArrayList<FuncSpec>();
      funcList.add(new FuncSpec(this.getClass().getName(),
          new Schema(new Schema.FieldSchema(null, DataType.CHARARRAY))));

      return funcList;
    }

    @Override
    public Boolean exec(Tuple t) throws IOException {
      if (t == null || t.size() == 0)
        return false;

      String address = extractFieldAsString(t, 0);
      return address != null && matchesIp(ipToInt(address));
    }
    ...
```

Your UDF constructor creates and populates a list of private IP ranges.

This method is used to specify the expected input type for your UDF. You're expecting that your input is a string,

This method is called once per tuple. With a FilterFunc this must return a Boolean indicating whether the condition this UDF represents holds true. In your implementation you're converting the IP address into numeric form and then comparing it with all the IP ranges.

---

[5] **GitHub source**—https://github.com/alexholmes/hadoop-book/blob/master/src/main/java/com/manning/hip/ch11/IsPrivateIP.java

To call your filter function you need to register your JAR, define an alias for your class, and then use it with the FILTER operator:

```
REGISTER target/hadoop-book-1.0.0-SNAPSHOT-jar-with-dependencies.jar;
DEFINE LogLoader com.manning.hip.ch11.TypedCommonLogLoader();
DEFINE IsPrivateIP com.manning.hip.ch11.IsPrivateIP();

logs = LOAD 'apachelog.txt' USING LogLoader;
filtered_logs = FILTER logs BY NOT IsPrivateIP(remoteAddr);
DUMP filtered_logs;
```

Outside of the FILTER operator, other mechanisms that can be employed for the same effect are Pig streaming, and MapReduce in conjunction with Pig.

Summary

A popular use of filters is to remove tuples that contain a NULL value for a field. The following example removes all log tuples that don't have a user ID:

```
A = FILTER logs by userid is not null;
```

This completes the first data manipulation step in your pipeline, which you used to remove private IP addresses.

11.2.3 *Grouping and aggregate UDFs*

Grouping allows you to collect data together for downstream processing. Grouping can occur based on individual or multiple fields in your tuples. The downstream processing can be in the form of aggregate functions, or any other data-related analysis that you want to perform over your grouped data.

PigLatin contains numerous functions that work with aggregate data. Aggregate functions are functions that let you perform operations over a collection of items. They're typically used for summarization operations, such as determining the number of requests that resulted in unsuccessful HTTP status codes, or finding the most popular URL.

TECHNIQUE 69   **Grouping and counting IP addresses**

After the filter operation, you now want to group log entries together by IP address, and then provide counts.

Problem

How do you group tuples together in Pig and apply aggregate functions on them?

Solution

Use the GROUP and COGROUP operators, and learn how they relate to JOIN and FLATTEN.

Discussion

The filter technique produced a filtered_logs relation, which you'll now use to group logs with identical IP address and status code together:

```
grunt> ip_group = GROUP filtered_logs BY (remoteAddr, statusCode);
```

The group command generates a tuple per unique field being grouped, with the resulting tuple containing two fields. The first field contains all the fields that were used in the group operator, and its name is always group. The second field is an inner bag[6] containing all the tuples from the original relation which matched the group field. The field name of the inner bag is the same as that of the original relation, in your case filtered_logs. You can use the DESCRIBE command to show this information:

```
grunt> DESCRIBE ip_group;
ip_group: {
  group: (remoteAddr: chararray, statusCode: long),
  filtered_logs: {
    remoteAddr: chararray,
    statusCode: long,
    resource: chararray
  }
}
```

With your data grouped together, you now want to count the number of occurrences of the combination of IP address and status code. To operate on grouped data you need to use the FOREACH operator, which lets you perform functions over each row of the group relation:

```
grunt> addrstatus_counts = FOREACH ip_group
                 GENERATE FLATTEN(group), COUNT(filtered_logs);
grunt> DESCRIBE addrstatus_counts;
addrstatus_counts: {
  group::remoteAddr: chararray,
  group::statusCode:long,
  long
}
```

In the preceding example you used the COUNT aggregate function to count the number of log entries for each unique combination of IP address and HTTP status code.

Summary

The power of groups in Pig is that you can group on multiple fields, and you're not restricted with what you do in your data pipeline with your grouped tuple.

The GROUP keyword can only operate on a single relation. If you want to group multiple relations together, the COGROUP keyword provides that functionality. This may prompt the question: what's the difference between a cogroup and a join? With a join, the results won't be grouped together by the join key, but with a cogroup they will be. Let's look at a simple example to better understand this difference:

```
employees = LOAD 'data' AS (name:chararray, department: int);
departments = LOAD 'data' AS (department: int, name:chararray );
```

---

[6] An inner bag is simply a bag that's contained within a tuple. An outer bag, which is referred to as *bag* generally in this text, is the overall container for tuples (outer bags are also referred to as *relations*).

```
join_result = JOIN employees BY department, departments BY department;
DESCRIBE join_result;
join_result: {
  employees::name: chararray,
  employees::department: int,
  departments::department: int,
  departments::name: chararray
}
cogroup_result = COGROUP employees BY department,
                         departments BY department;
DESCRIBE cogroup_result;
cogroup_result: {
  group: int,
  employees: {
    name: chararray,
    department: int},
  departments: {
    department: int,
    name: chararray
  }
}
```

Therefore, a JOIN is analogous to a COGROUP combined with a FLATTEN.

Pig performs a group or cogroup in the reduce phase of MapReduce because it needs to gather together all the tuples for a given grouped field. As a result, group operations can be parallelized, which we'll look at in section 11.4.

Each unique grouped field value will be fed to a single reduce function, along with all the tuples that contain the same field value. This can lead to data skew if some grouped fields have a significantly larger number of matching tuples than others. This can be exacerbated in situations where aggregation functions being performed on the grouped data aren't algebraic, because this means that the entire input relation tuples are fed to the reducer.

All the built-in PigLatin aggregate functions such as COUNT are algebraic. An algebraic function is a special kind of function in Pig, which can be decomposed into subfunctions corresponding to, and invoked from, each of the MapReduce phases (map, combine, and reduce). Algebraic functions must implement the Algebraic interface, as seen in figure 11.5, and provide UDF EvalFuncs corresponding to each MapReduce phase. Functions such as COUNT, SUM, and MAX can be algebraic because they can be broken down into multiple steps. They don't need to have all the tuples in a group at one time to perform their operations, and they can work on subsets of the data and produce intermediate values that can be aggregated in the reducer.

How do you determine how efficient a function is and whether it has algebraic properties that can optimize

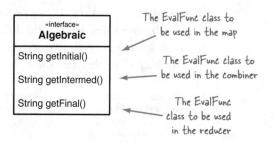

Figure 11.5 Pig's Algebraic interface

and cut down on the data being sent to the reduce phase? The explain command can be used to view how functions are distributed across the map and reduce phases for a given relation. Let's compare the output of explain against a relation generated with an algebraic built-in function (COUNT), and contrast it with a contrived UDF I created that isn't algebraic. We'll start with my inefficient UDF first:

```
grunt> DEFINE NonAlgebraic com.manning.hip.ch11.NonAlgebraic();
grunt> result = FOREACH ip_group
                GENERATE group, NonAlgebraic(filtered_logs);
grunt> explain result;

Map Plan
|---logs: Load(hdfs://apachelog.txt:TypedCommonLogLoader)


Reduce Plan
result: Store(fakefile:org.apache.pig.builtin.PigStorage)
|
|---result: New For Each(false,false)[bag]
    |   |
    |   POUserFunc(com.manning.hip.ch11.NonAlgebraic)[chararray]
```

Notice that your UDF is only invoked in the reduce phase, not in the map phase. Contrast this with the explain result you see when applied to the algebraic count function:

```
grunt> result = FOREACH ip_group
                GENERATE group, COUNT(filtered_logs);
grunt> explain result;

Map Plan
|---result: New For Each(false,false)[bag]
    |   |
    |   POUserFunc(org.apache.pig.builtin.COUNT$Initial)[tuple]
    |
    |---Pre Combiner Local Rearrange[tuple]{Unknown}
        |
        |---logs: Load(hdfs://apachelog.txt:TypedCommonLogLoader)

Combine Plan
|---result: New For Each(false,false)[bag]
    |   |
    |   POUserFunc(org.apache.pig.builtin.COUNT$Intermediate)[tuple]

Reduce Plan
result: Store(fakefile:org.apache.pig.builtin.PigStorage)
|
|---result: New For Each(false,false)[bag]
    |   |
    |   POUserFunc(org.apache.pig.builtin.COUNT$Final)[long]
```

Here you see the function being applied in the map, combine, and reduce phases. Because COUNT emits a single number in all these phases, it results in less data transfer

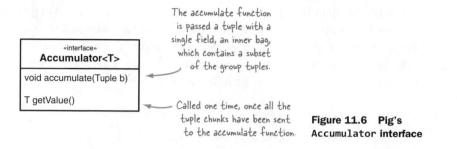

The accumulate function is passed a tuple with a single field, an inner bag, which contains a subset of the group tuples.

Called one time, once all the tuple chunks have been sent to the accumulate function.

Figure 11.6   Pig's Accumulator interface

between the map and reduce tasks. That's an overall win for the efficiency and execution time of your MapReduce job!

Not all functions can be algebraic, such as cases where the ordering of the tuples in the group is significant. If a function can't be algebraic but can operate on subsets of the data, it's recommended to implement the Accumulator interface, which can be seen in figure 11.6. The accumulator is a reduce-side optimization, where rather than feed the UDF a single bag containing all the group tuples, the group tuples are fed to the accumulator in chunks, and at the end the accumulator is asked for the final result.

11.2.4   Geolocation with UDFs

At this point in your pipeline, you've loaded some log files, you filtered out entries that contained private IP addresses and had good HTTP response codes, and you grouped them by IP address and HTTP response code. Your next step is to geolocate the IP addresses that will be useful to identify if attacks on your website are originating from specific countries. Geolocation isn't a built-in function with Pig, so you'll need to write your own using an evaluation UDF.

Evaluation UDFs, or EvalFuncs, are a mechanism that allow custom functions to be performed on a bag of tuples. They can only be used in conjunction with the FOREACH ... GENERATE operators. Generally, EvalFuncs fall into one of the broad categories in table 11.1.

We'll take a look at implementing a simple EvalFunc in the following technique.

Table 11.1   UDF types in Pig

Type of function	Description
Simple	These are functions that simply extend the EvalFunc class. They operate individually on each tuple in a bag, and generate a single result for each input tuple.
Aggregate	These functions also extend the EvalFunc class, but they differ from the simple functions due to the fact they operate over results generated by a GROUP operator. If you recall from the overview earlier in the chapter, a group operator results in a single tuple per unique group field, where the first field in the tuple is the unique group field, and the second field is a bag of tuples containing all the tuples that matched the group field. Therefore, group tuples can be large. It's advised that your functions be algebraic or accumulator if you are working with group tuples to help with memory utilization and to break up the work.

Table 11.1 UDF types in Pig *(continued)*

Type of function	Description
Algebraic	These implement the Algebraic interface and provide a mechanism to perform an operation over the entire bag. The result must always be a scalar type, for example, the result of an algebraic function can't be a tuple, bag, or map. What's special about these functions is that they can only work on an unordered subset of the over-all data. These functions are essentially invoked initially in the map phase, subse-quently in the combine phase, and finally in the reduce phase to produce the final result. Built-in examples include COUNT, MIN, MAX, AVG.
Accumulator	These implement the Accumulator interface, which provides a memory-efficient mechanism to operate over a bag of data. It's applicable to operations that typically can't be expressed in algebraic form. For example, this would apply if your function needs to run in the reducer so that all the input data is sorted. Data is fed to the accumulator in chunks (typically one or more times for each reducer key).

TECHNIQUE 70   **IP Geolocation using the distributed cache**

You want to geolocate IPs in your log files for data analytics, data mining, or poten-tially security reasons.

Problem

How do you write an evaluation function in Pig? And how do you join your log data with geolocation data?

Solution

Write an EvalFunc that uses the Distributed Cache to perform IP geolocation using the MaxMind library and data. Learn how to register multiple UDFs that can support dif-ferent input types.

Discussion

This technique will highlight how you write a custom evaluation function, and also how you can use the distributed cache in Pig. The distributed cache is a MapReduce mechanism that allows local files and files in HDFS to be made available to MapReduce code. Pig supports the distributed cache, and we'll use it to make your geolocation data available to your evaluation functions.

If you want to write your own function to manipulate some data, you'll need to extend Pig's EvalFunc class as shown in the following code. You indicate the return type of your EvalFunc when you extend EvalFunc, and the same type is returned in the exec method.

To perform the actual geolocation, you use MaxMind's GeoLite Country Lite binary file, which is free. You'll also use their Java client code. You need to somehow transport the geolocation data file to the DataNodes so that you can load the file with your MaxMind Java client. Luckily, Pig has support for working with the distributed cache, and if you override the getCacheFiles method, you can specify what local files should be copied into the distributed cache. Your exec method then can assume that the files are available locally on the DataNode on which they are operating.

Let's take a look at your geolocation `EvalFunc` in this listing.[7]

A Pig UDF for geolocation

You're using the MaxMind geolocation library, and here you're storing a reference to their Java class.

```
public class PigGeolocationUDF extends EvalFunc<String> {
private LookupService geoloc;
private static final String COUNTRY = "country";
private final static String DIST_CACHE_GEOIP_NAME = "geoip";
private final List<String> distributedCacheFiles;

public String exec(Tuple input) throws IOException {

  if (input == null || input.size() == 0) {
    return null;
  }

  Object object = input.get(0);
  if (object == null) {
    return null;
  }

  String ip = (String) object;

  return lookup(ip);
}

protected String lookup(String ip) throws IOException {
  if (geoloc == null) {
    geoloc =
    new LookupService
    ("./" + DIST_CACHE_GEOIP_NAME, LookupService.GEOIP_MEMORY_CACHE);
  }

  String country = geoloc.getCountry(ip).getName();

  if ("N/A".equals(country)) {
    return null;
  }

  return country;
}
```

This method is called for each tuple in the relation that the UDF is operating on.

Handle the case where you're passed a NULL or empty tuple.

Get the first field in the tuple, which you assume to be the IP address.

Create the MaxMind geolocation class and specify the file (in the distributed cache) which contains the geolocation data.

Perform the geolocation and extract the country from the result.

MaxMind uses N/A to indicate no data for an IP.

Before getting into the PigLatin code to run the geolocation, let's quickly recap where you're at in the pipeline. At this stage you have a relation called `addrstatus_counts` that contains a unique combination of IP address and HTTP status code, and a count of log entries for each combination:

```
grunt> DESCRIBE addrstatus_counts;
addrstatus_counts: {
  group::remoteAddr: chararray,
```

---

[7] **GitHub source**—https://github.com/alexholmes/hadoop-book/blob/master/src/main/java/com/manning/hip/ch11/PigGeolocationUDF.java

```
    group::statusCode: long,
    long
}
```

Now let's run your UDF against the IPs in your log file. You'll need to download the Max-Mind binary geolocation file from http://www.maxmind.com/app/geoip_country and extract the GeoIP.dat file into the local filesystem at /tmp/GeoIP.dat.

You'll geolocate the IP address contained in the remoteAddr field, but you also want to make sure that you retain all the other fields in the resulting tuple too.

You'll need to manually set a config setting to specify the file to load into the distributed cache:

Tell Hadoop that you want it to set up a symbolic link.

Update the Hadoop configuration indicating where a file exists that should be copied into the distributed cache. If the file exists on the local filesystem, you must use the file scheme, as in the example. If the file already exists in HDFS, you don't need to specify a scheme. Also note the #geoip at the end of the path. This indicates that you want Hadoop to create a symbolic link with that name. If you recall, in your UDF code earlier you use this link name to load the file from the distributed cache.

```
grunt> SET mapred.cache.files file:/tmp/GeoIP.dat#geoip;
grunt> SET mapred.create.symlink yes;

grunt> DEFINE GeoIP com.manning.hip.ch11.PigGeolocationUDF();

grunt> countries =
         FOREACH addrstatus_counts
         GENERATE *, GeoIP(remoteAddr);

grunt> DUMP countries;
```

With UDFs you can optionally define both input and output type information. The advantage of doing this is that the Pig framework will perform validations, which will let the user know if there's a type mismatch. In your code you specified the output type as String, but you assumed that your input would be a tuple with a single String field.

What would you do if you wanted your UDF to specify what you expect your input type to be? And is there a way to support different input data types? In the example, you may want to be able to support both the dot-separated string form of an IP, and the numeric form of the IP. You have two options available: you can either determine the type (using instanceof) in your exec method, or you can specify in your UDF type-specific alternative implementations, which is neater and removes ugly type-switching code.

If you want to switch between UDF implementations based on the input type, you can override the getArgToFuncMapping method, which returns a list of mappings from input types to UDF implementations that can handle that input type. If this function isn't supplied, the original UDF will always be used regardless of input type. In the example, you want to use your existing UDF to process IP addresses in string form, but use a different UDF to process IP addresses in numeric form:[8]

```
@Override
public List<FuncSpec> getArgToFuncMapping()
throws FrontendException {
List<FuncSpec> funcList = new ArrayList<FuncSpec>();
funcList.add(new FuncSpec(this.getClass().getName(),
```

Indicate that for the current class you expect a tuple with a single field, which is a chararray, also known as String.

---

[8] **GitHub source**—https://github.com/alexholmes/hadoop-book/blob/master/src/main/java/com/manning/hip/ch11/PigGeolocationUDF.java

```
    new Schema(new Schema.FieldSchema(null, DataType.CHARARRAY))));
  funcList.add(new FuncSpec(PigLongGeolocationUDF.class.getName(),
    new Schema(new Schema.FieldSchema(null, DataType.LONG))));
return funcList;
}
```

Specify a different EvalFunc class, PigLongGeolocationUDF, if the input is a tuple containing a Long.

What happens if you try and use your UDF with a type that's not supported by your `getArgToFuncMapping`, which only supports `Strings` and `Longs`? Pig will throw an error complaining that you must use an explicit cast and cast the field to a type supported by the UDF.

Summary

Are there any other approaches you could have used to geolocate your log data? You could have written a regular MapReduce job and called that directly from Pig. But your Pig function was vastly simpler than your MapReduce code would have been.

Your geolocation database was around 1 MB in size, but if you tried to use this methodology to work with very large data files (hundreds of MBs or larger), you probably want to rethink your strategy and consider moving your data into HDFS and performing a native join.

11.2.5 *Streaming*

Streaming is a process by which Pig will pipe relations to standard input of a process and collect the output relation from the process's standard output. It's useful in situations where you have existing applications or utilities that you want to use to perform some manipulation on your data.

TECHNIQUE 71 **Combining Pig with your scripts**

In this technique you'll write a very simple Python script that will simulate calling out to an external security system. Your simulated security system will return a score representing the *riskiness* of the IP address. You'll see how this script can be integrated into a Pig pipeline.

Problem

How do you integrate Pig with existing scripts and utilities?

Solution

Use the `STREAM THROUGH` operator to stream your Pig tuples through some Python code.

Discussion

Figure 11.7 shows how Pig streaming works in the context of MapReduce. Pig has the `PigToStream` interface, which defines a method to marshall tuples into byte form, and `StreamToPig` to perform the reverse. By

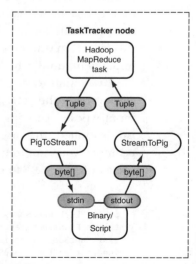

Figure 11.7 How Pig streaming works in combination with MapReduce

default Pig provides the PigStreaming class, which performs both duties, but you're able to define your own marshalling class if you desire.

The power of Pig's streaming is that you have complete control over what you output. While with UDFs you're limited to either filtering or evaluating, in streaming you can do both. In the example, you'll write a simple Python script that echoes back the input data, in addition to a new field that indicates the danger associated with an IP, as a number between 1 and 10:

```
import sys, random

for line in sys.stdin:
  fields = line.rstrip("\n\r")
  sys.stdout.write("%s,%s\n" % (fields, random.randint(1, 10)))
```

With Pig streaming, tuples are by default separated by lines, and tuple fields are separated by the tab character. This is for both input and output. The tuple field delimiter can be overridden by specifying an alternate delimiter in the PigStreaming constructor for input and output. In this example, you'll specify that the comma character should be the input and output delimiter:

```
grunt> DEFINE cmd `python ip_security.py`
        INPUT(stdin using PigStreaming(','))
        OUTPUT(stdout using PigStreaming(','))
        SHIP('/tmp/ip_security.py');

grunt> ip_metadata = STREAM countries
                    THROUGH cmd
                    AS (remoteAddr: chararray,
                        statusCode: long,
                        count: long,
                        country: chararray,
                        severity: int);
```

Your script must be available on the Hadoop cluster for Pig to call it during the MapReduce job. If you use the DEFINE command, this activates Pig's *auto-ship* mechanism, and it will copy the script from the local host to the cluster nodes. If your script has multiple dependencies beyond the name of the script provided in the DEFINE statement, you can specify a SHIP option, which can take more filename arguments and will copy them to the cluster. If you don't use DEFINE, it's your responsibility to ensure the scripts are available on your cluster hosts.

Summary
Pig streaming is a useful way to manipulate data. It allows any programming or scripting language to interact with your data in Pig.

11.2.6 Joining

Joins are one of the most important features in a data processing pipeline because they allow multiple relations to be combined together. You'll leverage Pig's joining support to join your IP addresses with a aggregated dataset that includes details on how many times you've flagged the IP address as suspicious in the past.

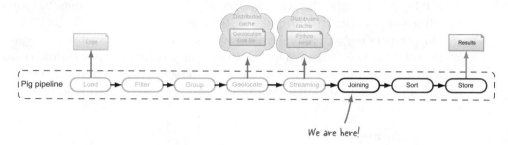

Figure 11.8   Current position in the Pig pipeline

Before you get started, let's see where you are in your Pig pipeline, which you can see in figure 11.8.

TECHNIQUE 72   Combining data in Pig

In this technique we'll look at how to take data from multiple data sources and join them together.

Problem

How do you combine data in Pig?

Solution

Use the JOIN operator to perform joins, and also learn how to perform full and outer joins.

Discussion

You'll load another relation from a file containing historical information about the number of times an IP has been classified as *bad*.

```
grunt> fs -put test-data/ch11/bad-ip-history.txt .
grunt> bad_ips = LOAD 'bad-ip-history.txt'
                 USING PigStorage(' ') AS
                 (ip: chararray, bad_instances: int);

grunt> joined_ips = JOIN ip_metadata BY remoteAddr, bad_ips BY ip;

grunt> DESCRIBE joined_ips;
joined_ips: {
  ip_metadata::remoteAddr: chararray,
  ip_metadata::statusCode: long,
  ip_metadata::count: long,
  ip_metadata::country: chararray,
  ip_metadata::severity: int,
  bad_ips::ip: chararray,
  bad_ips::bad_instances: int
}
```

As you can see, the joined relation qualifies each field with the appropriate original relation name.

Summary

By default the undecorated join keyword results in an inner join, which means that only IPs that were in both relations exist in the resulting relation. What if you wanted to include all the IPs in both relations? This is called a FULL join:

```
grunt> joined_ips = JOIN ip_metadata BY remoteAddr FULL, bad_ips BY ip;
```

You can also use the LEFT and RIGHT keywords to always include one side of the relation, even if the other doesn't have a matching field:

```
grunt> joined_ips = JOIN logs BY remoteAddr LEFT, bad_ips BY ip;
grunt> joined_ips = JOIN logs BY remoteAddr RIGHT, bad_ips BY ip;
```

Joins in Pig require that all the tuples for a given instance of the field being joined can fit in memory. This may not work well for cases where a relation contains many entries for the same field. Section 11.4 provides some performance tips to optimize joins.

Pig supports a repartition map-side join by appending USING 'replicated' to the end of the JOIN statement. It also supports a merge sort, where both relations are presorted by the join key.[9]

11.2.7 Sorting

Pig supports ordering relations on any tuple fields, as long as the fields are scalar data types. It orders numeric data numerically, Strings (chararray) lexicographically, and bytearray as binary data.

TECHNIQUE 73 **Sorting tuples**

We'll sort your data by the count of log entries for each IP address and HTTP status code combination.

Problem

How do you sort data in Pig?

Solution

Use the ORDER BY operator to sort your tuples.

Discussion

Relations can be sorted with the ORDER ... BY operator. You want to sort your URL path counts in ascending order, which you would do as follows;

```
grunt> sorted_ips = ORDER joined_ips BY count DESC;
```

---

[9] See http://wiki.apache.org/pig/PigMergeJoin.

Summary

There's a gotcha to watch out for with sorting in Pig. Pig breaks the normal Map-Reduce pattern and doesn't guarantee that only a single reducer will receive all of the map values for a map key. Pig attempts to optimize the reduce phase by balancing all the map output across all the reducers, which means a key can exist in multiple reducer output files. This may be bad news if you have downstream MapReduce code which assumes that only a single part file contains a key.

The other gotcha to be aware of is that the ordering of tuples that have the same sort value is nondeterministic. For example, if you were sorting on HTTP status code, and multiple log entries contained the same status code, their ordering in the result tuple may vary across different runs.

Sorting is the second-last item in your pipeline, and your final step is to store your results into HDFS.

11.2.8 Storing data

After you've loaded data into Pig and performed some interesting operations on your data, you'll want to store results. We'll take a look at how you can use Pig's built-in storage capabilities, and also write your own storage function.

TECHNIQUE 74   **Storing data in SequenceFiles**

What if you wanted to store your Pig output in a SequenceFile? One reason that you may want to do this is because your output size would be more compact (due to SequenceFile's binary data format and optional compression).

Problem

Pig already has a `LoadFunc` for reading SequenceFiles (`SequenceFileLoader` in Piggy-bank), but unfortunately doesn't have a `StoreFunc`. Therefore, if you're looking for built-in support in Hadoop for writing SequenceFiles, you're out of luck.

Solution

Write a `StoreFunc` that will be used to write tuples in SequenceFile form in HDFS. This technique also covers how to load them back into Pig.

Discussion

I described SequenceFiles in detail in chapter 3. They're essentially a key/value-based binary serialization file format, where internally records or blocks can be compressed and split across multiple input splits. The key and value types are typically `Writable` instances. The challenge with this technique is that you want to write out your log Pig tuples into your SequenceFile, and each tuple contains multiple fields. The only built-in `Writable` array type in Hadoop, `ArrayWritable`, can only store one type of `Writable`, so it's not a good fit for storing your tuple, which contains a variety of field types. Luckily, all tuples in Pig are `Writable` classes, so you can use the `DefaultTuple` class to handle reading and writing your tuple and fields to the SequenceFile.

Let's roll your own Pig StoreFunc, which can write data to SequenceFiles. To do so you need to extend the StoreFunc class. You want to allow users to specify if compression should be used, and the compression codec, so you provide a constructor which takes this information as input. This code is shown next.[10]

A Pig StoreFunc that will write output using Hadoop's SequenceFile format

```
public class SequenceFileTupleStoreFunc extends StoreFunc {

    protected RecordWriter writer;

    private final String compressionType;

    private final String compressionCodecClass;

    public SequenceFileTupleStoreFunc() {
        this(null, null);
    }

    public SequenceFileTupleStoreFunc(String compressionType,
                                      String compressionCodecClass) {
        this.compressionType = compressionType;
        this.compressionCodecClass = compressionCodecClass;
    }

    @Override
    public OutputFormat getOutputFormat() throws IOException {
        return new SequenceFileOutputFormat();
    }

    @Override
    public void setStoreLocation(String location, Job job)
            throws IOException {

        job.setOutputKeyClass(NullWritable.class);

        job.setOutputValueClass(DefaultTuple.class);

        if (compressionType != null && compressionCodecClass != null) {
            Class<? extends CompressionCodec> codecClass =
                FileOutputFormat.getOutputCompressorClass(job,
                    DefaultCodec.class);
            SequenceFileOutputFormat.
                setOutputCompressorClass(job, codecClass);

            SequenceFileOutputFormat.setOutputCompressionType(job,
                SequenceFile.CompressionType.valueOf(compressionType));
        }
        FileOutputFormat.setOutputPath(job, new Path(location));
    }
}
```

Store the optional compression type for the SequenceFile. Can be NULL or one of SequenceFile.CompressionType (NONE, RECORD, BLOCK). I discussed these in more detail in chapter 3.

The optional compression codec used by the SequenceFile.

Constructor where the type of compression and codec are specified.

Pig StoreFuncs are tightly integrated into Hadoop; therefore they use Hadoop's OutputFormats for serialization. Here you indicate that the SequenceFile output format should be used.

This is an initialization function called once before the job is started.

You're specifying that you're writing a NullWritable as the SequenceFile key. You do this since the value will contain the entire tuple.

Set the value type for the SequenceFile as DefaultTuple.

Set the compression codec for the SequenceFile.

Set the compression type for the SequenceFile.

---

[10] **GitHub source**—https://github.com/alexholmes/hadoop-book/blob/master/src/main/java/com/manning/hip/ch11/SequenceFileTupleStoreFunc.java

When creating the SequenceFileOutputFormat, you need to specify the SequenceFile key and value types. You can't specify the Tuple interface as your type because the type needs to be a concrete class with a default constructor. Because you don't know the concrete tuple class ahead of time, you specify the value type as DefaultTuple, and therefore have to convert between the relation tuple and a DefaultTuple when writing individual records to the SequenceFile.

Let's look at how you'll use your new StoreFunc to write your output:

```
grunt> fs -rmr seqfile-output;

grunt> STORE sorted_ips
       INTO 'seqfile-output'
       USING com.manning.hip.ch11.SequenceFileTupleStoreFunc('BLOCK',
       'org.apache.hadoop.io.compress.DefaultCodec');
```

In your SequenceFileTupleStoreFunc constructor, you're specifying that you use block-based compression using the default compression codec, which is gzip. Now that you've successfully written your SequenceFile, how can you read it back in?

The Piggybank SequenceFile LoadFunc unfortunately only supports simple built-in Writable types and won't work with your values, which are DefaultTuple types. Therefore, you have to write your own. I won't show the code here, but it's available on GitHub. The DefaultTuple doesn't store any information about the field names, so you need to specify them when you load your data:

```
grunt> logs2 = LOAD 'seqfile-output/part-*'
           USING com.manning.hip.ch11.SequenceFileTupleLoader()
           AS (remoteAddr: chararray,
               statusCode: long,
               count: long,
               country: chararray,
               severity: int,
               ip: chararray,
               bad_instances: int);

grunt> dump logs2;
(242.0.22.2,404,4,,8,242.0.22.2,43)
(212.76.137.2,404,2,Russian Federation,10,212.76.137.2,5)
(212.76.137.2,404,2,Russian Federation,10,212.76.137.2,8)
(74.125.113.104,404,2,United States,3,74.125.113.104,4)
(242.0.22.2,500,1,,3,242.0.22.2,43)
(89.151.85.133,404,1,United Kingdom,5,89.151.85.133,34)
```

Summary

I chose to use SequenceFiles for data storage since they're easy to use and offer a compressed binary file format. Efficiency is important not only when you process data, but also when you decide how you store data, and this technique exemplifies the use of a compact data store for your data.

Avro would have been another contender for a compact data format. Piggybank comes with AvroStorage, which could have been used for this technique. But the goal was to fill in a gap in the Pig ecosystem, and at the same time showcase how you go about writing a `StoreFunc`.

In this section we covered various ways you can save your useful data that you've computed. Saving data as text is easy, but often not the most efficient use of your storage tier, and the focus here was how to make better use of your valuable storage.

We've now covered the entire Pig data pipeline. The next question you may have is, how do I streamline the process by which I work in Pig?

11.3   *Optimizing user workflows with Pig*

Working with large datasets in Pig frequently results in the following situation: write a number of data flow statements, execute a store or dump, and then wait for long period of time as the data pipeline is executed and produces results you can evaluate. At this time it's likely you'll need to go back, make some tweaks, and repeat the process. *Efficient* this process is *not*.

The above scenario begs the question, how can you work in a rapid manner and quickly iterate over your PigLatin with large datasets?

TECHNIQUE 75   A four-step process to working rapidly with big data

We'll cover four keywords in Pig that will help you work effectively with your large datasets.

Problem

Working with large datasets can result in long pauses in your workflow as you wait for results to be generated.

Solution

Learn how the `LIMIT`, `SAMPLE`, and `ILLUSTRATE` operators can be used to speed-up your Pig workflow. This technique also covers use of the `EXPLAIN` operator and looks at the output, and how it can be interpreted to understand how Pig is executing your pipelines in MapReduce.

Discussion

The four Pig operators that we'll cover are summarized below:

- `LIMIT`—To reduce the number of tuples in the result to a fixed size
- `SAMPLE`—To select a random selection of tuples from a relation
- `EXPLAIN`—To evaluate the execution plan for inefficiencies
- `ILLUSTRATE`—To show the results of each statement in a given data flow

`DESCRIBE` is another useful tool in your arsenal to help you understand your data pipeline by providing schema information about relations. We've used it throughout this chapter to examine the schema of relations.

The first operator that we'll cover is `LIMIT`.

LIMIT

With the LIMIT operator you can reduce the size of a relation to a more manageable size, which is useful when you're developing a new data pipeline in Pig and want to work quickly with your data.

The following series of PigLatin statements will serve as your starting point:

```
grunt> fs -put test-data/ch10/logs-simple-large.txt .
grunt> logs = LOAD 'logs-simple-large.txt' AS (ip, date, status);
grunt> status_group = GROUP logs BY status;
grunt> status_counts = FOREACH status_group
                          GENERATE group, COUNT(logs);
grunt> STORE status_counts INTO 'status-counts.txt';
```

To drop the overall runtime of this pipeline for testing purposes, you'd inject a LIMIT as early on in the pipeline as possible. This code shows the modified pipeline:

```
grunt> logs = LOAD 'logs-simple-large.txt' AS (ip, date, status);
grunt> limited_logs = LIMIT logs 10;
grunt> status_group = GROUP limited_logs BY status;
grunt> status_counts = FOREACH status_group
                          GENERATE group, COUNT(limited_logs);
grunt> STORE status_counts INTO 'status-counts.txt';
```

Note that you applied the LIMIT immediately after the LOAD to cut down on the dataset being pushed through the pipeline.

SAMPLE

The SAMPLE operator will randomly pick a subset of a relations tuple. You need to indicate the percentage of records you want in your sample relation:

```
grunt> logs = LOAD 'logs-simple-large.txt' AS (ip, date, status);
grunt> sampled_logs = SAMPLE logs 0.15;
...
```

The amount to be sampled is expressed as a percentage, 0 to 1, of the overall number of tuples in the relation. In your example you're extracting just 15 percent.

Another option available is to use the RandomSampleLoader, which encapsulates an actual Pig loader and provides some sampling capabilities as tuples are produced from the embedded loader. The following example shows how it would be used:

```
grunt> logs = LOAD 'logs-simple-large.txt'
             USING RandomSampleLoader('PigStorage', '50')
             AS (ip, date, status);
```

The first argument to the RandomSampleLoader is the class name of the Pig LoadFunc, and the second argument is the number of tuples that should be randomly extracted.

ILLUSTRATE

The challenge that arises with LIMIT and SAMPLE is that, depending on your data pipeline and the data filtered by these operators, you may not get data flowing through some of your pipes. The ILLUSTRATE operator actually examines your pipeline and generates data to ensure that each pipe will have data fed through it. It's a useful mechanism to exercise your whole pipeline with a small generated dataset prior to running it against real data.

In the example your input data doesn't have any logs with an HTTP status code of 400, as evidenced by the output of dump. But using ILLUSTRATE will generate data for that data pipe:

```
grunt> logs = LOAD 'logs-simple-large.txt' AS (ip, date, status);
grunt> bad_request = filter logs by status == 400;
grunt> dump bad_request;

Input(s):
Successfully read 200 records (5867 bytes) from: "hdfs://..."

Output(s):
Successfully stored 0 records in: "hdfs://..."

grunt> illustrate bad_request;
```

```
-----------------------------------------------------------------
| logs      | ip: bytearray | date: bytearray | status: bytearray |
-----------------------------------------------------------------
|           | 127.0.0.1     | 10/Apr/2007     | 400             |
|           | 127.0.0.1     | 10/Apr/2007     | 404             |
-----------------------------------------------------------------

-----------------------------------------------------------------
| bad_request | ip: bytearray | date: bytearray | status: bytearray |
-----------------------------------------------------------------
|             | 127.0.0.1     | 10/Apr/2007     | 400             |
-----------------------------------------------------------------
```

Illustrate will actually sample a small subset of data from the input file, and then manipulate it as it goes through the data pipeline to ensure that each relation receives at least one tuple.

You must supply relation field names in order for ILLUSTRATE to work, but it doesn't need type details for fields.

EXPLAIN

Explains are a way to get insight into Pig's execution plan for your data pipelines. The output of explain contains three sections: a logical plan, which shows the pipeline and the sequence of operators that are applied to it; a physical plan, which shows the plan in the context of data sources and sinks; and, finally, the MapReduce plan which shows where operators are applied in MapReduce.

Explains are a very useful guide to gauge the efficiency of a data pipeline. You saw an example of that in technique 69, where you used explain to determine whether an aggregate function was algebraic.

The output of explain quickly gets verbose, so we'll take a simple load and filter sequence and make sense of the explain output:

```
grunt> logs = LOAD 'logs-simple-large.txt' AS (ip, date, status);
grunt> not_found = filter logs by status == 404;
grunt> explain not_found;
```

The first piece of information that the explain plan gives you is the logical plan. The logical plan is focused on the operations, input and output types for each operation, and type conversions required for the operation to function. The plan layout contains the end result at the top, and the starting point at the bottom-most node:

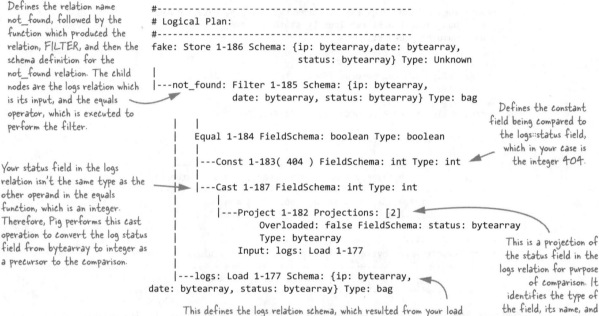

Defines the relation name not_found, followed by the function which produced the relation, FILTER, and then the schema definition for the not_found relation. The child nodes are the logs relation which is its input, and the equals operator, which is executed to perform the filter.

Your status field in the logs relation isn't the same type as the other operand in the equals function, which is an integer. Therefore, Pig performs this cast operation to convert the log status field from bytearray to integer as a precursor to the comparison.

```
#------------------------------------------------
# Logical Plan:
#------------------------------------------------
fake: Store 1-186 Schema: {ip: bytearray,date: bytearray,
                                status: bytearray} Type: Unknown
|
|---not_found: Filter 1-185 Schema: {ip: bytearray,
            date: bytearray, status: bytearray} Type: bag
        |   |
        |   Equal 1-184 FieldSchema: boolean Type: boolean
        |   |
        |   |---Const 1-183( 404 ) FieldSchema: int Type: int
        |   |
        |---Cast 1-187 FieldSchema: int Type: int
        |       |
        |       |---Project 1-182 Projections: [2]
        |           Overloaded: false FieldSchema: status: bytearray
        |               Type: bytearray
        |           Input: logs: Load 1-177
        |
        |---logs: Load 1-177 Schema: {ip: bytearray,
    date: bytearray, status: bytearray} Type: bag
```

Defines the constant field being compared to the logs::status field, which in your case is the integer 404.

This is a projection of the status field in the logs relation for purpose of comparison. It identifies the type of the field, its name, and also the source relation.

This defines the logs relation schema, which resulted from your load statement. You can see your fields, and the default Pig types for untyped fields, bytearray. If you follow the tree edge to the parent you can see that this is the input to the not_found relation (via the FILTER operation).

Next up is the physical plan, which looks at the pipeline execution from the perspective of input and output data sources for the operators. Just like with the logical plan, you read it starting from the bottom:

```
#------------------------------------------------
# Physical Plan:
#------------------------------------------------
not_found: Store(fakefile:org.apache.pig.builtin.PigStorage)
|
|---not_found: Filter[bag] - scope-17
        |   |
        |   Equal To[boolean] - scope-21
        |   |
        |   |---Cast[int] - scope-19
        |   |   |
```

```
|   |   |---Project[bytearray][2] - scope-18
|   |
|   |---Constant(404) - scope-20
|
|---logs: Load(
              hdfs://localhost/user/aholmes/logs-simple-large.txt
              :org.apache.pig.builtin.PigStorage) - scope-16
```

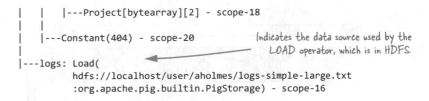

Indicates the data source used by the LOAD operator, which is in HDFS.

Lastly, the MapReduce explain plan shows the various MapReduce jobs that are executed for your data pipeline, and how your operations are distributed across the various map, combine, and reduce phases. With your simple Pig data flow, you only have a single MapReduce job, employing just the map phase:

```
#----------------------------------------------------
# Map Reduce Plan
#----------------------------------------------------
MapReduce node scope-23
Map Plan
not_found: Store(fakefile:org.apache.pig.builtin.PigStorage)
|
|---not_found: Filter[bag] - scope-17
|   |
|   |   Equal To[boolean] - scope-21
|   |
|   |---Cast[int] - scope-19
|   |   |
|   |   |---Project[bytearray][2] - scope-18
|   |
|   |---Constant(404) - scope-20
|
|---logs: Load(
              hdfs://localhost/user/aholmes/logs-simple-large.txt:
              org.apache.pig.builtin.PigStorage) - scope-16--------
Global sort: false
----------------
```

Indicates that the following plan applies to the map phase.

Your filter operator, executed in the map phase.

Your load operator, also executed in the map phase.

If you run explain with the -dot option, it will generate representations for the physical and MapReduce plans in DOT format. DOT files (http://en.wikipedia.org/wiki/DOT_language) can be read and saved as image files using Graphiv, graph visualization software available under the Eclipse Public License from http://www.graphviz.org/. Figure 11.9 shows the image produced in Graphiv for the MapReduce explain output.

Summary
The four operators identified in this technique are useful tools to help expedite your workflow process. For more robust and repeatable testing, I recommend taking a look at PigUnit, a Pig unit testing framework. More details can be found at http://pig.apache.org/docs/r0.9.1/test.html#pigunit.

After you have a data pipeline that performs the function that you need, it's time to turn your attention to performance aspects of Pig that can help reduce the execution time of your data flows.

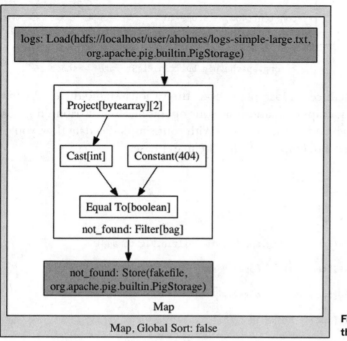

Figure 11.9   Graphical view of the MapReduce explain plan

11.4 Performance

In computer science you're taught to avoid premature optimization, since many assumptions around what's efficient and what's not efficient are quite often incorrect. With big data, efficiency and performance become a core part of your work and thought processes. When you're executing the same code on billions of records, even the smallest nonoptimal code can have big consequences. The single act of using regular expressions, either directly or indirectly (by using String.split, for example) is an example of code use that at face value sounds reasonable, yet can have some negative performance results when applied to large datasets. This was one of the reasons that your log file LoadFunc earlier in this chapter avoided the use of regular expressions (the use of regular expressions seems to be prevalent in most log file LoadFuncs).

Therefore, with MapReduce and Pig there are certain data and network patterns that are almost guaranteed to help reduce the runtime of your MapReduce jobs.

TECHNIQUE 76 **Pig optimizations**

Let's review some data and network performance patterns to help make your Pig jobs go from a trot to a sprint.

Problem

When you're working with very large datasets you'll often find that your jobs take longer than you expect.

Solution

Look at how filtering, reducer parallelism, sampling, and other patterns can be used to squeeze the maximum performance out of Pig and your Hadoop cluster.

Discussion

The solution will be composed of bite-sized recipes that you should keep in mind when working with Pig.

FILTER, FILTER, FILTER

A key pattern with MapReduce is to discard data as soon as you don't need to work with it anymore. This is exemplified by a map reducing the input data and emitting a subset to the reducer. With Pig, the same effect can be achieved with use of the FILTER operator to reduce data that you're working with.

Try to use FILTER as early in your data pipeline as possible, preferably immediately after a LOAD, if possible. The following example shows discarding logs that are from the loopback address:

```
logs = LOAD 'apachelog.txt' USING LogLoader;
A = filter logs by (remoteAddr != '127.0.0.1');
```

Another application of this pattern is as a join optimization. Joins that operate on NULL fields are wasteful since they're dropped. You can apply your filter pattern to discard tuples that contain a NULL field value prior to a join:

```
logs = LOAD 'apachelog.txt' USING LogLoader;
A = filter logs by remoteLogname is not null;
C = join A by remoteLogname, Users by name;
```

SAMPLING AND LIMITING

You can use the RandomSampleLoader to load a random subset of your file if you want to perform work on a sample of your data. You can also use the LIMIT keyword to reduce the number of tuples in your relation, as follows:

```
logs = LOAD 'apachelog.txt' USING LogLoader;
A = LIMIT logs 1000;
```

ALGEBRAIC AND ACCUMULATIVE UDFS

If your UDF is an aggregate function (meaning that it needs to operate on a relation that's the result of a GROUP operation), then it's highly encouraged that you define your function to be algebraic and/or accumulative. By default, if you don't and your group tuples are large, there may be overhead associated with spilling data to disk when working with your data. To avoid, this the Algebraic/Accumulative interfaces can be implemented which allow you to cut down the data being transmitted between the map and reduce phase (in the case of the algebraic functions), and also allow you to operate on smaller subsets of the grouped data (in the case of accumulator functions).

COMBINING OPERATIONS

Combining statements into a single statement will help ensure that a single Map-Reduce job is used to execute the statement.

REPLICATED JOINS AND SKEWED JOINS

Joins in Pig involve the reducer loading all the left-side relation tuples into memory, and then combining each left-side relation with each right-side relation to produce the joined relations. This is a memory-intensive operation. If you know that one relation contains more tuples for a join than the other, you would want to have that as your right-side relation.

Pig has the notion of replicated joins, where if one of the relations fits into memory, it can load the entire relation and perform the join in the map phase. The USING 'replicated' decoration can be added after the relation field name to enable this behavior.

Skewed joins can be used if the default MapReduce key partitioned distributes the majority of tuples to a small number of reducers. Skewed joins employ some key sampling to predetermine a more even distribution of keys across all the reducers. The USING 'skewed' decoration can be added after the relation field name to enable this behavior.

MULTIPLE REDUCERS

Some operators can be executed with multiple reducers in MapReduce, and it's useful to understand how to control the parallelism of these reducers, and also which operators this applies to.

There are a number of operators[11] in Pig that result in both a map and a reduce phase. In such cases, it's important that the reduce phase is parallelized; otherwise the reducer will run as a sequential operation in a single reduce task, which will be slow. Pig will determine the number of reducers to be used for each operator usage in order of precedence, as follows:

1 The PARALLEL keyword decorating the operator. For example, to run a group operator using 50 reducers you would do something like the following:

```
grunt> A = load 'mydata' using PigStorage() as (a, b, c);
grunt> B = group A by a PARALLEL 50;
```

2 The session-wide default_parallel setting. This is useful in situations where you have a default parallelism that you want applied to all operators that support parallelism. An example of setting this to 50 would be as follows:

```
grunt> set default_parallel 50;
```

3 The value of mapred.reduce.tasks in mapred-site.xml. This is the Hadoop-wide MapReduce default for the number of reducers. This should almost always be set to a number higher than 1, which is the default setting in mapred-default.xml.

---

[11] See http://pig.apache.org/docs/r0.9.1/perf.html#parallel.

The following operators in Pig use reducers:

- `COGROUP`
- `CROSS`
- `DISTINCT`
- `GROUP`
- `JOIN` (inner and outer)
- `ORDER ... BY`

Summary

I've outlined some approaches which will help optimize your data pipelines. As with any performance optimizations, you should always prove to yourself that an optimization actually yielded an improved or more efficient result.

11.5 *Chapter summary*

Pig is a tremendously useful tool for use by programmers, data analysts, and data scientists. It offers a high level of abstraction on top of MapReduce, with the flexibility to bump down to the Java and even lower to the MapReduce layers if custom functions and/or performance improvements are required.

In this chapter I showed you a number of useful techniques related to loading, manipulating, and storing your data:

- How to write your own Apache web server log file loader to simplify downstream data processing
- Aggregate and relational data manipulation techniques to mine basic analytics from your logs
- Storing your data in schema-rich SequenceFiles
- User workflow suggestions to optimize your workflow efficiency
- Practical performance tips to speed up your pipeline execution times

At this point, you're a fearless Pig warrior, ready to tackle any big data problem with your Pig skills!

12

Crunch and
other technologies

This chapter covers

- An exploration of Crunch basics
- Using Crunch for data analysis
- A comparison of Crunch and Cascading

Up until now we've looked at Pig and Hive, which are high-level MapReduce abstractions. Our final foray into MapReduce abstractions is Crunch, which is a Java library that makes it easy to write and execute MapReduce jobs. Much like Pig, it's a pipeline-based framework but, because it's a Java library, it offers a higher level of flexibility than you get with Pig.

Crunch is compelling in that it allows you to model MapReduce pipelines in Java without having to use MapReduce constructs such as Map/Reduce functions or Writables. Crunch also benefits from not forcing its own type system onto programmers wishing to hook into the framework, unlike Pig and Hive, which impose their own data types if you want to write UDFs. For programmers, this means you spend less time wrestling with MapReduce and Pig/Hive concepts, and instead focus on solving your actual problems. It should be noted that Crunch shares a lot in common with Cascading, which we'll briefly look at towards the end of this chapter.

Because Crunch is a newcomer to the MapReduce scene, we'll spend a little time introducing the basic Crunch concepts before looking at some techniques. In the techniques, we'll look at how you can use Crunch to find popular URLs in your log files, and we'll also look at some advanced Crunch use cases such as joining your logs with a user dataset.

12.1 What is Crunch?

In this section we'll first take a brief look at the history of Crunch, and then go over some of the fundamentals. After you have a handle on the fundamentals, you'll apply them to a simple example of how Crunch can be used to tokenize strings.

12.1.1 Background and concepts

Crunch is an implementation based on FlumeJava,[1] a paper published by Google detailing their data pipeline library for working with MapReduce. FlumeJava, like Crunch, is a Java library that makes it easy to create MapReduce pipelines using an abstracted MapReduce API. Much like Pig and Hive, FlumeJava and Crunch were created to provide a low-cost entry into MapReduce.

Crunch was written by Josh Wills, a former Google employee who used FlumeJava and decided to write an implementation that would work with Hadoop. At a basic level, Crunch has the following concepts:

1 A collection of data, representing data loaded from a data source such as HDFS, or a derivation of that data based on operations in Crunch

2 A type mapping system, which allows data stored in HDFS (or any other data store) to be mapped to types used in Crunch.

3 Operations that manipulate collections, and which Crunch maps into a series of MapReduce jobs

Crunch comes bundled with a number of built-in operations to perform aggregate and join functions. Crunch is extensible, so you can write and build a library of reusable custom functions for use in your Crunch pipelines.

The next section examines these concepts in more detail.

12.1.2 Fundamentals

Let's look at the basic concepts in Crunch, including its type system and pipelined architecture.

DATA PIPELINES

The Crunch pipeline is represented with the `Pipeline` interface and `MRPipeline` implementation class, which you can see in figure 12.1.

As you can see, the `Pipeline` class contains methods to read and write collections. These collection classes have methods to perform operations on the contents of the

---

[1] See http://dl.acm.org/citation.cfm?id=1806596.1806638.

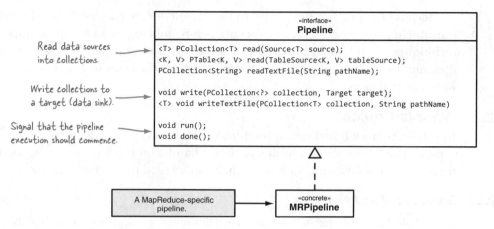

Figure 12.1   Crunch `Pipeline` **class diagram**

collections to produce a new result collection. Therefore, a pipeline consists of the definition of one or more input collections, a number of operations on these and intermediary collections, and the writing of the collections to data sinks. The execution of all the actual pipeline operations is delayed until the run or done methods are called, at which point Crunch translates the pipeline into one or more MapReduce jobs and starts their execution.

COLLECTIONS

In Crunch the collection interfaces represent a distributed set of elements. A collection can be created in one of two ways: as a result of a read method invocation on the Pipeline class, or as a result of an operation on another collection. There are three types of collections in Crunch, as seen in figure 12.2.

The PGroupedTable is a special collection that's a result of calling groupByKey on the PTable. This results in a reduce phase being executed to perform the grouping.

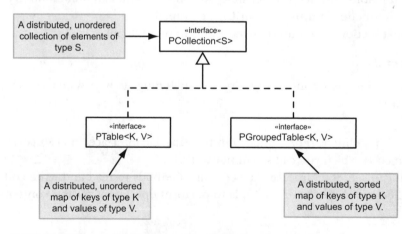

Figure 12.2   Crunch `Collections` **class diagram**

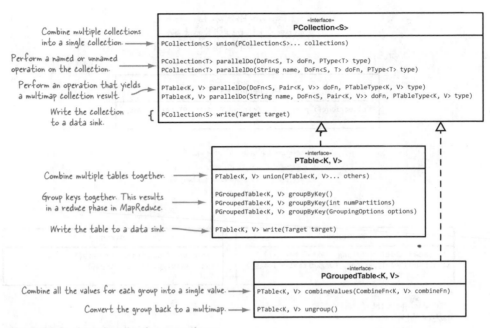

Figure 12.3   Crunch collection operations

Collection classes contain a number of methods, which operate on the contents of the collections, as seen in figure 12.3. These operations are executed in either the map or reduce phase.

DATA FUNCTIONS

Functions can be applied to the collections that you just saw using the `parallelDo` method in the collection interfaces. All the `parallelDo` methods take a `DoFn` implementation, which performs the actual operation on the collection in MapReduce. You can see the `DoFn` class in figure 12.4.

Crunch comes with a number of built-in operations (such as joining, grouping, and counting), which, as you've seen throughout the book in various guises, represent

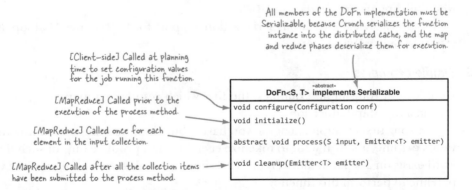

Figure 12.4   Crunch data functions class diagram

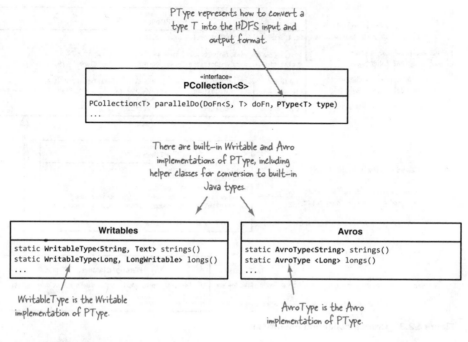

Figure 12.5   Crunch types

MapReduce operations that you commonly perform on your data. Because Crunch already has these operations defined, you don't need to wrestle with MapReduce to write your own. Crunch also lets you define your own custom operations, which you'll use later in this chapter.

TYPES AND SERIALIZATION

As you can see in figure 12.5, the parallelDo methods that you saw on the PCollection interface all take either a PType or PTableType argument, depending on whether the result was a PCollection or PTable. These interfaces are used by Crunch to map between the data types used in the Crunch pipeline, and the serialization format used when reading or writing data in HDFS.

As you can see, Crunch has serialization support for both native Hadoop Writable classes as well as Avro types.

12.1.3   *Simple examples*

We'll look at two simple examples, the first which results in a map-only job, and the second a full MapReduce job.

For your first example, imagine you have a bunch of text files containing multiple words per line, and you want to tokenize each line and produce output such that each word exists on a separate line. Figure 12.6 shows a visual representation of the Crunch pipeline to perform this function.

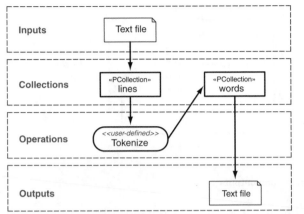

Figure 12.6   Crunch pipeline for text file tokenization

The code for this Crunch pipeline can be seen here:[2]

The MRPipeline class represents the overall Crunch pipeline, which consists of a number of operations. The MRPipeline class knows how to translate the overall pipeline into one or more MapReduce jobs.

A name for the pipeline operation.

A pipeline operation is implemented according to the DoFn interface.

Information about how values in the output collection should be serialized. Crunch has built-in support for Avro and Writables, and here you're using the Writables helper to tell Crunch to use the Writable Text class for serialization.

The first thing you need to do with a pipeline is to specify your input data. In Crunch the input data can be represented as any Java type and needs to be contained in either a PCollection or a PTable.

The parallelDo method is a way that you can inject an operation into the Crunch data pipeline.

The process method is called once per entry in the input collection, which in your case contains the lines from the input files. Depending on the state of the pipeline, this method is called either in the map or reduce side.

Specify that the words collection should be written out to the specified path.

Start execution of the Crunch pipeline. The run and done methods trigger the creation and execution of the MapReduce jobs.

```java
Pipeline pipeline = new MRPipeline(SimpleTokenize.class, conf);
PCollection<String> lines = pipeline.readTextFile(args[0]);
PCollection<String> words = lines.parallelDo(
    "tokenize",
    new DoFn<String, String>() {
      @Override
      public void process(String line,
                          Emitter<String> emitter) {
        for (String word : StringUtils.split(line)) {
          emitter.emit(word);
        }
      }
    }, Writables.strings());
pipeline.writeTextFile(words, args[1]);

pipeline.done();
```

You didn't use the groupBy method in your pipeline, which means that this will be a map-only job (groupBy is a trigger for the reduce phase to be used in a pipeline).

For the second example, you'll look at a full-blown MapReduce job with Crunch. You'll take the inverted index example you wrote in chapter 1 and write a Crunch version of it. As a reminder, the inverted index job takes a number of text files as input and produces output such that each line contains a unique word followed by a list of unique filenames that it occurs in, as seen in figure 12.7.

---

[2]   **GitHub source**—https://github.com/alexholmes/hadoop-book/blob/master/src/main/java/com/manning/hip/ch12/crunch/SimpleTokenize.java

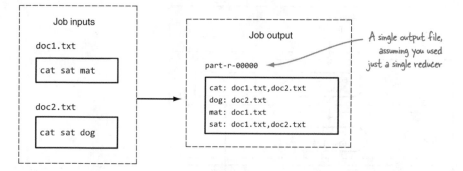

Figure 12.7   Inverted index inputs and outputs

Let's look at the Crunch code to create the inverted index:[3]

```
Pipeline pipeline = new MRPipeline(InvertedIndex.class, conf);
PCollection<String> lines = pipeline.readTextFile(args[0]);

PTable<String, String> wordDocs =
  CrunchUtils.extractWordFileTable(lines);

PTable<String, String> result =
  CrunchUtils.uniqueValues(wordDocs);

pipeline.writeTextFile(result, args[1]);
pipeline.done();
```

Use a helper method to convert the collection of lines into a multimap, where the key is a word in a line and the value is the filename that contained the word.

You call a helper function, which will produce a unique set of filenames for each word.

Let's look at the two helper functions, starting with the first one, which creates a map of words to the filenames from which they originated. The PTable is a multimap, which means that the same key can occur multiple times with different values:[4]

```
PTypeFamily tf = lines.getTypeFamily();
return lines.parallelDo(
    "inverted-index",
    new DoFn<String, Pair<String, String>>() {
      String filename;

      @Override
      public void setContext(TaskInputOutputContext<?, ?, ?, ?>
                             context) {
        super.setContext(context);

        filename = ((FileSplit)
            ((MapContext) context).getInputSplit()).getPath().getName();
      }
```

Extract the type information from the lines collection so that you can use it later.

This time you're using the PTable version of the parallelDo method, since you want to perform table-related operations on the result.

Extract the input split filename and cache it.

---

[3] **GitHub source**—https://github.com/alexholmes/hadoop-book/blob/master/src/main/java/com/manning/hip/ch12/crunch/InvertedIndex.java

[4] **GitHub source**—https://github.com/alexholmes/hadoop-book/blob/master/src/main/java/com/manning/hip/ch12/crunch/CrunchUtils.java

```
                    @Override
                    public void process(String line,
                                       Emitter<Pair<String, String>> emitter) {
                      for (String word : StringUtils.split(line)) {
                        Pair<String, String> pair =
                          Pair.of(word.toLowerCase(), filename);
                        emitter.emit(pair);
                      }
                    }
                  }, tf.tableOf(tf.strings(), tf.strings())));
```

Emit the word and filename as a key/value tuple.

Specify the type information to serialize the result collection. Here you're using the type information that you extracted from the original lines collection.

DoFn implementations can access the job configuration via the DoFn.getConfiguration method. In the previous example, you went a step further and overrode the setContext so that you could extract the input split filename from the context.

Let's take a look at the uniqueValues helper method that you wrote, which calls groupByKey (which means the reducer is used) to group the keys in the PTable together, and uses a CombineFn to iterate over all the values for each unique key. Your CombineFn anonymous inner class then produces a single output tuple for each unique key:[5]

```
        return collect.groupByKey()
                .combineValues(new CombineFn<K, String>() {

          @Override
          public void process(Pair<K, Iterable<String>> input,
                             Emitter<Pair<K, String>> emitter) {

            Set<String> filenames = new HashSet<String>();

            for (String filename : input.second()) {
              filenames.add(filename);
            }

            Pair<K, String> pair =
                Pair.of(input.first(),
                        StringUtils.join(filenames, ","));
            emitter.emit(pair);
          }
        });
```

You use the groupBy method to group all the keys in the collection together. Crunch fulfills a groupBy with a reduce phase in a job.

A combine function is one where the process method is called once per unique key in the group, and all the values of the key are streamed with an Iterable.

Create a set to store the unique filenames.

Add each filename into the set.

Produce output such that the key is the word, and the value is all the filenames concatenated together.

This concludes the introduction to Crunch. In this section you learned the basics about the Crunch API and implemented two examples in Crunch. Next we'll look at some real-life usages of Crunch for log processing.

12.2 Finding the most popular URLs in your logs

In this section we'll look at a practical example of using Crunch to perform some simple analytics on Apache log files. Working with log files is a common use of Hadoop, and by doing so you'll gain additional familiarity with Crunch. You'll use this work to

---

[5] **GitHub source**—https://github.com/alexholmes/hadoop-book/blob/master/src/main/java/com/manning/hip/ch12/crunch/CrunchUtils.java

highlight more advanced DoFn features, such as working with complex Writable structures, and implementing combiner functionality in Crunch.

TECHNIQUE 77   Crunch log parsing and basic analytics

In this technique you'll look at how you can work with log file data to produce the most popular resources (URL paths).

Problem

You want to work with complex data such as log file formats in Crunch.

Solution

Learn how to parse Apache log files, and how filtering, projection, and combiners can be used in Crunch.

Discussion

You'll write a Crunch pipeline which will read data from Apache log files, extract the resource, and then count the number of occurrences of each unique URL to give you basic usage analytics for your website. Figure 12.8 shows this Crunch pipeline.

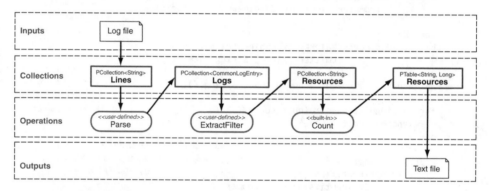

Figure 12.8   Crunch pipeline to extract resource

The following code creates and executes this pipeline:[6]

```
Pipeline pipeline = new MRPipeline(PopularLinks.class, conf);

PCollection<String> lines = pipeline.readTextFile(args[0]);

PCollection<CommonLogEntry> logs = CrunchUtils.logs(lines);

PCollection<String> resources = extractFilterResources(logs);

PTable<String, Long> counts = Aggregate.count(resources);

pipeline.writeTextFile(counts, args[1]);
pipeline.done();
```

Call a helper function to engineer a collection of CommonLogEntry.

Call a method to filter out records you want to ignore and also extract just the resource from each log entry.

Write the aggregated results to HDFS.

Call a built-in Crunch aggregation helper method, which counts each element in the collection.

---

[6] **GitHub source**—https://github.com/alexholmes/hadoop-book/blob/master/src/main/java/com/manning/hip/ch12/crunch/PopularLinks.java

PARSING LOG FILES

For this technique you'll leverage some code you wrote in chapter 11, which was about Pig. In that chapter you were also working with logs, and you wrote a `CommonLogEntry-Writable` to represent an entry in the log file, and an Apache log parser that engineered a `CommonLogEntry` from a log file line. You'll leverage both of these classes in your first DoFn:[7]

```java
public static PCollection<CommonLogEntry> logs(
                              PCollection<String> lines) {
  PTypeFamily tf = lines.getTypeFamily();
  return lines
      .parallelDo(new DoFn<String, CommonLogEntry>() {
      transient ApacheCommonLogReader logReader;
      transient Logger log;

      @Override
      public void initialize() {
        logReader = new ApacheCommonLogReader();
        log = LoggerFactory.getLogger(CrunchUtils.class);
      }

      @Override
      public void process(String input,
                      Emitter<CommonLogEntry> emitter) {
        try {
          CommonLogEntry log = logReader.decodeLine(input);

          if(log != null) {
            emitter.emit(log);
          } else {
            processingError(input, null);
          }
        } catch (IOException e) {
          processingError(input, e);
        }
      }

      void processingError(String line,
                        @Nullable Throwable t) {
        super.getCounter(LogCounters.LOG_LINE_ERRORS).increment(1);
        log.error("Hit exception parsing line '" + line + "'", t);
      }
    }, tf.records(CommonLogEntry.class));
}
```

Declare your ApacheCommonLogReader as transient so that you don't have to make it serializable.

Because your ApacheCommonLogReader is transient, you can't construct it at declaration time. Therefore, leverage the initialization method to create it.

Parse the line and convert it to a CommonLogEntry.

You don't want to abort processing the file if a line is malformed, so you update a counter and dump the error to the log file. On a related note, Crunch doesn't support throwing checked exceptions in the DoFn process method, but an unchecked exception can be thrown to cause the overall MapReduce job to fail if that's the desired result.

If you hit a parsing issue, update a counter and dump the error to the log file.

For complex Writables, there's a records method to identify type and serialization details.

Remember that Crunch serializes all the DoFn instances, which means that all nontransient member variables also need to implement java.io.Serializable. Your ApacheCommonLogReader wasn't a Serializable, but you didn't need to preserve any client-side state in the MapReduce code, so you declared it transient and constructed it in the initialize method.

---

[7] **GitHub source**—https://github.com/alexholmes/hadoop-book/blob/master/src/main/java/com/manning/hip/ch12/crunch/CrunchUtils.java

FILTERING AND PROJECTION

Next up is the second operation in your pipeline, which is a filtering and projection operation. You ignore log entries that originated from the localhost IP address, and you also extract just the resource from the log entry:[8]

```java
public static PCollection<String> extractFilterResources(
                              PCollection<CommonLogEntry> logs) {
  PTypeFamily tf = logs.getTypeFamily();
  return logs.parallelDo(
      "resource-extract-filter",
      new DoFn<CommonLogEntry, String>() {
        @Override
        public void process(CommonLogEntry input,
                            Emitter<String> emitter) {
          if (!"127.0.0.1".equals(input.getRemoteAddress())) {
            emitter.emit(input.getResource());
          }
        }
      }, tf.strings());
}
```

COMBINER

Finally, you leverage one of Crunch's built-in functions, `SUM_LONGS`, to count each resource occurrence:

```java
public static <S> PTable<S, Long> count(PCollection<S> collect) {
  PTypeFamily tf = collect.getTypeFamily();
  return collect.parallelDo(
    "Aggregate.count",
    new MapFn<S, Pair<S, Long>>() {
      @Override
      public Pair<S, Long> map(S input) {
        return Pair.of(input, 1L);
      }
  }, tf.tableOf(collect.getPType(), tf.longs()))
  .groupByKey()
  .combineValues(CombineFn.<S> SUM_LONGS());
}
```

Convert a PCollection to a PTable by emitting a count of 1 for each element.

Group all the keys together (on the reduce side).

Run a built-in combiner function which sums all the values together.

When a `CombineFn` is executed on a `PGroupedTable` (which is the result of calling the group-ByKey), this is a signal to Crunch that the operation being performed is distributive and can be executed on both the map side (as a combiner) and in the reduce side. If the function being implemented isn't distributive (such as calculating a mean), you'd want to call the regular `parallelDo` method rather than call `combineValues`.

Let's run the code against your Apache logs file and examine the output:

```
$ hadoop fs -put test-data/apachelog.txt apachelog.txt
$ bin/run.sh com.manning.hip.ch12.crunch.PopularLinks \
  apachelog.txt output
```

---

[8] **GitHub source**—https://github.com/alexholmes/hadoop-book/blob/master/src/main/java/com/manning/hip/ch12/crunch/PopularLinks.java

```
$ hadoop fs -cat output/part*
/              3
/blog          1
/cgi/pti.pl    1
/favicon.ico   2
/unix.html     1
```

The output shows the results you would expect.

Summary

In this technique we looked at how you could work with a complex data type representing log data and perform a basic analytics function.

In the next section we'll look at how you can join together two separate datasets.

12.3 Joins

Imagine you have two datasets that you wish to combine, such as log data and user data, so that you can understand how your users are using your website. Joining, which can be used to combine these datasets together, is a powerful capability you get with MapReduce. In previous chapters, we looked at how you can join in native MapReduce, Pig, and Hive, and now it's time to do the same with Crunch. Crunch doesn't require you to implement your own join logic, and it contains some code to make joins easy. In this section we'll look at how to leverage this code to join together the IP addresses in your logs with another dataset which contains IP and user details. We'll also look at how you can access the Crunch pipeline results directly from your Java code.

TECHNIQUE 78   Crunch's repartition join

We'll look at how you can use Crunch's built-in joining capabilities to join logs and user data together.

Problem

You have two distinct datasets that you want to join in Crunch.

Solution

See how the Join.join method can be used to join datasets together.

Discussion

Crunch has a Join class that provides support for a reduce-side repartition join. In this technique you'll join your log data with some user data. The user data contains IP addresses and users that are associated with each IP address.

Figure 12.9 shows the pipeline that you'll execute for this technique.

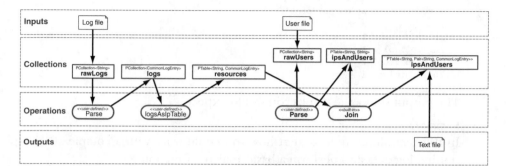

Figure 12.9 Crunch join pipeline

Let's look at the high-level series of collections and operations:[9]

```
Pipeline pipeline = new MRPipeline(JoinLogsAndUsers.class, conf);

PCollection<String> rawLogs = pipeline.readTextFile(args[0]);
```
Represent the logs as a collection of strings.

```
PCollection<String> rawUsers = pipeline.readTextFile(args[1]);
```
Represent the user details as a collection of strings.

```
PTable<String, CommonLogEntry> logs =
    logsAsIpTable(CrunchUtils.logs(rawLogs));
```
Call a function to convert the log strings into a table where the key is the IP address and the value is the CommonLogEntry instance.

```
PTable<String, String> ipsAndUsers = ipsAndUsers(rawUsers);
```
Load the users file into a table where the key is the IP address and the value is the user name.

```
PTable<String, Pair<String, CommonLogEntry>> joined =
    Join.join(ipsAndUsers, logs);
```
Join the log and users together.

You write out the IP address and the user name.

```
for(Pair<String, Pair<String, CommonLogEntry>> j:
    joined.materialize()) {
    System.out.println(j.first() + " " + j.second().first());
}
```
The materialize method causes the pipeline to execute and also streams the collection contents to the client process.

It's important that the smaller dataset is supplied as the first argument in the join function because data from this dataset will be cached to perform the join.

The two functions that you wrote to convert the logs into a table and to load the users file into a table are shown here:[10]

---

[9] **GitHub source**—https://github.com/alexholmes/hadoop-book/blob/master/src/main/java/com/manning/hip/ch12/crunch/JoinLogsAndUsers.java

[10] **GitHub source**—https://github.com/alexholmes/hadoop-book/blob/master/src/main/java/com/manning/hip/ch12/crunch/JoinLogsAndUsers.java

```
public static PTable<String, CommonLogEntry> logsAsIpTable(
                    PCollection<CommonLogEntry> logs) {
  PTypeFamily tf = logs.getTypeFamily();
  return logs.parallelDo(
      "logs-to-ip-table",
      new DoFn<CommonLogEntry, Pair<String, CommonLogEntry>>() {
        @Override
        public void process(CommonLogEntry input,
                    Emitter<Pair<String, CommonLogEntry>> emitter) {
          emitter.emit(Pair.of(input.getRemoteAddress(), input));
        }
      }, tf.tableOf(tf.strings(), tf.records(CommonLogEntry.class)));
}
```

You're creating a table where the key is the IP address and the value is the CommonLogEntry instance.

```
public static PTable<String, String> ipsAndUsers(
                    PCollection<String> ipUsers) {
  PTypeFamily tf = ipUsers.getTypeFamily();
  return ipUsers.parallelDo(
      "extract-users",
      new DoFn<String, Pair<String, String>>() {
        @Override
        public void process(String input,
                        Emitter<Pair<String, String>> emitter) {
          String[] parts = StringUtils.split(input);
          emitter.emit(Pair.of(parts[0], parts[1]));
        }
      }, tf.tableOf(tf.strings(), tf.strings()));
}
```

The first token in the line is the IP address, and the second token is the username.

You'll copy the users file into HDFS and run your job:

```
$ hadoop fs -put test-data/ch12/apachelog-users.txt .
$ hadoop fs -cat apachelog-users.txt
240.12.0.2 beth
127.0.0.1 ops

$ bin/run.sh com.manning.hip.ch12.crunch.JoinLogsAndUsers \
  apachelog.txt apachelog-users.txt output
240.12.0.2 beth
240.12.0.2 beth
```

Because you used the materialize method to get access to the result in the client side, you're able to write the results to the console.

Summary

There were two areas we covered in this technique: first, how to perform a join, and second, how Crunch can support accessing collection elements in the client process.

At the time of writing, the built-in support for joins in Crunch are limited to a two-table repartition join. But Crunch is very powerful and writing joins such as semi-joins and replicated joins is feasible.

12.4   Cascading

Cascading is a data pipeline framework similar to Crunch. Cascading abstracts Map-Reduce into a logical model comprised of tuples, pipes, and taps. Tuples represent the data in the pipeline; the pipes represent operations being performed on tuples; and taps are data sources and data sinks.

To get a sense of how Cascading works, let's look at how the log parser and resource count that you wrote in section 12.2 looks when implemented using Cascading in the next listing.[11]

Cascading implementation of Apache log parser and resource counting

```
String inputPath = args[0];
String outputPath = args[1];
```

TextLine represents a tuple stream, where each tuple represents a line of text. The tuple consists of two fields: the byte offset in the file for the line that will be contained in a field labeled offset, and the contents in the line contained in field line.

```
TextLine input = new TextLine(new Fields("offset", "line"));
```

```
Tap logTap = new Hfs(input, inputPath);
```

Define the data source that will be used to add tuples to the TextLine.

```
Fields apacheFields = new Fields("resource");
```

Define the field name that you'll extract from the log line. You only want to extract the resource, so this contains just a single field labeled resource.

The regular expression used to parse lines in the log file.

```
String apacheRegex = "^([^ ]*) +[^ ]* +[^ ]* +\\[([^]]*)\\] " +
  "+\\\"([^ ]*) ([^ ]*) [^ ]*\\\" ([^ ]*) ([^ ]*).*$";
```

```
int[] allGroups = {4};
```

Define the regular expression group that will be mapped to the fields you defined in apacheFields. The fourth group in the regular expression is the resource.

```
RegexParser parser =
  new RegexParser(apacheFields, apacheRegex, allGroups);
```

Define a regular expression parser.

```
Pipe pipeline = new Each("import",
  new Fields("line"), parser, Fields.RESULTS);
```

Create a new pipeline where the first pipe (operation) is Each, which is an operator that's applied to each tuple in the input tuple stream.

```
pipeline = new GroupBy(pipeline, new Fields("resource"));
```

Define the second operation in the pipeline, which groups all the resources.

```
Aggregator count = new Count(new Fields("count"));
```

Define the third pipeline operation that applies the count operation on the grouped resources.

```
pipeline = new Every(pipeline, count);
```

Count is an aggregation operation that's applied on grouped data. Here you specify the field (resource) on which the count should operate.

```
Tap remoteLogTap = new Hfs(new TextLine(),
  outputPath, SinkMode.REPLACE);
```

Create the data sink to write the results.

```
Properties properties = new Properties();
FlowConnector.setApplicationJarClass(properties,
  PopularLogResources.class);
```

```
Flow parsedLogFlow = new FlowConnector(properties)
  .connect(logTap, remoteLogTap, pipeline);
```

A FlowConnector links together a data source, a data sink, and a number of pipes.

Start the pipeline execution.

```
parsedLogFlow.start();
```

```
parsedLogFlow.complete();
```

Wait for the pipeline to finish executing.

---

[11] **GitHub source**—https://github.com/alexholmes/hadoop-book/blob/master/src/main/java/com/manning/hip/ch12/cascading/PopularLogResources.java

COMPARING CRUNCH AND CASCADING

So how does Cascading compare to other pipeline-based technologies such as Crunch and Pig? The advantage of Pig is that it contains a shell that makes it easy for ad hoc usage. But you could ostensibly use the Groovy or Scala shell to work with Crunch and Cascading too. Cascading and Crunch can also be more easily incorporated into existing Java applications because they're Java technologies. From a feature perspective the differences between them aren't significant other than the maturity of the project and the data model. A comparison of the two projects can be seen in table 12.1.

Table 12.1   Comparison of Crunch and Cascading

Item	Crunch	Cascading
Licensing	Apache 2.0.	Apache 2.0.
Language	Java.	Java.
Data model	Facilitates compile-time type checking of user-defined functions. The data model is independent of the serialization format.	Dynamically typed, using tuple-like model similar to Pig.
Support user-defined functions?	Yes.	Yes.
Comprehensiveness of built-in operations	Basic aggregations, join, cogroup. Still in early stages due to newness of project.	Comprehensive set of functions to work with Cascading's tuple model.
Project history	Public releases commenced October 2011.	Releases commenced early 2008.
Mailing list activity in January 2012	2 messages.	65 messages.
Literature	Low.	High.

The authors of Crunch have written about differences between Crunch and Cascading at http://goo.gl/cKC4y and http://goo.gl/LH1PE.

12.5   *Chapter summary*

The goal with this chapter was to introduce Crunch, a recent and promising high-level MapReduce library. Crunch's emphasis is to lower the barrier to using MapReduce in Java, and abstract away MapReduce concepts in favor of working with more familiar Java built-in types.

We looked at how you could use Crunch to work with log data, and along the way you learned how to perform join operations and how to use the combiner. We also briefly looked at Cascading and compared it to Crunch.

The next chapter looks at methods to help test and debug Java MapReduce applications.

Testing and debugging

13

When you're running MapReduce in production you can guarantee that some day you'll receive a call about a failing job. The goal of this chapter is to help you put in as many measures as possible to avoid the chance of this happening. We'll look at how to provide adequate unit testing for MapReduce code and examine some defensive coding techniques to minimize badly behaving code.

All the preparation and testing in the world doesn't guarantee you won't encounter any problems, and in the event that you do, we'll look at how to debug your job to figure out what went wrong. In this chapter we'll focus on testing and debugging user space MapReduce.

13.1 Testing

In this section we'll look at the best methods to test your MapReduce code, and also look at some design aspects to consider when writing MapReduce to help in your testing efforts.

13.1.1 *Essential ingredients for effective unit testing*

It's important to make sure unit tests are easy to write, and to ensure that they cover a good spectrum of positive and negative scenarios. Let's take a look at the impact that test-driven development, code design, and data have on writing effective unit tests.

TEST-DRIVEN DEVELOPMENT

When it comes to writing Java code, I'm a big proponent of test-driven development (TDD),[1] and with MapReduce things are no different. Test-driven development emphasizes writing unit tests ahead of writing the code, and recently has gained in importance as quick development turnaround times become the norm rather than the exception. Applying test-driven development to MapReduce code is crucial, particularly when such code is part of a critical production application.

Writing unit tests prior to writing your code forces your code to be structured in a way that easily facilitates testing.

CODE DESIGN

When you write code, it's important to think about the best way to structure it so you can easily test it. Leveraging concepts such as abstraction and dependency injection[2] will go a long way to reaching this goal.

When you write MapReduce code, it's a good idea to abstract away the code doing the work, which means you can test that code in regular unit tests without having to think about how to work with Hadoop-specific constructs. This is true not only for your map and reduce functions, but also for your InputFormats, OutputFormats, data serialization, and partitioner code.

Let's look at a simple example to better illustrate this point. The following code shows a reducer that calculates the mean for a stock:

```
public static class Reduce
    extends Reducer<Text, DoubleWritable, Text, DoubleWritable> {

  DoubleWritable outValue = new DoubleWritable();
  public void reduce(Text stockSymbol, Iterable<DoubleWritable> values,
                     Context context)
      throws IOException, InterruptedException {

    double total = 0;
    int instances = 0;
    for (DoubleWritable stockPrice : values) {
      total += stockPrice.get();
      instances++;
    }
    outValue.set(total / (double) instances);
    context.write(stockSymbol, outValue);
  }
}
```

This is a trivial example, but the way the code is structured means you can't easily test this in a regular unit test because MapReduce has constructs such as Text, DoubleWritable,

---

[1] See http://en.wikipedia.org/wiki/Test-driven_development.
[2] See http://en.wikipedia.org/wiki/Dependency_injection.

and the Context class that get in your way. If you were to structure the code to abstract away the work, you could easily test the user space code that's doing your work, as the following code shows:

```
public static class Reduce2
    extends Reducer<Text, DoubleWritable, Text, DoubleWritable> {

  SMA sma = new SMA();
  DoubleWritable outValue = new DoubleWritable();
  public void reduce(Text key, Iterable<DoubleWritable> values,
                     Context context)
      throws IOException, InterruptedException {
    sma.reset();
    for (DoubleWritable stockPrice : values) {
      sma.add(stockPrice.get());
    }
    outValue.set(sma.calculate());
    context.write(key, outValue);
  }
}

public static class SMA {
  protected double total = 0;
  protected int instances = 0;

  public void add(double value) {
    total += value;
    instances ++;
  }

  public double calculate() {
    return total / (double) instances;
  }

  public void reset() {
    total = 0;
    instances = 0;
  }
}
```

With this improved code layout you can now easily test the SMA class that's adding and calculating the simple moving average, without the Hadoop code getting in your way.

IT'S THE DATA, STUPID

When you write unit tests, you try to discover how your code handles both positive and negative input data. In both cases it's best if the data you're testing with is a representative sample from production.

Often, no matter how hard you try, issues in your code in production will arise from unexpected input data. Later, in section 13.2.2, we'll look at how to identify when this occurs in production jobs. It's important that when you do discover input data that causes a job to blow up, you not only fix the code to handle the unexpected data, but you also pull the data that caused the blowup and use it in a unit test to prove that the code can now correctly handle that data.

13.1.2 *MRUnit*

MRUnit is a test framework you can use to unit test MapReduce code. It was developed by Cloudera (a vendor with its own Hadoop distribution) and is currently an Apache project in incubator status. It should be noted that MRUnit supports both the old (org.apache.hadoop.mapred) and new (org.apache.hadoop.mapreduce) MapReduce APIs.

TECHNIQUE 79   Unit Testing MapReduce functions, jobs, and pipelines

In this technique we'll look at writing unit tests that leverage each of the four types of tests provided by MRUnit:

1 A map test that only tests a map function (supported by the MapDriver class).
2 A reduce test that only tests a reduce function (supported by the ReduceDriver class).
3 A map and reduce test that tests both the map and reduce functions (supported by the MapReduceDriver class).
4 A pipeline test that allows a series of MapReduce functions to be exercised (supported by the TestPipelineMapReduceDriver class).

Problem

You want to test map and reduce functions, as well as MapReduce pipelines.

Solution

Learn how MRUnit's MapDriver, ReduceDriver, MapReduceDriver and PipelineMapReduce-Driver classes can be used as part of your unit tests to test your MapReduce code.

Discussion

MRUnit has four types of unit tests—we'll start with a look at the map tests.

MAP TESTS

Let's kick things off by writing a test to exercise a map function. Before starting, let's look at what you need to supply to MRUnit to execute the test, and in the process learn about how MRUnit works behind the scenes.

Figure 13.1 shows the interactions of the unit test with MRUnit, and how, in turn, it interacts with the mapper you're testing.

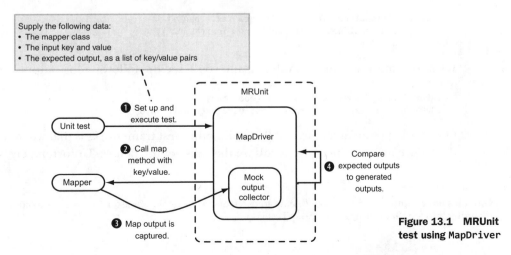

Figure 13.1   MRUnit test using MapDriver

The following[3] code is a simple unit test of the (identity) mapper class in Hadoop:

```java
public class IdentityMapTest extends TestCase {

    private Mapper<Text, Text, Text, Text> mapper;
    private MapDriver<Text, Text, Text, Text> driver;

    @Before
    public void setUp() {
      mapper = new Mapper<Text, Text, Text, Text>();
      driver = new MapDriver<Text, Text, Text, Text>(mapper);
    }

    @Test
    public void testIdentityMapper() {
      driver.withInput(new Text("foo"), new Text("bar"))
            .withOutput(new Text("foo"), new Text("bars"))
            .runTest();

    }
}
```

Create the map object you're testing. Here you're using Hadoop's built-in IdentityMapper, which outputs the input data without any transformations.

The MRUnit driver class you'll use in your test. This is the MapDriver, and as such you need to specify the key/value input and output types for the mapper you're testing in this class.

The withInput method is used to specify an input key/value, which will be fed to the IdentityMapper.

Run the test. If a failure's encountered, it logs the discrepancy, and throws an exception.

The withOutput method is used to specify the output key/value, which MRUnit will compare against the output generated by the mapper being tested.

> **Multiple input support**
>
> Be aware that MRUnit doesn't support multiple input records. If you call the withInput method more than once, it will overwrite the key and value from the previous call to withInput.

MRUnit is not tied to any specific unit testing framework, so if it finds an error it logs the error and throws an exception. Let's see what would happen if your unit test had specified output that didn't match the output of the mapper, as in the following code:

```java
driver.withInput(new Text("foo"), new Text("bar"))
      .withOutput(new Text("foo"), new Text("bar2"))
      .runTest();
```

If you run this test, your test will fail, and you'll see the following log output:

```
ERROR Received unexpected output (foo, bar)
ERROR Missing expected output (foo, bar2) at position 0
```

One of the powerful features of JUnit and other test frameworks is that when tests fail, the failure message includes details on the cause of the failure. Unfortunately, MRUnit

---

[3] **GitHub source**—https://github.com/alexholmes/hadoop-book/blob/master/src/test/java/com/manning/hip/ch13/mrunit/IdentityMapTest.java

Logging configuration

Because MRUnit uses the Apache Commons logging, which defaults to using log4j, you'll need to have a log4j.properties file in the classpath that's configured to write to standard out, similar to the following:

```
log4j.rootLogger=WARN, stdout
log4j.appender.stdout=org.apache.log4j.ConsoleAppender
log4j.appender.stdout.layout=org.apache.log4j.PatternLayout
log4j.appender.stdout.layout.ConversionPattern=
    %-5p [%t][%d{ISO8601}] [%C.%M] - %m%n
```

logs and throws a nondescriptive exception, which means you need to dig through the test output to determine what failed.

What if you wanted to leverage the power of MRUnit, and also leverage the informative errors that JUnit provides when assertions fail? You could modify your code[4] to do that, and bypass MRUnit's testing code:

```
@Test
public void testIdentityMapper() throws IOException {
    List<Pair<Text, Text>> results = driver
        .withInput(new Text("foo"), new Text("bar"))
        .run();

    assertEquals(1, results.size());
    assertEquals(new Text("foo"), results.get(0).getFirst());
    assertEquals(new Text("bar"), results.get(0).getSecond());
}
```

You assert the size and contents of the records.

The run method executes the map function and returns a list of all the output records emitted by the function. Also note that there was no need to call the withOutput method, because you'll do the validation yourself.

With this approach, if there's a mismatch between the expected and actual outputs, you get a more meaningful error message, which report-generation tools can use to easily describe what failed in the test:

```
junit.framework.AssertionFailedError: expected:<bar2> but was:<bar>
```

To cut down on the inevitable copy-paste activities with this approach, I wrote a simple helper class[5] to use JUnit asserts in combination with using the MRUnit driver. Your JUnit test now looks like this:

You're calling withOutput because the helper function can extract the outputs directly from the driver.

```
@Test
public void testIdentityMapper() throws IOException {
    List<Pair<Text, Text>> results = driver
        .withInput(new Text("foo"), new Text("bar"))
        .withOutput(new Text("foo"), new Text("bar"))
        .run();

    MRUnitJUnitAsserts.assertOutputs(driver, results);
}
```

Call the helper function that uses JUnit asserts to test the contents of the expected output with the generated output.

This is much cleaner and removes any mistakes that arise from the copy-paste anti-pattern.

---

[4] **GitHub source**—https://github.com/alexholmes/hadoop-book/blob/master/src/test/java/com/manning/hip/ch13/mrunit/IdentityMapJUnitTest.java

[5] **GitHub source**—https://github.com/alexholmes/hadoop-book/blob/master/src/test/java/com/manning/hip/ch13/mrunit/IdentityMapJUnitAssertsTest.java

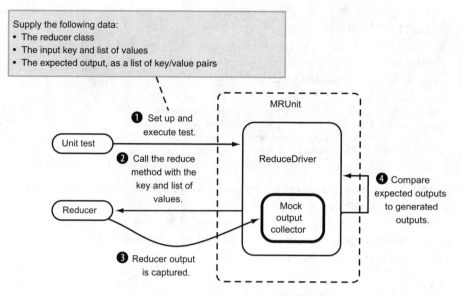

Figure 13.2   MRUnit test using `ReduceDriver`

REDUCE TESTS

Now that we've looked at map function tests, let's look at reduce function tests. The MRUnit framework takes a similar approach for reduce testing. Figure 13.2 shows the interactions of your unit test with MRUnit, and how it in turn interacts with the reducer you're testing.

The following code[6] is a simple unit test for testing the (identity) reducer class in Hadoop:

```
public class IdentityReduceTest extends TestCase {

  private Reducer<Text, Text, Text, Text> reducer;
  private ReduceDriver<Text, Text, Text, Text> driver;

  @Before
  public void setUp() {
    reducer = new Reducer<Text, Text, Text, Text>();
    driver = new ReduceDriver<Text, Text, Text, Text>(reducer);
  }

  @Test
  public void testIdentityMapper() throws IOException {
    List<Pair<Text, Text>> results = driver
      .withInput(new Text("foo"),
        Arrays.asList(new Text("bar1"), new Text("bar2")))
      .withOutput(new Text("foo"), new Text("bar1"))
        .withOutput(new Text("foo"), new Text("bar2"))
```

With the identity reducer you specified two value inputs so you expect two outputs.

When testing the reducer you specify a list of values that MRUnit sends to your reducer.

Add the expected output for the second value.

---

[6]   **GitHub source**—https://github.com/alexholmes/hadoop-book/blob/master/src/test/java/com/manning/hip/ch13/mrunit/IdentityMapJUnitAssertsTest.java

```
        .run();

    MRUnitJUnitAsserts.assertOutputs(driver, results);
  }
}
```

Use the helper class you wrote earlier in the map section.

Now that we've completed our look at the individual map and reduce function tests, let's look at how to test a map and reduce function together.

MAPREDUCE TESTS

MRUnit also supports testing the map and reduce functions in the same test. You feed MRUnit the inputs, which in turn are supplied to the mapper. You also tell MRUnit what reducer outputs you expect.

Figure 13.3 shows the interactions of your unit test with MRUnit, and how, in turn, it interacts with the mapper and reducer you're testing.

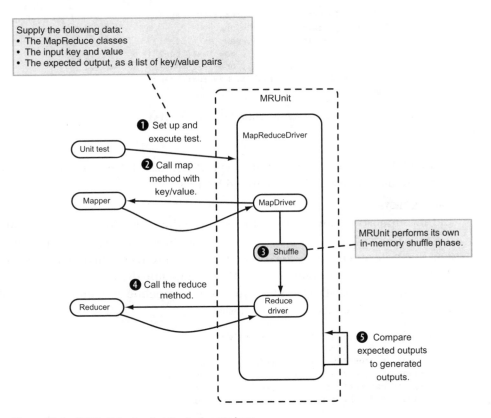

Figure 13.3 MRUnit test using `MapReduceDriver`

The following code[7] is a simple unit test for testing the (identity) mapper and reducer classes in Hadoop:

```java
public class IdentityMapReduceTest extends TestCase {

    private Reducer<Text, Text, Text, Text> reducer;
    private Mapper<Text, Text, Text, Text> mapper;
    private MapReduceDriver<Text, Text, Text, Text, Text, Text> driver;

    @Before
    public void setUp() {
      mapper = new Mapper<Text, Text, Text, Text>();
      reducer = new Reducer<Text, Text, Text, Text>();
      driver =
        new MapReduceDriver<Text, Text, Text, Text, Text, Text>(
        mapper, reducer);
    }

    @Test
    public void testIdentityMapper() throws IOException {
      List<Pair<Text, Text>> results = driver
          .withInput(new Text("foo"), new Text("bar"))
          .withInput(new Text("foo2"), new Text("bar2"))
          .withOutput(new Text("foo"), new Text("bar"))
          .withOutput(new Text("foo2"), new Text("bar2"))
          .run();

      MRUnitJUnitAsserts.assertOutputs(driver, results);
    }
}
```

With the MapReduce driver you need to specify six types, the map input and output key/value types, as well as the reducer key/value output types.

Supply the map inputs. In contrast to the MapDriver and ReduceDriver, the MapReduceDriver supports multiple inputs.

Set the expected reducer outputs.

Now we'll look at our fourth and final type of test that MRUnit supports, pipeline tests, which are used to test multiple MapReduce jobs.

PIPELINE TESTS

MRUnit supports testing a series of map and reduce functions—these are called *pipeline tests*. You feed MRUnit one or more MapReduce functions, the inputs to the first map function, and the expected outputs of the last reduce function. Figure 13.4 shows the interactions of your unit test with MRUnit pipeline driver.

The following code[8] is a unit test for testing a pipeline containing two sets of (identity) mapper and reducer classes in Hadoop:

```java
public class PipelineTest extends TestCase {

    private Mapper<Text, Text, Text, Text> mapper1;
    private Reducer<Text, Text, Text, Text> reducer1;
    private Mapper<Text, Text, Text, Text> mapper2;
    private Reducer<Text, Text, Text, Text> reducer2;
```

---

[7] **GitHub source**—https://github.com/alexholmes/hadoop-book/blob/master/src/test/java/com/manning/hip/ch13/mrunit/IdentityMapReduceTest.java

[8] **GitHub source**—https://github.com/alexholmes/hadoop-book/blob/master/src/test/java/com/manning/hip/ch13/mrunit/PipelineTest.java

```
private PipelineMapReduceDriver<Text, Text, Text, Text> driver;

@Before
public void setUp() {
  mapper1 = new IdentityMapper<Text, Text>();
  reducer1 = new IdentityReducer<Text, Text>();
  mapper2 = new IdentityMapper<Text, Text>();
  reducer2 = new IdentityReducer<Text, Text>();
  driver = new PipelineMapReduceDriver<Text, Text, Text, Text>();
  driver.addMapReduce(
    new Pair<Mapper, Reducer>(mapper1, reducer1));
  driver.addMapReduce(
    new Pair<Mapper, Reducer>(mapper2, reducer2));
}

@Test
public void testIdentityMapper() throws IOException {
  List<Pair<Text, Text>> results = driver
      .withInput(new Text("foo"), new Text("bar"))
      .withInput(new Text("foo2"), new Text("bar2"))
      .withOutput(new Text("foo"), new Text("bar"))
      .withOutput(new Text("foo2"), new Text("bar2"))
      .run();

  MRUnitJUnitAsserts.assertOutputs(driver, results);
}
}
```

Add the first map and reduce pair to the pipeline.

Add the second map and reduce pair to the pipeline.

As with the MapReduceDriver, the PipelineMapReduceDriver supports multiple input records.

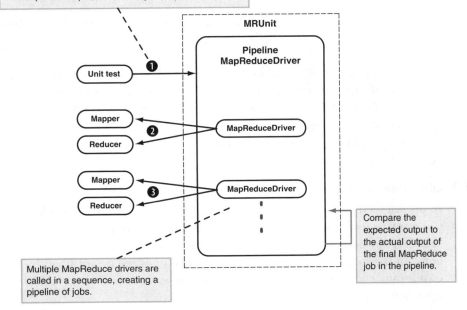

Supply the following data:
- The MapReduce classes
- The input key and value
- The expected output, as a list of key/value pairs

MRUnit

Pipeline MapReduceDriver

Unit test ❶

Mapper
Reducer ❷ **MapReduceDriver**

Mapper
Reducer ❸ **MapReduceDriver**

Compare the expected output to the actual output of the final MapReduce job in the pipeline.

Multiple MapReduce drivers are called in a sequence, creating a pipeline of jobs.

Figure 13.4   MRUnit test using `PipelineMapReduceDriver`

Note that the `PipelineMapReduceDriver` is the only driver in MRUnit that doesn't come in both old and new MapReduce API versions, which is why the previous code uses the old MapReduce API.

Summary

What type of test should you use for your code? Take a look at table 13.1 for some pointers. MRUnit has a few limitations, some of which we touched upon in this technique:

- The MapDriver and ReduceDriver support only a single key as input, which can make it more cumbersome to test map and reduce logic that requires multiple keys, such as those that cache the input data.

- MRUnit isn't integrated with unit test frameworks that provide rich error-reporting capabilities for quicker determination of errors.

- The pipeline tests only work with the old MapReduce API, so MapReduce code that uses the new MapReduce API can't be tested with the pipeline tests.

- There's no support for testing data serialization, or `InputFormat`, `RecordReader`, `OutputFormat`, or `RecordWriter` classes.

Table 13.1 MRUnit tests and when to use them

Type of test	Works well in these situations
Map	You have a map-only job, and you want low-level unit tests where the framework takes care of testing the expected map outputs for your test map inputs.
Reduce	Your job has a lot of complexity in the reduce function and you want to isolate your tests to only that function.
MapReduce	You want to test the combination of the map and reduce functions. These are higher-level unit tests.
Pipeline	You have a MapReduce pipeline where the input of each MapReduce job is the output from the previous job.

Notwithstanding these limitations, MRUnit is an excellent test framework to help you test at the granular level of individual map and reduce functions; MRUnit also can test a pipeline of MapReduce jobs. And because it skips the `InputFormat` and `OutputFormat` steps, your unit tests will execute quickly.

Next we'll look at how you can use the `LocalJobRunner` to test some MapReduce constructs that are ignored by MRUnit.

13.1.3 *LocalJobRunner*

In the last section we looked at MRUnit, a great lightweight unit test library. But what if you want to test not only your map and reduce functions, but also the `InputFormat`, `RecordReader`, `OutputFormat`, and `RecordWriter` code as well as the data serialization between the map and reduce phases? This becomes important if you've written your own input/output format classes because you want to make sure you're testing that code, too.

Hadoop comes bundled with the LocalJobRunner class, which Hadoop and related projects (such as Pig and Avro) use to write and test their MapReduce code. LocalJobRunner allows you to test all the aspects of a MapReduce job, including the reading and writing of data to and from the filesystem.

TECHNIQUE 80   **Heavyweight job testing with the LocalJobRunner**

Tools like MRUnit are useful for low-level unit tests, but how can you be sure that your code will play nicely with the whole Hadoop stack?

Problem

You want to test the whole Hadoop stack in your unit test.

Solution

Leverage the LocalJobRunner class in Hadoop to expand the coverage of your tests to include code related to processing job inputs and outputs.

Discussion

Using the LocalJobRunner makes your unit tests start to feel more like integration tests, because what you're doing is testing how your code works in combination with the whole MapReduce stack. This is great because you can use this to test not only how your user space MapReduce code plays with MapReduce, but also to test InputFormats, OutputFormats, partitioners, and advanced sort mechanisms. The code in the next listing[9] shows an example of how you can leverage the LocalJobRunner in your unit tests.

Using LocalJobRunner to test a MapReduce job

```
public class IdentityTest {

    @Test
    public void run() throws Exception {
        Path inputPath = new Path("/tmp/mrtest/input");
        Path outputPath = new Path("/tmp/mrtest/output");

        Configuration conf = new Configuration();
        conf.set("mapred.job.tracker", "local");

        conf.set("fs.default.name", "file:///");

        FileSystem fs = FileSystem.get(conf);
        if (fs.exists(outputPath)) {
          fs.delete(outputPath, true);
        }
        if (fs.exists(inputPath)) {
          fs.delete(inputPath, true);
        }
        fs.mkdirs(inputPath);

        String input = "foo\tbar";
        DataOutputStream file = fs.create(new Path(inputPath, "part-" + 0));
```

You force use of the LocalJobRunner by setting mapred.job.tracker to local (which is the default).

Force the filesystem to be local (which is the default).

Retrieve the filesystem. By default this will be the local filesystem. The next few lines of code delete the output and input directories to remove any lingering data from other tests.

Write the job inputs into a file.

---

[9] **GitHub source**—https://github.com/alexholmes/hadoop-book/blob/master/src/test/java/com/manning/hip/ch13/localjobrunner/IdentityTest.java

Read the job
output from
the filesystem.

```
        file.writeBytes(input);
        file.close();
                                                        Run an identity MapReduce job.
        Job job = runJob(conf, inputPath, outputPath);
                                                              Assert that the job
        assertTrue(job.isSuccessful());                      completed successfully.

        List<String> lines =
            IOUtils.readLines(fs.open(new Path(outputPath, "part-r-00000")));

        assertEquals(1, lines.size());
        String[] parts = StringUtils.split(lines.get(0), "\t");
        assertEquals("foo", parts[0]);
        assertEquals("bar", parts[1]);
    }                                            Verify the job output.

    public Job runJob(Configuration conf, Path inputPath, Path outputPath)
        throws ClassNotFoundException, IOException, InterruptedException {
        Job job = new Job(conf);
        job.setInputFormatClass(KeyValueTextInputFormat.class);
        job.setMapOutputKeyClass(Text.class);
        FileInputFormat.setInputPaths(job, inputPath);
        FileOutputFormat.setOutputPath(job, outputPath);
        job.waitForCompletion(false);
        return job;
    }
}
```

Writing this test is more involved because you need to handle writing the inputs to the filesystem, and also reading them back out. That's a lot of boilerplate code to have to deal with for every test, and probably something that you want to factor out into a reusable helper class.

Here's an example of a utility class to do that; the following code[10] shows how IdentityTest code can be condensed into a more manageable size:

```
    @Test
    public void run() throws Exception {
                                                        Set the job inputs.
        TextIOJobBuilder builder = new TextIOJobBuilder()
            .addInput("foo", "bar")
            .addExpectedOutput("foo", "bar")
            .writeInputs();

                                            Write the inputs to
        Job job = runJob(                       the filesystem.
            builder.getConfig(),
            builder.getInputPath(),
            builder.getOutputPath());

        assertTrue(job.isSuccessful());
                                            Delegate testing the expected results with
        builder.verifyResults();                    the results to the utility class.
    }
```

Set the expected
job outputs.

---

[10] **GitHub source**—https://github.com/alexholmes/hadoop-book/blob/master/src/test/java/com/manning/hip/ch13/localjobrunner/IdentityWithBuilderTest.java

Summary

So what are some of the limitations to be aware of when using LocalJobRunner?

- LocalJobRunner runs only a single reduce task, so you can't use it to test partitioners.
- As you saw, it's also more labor intensive; you need to read and write the input and output data to the filesystem.
- Jobs are also slow because much of the MapReduce stack is being exercised.
- Finally, it'll be tricky to use this approach to test InputFormats and OutputFormats that aren't file-based.

Despite these limitations, LocalJobRunner is the most comprehensive way to test your MapReduce code, and as such will provide the highest level of assurance that your jobs will run the way you expect them to in Hadoop clusters.

13.1.4   Integration and QA testing

Using the TDD approach, you wrote some unit tests using the techniques in this section. You next wrote the MapReduce code and got it to the point where the unit tests were passing. Hurray. Before you break out the champagne, you still want assurances that the MapReduce code is working prior to running it in production. The last thing you want is your code to fail in production and have to debug it over there. But why, you ask, would my job fail if all of my unit tests pass? Good question, and it could be due to a variety of factors:

- The data you used for your unit tests doesn't contain all of the data aberrations and variances of the data used in production.
- The volume and/or data skew issues cause side effects in your code.
- Differences in Hadoop and other libraries result in behaviors different from those in your build environment.
- Hadoop and operating system configuration differences between your build host and production cause problems.

Because of these factors, when you build integration or QA test environments it's crucial to ensure that the Hadoop version and configurations mirror those of the production cluster. Different versions of Hadoop will behave differently, as will the same version of Hadoop configured in different ways. When you're testing changes in test environments, you want to ensure a smooth transition to production, so do as much as you can to make sure that version and configuration are as close as possible to production.

After your MapReduce jobs are successfully running in integration and QA, you can push them into production, knowing there's a much higher probability that your jobs will work as expected.

This wraps up our look at testing MapReduce code. We looked at some TDD and design principles to help write and test your Java code, and also covered some unit test libraries that make it easier to unit test MapReduce code. Next we'll move into the complex world of debugging problems in MapReduce jobs.

13.2 Debugging user space problems

In this section we'll walk through the steps to isolate and fix problems in your MapReduce user space code. What's meant by *user space code* is code that developers write.

Your MapReduce jobs can fail due to a number of problems, including the following:

- You can run out of memory because you're caching too much data.
- Your logic, which parses input records, may not handle all inputs correctly.
- A logic error exists in your code or in a third-party library.
- Your custom RecordReader or RecordWriter code may have a serialization or deserialization bug.
- Your custom partitioner isn't partitioning records correctly.
- Your custom comparator for primary or secondary sort isn't working as expected.

The list goes on and on. You'll need to take a structured approach to debugging a problem MapReduce job. Figure 13.5 shows a decision tree you can use to narrow down a problem in your MapReduce code.

In the remainder of this section, we'll address the three areas highlighted in figure 13.5 to help with your debugging efforts:

- Examining task logs for details on what's causing the problems
- Finding the inputs that are breaking your code
- Looking at logging and coding guidelines to help you effectively debug your code

We'll kick things off with a look at the task logs.

13.2.1 Accessing task log output

Accessing your task logs is the first step to figuring out what issues you're having with your MapReduce job. Depending on the exact issue, the logs in their current form may or may not help you. For example, if there's a subtle serialization bug in your code, unless the steps in section 13.2.4 were followed, there's a good chance the logs won't be much help in pinpointing serialization as the problem.

<hr>

TECHNIQUE 81 **Examining task logs**

In this technique we'll look at ways to access task logs in the event that you have a problem MapReduce job you want to debug.

Problem

Your MapReduce job is failing, or generating unexpected outputs, and you want to determine if the logs can help you figure out the problem.

Solution

Learn how to use the JobTracker UI to view task logs. You will also look at how you can SSH to individual TaskTracker nodes and examine the logs directly.

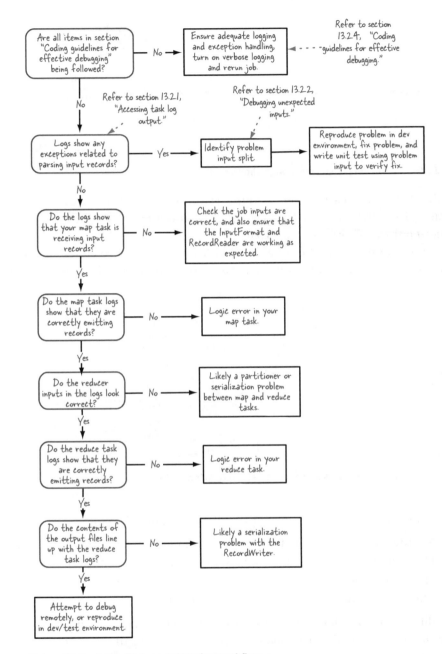

Figure 13.5 A MapReduce debugging workflow

Discussion

So, a job has failed and you want to find out information about the cause of the failure. When a job fails, it's useful to look at the logs to see if they tell you anything about the failure. Each map and reduce task has its own logs, so you need to identify the

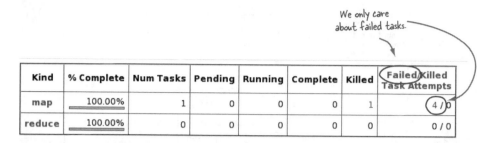

Figure 13.6   JobTracker job summary page showing tasks

tasks that failed. The easiest way to do this is to use the JobTracker UI. Select the job that failed from the main JobTracker page, and you'll be presented with some statistics about tasks, as shown in figure 13.6.

If you click on the number of a failed task you'll see a page containing all of the failed tasks and a stack trace for each task, an example of which is shown in figure 13.7.

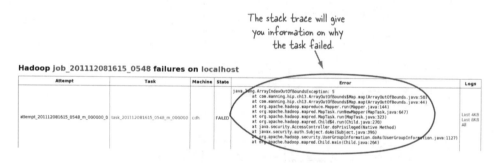

Figure 13.7   JobTracker task summary page showing failed tasks

A number of scenarios under which tasks will fail include following:

- A hardware problem related to the network or the local host running the task exists.
- The HDFS quota for the account running the job has been exceeded.
- Application caching caused the JVM to run out of memory.
- Unexpected input caused the application to fail.

Depending on the problem, you may find additional useful information in the logs, or in the standard out (stdout) or standard error (stderr) of the task process. You can view all three outputs easily by selecting the All link under the Logs column, as shown in figure 13.8.

This is all fine and dandy, but what if you don't have access to the UI? How do you figure out the failed tasks and get at their output files? The job history command-line

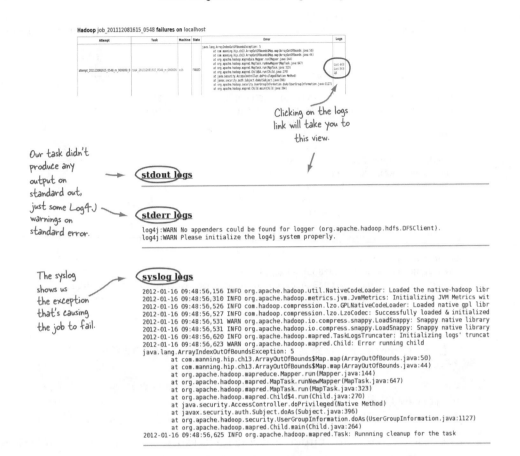

Clicking on the logs link will take you to this view.

Our task didn't produce any output on standard out, just some Log4J warnings on standard error.

stdout logs

stderr logs

```
log4j:WARN No appenders could be found for logger (org.apache.hadoop.hdfs.DFSClient).
log4j:WARN Please initialize the log4j system properly.
```

The syslog shows us the exception that's causing the job to fail.

syslog logs

```
2012-01-16 09:48:56,156 INFO org.apache.hadoop.util.NativeCodeLoader: Loaded the native-hadoop libr
2012-01-16 09:48:56,310 INFO org.apache.hadoop.metrics.jvm.JvmMetrics: Initializing JVM Metrics wit
2012-01-16 09:48:56,526 INFO com.hadoop.compression.lzo.GPLNativeCodeLoader: Loaded native gpl libr
2012-01-16 09:48:56,527 INFO com.hadoop.compression.lzo.LzoCodec: Successfully loaded & initialized
2012-01-16 09:48:56,531 WARN org.apache.hadoop.io.compress.snappy.LoadSnappy: Snappy native library
2012-01-16 09:48:56,531 INFO org.apache.hadoop.io.compress.snappy.LoadSnappy: Snappy native library
2012-01-16 09:48:56,620 INFO org.apache.hadoop.mapred.TaskLogsTruncater: Initializing logs' truncat
2012-01-16 09:48:56,623 WARN org.apache.hadoop.mapred.Child: Error running child
java.lang.ArrayIndexOutOfBoundsException: 5
        at com.manning.hip.ch13.ArrayOutOfBounds$Map.map(ArrayOutOfBounds.java:50)
        at com.manning.hip.ch13.ArrayOutOfBounds$Map.map(ArrayOutOfBounds.java:44)
        at org.apache.hadoop.mapreduce.Mapper.run(Mapper.java:144)
        at org.apache.hadoop.mapred.MapTask.runNewMapper(MapTask.java:647)
        at org.apache.hadoop.mapred.MapTask.run(MapTask.java:323)
        at org.apache.hadoop.mapred.Child$4.run(Child.java:270)
        at java.security.AccessController.doPrivileged(Native Method)
        at javax.security.auth.Subject.doAs(Subject.java:396)
        at org.apache.hadoop.security.UserGroupInformation.doAs(UserGroupInformation.java:1127)
        at org.apache.hadoop.mapred.Child.main(Child.java:264)
2012-01-16 09:48:56,625 INFO org.apache.hadoop.mapred.Task: Runnning cleanup for the task
```

Figure 13.8 TaskTracker page showing output from standard output, standard error, and the logs

interface (CLI) can help because it will include in its output a list of all the failed map and reduce tasks, and for each task the thrown exception:

```
$ hadoop job -history all output
...
FAILED MAP task list for job_201112081615_0548
TaskId          StartTime     FinishTime     Error         InputSplits
===================================================
task_201112081615_0548_m_000000
java.lang.ArrayIndexOutOfBoundsException: 5
        at com.manning.hip.ch13.ArrayOutOfBounds$Map.map(ArrayOutOfBo...
        at com.manning.hip.ch13.ArrayOutOfBounds$Map.map(ArrayOutOfBo...
        at org.apache.hadoop.mapreduce.Mapper.run(Mapper.java:144)
        at org.apache.hadoop.mapred.MapTask.runNewMapper(MapTask.java...
        ...
        http://cdh:50060/tasklog?attemptid=attempt_.
```

The last argument is the output directory of the job, which is used to extract the job history details. The all option gives you verbose output for all tasks.

The failed task name.

A URL that can be used to retrieve all the outputs related to the task. You can also figure out the host that executed the task by examining the host in the URL.

This output is informative: not only do you see the exception, but you also see the task name and the host on which the task was executed. The only data related to the task output you see here is the exception, so to view all of the task outputs you'll need to use the URL in this output:

```
$ curl http://cdh:50060/tasklog?attemptid=attempt_...
```
Using curl to download the outputs from the TaskTracker URL

```
<html> <title>Task Logs: 'attempt_201112081615_0548_m_000000_0'</title>
<body> <h1>Task Logs: 'attempt_201112081615_0548_m_000000_0'</h1><br>
<br><b><u>stdout logs</u></b><br>
<pre>
</pre></td></tr></table><hr><br>
<br><b><u>stderr logs</u></b><br>
<pre> log4j:WARN No appenders could be found ...
log4j:WARN Please initialize the log4j system properly.
</pre></td></tr></table><hr><br>
<br><b><u>syslog logs</u></b><br>
<pre> ...
2012-01-16 09:48:56,623 WARN org.apache.hadoop.mapred.Child:

Error running child
java.lang.ArrayIndexOutOfBoundsException: 5
    at com.manning.hip.ch13.ArrayOutOfBounds$Map.map(ArrayOutOfBounds...
    at com.manning.hip.ch13.ArrayOutOfBounds$Map.map(ArrayOutOfBounds...
...
</pre></td></tr></table><hr><br> </body></html>
```

An HTML tag indicating the start of the standard output.

The start of the standard error.

The start of the logs.

> **TaskTracker accessibility**
>
> For the curl command to work you'll need to run it from a host that has access to the TaskTracker node.

It'll be easier to parse the output by saving the HTML to a file (by adding `-o [filename]` to the curl command), copying that file to your local host, and using a browser to view the file.

What if you're working in an environment where you don't have access to the Job-Tracker or TaskTracker UI? This may be the case if you're working in clusters that have firewalls blocking access to the UI ports from your laptop or desktop. What if you only have SSH access to the cluster? One option is to run Lynx, a text-based web browser, from inside your cluster. If you don't have Lynx you'll have to know how to access the task logs directly. You know the hostname from the URL, so you'll need to first SSH to that host. The logs for each task are contained in the Hadoop logs directory.

> **Location of Hadoop logs**
>
> By default this directory is $HADOOP_HOME/logs, but check your `hadoop-env.xml`, because this can be overridden with the `HADOOP_LOG_DIR` environment variable.

In the example, you're running on a packaged CDH installation and CDH doesn't override the default logs directory, so because HADOOP_HOME is `/usr/lib/hadoop`,

/usr/lib/hadoop/logs/userlogs/job_201112081615_0548/attempt_201112081615_0548_m_000000_0

| Hadoop logs directory | MapReduce job logs | Logs for a specific job | Logs for a specific task attempt |

Figure 13.9   Location of task output files on the TaskTracker node

your logs are under /usr/lib/hadoop/logs.[11] Figure 13.9 shows the entire path to your failed task.

Under this directory you'll find at least the following three files:

- stderr, containing standard error output
- stdout, containing standard output
- stdlog, containing the logs

You can use your favorite editor or simple tools like cat or less to view the contents of these files.

Summary
Often, when things start going wrong in your jobs the task logs will contain details on the cause of the failure. This technique looked at how you could use the JobTracker and, alternatively, the Linux shell to access your logs.

If the data in the logs suggests that the problem with your job is with the inputs (which can be manifested by a parsing exception), you need to figure out what kind of input is causing the problem.

13.2.2   *Debugging unexpected inputs*

In the previous section, you saw how to access failed task output files to help you figure out the root cause of the failure. In the example, the outputs didn't contain any additional information, which means that you're dealing with some MapReduce code that wasn't written to handle error conditions.

If it's possible to easily modify the MapReduce code that's failing, go ahead and skip to section 13.2.4 and look at the strategies to update your code to better handle and report on broken inputs. Roll these changes into your code, push your code to the cluster, and rerun the job. Your job outputs now will contain enough details for you to be able to update your code to better handle the unexpected inputs.

If this isn't an option, read on; we'll look at what to do to isolate the input data that's causing your code to misbehave.

TECHNIQUE 82   **Pinpointing a problem Input Split**

Imagine you have a job that's reading Twitter tweets from a number of input files. Some of the tweets aren't formed correctly (could be a syntax problem or an unexpected value that you're unaware of in your data dictionary), which leads to failure in your processing logic.

---
[11] /usr/lib/hadoop/logs is a symbolic link that points to /var/log/hadoop-[version].

By examining the logs, you're able to determine that there's some data in your input files which is causing your parsing code to fail. But your job has numerous input files and they're all large, so your challenge is to narrow down where the problem inputs exist.

Problem

You want to identify the specific input split that's causing parsing issues.

Solution

Use the `keep.failed.task.files` MapReduce configuration parameter to stop Hadoop from cleaning-up task metadata, and use this metadata to understand information about the input splits for a failing task.

Discussion

Take the following three steps to fix the situation:

1   Identify the bad input record(s).
2   Fix your code to handle the bad input records.
3   Add additional error handling capabilities to your code to make this easier to debug in the future.

In this technique we'll focus on the first item, because it will help you to fix your code. We'll cover future-proofing your code for debugging in section 13.2.4.

The first step you need to do is determine what file contains the bad input record, and even better, find a range within that file, if the file's large. Unfortunately, Hadoop by default wipes out task-level details, including the input splits after the tasks have completed. You'll need to disable this by setting the `keep.failed.task.files` to `true`. You'll also have to rerun the job that failed, but this time you'll be able to extract additional metadata about the failing task.

After rerunning the failed job you'll once again need to use the `hadoop job -history` command discussed in the previous section to identify the host and job or task IDs. With this information in hand, you'll need to use the shell to log into the TaskTracker node, which ran the failed task, and then navigate to the task directory, which contains information about the input splits for the task. Figure 13.10 shows how to do that.

The trick here is, if you have multiple directories configured for `mapred.local.dir`, you'll need to find which directory contains the task directory. This can be easily accomplished with a `find`, as follows:

```
$ cd <mapred.local.dir>
$ find <task-attempt-id>
```

When you've located this directory, you'll see a number of files related to the task, including a file called split.info. This file contains information about the location of the input split file in HDFS, as well as an offset that's used to determine which of the input splits this task is working on. Both the task and job split files are a mixture of text and binary content, so unfortunately, you can't crack out your command-line editor to easily view their contents.

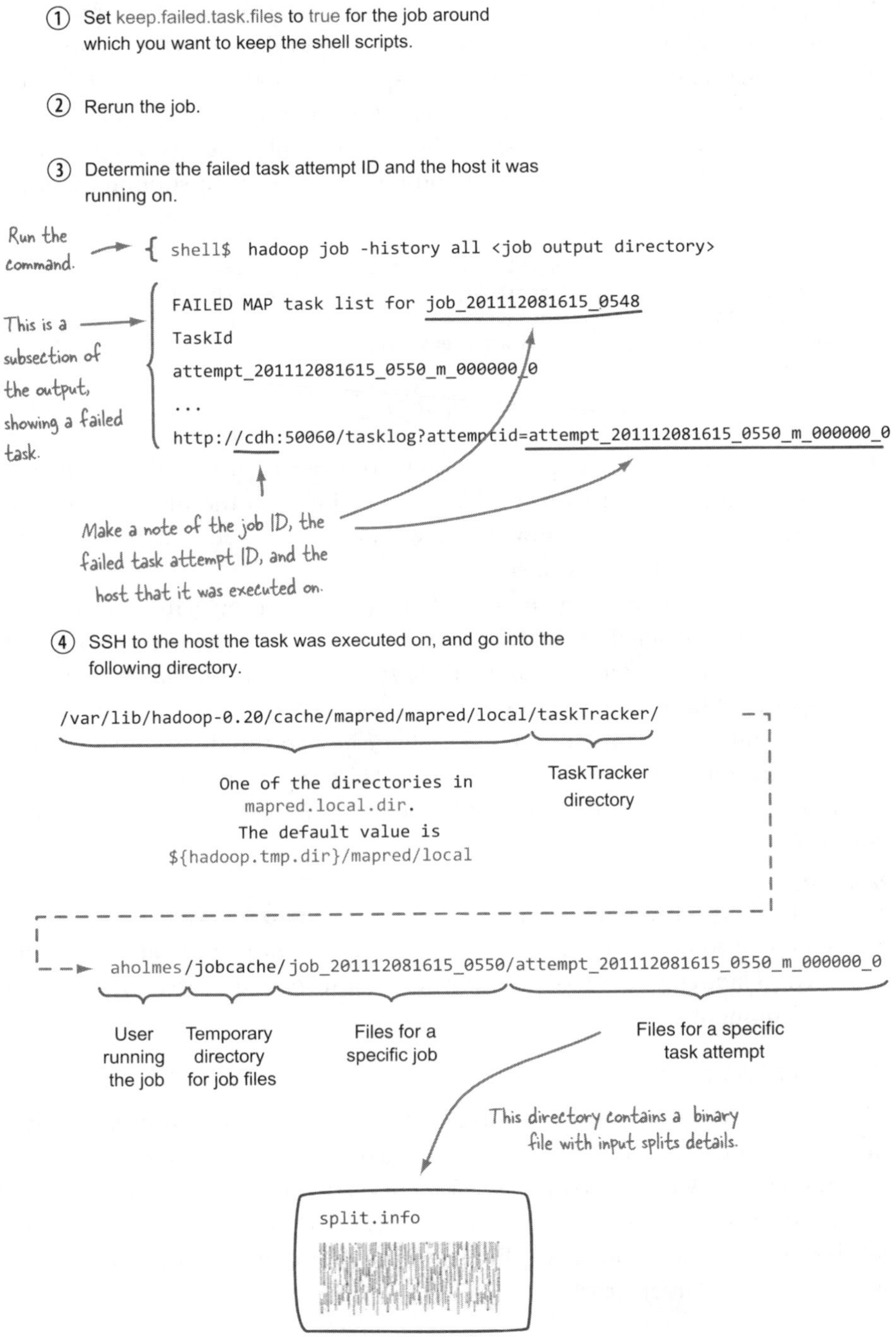

① Set keep.failed.task.files to true for the job around
which you want to keep the shell scripts.

② Rerun the job.

③ Determine the failed task attempt ID and the host it was
running on.

Run the
command. ⟶ { shell$ hadoop job -history all <job output directory>

This is a ⟶
subsection of
the output,
showing a failed
task.

FAILED MAP task list for job_201112081615_0548
TaskId
attempt_201112081615_0550_m_000000_0
...
http://cdh:50060/tasklog?attemptid=attempt_201112081615_0550_m_000000_0

Make a note of the job ID, the
failed task attempt ID, and the
host that it was executed on.

④ SSH to the host the task was executed on, and go into the
following directory.

/var/lib/hadoop-0.20/cache/mapred/mapred/local/taskTracker/

One of the directories in
mapred.local.dir.
The default value is
${hadoop.tmp.dir}/mapred/local

TaskTracker
directory

aholmes/jobcache/job_201112081615_0550/attempt_201112081615_0550_m_000000_0

User
running
the job

Temporary
directory
for job files

Files for a
specific job

Files for a specific
task attempt

This directory contains a binary
file with input splits details.

split.info

Figure 13.10   Accessing the files related to a task on a TaskTracker node

To help with this situation, I've written a utility that can read the input split file for a task and use that information to open the job split file in HDFS, jump into the task-specific offset, and read the task-specific split information. Be warned that there's a good chance this won't work with versions other than Hadoop 0.20.x.

If you run this on the input.split file for your failed task you'll gain some insight into the file and data about the start and end of the split (assuming the input for the task is a file):

```
$ bin/run.sh com.manning.hip.ch13.TaskSplitReader split.info
ToString on split = hdfs://localhost/user/aholmes/users.txt:0+110
Reflection fields = FileSplit[
file=hdfs://localhost/user/aholmes/users.txt,
start=0,
length=110,
hosts=<null> ]
```

At this point you have a couple of options: you can copy the file into your local box and write a unit test that runs the MapReduce job with the file. You also can modify your code to catch an exception, which will allow you to set a breakpoint in your IDE and observe the input that's causing your exception.

Alternatively, depending on the Hadoop distribution you're running, Hadoop comes with a tool called IsolationRunner, which can re-execute a specific task with its input split. Unfortunately, IsolationRunner is broken on 0.20.x[12] and on older Hadoop distributions, but it should work on versions 0.21 and newer. *Hadoop in Action* by Chuck Lam contains an example of how to use the IsolationRunner, as does the Hadoop tutorial at http://goo.gl/FRv1H. You can enable some options so that the task JVM runs with the Java debug agent enabled, and connect to the task via your IDE or jdb.

Summary

We used this technique to identify the input splits for a task that's failing due to a problem with some input data. Next we'll look at how you get at the JVM arguments you used to launch your task—useful when you suspect there's an issue related to the JVM environment.

13.2.3 *Debugging JVM settings*

This technique steps somewhat outside of the realm of your user space MapReduce debugging, but it's a useful technique in situations where you suspect there's an issue with the startup JVM arguments for tasks. For example, sometimes the classpath ordering of JARs is significant and issues with it can cause class loading problems. Also, if a job has dependencies on native libraries, the JVM arguments can be used to debug issues with java.library.path.

---

[12] If you're feeling adventurous, there's a 0.20 patch in the JIRA ticket https://issues.apache.org/jira/browse/HADOOP-4041.

Figuring out the JVM startup arguments for a task

The ability to examine the various arguments used to start a task can be helpful in debugging task failures. For example, let's say you're trying to use a native Hadoop compression codec, but your MapReduce tasks are failing and the errors complain that the native compression libraries can't be loaded. In this case review the JVM startup arguments to determine if all of the required settings exist for native compression to work.

Problem

You suspect that a task is failing due to missing arguments when a task is being launched, and want to examine the JVM startup arguments.

Solution

Use the `keep.failed.task.files` MapReduce configuration parameter to stop Hadoop from cleaning-up task metadata, and use this metadata to view the shell script used to launch the MapReduce map and reduce tasks.

Discussion

As the TaskTracker prepares to launch a map or reduce task, it also creates a shell script that's subsequently executed to run the task. The problem is that MapReduce by default removes these scripts after a job has completed. So, during the executing of a long-running job or task, you'll have access to these scripts, but if tasks and the job are short-lived (which they may well be if you're debugging an issue that causes the task to fail off the bat), you will once again need to set `keep.failed.task.files` to true. Figure 13.11 shows all of the steps required to gain access to the task shell script.

If you were investigating an issue related to the native Hadoop compression, there's a good chance that when you viewed the taskjvm.sh file, you'd notice that it's missing the necessary `-Djava.library.path`, which points to the directories containing the native Linux compression libraries. If this is the case, you can remedy the problem by adding the native path, which you do by exporting `JAVA_LIBRARY_PATH` in `hadoop-env.sh`.

Summary

This technique is useful in situations where you want to be able to examine the arguments used to launch the task JVM. Next we'll look at some coding practices that can help with debugging activities.

13.2.4 Coding guidelines for effective debugging

Debugging MapReduce code in production can be made a whole lot easier if you follow a handful of logging and exception-handling best practices.

Debugging and error handling

Debugging a poorly written MapReduce job consumes a lot of time, and can be challenging in production environments where access to cluster resources is limited.

Problem

You want to know the best practices to follow when writing MapReduce code.

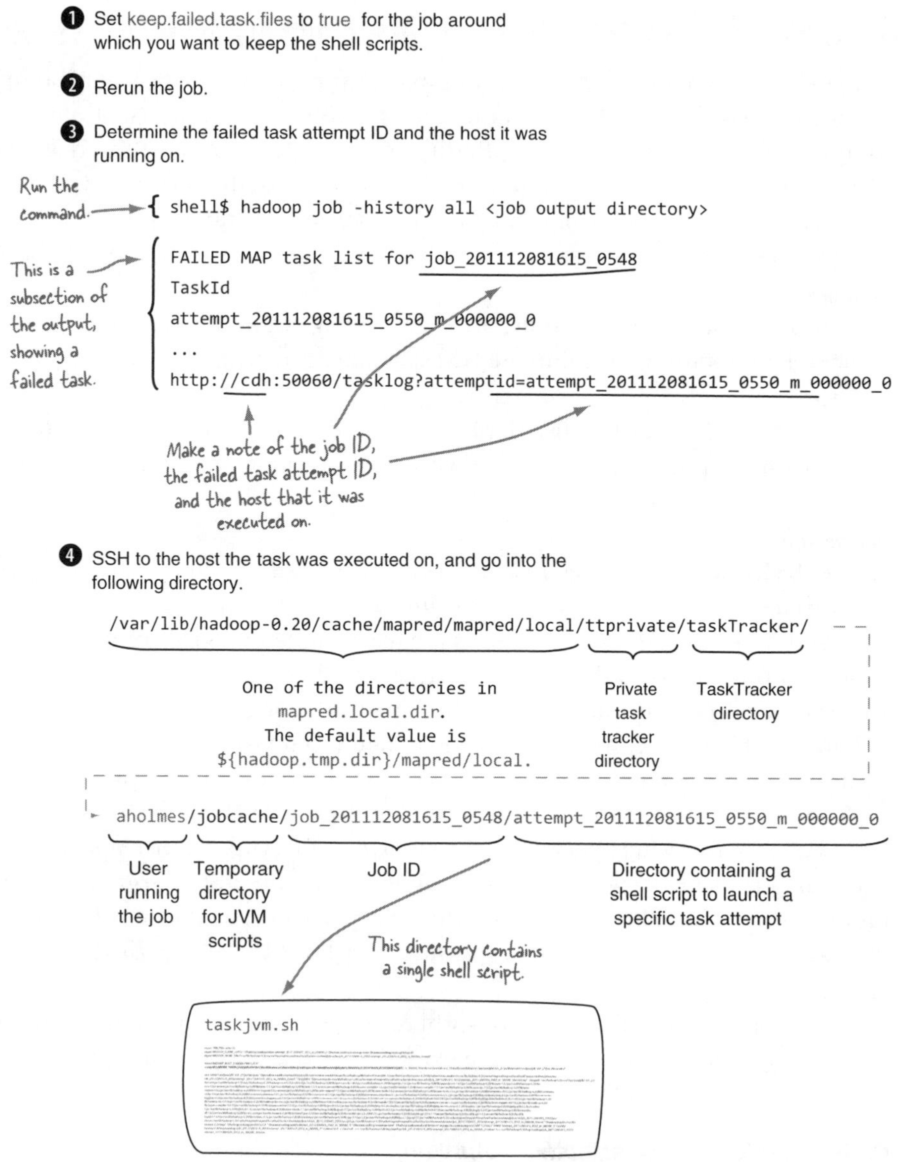

1 Set keep.failed.task.files to true for the job around
which you want to keep the shell scripts.

2 Rerun the job.

3 Determine the failed task attempt ID and the host it was
running on.

Run the
command.────►{ shell$ hadoop job -history all <job output directory>

This is a ────► FAILED MAP task list for job_201112081615_0548
subsection of
the output,   TaskId
showing a   attempt_201112081615_0550_m_000000_0
failed task.   ...
              └─ http://cdh:50060/tasklog?attemptid=attempt_201112081615_0550_m_000000_0

Make a note of the job ID,
the failed task attempt ID,
and the host that it was
executed on.

4 SSH to the host the task was executed on, and go into the
following directory.

/var/lib/hadoop-0.20/cache/mapred/mapred/local/ttprivate/taskTracker/

One of the directories in   Private   TaskTracker
mapred.local.dir.   task   directory
The default value is   tracker
${hadoop.tmp.dir}/mapred/local.   directory

aholmes/jobcache/job_201112081615_0548/attempt_201112081615_0550_m_000000_0

User   Temporary   Job ID   Directory containing a
running   directory   shell script to launch a
the job   for JVM   specific task attempt
             scripts
                            This directory contains
                            a single shell script.

taskjvm.sh

Figure 13.11 How to get to the private directory for a task attempt

Solution
Look at how counters and logs can be used to enhance your ability to effectively
debug and handle problem jobs.

Discussion
Add the following features into your code:

- Include logs to capture data related to inputs and outputs to help isolate where problems exist.
- Catch exceptions and provide meaningful logging output to help track down problem data inputs and logic errors.
- Think about whether you want to rethrow or swallow exceptions in your code.
- Leverage counters and task statuses that can be utilized by driver code and humans alike to better understand what happened during the job execution.

In the following code,[13] you'll see applied a number of the previously described principles.

A mapper job with some best practices applied to assist debugging

```java
public static class Map
    extends Mapper<Text, Text, Text, Text> {
  protected Text outputValue = new Text();
  protected int failedRecords;
  public static enum Counters {
    FAILED_RECORDS
  }

  @Override
  protected void setup(Context context)
      throws IOException, InterruptedException {
    super.setup(context);
    log.info("Input split = {}", context.getInputSplit());
  }


  @Override
  protected void map(Text key, Text value, Context context)
      throws IOException, InterruptedException {

    if(log.isDebugEnabled()) {
      log.debug("Input K[{}],V[{}]", key, value);
    }

    try {
      String id = StringUtils.split(value.toString())[5];
      outputValue.set(id);
      if(log.isDebugEnabled()) {
        log.debug("Output K[{}],V[{}]", key, value);
      }
      context.write(key, outputValue);
    } catch(Exception t) {
      processError(context, t, key, value);
    }
  }

  protected void processError(Context c, Throwable t, Text k, Text v) {
    log.error("Caught exception processing key[" +
      k + "], value[" + v + "]", t);
```

When the task starts, write the input split details to the log. This will tell you the input file for each specific task and the byte offset within that input file that was used to read map input records.

If the logger's in debug mode (which it should never be in production environments unless you're debugging a job), write out the input record key and value. You wouldn't want this to be a System.out or log.info since that would dramatically slow down your job. Note that you enclose both the key and value with square brackets so you can easily identify leading and trailing whitespaces. Also note that this is important because it helps isolate potential problems in your input data, or InputFormat/ RecordReader classes.

You also log the map output key and value. This can be compared to reducer inputs to help determine if there's a serialization or partitioning problem between map and reduce tasks.

Catch any exceptions thrown in your code.

Write out the key and value to the logs. Note that you enclosed both strings with square brackets to easily track down leading or trailing whitespaces.

[13] **GitHub source**—https://github.com/alexholmes/hadoop-book/blob/master/src/main/java/com/ manning/hip/ch13/OptimizedMRForDebugging.java

```
c.getCounter(Counters.FAILED_RECORDS).increment(1);

c.setStatus("Records with failures = " +
    (++failedRecords));
}
}
```

Increment a counter to signal that you hit an error.

Set that task status to indicate you hit an issue with a record, including a count of the total number of failed records this task encountered.

The reduce task should have similar debug log statements added to write out each reduce input key and value, and the output key and value. Doing so will help identify any issues between the map and reduce side, in your reduce code, or a problem with the OutputFormat/RecordWriter.

You used counters to count the number of bad records you encountered. The Job-Tracker UI can be used to view the counter values, as shown in figure 13.12.

| com.manning.hip.ch13.ArrayOutOfBoundsImprovedMapCounters | FAILED_RECORDS | | 10 | 0 | 10 |

Figure 13.12   Screenshot of the counter in JobTracker's job summary page

Depending on how you executed the job, you'll see the counters dumped on standard out. You have programmatic access to counters, and the job history command will also include the counters:

```
$ hadoop job -history all output

Counters:

|Group Name                     |Counter name                  |

Map Value |Reduce Value|Total Value|
----------------------------------------------------------------
...
|com.manning.hip.ch13.ArrayOutOfBoundsImproved$Map$Counters|

FAILED_RECORDS                  |10        |0        |10
...
```

If you look at the logs for your tasks, you'll also see some informative data related to the task:

This tells you what file the task was working on, as well as the input split range.

```
Input split = hdfs://localhost/user/aholmes/users.txt:0+110

Caught exception processing key[anne], value[22 NY]
```

Write out the key and value. Note that because you used square brackets to encapsulate your strings, any leading or whitespace issues will be easily identified.

Because you also updated the task status in your code, you can use the JobTracker UI to easily identify the tasks that had failed records, as shown in figure 13.13.

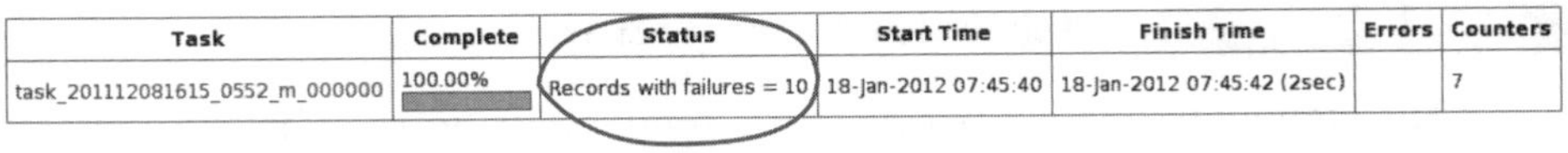

Task	Complete	Status	Start Time	Finish Time	Errors	Counters
task_201112081615_0552_m_000000	100.00%	Records with failures = 10	18-Jan-2012 07:45:40	18-Jan-2012 07:45:42 (2sec)		7

Figure 13.13 JobTracker UI showing map task and status

Summary

We looked at a handful of simple yet useful coding guidelines for your MapReduce code. If they're applied and you hit a problem with your job in production, you'll be in a great position to quickly narrow down possibilities on the root cause of the issue. If the issue's related to the input, your logs will contain details about how the input caused your processing logic to fail. If the issue is related to some logic error, or errors in serialization/deserialization, you can enable debug-level logging and better understand where things are going awry.

Should exceptions be swallowed?

In the previous code example you caught any exception in your code and then made sure to write the exception to the logs along with as much contextual information as possible (such as the current key and value that the reducer was working on). The big question is, should you rethrow the exception, or swallow it?

Rethrowing the exception is tempting because you'll be immediately aware of any issues in your MapReduce code. But if your code is running in production and fails every time it encounters a problem such as some input data that's not handled correctly, ops, dev, and QA will be spending quite a few cycles addressing each issue as it comes along.

Writing code as you did to swallow exceptions has its own problems—for example, what if you encounter an exception on all inputs to the job? If you write code to swallow exceptions, the correct approach is to increment a counter (as in the code example), which the driver class should use after job completion to ensure that most of the input records within some tolerable threshold were successfully processed. If they weren't, the workflow being processed should probably be terminated and the appropriate alerts be sent to notify operations.

Another approach is to not swallow exceptions and to configure record skipping with a call to setMapperMaxSkipRecords and/or setReducerMaxSkipGroups, indicating the number of records that you can tolerate losing if an exception is thrown when they're processed. This is covered in more detail in *Hadoop in Action* by Chuck Lam.

13.3   *MapReduce gotchas*

To complete this chapter we'll examine some common missteps in MapReduce that often lead to hours of debugging. The intent here is to learn by examining practices that should be avoided in MapReduce.

TECHNIQUE 85   **MapReduce anti-patterns**

Throughout this book I've covered a number of patterns to help you write and execute MapReduce jobs. It can be just as useful to learn from anti-patterns, which are patterns that are commonly used but are either ineffective or worse, detrimental in practice.

Problem

You want to learn some MapReduce anti-patterns so you'll be aware of what practices you should avoid.

Solution

Learn and laugh at mistakes that I've made in MapReduce on production clusters, which range from loading too much data into memory in tasks to going crazy with counters and bringing down the JobTracker.

Discussion

Here are some practices that are best avoided.

TOO MUCH CACHE

Caching data in map and reduce tasks is required for many kinds of operations, such as data joins. But in Java the memory overhead of caching is significant (see chapter 6 for specific details), and if your cache becomes too large to fit in Java's heap, your task will fail with an OutOfMemoryError exception.

Data join packages that perform caching (such as the Hadoop contribution org.apache.hadoop.contrib.utils.join package) attempt to mitigate this by limiting the maximum number of records that will be cached. This is an approach worth considering, albeit it assumes the records are not overly large (bear in mind that even if you cap the number of records to a small size, it only takes a handful of large records to blow out your memory).

If you're implementing some strategies (such as capping how many records are being cached), make sure you use counters to identify that you're performing that capping, and ideally, by how much (count how many records aren't being cached), so you can better understand data that's being skipped. If you're working with variable-length records, it may be useful to log records over a certain size—again, to better understand your data and to help you make future caching decisions.

LARGE INPUT RECORDS

Stop to think about the input data to your MapReduce jobs. If each input record isn't a fixed size, there's a chance you could encounter records that are possibly too large to fit into memory. Take, for example, a simple case of a job that reads lines from a text file. You'll likely be using TextInputFormat (the default InputFormat in MapReduce) or KeyValueTextInputFormat. In either case there's no cap on the maximum length of a line, so if you have a line that's millions of characters in length, there's a chance it won't fit into memory (or if it does, any operation you attempt to perform on that string will exhaust your memory).

Luckily, `TextInputFormat` and `KeyValueTextInputFormat` use the same `RecordReader` class, which contains a configuration you can set that limits the maximum line size, `mapred.linerecordreader.maxlength`. It will also log cases where it encountered lines that are over this length, including the byte offset in the input file.

If you're working with other `InputFormats`, you should check to see if they have any mechanisms to limit the size of input records. Similarly, if you're writing an `InputFormat`, think about adding support for limiting the size of records you feed to a map task.

OVERWHELMING EXTERNAL RESOURCES

There's nothing that can stop you from writing MapReduce jobs to pull data from databases, or web servers, or any other data source external to HDFS. Keep in mind, though, the use of these external data sources, both by other users as well as by the MapReduce job. It's possible that the data source you're working with doesn't scale to support hundreds or thousands of concurrent reads or writes, and your single MapReduce job may bring it to its knees. I recommend you limit the number of map and/ or reduce tasks to a small number to minimize the likelihood of this occurring.

SPECULATIVE EXECUTION RACE CONDITIONS

Speculative execution is a mechanism used in MapReduce to guard against slow nodes in a cluster. As the map and reduce phases of a job near completion, MapReduce will launch duplicate tasks that work off of the same inputs as the remaining tasks.

This is fine if your job is writing its outputs using the standard MapReduce output mechanism (and assuming the `InputFormat` being used is correctly handling output committing (see chapter 3 for more details). But what if your job is writing to a database or some other external resource, or directly to a file in HDFS? Now you have multiple tasks both writing the same data, which is probably not what you want.

One approach that tools such as distCp[14] and Sqoop[15] use to guard against this is to disable speculative execution:

```
conf.set("mapred.map.tasks.speculative.execution", "false");
conf.set("mapred.reduce.tasks.speculative.execution", "false");
```

If you're using an `OutputFormat` that's based on the `FileOutputFormat`, and you want to write additional output to HDFS, the best approach is to write into the task's attempt directory. Each task's reduce (or map if a no-reduce job is being run) is written to a temporary attempt directory, and only if the task succeeds are the files moved into the job output directory. The following code[16] shows a map-only job that is writing output to a side-effect file:

```
public static class Map
    extends Mapper<Text, Text, Text, Text> {
```

---

[14] DistCp is a useful tool for copying HDFS data between clusters; see http://hadoop.apache.org/docs/r1.0.3/distcp.html.

[15] Sqoop is a tool to import and export database data to and from HDFS. More details on Sqoop can be found in chapter 2.

[16] **GitHub source**—https://github.com/alexholmes/hadoop-book/blob/master/src/main/java/com/manning/hip/ch13/SideEffectJob.java

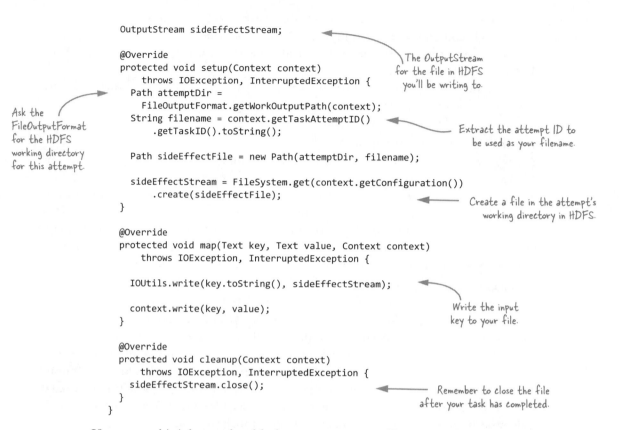

```
OutputStream sideEffectStream;
```
The OutputStream for the file in HDFS you'll be writing to.

```
@Override
protected void setup(Context context)
    throws IOException, InterruptedException {
  Path attemptDir =
    FileOutputFormat.getWorkOutputPath(context);
  String filename = context.getTaskAttemptID()
    .getTaskID().toString();
```
Ask the FileOutputFormat for the HDFS working directory for this attempt.

Extract the attempt ID to be used as your filename.

```
  Path sideEffectFile = new Path(attemptDir, filename);

  sideEffectStream = FileSystem.get(context.getConfiguration())
    .create(sideEffectFile);
}
```
Create a file in the attempt's working directory in HDFS.

```
@Override
protected void map(Text key, Text value, Context context)
    throws IOException, InterruptedException {

  IOUtils.write(key.toString(), sideEffectStream);

  context.write(key, value);
}
```
Write the input key to your file.

```
@Override
protected void cleanup(Context context)
    throws IOException, InterruptedException {
  sideEffectStream.close();
}
}
```
Remember to close the file after your task has completed.

If you run this job you should observe two output files, one written to be the Record-Writer, and the other written by you directly from your map task:

```
$ bin/run.sh com.manning.hip.ch13.SideEffectJob users.txt output

$ hadoop fs -ls output

/user/aholmes/output2/_SUCCESS
/user/aholmes/output2/_logs
/user/aholmes/output2/part-m-00000
/user/aholmes/output2/task_201112081615_0558_m_000000
```

NOT HANDLING BAD INPUT

Working with bad input is often the norm in MapReduce, but if you have code that doesn't expect the unexpected, it may start failing when it sees data it doesn't expect. Ideally, the code should be able to handle these situations, but there is a workaround, without having to touch the code, via the SkipBadRecords class.[17] *Hadoop in Action* by Chuck Lam has more details on how to use this class, but at a basic level this feature allows you to specify the tolerance for the number of records surrounding a bad record that can be discarded.

---

[17] See http://hadoop.apache.org/common/docs/r1.0.0/api/org/apache/hadoop/mapred/SkipBadRecords.html.

CLUSTERS WITH DIFFERENT HADOOP VERSIONS AND CONFIGURATION SETTINGS

It's not uncommon for code that works in unit tests to fail in a cluster. But if you're running multiple clusters, make an effort to ensure that the Hadoop versions, and Hadoop configurations, align as closely as possible. Hadoop's many configuration settings can cause jobs to behave differently, and keeping discrepancies down to a minimum will ensure that a job succeeding on one cluster will work on another cluster.

TESTING AND DEBUGGING WITH LARGE DATASETS

When you're developing and testing MapReduce, Pig, or Hive scripts, it's tempting to work directly with the full set of input data. But doing so flies in the face of rapid development—rather than quickly iterating the development and test cycles, you'll be sitting around waiting for the results of your job, and at the same time needlessly chewing up cluster resources. Instead, look at the sampling techniques presented in chapters 4, 10, and 11 to work on a subset of the input data, and leave the execution against the full set of data until such a time as you're happy with the results using the smaller dataset.

NOT HANDLING PARSING OR LOGIC ERRORS

We already covered this topic in section 13.2.4, but I want to reemphasize that a high percentage of problems you'll encounter in your job are due to unexpected input, and can be as simple an issue as leading or trailing whitespace characters that cause parsing issues. Including measures to be able to quickly debug these issues is crucial.

TOO MANY COUNTERS

Counters are a great mechanism to communicate numerical data to some driver code that's running your MapReduce job. Be warned that each counter incurs some amount of memory overhead in the JobTracker. For each individual counter the memory footprint may be small, but if you use counters carelessly this could lead to memory exhaustion in the JobTracker. An example of this situation would be where you dynamically created a counter for each input record in the map task—it would only take a few million records for there to be a noticeable memory impact and overall slowdown in the JobTracker.

Summary

We covered a few of the bumps you'll face when you work with MapReduce. You'll never be able to foresee all of the potential problems you could encounter, but understanding some of the more common issues we've highlighted in this technique, coupled with a well-thought-out implementation of your MapReduce functions, can go a long way to avoiding those 2 a.m. production debugging sessions.

13.4 *Chapter summary*

This chapter only scratched the surface when it comes to testing and debugging. We laid the groundwork for how to test and debug user space MapReduce, but there's much more to testing and debugging outside of the scope of user space MapReduce.

If you're running any critical MapReduce code in production, it's crucial to follow at least the steps in the testing section of this chapter, where I showed you how to best design your code so it easily lends itself to basic unit testing methodologies outside the scope of Hadoop. We also covered how the MapReduce-related parts of your code could be tested in both lightweight (without MapReduce stack involvement via MRUnit) and more heavyweight (with `LocalTestRunner`) setups.

We also emphasized how to debug issues that result in failing MapReduce jobs, as well as jobs that aren't generating the results you'd expect. We wrapped things up with some examples of badly written MapReduce jobs with the hope that we all can learn from the mistakes of others (including the author).

appendix A
Related technologies

This appendix contains background information on all the related Hadoop technologies in the book. Where applicable, I also include instructions on how to build, install, and configure related projects.

A.1 Hadoop 1.0.x and 0.20.x

This section covers installing, configuring, and running the Cloudera and Apache distributions of Hadoop.

A.1.1 Getting more information

Table A.1 Useful resources

Description	URL
Hadoop in Action by Chuck Lam, geared to helping those that are new to Hadoop	http://www.manning.com/lam/
Apache Hadoop project home	http://hadoop.apache.org
Apache Hadoop releases	http://hadoop.apache.org/common/releases.html
"CDH3 Installation Guide"	http://goo.gl/qiaWA
CDH3 downloads	https://ccp.cloudera.com/display/SUPPORT/Downloads
CDH3 tarballs	http://goo.gl/asj6Y
Michael Noll's guide to install Hadoop 0.20.x on a single host	http://goo.gl/8ogSk
Michael Noll's guide to install Hadoop 0.20.x on multiple hosts (a full cluster setup)	http://goo.gl/NIWoK

A.1.2   *Apache and CDH tarball installation*

The following instructions are for users wanting to install the tarball versions of CDH or the vanilla Apache Hadoop distribution. These instructions are for installing Hadoop on your desktop or laptop in pseudo-distributed mode, and not for a full-blown cluster.

First you'll need to download the tarballs from their respective locations. For Cloudera, go to http://goo.gl/DNztO, click on the tarball download link, and download the tarball called Hadoop 0.20.2+923.142 (the version may be different). For Apache, go to http://hadoop.apache.org/common/releases.html#Download and download the most recent stable 0.20.x release.

Extract the tarball under /usr/local.

> **Installation directory for users that don't have root privileges**
>
> If you don't have root permissions on your host, you can install Hadoop under a different directory, and substitute instances of /usr/local in the following instructions with your directory name.

```
$ cd /usr/local
$ sudo tar -xzf <path-to-cdh-or-apache-tarball>

$ sudo ln -s hadoop-<version> hadoop

$ sudo chown -R <user>:<group> /usr/local/hadoop*
$ mkdir /usr/local/hadoop/tmp
```

CONFIGURATION FOR PSEUDO-DISTRIBUTED MODE

Edit the file /usr/local/hadoop/conf/core-site.xml and make sure it looks like the following:

```
<?xml version="1.0"?>
<?xml-stylesheet type="text/xsl" href="configuration.xsl"?>

<configuration>

  <property>
    <name>hadoop.tmp.dir</name>
    <value>/usr/local/hadoop/tmp</value>
  </property>

  <property>
    <name>fs.default.name</name>
    <value>hdfs://localhost:8020</value>
  </property>

</configuration>
```

Edit the file /usr/local/hadoop/conf/hdfs-site.xml and make sure it looks like the following:

```
<?xml version="1.0"?>
<?xml-stylesheet type="text/xsl" href="configuration.xsl"?>

<configuration>
  <property>
    <name>dfs.replication</name>
    <value>1</value>
  </property>
  <property>
      <!-- specify this so that running 'hadoop namenode -format'
          formats the right dir -->
      <name>dfs.name.dir</name>
      <value>/usr/local/hadoop/cache/hadoop/dfs/name</value>
  </property>
</configuration>
```

Edit the file /usr/local/hadoop/conf/mapred-site.xml and make sure it looks like the following:

```
<?xml version="1.0"?>
<?xml-stylesheet type="text/xsl" href="configuration.xsl"?>

<configuration>
  <property>
    <name>mapred.job.tracker</name>
    <value>localhost:8021</value>
  </property>
</configuration>
```

SSH SETUP

Hadoop uses Secure Shell (SSH) to remotely launch processes such as the Data-Node and TaskTracker, even when everything is running on a single node in pseudo-distributed mode. If you don't already have an SSH key pair, create one with the following command:

```
$ ssh-keygen -b 2048 -t rsa
```

You'll need to copy the .ssh/id_rsa file to the authorized_keys file:

```
$ cp ~/.ssh/id_rsa.pub  ~/.ssh/authorized_keys
```

You'll also need an SSH agent running so that you aren't prompted to enter your password a bazillion times when starting and stopping Hadoop. Different operating systems have different ways to run an SSH agent, and there are links for CentOS and other RedHat derivatives (http://goo.gl/Nffty) and OSX (http://goo.gl/dbdNb). Google is your friend if you're running on a different system.

To verify the agent is running and has your keys loaded, try opening an SSH connection to the local system:

```
$ ssh 127.0.0.1
```

If you're prompted for a password, the agent's not running or doesn't have your keys loaded.

JAVA

You need a current version of Java (1.6 or newer) installed on your system. You'll need to ensure that the system path includes the binary directory of your Java installation. Alternatively, you can edit /usr/local/hadoop/conf/hadoop-env.sh, uncomment out the JAVA_HOME line, and update the value with the location of your Java installation.

ENVIRONMENT SETTINGS

For convenience purposes, it's recommended to add the Hadoop binary directory to your path. The following code shows what you can add to the bottom of your bash shell profile file in ~/.bash_profile (assuming you're running bash):

```
HADOOP_HOME=/usr/local/hadoop
PATH=$PATH:$HADOOP_HOME/bin
export PATH
```

HFDS FORMATTING

Next you need to format HDFS. The rest of the commands in this section assume that the Hadoop binary directory exists in your PATH, as per the instructions in the previous section:

```
$ hadoop namenode -format
```

After HDFS has been formatted, you can start Hadoop with the following script:

```
$ start-all.sh
```

After running the start script, you should use the jps Java utility to check that all the processes are running. You should see the same output as follows (with the exception of the process IDs, which will be different):

```
$ jps
23836 JobTracker
23475 NameNode
23982 TaskTracker
23619 DataNode
24024 Jps
23756 SecondaryNameNode
```

If any of these processes aren't running, you should check the logs directory under /usr/local/hadoop/logs to see why the processes didn't start correctly. Each of the above processes has two output files that can be identified by name and should be checked for errors.

The most common error is that the HDFS formatting step, which I showed earlier, was skipped.

VERIFYING THE INSTALLATION

The following commands can be used to test your Hadoop installation. The first two commands create a directory in HDFS and upload the contents of the Hadoop configuration into HDFS. The third command runs a MapReduce job, and the final command dumps the contents of the job output:

```
$ hadoop fs -mkdir input
$ hadoop fs -put /usr/local/hadoop/conf/*.xml input

$ hadoop jar /usr/local/hadoop/*-examples*.jar grep \
  input output 'dfs[a-z.]+'
$ hadoop fs -cat output/part*
1    dfs.name.dir
1    dfs.replication
1    dfsadmin
```

STOPPING HADOOP

To stop Hadoop use the following command:

```
$ stop-all.sh
```

A.1.3 Hadoop UI ports

There are a number of UIs in Hadoop. Here's a list of them, including the ports that they run on, and URLs that assume they're running on the local host (as is possibly the case if you have a pseudo-distributed installation running).

Table A.2 Hadoop UIs and ports

Component	Default port	Config parameter	Local URL
MapReduce JobTracker	50030	`mapred.job.tracker.http.address`	http://127.0.0.1:50030/
MapReduce TaskTracker	50060	`mapred.task.tracker.http.address`	http://127.0.0.1:50060/
HDFS NameNode	50070	`dfs.http.address`	http://127.0.0.1:50070/
HDFS DataNode	50075	`dfs.datanode.http.address`	http://127.0.0.1:50075/
HDFS SecondaryNameNode	50090	`dfs.secondary.http.address`	http://127.0.0.1:50090/
HDFS Backup and Checkpoint Node	50105	`dfs.backup.http.address`	http://127.0.0.1:50105/

Each of these URLs support the following common paths:

- */logs*—This shows a listing of all the files under hadoop.log.dir. By default this is under $HADOOP_HOME/logs on each Hadoop node.
- */logLevel*—This can be used to view and set the logging levels for Java packages.
- */metrics*—This shows JVM and component-level statistics. Only available in 0.21 and newer (not in 1.0, 0.20.x, or earlier).
- */stacks*—This shows a stack dump of all the current Java threads in the daemon.

A.2   *Flume*

Flume is a log collection and distribution system that can transport log files across a large number of hosts into HDFS. It's an Apache project in incubator status, originally developed and currently maintained and supported by Cloudera.

Chapter 2 contains a section on Flume and how it can be used.

A.2.1   *Getting more information*

Table A.3   Useful resources

Description	URL
Flume Apache incubator web page	http://incubator.apache.org/flume/
"CDH3 Installation Guide" (which covers Flume)	https://ccp.cloudera.com/display/CDHDOC/CDH3+Installation+Guide
An excellent Flume user guide with a high level of detail.	http://archive.cloudera.com/cdh/3/flume-0.9.1+1/UserGuide.html
"Flume Cookbook"	http://archive.cloudera.com/cdh/3/flume-0.9.1+1/Cookbook.html
Cloudera article on how to use Flume to collect Apache web server logs	http://goo.gl/zJEX7

A.2.2   *Installation on CDH*

The resource link titled "CDH3 Installation Guide" shows how to install Flume on CDH. For the purpose of the book, the Flume Master and Flume Node packages should be installed.

A.2.3   *Installation on non-CDH*

Because Flume is currently in incubator status, there aren't any installation instructions for non-CDH Hadoop distributions.

A.3   *Oozie*

Oozie is an Apache project which started life inside Yahoo. It's a Hadoop workflow engine that manages data processing activities.

A.3.1 Getting more information

Table A.4 Useful resources

Description	URL
Oozie Apache incubator web page	http://incubator.apache.org/oozie/
"CDH3 Installation Guide" (which covers Oozie)	https://ccp.cloudera.com/display/CDHDOC/CDH3+Installation+Guide
CDH3 copy of Oozie documentation	http://archive.cloudera.com/cdh/3/oozie/

A.3.2 Installation on CDH

The previous resource link titled "CDH3 Installation Guide" shows how to install Oozie on CDH.

A.3.3 Installation on non-CDH

Oozie is currently in incubator status, so there aren't any download packages or instructions from Apache.

A.4 Sqoop

Sqoop is a tool for importing data from relational databases into Hadoop, and vice versa. It can support any JDBC-compliant database, and also has native *connectors* for efficient data transport to and from mySQL and PostgreSQL.

Chapter 2 contains details on how imports and exports can be performed with Sqoop.

A.4.1 Getting more information

Table A.5 Useful resources

Description	URL
Apache Incubator project page	http://goo.gl/yl4JX
Sqoop JIRA	https://issues.apache.org/jira/browse/SQOOP
Cloudera Sqoop overview	http://goo.gl/aQ1Dd
"Sqoop Installation"	http://goo.gl/c4vN4
"Sqoop User Guide"	http://goo.gl/Ldyn2

A.4.2 Installation on CDH

The resource link above titled "Sqoop Installation" shows how to install Sqoop on CDH.

On RedHat systems run the following command:

```
$ yum install sqoop
```

If you're planning on using Sqoop with MySQL, you'll need to download the MySQL JDBC driver tarball from http://dev.mysql.com/downloads/connector/j/, explode it into a directory, and then copy the JAR file into the Sqoop lib directory:

```
$ tar -xzf mysql-connector-java-5.1.18.tar.gz
$ cd mysql-connector-java-5.1.18
$ sudo cp mysql-connector-java-5.1.18-bin.jar /usr/lib/sqoop/lib
```

A.4.3   *Installation on Apache Hadoop*

Download the Sqoop 1.3.0 tarball from Cloudera's GitHub http://goo.gl/mxckw. Explode the tarball in a directory. The tarball includes prebuilt Sqoop JARs. You'll need to set the following environment variables for Sqoop.

The following instructions assume that you're installing under /usr/local:

```
$ wget --no-check-certificate \
  https://github.com/downloads/cloudera/sqoop/sqoop-1.3.0.tar.gz

$ sudo tar -xzf sqoop-1.3.0.tar.gz -C /usr/local/
```

If you're planning on using Sqoop with MySQL, you'll need to download the MySQL JDBC driver tarball from http://dev.mysql.com/downloads/connector/j/, explode it into a directory, and then copy the JAR file into the Sqoop lib directory:

```
$ tar -xzf mysql-connector-java-5.1.18.tar.gz
$ cd mysql-connector-java-5.1.18
$ sudo cp mysql-connector-java-5.1.18-bin.jar \
  /usr/local/sqoop-1.3.0/lib
```

To run Sqoop there are a few environment variables that you may need to set.

Table A.6   Sqoop environment variables

Environment variable	Description
JAVA_HOME	The directory where Java is installed. If you have the Sun JDK installed on RedHat this would be /usr/java/latest.
HADOOP_HOME	The directory of your Hadoop installation.
HIVE_HOME	Only required if you're planning on using Hive with Sqoop. Refers to the directory where Hive was installed.
HBASE_HOME	Only required if you're planning on using HBase with Sqoop. Refers to the directory where HBase was installed.

The /usr/local/sqoop-1.3.0/bin directory contains the binaries for Sqoop. Chapter 2 contains a number of techniques that show how the binaries are used for imports and exports.

A.5 HBase

HBase is a real-time key/value distributed column-based database modeled after Google's BigTable.

A.5.1 Getting more information

Table A.7 Useful resources

Description	URL
Apache HBase project page	http://hbase.apache.org/
Apache HBase getting started	http://hbase.apache.org/book/quickstart.html
"Apache HBase Reference Guide"	http://hbase.apache.org/book/book.html
"CDH3 Installation Guide" (which covers HBase)	https://ccp.cloudera.com/display/CDHDOC/CDH3+Installation+Guide
Cloudera blog post on HBase Do's and Dont's	http://goo.gl/kAqPB

A.5.2 Installation on CDH

The resource link titled "CDH3 Installation Guide" shows how to install HBase on CDH. For the purpose of the book, it's sufficient to install HBase in *standalone mode* (http://goo.gl/1Y6Bi).

A.5.3 Installation on non-CDH

The previous resource links titled "Apache HBase getting started" and "Apache HBase Reference Guide" have comprehensive installation and configuration instructions for HBase.

A.6 Avro

Avro is a data serialization system that provides features such as compression, schema evolution, and code generation. It can be viewed as a more sophisticated version of a SequenceFile, with additional features such as schema evolution.

Chapter 3 contains details on how Avro can be used in MapReduce as well as with basic input/output streams.

A.6.1   *Getting more information*

Table A.8   Useful resources

Description	URL
Apache project page	http://avro.apache.org/
Avro Apache issue tracking page	https://issues.apache.org/jira/browse/AVRO
Cloudera blog about Avro use	http://goo.gl/K8YyH
CDH usage page for Avro	https://ccp.cloudera.com/display/CDHDOC/Avro+Usage
Avro 1.5.4 Javadocs with instructions on how Avro can be used in MapReduce	http://goo.gl/IY2Kb

A.6.2   *Installation*

Avro is a full-fledged Apache project, so you can download the binaries from the downloads link from the previous Apache project page link.

A.7   *Protocol Buffers*

Protocol Buffers is Google's data serialization and Remote Procedure Call (RPC) library, which is used extensively at Google. In this book we'll use it in conjunction with Elephant Bird and Rhipe. Elephant Bird requires version 2.3.0 of Protocol Buffers (and won't work with any other version), and Rhipe only works with Protocol Buffers version 2.4.0 and newer.

A.7.1   *Getting more information*

Table A.9   Useful resources

Description	URL
Protocol Buffers project page	http://code.google.com/p/protobuf/
"Developer Guide"	http://bit.ly/JIXlv
Downloads page, containing a link for version 2.3.0 (required for use with Elephant Bird)	http://code.google.com/p/protobuf/downloads/list

A.7.2   *Building Protocol Buffers*

We'll cover how to build and install Protocol Buffers.

BUILDING

Download the 2.3 or 2.4 (2.3 for Elephant Bird, and 2.4 for RHIPE) source tarball from http://code.google.com/p/protobuf/downloads and extract the contents.

You'll need a C++ compiler, which can be installed on 64-bit RHEL systems with the following command:

```
sudo yum install gcc-c++.x86_64
```

Build and install the native libraries and binaries:

```
$ cd protobuf-<version>/
$ ./configure
$ make
$ make check
$ sudo make install
```

Build the Java library:

```
$ cd java
$ mvn package install
```

Copy the Java JAR into Hadoop's lib directory. The following instructions are for CDH:

```
# replace the following path with your actual
# Hadoop installation directory
#
# the following is the CDH Hadoop home dir
#
export HADOOP_HOME=/usr/lib/hadoop


$ cp target/protobuf-java-2.3.0.jar $HADOOP_HOME/lib/
```

A.8   Apache Thrift

Apache Thrift is essentially Facebook's version of Protocol Buffers. It offers very similar data serialization and RPC capabilities. We'll use it with Elephant Bird to support Thrift in MapReduce. Elephant Bird only works with Thrift version 0.5.

A.8.1   Getting more information

Thrift documentation is lacking, something which the project page attests to.

Table A.10   Useful resources

Description	URL
Project page	http://thrift.apache.org/
Blog post with a tutorial	http://bit.ly/vXpZOz
Downloads page, containing a link for version 0.5 (required for use with Elephant Bird)	http://bit.ly/vsmlhJ

A.8.2   Building Thrift 0.5

We'll cover how to build and install Thrift.

BUILDING

Download the 0.5 source tarball from http://bit.ly/vsmIhJ and extract the contents. Install some Thrift dependencies:

```
$ sudo yum  install automake libtool flex bison pkgconfig gcc-c++ \
   boost-devel libevent-devel zlib-devel python-devel \
   ruby-devel php53.x86_64 php53-devel.x86_64
```

Build and install the native and Java/Python libraries and binaries:

```
$ ./configure
$ make
$ make check
$ sudo make install
```

Build the Java library. This step requires Ant to be installed, instructions for which are available at http://ant.apache.org/manual/index.html.

```
$ cd lib/java
$ ant
```

Copy the Java JAR into Hadoop's lib directory. The following instructions are for CDH:

```
# replace the following path with your actual
# Hadoop installation directory
#
# the following is the CDH Hadoop home dir
#
export HADOOP_HOME=/usr/lib/hadoop

$ cp lib/java/libthrift.jar $HADOOP_HOME/lib/
```

A.9   Snappy

Snappy is a native compression codec developed by Google, which offers fast compression and decompression times. It can't be split (as opposed to LZOP compression). In the book code examples where we don't need splittable compression, we'll use Snappy because of its time efficiency. In this section we'll cover how to build and set up your cluster to work with Snappy.

A.9.1   Getting more information

Table A.11   Useful resources

Description	URL
Google's project page on Snappy	http://code.google.com/p/snappy/
Snappy integration with Hadoop	http://code.google.com/p/hadoop-snappy/
CDH Snappy installation instructions	https://ccp.cloudera.com/display/CDHDOC/Snappy+Installation

A.9.2 *Install Hadoop native libraries on CDH*

CDH includes Snappy in its hadoop-0.20-native package, as well as the CDH tarball. If you're running from the tarball, you already have Snappy, and if you're running packaged CDH, you'll simply need to follow the instructions at https://ccp.cloudera.com/display/CDHDOC/Snappy+Installation.

A.9.3 *Building Snappy for non-CDH*

The following steps will walk you through the process to build, install, and configure Snappy compression. Before you do this, I should mention a few key considerations as you're performing these steps:

- It's highly recommended that you build the libraries on the same hardware that you have deployed in production.
- All of the installation and configuration steps will need to be performed on any client hosts that will be using Snappy, as well as *all* the DataNodes in your cluster.

INSTALL HADOOP NATIVE LIBRARIES

If you're using the vanilla Apache Hadoop distribution, it already comes bundled with Linux 32-bit and 64-bit native libraries under $HADOOP_HOME/lib/native. For other Hadoop distributions, please consult your vendor about how to install native Hadoop libraries. You can also build the native libraries yourself by following the instructions at http://hadoop.apache.org/common/docs/r1.0.0/native_libraries.html.

BUILDING SNAPPY

Download and explode a release of the Snappy sources from http://code.google.com/p/snappy/downloads/list.

   If you don't already have the GCC compiler installed, you can install it with the following command (on RHEL-based Linux systems):

```
$ sudo yum install gcc-c++.x86_64


$ cd snappy-<version>
$ ./configure
$ make
$ sudo make install
```

BUILDING HADOOP-SNAPPY

You'll need to use a Subversion client to download the source for Hadoop-Snappy:

```
$ svn checkout http://hadoop-snappy.googlecode.com/svn/trunk/ \
  hadoop-snappy
```

You'll also need to have Maven installed and the automake and libtool packages installed to build it:

```
$ sudo yum install automake libtool

$ cd hadoop-snappy/
$ mvn package
```

After it's built, copy the libraries into your Hadoop lib directory:

```
# replace the following path with your actual
# Hadoop installation directory
#
# the following is the CDH Hadoop home dir
#
export HADOOP_HOME=/usr/lib/hadoop

$ cp -R \
target/hadoop-snappy-<version>-tar/hadoop-snappy-<version>/lib/* \
$HADOOP_HOME/lib
```

CONFIGURING HADOOP

Next you need to configure Hadoop core to be aware of your new compression codec. Add the following lines to your core-site.xml (in CDH it's located in /etc/hadoop/conf/core-site.xml). Make sure you remove the newlines and spaces such that there are no whitespace characters between the commas.

The following codecs also assume that you have the LZO/P codecs available. If you don't, simply remove the two class names from the value part of the io.compression.codecs property, as well as removing the entire io.compression.codec.lzo.class property:

```
<property>
  <name>mapred.compress.map.output</name>
  <value>true</value>
</property>
<property>
  <name>mapred.map.output.compression.codec</name>
  <value>org.apache.hadoop.io.compress.SnappyCodec</value>
</property>
<property>
  <name>io.compression.codecs</name>
  <value>org.apache.hadoop.io.compress.GzipCodec,
  org.apache.hadoop.io.compress.DefaultCodec,
  org.apache.hadoop.io.compress.BZip2Codec,
  com.hadoop.compression.lzo.LzoCodec,
  com.hadoop.compression.lzo.LzopCodec,
  org.apache.hadoop.io.compress.SnappyCodec
  </value>
</property>
<property>
  <name>io.compression.codec.lzo.class</name>
  <value>com.hadoop.compression.lzo.LzoCodec</value>
</property>
```

The CDH /usr/lib/hadoop/bin/hadoop script will automatically add the native directories to the JVM's java.library.path. However, if you're running client-side Hadoop code that's not being invoked via this script, you'll need to add the following to your Java command line (there should be no whitespace after the colon and the */usr...* part):

```
-Djava.library.path=/usr/lib/hadoop/lib/native/Linux-amd64-64:/usr/lib64
```

The bin/run.sh which you use to launch your example code also will ensure that the -Djava.library.path is set correctly to include the native directory appropriate for your platform.

A.10 *LZOP*

LZOP is a compression codec that can be used to support splittable compression in MapReduce. Chapter 5 has a section dedicated to working with LZOP. In this section we'll cover how to build and set up your cluster to work with LZOP.

A.10.1 *Getting more information*

Table A.12   Useful resources

Description	URL
Blog post from Twitter about why they use LZO, including some statistics and setup instructions.	http://bit.ly/dfEvGn
Todd Lipcon's LZO GitHub repository, which is what we'll use to build the native and Java libraries. Todd Lipcon is a Cloudera employee (and Hadoop committer) who maintains this code for compatibility with CDH.	https://github.com/toddlipcon/hadoop-lzo

A.10.2 *Building LZOP*

The following steps walk you through the process to build, install, and configure LZOP compression. Before you do this, I should mention a few key considerations as you're performing these steps:

- It's highly recommended that you build the libraries on the same hardware that you have deployed in production.
- All of the installation and configuration steps will need to be performed on any client hosts that will be using LZOP, as well as *all* the DataNodes in your cluster.

INSTALL HADOOP NATIVE LIBRARIES ON CDH

LZOP has a dependency on Hadoop running with native libraries, so you'll first need to get the Hadoop native libraries set up. Luckily, with CDH this is simple:

```
$ yum install hadoop-0.20-native.x86_64
```

This results in the following files being installed:

```
$ rpm -ql hadoop-0.20-native-0.20.2+923.97-1
/usr/lib/hadoop-0.20/lib/native
/usr/lib/hadoop-0.20/lib/native/Linux-amd64-64
/usr/lib/hadoop-0.20/lib/native/Linux-amd64-64/libhadoop.a
/usr/lib/hadoop-0.20/lib/native/Linux-amd64-64/libhadoop.la
/usr/lib/hadoop-0.20/lib/native/Linux-amd64-64/libhadoop.so
/usr/lib/hadoop-0.20/lib/native/Linux-amd64-64/libhadoop.so.1
/usr/lib/hadoop-0.20/lib/native/Linux-amd64-64/libhadoop.so.1.0.0
```

```
/usr/lib/hadoop-0.20/lib/native/Linux-amd64-64/libsnappy.a
/usr/lib/hadoop-0.20/lib/native/Linux-amd64-64/libsnappy.la
/usr/lib/hadoop-0.20/lib/native/Linux-amd64-64/libsnappy.so
/usr/lib/hadoop-0.20/lib/native/Linux-amd64-64/libsnappy.so.1
/usr/lib/hadoop-0.20/lib/native/Linux-amd64-64/libsnappy.so.1.1.1
```

INSTALL HADOOP NATIVE LIBRARIES ON NON-CDH

If you're using the vanilla Apache Hadoop distribution, it already comes bundled with Linux 32-bit and 64-bit native libraries under $HADOOP_HOME/lib/native. For other Hadoop distributions please consult your vendor about how to install native Hadoop libraries. You can also build the native libraries yourself by following the instructions at http://hadoop.apache.org/common/docs/r1.0.0/native_libraries.html.

INSTALL THE LZOP NATIVE LIBRARIES

To use LZOP you must install the native LZOP libraries. On RedHat this is as simple as the following:

```
$ yum install liblzo-devel
```

On CentOS you must download the 64- or 32-bit lzo and lzo-devel RPMs from http://pkgs.repoforge.org/lzo/ for your OS version and architecture.

BUILD, INSTALL, AND CONFIGURE LZOP LIBRARIES FOR HADOOP

There are two separate GitHub repositories that are maintaining LZOP libraries. Todd Lipcon maintains a version that's tested for compatibility with CDH at https://github.com/toddlipcon/hadoop-lzo, and Twitter manages another version that contains more recent changes at https://github.com/kevinweil/hadoop-lzo. For the latest and greatest, go with the Twitter, unless you're running CDH and you want a version that's been baked and tested to work with CDH.

This code contains the sources for both a native and Java LZOP library. Prebuilt versions of the libraries aren't bundled, so you'll need to build them yourself. After you've downloaded and exploded the tarball, change into the directory that was just exploded and run the build to generate both the native and Java libraries:

```
$ ant package
```

After you're done, copy the resulting libraries into the Hadoop library directives:

```
# replace the following path with your actual
# Hadoop installation directory
#
# the following is the CDH Hadoop home dir
#
export HADOOP_HOME=/usr/lib/hadoop
$ cp ./build/hadoop-lzo-<version>.jar $HADOOP_HOME/lib/
$ cp -R build/hadoop-lzo-<version>/lib/native/* \
      $HADOOP_HOME/lib/native/
```

CONFIGURING HADOOP

Next you need to configure Hadoop core to be aware of your new compression codecs. Add the following lines to your core-site.xml (in CDH it's located in /etc/hadoop/conf/core-site.xml). Make sure you remove the newlines and spaces such that there are no whitespace characters between the commas.

The value for io.compression.codecs assumes that you have the Snappy compression codec already installed. If you don't, simply remove org.apache.hadoop.io.compress .SnappyCodec from the value:

```
<property>
  <name>mapred.compress.map.output</name>
  <value>true</value>
</property>
<property>
  <name>mapred.map.output.compression.codec</name>
  <value>com.hadoop.compression.lzo.LzoCodec</value>
</property>
<property>
  <name>io.compression.codecs</name>
  <value>org.apache.hadoop.io.compress.GzipCodec,
  org.apache.hadoop.io.compress.DefaultCodec,
  org.apache.hadoop.io.compress.BZip2Codec,
  com.hadoop.compression.lzo.LzoCodec,
  com.hadoop.compression.lzo.LzopCodec,
  org.apache.hadoop.io.compress.SnappyCodec</value>
</property>
<property>
  <name>io.compression.codec.lzo.class</name>
  <value>com.hadoop.compression.lzo.LzoCodec</value>
</property>
```

The CDH /usr/lib/hadoop/bin/hadoop script will automatically add the native directories to the JVM's java.library.path. But if you're running client-side Hadoop code that's not being invoked via this script, you'll need to add the following to your Java command line (there should be no whitespace after the colon and the */usr...* part).

```
-Djava.library.path=/usr/lib/hadoop/lib/native/Linux-amd64-64:/usr/lib64
```

The bin/run.sh that you use to launch your example code also will ensure that the -Djava.library.path is set correctly to include the native directory appropriate for your platform.

A.11 *Elephant Bird*

Elephant Bird is a project that provides utilities for working with LZOP-compressed data. It also provides a container format that supports working with Protocol Buffers and Thrift in MapReduce.

A.11.1   Getting more information

Table A.13   Useful resource

Description	URL
Project page	https://github.com/kevinweil/elephant-bird

A.11.2   Installation

For Elephant Bird to work, you need to build and install LZO, Protocol Buffers, and Thrift. Please refer to their respective sections in this appendix for instructions.

After this is done, copy the Elephant Bird JAR from your Maven repository located at http://goo.gl/C6nPp and copy it into your Hadoop lib directory. The following instructions work for CDH (substitute /usr/lib/hadoop/lib/ with your Hadoop lib directory for other Hadoop distributions):

```
$ wget http://goo.gl/C6nPp
$ sudo cp elephant-bird-2.0.5.jar /usr/lib/hadoop/lib/
```

Elephant Bird version

The code in the book is compiled against version 2.0.5 of Elephant Bird. The installation instructions above ensure that the 2.0.5 Elephant Bird JAR is placed into the Hadoop lib directory. If a newer version of the Elephant Bird JAR is copied into the Hadoop lib directory there's a chance that some of the examples in this book will fail.

A.12   Hoop

Hoop is an HTTP/S server which provides access to all the HDFS operations.

A.12.1   Getting more information

Table A.14   Useful resources

Description	URL
GitHub project page	https://github.com/cloudera/hoop
Cloudera introduction to Hoop	http://goo.gl/ZnADQ
Hoop REST API details	http://goo.gl/qVyTf
Getting started (download, build, install, configure, run)	http://goo.gl/9CjVZ

A.12.2   Installation

The "Getting started" resource link has comprehensive instructions on how to download, configure, and run the Hoop server.

A.13 MySQL

MySQL (or another JDBC-compliant database) is needed by some projects such as Sqoop and Oozie.

A.13.1 MySQL JDBC drivers

The JDBC driver for MySQL can be downloaded from http://dev.mysql.com/downloads/connector/j/.

A.13.2 MySQL server installation

MySQL packages are usually available for most Linux systems and can be downloaded using the normal package installation scripts. For non-Linux systems, consult the MySQL project page at www.mysql.com for download and installation instructions.

CENTOS
For CentOS, MySQL can be installed via Yum:

```
$ sudo yum install  mysql.x86_64 mysql-server.x86_64
```

It's generally a good idea to run the mysql_secure_installation script to harden the MySQL installation. Get more details at http://goo.gl/WHQMO:

```
$ sudo /usr/bin/mysql_secure_installation
```

Now you can run mysql:

```
$ sudo /sbin/service mysqld start
```

A.14 Hive

Apache Hive is a data warehouse project that provides a simplified and SQL-like abstraction on top of Hadoop.

Chapter 10 is dedicated to techniques using Hive.

A.14.1 Getting more information

Table A.15 Useful resources

Description	URL
Apache project page	http://hive.apache.org/
Apache release and downloads	http://hive.apache.org/releases.html
"CDH3 Installation Guide" (which covers Hive)	https://ccp.cloudera.com/display/CDHDOC/CDH3+Installation+Guide
Apache Hive wiki	https://cwiki.apache.org/confluence/display/Hive/Home

Table A.15 Useful resources *(continued)*

Description	URL
"Hive Mailing Lists"	http://hive.apache.org/mailing_lists.html
Hive language manual	https://cwiki.apache.org/confluence/display/Hive/LanguageManual
Hive DDL manual	https://cwiki.apache.org/confluence/display/Hive/LanguageManual+DDL
Hive DML manual	https://cwiki.apache.org/Hive/languagemanual-dml.html
Hive UDFs (for common arithmetic, relation, and string functions)	https://cwiki.apache.org/confluence/display/Hive/LanguageManual+UDF
Hive joins	https://cwiki.apache.org/confluence/display/Hive/LanguageManual+Joins
Default Hive configuration settings	http://goo.gl/18oyT

A.14.2 Installation on CDH

The resource link titled "CDH3 Installation Guide" shows how to install Hive on CDH.

A.14.3 Installation on non-CDH

The resource link titled "Apache release and downloads" contains a download link to get to the Hive tarball. The tarball can be extracted on any node that has access to a Hadoop instance. The following shows instructions on installation into the /usr/local directory:

```
$ cd /usr/local
$ sudo tar -xzf <path/to/download/dir>/hive-<version>.tar.gz
$ sudo ln -s hive-<version> hive
```

A.14.4 Configuring MySQL for metastore storage

Out of the box, Hive is configured to use an embedded database (Derby) to store metadata. This means that each individual user account would have their own Derby database and couldn't share Hive database metadata. To remedy this, it's recommended to install a database such as MySQL to store the metadata. This appendix includes a separate section with MySQL installation instructions.

After there's a MySQL server accessible from the Hive installation, you need to configure Hive to use that database. This involves updating the hive-site.xml file to add lines similar to the following example. These instructions were modeled after the Hive wiki entry at http://goo.gl/IWioT. We'll assume that MySQL is running on the local host, and that the database name is called *hive*, and the MySQL username and password for accessing the hive database are hive_user and hive_pwd. Please replace these values with the actual values in your setup.

```
<?xml version="1.0"?>
<?xml-stylesheet type="text/xsl" href="configuration.xsl"?>

<configuration>
```

```
  <property>
    <name>javax.jdo.option.ConnectionURL</name>
    <value>
      jdbc:mysql://127.0.0.1/hive?createDatabaseIfNotExist=true
    </value>
  </property>

  <property>
    <name>javax.jdo.option.ConnectionDriverName</name>
    <value>com.mysql.jdbc.Driver</value>
  </property>

  <property>
    <name>javax.jdo.option.ConnectionUserName</name>
    <value>hive_user</value>
  </property>

  <property>
    <name>javax.jdo.option.ConnectionPassword</name>
    <value>hive_pwd</value>
  </property>

</configuration>
```

ConnectionURL **whitespace**

Because of the line length limitations in the code segments, the value for javax.jdo.option.ConnectionURL is on a separate line. When you copy the following XML, you'll need to remove any whitespace between the start and end tags and the actual value.

The username and password must have already been created in MySQL, using commands similar to those below:

```
$ mysql -u root -p

CREATE DATABASE hive;
CREATE USER 'hive_user'@'localhost' IDENTIFIED BY 'hive_pwd';
GRANT ALL PRIVILEGES ON hive.* TO 'hive_user'@'localhost';
FLUSH PRIVILEGES;
```

You'll also need to copy the MySQL JDBC driver JAR into the Hive lib directory. The MySQL section in this appendix includes a link for obtaining the JAR. This file should be copied into [HIVE-HOME]/lib.

A.14.5 *Hive warehouse directory permissions*

In a multiuser environment, you need to make sure that the directories used by Hive have been opened up:

```
$ hadoop fs -mkdir /tmp
$ hadoop fs -chmod 777 /tmp
```

```
$ hadoop fs -mkdir /user/hive/warehouse
$ hadoop fs -chmod 777 /user/hive/warehouse
```

A.14.6 *Testing your Hive installation*

Before running Hive, you should add the Hive binary directory to your path, as well as HADOOP_HOME (ideally you'd add this to your ~/.bash_profile file). The following lines assume Hive is installed under /usr/local/hive, and that Hadoop is installed under /usr/local/hadoop:

```
$ export HIVE_HOME=/usr/local/hive
$ export HADOOP_HOME=/usr/local/hadoop

$ echo "val1-val2" > /tmp/foobar.txt

$ hive

hive> CREATE TABLE pokes (foo STRING, bar STRING)
      ROW FORMAT DELIMITED FIELDS TERMINATED BY '-'
      STORED AS TEXTFILE;

hive> LOAD DATA LOCAL INPATH '/tmp/foobar.txt'
      OVERWRITE INTO TABLE pokes;

hive> SELECT * FROM pokes;
OK
val1    val2
```

A.15   Pig

Apache Pig is a MapReduce pipeline project that provides a simplified abstraction on top of Hadoop.

Chapter 11 is dedicated to techniques using Pig.

A.15.1 *Getting more information*

Table A.16   Useful resources

Description	URL
Apache project page	http://pig.apache.org/
Apache release and downloads	http://pig.apache.org/releases.html
"CDH3 Installation Guide" (which covers Pig)	https://ccp.cloudera.com/display/CDHDOC/CDH3+Installation+Guide
Apache Pig wiki	https://cwiki.apache.org/confluence/display/PIG/Index
Pig mailing lists	http://pig.apache.org/mailing_lists.html
"Pig Latin Basics"	http://pig.apache.org/docs/r0.9.2/basic.html

A.15.2 Installation on CDH

The resource link titled "CDH3 Installation Guide" shows how to install Pig on CDH.

A.15.3 Installation on non-CDH

The resource link titled "Apache release and downloads" contains a download link to get to the Hive tarball. Download the tarball and then extract to a local directory. The following shows instructions on installation into the /usr/local directory:

```
$ cd /usr/local
$ sudo tar -xzf <path/to/download/dir>/pig-<version>.tar.gz
$ sudo ln -s pig-<version> pig
```

A.15.4 Building PiggyBank

There are many useful user-defined functions in PiggyBank, which is a Pig contrib. With CDH, the PiggyBank JAR already exists, but if you're working with Apache Hadoop, you'll need to build it using the following instructions. The instructions assume that Pig is installed under /usr/local/pig, and that the Oracle JDK is installed under /usr/java/latest:

```
$ export JAVA_HOME=/usr/java/latest
$ cd /usr/local/pig
$ ant
$ cd contrib/piggybank/java
$ ant
```

This will generate /usr/local/pig/contrib/piggybank/java/piggybank.jar.

A.15.5 Testing your Pig installation

Before running Pig, you should add the Pig binary directory to your path, as well as HADOOP_HOME (ideally you'd add this to your ~/.bash_profile file). The following lines assume Pig is installed under /usr/local/pig, and that Hadoop is installed under /usr/local/hadoop:

```
$ export PIG_HOME=/usr/local/pig
$ export HADOOP_HOME=/usr/local/hadoop
$ pig
grunt> copyFromLocal /etc/passwd /tmp/passwd
grunt> A = load '/tmp/passwd' using PigStorage(':');
grunt> B = foreach A generate $0 as id;
grunt> DUMP B;
(root)
(bin)
(daemon)
(adm)
...
```

A.16   Crunch

Crunch is a pure Java library that lets you write code that's executed in MapReduce without having to actually use MapReduce specific constructs.

A.16.1 Getting more information

Table A.17   Useful resources

Description	URL
GitHub project page	https://github.com/cloudera/crunch
Cloudera's "Crunch for Dummies"	http://goo.gl/3HbOT

A.16.2 Installation

The following instructions can be used to download and build Crunch:

```
$ git clone https://github.com/cloudera/crunch.git
$ cd crunch
$ mvn install
$ cd examples/
$ mvn package
```

A.17   R

R is an open source tool for statistical programming and graphics.

Chapter 8 contains details on how R can be used in conjunction with Hadoop.

A.17.1 Getting more information

Table A.18   Useful resources

Description	URL
R project page	http://www.r-project.org/
R function search engine	http://rseek.org/

A.17.2 Installation on RedHat-based systems

Installing R from Yum makes things easy: it will figure out RPM dependencies and install them for you.

Go to http://www.r-project.org/, click on CRAN, select a download region that's close to you, select RedHat, and pick the version and architecture appropriate for your system. Replace the URL in baseurl in the following code and execute the command to add the R mirror repo to your Yum configuration:

```
$ sudo -s
$ cat << EOF > /etc/yum.repos.d/r.repo
# R-Statistical Computing
```

```
[R]
name=R-Statistics
baseurl=http://cran.mirrors.hoobly.com/bin/linux/redhat/el5/x86_64/
enabled=1
gpgcheck=0
EOF
```

A simple Yum command can be used to install R on 64-bit systems:

```
$ sudo yum install R.x86_64
```

perl-File-Copy-Recursive RPM

On CentOS, the Yum install may fail, complaining about a missing dependency. In this case, you may need to manually install the perl-File-Copy-Recursive RPM (for CentOS you can get it from http://goo.gl/grfDP).

A.17.3 Installation on non-RedHat systems

Go to http://www.r-project.org/, click on CRAN, select a download region that's close to you, and select the binaries appropriate for your system.

A.18 RHIPE

RHIPE is a library that improves the integration between R and Hadoop.

Chapter 8 contains details on how RHIPE can be used in conjunction with Hadoop.

A.18.1 Getting More Information

Table A.19 Useful resources

Description	URL
RHIPE GitHub page	https://github.com/saptarshiguha/RHIPE
RHIPE documentation	http://saptarshiguha.github.com/RHIPE/

A.18.2 Dependencies

Each node in your Hadoop cluster will require the following components:

- RHIPE requires Protocol Buffers version 2.4 or newer. Refer to section A.7 for details on how to build and install Protocol Buffers.
- R must be installed. Installation instructions are in section A.17.

A.18.3 *Installation on CentOS*

Unfortunately, Rhipe isn't integrated with CRAN, the R repository that's used to quickly download and install R packages. The following instructions have been tested on CentOS 5.7.

These instructions will need to be executed on all your Hadoop nodes and any client-side nodes using Rhipe.

Download RHIPE from https://github.com/saptarshiguha/RHIPE/downloads:

```
$ sudo -s
$ export PKG_CONFIG_PATH=/usr/local/lib/pkgconfig
$ export HADOOP = <your Hadoop installation directory>
$ export HADOOP_LIB = $HADOOP/lib
$ export HADOOP_CONF_DIR=$HADOOP/conf
$ /sbin/ldconfig
$ cat << EOF > /etc/ld.so.conf.d/Protobuf-x86.conf
/usr/local/lib
EOF
$ R CMD INSTALL Rhipe_<version>.tar.gz
```

Test the Rhipe installation:

```
$ R
> library(Rhipe)
---------------------------------------------------------
| IMPORTANT: Before using Rhipe call rhinit() |
| Rhipe will not work or most probably crash        |
---------------------------------------------------------
```

A.19 *RHadoop*

RHadoop is an open source tool developed by Revolution Analytics for integrating R with MapReduce.

Chapter 8 contains details on how RHadoop can be used in conjunction with Hadoop.

A.19.1 *Getting more information*

Table A.20   Useful resources

Description	URL
RHadoop project page	https://github.com/RevolutionAnalytics/RHadoop
RHadoop downloads and prerequisites	https://github.com/RevolutionAnalytics/RHadoop/wiki/Downloads
rmr wiki including prerequisites	https://github.com/RevolutionAnalytics/RHadoop/wiki/rmr
RHadoop wiki	https://github.com/RevolutionAnalytics/RHadoop/wiki
RHadoop tutorial	https://github.com/RevolutionAnalytics/RHadoop/blob/master/rmr/pkg/docs/tutorial.md

A.19.2 *Dependencies*

Each node in your Hadoop cluster will require the following components:

- R Installation instructions are in section A.17.
- Three R packages need to be installed: RJSONIO (0.95-0 or later recommended), itertools, and digest:

```
$ sudo -s
$ R
> install.packages("RJSONIO")
> install.packages("itertools")
> install.packages("digest")
> install.packages("rJava")
```

If you get an error installing rJava, you may need to set JAVA_HOME and reconfigure R prior to running the rJava installation:

```
$ sudo -s
$ export JAVA_HOME=/usr/java/latest
$ R CMD javareconf
$ R
> install.packages("rJava")
```

A.19.3 *rmr/rhdfs installation*

These instructions will need to be executed on all your Hadoop nodes and any client-side nodes using rmr/rhdfs.

RHadoop comes with three packages, but we'll focus on the rmr and rhdfs packages which provide MapReduce and HDFS integration with R. The other package in RHadoop is rhbase for HBase integration.

Click on the rmr and rhdfs download links on https://github.com/RevolutionAnalytics/RHadoop/wiki/Downloads. Then execute the following commands:

```
$ sudo R CMD INSTALL rmr_<version>.tar.gz
$ sudo R CMD INSTALL rhdfs_<version>.tar.gz
```

Test that the rmr package was installed correctly:

```
$ R
> library(rmr)
Loading required package: RJSONIO
Loading required package: itertools
Loading required package: iterators
Loading required package: digest
```

A.20 *Mahout*

Mahout is a predictive analytics project that offers in-JVM as well as MapReduce implementations for some of its algorithms.

Chapter 9 contains details on how Mahout can be used in conjunction with Hadoop.

A.20.1 *Getting more information*

Table A.21   Useful resources

Description	URL
Mahout project page	http://mahout.apache.org/
Mahout downloads	https://cwiki.apache.org/confluence/display/MAHOUT/Downloads
Mahout wiki	https://cwiki.apache.org/confluence/display/MAHOUT/Mahout+Wiki
Mahout algorithms	https://cwiki.apache.org/confluence/display/MAHOUT/Algorithms

A.20.2 *Mahout installation*

Mahout should be installed on a node which has access to your Hadoop cluster. Mahout is a client-side library and doesn't need to be installed on your Hadoop cluster.

Mahout is packaged as a tarball. The following instructions will work on most Linux Operating Systems.

Click on the "official release" links on the Mahout download page on https://cwiki.apache.org/confluence/display/MAHOUT/Downloads and select the current release (this book was tested on release 0.6). Download the Mahout distribution tarball and then execute the following instructions:

```
$ cd /usr/local
$ sudo tar -xzf <path-to-mahout-tarball>

$ sudo ln -s mahout-distribution-<version> mahout

$ sudo chown -R <user>:<group> /usr/local/mahout*
```

For convenience it's worthwhile updating your ~/.bash_profile to export an environment variable MAHOUT_HOME to your installation directory. The following command shows how this can be performed on the command line (the same command can be copied into your bash profile file):

```
$ export MAHOUT_HOME=/usr/local/mahout
```

appendix B
Hadoop built-in
ingress and egress tools

In this appendix, we'll look at built-in mechanisms to read and write to HDFS, including the NameNode's embedded HTTP server, and Hoop, a REST-based HDFS proxy. This will help you understand what tools Hadoop provides out of the box. Chapter 2 provides higher-level techniques and approaches for data ingress and egress.

B.1 Command line

It's easy to copy files to and from HDFS using the command-line interface (CLI). The put and get options will perform these tasks for you. The put option is more useful than the copyFromLocal option because it supports multiple file sources and it can also work with standard input. For example, to read from standard input and write to a file in HDFS, you'd do the following:

```
$ echo "the cat sat on the mat" | hadoop fs -put - /stdin-example.txt
$ hadoop fs -cat /stdin-example.txt
the cat sat on the mat
```

There are also moveFromLocal and moveToLocal options that can be useful for ingress/egress operations where you want to remove the source after the copy has completed.

B.2 Java API

Hadoop has an org.apache.hadoop.fs package that contains the filesystem classes. The FileSystem class is the abstracted class that has several implementations including DistributedFileSystem for HDFS. It exposes basic filesystem operations such as create, open, and delete, among others. Chapter 2 contains examples of how to read and write to HDFS in Java.

B.3   *Python/Perl/Ruby with Thrift*

Apache Thrift is an open source client-server RPC protocol library. Hadoop has a contrib project (contributed in JIRA ticket HADOOP-3754) that contains a Thrift server and bindings for various client languages including Python, Ruby, and Perl. Figure B.1 shows the Thrift HDFS interface architecture.

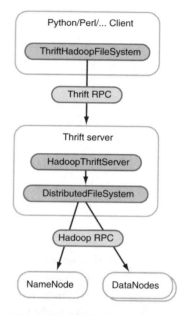

Figure B.1   Thrift client and server HDFS architecture

The Thrift client, Thrift server, and NameNode components can all exist on separate hosts. For convenience sake, you would likely want to co-locate the Thrift server on the same node as the NameNode. The Thrift interface is useful in situations where programming languages other than Java need access to HDFS.

Getting the Thrift HDFS interface to work is a two-step process: running the server, and then writing and running a client to perform filesystem operations.

CDH in RPM form doesn't come with all the JARs needed to run Thrift, so you'll need to download the CDH tarball (from https://ccp.cloudera.com/display/DOC/CDH+Version+and+Packaging+Information), which contains everything you need. Explode the tarball into a directory on your pseudo-distributed host. There's a script that's supposed to launch the Thrift server, but it doesn't work, so you'll quickly write your own. Create a start_thrift_server_cdh.sh file in the ./src/contrib/thriftfs/scripts path relative to your CDH tarball directory. It should contain the contents seen here:

```
$ cd <CDH_TARBALL_DIR>/src/contrib/thriftfs/scripts
$ cat start_thrift_server_cdh.sh
#!/bin/sh

TOP=../../../..

CLASSPATH=$CLASSPATH:$TOP/*
CLASSPATH=$CLASSPATH:$TOP/lib/*
CLASSPATH=$CLASSPATH:$TOP/src/contrib/thriftfs/lib/*
CLASSPATH=$CLASSPATH:$TOP/contrib/thriftfs/*

CLASS=org.apache.hadoop.thriftfs.HadoopThriftServer

java -Dcom.sun.management.jmxremote -cp $CLASSPATH $CLASS $*
```

After you've created the start_thrift_server_cdh.sh script, make it an executable and then run the server:

```
$ chmod +x start_thrift_server_cdh.sh
$ ./start_thrift_server_cdh.sh
Starting the hadoop thrift server on port [51322]...
```

Now that your server's running, you need to tackle the client side. I wrote a simple Python script that uses the Thrift-generated HDFS client API to perform a simple read of a file in HDFS, which is available at GitHub at http://goo.gl/MYqFZ. The main Python function that performs the copy from HDFS to local disk can be seen here:

```
def get(self, hdfs, local):

  output = open(local, 'wb')

  path = Pathname();
  path.pathname = hdfs;
  input = self.client.open(path)

  # find size of hdfs file
  filesize = self.client.stat(path).length

  # read 1MB bytes at a time from hdfs
  offset = 0
  chunksize = 1024 * 1024
  while True:
    chunk = self.client.read(input, offset, chunksize)
    if not chunk: break
    output.write(chunk)
    offset += chunksize
    if (offset >= filesize): break

  self.client.close(input)
  output.close()
```

When you run your Python client, you need to specify the Thrift server port that it dumped on standard out when it started. You'll write a file in HDFS and then use your Thrift Python client to copy it back to the local filesystem:

```
$ echo "the cat sat on the mat" | hadoop fs -put - /stdin-example.txt
$ python ./hdfs-get.py --port 51322 \
    --source /stdin-example.txt --dest /tmp/stdin-example.txt
$ cat /tmp/stdin-example.txt
the cat sat on the mat
```

It worked!

The disadvantage of using the Thrift server is that it adds another layer of indirection on top of HDFS, which means that your reads and writes won't be as fast as they could be. Also, because the Thrift server is the one performing all the interactions with HDFS, you've lost any client-side data locality that may result when a Thrift client is running on a DataNode.

You can see more examples of HDFS operations with Thrift in Python in the Hadoop source code under src/contrib/thriftfs/scripts/hdfs.py.

B.4   *Hadoop FUSE*

Hadoop comes with a component called FuseDFS, which allows HDFS to be mounted as a Linux volume via Filesystem in Userspace (FUSE). Figure B.2 shows its architecture.

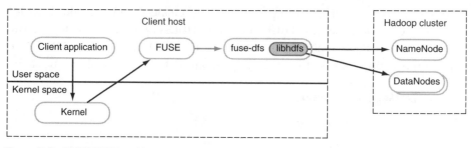

Figure B.2 HDFS FUSE architecture

Because FUSE is a user space filesystem, there are quite a number of hops between the client application and HDFS.

The first step to getting things going is to install FuseDFS:

```
$ sudo yum install hadoop-0.20-fuse
```

If you wanted to mount HDFS on /app/hdfs-fuse, you would do the following:

```
$ mkdir /app/hdfs-fuse
$ hadoop-fuse-dfs dfs://localhost:8020 /app/hdfs-fuse -d
```

Now you can interact with HDFS with your normal filesystem utilities. When you are finished using Hadoop FUSE, you can kill the hadoop-fuse-dfs application and then unmount the directory:

```
$ umount /app/hdfs-fuse
```

The convenience offered by using Hadoop FUSE is overshadowed by issues that make it not recommended for general use. The main issues are around performance and consistency. Hadoop FUSE is executed in user space and involves many layers between the client and the eventual HDFS operation, which results in poor performance. It also can't support use by any tools or applications that perform random writes. And if you write a file, there's no guarantee that the subsequent read will result in the contents you just wrote, so its consistency model is much worse than that of HDFS. This is shown in the following example, where you write a file into HDFS and immediately read it, only to find that it seems to contain no contents:

The file appears to be empty.

You write a file to HDFS and immediately attempt to concatenate it to standard output.

```
$ echo "asdadafsdfasgsfg" > alex; cat alex
$
$ cat alex
asdadafsdfasgsfg
```

If you wait a second or two and reissue the cat command, you'll now see the contents of the file.

In conclusion, although Hadoop FUSE sounds like an interesting idea, it's not ready for use in production environments.

B.5 NameNode embedded HTTP

The advantage of using HTTP to access HDFS is that it relieves the burden of having to have the HDFS client code installed on any host that requires access. Further, HTTP is ubiquitous and many tools and most programming languages have support for HTTP, which makes HDFS that much more accessible.

The NameNode has an embedded Jetty HTTP/HTTPS web server, which is used for the SecondaryNameNode to read images and merge them back. It also supports the HTFP filesystem, which utilities such as distCp use to enable cross-cluster copies when Hadoop versions differ. It supports a handful of operations and only read operations (HDFS writes aren't supported). The web server can be seen in figure B.3.

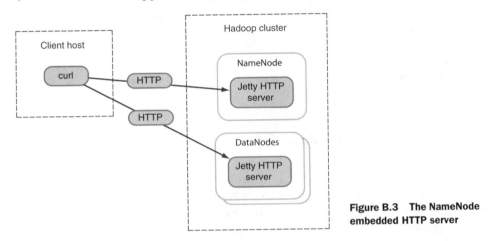

Figure B.3 The NameNode embedded HTTP server

Let's look at a handful of basic filesystem operations that can be made with the embedded HTTP server. The following shows an example of using curl, a client HTTP utility, to perform a directory listing:

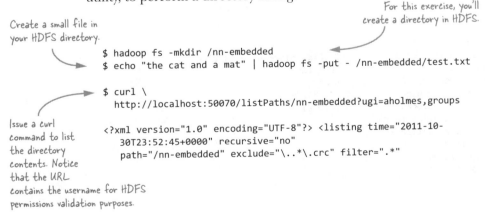

Create a small file in your HDFS directory.

For this exercise, you'll create a directory in HDFS.

```
$ hadoop fs -mkdir /nn-embedded
$ echo "the cat and a mat" | hadoop fs -put - /nn-embedded/test.txt

$ curl \
    http://localhost:50070/listPaths/nn-embedded?ugi=aholmes,groups

<?xml version="1.0" encoding="UTF-8"?> <listing time="2011-10-
    30T23:52:45+0000" recursive="no"
    path="/nn-embedded" exclude="\..*\.crc" filter=".*"
```

Issue a curl command to list the directory contents. Notice that the URL contains the username for HDFS permissions validation purposes.

```
    version="0.20.2-cdh3u2">
      <directory path="/nn-embedded"
      modified="2011-10-30T23:52:39+0000"
      accesstime="1970-01-01T00:00:00+0000"
      permission="drwxr-xr-x"
      owner="aholmes"
      group="supergroup"/>
    <file path="/nn-embedded/test.txt"
      modified="2011-10-30T23:52:39+0000"
      accesstime="2011-10-30T23:52:39+0000"
      size="23"
      replication="1"
      blocksize="67108864"
      permission="-rw-r--r--"
      owner="aholmes"
      group="supergroup"/> </listing>
```

⟵ The response contains a listing element with two child elements, the first one being the element representing the directory.

⟵ This element represents the file.

Files can be downloaded from the embedded HTTP NameNode server too. In the following example you're downloading the file you uploaded in the last step (/nn-embedded/test.txt):

```
$ wget \
http://localhost:50070/data/nn-embedded/test.txt?ugi=aholmes,groups \
  -O test.txt
$ cat test.txt
the cat and a mat
```

That's pretty much all that the embedded HTTP server currently supports in terms of file-level operations.

What's interesting with the implementation of this servlet is that it redirects the actual file download to one of the DataNodes that contains the first block of the file. That DataNode then streams back the entire file to the client.

There are a few other operations that can be performed via the HTTP interface, such as fsck for retrieving any issues with the filesystem, and contentSummary, which returns statistical information about a directory, such as quota limits, size, and more:

```
$ curl http://localhost:50070/fsck?ugi=aholmes,groups
.Status: HEALTHY
Total size:    1087846514 B
Total dirs:    214
Total files:   315
Total blocks (validated):    1007 (avg. block size 1080284 B)
Minimally replicated blocks:    1007 (100.0 %)
Over-replicated blocks:      0 (0.0 %)
Under-replicated blocks:    360 (35.749752 %)
Mis-replicated blocks:       0 (0.0 %)
Default replication factor:    1
Average block replication:    1.0
Corrupt blocks:         0
Missing replicas:      3233 (321.05264 %)
Number of data-nodes:       1
Number of racks:         1
```

```
$ curl http://localhost:50070/contentSummary/?ugi=aholmes,groups
<?xml version="1.0" encoding="UTF-
    8"?> <org.apache.hadoop.fs.ContentSummary length="23" fileCount="1"
directoryCount="1" quota="-1" spaceConsumed="23" spaceQuota="-1"/>
```

These three operations combined together can be used to read information from HDFS, but that's about it.

B.6 HDFS proxy

The HDFS proxy is a component in the Hadoop contrib that provides a web app proxy frontend to HDFS. Its advantages over the embedded HTTP server are an access-control layer and support for multiple Hadoop versions. Its architecture can be seen in figure B.4.

Because the HDFS proxy leverages the embedded HTTP Jetty server in the NameNode, it has the same limitations that you saw in that section, primarily around only being able to support file reads. Details about how to install and use the HDFS proxy are available at http://goo.gl/A9dYc.

B.7 Hoop

Hoop is a REST, JSON-based HTTP/HTTPS server that provides access to HDFS, as seen in figure B.5. Its advantage over the current Hadoop HTTP interface is that it supports writes as well as reads. It's a project created by Cloudera as a full replacement for the existing Hadoop HTTP service, and it's planned for contribution into Hadoop. Hoop will be included in the 2.x Hadoop release (see https://issues.apache.org/jira/browse/HDFS-2178).

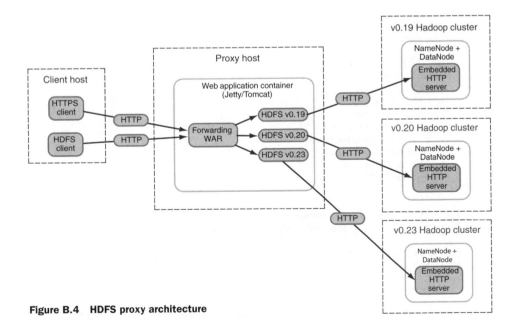

Figure B.4   HDFS proxy architecture

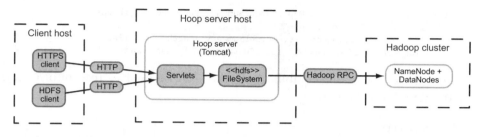

Figure B.5   Hoop architecture

Installation is documented at https://github.com/cloudera/hoop. After you have the Hoop server up and running, it's simple to perform filesystem commands via curl:[1] Let's go through a sequence of basic filesystem manipulations, where you create a directory, write a file, and then list the directory contents:

Create a directory, /hoop-test.

```
$ curl -X POST \
    "http://localhost:14000/hoop-test?op=mkdirs&user.name=aholmes"
{"mkdirs":true}

$ url="http://localhost:14000/hoop-test/example.txt"
$ url=$url"?op=create&user.name=aholmes"
```

Write a local file, /tmp/example.txt into /hoop-test/example.txt.

```
$ curl -X POST $url \
  --data-binary @/tmp/example.txt \
  --header "content-type: application/octet-stream"
```

```
$ curl -i \
"http://localhost:14000/hoop-test?op=list&user.name=aholmes"
[{
  "path":"http:\/\/cdh:14000\/hoop-test\/example.txt",
  "isDir":false,
  "len":23,
  "owner":"aholmes",
  "group":"supergroup",
  "permission":"-rw-r--r--",
  "accessTime":1320014062728,
  "modificationTime":1320014062728,
  "blockSize":67108864,
  "replication":3
}]
```

Perform a directory listing of /hoop-test, which shows the file you just created.

```
$ url="http://localhost:14000/hoop-test"
$ url=$url"?op=delete&recursive=true&user.name=aholmes"

$ curl -X DELETE $url
{"delete":true}
```

Perform a recursive delete of /hoop-test.

---

[1] All the REST operations are documented at http://cloudera.github.com/hoop/docs/latest/HttpRestApi.html.

Hoop, as with any HDFS proxy, will suffer from adding hops between a client and HDFS, as well as circumventing data locality features available when using the Java HDFS client. But it's a huge improvement over the HDFS proxy, primarily because it can support writes due to its use of the Java HDFS client.

B.8 WebHDFS

WebHDFS, which is included in Hadoop versions 1.x and 2.x, is a whole new API in Hadoop providing REST/HTTP read/write access to HDFS. Figure B.6 shows that it coexists alongside the existing HDFS HTTP services.

You'll use WebHDFS to create a directory, write a file to that directory, and finally remove the file. WebHDFS may be turned off by default; to enable it you may have to set dfs.webhdfs.enabled to true in hdfs-site.xml and restart HDFS.

Your first step is to create a directory, /whdfs, in HDFS. Table B.1 shows the URL constructs, and optional parameters that can be supplied.

Table B.1   WebHDFS optional arguments for directory creation

Option	Description
permission	The octal code of the directory permission. For example, the default in HDFS is the three digit octal 755, equivalent to -rwxr-xr-x.

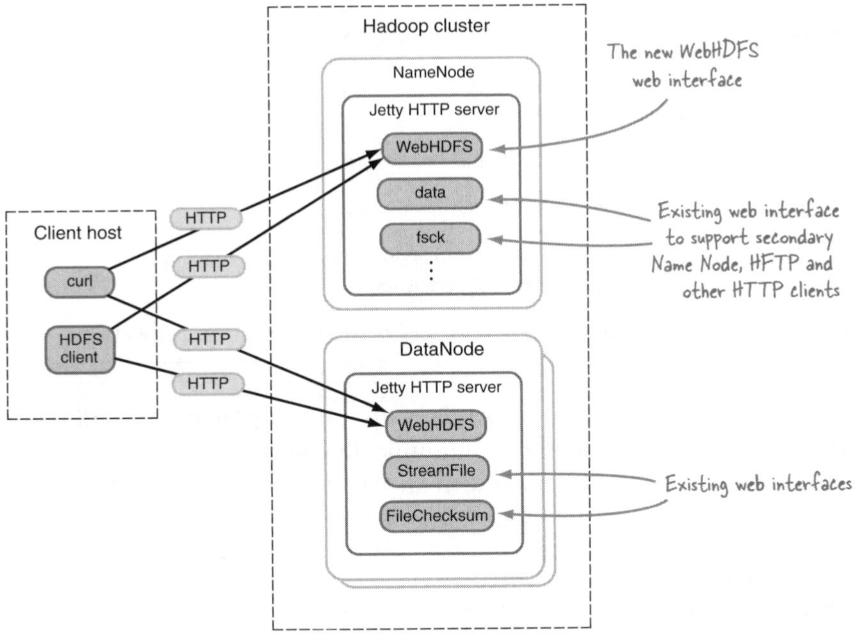

Figure B.6   WebHDFS architecture

> **Bash shell, URLs, and ampersands**
>
> Take care when working with URLs in bash. The ampersand (&) in bash is a control character that's used to launch a process in the background. Because URLs frequently contain ampersands, it's best to always enclose them in double quotes.

You'll create your directory without specifying the optional permissions:

```
$ curl -i -X PUT "http://localhost:50070/webhdfs/v1/whdfs?op=MKDIRS"

HTTP/1.1 200 OK
Content-Type: application/json
Transfer-Encoding: chunked
Server: Jetty(6.1.26)

{"boolean":true}
```

Next you'll create a file called test.txt under your newly created /whdfs directory. You should quickly examine the options you have available when creating the file in table B.2.

Table B.2 WebHDFS optional arguments for file creation

Option	Description
overwrite	What the action should be if a file already exists with the same name. Valid values are true or false.
blocksize	The HDFS block size for the file, in bytes.
replication	The replication count for the file blocks.
permission	The octal code of the file permission. For example, the default in HDFS is the three digit octal 755, equivalent to -rwxr-xr-x.
buffersize	The internal buffer size when streaming writes to other DataNodes.

Again, you'll run the command without any optional arguments. Creation of a file is a two-step process. You first need to communicate your intent to create a file with the NameNode. The NameNode replies with an HTTP redirect to a DataNode URL, which you must use to actually write the file content:

```
$ curl -i -X PUT \                                           Notify the NameNode of your
    "http://localhost:50070/webhdfs/v1/whdfs/test.txt?op=CREATE"    intent to create a file.

HTTP/1.1 307 TEMPORARY_REDIRECT                          The response is an HTTP temporary
Location: http://localhost.localdomain:50075/           redirect with a location field containing
webhdfs/v1/whdfs/test.txt                               the DataNode URL to be used for the
?op=CREATE&user.name=webuser&overwrite=false            actual write of the file.
```

```
Content-Type: application/json
Content-Length: 0
Server: Jetty(6.1.26)

$ echo "the cat sat on the mat" > /tmp/test.txt

$ url="http://localhost.localdomain:50075/webhdfs/v1/whdfs/test.txt"
$ url=$url"?op=CREATE&user.name=webuser&overwrite=false"

$ curl -i -X PUT -T /tmp/test.txt $url
HTTP/1.1 100 Continue

HTTP/1.1 201 Created
Location: webhdfs://0.0.0.0:50070/whdfs/test.txt
Content-Type: application/json
Content-Length: 0
Server: Jetty(6.1.26)

$ hadoop fs -cat /whdfs/test.txt
the cat sat on the mat
```

Create a small file on your local filesystem.

Construct the DataNode URL (it's too long to fit on a single line in the book).

Write the file content to the DataNode.

Use the HDFS concatenate command to view the contents of the file.

APPEND works in the same way, first getting the DataNode URL from the NameNode, and then communicating the appended data to the DataNode. The options for APPEND are the same as for the creation operation; refer to table B.2 for more details:

```
$ curl -i -X POST \
  "http://localhost:50070/webhdfs/v1/whdfs/test.txt?op=APPEND"
HTTP/1.1 307 TEMPORARY_REDIRECT
Location: http://localhost.localdomain:50075/webhdfs/v1/whdfs/test.txt
?op=APPEND&user.name=webuser
Content-Type: application/json
Content-Length: 0
Server: Jetty(6.1.26)

$ url="http://localhost.localdomain:50075/webhdfs/v1/whdfs/test.txt"
$ url=$url"?op=APPEND&user.name=webuser"

$ curl -i -X POST -T /tmp/test.txt $url
HTTP/1.1 100 Continue

HTTP/1.1 200 OK

$ hadoop fs -cat /whdfs/test.txt
the cat sat on the mat
the cat sat on the mat
```

Your next operation is to perform a directory listing in your directory:

```
$ curl -i "http://localhost:50070/webhdfs/v1/whdfs?op=LISTSTATUS"
{
  "HdfsFileStatuses": {
    "HdfsFileStatus": [
      {
        "accessTime":1322410385692,
        "blockSize":67108864,
        "group":"supergroup",
```

```
            "isDir":false,
            "isSymlink":false,
            "len":23,
            "localName":"test.txt",
            "modificationTime":1322410385700,
            "owner":"webuser",
            "permission":"644",
            "replication":1
        }
    ]
  }
}
```

A file status operation returns some statistics around a file or directory:

```
$ curl -i \
  "http://localhost:50070/webhdfs/v1/whdfs/test.txt?op=GETFILESTATUS"
{
  "HdfsFileStatus": {
    "accessTime":1322410385692,
    "blockSize":67108864,
    "group":"supergroup",
    "isDir":false,
    "isSymlink":false,
    "len":23,
    "localName":"",
    "modificationTime":1322410385700,
    "owner":"webuser",
    "permission":"644",
    "replication":1
  }
}
```

Finally, you'll recursively remove the whdfs directory:

```
$ curl -i -X DELETE \
  "http://localhost:50070/webhdfs/v1/whdfs?op=DELETE&recursive=true"

HTTP/1.1 200 OK
Content-Type: application/json
Transfer-Encoding: chunked
Server: Jetty(6.1.26)

{"boolean":true}
```

WebHDFS is a big step forward for HDFS in allowing rich client-side access to HDFS via HTTP.

B.9 *Distributed copy*

Hadoop has a command-line tool for copying data between Hadoop clusters called distCp. It performs the copy in a MapReduce job, where the mappers copy from one filesystem to another.

The following example shows a copy within the same cluster. To copy between clusters running the same Hadoop version, change the URLs to point to the source and destination NameNode URLs:

```
$ hadoop fs -mkdir /distcp-source
$ echo "the cat sat on the mat" | hadoop \
  fs -put - /distcp-source/test.txt
$ hadoop distcp hdfs://localhost:8020/distcp-source \
              hdfs://localhost:8020/distcp-dest
$ hadoop fs -cat /distcp-dest/test.txt
the cat sat on the mat
```

One of the useful characteristics of distCp is that it can copy between multiple versions of Hadoop. To support this, it uses the NameNode and DataNode HTTP interfaces to read data from the source cluster. Because the Hadoop HTTP interfaces don't support writes, when you're running distCp between clusters of differing versions, you must run it on the destination cluster. Notice in the following example that the source argument uses hftp as the scheme:

```
$ hadoop distcp hftp://source-nn:8020/distcp-source \
              hdfs://localhost:8020/distcp-dest
```

Because Hadoop version 1.x and 2.x offer the WebHDSF HTTP interfaces that support writes, there will no longer be any restrictions over what cluster the distCp must run on.

distCp does support FTP as a source, but unfortunately not HTTP.

B.10 WebDAV

Web-based Distributed Authoring and Versioning (WebDAV) is a series of HTTP methods that offer file collaboration facilities, as defined in RFC 4918 (HTTP Extensions for Web Distributed Authoring and Versioning (WebDAV)). A JIRA ticket (HDFS-225) was created in 2006 to add this capability to HDFS, but as of yet it hasn't been committed to any HDFS release.

A GitHub project at https://github.com/huyphan/HDFS-over-Webdav claims to have WebDAV running against Hadoop 0.20.1.

B.11 MapReduce

MapReduce is a great mechanism to get data into HDFS. Unfortunately, other than distCp, there's no other built-in mechanism to ingest data from external sources. Let's look at how to write a MapReduce job to pull data from an HTTP endpoint:

```
public final class HttpDownloadMap
    implements Mapper<LongWritable, Text, Text, Text> {
...
  public static final String CONN_TIMEOUT =
      "httpdownload.connect.timeout.millis";

  public static final String READ_TIMEOUT =
```

Get the job output
directory in HDFS.

```
                  "httpdownload.read.timeout.millis";

    @Override
    public void configure(JobConf job) {
      conf = job;
      jobOutputDir = job.get("mapred.output.dir");

      taskId = conf.get("mapred.task.id");

      if (conf.get(CONN_TIMEOUT) != null) {
        connTimeoutMillis = Integer.valueOf(conf.get(CONN_TIMEOUT));
      }

      if (conf.get(READ_TIMEOUT) != null) {
        readTimeoutMillis = Integer.valueOf(conf.get(READ_TIMEOUT));
      }
    }

    @Override
    public void map(LongWritable key, Text value,
                    OutputCollector<Text, Text> output,
                    Reporter reporter) throws IOException {
      Path httpDest =
        new Path(jobOutputDir, taskId + "_http_" + (file++));

      InputStream is = null;
      OutputStream os = null;
      try {
        URLConnection connection =
          new URL(value.toString()).openConnection();
        connection.setConnectTimeout(connTimeoutMillis);
        connection.setReadTimeout(readTimeoutMillis);
        is = connection.getInputStream();

        os = FileSystem.get(conf).create(httpDest);

        IOUtils.copyBytes(is, os, conf, true);
      } finally {
        IOUtils.closeStream(is);
        IOUtils.closeStream(os);
      }

      output.collect(new Text(httpDest.toString()), value);
    }
  }
```

Get the job's task ID, which is
unique across all the tasks.

Get the connection timeout or
use a default if not supplied.

Get the read timeout
or use a default if
not supplied.

Create the path to the file
that you'll use to write the
URL contents. You create
the file in the job output
directory, and use the
unique task ID in conjunction
with a counter (because the
map task can be called with
multiple URLs).

Create a
connection object.

Set the read
timeout.

Copy the contents of the HTTP
body into the HDFS file.

You emit the location of the URL file
in HDFS, as well as the URL that was
downloaded, so that they can be correlated.

You can run the MapReduce job and examine the contents of HDFS after it completes:

```
$ echo "http://www.apache.org/dist/avro/KEYS
http://www.apache.org/dist/maven/KEYS" | \
hadoop fs -put - /http-lines.txt

$ hadoop fs -cat /http-lines.txt
http://www.apache.org/dist/avro/KEYS
```

Create a file in HDFS containing a
list of URLs you want to download.

Verify the contents of the file.

```
http://www.apache.org/dist/maven/KEYS
```

Run your MapReduce job, specifying the input file and the output directory.

```
$ bin/run.sh com.manning.hip.ch2.HttpDownloadMapReduce \
  /http-lines.txt /http-download
```

List the contents of the job directory after the job completes.

```
$ hadoop fs -ls /http-download
/http-download/_SUCCESS
/http-download/_logs
/http-download/part-m-00000
/http-download/task_201110301822_0008_m_000000_http_0
/http-download/task_201110301822_0008_m_000000_http_1
```

View the metadata file of one of the mappers. The first field in the file is the HDFS location of the URL, and the second field is the URL you downloaded.

```
$ hadoop fs -cat /http-download/part-m-00000
/http-download/task_201110301822_0008_m_000000_http_0    http://www....
/http-download/task_201110301822_0008_m_000000_http_1    http://www...
```

```
$ hadoop fs -cat /http-download/<filename in part-m-00000>
pub   1024D/A7239D59 2005-10-12
Key fingerprint = 4B96 409A 098D BD51 1DF2  BC18 DBAF 69BE A723 9D59
uid              Doug Cutting (Lucene guy) <cutting@apache.org> ...
```

View the contents of one of the filenames contained in part-m-00000.

A few notes about your implementation: It's speculative-execution safe, as opposed to distCp, because you always write output based on the task attempt. If you want multiple mappers to be run, then simply create separate input files, and each one will be processed by a separate mapper. The connection and read timeouts can be controlled via the httpdownload.connect.timeout.millis and httpdownload.read.timeout.millis configuration settings, respectively.

We've gone through a number of Hadoop built-in mechanisms to read and write data into HDFS. If you were to use them, you'd have to write some scripts or code to manage the process of the ingress and egress because all the topics we covered are low-level.

appendix C
HDFS dissected

If you're using Hadoop you should have a solid understanding of HDFS so that you can make smart decisions about how to manage your data. In this appendix we'll walk through how HDFS reads and writes files to help you better understand how HDSF works behind the scenes.

C.1   What is HDFS?

HDFS is a distributed filesystem modeled on the Google File System (GFS), details of which were published in a 2003 paper.[1] Google's paper highlighted a number of key architectural and design properties, the most interesting of which included optimizations to reduce network input/output (I/O), how data replication should occur, and overall system availability and scalability. Not many details about GFS are known beyond those published in the paper, but HDFS is a near clone[2] of GFS, as described by the Google paper.

HDFS is an optimized filesystem for streaming reads and writes. It was designed to avoid the overhead of network I/O and disk seeks by introducing the notion of data locality (the ability to read/write data that's closest to the client), and by using large block sizes. Files in HDFS are stored across one or more blocks, and each block is typically 64 MB or larger. Blocks are replicated across multiple hosts in your cluster (as shown in figure C.1) to help with availability and fault tolerance.

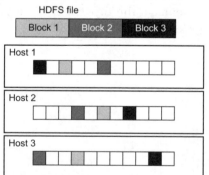

Figure C.1   An example of a single file occupying three blocks and the block distribution and replication across multiple HDFS storage hosts

---

[1] See http://research.google.com/archive/gfs.html.

[2] They differ from an implementation language perspective; GFS is written in C and HDFS is written mostly in Java, although critical parts are written in C.

HDFS is also a checksummed filesystem. Each block has a checksum associated with it, and if a discrepancy between the checksum and the block contents is detected (as in the case of bit rot), this information is sent to the HDFS master. The HDFS master coordinates the creation of a new replica of the bad block as well as the deletion of the corrupted block.

> **Beyond 0.20.x**
>
> The 2.x release will eventually include High Availability (HA) support for the NameNode.
>
> Also included in 2.x are the additions of a Backup Node and Checkpoint Node, which serve as replacements of the SecondaryNameNode (although the SNN still exists). The Checkpoint Node performs the same functions as the SecondaryNameNode; it downloads from the NameNode the current image file and subsequent edits, merges them together to create a new image file, and then uploads the new image to the NameNode. The Backup Node is a superset of the Checkpoint Node, also providing that checkpointing mechanism, as well as acting as a NameNode in its own right. This means if your primary NameNode goes down, you can immediately start using your Backup NameNode.

C.2 How HDFS writes files

A look at how HDFS writes files will bootstrap your HDFS knowledge and help you make smart decisions about your data and cluster, and how you work with your data. The first step is to use the command-line interface (CLI) to copy a file from local disk to HDFS:

```
$ hadoop -put /etc/hadoop/conf/hdfs-site.xml /tmp/hdfs-site.xml
```

Now let's look at how to achieve the same effect using Java:

Initialize a new configuration object. By default it loads core-default.xml and core-site.xml from the classpath.

Create a stream for the file in HDFS. This involves a round trip communication with the NameNode to determine the set of DataNodes that will be used to write to the first block in HDFS.

```java
public class StreamToHdfs {
    public static void main(String... args) throws Exception {
        Configuration config = new Configuration();

        FileSystem hdfs = FileSystem.get(config);

        OutputStream os = hdfs.create(new Path(args[0]));

        IOUtils.copyBytes(System.in, os, config, true);

        IOUtils.closeStream(os);
    }
}
```

Gets a handle to the filesystem, using the default configuration. This is most likely to be HDFS.

Copy the contents of the local file to the file in HDFS. As each block is filled, the NameNode is communicated with to determine the next set of DataNodes for the next block.

The previous code example is for illustrative purposes only; in real life you'd probably replace this code with a function call to Hadoop's utility class, `org.apache.hadoop` `.fs.FileUtil`, which contains a `copy` method for copying files, in addition to a number of other common filesystem operations.

Don't forget to set your classpath

If you run the previous example and don't include the Hadoop configuration directory in your classpath, Hadoop uses default settings for all of its configuration. By default `fs.default.name` is set to `file:///`, which means the local filesystem will be used for storage, not HDFS.

Now that you know how to copy a file using the CLI and Java, let's look at what HDFS is doing behind the scenes. Figure C.2 shows the components and how they interact when you write a file in HDFS.

DETERMINING THE FILESYSTEM

I mentioned earlier that the filesystem is abstracted, so Hadoop's first action is to figure out the underlying filesystem that should be used to perform the write. This is determined by examining the configured value for `fs.default.name`, which is a URI, and extracting the scheme. In the case of an HDFS filesystem, the value for `fs.default.name` would look something like `hdfs://namenode:9000`, so the scheme is *hdfs*. When the scheme is in hand, an instance of the concrete filesystem is created by reading the configuration value for `fs.[scheme].impl`, where *[scheme]* is replaced by the scheme, which in this example is hdfs. If you look at `core-default.xml`, you'll see that `fs.hdfs.impl` is set to `org.apache.hadoop.hdfs.DistributedFileSystem`, so that's the concrete filesystem you'll use.

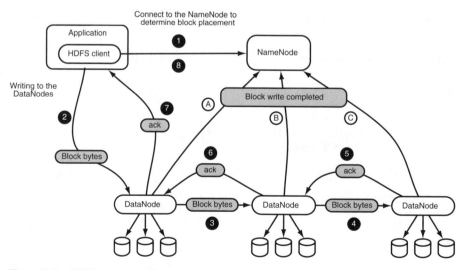

Figure C.2   HDFS write data flow

CONNECT TO THE NAMENODE TO DETERMINE BLOCK PLACEMENT

Hadoop's `DistributedFileSystem` class creates a `DFSClient` instance to manage all communication with the NameNode and DataNodes when performing the file write. `DFSClient` reads a number of configuration items, including the block size (`dfs.block.size`) and replication factor (`dfs.replication`). It also sets up a connection to the NameNode using Hadoop's transparent RPC mechanism, as you saw in figure C.2 in step 1.[3, 4]

HDFS stores files across one or more blocks, so for each block the NameNode is consulted to determine which DataNodes will hold the data for the block. When determining what DataNodes should be used for a block, the NameNode first attempts to pick the local node, if the client is running on a DataNode. Nodes are prioritized in the following order:

1 *Local disk*—Network I/O is expensive, so reading from local disk is always preferred over any network I/O.
2 *Rack-local*—Typically network speeds between nodes in a rack are faster than across racks.
3 *Other*—The data is resident on a separate rack, which makes it the slowest I/O of the three nodes (generally due to the additional network hops between the client and data).

In a rack-aware environment, the NameNode will ensure that at least one copy of the replica is on a rack separate from the other replicas. If you're using a high replication value, it also ensures that no one rack has too many replicas. The list of DataNodes for the block are returned to the client ordered by proximity to the client, which means if the client is running on a DataNode, it will write to the local DataNode first.

There are two ways to enable rack awareness in Hadoop. First, there's a Java interface, `DNSToSwitchMapping`, that you can implement. Alternatively, you can specify that Hadoop use your configuration by setting `topology.node.switch.mapping.impl`. An alternative (and simpler) mechanism would be to write a script and locate it on your NameNode. Configure the location of your script with `topology.script.file.name`; see class `ScriptBasedMapping` for more details. The following code is a brief example of how you'd write a shell script:

```
#!/bin/bash4
# fetch_rack.sh

declare -A rack_map
#        -A option declares associative array.

rack_map[10.0.0.2]="/datacenter-dallas/rack1"
```

---

[3] Prior to 2.x, Hadoop internally used its own RPC mechanism for components to communicate with each other. This RPC mechanism uses Java's proxy mechanism coupled with a simple marshalling framework (which marshalls `Writable` and Java primitives).

[4] For Hadoop 2.x, Hadoop's custom RPC framework was replaced with Protocol Buffers—please read https://issues.apache.org/jira/browse/HDFS-2058 for more details.

```
rack_map[10.0.0.3]="/datacenter-dallas/rack1"
rack_map[10.0.0.4]="/datacenter-dallas/rack2"

default_rack=10.0.0.1

if [ $# -eq "0" ]; then
  echo $default_rack
else
  result="
  for i in $*; do
    result="$result ${default_rack[$i]}"
  done
  echo $result
fi
```

WRITING TO THE DATANODES

HDFS uses pipelining to achieve its replicated writes. When the client receives the list of DataNodes from the NameNode, the client streams the block data to the first DataNode (in step 2 in figure C.2), which in turn mirrors the data to the next DataNode (in step 3 of the same figure), and so on until the data has reached all of the DataNodes (in step 4). Acknowledgements from the DataNodes are also pipelined in reverse order. After the last DataNode has completed processing a packet, it sends an ack back to the previous DataNode and so on until it reaches the client (in steps 5, 6, and 7). The client only moves on to writing the next block after all acks for packets sent for the block have been received. When each DataNode has completed writing the block locally, the blocks are moved from temporary storage into permanent storage, and each DataNode asynchronously notifies the NameNode of their block storage (steps A, B, and C).

Finally, when all the blocks have been written and the client closes the stream, the NameNode is notified that it should persist the blocks related to the file (last step, 8).

Walking through how HDFS writes files helps you to understand HDFS internals, which in turn will let you make better decisions related to your data and your environment. We looked at how HDFS components work, and how they relate and communicate with each other. You also learned how HDFS makes decisions about where to place your file blocks, and how you can set up your cluster to be rack aware. Now that you have a handle on how HDFS writes, let's move on to file reads.

C.3   *How HDFS reads files*

Typically, you'll read a file many more times than you'll write it, so it's equally important to know how HDFS reads your files. Let's first take a look at how you read (or view) the contents of a file using the CLI:

```
$ hadoop fs -cat hdfs-site.xml
```

In Java it's a little more work but straightforward nonetheless:

```
public static void main(String... args) throws Exception {
  Configuration config = new Configuration();

  FileSystem hdfs = FileSystem.get(config);

  InputStream is = hdfs.open(new Path(args[0]));

  IOUtils.copyBytes(is, System.out, config, true);

  IOUtils.closeStream(is);
}
```

Opens a stream based on a file in HDFS. This involves a request to the NameNode, which sends back the block details for up to the first ten blocks of the file to the client.

Reads the contents of the file and writes them to standard output. After the first ten blocks have been read, the NameNode will be contacted to return details on the next ten blocks.

The interactions between Hadoop components for reading a file are detailed in figure C.3, which shows the interactions involved in reading a file from HDFS.

CONNECT TO THE NAMENODE TO DETERMINE BLOCK LOCATIONS

As you saw with writes, the DFSClient contains all of the client-side logic related to communicating with the NameNode and DataNodes. When a stream to an existing HDFS file is requested, the DFSClient creates a DFSInputStream, which in turn asks the NameNode for metadata about the first ten blocks of the file, as shown in step 1 in figure C.3. For each block, the NameNode orders the DataNodes by proximity to the client; a local DataNode (on the same physical host) is favored over a remote DataNode, which incurs the overhead of network I/O. Rack-local DataNodes are also favored over nodes on different racks.

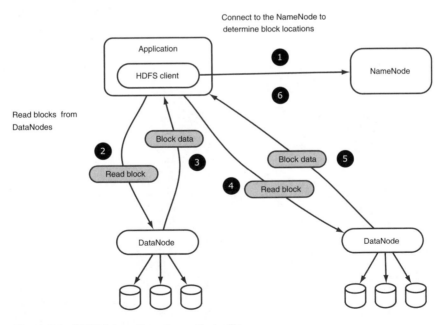

Figure C.3   HDFS interactions for reading a file

READING FROM DATANODES

When the client receives the list of blocks from the NameNode, it picks the first Data-Node for each block and opens a stream with that DataNode (in step 2 of figure C.3). As the client requests bytes from the stream, the DFSInputStream in turn reads from the DataNode's stream until the end of the block is reached (in step 3 of the same figure). It then closes the connection with that DataNode, and repeats the process for the next DataNode (in steps 4 and 5). If the file is larger than ten blocks, it once again asks the NameNode for block details on the next ten blocks (in step 6), and continues this pattern until all the blocks for the file have been read.

Now that you understand how HDFS reads data, you can see that it's optimized for local reads, which is an important characteristic of a distributed system. MapReduce leverages this knowledge and intelligently schedules its map tasks to execute on nodes such that the map reads the data from local disk and not over the network.[5] You can also leverage this knowledge when making decisions about the architecture of your application.

---

[5] Whether or not MapReduce can schedule a map task on a node that has all of its data local is dependent on a variety of factors.

appendix D
Optimized MapReduce
join frameworks

In this appendix we'll look at the two join frameworks we used in chapter 4. The first is the repartition join framework, which lessens the required memory footprint of the Hadoop join implementation in the `org.apache.hadoop.contrib.utils.join` package. The second is a framework provided to perform a replicated join, and you'll build in some smarts that will allow you to cache the smaller of the datasets being joined.

D.1 An optimized repartition join framework

The Hadoop contrib join package requires that all the values for a key be loaded into memory. How can you implement a reduce-side join without that memory space overhead? In this optimization you'll cache the dataset that's smallest in size, and then perform a join as you iterate over data from the larger dataset. This involves performing a secondary sort over the map output data so that the reducer will receive the data from the smaller dataset ahead of the larger dataset. Figure D.1 shows the improved repartition join in action.

Figure D.2 shows a class diagram broken into two parts, with a generic framework, and some sample implementation classes.

THE JOIN FRAMEWORK

We'll craft the join code in a similar fashion to that of the Hadoop contrib join package. The goal is to create a generic repartition join mechanism that can work with any datasets. For the sake of brevity we'll highlight the main elements of the package.

We'll kick things off with a look at the `OptimizedDataJoinMapperBase` class. The goals of this class are to classify one dataset as the smaller dataset, and to generate the output key and value. First we'll look at the `configure` method, which is called at

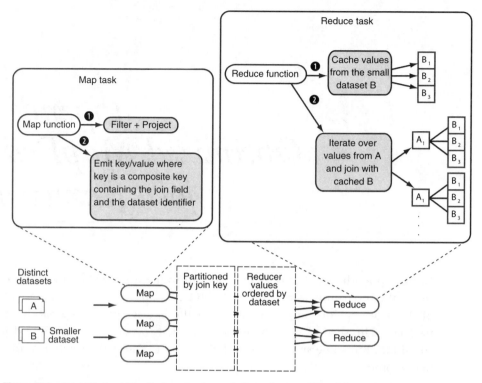

Figure D.1   An optimized MapReduce implementation of a repartition join

mapper construction time. The goal here is to label each dataset so the reducer can distinguish between both datasets, and also to determine whether the input split you're processing is the smaller or larger dataset:

An abstract method that should return a unique identifier representing the dataset.

```
protected abstract Text generateInputTag(String inputFile);

protected abstract boolean isInputSmaller(String inputFile);

public void configure(JobConf job) {
  this.inputFile = job.get("map.input.file");

  this.inputTag = generateInputTag(this.inputFile);

  if(isInputSmaller(this.inputFile)) {
    smaller = new BooleanWritable(true);
    outputKey.setOrder(0);
  } else {
    smaller = new BooleanWritable(false);
    outputKey.setOrder(1);
  }
}
```

An abstract method that must determine if the current dataset is the smallest.

Store the logical identifier for this input split.

Read the input split filename.

Store the results about whether this dataset is smaller.

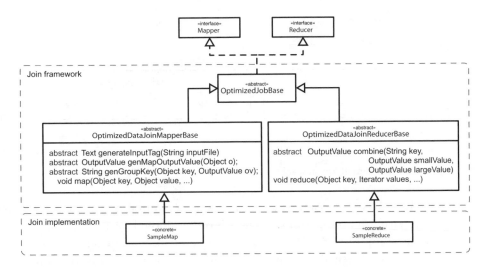

Figure D.2 Class diagram showing main classes in the framework and a sample implementation

The map method first asks the implementing class to engineer an OutputValue object, which contains the value that the implementing class wants to use in the join (and presumably include in the final output), and a boolean indicating whether the value is being materialized from the smaller dataset. If the map method then asks the implementing class to engineer the key that will be used for the join, this will make it the output key for the map:

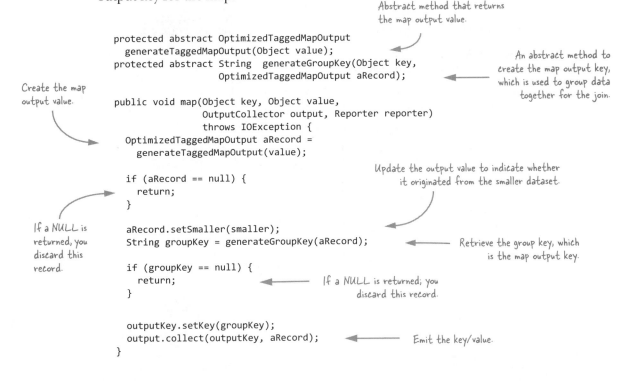

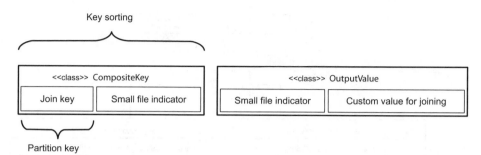

Figure D.3 Map output key and value

Figure D.3 shows the composite key and values emitted by the map. The secondary sort will partition on the join key, but will order all the keys for a single join key using the whole composite key. The composite key contains an integer indicating if the data source is from the small file, and as such can be used to ensure that values from the small file are passed to the reducer before records for the large file.

The next step is to look at the reducer. Because you have a guarantee that the small file values will arrive at the reducer ahead of the large file values, you can cache all of the values from the small dataset, and when you start seeing values from the large dataset, join each one with the cached values:

```
public void reduce(Object key, Iterator values,
                   OutputCollector output, Reporter reporter)
    throws IOException {

  CompositeKey k = (CompositeKey) key;                    ← Create a structure to store
                                                            the cached values from the
  List<OptimizedTaggedMapOutput> smaller =                 small dataset.
     new ArrayList<OptimizedTaggedMapOutput>();

  while (values.hasNext()) {                               ← Clone the value because it's reused
    Object value = values.next();                           by the MapReduce code to store
                                                             subsequent reducer values.

    OptimizedTaggedMapOutput cloned =                     ←
        ((OptimizedTaggedMapOutput) value).clone(job);

    if (cloned.isSmaller().get()) {
      smaller.add(cloned);
    } else {
      joinAndCollect(k, smaller, cloned, output, reporter); ←
    }
  }
}
```

Cache it if it's from the small dataset.

Perform the join if it's from the large dataset.

The joinAndCollect method combines values from the two datasets together and emits them:

```
protected abstract OptimizedTaggedMapOutput combine(   ◄────
                     String key,
                     OptimizedTaggedMapOutput value1,
                     OptimizedTaggedMapOutput value2);

private void joinAndCollect(CompositeKey key,
                     List<OptimizedTaggedMapOutput> smaller,
                     OptimizedTaggedMapOutput value,
                     OutputCollector output,
                     Reporter reporter)

    throws IOException {
    if (smaller.size() < 1) {
      OptimizedTaggedMapOutput combined =
          combine(key.getKey(), null, value);       ◄────────
      collect(key, combined, output, reporter);

    } else {
      for (OptimizedTaggedMapOutput small : smaller) {
        OptimizedTaggedMapOutput combined =
            combine(key.getKey(), small, value);    ◄───
        collect(key, combined, output, reporter);   ◄───
      }
    }
}
```

An abstract method that must be implemented to perform the combination of dataset values and return the value to be emitted by the reducer.

Even if no data was collected from the small dataset, calling the combine method allows implementations to perform an outer join.

For each small dataset value combine it with the large dataset value.

Call the collect method, which emits the combined record if it isn't NULL.

Now you have the main guts of the framework uncovered. Chapter 4 shows how you can use the framework.

D.2   *A replicated join framework*

A replicated join is a map-side join, and gets its name from the fact that the smallest of the datasets is replicated to all the map hosts. The implementation of the replicated join is straightforward and is demonstrated in Chuck Lam's *Hadoop in Action*.

The goal in this section is to create a generic replicated join framework that can work with any datasets. I'll also provide an optimization that will dynamically determine if the distributed cache contents are larger than the input split, in which case you'd cache the map input and execute the join in the mapper cleanup method.

The class diagram for this framework is shown in figure D.4. Rather than provide an abstract Join class, I'll instead provide an implementation of the join (class Generic-ReplicatedJoin), which out of the box works with KeyValueTextInputFormat and Text-OutputFormat, and assumes that the first token in each file is the join key. But the join class can be extended to support any input and output formats.

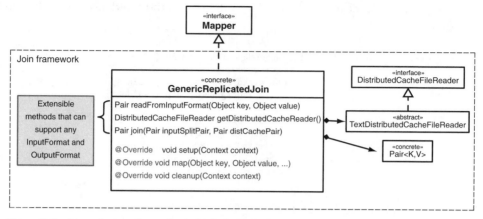

Figure D.4   Class diagram for replicated join framework

Figure D.5 shows the algorithm for the join framework. The mapper setup method determines if the map's input split is larger than the distributed cache, in which case it loads the distributed cache into memory. The map function either performs a join or caches the key/value pairs, based on whether the setup method loaded the cache. If the input split is smaller than the distributed cache, the map cleanup method will read the records in the distributed cache and join them with the cache created in the map function.

Job.Driver
1: add small data set to the Distributed Cache

Map.Setup
1: $distCacheSmaller \leftarrow distCacheFileLenghts < inputSplitSize$
2: **if** $distCacheSmaller$ **then**
3:     $smallDatasetHash \leftarrow distributedCache$

Map.Map(key, value)
1: **if** $distCacheSmaller$ **then**
2:     **for all** $smallData \in smallDatasetHash$ **do**
3:         $combined = combine(value, smallData.value)$
4:         **if** $combined \neq NULL$ **then**
5:             $emit(key, combined)$
6: **else**
7:     $smallDatasetHash = smallDatasetHash \cup \{(key, value)\}$

Map.Cleanup
1: **if** $distCacheSmaller = false$ **then**
2:     **for all** $largeData \in distributedCache$ **do**
3:         **for all** $smallData \in smallDatasetHash$ **do**
4:             $combined = combine(smallData.value, largeData.value)$
5:             **if** $combined \neq NULL$ **then**
6:                 $emit(smallData.key, combined)$

Figure D.5   Algorithm for optimized replicated join

The setup method in the GenericReplicatedJoin is called at map initialization time. It determines if the size of the files in the distributed cache are smaller than the input split, and if they are, loads them into a HashMap:

```
@Override
protected void setup(
    Context context)
    throws IOException, InterruptedException {

  distributedCacheFiles = DistributedCache.getLocalCacheFiles(
    context.getConfiguration());

  int distCacheSizes = 0;
  for (Path distFile : distributedCacheFiles) {
    File distributedCacheFile = new File(distFile.toString());

    distCacheSizes += distributedCacheFile.length();
  }

  if(context.getInputSplit() instanceof FileSplit) {
    FileSplit split = (FileSplit) context.getInputSplit();

    long inputSplitSize = split.getLength();

    distributedCacheIsSmaller =
      (distCacheSizes < inputSplitSize);

  } else {
    distributedCacheIsSmaller = true;
  }

  if (distributedCacheIsSmaller) {
    for (Path distFile : distributedCacheFiles) {
      File distributedCacheFile = new File(distFile.toString());
      DistributedCacheFileReader reader =
          getDistributedCacheReader();
      reader.init(distributedCacheFile);

      for (Pair p : (Iterable<Pair>) reader) {
        addToCache(p);
      }
      reader.close();
    }
  }
}
```

Tally up sizes of all the files in the distributed cache.

If the input split is from a file, determine whether the distributed cache files are smaller than the length of the input split.

If the input split is not from a file, assume that the distributed cache is smaller, because you have no way of knowing the length of the input split.

Call a method to engineer a DistributedCacheFileReader to read records from the distributed cache file.

Add each record to your local HashMap.

Your map method chooses its behavior based on whether the setup method cached the distributed cache. If the distributed cache was loaded into memory, then it proceeds to join the tuple supplied to the map method with the cache. Otherwise, it caches the map tuple for use later in the cleanup method:

```
@Override
protected void map(Object key, Object value, Context context)
    throws IOException, InterruptedException {
  Pair pair = readFromInputFormat(key, value);
```

```
        if (distributedCacheIsSmaller) {
          joinAndCollect(pair, context);
        } else {
          addToCache(pair);
        }
    }
```

Join the map tuple with the distributed cache.

Cache the map tuple.

```
    public void joinAndCollect(Pair p, Context context)
        throws IOException, InterruptedException {
      List<Pair> cached = cachedRecords.get(p.getKey());
      if (cached != null) {
        for (Pair cp : cached) {
          Pair result;
          if (distributedCacheIsSmaller) {
            result = join(p, cp);
          } else {
            result = join(cp, p);
          }
          if (result != null) {
            context.write(result.getKey(), result.getData());
          }
        }
      }
    }
```

Ensure the join method is called with records in a predictable order: the record from the input split first, followed by the record by the distributed cache.

If the result of the join was a non–NULL object, emit the object.

```
    public Pair join(Pair inputSplitPair, Pair distCachePair) {
      StringBuilder sb = new StringBuilder();
      if (inputSplitPair.getData() != null) {
        sb.append(inputSplitPair.getData());
      }
      sb.append("\t");
      if (distCachePair.getData() != null) {
        sb.append(distCachePair.getData());
      }
      return new Pair<Text, Text>(
          new Text(inputSplitPair.getKey().toString()),
          new Text(sb.toString()));
    }
```

The default implementation of the join, which can be overridden to support other InputFormat and OutputFormat classes, concatenates the string forms of the values together.

After all of the records have been fed to the map method, the MapReduce framework will call the cleanup method. If the contents of the distributed cache were larger than the input split, it is here where you perform the join between the map function's cache of the input split tuples with the records contained in the distributed cache:

```
@Override
protected void cleanup(
    Context context)
    throws IOException, InterruptedException {
  if (!distributedCacheIsSmaller) {
    for (Path distFile : distributedCacheFiles) {
      File distributedCacheFile = new File(distFile.toString());
      DistributedCacheFileReader reader =
          getDistributedCacheReader();
```

```
        reader.init(distributedCacheFile);
        for (Pair p : (Iterable<Pair>) reader) {
          joinAndCollect(p, context);
        }
        reader.close();
      }
    }
  }
```

Finally, the job driver code must specify the files that need to be loaded into the distributed cache. The following code works with a single file, as well as a directory containing the results of a MapReduce job:

```
Configuration conf = new Configuration();

FileSystem fs = smallFilePath.getFileSystem(conf);

FileStatus smallFilePathStatus = fs.getFileStatus(smallFilePath);

if(smallFilePathStatus.isDir()) {
  for(FileStatus f: fs.listStatus(smallFilePath)) {
    if(f.getPath().getName().startsWith("part")) {
      DistributedCache.addCacheFile(f.getPath().toUri(), conf);
    }
  }
} else {
  DistributedCache.addCacheFile(smallFilePath.toUri(), conf);
```

The assumption with this framework is that either the distributed cache or the input split contents can be cached in memory. The advantage of this framework is that it will cache the smaller of the distributed cache and the input split.

In the paper "A Comparison of Join Algorithms for Log Processing in MapReduce,"[1] you can see a further optimization of this approach in cases where the distributed cache contents are larger than the input split. In their optimization they further partition the distributed cache into N partitions, and likewise cache the map tuples into N hashtables, which process provides a more optimal join in the map cleanup method.

A downside to the replicated join is that each map task must read the distributed cache on startup. A potential optimization suggested by the paper referenced in the previous paragraph is to override the FileInputFormat splitting such that input splits that exist on the same host are combined into a single split, thereby cutting down on the number of map tasks that need to load the distributed cache into memory.

On a final note, Hadoop comes with a built-in map-side join in the org.apache .hadoop.mapred.join package. But it requires that the input files of both datasets be sorted and distributed into identical partitions, which requires a good amount of preprocessing prior to leveraging their join mechanism.

---

[1] See http://pages.cs.wisc.edu/~jignesh/publ/hadoopjoin.pdf.

index

RELATED MANNING TITLES

Hadoop in Action
by Chuck Lam

ISBN: 978-1-935182-19-1
336 pages, $44.99
December 2010

HBase in Action
by Nick Dimiduk and Amandeep Khurana

ISBN: 978-1-617290-52-7
350 pages, $39.99
November 2012

Machine Learning in Action
by Peter Harrington

ISBN: 978-1-617290-18-3
384 pages, $44.99
April 2012

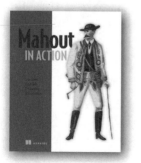

Mahout in Action
by Sean Owen, Robin Anil, Ted Dunning,
and Ellen Friedman

ISBN: 978-1-935182-68-9
416 pages, $44.99
October 2011

For ordering information go to www.manning.com